- **Dynamic Study Modules** help students study chapter topics and the language ~~~ on their own by continuously assessing their knowledge application and performance in real time. These are available as graded assignments prior to class, and are accessible on smartphones, tablets, and computers.

- **Learning Catalytics™** is a student response tool that helps you generate class discussion, customize your lecture, and promote peer-to-peer learning based on real-time analytics. Learning Catalytics uses students' smartphones, tablets, or laptops to engage them in more interactive tasks.

- The **Gradebook** offers an easy way for you and your students to see their performance in your course.

  Item Analysis lets you quickly see trends by analyzing details like the number of students who answered correctly/incorrectly, time on task, and more.

  And because it's correlated with the AACSB Standards, you can track students' progress toward outcomes that the organization has deemed important in preparing students to be leaders.

- **Pearson eText** enhances learning — both in and out of the classroom. Students can take notes, highlight, and bookmark important content, or engage with interactive lecture and example videos that bring learning to life anytime, anywhere via MyLab or the app.

- **Accessibility (ADA)**—Pearson is working toward WCAG 2.0 Level AA and Section 508 standards, as expressed in the **Pearson Guidelines for Accessible Educational Web Media.** Moreover, our products support customers in meeting their obligation to comply with the Americans with Disabilities Act (ADA) by providing access to learning technology programs for users with disabilities.

  Please email our Accessibility Team at **disability.support@pearson.com** for the most up-to-date information.

- With **LMS Integration**, you can link your MyLab course from Blackboard Learn™, Brightspace® by D2L®, Canvas™, or Moodle®.

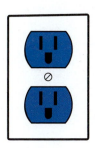

http://www.pearsonmylabandmastering.com

PROCESSES, SYSTEMS, AND INFORMATION

An Introduction to MIS

PROCESSES, SYSTEMS, AND INFORMATION
An Introduction to MIS

THIRD EDITION

EARL McKINNEY JR.
Bowling Green State University

DAVID M. KROENKE

Pearson

330 Hudson Street, NY NY 10013

Vice President, IT & Careers: Andrew Gilfillan
Senior Portfolio Manager: Samantha Lewis
Managing Producer: Laura Burgess
Associate Content Producer: Stephany Harrington
Portfolio Management Assistant: Madeline Houpt
Director of Product Marketing: Brad Parkins
Product Marketing Manager: Heather Taylor
Product Marketing Assistant: Jesika Bethea
Field Marketing Manager: Molly Schmidt
Field Marketing Assistant: Kelli Fisher
Cover Image: RedlineVector/Shutterstock; bluebay/Shutterstock

Vice President, Product Model Management: Jason Fournier
Senior Product Model Manager: Eric Hakanson
Lead, Production and Digital Studio: Heather Darby
Digital Studio Course Producer: Jaimie Noy
Program Monitor: SPi Global
Full-Service Project Management and Composition:
Katie Ostler, Cenveo® Publisher Services
Printer/Binder: LSC Communications
Cover Printer: Phoenix
Text Font: 10/12 Times LT Pro Roman

Library of Congress Cataloging-in-Publication Data

On file with the library of Congress.

ISBN   10: 0-13-482700-7
ISBN 13: 978-0-13-482700-1

1 18

Brief Contents

Contents

Preface

Since the emergence of ERP and EAI systems in the early 1990s, the MIS discipline has undergone a slow but persistent change. Whereas the early emphasis of MIS was on the management and use of information systems *per se,* emerging cross-functional systems began to place the focus on processes that utilize such systems. We believe that existing MIS textbooks, particularly those at the introductory level, do not sufficiently recognize this change in emphasis. Hence, we offer this textbook that provides a strong process orientation.

Why This Third Edition?

We have made a number of changes to this third edition; these are listed in Table 1. While Table 1 spells out the changes in detail, there are several significant changes that warrant a short explanation.

First, the technology landscape has changed rapidly from the time the second edition was written. At that time, Uber, Blockchain, Smartphone payments, group messaging, and the Internet of Things were not on the scene. Robotics, Big Data, and SAP HANA S/4 were just beginning. Further, security was not the priority it is now. These changes led to updates of many of the chapters. In addition, we decided to introduce Extensions in this third edition to provide more coverage of new topics without making existing chapters too long.

These Extensions include completely new discussions of technologies such as Location Based Data, AI, and Robots. They also include some topics that no longer fit in chapters such as hardware, software, and systems development. Finally the extensions include a discussion of IS careers.

We also wanted to expand the opportunity for students to gain more first-hand practice with SAP. We added a Production tutorial in Appendix A based on the same Chuck's Bikes case used in the Procurement and Sales tutorials.

One of the biggest challenges to any SAP tutorial is ensuring students understand the underlying business processes, that they not blindly enter data into on-screen forms. To that end, Pearson has introduced a new app called MySAP Lab. This browser app runs independently from SAP but is synced to the tutorial so that as a student works through the tutorial this app periodically poses questions about the underlying process. It also provides the instructor an opportunity to passively observe assignment completion, notice where students encounter difficulty, and record student responses to questions.

Another significant change is our coverage of security. Security is becoming more essential for all business students. Often the only exposure business students get to security is in an MIS class. For this reason we greatly expanded our discussion of security, gave it its own chapter, and moved it earlier in the semester next to the other technical topics.

Another change is that MyLab MIS is now integrated with the 3rd Edition. At the end of each chapter students are directed to MyLab MIS for short answer questions as well as essay questions.

Many colleagues have told us they are "flipping" their class rooms and are using more student engagement activities during class meeting times. As a result, we updated half of the MIS InClass exercises and improved the instructions on the others.

At times introductory classes like MIS can devolve into a mastery of vocabulary lists. We've tried to counter this by helping the student see the value of using the vocabulary and the usefulness of the models presented in the text by consistently applying the course vocabulary to familiar domains such as a hospital, a bicycle company, and a university. We also ask students to self-inspect; we don't ask them to memorize the definition of collaboration and experimentation—we ask them to evaluate themselves and find ways to improve. Just as important, we tried to identify key themes for entire chapters highlighting them in the introduction and returning to them at various points in the chapters. For example, the security chapter theme is that security is a tradeoff; a tradeoff between freedom and security and between cost and security. All these changes seek to make student engagement more natural and frequent.

Finally, to improve currency and readability all the chapters were updated, and many new figures added or repurposed. In addition, 8 opening vignettes, 10 end of chapter cases, and 7 application exercises were completely rewritten. We also tried to be more efficient with page use, reducing the length of chapter opening vignettes, cases, and ethical guides.

TABLE 1 Changes in the 3rd Edition

Chapter	Change
1	New Figure on Data and Internet rapid expansion
	New Figure on IS job history and growth
	Updated and simplified the definition of MIS
	New MIS InClass on student skills
	New Tesla Case Study
2	6 new Figures
	New chapter opening vignette highlights hospital process
	Expanded discussion of importance of processes
	Definitions of IS components more specific
	Expanded discussion of the value of internal information
	New MIS InClass on information
	New concluding question applying book topics to work
	New Coffee Shop Case Study
3	10 new Figures
	New chapter opening vignette describes cloud issues
	Hardware and Software updated and moved to Extension
	Expanded discussion of Cloud, recent growth, most popular uses
	MIS InClass moved here from Chapter 2
	Key Terms and Concepts reduced
	New vocabulary: PAN, handover, net neutrality, peering
	New discussion of cellular networks
	Three questions replace one on how networks work
	A single continuous example of image upload to Snapchat
	Added discussion of Tier 1 network providers
	New McDonalds Case Study
4	New chapter opening vignette on database issues at a hospital
	Updated discussion of NoSQL
	New case study on personal DBMS
	New discussion on how hospital database should be corrected
5	New Security chapter, previously half a chapter
	9 new figures
	New chapter opening vignette describes a security lapse
	New end of chapter collaboration exercise
	New MIS InClass
	New WikiLeaks case
	New vocabulary: APT, BYOD, brute force, CAPTCHA, forensics, hash, malware, overflow
	New vocabulary: Ransomware, risk, audit, session hijacking, usurpation, VPN
	Updated discussion of implications from IoT, cloud, mobile, and Big Data
	Current security failures and scope of challenges updated
	Emphasis on tradeoff expanded
	Figure on Threat vs Loss updated and simplified
	Suggestions for personal security updated and expanded
	Expanded discussion on passwords, 2 factor, VPN and others
6	7 new figures
	New chapter opening vignette describes poor hospital process
	Expanded discussion of importance of processes to business
	New end of chapter collaboration exercise
	New ethics guide on the ethics of automation
	New Electronic Dance Music case
	Emphasis on KPI rather than measures for processes
	New discussion of the importance of process feedback

Chapter	Change
7	10 new figures
	New chapter opening vignette on ERP cutover at CBI
	Added personal examples to motivate students
	New end of chapter collaboration exercise
	New MIS InClass
	New AF ERP Bonfire case describes implementation disaster
	New emphasis on upgrades not initial implementation of ERP
	Removed discussion of EAI
	Discussion of new concepts—Fiori, SAP HANA S/4
	Expanded discussion of ERP system challenges
	Updated goals of Tier 1 ERP vendors
8	11 new figures
	Expanded discussion of supply chain early to provide procurement ERP context
	Implications for student job skills added
	New 2028–A/R, robots, 3-D printing, and Worldwide Internet
9	14 new figures
	Expanded discussion of marketing early to provide sales ERP context
	A consideration of Salesforce discussion added
	Implications for student job skills added
	New 2028—Blockchain, Amazon buttons, darknet, and smartphone payment
10	New chapter opening vignette hospital collaboration
	New end of chapter collaboration exercise on Kata
	Updated descriptions of Google Drive and Microsoft OneDrive
	New MIS InClass
	New Miracle on the Hudson case
	New 2028—collaboration with AI and robots
	Expanded motivation to students to apply collaboration topics
11	7 new Figures
	New chapter opening vignette examines negative social media posts
	New Airbnb case
	New section on the sharing economy and trust added
	Added new section on group messaging apps and Reddit
	New vocabulary: Reddit, sharing economy, unicorns, collaborative consumption
	New vocabulary: click-through rate, conversion rate, Enterprise 2.0, privacy
	Expanded discussion of common social media measures
	Updated business uses of social media
	New 2028—analysis of social media data and privacy
	Impact of social media on hiring process added
	Expanded discussion of challenge of measuring financial results
12	9 new Figures
	New discussion of data marts, Excel PowerPivot, text mining
	Expanded descriptions of prediction markets, urban applications
	New Privacy case
	New 2028—mobile BI, unstructured data, IoT, and privacy
	New vocabulary: data marts, text mining, sentiment analysis, IoT, GDPR
	Big Data section updated on NoSQL, MapReduce, Hadoop, SAP HANA
	New discussion on skepticism of analysis added
New	Extensions
	1 IS Careers
	2 Software and Hardware
	3 Process Management and IS Design
	4 Robots and AI
	5 Location Based Data Information Systems
	Appendix A: SAP Production Tutorial

Importance of MIS

Chapter 1 claims that MIS is the most important class in the business curriculum. That's a bold statement, and every year we ask whether it remains true. Is there any discipline having a greater impact on contemporary business and government than IS? We continue to doubt there is. Every year brings important new technology to organizations, and many of these organizations respond by creating innovative applications that increase productivity and otherwise help them accomplish their strategies. In the past year, Blockchain, IoT, and new security challenges are posing new opportunities and requirements on organizations. More sophisticated and demanding users push organizations into a rapidly changing future, one that requires continual adjustments in business planning. To participate, our graduates need to know how to apply emerging technologies to better achieve their organizations' strategies. Knowledge of MIS is critical to this application.

The effects of changing technology and new user demands fall on processes and information systems at all levels—workgroup, organizational, and inter-enterprise. The impact on the latter is especially dramatic because cloud-based hosting and mobile devices enable independent organizations to work together in ways previously unimaginable.

As stated, we continue to believe we can enter the classroom with the confidence that we are teaching the single most important course in the business school—an argument that relies on two observations. First, because of nearly free data storage and data communications, businesses are increasingly finding and, more important, increasingly *required* to find innovative applications for information systems. The incorporation of Facebook and Twitter into marketing systems is an obvious example, but this example is only the tip of the iceberg. For at least the next 10 years, every business professional will, at a minimum, need to assess the efficacy of proposed IS applications. To excel, business professionals will need to not only assess but define innovative IS applications. These applications will increasingly take advantage of advances in Big Data and analytical software.

Such skills will not be optional. Businesses that fail to create systems that take advantage of nearly free data storage and communication will fall prey to the competition that can create such systems. So, too, will business professionals.

The second premise for the singular importance of the MIS class relies on the work of Robert Reich, former Secretary of Labor for the Clinton administration. In *The Work of Nations*,[1] Reich identifies four essential employability skills for knowledge workers in the 21st century:

- Abstract reasoning
- Systems thinking
- Collaboration
- Experimentation

For reasons set out in Chapter 1, beginning on page 2, we believe the MIS course is the single best course in the curriculum for learning these four key skills.

While most Introduction to MIS textbooks address technical innovation and nonroutine skills, *Processes, Systems, and Information, Third Edition,* uniquely enables the Intro course to also address business processes. The process view of business is the dominant view of business today; students need a consistent, extended opportunity to master the language and apply it. The Introduction to MIS class that uses this textbook can expose both IS and non-IS students to process concepts and appropriately place IS in its vital role of supporting and improving processes. With this process foundation, students are better able to understand the benefits and challenges of ERP systems.

Background on Processes and IS

The relationship between business processes and information systems is complex. They are not one and the same; a given process might use several different information systems, and, at the same time, a given information system might support many different processes. So, we cannot

---

[1]Robert B. Reich, *The Work of Nations* (New York: Alfred A. Knopf, 1991), p. 229.

say that a process encapsulates all of its information systems, nor can we say that an information system encapsulates all of its processes.

In part because of this complex relationship, we define *MIS* as creating, monitoring, and adapting *processes, information systems, and information* to help organizations achieve their strategy (Chapter 1). The fabric of this text is woven around and through these definitions.

Potential adopters of this textbook are departments that make business processes a key component or thread throughout their curricula. This group includes all of the universities that are part of the SAP University Alliance, those that are part of the Microsoft Dynamics Academic Alliance, and other institutions for which a business process orientation is important. Chapters 8 and 9 provide specific examples of the use of SAP, and the cases that conclude each of those chapters provide tutorial exercises that use the SAP University Alliance's Global Bikes Inc. (GBI) case. This is the same case and client data used in University Alliance training, so it will be familiar to many instructors.

In our opinion, a text must go beyond the operational processes that comprise Chapters 8 and 9. Of course, operational processes are most important, and five chapters and an Appendix of our text include or are devoted to them. However, other dynamic processes, such as collaboration, project management, problem solving, business intelligence, and social networking, are also important. Hence, we -believe that this text should include much more than SAP-oriented processes.

Text Features

A challenge of teaching the Introduction to MIS course from a process orientation is the lack of business knowledge and experience on the part of most students. Many universities offer the Introduction to MIS course at the sophomore and even freshman levels. Most of these students have completed few business courses. Even when this course is taught to higher-level students, however, few of them have significant business or process experience. They have been lifeguards or baristas. When we attempt to talk about, for example, the impact of process change on departmental power, that discussion goes over the heads of students. They may memorize the terms, but they often lose the essence of the discussion. The features of this text are designed, in part, to address this problem.

Question-Based Pedagogy

Research by Marilla Svinicki in the Psychology Department of the University of Texas indicates that today's students need help managing their time. She asserts that we should never give homework assignments such as "read pages 75–95." The problem, she says, is that students will fiddle with those pages for 30 minutes and not know when they're done. Instead, she recommends that we give our students a list of questions and the assignment that they be able to answer those questions. When they can answer the questions, they're done studying. We have used this approach in our classrooms, and we believe that it is most effective. Students like it as well. Hence, we have organized each chapter as a list of questions.

Opening Vignettes

Each chapter opens with a short vignette of a business situation and problem that necessitates knowledge of that chapter. We use two different fictitious organizational settings:

1. Wood Hospital, a local hospital
2. Chuck's Bikes, Inc., a bicycle manufacturer that competes with Global Bikes

Each of these vignettes presents a situation that illustrates the use of the chapter's contents in an applied setting. Most contain a problem that requires knowledge of the chapter to understand and solve.

MIS InClass Exercises

Every chapter includes a student group exercise that is intended to be completed during class. These exercises are designed for teachers who seek to use active learning exercises, also called flipping the classroom. The purpose of the exercise is to engage the student with knowledge gained from the chapter. These exercises are part lab and part case study in nature. In our experience, some of them lead to spirited discussions, and we could have let them run on for two or three class periods, had we had that luxury.

SAP Tutorial Exercises

The appendices to Chapters 8 and 9 as well as Appendix A contain process exercises that involve the SAP Alliance's Global Bike case. Professors at institutions that are members of the alliance can use these with their students. Because not every department that uses this book is a member of that alliance, we have made these exercises optional appendices. You can omit the exercises without any loss of continuity.

The exercises are, we hope, purposeful yet simple to do. Our goal is to make it possible for them to be conducted by teaching assistants and faculty who have not yet attended the SAP university training. To that end, we provide extensive instructor support materials. Instructors who have had training by the SAP University Alliance will immediately recognize that these tutorials use exactly the same data and screens they used during training.

Earl McKinney, the author of the tutorial exercises, has been teaching SAP for 12 years at Bowling Green State University. The tutorial exercises included in this book have been tested extensively with Introduction to MIS students in a BGSU lab setting. In addition to the exercises, Earl has written a detailed teaching guide on how to best use the exercises as well as tips and pointers about their use and his experience about where students are most likely to struggle.

A fourth tutorial is offered at the end of the Chapter 12 on Business Intelligence. This tutorial uses SAP's Lumira to analyze Global Bike Inc. data. While a particular set of data is specified in the tutorial, students and instructors can also simply read the tutorial, learn how the operations like slicing and filtering are done, and use these skills on any dataset.

Over these years, Earl learned that when doing SAP exercises, it is far too easy for students to slip into "monkey-see, monkey-do" mode without any clear understanding of what they are doing or why. Based on this classroom experience, we believe that the setup to procurement and sales in Chapters 8 and 9, together with the exercises themselves, help students move beyond simple copy mode, in which they learn the SAP keystrokes, to learn the nature of process--oriented software and its role in organizations.

Like all who have used the GBI case, we are grateful to the SAP Alliance and to the case's authors. In accordance with both the letter and spirit of the SAP Alliance community's policy, we have placed these exercises on the SAP University Alliance Web site. We hope you will find sufficient value in this text to use it in your classroom, but please feel free to use these exercises even if you do not adopt this text.

By the way, the body of Chapters 8 and 9 uses the example of Chuck's Bikes, Inc., rather than GBI. We made this change at the request of the SAP Alliance. The alliance prefers that authors not add new material to GBI, change any characters, make videos, and so forth. We created CBI so as to comply with that request while at the same time providing more detailed business scenarios that are compatible with GBI.

Ethics Guides

We believe that business ethics are a critically important component of the Introduction to MIS course and that the best way to teach ethics is in the context of case-like situations. We also believe that ethics ought not to be relegated to a single chapter or chapter section. Including ethics in one place leads to the inoculation theory of education: "We don't need to discuss ethics, we've already done that." Accordingly, each chapter contains one two-page spread called an Ethics Guide. They are shown in the table of contents; to sample just one of them, turn to page 20.

In recent years, we believe there has been a shift in students' attitudes about ethics. Many students seem to be increasingly cynical and callous about ethical issues. As a result, when we try to raise interest with them about unethical behavior, we find ourselves interjecting and defending a particular set of values, a role that strikes many students as inappropriate. A common attitude seems to be, "We should think for ourselves, thank you anyway."

In frustration about the situation, we turned to a good friend of many years, Dr. Chuck Yoos, emeritus professor from the U.S. Air Force Academy. We told him our goals for presenting the Ethics Guides and asked him what criteria he would use with his students if he only had 20 minutes per guide. His response was that while there are many ways of addressing ethics in business, Kant's categorical imperative and the utilitarianism of Bentham and Mill would be at the top of his list. We investigated both and decided to use them with this edition.

Our goal in doing so is to ask students, whose ethical standards may be immature, to learn and apply the categorical imperative and utilitarianism perspectives. By doing so, students are asked to "try on" those perspectives and in the process think more deeply about ethical principles than they do when we allow them simply to apply their personal ethical standards.

The Ethics Guide in Chapter 1 introduces the categorical imperative, whereas the Ethics Guide in Chapter 2 introduces utilitarianism. If you choose to use these perspectives, you will need to assign both of those guides.

Collaboration Exercises

As stated in Chapter 1, collaboration is a key skill for today's business professionals. Accordingly, we believe that teaching collaboration, collaboration processes, and collaboration information systems is an important component of this course. To that end, each chapter includes a collaboration exercise to be accomplished by a student team. In our opinion, it is not possible for students to complete all of these in one term. Instead, we recommend using three or four of them throughout the term.

In doing these exercises, we recommend that students not meet face to face, at least not most of the time, but use modern collaboration tools for their meetings. Google Docs and related tools are one possibility. We prefer requiring students to use Microsoft OneDrive.

End-of-Chapter Cases

The chapter-opening vignettes are based on real-life experience, but the organizations they describe are fictitious. We use fictitious companies because we want students to learn from organizational mistakes and, at times, even organizational foolishness. We have not found many real companies that will allow us to share their laundry in this way, and, in any case, it seems unfair to ask for an organization's cooperation and then turn around and publish its problems.

However, we do believe students need to see examples of the role of MIS in actual organizations to help them bridge the chapter content to the real world. Hence, each chapter concludes with a case that illustrates some aspect of the chapter's contents in a real-world company.

Active Reviews

Each chapter includes an Active Review at the end. These reviews help students ensure that they have learned the most essential material. They also serve as a list of potential exam questions and thus help students prepare for exams.

Application Exercises

For courses that involve a Microsoft Office component, we have developed a set of Excel and Access exercises for all chapters. These exercises, which assume the student has beginner's level expertise with these products, appear beginning on page 448. They are listed approximately in increasing order of difficulty.

What We Left Out

We chose to keep this book to the traditional 12-chapter length because we find that this number of chapters fits best into the number of class lessons of most courses. Because we are adding substantial process-oriented material, however, that meant we needed to remove some content from the typical Introduction to MIS text.

In this text, we have reduced and simplified the discussions of hardware, software, and data communications. Furthermore, we simplified and shortened the discussion of information systems development. Finally, you will find no mention of IS departmental management in this text. It is not that we believe the shortened and omitted content is unimportant; rather, we think the opportunity cost is the least for these topics.

This text includes some material that has been previously published in David Kroenke's text *Using MIS*. The two texts differ in that *Using MIS* makes information systems primary, whereas this text makes business processes primary. Both texts will continue to be published. Because of this difference, however, every sentence that was brought over was examined from the perspective of business processes and much of that content was changed in both minor and major ways. The discussion of collaboration, for example, is reframed into the context of dynamic business processes. That said, the majority of the material in this text is new.

Chapter Outline

This text is organized into four parts: Introduction, Technology, Structured Processes, and Dynamic Processes.

Introduction

Chapter 1 sets the stage by illustrating the need for this course and especially for the behaviors and skills that students gain in the course. It defines *MIS* and summarizes the means by which organizations obtain goals and objectives. Porter's industry, five forces, and value chain models are presented.

Chapter 2 defines and illustrates processes, information systems, and information. It uses a common fast food restaurant to illustrate the relationship of processes and information systems. It also defines information using the Gregory Bateson definition that *information* is a difference that makes a difference.

Technology

Chapters 3, 4 and 5 address technology. Chapter 3 provides a quick summary of networks and the cloud. Chapter 4 discusses database processing. Security is the topic of Chapter 5. These chapters serve as a technology platform for the discussions in the remaining chapters.

Structured Processes

Chapters 6 through 9 discuss structured processes and related information systems and information. Chapter 6 provides an overview of the scope and objectives of business processes. It also discusses process adaptation and improvement and the use of process objectives and measures in making process changes. Chapter 7 is a survey of ERP information systems, their benefits, and their challenges.

Chapters 8 and 9 are "applied" chapters. They show how SAP is used in two representative processes: procurement and sales. Two processes were chosen so that students could begin to see what is common to all processes and what might differ between processes. These two processes, buying and selling, are fundamental to business and are widely used. Each chapter includes a student lab exercise appendix that uses the Global Bikes case from the SAP Alliance's curriculum.

Dynamic Processes

Chapters 10 through 12 address what we term *dynamic processes*. Such processes are neither as structured nor as rigid as the more structured operational processes. We dislike the term *unstructured processes* because we believe that such processes do have structure, at least at a meta-level. Each of the three chapters follows a similar flow: The IS that supports each process is discussed first, followed by the activities in the process, and concluding with the business processes supported by the dynamic process.

Chapter 10 discusses collaboration processes for both project management and workflow applications. Chapter 11 addresses the use of social media in organizations. We discuss Lin's theory of social capital, apply that theory to organizational use of social media systems, and survey the processes supported by social media systems. Chapter 12 considers business processes supported by business intelligence (BI) systems and discusses BI systems, data warehouses, data mining, and Big Data.

Extensions

We added 5 new Extensions to this edition of the textbook. These extensions discuss, in order, IS Careers, Software and Hardware, Process Management and IS Design, Robots and AI, and Location Based Data IS.

Appendix

With this edition we added a third structured process SAP tutorial. This tutorial takes a student through the SAP inputs required to accomplish the Production process.

Supplements

The following supplements are available at the Online Instructor Resource Center, accessible through *www.pearsonhighered.com/kroenke*.

Instructor's Manual

The Instructor's Manual, prepared by Hasan Bassam of the University of Toledo, includes a chapter outline, list of key terms, suggested answers to the MIS InClass questions, and answers to all end-of-chapter questions.

Test Item File

This Test Item File, prepared by Noreen Power of Bentley University, contains more than 1,500 questions, including multiple-choice, true/false, and essay questions. Each question is followed by the correct answer, the learning objective it ties to, page reference, AACSB category, and difficulty rating.

PowerPoint Presentations

The PowerPoints, prepared by Nancy Lamm of N. Lamm Consulting Associates, Ltd., highlight text learning objectives and key topics and serve as an excellent aid for classroom presentations and lectures.

Image Library

This collection of the figures and tables from the text offers another aid for classroom presentations and PowerPoint slides.

TestGen

Pearson Education's test-generating software is available from *www.pearsonhighered.com/irc*. The software is PC/MAC compatible and preloaded with all of the Test Item File questions. You can manually or randomly view test questions and drag and drop to create a test. You can add or modify test bank questions as needed. Our TestGens are converted for use in BlackBoard, WebCT, Moodle, D2L, and Angel. These conversions can be found on the Instructor's Resource Center. The TestGen is also available in Respondus and can be found on *www.respondus.com*.

CourseSmart

CourseSmart eTextbooks were developed for students looking to save on required or recommended textbooks. Students simply select their eText by title or author and purchase immediate access to the content for the duration of the course using any major credit card. With a CourseSmart eText, students can search for specific keywords or page numbers, take notes online, print out reading assignments that incorporate lecture notes, and bookmark important passages for later review. For more information or to purchase a CourseSmart eTextbook, visit *www.coursesmart.com*.

Acknowledgments

First, we thank the numerous fellow-traveler professors and professionals who encouraged the development of this text and who have helped us in many ways along our path. In particular, we thank:

Yvonne Antonucci, *Widener University*

Cynthia Barnes, *Lamar University*

John Baxter, *SAP*

William Cantor, *Pennsylvania State University–York Campus*

Thomas Case, *Georgia Southern University*

Gail Corbitt, *SAP*

Darice Corey, *Albertus Magnus College*

Mike Curry, *Oregon State University*

Heather Czech, *SAP*

Peter Daboul, *Western New England University*

Janelle Daugherty, *Microsoft Dynamics*

Peter DeVries, *University of Houston, Downtown*

Lauren Eder, *Rider University*

Kevin Elder, *Georgia Southern University*

John Erickson, *University of Nebraska at Omaha*

Donna Everett, *Morehead State University*

David Firth, *The University of Montana*

Jerry Flatto, *University of Indianapolis*

Kent Foster, *Microsoft*

Biswadip Ghosh, *Metropolitan State College of Denver*

Bin Gu, *University of Texas at Austin*

William Haseman, *University of Wisconsin–Milwaukee*

Jun He, *University of Michigan–Dearborn*

Mark Hwang, *Central Michigan University*

Gerald Isaacs, *Carroll University*

Stephen Klein, *Ramapo University*

Ben Martz, *University of Northern Kentucky*

William McMillan, *Madonna University*

Natalie Nazarenko, *SUNY College at Fredonia*

Timothy O'Keefe, *University of North Dakota*

Tony Pittarese, *East Tennessee State University*

Martin Ruddy, *Bowling Green State University*

James Sager, *California State University–Chico*

Narcissus Shambare, *College of Saint Mary*

Robert Szymanski, *Georgia Southern University*

Lou Thompson, *University of Texas, Dallas*

Ming Wang, *California State University*

Harold Webb, *University of Tampa*

We wish to thank the unique production team that helped us bring this book into existence. First and foremost, we thank Samantha Lewis, our editor, for her vision for a process-oriented introductory MIS text, for her untiring support throughout the process and her many excellent additions. Thanks, too, to Nancy Lamm, our developmental editor, whose direction, guidance, and patient efforts brought these ideas to life. We thank Janelle Rogers, who helped us marshal this text and all its supplements through the Pearson production process and Katie Ostler of Cenveo for her management of the project as well.

We thank our friend and colleague, Chuck Yoos, of Fort Lewis College, for hours and hours and hours of conversation on the meaning of information, the role of information in organizations today, and how to address the instruction of business ethics. Chuck is responsible for the helpful distinction between *perceiving data* and *conceiving information* and many other insights that have shaped this text's material. Chuck's Bikes is named in honor of him.

Finally, we are most grateful to our families, who have lovingly supported us through these processes; to them we dedicate this book.

Earl McKinney Jr.
Bowling Green, Ohio

David Kroenke
Whidbey Island, Washington

About the Authors

Earl McKinney Jr. Teaching the introduction to MIS course has been Earl McKinney's passion for 20 years. He first caught the bug at his alma mater, the U.S. Air Force Academy, and has continued his addiction during his tenure at Bowling Green State University. While teaching that class and other undergraduate and graduate classes, Earl has also introduced a half dozen new courses on security, social media, ERP, and information. He has been awarded a number of department and college teaching awards by students and fellow faculty. His interest in the broader context of the business curriculum is reflected in several of his publications and by the Decision Science Institute's National Instructional Innovation Award.

Earl's research in e-commerce, small team communication during a crisis, and theoretical work on the notion of information has been published in *Behaviour and Information Technology, Human Factors, Information and Management,* and *MIS Quarterly.* He consults with James Hall, the former head of the NTSB for British Petroleum, the U.S. Forest Service, and several Air Force agencies on human factors and aviation communication issues.

He holds an undergraduate economics degree from the Air Force Academy, a Master's of Engineering from Cornell University, and a PhD in MIS from the University of Texas. A former Air Force fighter pilot, Earl lives in Bowling Green with his wife and has two grown sons.

David Kroenke David Kroenke has many years of teaching experience at Colorado State University, Seattle University, and the University of Washington. He has led dozens of seminars for college professors on the teaching of information systems and technology; in 1991 the International Association of Information Systems named him Computer Educator of the Year. In 2009, David was named Educator of the Year by the Association of Information Technology Professionals-Education Special Interest Group (AITP-EDSIG).

David worked for the U.S. Air Force and Boeing Computer Services. He was a principal in the start-up of three companies. He also was vice president of product marketing and development for the Microrim Corporation and was chief of technologies for the database division of Wall Data, Inc. He is the father of the semantic object data model. David's consulting clients have included IBM, Microsoft, and Computer Sciences Corporations, as well as numerous smaller companies. Recently, David has focused on using information systems for collaboration in education and industry.

His text *Database Processing* was first published in 1977 and is now in its 13th edition. He has published many other textbooks, including *Database Concepts,* 6th ed. (2013), *Using MIS,* 7th ed. (2015), *Experiencing MIS,* 5th ed. (2015), *MIS Essentials,* 4th ed. (2015), *SharePoint for Students* (2012), and *Office 365 in Business* (2012). David lives on Whidbey Island, Washington. He has two children and three grandchildren.

To Susan, James, and Daniel   —Earl McKinney

To C.J., Carter, and Charlotte   —David Kroenke

Part 1

Why MIS?

Knowledge of information systems will be critical to your success in business. If you major in accounting, marketing, management, or another major, you may not yet know how important such knowledge will be to you. The purposes of Part 1 of this textbook are to demonstrate why this subject is so important to every business professional today and to introduce important terms and concepts that you will need to succeed in business.

Chapter 1 lays the foundation. First, we discuss why this course is of critical importance to every business student today. We claim, in fact, that it is the most important course you will take. Then we define *MIS* and explain how organizational strategy determines the structure and functions of MIS components.

In Chapter 2, we will define and illustrate business processes, information systems, and information. As you will see, these three constructs are closely interwoven. Understanding the relationships among them sets the foundation for the rest of this text.

We begin each chapter with a short business vignette to help you relate the chapter's concepts to the business world. Chapter 1 begins with Chuck's Bikes, Inc. (CBI), a bicycle wholesaler that also assembles its own line of bicycles. Throughout the text, we'll meet various employees of CBI; in Chapter 1, we see Kelly terminating an employee, for reasons that you will soon learn.

In Chapter 2, we will investigate the processes of a hospital. At the hospital we'll meet Jake and see how he puts the ideas of this textbook to work.

The Importance of MIS

"Fired? You're firing me?"

"Well, *fired* is a harsh word, but…well, Chuck's Bikes has no further need for your services."

"But, Kelly, I don't get it. I really don't. I worked hard, and I did everything you told me to do."

"Jennifer, that's just it. You did everything *I* told you to do."

"I put in so many hours. How could you fire me?"

"Your job was to find ways we can generate additional revenue from our existing retailers."

"Right! And I did that."

"No, you didn't. You followed up on ideas *that I gave you*. But we don't need someone who can follow up on my plans. We need someone who can figure out what we need to do, create her own plans, and bring them back to me…and others."

"How could you expect me to do that? I've only been here 4 months!"

"It's called teamwork. Sure, you're just learning our business, but I made sure all of our best salespeople would be available to you…"

"I didn't want to bother them."

"Well, you succeeded. I asked Jason what he thought of the plans you're working on. 'Who's Jennifer?' he asked."

"But doesn't he work out of our other office?"

"Right…and 37 percent of our sales come out of that office. Probably worth talking to him."

"I'll go do that!"

"Jennifer, do you see what just happened? I gave you an idea, and you said you'll do it. That's not what I need. I need you to find solutions on your own."

"I worked really hard. I put in a lot of hours. I've got all these sales reports written."

"Has anyone seen them?"

"I talked to you about some of them, but I was waiting until I was satisfied with them."

"Right. That's not how we do things here. We develop ideas and then kick them around with each other. Nobody has all the answers. Our plans get better when we discuss and rework them…I think I told you that."

"Maybe you did. But I'm just not comfortable with that."

"Well, it's a required skill here."

"I know I can do this job."

"Jennifer, you've been here almost 4 months; you have a degree in business. Several weeks ago, I asked you for your first idea about how to up-sell our customers. Do you remember what you said?"

"Yes, I wasn't sure how to proceed. I didn't want to just throw something out that might not work."

"But how would you find out if it would work?"

"I don't want to waste money…"

"No, you don't. So, when you didn't get very far with that task, I backed up and asked you to send me a diagram of the life cycle for new

Q1-1. Why is Introduction to MIS the most important class in the business school?

Q1-2. What is MIS?

Q1-3. How does MIS relate to organizational strategy?

Q1-4. What five forces determine industry structure?

Q1-5. What is competitive strategy?

Q1-6. How does competitive strategy determine value chain structure?

Q1-7. How does competitive strategy determine business processes and information systems?

PSI BIG PICTURE

PROCESS: A way of doing something

IS: A collection of components that produces information

INFORMATION: Meaningful insight in a person

---

clients…how we first contact them, how we make our first sale, how we grow our sales to them…"

"Yes, I sent you that diagram."

"Jennifer, it made no sense. Your diagram had clients talking to Neil in accounts receivable before they were even customers."

"I know that process; I just couldn't put it down on paper. But I'll try again!"

"Well, I appreciate that attitude, but times are tight. We don't have room for trainees. When the economy was strong, I'd have been able to look for a spot for you, see if we can bring you along. But we can't afford to do that now."

"What about my references?"

"I'll be happy to tell anyone that you're reliable, that you work 40 to 45 hours a week, and that you're honest and have integrity."

"Those are important!"

"Yes, they are. But today, they're not enough."

For a similar story, see also *www.youtube.com/watch?v=8UQx-zUuGf4.*

PREVIEW

"But today, they're not enough."

Do you find that statement sobering? And if timely hard work isn't enough, what is? We will begin this book by discussing the key skills that Jennifer (and you) needs and explain why this course is the single best course in all of the business school for teaching you those key skills.

You may find that last statement surprising. If you are like most students, you have no clear idea what your MIS class will be about. If someone were to ask you, "What do you study in that class?" you might respond that the class has something to do with computers and maybe computer programming. Beyond that, you might be hard-pressed to say more. You might add, "Well, it has something to do with computers in business," or maybe, "We are going to learn to solve business problems with computers using spreadsheets and other programs." So, how could this course be the most important one in the business school?

We begin with that question. Once you have gained an understanding of how important this class will be to your career, we will discuss fundamental concepts.

MyLab MIS

- Using Your Knowledge Questions 1-1, 1-2, 1-3
- Essay Questions 1-11, 1-12
- Excel and Access Application Questions 1-1, 1-2

Q1-1 ▸ Why Is Introduction to MIS the Most Important Class in the Business School?

Introduction to MIS is the most important class in the business school. That statement was not true in 2005, and it may not be true in 2028. But it is true in 2018.

Why?

The ultimate reason lies in a principle known as **Moore's Law**. In 1965, Gordon Moore, cofounder of Intel Corporation, stated that because of technology improvements in electronic chip design and manufacturing, "The number of transistors per square inch on an integrated chip doubles every 18 months." His statement has been commonly misunderstood to be "The speed of a computer doubles every 18 months," which is incorrect but captures the essence of his principle.

Because of Moore's Law, the ratio of price to performance of computers has fallen from something like $4,000 for a standard computing device to a fraction of a penny for that same computing device.[1] See Figure 1-1.

As a future business professional, however, you needn't care how fast a computer your company can buy for $100. That's not the point. Here's the point:

> Because of Moore's Law, the cost of data processing, communications, and storage is essentially zero.

Moore's Law is relentlessly driving down the cost of computing. As a result, computers are everywhere in business—every job requires extensive computer use, and every product you see needed IT to make it, deliver it, market it, and sell it. Seriously, every product. Look around.

This avalanche is not stopping. Moore's Law will continue to reduce costs, so Moore and Moore technology will flood business, and new opportunities will arise all the time as what was once too expensive becomes a very real possibility.

What happens when the cost of technology is essentially zero? Here are some of the recent consequences:

SoundCloud	selfies	Airbnb	Apply Pay	3D printers
Siri	FitBits	Pandora	WhatsApp	self driving cars
FaceTime	Uber	Internet of Things	the cloud	virtual reality
Snapchat	Venmo	Spotify	Big Data	Echo

FIGURE 1-1

Changes in Price/Performance of Processors

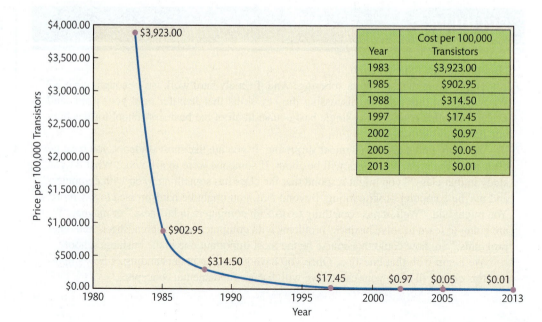

Year	Cost per 100,000 Transistors
1983	$3,923.00
1985	$902.95
1988	$314.50
1997	$17.45
2002	$0.97
2005	$0.05
2013	$0.01

These technologies and others before them have ushered in the **Information Age** where the production, distribution, and control of information are the primary drivers of the economy. Indicators of this age—the exploding quantities of data and the growth of Internet users—are shown in Figure 1-2.

There are two unique aspects of this age. First, the global world is *flat*. A new IT opportunity in India can quickly find the capital and connections needed to spread rapidly worldwide. Two, in such a flat and connected world, businesses must *adapt* quickly or be overtaken by those who do.

While the business world is driven by technology, so too are the people in it. Think about how many IT-enabled events you have participated in today—all the apps you have used, games you have played, music you have listened to, and videos you have watched as well as all your texts, posts, and tweets. In fact, the average adult spends more than 5 hours a day on their smartphones, social media, and laptops for work and entertainment.

Wherever we work or whatever we do, IT is there. Businesses need you to help them use IT wisely whether you are a graduate in MIS, accounting, marketing, or any other discipline. You need to use IT wisely to be effective at work, education, or even leisure. That's why MIS is the most important course in the business school today.

Jeff Bezos, CEO of Amazon, sees this unprecedented period of IT as the most exciting era of business: "It's pretty easy to wake up excited." We share Mr. Bezos's passion. It's an exciting time. We want you to be effective in it; we wrote this book for only that reason.

> Future business professionals need to be able to assess, evaluate, and apply emerging information technology to business.

You need the knowledge of this course to attain these skills, and having these skills will lead to greater job security.

How Can I Attain Job Security?

A wise and experienced business executive once said that the only job security that exists is "a marketable skill and the courage to use it." He continued, "There is no security in our company, there is no security in any government program, there is no security in your investments, and there is no security in Social Security." Alas, how right he turned out to be.

So, what is a marketable skill? Job seekers used to name particular skills, such as computer programming, tax accounting, or marketing. But today, because of Moore's Law, because the cost of data processing, storage, and communications is essentially zero, any routine skill can and will be outsourced to the lowest bidder. And if you live in the United States, Canada, Australia, Europe, and so on, that is unlikely to be you. Numerous organizations and experts have studied the question of what skills will be marketable during your career. Consider two of them.

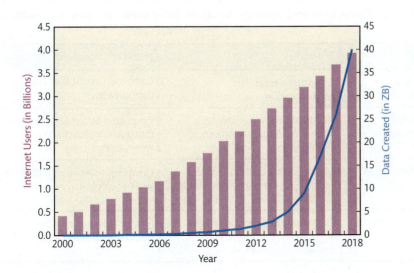

FIGURE 1-2

Data Created and Worldwide Internet Users

Source: https://recodetech.files. wordpress.com/2014/01/pimentel_ graphic-1.jpghttp://www.internetlivestats. com/internet-users/

First, the RAND Corporation, a think tank located in Santa Monica, California, has published innovative and groundbreaking ideas for more than 60 years, including the initial design for the Internet. Recently, RAND published a description of the skills that workers in the twenty-first century will need:

> Rapid technological change and increased international competition place the spotlight on the skills and preparation of the workforce, particularly the ability to adapt to changing technology and shifting demand. These shifts in the nature of organizations...favor strong nonroutine cognitive skills.[2]

Whether you are majoring in accounting or marketing or finance or information systems, you need to develop these strong nonroutine cognitive skills. These nonroutine skills will be increasingly important in the near future as robots and artificial intelligence replace more and more people doing routine work.

A second study by Robert Reich, former Secretary of Labor, enumerates these nonroutine cognitive skills, which we call the four employability skills:[3]

- Abstract reasoning
- Systems thinking
- Collaboration
- Ability to experiment

Figure 1-3 shows an example of each. Reread the CBI case that started this chapter, and you will see that Jennifer lost her job because of her inability to practice these skills.

How Can Intro to MIS Help You Learn Employability Skills?

The second reason Introduction to MIS is the best course in the business school is that it allows you to learn and practice these four key skills, because every topic will require you to apply and practice them. Here's how.

ABSTRACT REASONING **Abstract reasoning** is the ability to make and manipulate models. An abstraction is a simplification of an object; it is an idea, model or concept that can then be manipulated with a logical or reasonable thought process. You will work with one or more models in every course topic and book chapter. For example, in Chapter 2, you will learn ways to *model* business processes, and you will also learn a *model* of the five components of an information system.

In this course, you will not just manipulate models provided in this text or a model that your instructor has developed; you will also be asked to construct models of your own. In Chapter 4, for example, you will learn how to create data models, and in Chapter 5, you will learn how to make process models.

SYSTEMS THINKING Can you go to a grocery store, look at a can of green beans, and connect that can to U.S. immigration policy? Can you watch tractors dig up a forest of pulpwood trees and connect that woody trash to Moore's Law? Do you know why one of the major beneficiaries of YouTube is Cisco Systems? Answers to all of these questions require systems thinking.

FIGURE 1-3

Need for Employability Skills

Skill	Example	Jennifer's Problem
Abstract reasoning	Construct a model or representation.	Confusion about life cycle for new clients.
Systems thinking	See the whole and show how inputs and outputs relate to one another.	Confusion about when/how customers contact accounts receivable.
Collaboration	Develop ideas and plans with others. Provide and receive critical feedback.	Unwilling to work with others with work-in-progress.
Experimentation	Create and test promising new alternatives, consistent with available resources.	Fear of failure prohibited discussion of new ideas.

Systems thinking is the ability to see the whole, not just the parts; it is the ability to model the components of the system and to connect the inputs and outputs among those components into a sensible whole, one that explains the phenomenon observed. For example, why is Uber profitable as a whole, and how do inputs like riders and drivers get connected to create successful outcomes for both?

As you are about to learn, this class is about processes and information *systems*. Processes are parts of systems—the output of one process is the input to another process. For example, the process of acquiring the material to make bicycles is the input to the process of production; and the output of production is the input to the sales process. Systems thinking is also important to information systems. Throughout this book, we will discuss and illustrate systems. You will be asked to critique systems, compare alternative systems, and apply different systems to different situations. All of those tasks will prepare you for systems thinking as a professional.

COLLABORATION Here's a fact that surprises many students: Effective collaboration isn't about being nice. It includes planning discussions, anticipating reactions, being inquisitive and not defensive, educating, and influencing. Interestingly, surveys indicate the single most important skill for effective collaboration is to give and receive critical feedback. Advance a proposal in business that challenges the cherished program of the VP of marketing, and you will quickly learn that effective collaboration skills differ from party manners at the neighborhood barbeque. So, how do you advance your idea in the face of the VP's resistance? And without losing your job?

In this course, you can learn both skills and information systems that will be of use for such collaboration. Even better, you will have many opportunities to practice them. Chapter 9 will teach you collaboration skills and illustrate several sample collaboration information systems. In addition, every chapter of this book includes collaboration exercises that you may be assigned in class or as homework.

ABILITY TO EXPERIMENT

"I've never done this before."
"I don't know how to do it."
"But will it work?"
"Is it too weird for the market?"

The fear of failure is a major stumbling block that paralyzes so many good people and so many good ideas. In the days when business was stable, when new ideas were just different verses of the same song, professionals could allow themselves to be limited by the fear of failure.

But think again about the application of social networking to the oil change business. Is there a legitimate application of social networking there? If so, has anyone ever done it? Is there anyone in the world who can tell you what to do? How to proceed? No. As Reich says, professionals in the twenty-first century need to develop experimentation skills.

Successful experimentation is not throwing buckets of money at every crazy idea that enters your head. **Experimentation** is, however, making a careful and reasoned analysis of an opportunity, envisioning potential products or solutions or applications of technology, and then developing those ideas that seem to have the most promise, consistent with the resources you have. Successful experimentation also means learning from the experience: If it worked, why? If not, why not?

Experimentation is essential in a flat and connected global economy as the payoff for success in a global market is higher than ever. If a company does not experiment, it has lowered its chances of a breakthrough success. Experimentation is like drawing cards in poker or a game of cards. You do not know when a good card will come to you, but if you quit drawing cards, and your opponents continue, you're done.

In this course, you will be asked to use products with which you have no familiarity. Those products might be Microsoft Access, Visio, or something called SAP, or they might be features and functions of Blackboard that you have not used. You may be asked to collaborate using Microsoft Office 365 or Google Docs. Will your instructor explain every feature of those products that you will need? You should hope not. You should hope your instructor will leave it up to you to envision new possibilities on your own and to experiment with those possibilities, consistent with the time you have available.

FIGURE 1-4

IS Job History and Forecast Growth

Source: Bureau of Labor Statistics:
https://www.bls.gov/opub/btn/volume-2/
careers-in-growing-field-of-information-
technology-services.htm

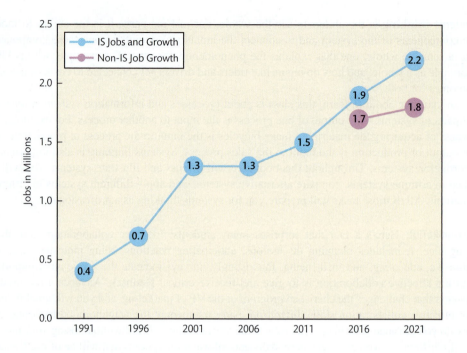

Jobs

Employment is the third reason the Introduction to MIS course is vitally important to you. During most of 2013, the U.S. unemployment rate averaged 7.5 percent over all ages and job categories; but according to the U.S. Bureau of Labor Statistics, unemployment of those ages 20 to 24 averaged over 13 percent. Employment was better for college graduates than for those without degrees, but even college grads had a high rate of unemployment. Hope Yen, writing for the Associated Press, said in April 2012 that one in two college graduates are either unemployed or underemployed.[4] But this is not the case in all job categories.

As shown in Figure 1-4, jobs in IS have grown rapidly over the past 25 years, from less than 0.5 million to now more than 2 million. The figure also shows that the anticipated growth of IS jobs for the next 5 years exceeds forecasts for job growth by all non-IS jobs.

However, information systems and computer technology provide job and wage benefits beyond just IS professionals. Acemoglu and Autor published an impressive empirical study of job and wages in the United States and parts of Europe from the 1960s to 2010.[5] They found that early in this period, education and industry were the strongest determinants of employment and salary. However, since 1990, the most significant determinant of employment and salary is the nature of work performed. In short, as the price of computer technology plummets, the value of jobs that benefit from it increases dramatically. For example, plentiful, high-paying jobs are available to business professionals who know how to use information systems to improve business process quality, interpret data mining results for improved marketing, enhance information security, or use 3D printing to create new products and address new markets.

What Is the Bottom Line?

The bottom line? This course is the most important course in the business school because:

1. It will give you the background you need to assess, evaluate, and apply emerging information systems technology to business.
2. It can give you the ultimate in job security—employability skills—by helping you learn abstract reasoning, systems thinking, collaboration, and experimentation.
3. Job opportunities.

Please give this course your best shot; we believe that effort will pay off handsomely. We understand everyone says this about their topic, so ask non-IS friends, teachers, friends of parents, and others how important is it for you to be able to use and understand how technology is employed by businesses. Think of it this way: If you were planning a future in Germany, wouldn't you want to be good with the German language? Same here—you're going into a high-tech business environment…so be good with technology language. With that introduction, let's get started![6]

Q1-2 What Is MIS?

We've used the term *MIS* several times, and you may be wondering what it is. **MIS** stands for **management information systems**, which we define as creating, monitoring, and adapting processes, information systems, and information to help organizations achieve their strategies. This definition has three key elements:

- Processes, information systems, and information
- Creating, monitoring, and adapting
- Achieve strategies

Consider each, starting with processes, information systems, and information.

Processes, Information Systems, and Information

Chapter 2 discusses these three terms and their interrelationships in detail. For now, however, consider the following intuitive definitions. A *process,* or, as it is sometimes called, a *business process,* is a way of doing something. CBI has a process for acquiring new customers. The process involves finding potential customers, contacting them, assigning a sales person, and so forth. Because organizations accomplish work via processes, focusing on them is key to improving organizational effectiveness and efficiency, as you will learn throughout this book.

An *information system* is a collection of components, including but not limited to a computer, that stores and retrieves data and produces information. Business processes and information systems are not the same things. A process may use multiple information systems, and an information system may touch many different processes. You can avoid considerable confusion by differentiating between these two concepts. Finally, *information* is a meaningful insight that helps employees do their jobs. But we're getting ahead of the story. In Chapter 2, we will formalize these definitions, explore them in detail, and investigate their relationships. Use these informal definitions as placeholders just to get started.

Creating, Monitoring, and Adapting

The next element in our definition of MIS is creating, monitoring, and adapting processes, information systems, and information, as shown in Figure 1-5.

Consider CBI's process for acquiring new customers. That process did not just pop up like a mushroom after a hard rain; it was constructed by someone to meet CBI's needs. Over time, requirements for that process will change; perhaps CBI will introduce a discount for first-time customers. CBI needs to monitor its processes to detect when a new customer places an order. When it does, the process will need to be adapted to meet the new requirements.

Similar statements apply to information systems. Information systems need to be created; computers, programs, databases, and other elements need to be constructed in such a way that they meet the requirements of the business processes that they serve. Like processes, they need to be monitored to ensure that they continue to meet their requirements, and they need to be adapted when they do not.

The same comments pertain to information. For example, managers at CBI have a set of reports that show bike sales. Over time, monitoring of manager decisions about sales may indicate that new information is needed to help managers improve those decisions. If so, the information system will need to be adapted to help managers find more meaningful insights.

At this point, you might be saying, "Wait a minute. I'm a finance (or accounting or management) major, not an information systems major. I don't need to know how to build or adapt

Processes	IS	Information
• Create	• Create	• Create
• Monitor	• Monitor	• Monitor
• Adapt	• Adapt	• Adapt

 Achieve Strategies

FIGURE 1-5
Scope of MIS

processes or information systems." If you are saying that, you are like a lamb headed for shearing. Like Jennifer, throughout your career, in whatever field you choose, you will work with processes, information systems, and information. To ensure these elements meet your needs, you need to take an *active role* in their management. Even if you are not a business analyst, a programmer, a database designer, or some other IS professional, you must take an active role in specifying process, system, and information requirements and in helping manage developmental projects to create or adapt them. Without active involvement on your part, it will only be good luck that causes processes, information systems, or information to meet your needs.

In addition to development tasks, you will also have important roles to play in the *use* of MIS. Of course, you will need to learn how to follow processes and employ information systems to accomplish your goals. But you will also have important ancillary functions as well. For example, when using an information system, you will have responsibilities for protecting the security of the system and its data. You may also have tasks for backing up data. When the system fails (most do, at some point), you will have tasks to perform while the system is down as well as tasks to accomplish to help recover the system correctly and quickly.

Achieve Strategies

The last part of the definition of MIS is that MIS exists to help organizations achieve their *strategies*. First, realize that this statement hides an important fact: Businesses themselves do not "do" anything. A business is not alive, and it cannot act. It is the people within a business who sell, buy, design, produce, finance, market, account, and manage. So, MIS exists to help people who work in a business achieve the strategies of that business.

At times, it can be difficult for organizations to stay focused on business strategy because information technology is seductive: "Our competitor is using Twitter to announce products; we better do the same." Because of the rapid pace of technology development, it can be tempting to construct information systems just to be "modern," so that the company can claim to be "world-class," or for some other reason. Constructing systems for such reasons is unwise and wasteful of both time and money. Processes, information systems, and information need to be created for the purpose of achieving the organization's strategy. Period. They are not created because the IS department thinks they need to be created or because the company is "falling behind the technology curve."

This point may seem so obvious that you wonder why we mention it. Every day, however, some business somewhere is developing an information system for the wrong reasons. Right now, somewhere in the world, a company is deciding to create a social networking site for the sole reason that "every other business has one." This company is not asking questions such as:

- "What is the purpose of our Facebook page?"
- "What is it going to do for us?"
- "What is our policy for employees' contributions to the page?"
- "What should we do about critical customer reviews?"
- "Are the costs of maintaining the page sufficiently offset by the benefits?"

Even more serious, somewhere right now an IS manager has been convinced by some vendor's sales team or by an article in a business magazine that his or her company must upgrade to the latest, greatest high-tech gizmo. This IS manager is attempting to convince his or her manager that this expensive upgrade is a good idea. We hope that someone somewhere in the company is asking questions like "What strategic goal or objective will be served by the investment in the gizmo?"

As a future business professional, you need to learn to look at information systems and technologies only through the lens of *business need*. Learn to ask, "All of this technology may be great, in and of itself, but what will it do for us? What will it do for our business and our particular strategy?"

Because strategy is so important to MIS, we will discuss the relationship between MIS and strategy in the next question and then, in the balance of this chapter, explore the relationship of MIS to value chains and related concepts.

Q1-3 ▸ How Does MIS Relate to Organizational Strategy?

According to the definition of MIS, information systems exist to help organizations achieve their strategies. As you will learn in your business strategy class, an organization's goals and objectives are determined by its *competitive strategy*. Thus, ultimately, competitive strategy

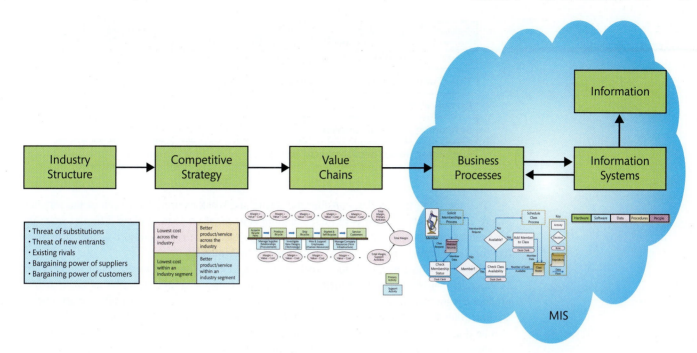

FIGURE 1-6
Organizational Strategy Determines MIS

determines the structure, features, and functions of every information system. Business processes can also influence the design of information systems. However, as you will learn in Chapter 2, the relationship between business processes and information systems is complex; in some cases, the information system's capabilities will be constrained. If so, the information system's features and functions may determine the structure of business processes as well. Finally, as shown in Figure 1-6, information systems produce information.

Michael Porter, one of the key researchers and thinkers in competitive analysis, developed three different models that can help you understand the elements in Figure 1-6. To understand this figure, we begin with Porter's five forces model.

Q1-4 ▶ What Five Forces Determine Industry Structure?

Organizational strategy begins with an assessment of the fundamental characteristics and structure of an industry. One model used to assess an industry structure is Porter's **five forces model**,[7] summarized in Figure 1-7. According to this model, five competitive forces determine industry profitability: threat of substitutes, threat of new entrants, existing rivals, bargaining power of suppliers, and bargaining power of customers. The intensity of each of the five forces determines the characteristics of the industry, how profitable it is, and how sustainable that profitability will be. Industries vary in profitability and business leaders must understand the forces that drive profitability.

FIGURE 1-7
Examples of Five Forces

Force	Example of Strong Force	Example of Weak Force
Threat of substitutions	Toyota's purchase of auto paint	Your power over the procedures and policies of your university
Threat of new entrants	Frequent traveler's choice of auto rental	Patients using the only drug effective for their type of cancer
Existing rivals	Students purchasing gasoline	Grain farmers in a surplus year
Bargaining power of suppliers	Corner latté stand	Professional football team
Bargaining power of customers	Used car dealers	Internal Revenue Service

FIGURE 1-8

Five Forces at Walmart

Force	Examples	Strength of Force
Threat of substitutes	e-commerce	Strong
Threat of new entrants	Regional chains that grow	Strong
Existing rivals	Target, Kmart, Sears	Medium
Bargaining power of suppliers	Procter & Gamble, Microsoft	Weak
Bargaining power of customers	You and I	Weak

To understand this model, consider the strong and weak examples for each of the forces in Figure 1-7. A good check on your understanding is to see if you can think of different examples for each category. Also, take a particular industry—say, auto repair—and consider how these five forces determine the competitive landscape of that industry.

Figure 1-8 illustrates how the five forces model can be applied to the retail industry and to Walmart in particular. A **substitute** performs the same or similar function as an industry's product by another means. Examples include email as a substitute for post office mail, ebooks as substitutes for traditional books, Uber for a taxi, or Airbnb for a hotel room. Substitutes can also be doing without, buying used, or doing it yourself. The threat of a substitute is stronger if the substitute's price is lower, if the benefits of the substitute are similar, and if it is easy for the buyer to switch products. For example, Walmart views e-commerce and used products as substitution threats. Walmart judges the threat from e-commerce to be high because switching costs are low and prices can be low.

The threat from new entrants is based on industry barriers to entry and the reaction new entrants can expect from established companies in the industry. **Barriers to entry** are factors that make it difficult for a new business to begin operating in an industry. Examples include high customer switching costs, large financial investments to get started, sales and distribution channels that are not accessible to new entrants, and government policies. Walmart views existing regional retailers that grow to become national retailers as a high new entrant threat because they face few barriers to entry.

The competition from industry rivals, also called copycats, is high when rivals compete with each other using price discounting, new products, and service improvements. Competition from rivals is particularly high when competitors are numerous, when industry growth is slow, and when exit barriers are high. Walmart considers Target, Kmart, and Sears to be rivals and the rivalry force medium.

The last two forces concern bargaining power forces from suppliers or from customers. The strength of these forces depends on the number of available suppliers and buyers, switching costs, the differentiation of the product, and the relative size of the firm (here Walmart) compared to the size of suppliers or customers. Walmart's suppliers include Procter & Gamble, Microsoft, and thousands of smaller players. Because there are many suppliers for Walmart to choose from, low switching costs for Walmart to switch from one to another, limited product differentiation by the suppliers, and the tremendous relative size advantage for Walmart, the bargaining power of suppliers is weak. People like you and me are Walmart's buyers, and because you have many suppliers and low switching costs and Walmart's products are not differentiated from other suppliers' products, you have some buyer power. However, that power is completely overcome by Walmart's size advantage. As a result, Walmart sees the bargaining power of its buyers as weak.

To summarize, Walmart concludes that its competitive strategy, and the IS that supports that strategy, should address e-commerce, regional threats, and industry rivals. An IS that addresses weak forces and attempts to lock in customers or prevent buyers from switching, while useful, will not be strategically aligned.

▶ Q1-5 ▶ What Is Competitive Strategy?

An organization responds to the structure of its industry by choosing a **competitive strategy**. Porter followed his five forces model with the model of four competitive strategies shown in Figure 1-9.[8] According to Porter, a firm can engage in one of four fundamental competitive

	Cost	Differentiation
Industry-wide	Lowest cost across the industry	Better product/service across the industry
Focus	Lowest cost within an industry segment	Better product/service within an industry segment

FIGURE 1-9

Porter's Four Competitive Strategies

strategies. An organization can be the cost leader and provide products at the lowest prices in the industry, or it can focus on adding value to its products to differentiate them from those of the competition. Further, the organization can employ the cost or differentiation strategy across an industry, or it can focus its strategy on a particular industry segment.

The key is for companies to commit to one of the four competitive strategies. It is always wrong to try to do more than one competitive strategy at a time. Too often a company will state a strategy of low cost leadership *and* a differentiation on customer service. The result is typically accomplishing neither, as these goals are often at odds and pursuing both sends mixed messages within the firm about which is most important. A second principle of strategy is that a competitive strategy must be distinctive and maintainable. If competitors are pursuing a similar strategy and do it better, the impact of this strategy on your company may be fatal.

Consider the car rental industry, for example. According to the first column of Figure 1-9, a car rental company can strive to provide the lowest-cost car rentals across the industry, or it can seek to provide the lowest-cost car rentals to a "focused" industry segment—say, U.S. domestic business travelers.

As shown in the second column, a car rental company can instead seek to differentiate its products from the competition. It can do so in various ways—for example, by providing a wide range of high-quality cars, by providing the best reservation system, by having the cleanest cars or the fastest check-in, or by some other means. The company can strive to provide product differentiation across the industry or within particular segments of the industry, such as U.S. domestic business travelers.

According to Porter, to be effective, the organization's goals, objectives, culture, and activities must be consistent with the organization's strategy. To those in the MIS field, this means that all processes, information systems, and information must be constructed to facilitate the organization's competitive strategy.

Consider the competitive strategy at Walmart. Walmart has chosen a low-cost strategy industry-wide. Walmart seeks to fight off threats from e-commerce, regional chains, and industry rivals by having the lowest cost structure in the industry. Keep in mind that cost is not price. Cost is what it takes to produce a product or service, while price is what people are willing to pay for it. You might also be thinking that cost leadership does not sound distinctive—couldn't several firms have this same strategy? Porter tells us that only one company in an industry can actually be the leader. If you attempt this strategy and your costs are actually higher than another firm, this may be your last strategy.

Q1-6 How Does Competitive Strategy Determine Value Chain Structure?

Organizations analyze the structure of their industry, and using that analysis, they formulate a competitive strategy. They then need to organize and structure the organization to implement that strategy. If, for example, the competitive strategy is to be the *cost leader*, then business activities should be developed to provide essential functions at the lowest possible cost.

A business that selects a *differentiation* strategy would not necessarily structure itself around least-cost activities. Instead, such a business might choose to develop more costly processes, but it would do so only if those processes provided benefits that outweighed their risks.

FIGURE 1-10

Primary Activities in the Value Chain

Primary Activity	Description
Inbound logistics	Receiving, storing, and disseminating inputs to products
Operations/manufacturing	Transforming inputs into final products
Outbound logistics	Collecting, storing, and physically distributing products to buyers
Sales and marketing	Inducing buyers to purchase products and providing a means for them to do so
Customer service	Assisting customers' use of products and thus maintaining and enhancing the products' value

Porter defined **value** as the amount of money that a customer is willing to pay for a resource, product, or service. The difference between the value that an activity generates and the cost of the activity is called the **margin**. A business with a differentiation strategy will add cost to an activity only as long as the activity has a positive margin.

A **value chain** is a network of value-creating activities. According to Porter, that generic chain consists of five primary activities and four support activities.

Primary Activities in the Value Chain

Figure 1-10 summarizes the primary activities of the value chain. **Primary activities** drive competitive advantage. Raw materials are obtained using inbound logistics activity, products and goods are produced in operations/manufacturing activity, and those products and goods are shipped to customers using outbound logistics activity. Additionally, organizations have sales and marketing as well as customer service activities.

To understand the essence of these activities, consider the bicycle wholesaler CBI (see Figure 1-11). First, CBI acquires bicycle parts (inbound logistics). This activity concerns the

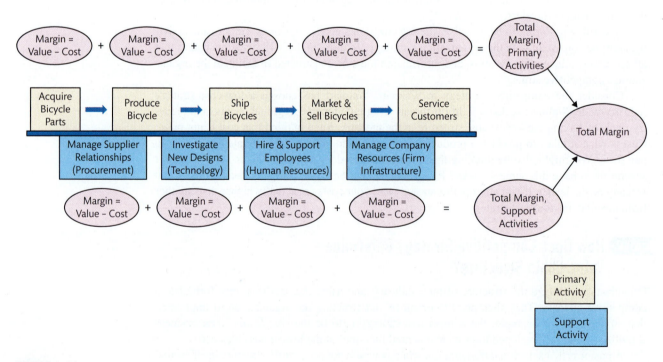

FIGURE 1-11

Bicycle Company's Value Chain

MIS InClass

Work Skills Exercise

In this chapter, we have asked you to think about work skills that are in demand in business today. For example, one might be good collaboration, another the ability to use software effectively. If you can do these skills well, you will have a better chance at finding and keeping a great job.

Step 1: In collaboration with teammates, write down six skills that you think are most in demand in business today. Each team member writes down the same list.

Step 2: In discussion with teammates, identify and circle four of these skills that your team believes are most often lacking in students.

Step 3: Evaluate yourself: On which of these four are you capable, and on which of these are you weakest?

Step 4: In discussion with teammates, decide which of these four are taught well by other classes at your school and which are not.

Step 5: Based on what you know about this class, which of the four skills can you practice in this class? How will you know that you are better at them?

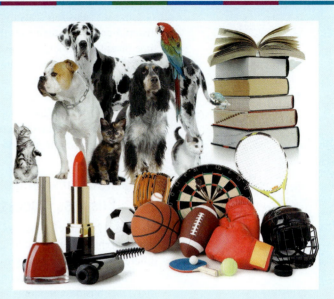

Source: monticello/Shutterstock; Eric Isselée/Shutterstock; Denis Pepin/ Shutterstock; gresei/Shutterstock.

receiving and handling of raw materials and other inputs. The accumulation of those materials adds value in the sense that even a pile of unassembled parts is worth something to some customer. A collection of the parts needed to build a bicycle is worth more than an empty space on a shelf. The value is not only the parts themselves, but also the time required to contact vendors for those parts, to maintain business relationships with those vendors, to order the parts, to receive the shipment, and so forth.

In the operations activity labeled Produce Bicycle, the bicycle maker transforms raw materials into a finished bicycle, a process that adds more value. Next, the company ships bicycles (outbound logistics) to customers. Of course, there is no customer to send the bicycle to without the marketing and sales activity. Finally, the customer service activity provides support to the bicycle users.

Each stage of this generic chain accumulates costs and adds value to the product. The net result is the total margin of the chain, which is the difference between the total value added and the total costs incurred.

Support Activities in the Value Chain

The **support activities** in the generic value chain contribute or facilitate the primary value chain activities. They include procurement, technology, human resources, and firm infrastructure.

Porter defined *procurement* as the processes of finding vendors, setting up contractual arrangements, and negotiating prices. He defined *technology* broadly. It includes research and development, but it also includes other activities within the firm for developing new techniques, methods, and procedures. He defined *human resources* as recruiting, compensation, evaluation, and training of full- and part-time employees. Finally, *firm infrastructure* includes general management, finance, accounting, legal, and government affairs.

Supporting functions add value, albeit indirectly, and they also have costs. Hence, as shown in Figure 1-11, supporting activities contribute to a margin. In the case of supporting activities, it would be difficult to calculate the margin because the specific value added of, say, the manufacturer's lobbyists in Washington, D.C., is difficult to know. But there is a value added, there are costs, and there is a margin, even if it is only in concept.

Value Chain Linkages

Porter's model of business activities includes **linkages**, which are interactions across value activities. For example, manufacturing systems use linkages to reduce inventory costs. Such a system uses sales forecasts to plan production; it then uses the production plan to determine raw material needs and then uses the material needs to schedule purchases. The end result is just-in-time inventory, which reduces inventory sizes and costs.

By describing value chains and their linkages, Porter started a movement to create integrated, cross-departmental business systems. Over time, Porter's work led to the creation of a new discipline called business process design. The central idea is that organizations should not automate or improve existing functional systems. Rather, they should create new, more efficient business processes that integrate the activities of all departments involved in a value chain. We will revisit this idea of activity integration throughout this book when we examine process improvement.

Q1-7 How Does Competitive Strategy Determine Business Processes and Information Systems?

Figure 1-12 shows a business process for renting bicycles. The value-generating activities are shown in the top of the table, and the implementation of those activities for two companies with different competitive strategies is shown in the rows that follow.

The first company has chosen a competitive strategy of low-cost rentals to students. Accordingly, this business implements business processes to minimize costs. The second company has chosen a differentiation strategy. It provides "best-of-breed" rentals to executives at a high-end conference resort. Notice that this business has designed its business processes to ensure superb service. To achieve a positive margin, it must ensure that the value added will exceed the costs of providing the service.

Now, consider the information systems required for these business processes. The processes used by the student rental business require minimal information systems support. The only computer/-software/data component in its business is the machine provided by its bank for processing credit card transactions.

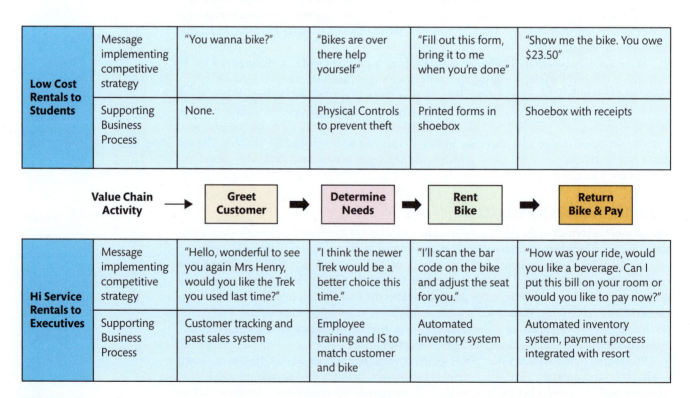

		Greet Customer	Determine Needs	Rent Bike	Return Bike & Pay
Low Cost Rentals to Students	Message implementing competitive strategy	"You wanna bike?"	"Bikes are over there help yourself"	"Fill out this form, bring it to me when you're done"	"Show me the bike. You owe $23.50"
	Supporting Business Process	None.	Physical Controls to prevent theft	Printed forms in shoebox	Shoebox with receipts
Value Chain Activity →		**Greet Customer**	**Determine Needs**	**Rent Bike**	**Return Bike & Pay**
Hi Service Rentals to Executives	Message implementing competitive strategy	"Hello, wonderful to see you again Mrs Henry, would you like the Trek you used last time?"	"I think the newer Trek would be a better choice this time."	"I'll scan the bar code on the bike and adjust the seat for you."	"How was your ride, would you like a beverage. Can I put this bill on your room or would you like to pay now?"
	Supporting Business Process	Customer tracking and past sales system	Employee training and IS to match customer and bike	Automated inventory system	Automated inventory system, payment process integrated with resort

FIGURE 1-12

Operations Value Chain and Business Processes for Bicycle Rental Companies

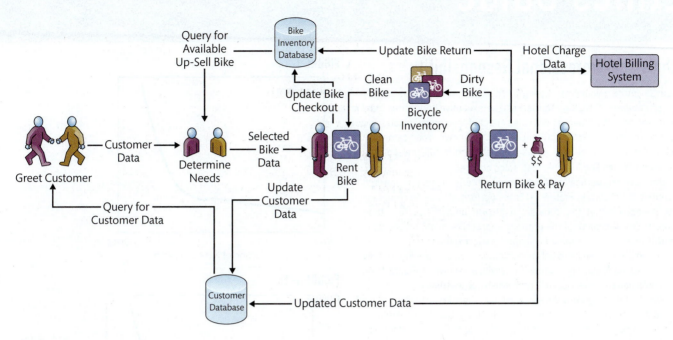

FIGURE 1-13

Business Process and Information Systems for High-Service Bike Rental

The high-service business uses processes that require more sophisticated information systems, as shown in Figure 1-13. It has a sales tracking database that tracks past customer rental activity and an inventory database that is used to select and up-sell bicycle rentals as well as control bicycle inventory with a minimum of fuss to its high-end customers.

To see how competitive strategy affects processes and information at a large firm, once again consider Walmart. Instead of the four simple value chain activities as shown in the top of Figure 1-12, Walmart would have hundreds of activities and hundreds of business processes. To be the low-cost leader in the industry, Walmart uses very sophisticated IS to link its activities and processes together to reduce cost and create value.

So the bottom line is this: Organizations analyze their industry and choose a competitive strategy. Given that strategy, they examine their value chain and design business processes that span value-generating activities. Those processes determine the scope and requirements of each organization's information systems. This textbook's main focus is to help you better understand business processes and the information systems that support them. In our next chapter, we examine processes and information systems in more depth and introduce the topic of information, the final element of Figure 1-6.

In general, IS can influence strategy by offering new opportunities to address the five forces. For example, IS can reduce the threat of new competitors or change bargaining power by raising switching costs for suppliers or customers. In addition to affecting the five forces, IS influences strategy when it offers new opportunities for differentiation. For example, a supplier can differentiate itself using IS to become a leader in customer responsiveness or to become the leader in ecological stewardship. Finally, IS can influence strategy when an organization uses IS to pursue a low-cost competitive strategy.

In this chapter, and in most of this textbook, we contend that IS should support strategy. However, in some cases, IS can also shape or influence strategy. For example, a firm may want to offer a new product or service that is highly dependent on an IS. A car manufacturer may decide to offer a self-driving vehicle, a university a new online curriculum, or a financial institution a new way to apply for a loan via a new technology. In these cases, new advancements in IT are influencing strategy. Without the IS, the strategy would be impossible.

Before closing, we must also point out that strategy continually evolves. Every organization periodically must assess its strategy and decide if it needs to be altered. Strategic planning should always ask what is next, which markets and products should we exit, and how is our industry changing.

Ethics Guide

Ethics and Professional Responsibility

Suppose you're a young marketing professional who has just taken a new promotional campaign to market. The executive committee asks you to present a summary of the sales effect of the campaign, and you produce the graph shown in Figure 1-14. As shown, your campaign was just in the nick of time; sales were starting to fall the moment your campaign kicked in. After that, sales boomed.

But note the vertical axis has no quantitative labels. If you add quantities, as shown in Figure 1-15, the performance is less impressive. It appears that the substantial growth amounts to less than 20 units. Still, the curve of the graph is impressive, and if no one does the arithmetic, your campaign will appear successful.

This impressive shape is only possible, however, because Figure 1-15 is not drawn to scale. If you draw it to scale, as shown in Figure 1-16, your campaign's success is, well, problematic, at least for you.

Which of these graphs do you present to the committee?

Each chapter of this text includes an Ethics Guide that explores ethical and responsible behavior in a variety of MIS-related contexts. In this chapter, we'll examine the ethics of data and information.

Centuries of philosophical thought have addressed the question "What is right behavior?" and we can't begin to discuss all of it here. You will learn much of it, however, in your business ethics class. For our purposes, we'll use two of the major pillars in the philosophy of ethics. We introduce the first one here and the second in Chapter 2.

The German philosopher Immanuel Kant defined the **categorical imperative** as the principle that one should behave only in a way that one would want the behavior to be a universal law. Stealing is not such a behavior because if everyone steals, nothing can be owned.

When you ask whether a behavior is consistent with this principle, a good litmus test is "Are you willing to publish your behavior to the world? If not, your behavior is not ethical, at least not in the sense of Kant's categorical imperative.

We will apply these principles in the chapters that follow. For now, use them to assess your beliefs about Figures 1-14 to 1-16 by answering the following questions.

Source: .shock/Fotolia

FIGURE 1-14

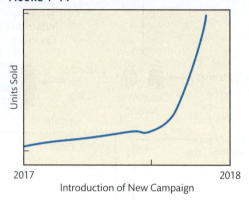

Units Sold

2017 — Introduction of New Campaign — 2018

FIGURE 1-15

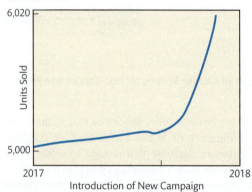

6,020

Units Sold

5,000

2017 — Introduction of New Campaign — 2018

FIGURE 1-16

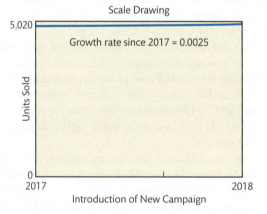

Scale Drawing

5,020

Growth rate since 2017 = 0.0025

Units Sold

0

2017 — Introduction of New Campaign — 2018

DISCUSSION QUESTIONS

1. Restate Kant's categorical imperative using your own words. Explain why cheating on exams is not consistent with the categorical imperative.

2. While there is some difference of opinion, most scholars believe that the Golden Rule ("Do unto others as you would have them do unto you.") is not as limiting to behavior as Kant's categorical imperative. Justify this belief.

3. Change roles. Assume now you are a member of the executive committee. A junior marketing professional presents Figure 1-14 to the committee and you object to the lack of labels and the scale. In response, the junior marketing professional says, "Sorry, I didn't know. I just put the data into Excel and copied the resulting graph." What conclusions do you, as an executive, make about the junior marketing professional in response to this statement?

4. As the junior marketing professional, which graph do you present to the committee?

5. According to Kant, lying is not consistent with the categorical imperative. Suppose you are invited to a seasonal BBQ at the department chair's house. You are served a steak that is tough, over-cooked, and so barely edible that you secretly feed it to the department chair's dog (who appears to enjoy it). The chairperson asks you, "How is your steak?" and you respond, "Excellent, thank you."
   a. Is your behavior consistent with Kant's categorical imperative?
   b. The steak seemed to be excellent to the dog. Does that fact change your answer to a?
   c. What conclusions do you draw from this example?

ACTIVE REVIEW

Use this Active Review to verify that you understand the material in the chapter. You can read the entire chapter and then perform the tasks in this review, or you can read the text material for just one question and perform the tasks in this review for that question before moving on to the next one.

Q1-1 Why is Introduction to MIS the most important class in the business school?

Define *Moore's Law* and explain why its consequences are important to business professionals today. Explain the trends in IT being driven by Moore's Law. Describe the key aspects of the Information Age. Give the text's definition of *job security*, and use Reich's enumeration of four key skills to explain how this course will help you attain that security. Summarize IS-related job opportunities.

Q1-2 What is MIS?

Define *MIS*. Describe, in the intuitive manner used in this chapter, the meaning of processes, information systems, and information. Explain the meaning of creating, monitoring and adapting, and summarize the reasons why this text claims it is important to all businesspeople, not just MIS professionals. Explain the confusion in the statement "organizations achieve their strategies." Summarize why it can be difficult for organizations to focus their MIS on organizational strategy.

Q1-3 How does MIS relate to organizational strategy?

Summarize the reasons that the Porter models are relevant to MIS. Diagram and explain the relationship among industry structure, competitive strategy, value chains, business processes, information systems, and information.

Q1-4 What five forces determine industry structure?

Name and briefly describe the five forces. Give your own examples of both strong and weak forces of each type, similar to Figure 1-7. Define *substitute, barrier to entry,* and *switching cost.* Explain how they are used by the five forces.

Q1-5 What is competitive strategy?

Describe four different competitive strategies, as defined by Porter. Give an example of four different companies that have implemented each of the strategies.

Q1-6 How does competitive strategy determine value chain structure?

Define the terms *value, margin,* and *value chain.* Explain why organizations that choose a differentiation strategy can use value to determine a limit on the amount of extra cost to pay for differentiation. Name the primary and support activities in the value chain and explain the purpose of each. Explain the concept of linkages.

Q1-7 How does competitive strategy determine business processes and information systems?

Describe the relationship between a value chain and a business process. Explain how business processes relate to competitive strategy. Explain how information systems relate to competitive strategy. Justify the comments in the two rows labeled "Supporting business process" in Figure 1-12.

KEY TERMS AND CONCEPTS

Abstract reasoning 6	Information Age 5	Primary activities 14
Barriers to entry 12	Linkages 16	Substitute 12
Categorical imperative 18	Management information systems	Support activities 15
Competitive strategy 12	(MIS) 9	Systems thinking 7
Experimentation 7	Margin 14	Value 14
Five forces model 11	Moore's Law 4	Value chain 14

USING YOUR KNOWLEDGE

1-1. One of life's greatest gifts is to be employed doing work
MyLab MIS   that you love. Reflect for a moment on a job that you
would find so exciting that you could hardly wait to get
to sleep on Sunday night so that you could wake up and
go to work on Monday.

a. Describe that job. Name the industry, the type of company or organization for whom you'd like to work, the
products and services it produces, and your specific
job duties.

b. Explain what it is about that job that you find so
compelling.

c. In what ways will the skills of abstract reasoning,
systems thinking, collaboration, and experimentation
facilitate your success in that job?

d. Given your answers to parts a–c, define three to five
personal goals for this class. None of these goals
should include anything about your GPA. Be as specific as possible. Assume that you are going to evaluate yourself on these goals at the end of the quarter
or semester. The more specific you make these goals,
the easier it will be to perform the evaluation. Use
Figure 1-3 for guidance.

1-2. Suppose you decide to start a business that recruits stu-
MyLab MIS   dents for summer jobs. You will match available students
with available jobs. You need to learn what positions
are available and what students are available for filling
those positions. In starting your business, you know
you will be competing with local newspapers, Craigslist
(*www.craigslist.org*), and your college. You will probably have other local competitors as well.

a. Analyze the structure of this industry according to
Porter's five forces model.

b. Given your analysis in part a, recommend a competitive strategy.

c. Describe the primary value chain activities as they
apply to this business.

d. Describe a business process for recruiting students.

e. Describe information systems that could be used to
support the business process in part d.

f. Explain how the process you described in part d and
the system you described in part e reflect your competitive strategy.

1-3. Consider the two different bike rental companies in
MyLab MIS   Figure 1-12. Think about the bikes they rent. Clearly,
the student bikes will be just about anything that can
be ridden out of the shop. The bikes for the business
executives, however, must be new, shiny, clean, and in
tip-top shape.

a. Compare and contrast the operations value chains of
these two businesses as they pertain to the management of bicycles.

b. Describe a business process for maintaining bicycles
for both businesses.

c. Describe a business process for acquiring bicycles for
both businesses.

d. Describe a business process for disposing of bicycles
for both businesses.

e. What roles do you see for information systems in your
answers to the earlier questions? The information systems can be those you develop within your company,
or they can be those developed by others, such as
Craigslist.

1-4. Using Monster.com or the Bureau of Labor Statistics
(www.bls.gov/bls/occupation.htm), read about a job you
are interested in pursuing after graduation. Specify:

a. What skills are required?

b. What education level is required?

c. What is the entry-level pay range?

d. Go to LinkedIn and create an account if you do not
already have one. Using search, find professionals
who are working at the job you specified. Write down
their career path, that is, the jobs they did prior to their
current job. Scroll down on their LinkedIn page and
record their experience and featured skills.

COLLABORATION EXERCISE 1

Collaborate with a group of fellow students to answer the following questions. For this exercise, do not meet face to face.
Your task will be easier if you coordinate your work with
SharePoint, Office, Google Docs or equivalent collaboration
tools. (See Chapter 10 for a discussion of collaboration tools
and processes.) Your answers should reflect the thinking of the
entire group, not just that of one or two individuals.

1. Abstract reasoning.

a. Define *abstract reasoning,* and explain why it is an
important skill for business professionals.

b. Explain how a list of items in inventory and their quantity on hand is an abstraction of a physical inventory.

c. Give three other examples of abstractions commonly
used in business.

d. Explain how Jennifer failed to demonstrate effective
abstract reasoning skills.

e. Can people increase their abstract reasoning skills? If
so, how? If not, why not?

2. Systems thinking.

a. Define *systems thinking,* and explain why it is an
important skill for business professionals.

b. Explain how you would use systems thinking to
explain why Moore's Law caused a farmer to dig up
a field of pulpwood trees. Name each of the elements
in the system, and explain their relationships to each
other.

c. Give three other examples of the use of systems thinking
with regard to consequences of Moore's Law.

d. Explain how Jennifer failed to demonstrate effective systems-thinking skills.
e. Can people improve their systems-thinking skills? If so, how? If not, why not?

3. Collaboration.
   a. Define *collaboration,* and explain why it is an important skill for business professionals.
   b. Explain how you are using collaboration to answer these questions. Describe what is working with regard to your group's process and what is not working.
   c. Is the work product of your team better than the product any one of you could have produced separately? If not, your collaboration is ineffective. If that is the case, explain why.
   d. Does the fact that you cannot meet face to face hamper your ability to collaborate? If so, how?
   e. Explain how Jennifer failed to demonstrate effective collaboration skills.
   f. Can people increase their collaboration skills? If so, how? If not, why not?

4. Experimentation.
   a. Define *experimentation,* and explain why it is an important skill for business professionals.
   b. Explain several creative ways you could use experimentation to answer this question.
   c. How does the fear of failure influence your willingness to engage in any of the ideas you identified in part b?
   d. Explain how Jennifer failed to demonstrate effective experimentation skills.

e. Can people increase their willingness to take risks? If so, how? If not, why not?
f. Do you think IS make experimentation easier or harder?

5. Job security.
   a. State the text's definition of *job security*.
   b. Evaluate the text's definition of job security. Is it effective? If you think not, offer a better definition of job security.
   c. As a team, do you agree that improving your skills on the four dimensions in Collaboration Exercise 1 will increase your job security?
   d. Do you think technical skills (accounting proficiency, financial analysis proficiency, and so on) provide job security? Why or why not? Do you think you would have answered this question differently in 1980? Why or why not?

6. Apply the models in Figure 1-6 to a company of your choosing. Specify the strength of each of the five forces, select a competitive strategy, identify value-adding activities, diagram a process, and describe the information system that will support your analysis.

7. Using Google, find out how to follow experts on Twitter. Discuss as a team one potential job area that some of you are interested in working in after graduation. Have one person on your team log into Twitter. Find an expert on Twitter in that job area. Record the Twitter handle and an interesting tweet from this account.

CASE STUDY 1

Tesla: Driving Competitive Strategy

On a bright, sunny afternoon in May 2016, Joshua Brown was driving down a divided highway in Florida. The 40-year-old entrepreneur from Ohio lost his life when his Tesla Model S crashed into a semitrailer that was turning onto the highway. This tragic accident was particularly significant as it was the first fatal car accident involving a self-driving car. Mr. Brown had engaged the Tesla's autopilot, which was designed to hold the car in its lane and to brake for obstacles, but the autopilot failed to apply brakes, and sadly, Mr. Brown failed to also.

Tesla has a short and dynamic history. It launched its first car, the Roadster, in 2009 with great hype and fanfare but failed to ignite excitement by financial experts, many of whom expected the company not to survive. The following year, despite these expectations of early failure, its IPO raised $225 million. By 2014, it had a market value of half of Ford Motor Co. Tesla now produces the Model S, for about $75,000 MSRP, and Model X, shown in Figure 1-17, for about $80,000. The company churns out 60,000 vehicles a year while leading the industry in battery life and car performance. In the coming years, Tesla intends to introduce much less expensive vehicles—in the range of $30,000 to $40,000. Tesla

has become both an automotive and battery storage company that designs, builds, and sells cars, power trains, and batteries.

The dream of self-driving cars first emerged in a 1939 World's Fair exhibit by General Motors. By 1958, Chevy was testing a car that could sense electrical current embedded in the road below it and adjust its driving to stay over top of the current. Twenty years later, Volkswagen developed a robotic cart, intended for the space program, that could navigate its way across a chair-filled room in the amazing time of five hours. Then, in 1995, a group of Carnegie Mellon University robotic experts drove a specially equipped Pontiac Trans Am across America, 98 percent of the time hands free.

Before the accident with Mr. Brown, Tesla cars had driven more than 130 million miles using the autopilot feature. Elon Musk, the billionaire CEO of Tesla, promoted the autopilot feature to differentiate his cars as high-tech within the electric car market. Tesla is also unique in the industry as it sells its cars directly to the customer without any dealerships. Tesla sees itself as an industry disruptor.

Tesla technology is world-class. The range and recharge time of its battery lead the market, its battery is as small as any in the

FIGURE 1-17

business, and its engine is more responsive and powerful than competitors. Tesla also seeks to lead the industry in self-driving features. The Tesla autopilot feature uses sensors, cameras, a front radar, and digitally controlled brakes. Tesla provides software updates to cars already in use when autopilot improvements pass initial safety tests.

Tesla calls its use of self-driving features its "public beta phase." Musk says those who participate during this phase of testing help Tesla improve its technology. Tesla contends that its autopilot features in the beta phase are thoroughly tested and evaluated before they are put in use by consumers. However, they contend that putting the technology to work on actual roads with actuals vehicles is the only way the software can learn, improve, and become highly reliable.

Tesla knows that its self-driving software has bugs in it, as every piece of software does. However, it contends that involving actual drivers to help them remove these bugs is faster and more effective than more in-company testing. Critics would claim that a company is responsible for ensuring safety before a product is released. Is Tesla releasing an unsafe product, or is it making the world safer by its approach? With new technology often come new questions.

Questions

1-5. What is their competitive strategy?

1-6. Which of the five forces affect the sports car industry the most? The least?

1-7. Do you think it is ethical to test new technology such as autopilot features on the public? How should a company decide when it is safe to release a new feature that will drive sales?

1-8. What other technology can or should Tesla use to make its cars safer?

1-9. Which of the four employability skills are Tesla engineers demonstrating when they develop their self-driving features?

1-10. Which of the company's value chain activities do you believe creates its greatest margin?

CHAPTER RESOURCES

1 These figures represent the cost of 100,000 transistors, which can roughly be translated into a unit of a computing device. For our purposes, the details don't matter. If you doubt any of this, just look at low-end smartphones for less than $250 and cell plans for less than $50 a month.

2 Lynn A. Karoly and Constantijn W. A. Panis, *The 21st Century at Work* (Santa Monica, CA: RAND Corporation, 2004), p. xiv.

3 Robert B. Reich, *The Work of Nations* (New York: Alfred A. Knopf, 1991), p. 229.

4 Hope Yen, "1 in 2 new graduates are jobless or underemployed," Associated Press April 23, 2012, http://news.yahoo.com/1-2-graduates-jobless-underemployed-140300522.html.

5 Daron Acemoglu and David Autor, "Skills, Tasks, and Technologies: Implications for Employment and Earnings" (working paper), National Bureau of Economic Research June 2010, www.nber.org/papers/w16082.

6 For another perspective on the importance of these skills, read www.nytimes.com/2011/07/13/opinion/13friedman.html?_r=1.

7 Michael Porter, *Competitive Strategy: Techniques for Analyzing Industries and Competitors* (New York: Free Press, 1980).

8 Michael Porter, *Competitive Strategy* (New York: Free Press, 1980).

MyLab MIS

Go to **MyLab MIS.com** for Auto-graded writing questions as well as the following Assisted-graded writing questions:

1-11. In the chapter we quote a business executive who said the only job security is a marketable skill and the courage to use it. We then outlined the four marketable skills on page 6. For each of the four marketable skills, rate yourself on a 5 point scale with 5 being the highest, then explain why you believe that is an accurate assessment.

1-12. The U.S. Department of Labor publishes descriptions of jobs, educational requirements, and the outlook for many jobs and professions. Go to its site at *www.bls.gov*. Search for the job title *systems analyst*. Describe the job and its growth projection. Use a search engine and find articles that describe the job of the systems analyst. Which aspects of this job are most attractive to you, and which aspects are least attractive to you?

Chapter 2

Business Processes, Information Systems, and Information

During his afternoon shift, Jake was walking back to his office in the hospital along a long, straight hallway, lost in thought. As he passed the X-ray waiting room, he was surprised to see the area was packed with patients. "Maybe we're having a sale on X-rays today," he mused. He stopped at the check-in desk to ask Sally, the long-suffering receptionist, if there was an explanation for the flash mob.

"Hi Sally, is it free pizza with your X-rays today?"

"Jake, it's good to see you. No, no free pizza. We've made this crowd ourselves. We're terribly disorganized."

"Is nobody working back in X-ray?"

"That's not it—there are three technicians back there. It's the stupid orderlies. We need them to take the patients back to the X-ray room, but they don't care as much as you did when you interned here. They don't care about the patients, just themselves." Sally is about explode.

"There are two on for today, but one got called away upstairs, and the other, well, I'm not sure. We haven't seen him in a while, maybe he's at lunch, maybe they needed him at pre-op, maybe he's outside smoking, he never tells us. I know you're a millennial, Jake, but good Lord, every one else in your generation is so lazy and self-centered. Maybe we should put a bell on them so we can hear them when they wander off. I give up."

"Well, let me put on a coat and take the patients back until my meeting. Who's next on the list?"

After substituting as an orderly for an hour, Jake heads off to his weekly staff meeting. As the meeting draws to a close, Joe Smit, the director of patient services, asks for other inputs, and Jake tells the group about his recent experience at X-ray and Sally's meltdown.

Joe asks, "Do you think this was just a one-time thing, or does this happen a lot?"

"You mean Sally insulting my generation? Well, that is fairly common. But if you mean the orderlies, Sally told me she sees this about once every couple of weeks. They get behind, and it just snowballs, and they can't call anyone to bail them out. She sees us wasting patients' time but doesn't know what to do."

Joe asks, "Maybe she's right. Maybe we should fire the orderlies and hire more motivated people. Why can't we find good orderlies? Is it an attitude problem? Or have we just spread them too thin?"

"Maybe we should require patients get appointments for X-ray to smooth things out," offers Mary from accounting.

"Have we tried keeping the X-ray orderlies in X-ray and have someone else move patients around upstairs?" suggests Bill.

Q2-1.   What is a business process?

Q2-2.   What is an information system?

Q2-3.   How do business processes and information systems relate?

Q2-4.   How do structured and dynamic processes vary?

Q2-5.   What is information?

Q2-6.   What are necessary data characteristics?

Q2-7.   How can I use these topics at work?

PSI BIG PICTURE

PROCESS: A sequence of activities to accomplish a function

IS: Five components: Hardware, Software, Data, Procedures, People

INFORMATION: A difference that makes a difference

After several other ideas are forwarded and withdrawn, Jake floats another idea. "Maybe it's not motivation. Maybe the orderlies are pulled away and don't know they should return. What if we put an app on the orderlies' phones so we could track their location and text them when we need them to return to X-ray?"

"What if they don't have smartphones? It costs too much to buy everyone a phone." Mary leads a chorus of naysayers.

Henry from HR chimes in, "I'm pretty sure we can't spy on their whereabouts using their phones anyway."

Jake takes another swing. "What about something like a FitBit or something that simple? Something that we could use to see their location and send them a text. We'd just have to buy three or four—that can't cost too much."

Surprised by the silence, Jake pushes on. "It wouldn't just make the X-ray unit better. By using the orderlies this way, we can better schedule them to discharge patients, send them to the psych ward when trouble breaks out there, and have them assist in pre-op when needed. Instead of having orderlies assigned to each of these places we pool the orderlies and text them when and where they are needed. We can test it out in X-ray, and if that little experiment works, we can just add in the other wards one at a time."

Mary is warming to the idea. "It seems to me that half of the time I see the orderlies they aren't busy, so this might make better use of them."

Joe concludes the meeting. "I did orderly work as an intern here. I'll do a couple of shifts next week, and we can use our smartphones to give it a try before we go any further. It's worth a shot, I think."

PREVIEW

In Chapter 1, we defined MIS as creating, monitoring, and adapting business processes, information systems, and information to help organizations achieve their strategies. This chapter extends that initial discussion by defining and describing that definition's three fundamental terms: business process, information system, and information. We begin by describing the features of business processes. Then we will introduce you to the standard way of documenting business processes. Because processes depend on information systems, we follow our discussion of business processes by defining information systems and describing their components. Then we explain how business processes and information systems relate. Next, we present several definitions of information to better understand where and how information is created. Finally, because information depends on data, we discuss factors that influence data quality.

MyLab MIS

- Using Your Knowledge Questions 2-1, 2-2, 2-3
- Essay Questions 2-15, 2-16
- Excel and Access Application Questions 2-1, 2-2

Q2-1 What Is a Business Process?

Processes are everywhere, but they are invisible, if that is possible. Look around the room you are sitting in. Do you see anything, any object that was not made by a business process? While the process is not visible, the result is. Every piece of furniture, the flooring, the lights, the technology, the decorations, the windows, the paint, the doors, the books; everything is the output of a business process. Every business has these processes, and whether you work in human resources, sales, accounting, supply chain, or IS you will play many roles in many processes every day.

Not only are they everywhere, they are essential to business success. Businesses compete with processes like sports teams compete with their plays. The hospital in the opening vignette did not have an effective process in the X-ray unit until Jake suggested one. We want you to be like Jake when you take your first job—you can look at a situation, determine the processes in play, and know how to make them better. Understanding processes, how they work with information systems, and information will help you in every business job you'll ever have.

A **business process** is a sequence of activities for accomplishing a function. For example, your university has business processes to:

- Add a class to the business curriculum
- Add a new section to a class schedule
- Assign a class to a classroom
- Drop a class section
- Record final grades

An **activity** is a task within a business process. Examples of activities that are part of the record final grades process are:

- Compute final grades
- Fill out grade reporting form
- Submit the grade reporting form to the departmental administrator

A process view is like systems thinking, described in Chapter 1. A business process is a system composed of activities that take inputs and create outputs.

Business processes also involve resources, such as people, computers, and data and document collections. To show how resources are connected to business processes, next we explain how processes and resources can be diagrammed using a typical Drive-Thru process at a fast food restaurant as our example.

An Example Business Process

DOCUMENTING BUSINESS PROCESSES To talk meaningfully about business processes, we need some way of documenting each process and activity. Documenting a process is like diagramming a play in a team sport; it helps everyone involved see their part and the whole. To use the terms from Chapter 1, a process document is an abstraction of an actual set of activities. The computer industry has created dozens of techniques for documenting business processes over the years, and this text will use one of them known as the **Business Process Model and Notation (BPMN) standard.** We use this technique because it is a global standard and is widely used in industry. Microsoft Visio Premium,[1] for example, includes templates for creating process drawings using BPMN symbols. We will use BPMN diagrams in many of the upcoming chapters.

Figure 2-1 is a BPMN model of the Drive-Thru process at a fast food restaurant. Each of the long columns is headed by a name such as *Cashier* and *Food Runner*. To begin the process, the *Cashier* greets the customer and asks for his or her order. The cashier records the order in a computer system called the *Order Tracker*. After the customer pays the *Cashier* at the first drive-thru window, the customer pulls forward and is given his or her order by the *Presenter*. The *Food Runner* is directed by the *Presenter* to bag the food items when the runner's assistance would help.

Each of the four columns in Figure 2-1 identifies a **role**, which is a subset of the activities in a business process that is performed by a particular actor. **Actors** can be people; an employee plays the role of *Food Runner* in the Drive-Thru process. As you will learn, actors can also be computers, such as the *Order Tracker*, but that's getting ahead of the story. Actors, whether they are people or computers, are expected to be able to perform all the activities assigned to them for a given role.

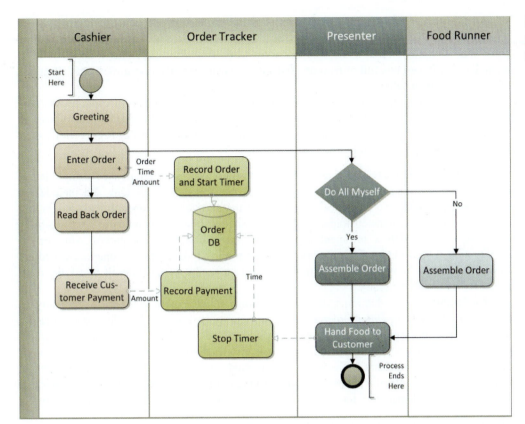

FIGURE 2-1

Fast Food Restaurant Drive-Thru BPMN Diagram

The long columns in Figure 2-1 are called **swimlanes**; each lane contains all the activities for a particular role. Swimlanes make it easy to determine which roles do what. According to the BPMN standard, the process starts at a circle with a narrow border and ends at a circle with a heavy border. Thus, in Figure 2-1, the business process starts at the top of the *Cashier* swimlane and ends at the heavy-bordered circle at the end of the *Presenter* swimlane.

The BPMN standard defines dozens of symbols; the symbols we will use in this text are summarized in Figure 2-2. Activities are shown in rectangles with rounded corners, and decisions are shown by diamonds. A solid arrow shows the flow of action; the solid arrow between Read Back Order and Receive Customer Payment in Figure 2-1 means that once the *Cashier* has finished reading back the order to the customer, the next activity in the process is the payment activity. Dotted arrows show the flow of the data named on the arrow. Thus, the dotted arrow between the Receive Customer Payment activity and the Record Payment activity means that the data named on that arrow (Amount) is sent from the Receive Customer Payment activity to the Record Payment activity.

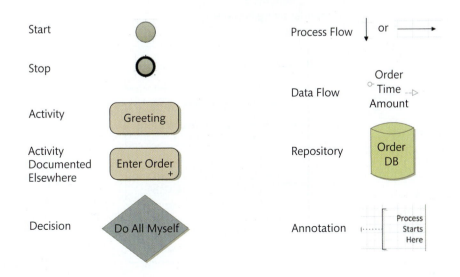

FIGURE 2-2

Summary of BPMN Symbols

A **repository** is a collection of something, usually a collection of records. In Figure 2-1, the symbol that looks like a small tin can represents a repository. Here we have a repository named *Order DB*. As hinted in that name, a repository is often a database (DB), but it need not be. It might be a cardboard box full of records. And some repositories, like inventories, are collections of things other than data.

Notice one thing about the activities in Figure 2-1. All the activities begin with a verb. This is an excellent rule for you to use as you begin to think of processes and activities. When you diagram a process or list activities, always ask yourself if each listed activity begins with a verb. If it does not, it is probably not an activity.

HOW MUCH DETAIL IS ENOUGH? As an abstraction, a business process diagram shows some details and omits others. It has to; otherwise it would be hundreds of pages long and include too many obvious details. We don't need to show that the *Cashier* must open the window before exchanging money with the customers or that he or she must turn on a computer before using it. However, we need to show sufficient detail so as to avoid ambiguity. The process with one big activity named Fulfill Drive-Thru Orders leaves out too much detail. Such a diagram would not show, for example, that the *Presenter* must choose to assemble orders himself or ask the *Food Runner* to assemble the order.

To simplify process diagrams, the details of some activities are documented separately. In Figure 2-1, consider the Enter Order activity. The activity is shown with a plus sign, indicating that the details of the Enter Order activity are documented elsewhere. As stated, such external documentation is used to simplify a diagram; it is also used when the details of the subprocess are unknown or unimportant to the process under study or when those details are documented elsewhere. For example, the details of the Enter Order activity such as repeating the order and concluding the exchange with totals and where to drive are unimportant to the overall process.

Why Do Organizations Standardize Business Processes?

Other than very small businesses, most businesses choose to standardize business processes. The benefits of standardizing processes are listed in Figure 2-3. Standardizing processes enables the business to enforce policies. For example, the fast food restaurant has a policy that all customer orders are to be recorded electronically, not just verbally, that customer orders are to be read back to the customer by the cashier, and that timing starts when the order is first recorded. By standardizing the process, these policies can be enforced. Second, standardized business processes produce consistent results. When every employee follows the same process steps, the results will be the same, regardless of who is staffing the cash window or assembling drinks. Third, standardized processes are scalable. If the owner creates a burger with new toppings, he then standardizes the process of making that burger so the other employees can use it. Finally, standardized business processes reduce risk. When every employee follows the same process,

FIGURE 2-3

Benefits of Standardizing Processes

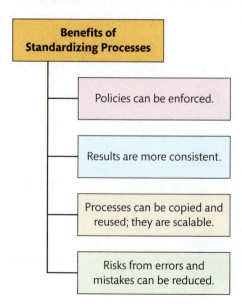

the opportunities for error and serious mistakes are greatly reduced. Standardizing processes requires collaboration; to standardize a fast food process, store employees and process experts must collaborate well.

Documenting and standardizing business processes is increasingly common in business. However, understanding how these processes interact with information systems is not common. We will more closely examine the relationship between processes and information systems after we discuss information systems.

Q2-2 ▶ What Is an Information System?

A **system** is a group of components that interact to achieve some purpose. As you might guess, an **information system (IS)** is a group of components that interact to produce information. That sentence, although true, raises another question: What are these components that interact to produce information?

Figure 2-4 shows the **five-component framework**—a model of the components of a functioning information system: computer hardware, software, data, procedures, and people. These five components are present in every information system, from the simplest to the most complex. **Hardware**, the physical parts of a computer, includes input and output devices as well as the computer processor and internal storage system. **Software** is organized instructions used by the computer to accomplish tasks. Hardware and software are discussed more completely in Extension 4. **Data** are facts or figures about things used in analysis and reasoning. **Procedures** are steps or instructions for people to follow when accomplishing an activity on a computer. **People** are the actors, the users that are accomplishing the activity on the computer, as well as those that service or support it. For example, when you use a computer to write a class report, you are using hardware (the computer, storage disk, keyboard, and monitor), software (Word, WordPerfect, or some other word-processing program), data (the words, sentences, and paragraphs in your report), procedures (the steps you use to start the program, enter your report, print it, and save and back up your file), and people (you).

Consider a more complex example, such as an airline reservation system. It, too, consists of these five components, even though each one is far more complicated. The hardware consists of dozens of computers linked together by data communications hardware. Further, hundreds of different programs coordinate communications among the computers, and still other programs perform the reservations and related services. Additionally, the system must store millions upon millions of characters of data about flights, customers, reservations, and other facts. Hundreds of different procedures—instructions for booking a flight, canceling a reservation, or selecting a seat—are followed by airline personnel, travel agents, and customers. Finally, the information system includes people, not only the users of the system, but also those who operate and service the computers, those who maintain the data, and those who support the networks of computers.

Notice the symmetry in these five components. Hardware and people do things. Programs and procedures are instructions. Programs tell hardware what to do, and procedures tell people what to do. Data is the bridge between the machine side (hardware and software) and the human side (procedures and people).

The important point here is that the five components in Figure 2-4 are common to all information systems, from the smallest to the largest. As you think about any information system, including the order IS at the fast food restaurant, learn to look for these five components.

Before we move forward, note that we have defined an information system to include a computer. Some people would say that such a system is a **computer-based information system**. They would note that there are information systems that do not include computers, such as a calendar hanging on the wall outside of a conference room that is used to schedule the room's use. Such systems have been used by businesses for centuries. Although this point is true, in this book we focus on computer-based information systems. To simplify and shorten the book, we will use the term *information system* as a synonym for *computer-based information system*. Please also note that not all computers are information systems; for example, robotic computers are not IS.

Five-Component Framework

Hardware	Software	Data	Procedures	People

FIGURE 2-4

Five Components of an Information System

FIGURE 2-5

How to Apply the Five-Component Model

Recognize that you are the key.

Make each component work.

Estimate the scope of a new IS.

Prioritize components by difficulty and disruption.

Appreciate that IS is more than technology.

How Can I Use the Five-Component Model?

Now that you understand the five components better, you're ready to apply your understanding and gain some valuable insights about information systems. To pique your interest, we believe there are at least four helpful ways to apply this idea, and they are listed in Figure 2-5.

RECOGNIZE THAT YOU ARE THE KEY You are part of every information system you use. Indeed, your mind and your thinking are not merely *a* component of the information systems you use; they are the *most important* component. Here's the point: Even if you have the perfect information system, if you do not know what to do with the data that it produces, the other components are a waste of time and money. The quality of your thinking determines in large part the quality of the information system.

MAKE EACH COMPONENT WORK Information systems often encounter problems—despite our best efforts, they don't always work right. All too often in these situations, blame is fixed on the wrong component. You will frequently hear that the culprit is the computer that doesn't work quite right, and certainly at times the hardware or software can be at fault. But with the five-component model, you have more suspects to interrogate. Sometimes the data is not in the right format, the procedures are not clear, or the people using the system are not trained or motivated. By using the five-component model, you can better locate the cause of a problem and pursue smarter solutions.

ESTIMATE THE SCOPE OF A NEW IS The five-component framework can also be used when assessing the scope of new systems. When a vendor pitches the need for a new technology to you, use the five components to assess how big of an investment that new technology represents. What new hardware will you need? What programs will you need to license? What databases and other data must you create? What procedures will need to be developed for both the use and administration of the information system? And, finally, what will be the impact of the new technology on people? Which jobs will change? Who will need training? How will the new technology affect morale? Will you need to hire new people? Will you need to reorganize? The five-component model helps you think more completely about the impact of new technology.

PRIORITIZE COMPONENTS BY DIFFICULTY AND DISRUPTION Finally, as you consider the five components, keep in mind that Figure 2-4 shows them in order of ease of change and the extent of organizational disruption. It is a simple matter to order additional hardware. Obtaining or developing new programs is more difficult. Creating new databases or changing the structure of existing databases is still more difficult. Changing procedures, requiring people to work in new ways, is even more difficult. Finally, changing personnel responsibilities and reporting relationships and hiring and terminating employees are very difficult and very disruptive to the organization.

APPRECIATE THAT INFORMATION SYSTEMS ARE MORE THAN TECHNOLOGY Without the five-component model, businesspeople think IS is IT—that IS is just the hardware, software, and data. As a result, they believe that when they buy or obtain the technology that is all they need to do to improve their process. They underestimate the need to specify procedures and train people to use the IS within their process. *A narrow view of IS as just IT results in poor procedures and undertrained people.*

Not everyone understands information systems this way; most businesspeople think of information systems as computers or applications. By understanding the five components, not only can you apply the lessons just mentioned, you can also apply the most important lesson found in our next topic—procedures link information systems to processes.

Q2-3 How Do Business Processes and Information Systems Relate?

Processes and information systems are the most important aspects of this book. Earlier we noted that everything you can see is the result of a business process. Now ask yourself if any of these things you can see were made by a process that did not use an IS. Every important business process is supported by an IS, so understanding IS and how they support processes is vital to your future career.

To begin to understand how processes and IS relate to each other think back to your last airline flight. Your smartphone, your IS, helped you accomplish many flight-related activities. It helped you find and purchase tickets, it helped you check in at the airport and at the gate, and it helped you get an Uber ride at your destination, to name just a few. Information systems and processes also have an important relationship at the fast food restaurant. The Order Tracker IS supports the Drive-Thru process, and it helps support a number of other processes at the restaurant as shown in Figure 2-6 such as the Hiring process and the Scheduling process as well as the In-Store Ordering, Revenue Totaling, and Reordering processes.

Notice that if a second IS is added to the Drive-Thru process, we then have a process that is supported by two IS. For example, the second IS might use a motion detection system to record traffic patterns of cars that join the drive-thru line. We could continue this example with a third or fourth IS for the Drive-Thru process. In general, we say that a process can be supported by any number of information systems—from zero to many.

Now let's look at it from the IS point of view and ask how many processes one IS can support. The Order Tracker IS supports the Drive-Thru process, but it also supports the process that adds up the revenue for the day and the process to reorder items from the warehouse. So, in this case, we see that one IS can support one or many processes. The relationship between IS and processes at the fast food restaurant is shown in Figure 2-6.

Starting from the right side of Figure 2-6, the processes used to open and close the store do not rely on any IS. These processes are a series of activities performed entirely by human actors. Moving left in the figure, we can see that the Drive-Thru, In-Store Ordering, Revenue Totaling, and Reordering processes are supported by the Order Tracker IS. At the other end of Figure 2-6, another IS, the Laptop IS, is used by the manager to exchange email in the Landscaping process as well as the Community Outreach process. Finally, two processes, Hiring and Scheduling, are supported by both IS. There are many other processes that occur at the restaurant, but you get the idea.

1. A process can be supported by zero to many IS.
2. An IS can support one or many processes.

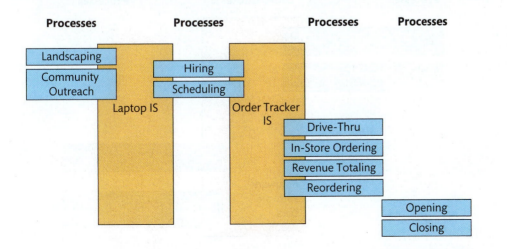

FIGURE 2-6

Processes and the Two IS at the Fast Food Restaurant

When business leaders misunderstand the relationship between IS and processes they tend to see the IS as supporting just one process, a monogamous marriage sort of relationship. As a result, they believe that if an IS needs to change to make a process better, just change the IS and be done with it. They fail to notice that the IS has a relationship with other processes as well, and the proposed change might make those processes worse. More polygamy than monogamy.

For example, the fast food chain wants to improve its hiring process, but the change in the process requires a change in the Order Tracker IS. The IS manager responsible for the Order Tracker IS must keep all the other processes in mind when he changes the IS to support the hiring change. Keep this process-IS relationship in mind. If you are a specialist in accounting, supply chain, finance, or marketing and you want to change an IS, realize that the IS must still support other processes. The IS is not yours alone; it belongs to other processes as well.

The Role of Procedures

There is one more item to discuss about the relationship between IS and processes—the important role of procedures. Procedures, one of the five components of an IS, anchor an IS to a process. A procedure is a set of instructions for a person to follow when operating an IS. For example, when you create a Facebook account, the Facebook IS gives you a procedure to follow in the form of instructions for filling out the on-screen application.

The importance of procedures is evident when we compare you and your grandmother on the lucky day she buys you each an identical smartphone. The phone arrives with exactly the same hardware, software, and data, but you know procedures your grandmother does not. Soon you'll be using your phone to improve dozens of processes in your daily life—communicating with friends, paying bills, finding reviews, taking photos, participating in social media, and finding airline flights and Uber drivers while your grandmother uses it as a phone and to FaceTime with your cousins. Same technology, but your knowledge of procedures makes you more productive. Likewise, businesses will need you to learn their procedures for using technology so you can accomplish their activities productively.

Each information system has a different procedure for every process the information system supports. The Facebook information system includes a procedure for each of its processes—there is a procedure for creating an account, posting a picture, searching for friends, and setting privacy preferences. Let's return to the fast food example. Figure 2-7 shows the processes supported by the Order Tracker IS. Notice that for each process, the Order Tracker IS has a unique procedure. For the Hiring process, the Hiring procedure is a series of instructions for entering new employee data into the Order Tracker IS. The Drive-Thru procedure is a series of instructions for inputting orders, changing orders, and calculating amount due. Again, a procedure links an IS to a process.

To wrap this up, an IS will have a different procedure for every process, and a process will have a different procedure for every IS that supports it. In many of the chapters that follow, we'll rely on these fundamental ideas about IS, processes, and procedures. But you might already

FIGURE 2-7

Procedures, Processes, and the Order Tracker IS

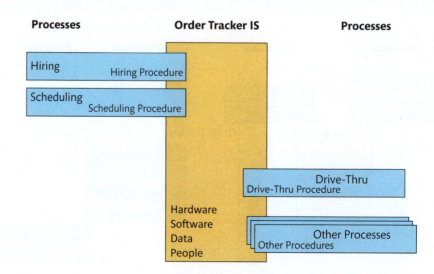

notice a few useful applications of this model. When you think about improving a process, make sure you identify all the IS that support it. When you make changes to an IS, make sure you anticipate all the processes that use that IS. Finally, when either the IS or the process changes, the procedure will also need to change. It might surprise you that many businesspeople are not aware of the distinction between procedures and processes, but you do.

Q2-4 How Do Structured and Dynamic Processes Vary?

Businesses have dozens, hundreds, even thousands of different processes. Some processes are stable, almost fixed, in the flow among their activities. For example, the daily processes of open-ing or closing the fast food restaurant are fixed—employees perform the same listed steps in the same order every time. These processes are highly standardized so that the procedures are done the same way each time regardless of who is working.

Other processes are less structured, less rigid, and sometimes creative. For example, how does the restaurant manager decide on landscaping improvements? The manager can look at other restaurants or visit a nursery, but the process for deciding what to do next is not nearly as structured as that for opening or closing the restaurant.

In this text, we divide processes into two broad categories. **Structured processes** are for-mally defined, standardized processes. Most structured processes support day-to-day operations: scheduling work shifts, calculating daily sales tax totals, and so forth. **Dynamic processes** are less specific, more adaptive, and even intuitive. Deciding whether to open a new store location and how best to solve a problem of poor employee training are examples of dynamic processes.

Characteristics of Structured Processes

Figure 2-8 summarizes the major differences between structured and dynamic processes and gives examples of each from the fast food restaurant. Structured processes are formally defined with specific detailed activities arranged into fixed, predefined sequences, like that shown in the BPMN diagram in Figure 2-1. Changes to structured processes are slow, made with deliberation, and difficult to implement. Control is critical in structured processes. Innovation of structured

Structured Processes	Dynamic Processes
Characteristics of Processes	
Formally defined process, fixed flow	Informal process
Process change slow and difficult	Process change rapid and expected
Control is critical	Adaptation is critical
Innovation not expected	Innovation required
Efficiency and effectiveness important	Effectiveness typically more important
IS procedures are prescriptive	IS procedures are supportive
Chapters in This Textbook	
Chapter 8: Procurement	Chapter 10: Collaboration
Chapter 9: Sales	Chapter 11: Social Media
	Chapter 12: Business Intelligence
	Extension 3: Systems Design
Examples at the Fast-Food Restaurant	
Scheduling	Landscaping
Drive-Thru	Community outreach
Opening & Closing	Hiring

FIGURE 2-8

Differences Between Structured and Dynamic Processes

processes is not expected, nor is it generally appreciated or rewarded. "Wow, I've got four different ways of closing the store at night" is not a positive accomplishment.

For structured processes, both efficiency and effectiveness are important, and we will define these aspects in Chapter 5. For now, assume that *efficiency* means accomplishing the process with minimum resources, and *effectiveness* means that the process contributes directly to the organization's strategy. Reducing average drive-thru time for customers by 5 seconds would be a huge efficiency gain. If the competitive strategy is getting every order correct, then a Drive-Thru process that leads to a decrease in errors is effective.

Finally, the procedures for structured processes are prescriptive. **Prescriptive procedures** clearly delimit what the users of the information system can do and under what conditions they can do it. In Chapters 8 and 9, you will see how procedures occur in procurement and sales. Variations on those procedures will not be tolerated, as you will learn.

Characteristics of Dynamic Processes

The second column of the table in Figure 2-8 summarizes characteristics of dynamic processes. First, such processes tend to be informal. This does not mean that they are unstructured; rather, it means that the process cannot be reduced to fixed activities done the same way every time. Instead, these processes are often created on the fly, their activities are fluid and intermingled with other processes, and they frequently include backtracking and repetition. As a result, BPMN diagrams of dynamic processes are always highly generic. They have activities with generalized names like "gather data," "analyze past sales," and "assess maintenance costs." Human intuition plays a big role in a dynamic process. Examples at the fast food restaurant include hiring, landscaping, and community outreach.

Dynamic processes, as their name implies, change rapidly as requirements and situations change. If structured processes are cast in stone, dynamic processes are written in sand on a windy beach. "We'll try it this way. If it works, great; if not, we'll do something else." A good example is the Community Outreach process at the fast food restaurant. Today, this process involves choosing which youth sports team to support, but tomorrow when an employee asks if the restaurant would like to be a sponsor for a new 5K run, the activities in the process change. Such change is expected. The need to try one method and revise it as needed reinforces the need to experiment—one of the four key employability skills for success, as discussed in Chapter 1.

Rather than being controlled, dynamic processes are adaptive; they must be so to evolve with experience. Dynamic process actors collaborate. As they give feedback to each other, the process evolves into one that no single person might have envisioned but that works better than anyone could have created on their own ahead of time.

Adaptation requires innovation. Whereas innovation on a structured process like computing sales revenue is likely to get you fired, innovating with Twitter to forecast sales will be highly rewarded. Another word for *innovation* is *experimentation*, which we described in Chapter 1.

For the most part, dynamic processes often have fewer well-accepted objectives than structured processes, and these objectives tend to emphasize effectiveness rather than efficiency. Did the process help us accomplish our strategy? This is not to say that efficient use of resources does not matter; rather, dynamic processes change so fast that it is often not possible to measure efficiency over time. Typically, costs are controlled by budget: "Get the best result you can with these resources."

Finally, procedures for dynamic processes are supportive rather than prescriptive. **Supportive procedures** allow end users to determine how to best use an IS. The instructions for using an information system are less rigid. The procedures for using email to coordinate a Landscaping process—the time between emails, the contents of the email, and other procedures—will change each time a Landscaping process is executed.

This structured–dynamic distinction is important. For one, the behavior you choose as a business professional depends on the type of process in which you are involved. Innovation will be expected in dynamic processes but discouraged in structured processes. For information systems, this process distinction is important in the nature and character of the system. As stated, the procedures of an IS used to support structured processes will restrict your behavior and readily (and successfully) frustrate any attempts at innovation. In contrast, an IS that supports a dynamic process supports innovation. For example, using text messaging to support a collaboration process is an open book. Put anything in it you want; control that content in whatever way you think is appropriate. As you learn about information systems this semester, understand that their procedures are a direct reflection of the kind of process they are intended to support.

Q2-5 What Is Information?

Earlier, we defined an information system as an assembly of hardware, software, data, procedures, and people that interact to produce information. The only term left undefined in that definition is information, and we turn to it next. The meaning of the term *information* is often taken for granted. We believe that behind this simple and common word are some very helpful distinctions that will be of help to you.

Definitions Vary

It is hard to imagine another word that is more frequently used in business than *information*; not only by itself, but in combination with other terms such as *information technology, information processing, information system,* and *information overload*. Although information is one of those common terms that we use every day, it turns out to be surprisingly difficult to define. Defining information is like defining words such as *love* and *truth*. We know how to use these words in normal conversation, but when we ask other people for a definition, we discover they mean different things.

A common definition for **information** *is knowledge derived from data*, whereas *data* is defined as recorded facts or figures. Thus, the facts that Jake earns $11.50 per hour at the hospital and that Sally earns $10.00 per hour are *data*. The statement that the average wage of all hourly wage employees is $10.37 per hour is *information*. Average wage is knowledge that is derived from the data of individual wages.

Another common definition is that *information is data presented in a meaningful context*. The fact that Jake earns $11.50 per hour is data. The statement that Jake earns more than the average hourly wage, however, is information. It is data presented in a meaningful context.

A third definition is that *information is processed data* or, sometimes, *information is data processed by sorting, filtering, grouping, comparing, summing, averaging, and other similar operations*. Figure 2-9 shows an example of how data is processed into information. The fundamental idea of this definition is that we do something to data to produce information.

The plot thickens with the fourth definition: *Information is any difference that makes a difference.*[2] For example, when you drive a car and glance down at your speed, you notice a difference between your speed and the speed limit, and this difference makes a difference to you—you adjust your speed. The first difference is something you notice that is different from something else, and the second difference is that you change your mind. Jake in the opening

	Drive-Thru		In-Store				
Date	Orders	Total Sales	Orders	Total Sales			
1	1213	$ 6,523.12	1012	5876.34			
2	1165	$ 5,789.23	1243	6823.45			
3	1376	$ 7,012.22	1325	7112.34			
4	1465	$ 7,376.23	1423	7145.98	a. Original data		
5	1543	$ 7,576.22	1254	6932.22			
6	2422	$ 11,543.67	2012	9238.88			
7	1865	$ 8,543.23	1743	8453.98			
Average	1578	$ 7,766.27	1430	$7,369.03	b. Information from processing data		

FIGURE 2-9

Data and Information from Data Processing

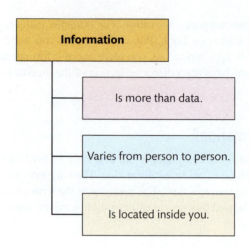

vignette provides us with an example. When he looked at the problem with the orderlies as a tracking issue and not as a motivation issue, this difference changed his mind about the nature of the problem and possible solutions.

Common Elements in the Definitions

For the purposes of this text, any of these definitions of information will do. None of these definitions is perfect or broadly accepted; each can be useful in certain circumstances. But in general, they agree about a few important things, and these similarities are listed in Figure 2-10. Also shown in Figure 2-10 are differences between data and information. These common elements are important to understanding information and using it to your advantage.

First, information is not data, it is something more. What makes information "more" is that it is meaningful; there is meaning in the average wage, a customer's order, and your driving speed. The magic of meaning is that it can change minds. The number 6 or October 4 are just data; they do not have meaning because they change no one's mind.

Second, because meaning is in the eye of the beholder, information varies from person to person—different people often have different information. For example, if you sat in the captain's chair on the flightdeck of an airliner and looked at all the data on the dials, instruments, and switches, you don't have information, but an airline captain would.

Now consider the data in Figure 2-11. You might say that the first column contains the name of a person, the second maybe the person's employee number, and the third the employee's age. Now, put that same data in front of someone who manages an IQ testing center for adults. Ask that person to interpret the data. She will most likely say the first column contains the name of a person, the second the person's IQ test score, and the third the person's age. Furthermore, she

FIGURE 2-11

Sample of Data

Christianson	140	42
Abernathy	107	25
Green	98	21
Moss	137	38
Baker	118	32
Jackson	127	38
Lloyd	119	29
Dudley	111	22
McPherson	128	33
Jefferson	107	24
Nielsen	112	33
Thomas	118	29

Assume it is hard to communicate.

Recognize that all new IS are frustrating at first.

Understand how to be effective on a team.

Stay curious.

Realize that people share data but believe it is information.

Take responsibility for your own learning.

FIGURE 2-12

How to Apply the Data/Information Distinction

may also find the information that, according to this data, IQ increases with age. We can continue this thought experiment to the manager of a bowling league and other contexts, but you get the point: In these cases, information varies from person to person based on experiences, education, and expectations. We further examine this in the Ethics Guide on page 42.

This leads to the final common element about information. Information resides in the head of the person looking at the data. If it's on a piece of paper or on a digital screen, it's data; if it's in the mind, it's information. An airline pilot looks at a screen of data on the instrument panel but the information he makes is in his mind.

How Can I Use These Ideas About Information?

At this point you might be asking, "What difference does all this make to me?" We think there are several important implications, as shown in Figure 2-12.

ASSUME IT IS HARD TO COMMUNICATE If information varies from person to person, we should no longer say, give me *the* information. I can try to give you *my* information, and you can try to give me *your* information, but in both cases what is given is not exactly what is received. To see this, consider two people in a romantic relationship. How often do you hear that the two create different meanings from the same data? For example, one person didn't respond to a text. To one person the meaning is clear—you don't want to spend time with me; to the other person, there was no message—my phone was dead. While the data is the same—no text response—the information created is very, very different. So if in business you and I are talking or exchanging data, expect that I will not have your information and you won't have my information, either. While you might want to tell me that I'm misinformed, I could say the same about you. We're all slightly misinformed all the time, as nobody knows *exactly* what anyone else means. With this outlook, you realize how hard it is to effectively communicate, you won't assume others understand what you mean, and you'll become a better communicator because you will work at it.

RECOGNIZE THAT ALL NEW INFORMATION SYSTEMS ARE FRUSTRATING AT FIRST If you make your own information from the differences you see on a screen and one day a new screen appears because the IS has changed, you will have to work harder for a while to create your information. For example, when an app changes on your phone or you buy a new computer with a different operating system, it is harder to identify your old familiar differences from which you can make information. Finding differences with the old system had become an easy habit; now you have to work at it. All new information systems initially make it harder on the end user to find their differences. Unfortunately, many companies do not anticipate this when they roll out a shiny new app and are surprised when employees want the old system back.

UNDERSTAND HOW TO BE EFFECTIVE ON A TEAM To help your teammates, provide data that is different from what they already know so they can create information for themselves. Ask them to share with you the differences that have meaning to them. Listen to these differences and see what meaning they create for you. Also, ask questions that reveal new differences. If your questions are original and insightful, then others on the team can use your questions to inform themselves.

STAY CURIOUS If information is inside of you, the only way to get it there is for you to put it there. Information can't be received; it has to be made. This creative effort is fueled by curiosity. When you quit being curious, you quit informing yourself. Realize every day that other people are informing themselves and seeing things you don't. The only way to keep up is to create information for yourself. Stay curious! You were born that way for a reason.

REALIZE THAT PEOPLE SHARE DATA BUT BELIEVE IT IS INFORMATION Most people do not distinguish between data and information; they naively believe the information inside them is the same as the data outside them. As a result, when they communicate they mistakenly believe they are communicating their information, their ideas, directly to other people. However, they are speaking data, not information. Information, meaning, only exists inside the mind; outside are data. Other individuals who are listening to them must create their own information from the spoken data. With this outlook, you are more open to feedback and discussion as you realize others are trying to make their own information from the data you speak, making you a better collaborator.

TAKE RESPONSIBILITY FOR YOU OWN LEARNING The information that you know wasn't given to you; you created it. Teachers, books, and life experiences provide data to your doorstep; you have to carry the data inside and make information out of it. Everything you will ever learn requires you to take this active step. So take responsibility for your lifelong learning. Set your expectations high.

Q2-6 ▶ What Are Necessary Data Characteristics?

You have just learned that humans conceive information from data. As stated, the quality of the information that you can create depends, in part, on your thinking skills. However, it also depends on the quality of the data that you are given. Figure 2-13 summarizes critical data characteristics.

Accurate

First, good information is conceived from accurate, correct, and complete data that has been processed correctly. Accuracy is crucial; business professionals must be able to rely on the results of their information systems. The IS function can develop a bad reputation in the organization if a system is known to produce inaccurate data. In such a case, the information system becomes a waste of time and money as users develop work-arounds to avoid the inaccurate data.

A corollary to this discussion is that you, a future user of information systems, ought not to rely on data just because it appears in the context of a Web page, a well-formatted report, or a fancy query. It is sometimes hard to be skeptical of data delivered with beautiful, active graphics. Do not be misled. When you begin to use a new information system, be skeptical. Cross-check the data you are receiving.

FIGURE 2-13

Factors That Affect Data Quality

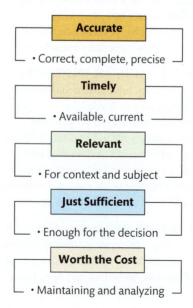

For data to be accurate, it must be trustworthy, coming from a reliable, credible source or technique. Data that appears accurate may be misleading if its source is unreliable. Survey data and self-reports by subjects such as polling results for elections may be unreliable if leading questions create biased answers. Data may be unreliable if data from different databases have been thrown together. A common example is combining data from different political polls—how to combine polls of likely voters and all voters or polls that allow undecided with those that do not.

Timely

Good information requires that data be timely—available in time for its intended use. A monthly report that arrives 6 weeks late is not timely and most likely useless. The data arrives long after the decisions have been made. An information system that sends you a poor customer credit report after you have shipped the goods is unhelpful and frustrating. Notice that timeliness can be measured against a calendar (6 weeks late) or against events (before we ship).

When you participate in the development of an IS, timeliness will be part of the requirements you specify. You need to give appropriate and realistic timeliness needs. In some cases, developing systems that provide data in near real time is much more difficult and expensive than producing data a few hours later. If you can get by with data that is a few hours old, say so during the requirements specification phase.

Consider an example. Suppose you work in marketing and you need to be able to assess the effectiveness of new online ad programs. You want an information system that will not only deliver ads over the Web but will also enable you to determine how frequently customers click on those ads. Determining click ratios in near real time will be very expensive; saving the data in a batch and processing it some hours later will be much easier and cheaper. If you can live with data that is a day or two old, the system will be easier and cheaper to implement.

Relevant

Data should be relevant both to the context and to the subject. Considering context, you, the CEO, need data that is summarized to an appropriate level for your job. A list of the hourly wage of every employee in the company is unlikely to be useful. More likely, you need average wage information by department or division. A list of all employee wages is irrelevant in your context.

Data should also be relevant to the subject at hand. If you want data about short-term interest rates for a possible line of credit, then a report that shows 15-year mortgage interest rates is irrelevant. Similarly, a report that buries the data you need in pages and pages of results is also irrelevant to your purposes.

Just Sufficient

Data needs to be sufficient for the purpose for which it is generated, but just barely so. We are inundated with data; one of the critical decisions that each of us has to make each day is what data to ignore. The higher you rise into management, the more data you will be given and, because there is only so much time, the more data you will need to ignore.

Worth Its Cost

Data is not free. There are costs for developing an information system, costs of operating and maintaining that system, and costs of your time and salary for reading and processing the data the system produces. For data to be worth its cost, an appropriate relationship must exist between the cost of data and its value. Consider an example. What is the value of a daily report of the names of the occupants of a full graveyard? Zero, unless grave robbery is a problem for the cemetery. The report is not worth the time required to read it. It is easy to see the importance of economics for this silly example. It will be more difficult, however, when someone proposes new technology to you. You need to be ready to ask, "What's the value of the information that I can conceive from this data?" "What is the cost?" "Is there an appropriate relationship between value and cost?" Information systems should be subject to the same financial analyses to which other assets are subjected.

Summary

Do not take data quality for granted. There is no shortage of data, but not all of this data is of good quality. Analysis and insight depend on having good data, but all too often the limitations of the data are overlooked. Be able to ask good questions about the accuracy, timeliness, relevancy, sufficiency, and cost of the data.

Q2-7 How Can I Use These Topics at Work?

We met Jennifer in the opening vignette of Chapter 1, and she sadly did not have the employability skills important for her job. She was fired for lacking the skills of abstract reasoning, systems thinking, collaboration, and experimentation. In this chapter, we met Jake who seems to display each of these skills in his work at the hospital. The differences between Jennifer and Jake are highlighted in Figure 2-14. We created these two characters to provide you as bright a contrast as possible and to confront you with a question—am I more like Jenn or Jake?

Jennifer demonstrated a limited ability to reason abstractly. She struggled to model the steps of the company's customer life cycle. On the other hand, Jake was able to reason that the X-ray problem had more to do with process than poorly motivated people. He reasoned that tracking the orderlies and communicating with them might solve the problem. In this chapter and in this textbook, we introduce abstract ideas about processes, IS, and information. These ideas are not intended for you to just write down or remember; they are intended to be used. The key question for you is can you *apply* these models? Can you think with them, and can you see things and do things you could not see and do before?

Systems thinking requires an individual to understand which inputs and outputs are required for the system and how they relate to each other. Jennifer struggled to create a sensible diagram of customer activities—how one activity fed into another. Jake could see the bigger picture. If he could fix the X-ray process the right way, this solution might also improve how orderlies are used in other places in the hospital. A process is a type of system, with inputs and outputs that affect other processes. As we explain processes in this book, ask yourself if you can see how these processes affect each other, how improving one can simultaneously improve or diminish another.

Jennifer was criticized for poor collaboration—she failed to work well with other employees and was unsuccessful contacting one of the lead salespeople at another office. Jake, on the other hand, shared his ideas knowing they were not facts and was open to feedback to improve them. Ask yourself, "What evidence do I have that I am a good collaborator like Jake? Do I join in the activities of others on teams and activities around campus? Or am I more like Jenn? Do I fail to remember teammates' names?"

FIGURE 2-14

Are You a Jake or a Jenn?

Abstract Reasoning
- Jenn: Could not model life cycle
- Jake: Track orderlies, don't fire them
- You: Can I apply models, think with them, see new things with them?

Systems Thinking
- Jenn: Could not diagram how one activity fed into the next activity
- Jake: X-ray solution could be applied to other processes
- You: Can you see how processes fit together?

Collaboration
- Jenn: Could not contact lead salesperson
- Jake: Shares ideas and is open to feedback
- You: When I share my ideas do I encourage feedback?

Experimentation
- Jenn: Expected to be told what to do
- Jake: Proposed trial run with X-ray orderlies
- You: Do you propose and try out new solutions?

MIS InClass 2

A Beautiful Mind

The purpose of this exercise is to examine beauty, determine where it exists, and apply it to information systems.

This activity has several phases. To begin, consider the pictures of famous buildings in Figure 2-15. Select two of these buildings as the most beautiful.

1. Record your vote for the two most beautiful buildings.
2. As a class, compile your votes for the most beautiful buildings.
   Class members should now discuss why they liked the buildings they chose. Be as specific as possible about the terms you use to describe a beautiful building.
3. Did any of your votes change after the discussion?
4. Record how others describe what beauty means to them. Are these terms similar or different from your own terms?
   The class should now review the distinction between data and information used in this chapter. By the definitions in this book, the images of buildings are data, external to each student. The beauty of the buildings is information, internal to each student. The data, the photo, is precisely the same for each student; however, the information the student forms is unique to each student.

5. In some ways a new IS is like a new building. Individuals other than the designer use it. Should the designer of either make the building or IS to suit their own description of beautiful?
6. Record which of the four employability skills listed in Chapter 1 and discussed in Chapter 2 is important for the architect and the IS designer.
   Finally, apply this data and information distinction more broadly than buildings and IS.
7. In what other settings do individuals have precisely the same data but differ on information?
8. If a person believes external data and internal information are the same thing, what will surprise them?
9. If you treat data and information as different, what employability skill will improve for you?

Beauty, and information, is in the eye of the beholder.

Paris Louvre

Source: Anna Ivanova

Frank Lloyd Wright Home

Source: Marco Lachmann

New York City Freedom Tower

Source: haveseen

Paris Notre Dame

Source: Iakov Kalinin

Vienna Opera House

Source: tomas1111

Sydney Opera House

Source: nerthuz

Chinese Forbidden City

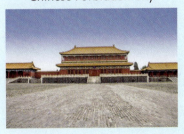

Source: Giancarlo Liguori

FIGURE 2-15
Famous Buildings

Finally, Jenn did not feel comfortable experimenting. She expected to be told what to do. On the other hand, Jake suggested a trial run with the X-ray orderlies before adopting his solution. Do you do things on your own? Do you try out new solutions?

While the rest of this book fills in the details in your understanding of IS and processes, our hope is that by the end of the semester you will have practiced using these four skills. The key will be practice and self-motivation. We think the topic of MIS provides plenty of opportunity to practice these skills; give it your best shot.

Ethics Guide

Informing About Misinforming

Earlier in the chapter, we concluded that information varies from person to person. One implication of people informing themselves differently is that inevitably some people will "misinform" themselves about events. For example, you know that Chapter 1 is on the exam, but your classmate was distracted when the teacher explained this and believes it is not. This exam misinforming is not an ethical issue, but in your future work environment, the ethics of misinforming will certainly appear.

Consider this example where misinforming hides a mistake you make. One of your jobs at a regional supermarket company is to work with potential suppliers. You have been corresponding with one potential new supplier, Green Foods, by email and have copied your boss on the important exchanges. On one email sent by Green Foods with the subject line "Remove Application," it asks about how to stop its application, as it would like to reapply later in the year. Unknown to you, your boss misreads this exchange and concludes Green Foods has decided to end its application. You knew the supplier was only asking about removing its application, but sadly, you got distracted and made a mistake—you failed to include Green Foods in the list of new applications to consider. Shortly afterward at a meeting of managers of the supermarket chain, you hear that your boss explained to the group that Green Foods withdrew its application. You know he is misinformed, that it did not withdraw, but clearly his misinforming has hidden your mistake.

The Ethics Guide in Chapter 1 introduced Kant's categorical imperative as one way of assessing ethical conduct. This guide introduces a second way, one known as utilitarianism. The basis of this theory goes back to early Greek philosophers, but the founders of the modern theory are considered to be Jeremy Bentham and John Stuart Mill, as you will learn in your business ethics class.

According to **utilitarianism**, the morality of an act is determined by its outcome. Acts are judged to be moral if they result in the greatest good to the greatest number or if they maximize happiness and reduce suffering.

Using utilitarianism as a guide, killing can be moral if it results in the greatest good to the greatest number. Killing Adolph Hitler would have been moral if it stopped the Holocaust. Lying to persons with a fatal illness is moral if it increases their happiness and decreases their suffering.

DISCUSSION QUESTIONS

1. You did nothing to misinform your boss, and in the long run, you expect everything to work out. You will finish what you failed to do and Green Foods will be considered at the next meeting. In all likelihood, no one will notice your boss's mistake. Should you tell your boss your mistake?
2. Is the decision to not tell your boss unethical? Consider both the categorical imperative (page 18) and utilitarianism (page 43) in your response. If you were the boss, what would you want your employee to do in this case (the Golden Rule)?
3. Consider the same situation as before except that you are expecting a promotion, and to make things interesting, you have pursued this promotion for a year and it will triple your salary. You think that if you admit your mistake about Green Foods, the promotion will be at risk. If this changes your answer to question 1, what does this change imply about your ethics?
4. What could go wrong if you decide not to tell the boss? Compare your answers to those of other students. Should the possible consequences of your decision affect what you decide to do?
5. A similar situation occurs when a teacher incorrectly totals your points on an exam. Can you describe another scenario that examines these issues in the context of an event in your own life?
6. For questions 1–3, how do your answers change if someone else was involved and not you, for example, if you observed the misinforming between another employee and a boss?

Source: auremar/Fotolia

ACTIVE REVIEW

Use this Active Review to verify that you understand the material in the chapter. You can read the entire chapter and then perform the tasks in this review, or you can read the text material for just one question and perform the tasks in this review for that question before moving on to the next one.

Q2-1 What is a business process?

Explain how businesses compete. Define *business process* and give an example of two business processes not in this text. Define *activity* and give examples of five activities. Explain the need for an abstraction of a business process and describe the purpose of the BPMN notation. Define *role* and *actor* and explain their relationship. Identify four swimlanes in Figure 2-1 and explain their utility. Explain the meaning of each of the symbols in Figure 2-2. Give an example of two repositories. Describe criteria for deciding how much detail is enough in a process diagram. Describe four reasons that organizations standardize business processes.

Q2-2 What is an information system?

Define *system* and *information system*. Name and describe the five components of an information system. Describe the five components of an information system required to buy a product online. Explain the five ways to apply the five-component model.

Q2-3 How do business processes and information systems relate?

Explain how an IS supports a process in your life. How many IS can support a process, and how many processes can be supported by one IS? What role do procedures play in linking processes and information systems? Explain what a procedure is, give an example, and describe why procedures are important.

Q2-4 How do structured and dynamic processes vary?

In your own words, describe and characterize structured processes. Describe and characterize dynamic processes. Describe the differences in expected employee behavior for each type of process. Summarize differences in the character of IS that support each category of process. Give several examples of structured processes and of dynamic processes.

Q2-5 What is information?

Give four different definitions for *information* and give an example of information for each definition. For the fourth definition, explain what the word *difference* means in each of its two uses. Describe the three common elements in the four definitions. Where does information exist, and where does data exist? Explain each of the benefits of understanding information.

Q2-6 What are necessary data characteristics?

Summarize the five critical data characteristics. For each of the five, give an example of data that has that characteristic.

Q2-7 How can I use these topics at work?

Describe the ways Jake and Jennifer are different. In which of these ways are you more like Jake or more like Jennifer?

KEY TERMS AND CONCEPTS

Activity 26	Dynamic processes 33	Repository 28
Actor 26	Five-component framework 29	Role 26
Business process 26	Hardware 29	Software 29
Business Process Model and Notation (BPMN) standard 26	Information 35	Structured processes 33
Computer-based information system 29	Information system (IS) 29	Supportive procedures 34
	People 29	Swimlane 27
Data 29	Prescriptive procedures 34	System 29
	Procedures 29	Utilitarianism 43

USING YOUR KNOWLEDGE

2-1. Practice learning new procedures for your smartphone (or laptop if you do not have a smartphone). Find a friend or classmate with a similar phone and find a software app that person uses that would be helpful to you. Download that app and learn how to use it. Identify the process that your new app supports. Write down three other apps you would like to learn to use and learn the procedures to use that app. Record the process supported, the app, and the steps in each procedure you learn. Don't write it down, but ask yourself an important question: Do I learn procedures rapidly? If not, why not?
MyLab MIS

2-2. Explain, in your own words, the relationship between business processes and information systems. Assume you are going to give your explanation to a business professional who knows little about information systems.
MyLab MIS

2-3. From your own life, choose three processes. These may be something like selecting a movie on Netflix, making breakfast, or registering for an account on a new social media platform. For each, specify:
   a. if the process is dynamic or structured
   b. process objectives
   c. the steps in one of the procedures if the process is supported by an IS
   d. several data items, and write down at least two interpretations for each data item.

2-4. Consider some of the ramifications of the way in which information is defined in this chapter.
   a. Why, according to this chapter, is it incorrect to say, "Consider the information in Figure 2-11"? Where is the information?
   b. When you read a news article on the Web, where is the news? When you and a friend read the same news, is it the same news? What is going on here?
   c. Suppose you are having a glass of orange juice for breakfast. As you look at the juice, where is it? Is the thing that you know as orange juice on the table, or is it in your mind? After you drink the orange juice, where is it?

   d. Consider the statement, "Words are just tokens that we exchange to organize our behavior; we don't know anything, really, about what it is they refer to, but they help us organize our social behavior. Reality is a mutual hallucination. It only looks the way it does because all of us have the same, more or less, mental apparatus, and we act as if it's there." Do you agree with this statement? Why or why not?
   e. Describe how you might use insights from this sequence of questions to become a better business professional.

2-5. Using Figure 2-8 as a guide, identify two structured processes and two dynamic processes at your university. Explain how the degree of structure varies in these processes. How do you think change to these processes is managed? Describe how the nature of the work performed in these processes varies. Explain how information systems are used to facilitate these processes. How do you think the character of the information systems supporting these processes varies?

2-6. Specify an e-commerce site where you have purchased something (e.g., Amazon, sports tickets, etc.).
   a. Write down your Buying process, including the activities you perform to buy the product.
   b. Specify the five components of the IS that is supporting your e-commerce purchase. One piece of software is the Web browser.
   c. How did you learn the necessary procedures?

2-7. Think about the processes used by your favorite coffee shop, fast food restaurant, or campus dining facility. Now imagine you are waiting in line.
   a. How do you improve the Customer Service process to make the line go faster?
   b. How are the process objectives being measured? Is your waiting time being measured?
   c. What IS would reduce waiting time—robots making the food, call-ahead ordering, kiosks to order food, and so on? List three and which would have the biggest impact on reducing waiting time.
   d. For your answer in c, what other processes would this IS also impact?

COLLABORATION EXERCISE 2

Collaborate with a group of fellow students to answer the following questions. For this exercise, do not meet face to face. Your task will be easier if you coordinate your work with SharePoint, Office, Google Docs or equivalent collaboration tools. (See Chapter 10 for a discussion of collaboration tools and processes.) Your answers should reflect the thinking of the entire group, not just that of one or two individuals.

The purpose of this exercise is to compute the cost of class registration. To do so, we will consider both class registration processes as well as information systems that support them.

1. Class Registration processes:
   a. List as many processes involved in class registration as you can. Consider class registration from the standpoint of students, faculty, departments, and the university. Consider resources such as classrooms, classroom sizes, and requirements for special facilities, such as audiovisual equipment, labs, and similar needs. Also consider the need for departments to ensure that classes are offered in such a manner that students can complete a major within a 4- or 5-year time period. For this exercise, ignore graduate schools.

b. For each process, identify human actors and the procedures they execute. Estimate the number of hours each actor spends in the roles that he or she plays per enrollment period. Interview, if possible, two or three actors in each role to determine the time they spend in that role per term.

c. Estimate the labor cost of the processes involved in class registration. Assume the fully burdened (wages plus benefits plus applicable taxes) hourly rate of clerical staff is $50 per hour and professorial staff is $80 per hour. Determine the number of departments involved in registration and estimate the number of clerical and professional actors involved in each. Use averages, but realize that some departments are much larger than others.

d. Do you consider the Class Registration process to be structured or dynamic? Why?

2. Information systems:

a. For each process identified in question 1, list supporting information systems. Consider information systems that are used university-wide, those used by departments, and those used by individuals.

b. For each information system identified in part a, describe the five components of that information system.

c. List sources of cost for each of the five components identified in part a. Consider both developmental and operational costs. Ensure you have included the cost of training employees to execute the procedures. Explain how some of the personnel costs in your answer here may overlap with the costs of actors in processes. Why will only some of those costs overlap? Do all of the costs of class registration information systems apply to the cost of class registration business processes? Why or why not?

d. Assume the university updates its universitywide IS that supports class registration. Put in rank order from easiest to most difficult to change the five components of the IS.

3. Effectiveness and efficiency:

a. What does the term *effectiveness* mean when applied to business processes? List as many pertinent effectiveness objectives for class registration as possible. List possible measures for each objective.

b. What does the term *efficiency* mean when applied to business processes? List as many pertinent efficiency objectives for class registration as possible. List possible measures for each objective.

4. The quarter system. Many universities operate on a four-term quarter system that requires class registration four times per year as opposed to semester systems that require class registration just three times per year. Recently, the state of Washington has experienced large tax revenue reductions and has severely cut the budget of state universities, resulting in substantial increases in student tuition and fees. Yet the University of Washington continues to operate on a quarter system.

a. Assume that you work for a university using a quarter system. Justify that system. Can your argument be based upon Registration process efficiency? Why or why not? Can it be based on Registration process effectiveness? Why or why not?

b. Assume you attend a university on a quarter system. Using your answers to questions 1 and 2, write a two-page memo explaining the advantages of converting to a semester system.

c. Considering your answers to questions 1 and 2, do you think it would be wise for universities to convert to semester systems? Why or why not? Would you recommend a national policy for universities to use the semester system?

d. If converting from a quarter system to a semester system is advantageous, why not convert to a one-term system? What would be the advantages and disadvantages of such a system? Would you recommend one if it reduced your tuition by 25 percent? 50 percent? 75 percent?

e. At present, there has been no public outcry to convert the University of Washington to a semester system. There has been, however, considerable public anguish about the increasing costs of tuition. Why do you suppose this situation exists?

f. Given all of your answers to these questions, which type of term system (e.g., quarter, semester, and year) does your team believe is best? Justify your answer.

CASE STUDY 2

One IS, Many Cups of Coffee

Ben Vollmar had a vision. His small college town needed a coffee shop, and he loved coffee. He was soon to graduate from the college and recognized an opportunity. Flatlands Coffee began, at least as a vision. To act on that vision, Ben set off to master the art of coffee making, discovering the many nuisances of coffee preparation, and deciding on his particular blend. Then it was time to turn his idea into a business.

Ben hunted for store locations around town as he began to develop his business plan. His first big challenge was going to be raising enough money to get started. He estimated that he needed $10,000. His MIS class gave him an idea; he might be able to raise his money with a Kickstarter campaign.

Kickstarter is a global crowdfunding platform. In its first 8 years, it raised more than $2 billion in funding for 250,000 different creative projects. Kickstarter projects range from films to video games to journalism to food and coffee shops. On Kickstarter, owners of the projects offer tangible rewards for investors willing to make an initial investment in the project. Eagerly, Ben launched his Kickstarter campaign, but his enthusiasm could not overcome poor planning, and his campaign fell short. A second lesson from his MIS class was then put to work—keep asking questions. What did he miss about how to make a Kickstarter project successful?

Ben discovered he did not adequately promote the Kickstarter campaign and did not offer the right rewards and incentives to investors. Kickstarter round two ended in success. Money in hand, Ben began to shape the store. Now on to the hard work of actually building the place.

Decisions about store layout, variety of coffees sold, furnishings, promotions, and a hundred other choices had to be made. One unexpected decision turned out to be one of his best choices. Ben had to decide how he was going to record purchases and keep track of employees, inventory, and all his accounting data. What technology might be of help with all these processes? Would he have to lease multiple platforms? One technology for each? After some research and discussion with other small business owners, Ben discovered Square.

Square, designed by Twitter cofounder Jack Dorsey, started about the same time as Kickstarter, in 2009. Square bills itself as a mobile payment company and merchant services aggregator. Square is now serving more than 2 million merchants and processing more than $10 billion in payments per quarter. While Square is an industry leader, other brands such as Clover Go, iZettle, and PayPal Here provide similar support to small merchants.

When you buy coffee at Flatlands, Ben or one of his baristas swipes your credit card on the Square point-of-sale reader. The reader records all sales and stores them in Square's cloud storage account. For each transaction, Square verifies the credit card and credits Ben's account for 98 percent of the value of the sale. But, in addition to supporting the sales process, the Square IS also support other processes at Flatlands.

To conduct a promotion, Ben sends emails to his best customers—not directly but through Square. Ben never had to ask for his customers' email addresses because Square has on file many of the email addresses of his verified customers. If he wants to give his frequent customers a discount, Square can tell him how much the promotion will cost and the expected use rate by his customers.

Square also supports Ben's accounting processes. Every employee swipes into Square when a shift starts and swipes out when it is complete. Square pays the employees from Ben's account on paydays. Square also creates tax forms for Ben's business and sends employees their W-2 forms.

Square helps the financing process as well. If cash runs low for a month, Ben can obtain a short-term loan from Square. Square has *all* of Ben's transactions and all of his labor costs so it knows how risky the loan to Ben will be. It charges a rate Ben can't beat with a banker, it requires no documentation from Ben, and the money is available the same day.

Source: Makistock/Shutterstock

FIGURE 2-16

Image of a Square POS Device Reading a Credit Card.

While Square is the most versatile IS system Ben uses, he also uses other IS. He watches and responds to customer comments on review sites such as Google, TripAdvisor, and Yelp. He also advertises the shop through Business Ads on Facebook and through AdWords on Google.

One year into his business, Ben reports his financials are in the black. A good way to serve coffee.

Questions

2-8. List the major activities in the Customer Service process (the sale of a cup of coffee). Include activities conducted by both the customer and barista roles.

2-9. Make a BPMN diagram of the Customer Service process at Flatlands. Show swimlanes for the customer, the barista, and the Square IS.

2-10. Using Figure 2-6 as an example, diagram the information systems and processes at Flatlands.

2-11. Describe at a high level the five components of the Square IS that supports the Customer Service process.

2-12. Based on the characteristics of structured and dynamic processes in Figure 2-8, which of the processes described in this case (not just the ones supported by Square) are structured and which are dynamic? Give reasons for each.

2-13. Is Ben more like Jennifer or Jake described at the end of the chapter? Are you more like Jennifer or Jake? Provide evidence for your decision.

2-14. Using the Internet, read about Business Ads on Facebook and AdWords on Google. Which method do you think would be best for a coffee shop in your university's setting? Why?

CHAPTER RESOURCES

[1] Visio is a diagram-drawing product licensed by Microsoft. If your university belongs to the Microsoft Academic Alliance (which is likely), you can obtain a copy of Visio for free. If you want to draw diagrams that use BPMN symbols, be certain that you obtain the Premium version of this product, which is available from the Academic Alliance.

[2] From Gregory Bateson, *Steps to an Ecology of Mind* (St. Albans, Australia: Paladin Books, 1973).

MyLab MIS

Go to **MyLab MIS.com** for Auto-graded writing questions as well as the following Assisted-graded writing questions:

2-15. Your smartphone is an IS with the same five components described in the chapter. One of your parents wants you to help them buy a smartphone. Using Figure 2-5 that explains how to apply the five-component framework. How will this knowledge help you assist your parent? In other words, how can your knowledge of the five-component framework help you assist your parent?.

2-16. The common elements of information are shown in shown in Figure 2-10; one of these common elements is that information varies from person to person. The benefits of understanding information in this way are summarized in Figure 2-12. Using a personal example explain two of the benefits in Figure 2-12.

Part 2

Information Technology

The three chapters in Part 2 address the information technology that is the foundation for MIS. You may think that such technology is unimportant to you as a business professional. However, today's managers and business professionals work frequently with information technology as purchasers and purchase approvers, if not in more involved ways.

Chapter 3 discusses computer networks and the cloud. It defines basic terms and fundamental computing concepts. You will need these terms so that when we refer to three-tier architecture later in this text, you will know what those terms mean. Also, you may someday work for (or own!) a small business and have important decisions to make about networks and using the cloud.

Chapter 4 describes database processing. You will learn the purpose and roles for databases and database applications. You will also learn how to create simple entity relationship data models, which are abstractions from which you can create database structure. We will illustrate database modeling and design using the database employed by a local hospital.

Chapter 5 explains information systems security. It describes the threats, responses by organizations, and types of safeguards used to reduce security losses. You will discover that many of the topics in the chapter can be put to use in your life as a student so that you build good habits before your professional life begins.

Extension 2 also discusses technology. It highlights important aspects of software and hardware that are useful for business students.

The purpose of these technology readings is to teach you the basics about technology to enable you to be an effective IT consumer. You will learn basic terms, fundamental concepts, and useful frameworks so that you will have the knowledge to ask good questions and make appropriate requests of the IS professionals who will serve you. Those concepts and frameworks will be far more useful to you than the latest technology trend, which may be outdated by the time you graduate.

Chapter 3

Networks and the Cloud

At Chuck's Bikes Inc. (CBI), the IT staff is assembled for their monthly meeting. Juan Bouzat, their director, is leading the discussion.

"Folks, I've got some tough news. The leadership committee has decided we need to migrate most of our storage and many of our apps to the cloud in the coming months," Juan begins.

After a stunned silence, Mark, an IT app developer, speaks up. "What reasons did they give you, Juan?"

Juan replied, "They said it was because of several things. They think it will be cheaper in the long run; they would rather pay a steady price for IT than have to replace all the infrastructure from time to time. And they want to invest less in IT and more in growing the business. They don't want to own all the hardware and pay to have licenses for all the software; by moving to the cloud, they think of it as renting rather than buying. In a way it is hard to argue with them."

Mark said, "What does that mean for us?"

"Well, it means we'll be really, really busy for next year or so."

"You know what I mean—when this is done, will we still be here?"

"Let's be honest—no, we all won't be. I don't know how it will be decided or when we'll downsize, but if we move as many of the apps to the cloud as they are intending to, several of us might have to go. Myself included."

"You'll be safe, Juan."

"There will be a leadership job for someone, but if we're 25 percent smaller in headcount, and we're not doing as much app development, the supervisory job may be much different and may be better suited for someone else. There are lots of jobs out there in tech. I'll trust the market to protect me, not CBI, and if I can suggest anything to you, please do the same. You're a very talented group. Each of you has a very good career in front of you even if it's not here. I mean that."

"What do they want to move to the cloud, Juan?" Mark asks.

"Most of the data storage, most of the internal apps like HR and pay, all the customer-facing things like CRM and billing, and most of the supply chain apps."

"And how much do they think they will save?"

"They think the first year will be a big change, but long term, about 20 percent in the out years."

"What will we be doing now that the decision has been made?"

"First we need to make a list of what goes and what stays. Which apps we think we should be doing and which ones we can move. Then we start looking for vendors for the apps and options they provide and writing contracts."

"But first we will need to start streamlining a lot of what we do. We need to find out what rogue apps everyone is running and get them off of those so when we go to a cloud vendor we aren't discovering all sorts of homegrown solutions that people have been using that won't be supported by the vendor. The whole process is expected to take a year to 18 months."

Mark continues to press but without enthusiasm. "Does anyone making these decisions know what we're giving up—we'll be locked into contracts, we won't have the staff to build things when marketing or supply chain comes up with a new idea, we'll lose our best people and corporate memory..."

"I think they know some of that. But we are a support function. No one buys bikes from us because our Web site is great or our ERP system is world-class. We're the roadies; customers come to the show because of the artist, and we aren't them. What we do is essential—the show can't go on without us—but if the bosses think they can save 20 percent year over year, it's hard to argue."

Q3-1. What do business professionals need to know about networks and the Internet?

Q3-2. How does data move over a network?

Q3-3. How does a typical Web server move data on a network?

Q3-4. Why is the cloud the future for most organizations?

Q3-5. What are the typical cloud options?

PSI BIG PICTURE

IS: IS are connected by networks; many IS use the Cloud

"But, Juan, hold on. What's going to happen to the sensitive corporate data? To be safe, that stuff needs to stay with us, right?"

Sensing some light in the darkness, Terry, a database admin, joins in, "And all the customer data is sensitive. It's safer here too."

Juan with sympathy replies, "I used to think so, but so did the people at Sony, Target, Tinder, Home Depot, Snap, Verizon, and Yahoo! And that doesn't include all the government agencies and healthcare providers who were also hacked in just 2 years."

Terry agrees. "That list keeps getting bigger each year, but who would want to hack us? We're pretty small potatoes here."

"True, but imagine the impact on our bottom line if hackers corrupted our data or wiped out our customer list."

Mark joins back in. "I hate to agree with Juan, but he's right. Cloud services on their systems are so locked down nothing gets in that shouldn't. They build their apps with security at the beginning; all our systems are wide open, and we secure them as we go. And their careers depend on security. If a cloud vendor suffered a hack, that would cost it huge market share, and heads would roll."

Juan concludes, "Thanks, gang. I'll be asking everyone in the coming weeks what they want to work on during the transition process. This is going to be a challenge. I am convinced, though, that everyone who wants to find employment someplace else will find it. This whole cloud thing is probably a net positive for our jobs. We just need to be willing to move as opportunities come."

PREVIEW

The Internet is the most significant technical advancement in the past 100 years. It is still a young, unruly teenager, upsetting business and society with some new thing every year. There are a great number of details about how the Internet works, but our goal is not to bury you with technospeak. Instead, we want you to learn important distinctions about networks that will help you use them effectively and securely in the business world. Also, please realize the Internet continues to evolve, new opportunities will emerge, and a solid understanding of how networks operate will help you understand these future changes.

As you are reading this chapter, you may think, "Well, I don't need to know that. I'll just rely on outside experts to tell me what to do." But that strategy will not work in the twenty-first century. Many of your peers will be able to effectively collaborate with IT professionals and gain a competitive advantage over you. In fact, today, basic knowledge of technology is a key component of any business professional's toolkit. So, let's get started with the two main components of the Internet: networks and the cloud.

You use networks and the cloud every time you text, use social media, listen to music, or use email. These daily activities seem simple, and in this chapter, we'll see how networks and the cloud do their magic to make them that way. To dispel some of this magic, we will highlight various types of networks, how data moves on those networks, how a Web server operates, how the cloud works, and cloud options for businesses.

MyLab MIS
- Using Your Knowledge Questions 3-1, 3-2, 3-3
- Essay Questions 3-21, 3-22
- Excel and Access Application Questions 3-1, 3-2, 3-3

Q3-1 What Do Business Professionals Need to Know About Networks and the Internet?

In this question, we will introduce types of computer networks and how they are connected. The subject can be quite technical, but we will only discuss the essential ideas in general terms.

Types of Networks

To begin, a computer **network** is a collection of computers that communicate with one another over transmission lines or wireless connections. As shown in Figure 3-1, the four basic types of networks are personal area networks, local area networks, wide area networks, and the Internet.

A **personal area network (PAN)** connects devices around a single person. Most of these devices connect wirelessly with other devices up to about 10 meters. An example of a PAN is a wearable device such as a Fitbit connected to a mobile device such as an iPhone.

A **local area network (LAN)** connects computers that reside in a single geographic location. The number of connected computers can range from two to several hundred. The distinguishing characteristic of a LAN is *a single location*. Figure 3-2 shows a LAN that is typical of those in a **small office** or a **home office (SOHO)**. Typically, such LANs support fewer than a dozen or so smartphones, computers, and printers. Computer 2 and printer 5 use wired connections, while computer 1 and the smartphones are connected to the LAN wirelessly. They are all connected to a **switch**, which is a special-purpose computer that receives and transmits wired traffic on the LAN. This switch is often mislabeled a router when it is used in a small home LAN. Many businesses, of course, operate LANs that are much larger than this one, but the principles are the same for a larger LAN.

Wide area networks (WANs) connect computers at different geographic locations. The computers in two separated company sites must be connected using a WAN. To illustrate, the computers for a College of Business located on a single campus can be connected via a LAN. The computers for a College of Business located on multiple campuses must be connected via a WAN. The single- versus multiple-site distinction is important. With a LAN, an organization can place communication lines wherever it wants because all lines reside on its premises. The same is not true for a WAN. A company with offices in Chicago and Atlanta cannot run a wire down the freeway to connect computers in the two cities. Instead, the company contracts with a communications vendor that is licensed by the government and that already has lines or has the authority to run new lines between the two cities.

An internet is a network of networks. Internets connect LANs, WANs, and other internets. The most famous internet is **"the Internet"** (with an uppercase letter *I*), the collection of networks that you use when you send email or access a Web site. In addition to the public Internet, private networks of networks, called *internets*, also exist. A private internet used exclusively within an organization is sometimes called an **intranet**.

Wireless Options for Networks

Networks, like the SOHO LAN in Figure 3-2 include some devices that connect wirelessly, such as computer 1 and the smartphones. Here we contrast three wireless network options: Bluetooth, Wi-Fi, and cellular.

FIGURE 3-1

Basic Network Types

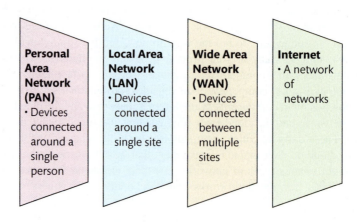

Personal Area Network (PAN)	Local Area Network (LAN)	Wide Area Network (WAN)	Internet
• Devices connected around a single person	• Devices connected around a single site	• Devices connected between multiple sites	• A network of networks

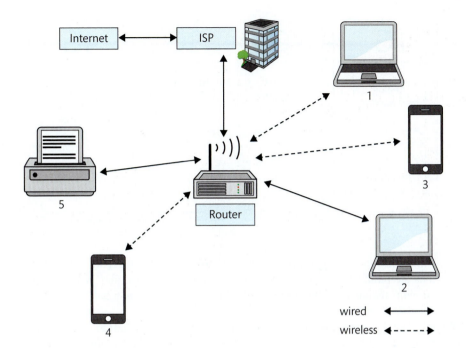

FIGURE 3-2
Typical Small Office/Home Office

Bluetooth is a common wireless communication method. It is designed for transmitting data over short distances. Some devices, such as wireless mice and keyboards, use Bluetooth to connect to the computer. Smartphones use Bluetooth to connect to automobile entertainment systems.

Wi-Fi (Wide Fidelity) is a technology that allows devices to connect wirelessly to a LAN. Common devices that use Wi-Fi are laptops and tablet computers, video game consoles, smartphones, and digital readers. Wi-Fi can be used up to about 65 feet indoors and slightly farther outdoors. It has its own set of communication rules called IEEE 802.11 and security methods.

A **cellular network**, also called a mobile network or wireless WAN (WWAN), is a communication network that uses radio signals to send and receive data to mobile users. The physical layout of a cellular network is shown in Figure 3-3. Users wirelessly connect to stationary base stations, also known as cell towers, using a variety of frequencies with low power. The base stations are connected to each adjoining station and to a mobile switching center (or MTSO). The switching center connects users to the Internet. Like Wi-Fi, cellular communication uses radio waves, but cellular radio range is greater than Wi-Fi and uses different frequencies.

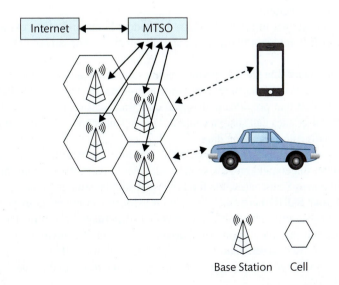

FIGURE 3-3
Cellular Network

FIGURE 3-4
Four Generations of Cellular
Networks

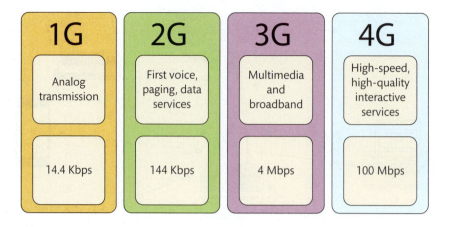

Cells in the network are typically hexagonal shapes as shown in Figure 3-3. Although most base stations are omnidirectional and located in the middle of cells, they can be directional as is common with stadiums and highways. Cells can vary in size from a half mile in diameter in urban settings to 25 miles in remote locations.

When a mobile user contacts a network a base station assigns a frequency to that user. If the user moves out of the original cell a **handover** or handoff is accomplished which switches the end user to an adjoining cell base station automatically. The gaining base station can reuse the original frequency or change to a new frequency.

Cellular networks have become more popular as they have grown in capabilities and capacities. This evolution in features, called generations, is shown in Figure 3-4. As these features have grown in utility and diminished in cost, mobile networks are now more popular than fixed networks in many countries and are the only method of digital communication in some countries, particularly in Africa.

Connecting a LAN to the Internet

When you connect to the Internet, you are actually connecting to an **Internet service provider (ISP)**. An ISP offers access to the Internet and other associated services. It has three important functions. First, it provides you with a legitimate Internet address. Second, it serves as your gateway to the Internet. The ISP receives the communications from your computer and passes them on to the Internet, and it receives communications from the Internet and passes them on to you. Finally, ISPs pay for the Internet. They collect money from their customers and pay access fees and other charges on your behalf.

Figure 3-5 shows the three common alternatives for connecting to the Internet. Notice that we are discussing how your computer connects to the Internet via a WAN; we are not discussing the structure of the WAN itself. Search the Web for *leased lines* or *PSDN* if you want to learn more about WAN architectures.

SOHO LANs (like that in Figure 3-2) and individual home and office computers are commonly wired to an ISP in one of two ways: a special telephone line called a DSL line or a cable TV line.

A **digital subscriber line (DSL)** operates on the same lines as voice telephones, but it operates so that its signals do not interfere with voice telephone service. A **cable line** is the second type of ISP connection that provides high-speed data transmission using cable television lines. Because up to 500 user sites can share a cable line, performance varies depending on how many other users are sending and receiving data.

To provide some context for networks, let's introduce an example we can use throughout the chapter to better understand how these network devices work together. In this example, you are posting an image to Snapchat, while the process would be similar for any social media. You are at home on your SOHO network; your laptop using Wi-Fi connects to your home router, which carries your data through a cable line to your ISP, perhaps Spectrum. These network and connection topics are the main points of Question 3-1. Your ISP then connects you over the Internet to Snapchat Web servers that we describe in Question 3-3. How the data that comprise your image get to Snapchat over this connection is explained next in Question 3-2.

Type	Topology	Transmission Line	Transmission Speed	Equipment Used	Protocol Commonly Used	Remarks
Local area network	Local area network	UTP or optical fiber	Common: 10/100/1000 Mbps Possible: 1 Gbps	Switch NIC UTP or optical	IEEE 802.3 (Ethernet)	Switches connect devices, multiple switches on all but small LANs.
	Local area network with wireless	UTP or optical for non-wireless connections	Up to 600 Mbps	Wireless access point Wireless NIC	IEEE 802.11n	Access point transforms wired LAN (802.3) to wireless LAN (802.11).
Connections to the Internet	DSL modem to ISP	DSL telephone	Personal: Upstream to 1 Mbps, downstream to 40 Mbps (max 10 likely in most areas)	DSL modem DSL-capable telephone line	DSL	Can have computer and phone use simultaneously. Always connected.
	Cable modem to ISP	Cable TV lines to optical cable	Upstream to 1 Mbps Downstream 300 Kbps to 10 Mbps	Cable modem Cable TV cable	Cable	Capacity is shared with other sites; performance varies depending on others' use.
	WAN wireless	Wireless connection to WAN	500 Kbps to 1.7 Mbps	Wireless WAN modem	One of several wireless standards	Sophisticated protocol enables several devices to use the same wireless frequency.

FIGURE 3-5
Summary of LAN Networks

Q3-2 How Does Data Move over a Network?

Having described the general types of networks and how they are connected, now we consider how data moves over these connected networks. We'll discuss protocols, addressing, languages, SOA, and carriers.

Protocols

The networks that comprise the Internet use a large variety of communication methods and conventions, and data must flow seamlessly across them. To provide seamless flow, protocols are used. A **protocol** is a set of rules used by two communicating devices. You are not a device, but you use protocols. You speak differently to your friends than your parents or a 3-year old. It's still English for all three, but the rules are different—you banter with friends, you exercise patience with your parents, and you fill in blanks with the 3-year old. You use and reuse these protocols in many different situations to communicate with many different types of people.

The same is true of devices on the Internet. We program them with many protocols so they can communicate in a wide variety of settings with a wide variety of other devices. To get an appreciation of how protocols are used, we next examine how protocols are used on a LAN and then how they work on the Internet.

The devices on a LAN use common protocols to talk with each other and accommodate new devices. The **IEEE 802.3 protocol** is used for wired LAN connections. This protocol standard, also called **Ethernet**, specifies hardware characteristics, such as which wire carries which signals. Wireless LAN connections use the **IEEE 802.11 protocol**. Several versions of 802.11 exist, and as of 2017 the most current one is IEEE 802.11ac. The differences among these versions are beyond the scope of this discussion. Just note that the current standard, 802.11ac, allows speeds of up to 1300 Mbps, a 100 percent increase in speed over the previous protocol in just over 4 years.

To illustrate how protocols work on the Internet, let's resume our example of posting an image to Snapchat as shown in Figure 3-6. Your communication with Snapchat Web servers involves nearly unimaginable complexity. Somehow, your smartphone communicates with these servers half a world away even though these devices most likely have not interacted before. This is the taken-for-granted marvel of Internet protocols—you can upload any image type, size, or format, and you don't have to care about any of the devices that will carry your image to

FIGURE 3-6

You, the Internet, and Snapchat

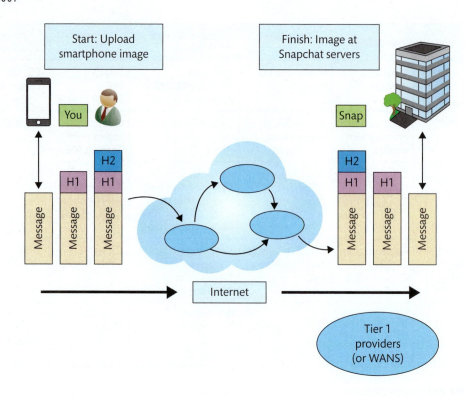

Snapchat. Your image might show up on a watch, a smartphone, or the side of a refrigerator, but it's your exact image, every time.

This process depends on two clever techniques. First, your upload, which is too big to travel in one piece, is broken up into parts called packets, and each packet passed along from WAN to WAN in such a way that it arrives intact. Then your original image is reassembled, any parts that were lost or damaged are resent, and the reconstructed image is delivered to the server for processing. In Figure 3-6, the message on the leftmost side is just one packet, one part of your original image. All the other packets that comprise your image are treated the same way.

The second technique is encapsulation. Each of your packets swimming their way from you to Snapchat is encapsulated, enveloped, inside a container of protocols. As shown in Figure 3-6 each packet, shown as *Message*, is contained within several containers, several layers of these protocols. In Figure 3-6, your original message is encapsulated within H1, then this message + H1 is encapsulated within H2. Your device and ISP wrap these layers on, and the Snapchat servers take them off, like Russian dolls or envelopes within envelopes.

These layers of protocols are organized according to the **TCP/IP Protocol architecture**, which is a scheme of protocol types arranged in layers. We will define the role of several important protocols here.

Hypertext Transport Protocol (http) is the protocol used between browsers and Web servers. When you use a browser like Edge, Safari, or Chrome to upload your image to Snapchat, you are using a program that implements the http protocol. At the other end, the Snapchat server also processes http, as you will learn in the next part of this chapter. Even though your browser and the Web server have never "met" before, they can communicate with one another because they both follow the rules of http. Your browser sends requests for service encoded in a predefined http *request format*. The server receives that request, processes the request (in this case to upload an image), and formats a response in a predefined http *response format*.

A secure version of http is available called **https**. Whenever you see *https* in your browser's address bar, you have a secure transmission and you can safely send sensitive data like credit card numbers. However, when you are on the Internet, unless you are using https, you should assume that all of your communication is open and could be published on every social media platform 5 minutes from now.

Two additional TCP/IP protocols are common. Smtp, or Simple Mail Transfer Protocol, is used for email transmissions (along with other protocols as well). Ftp, or File Transfer Protocol, is used to move large files over the Internet. Google Drive and Microsoft OneDrive use ftp to transmit files between their cloud servers and your computer.

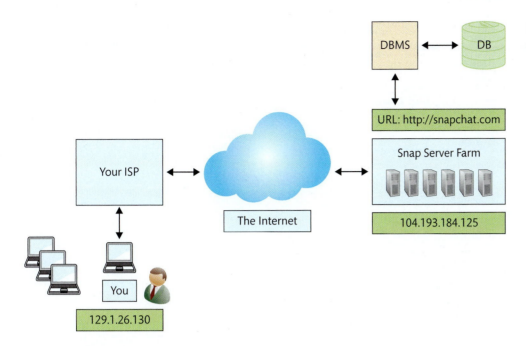

FIGURE 3-7
Network Addresses

A final protocol, IP (Internet Protocol), identifies an address for every device connected to the Internet. It also stamps a destination and sender IP address onto every packet moving on the Internet so that along its way to its destination the intermediate stops know where to send the packet. This protocol is discussed next.

Addressing

Every location on the Internet has an address, called an **IP address**, which is a number that uniquely identifies its location as shown in Figure 3-7. Two IP addresses are shown, one for your machine and one for the Snap server farm. To connect to the Internet every device needs an IP address. Public IP addresses identify a particular device on the public Internet. Private IP addresses identify a particular device on a private network, usually on a LAN. These private addresses are controlled within the LAN. When you connect to your LAN, your laptop receives a private IP address, and when you use the Internet, your ISP gives you an IP address, probably a temporary one while you use the Internet.

IP addresses have two formats; the older version is IPv4, which has a four-decimal dotted format such as 104.193.184.125 (a previous IP address for Snapchat). The more recent version, IPv6, is much longer. If you type into a browser the IP address, it will connect with the device at that address.

No one would want to remember these numbers, so common locations are given a **domain name**, a worldwide-unique name that is affiliated with a particular public IP address. Snapchat .com is an example of a domain name.

Note two important points: First, several domain names can point to the same Internet address. Second, the affiliation of domain names with Internet addresses is dynamic. The owner of the domain name can change the affiliated addresses at its discretion.

Languages

While protocols are rules for devices to follow, they don't specify a particular language. All sorts of computer languages are used on networks. One type of language, common on Web pages, is called a markup language. A **markup language** is a system for annotating a document in a way distinguishable from the text. It takes its name from "marking up" a written manuscript to show how it should be displayed. One markup would indicate that this is the title, center it on the page, and use 18-point font; another would say this text should be shown with an underline. A digital markup language does the same thing; it tells a browser how to display a document. A markup language provides instructions about the display, not a language used to write the content. The value of using markup languages is that the text can be written once but formatted dynamically as different devices retrieve the document from a Web server and display the text in a variety of ways—on a smartphone, on a tablet, or on a TV screen.

FIGURE 3-8

html Code

```
<!DOCTYPE html PUBLIC "-//W3C//DTD XHTML 1.0 Transitional//EN" "http://www.w3.org/TR/xhtml1/DTD/xhtml1-transitional.dtd">
<html xmlns="http://www.w3.org/1999/xhtml">
<head>
<meta content="en-us" http-equiv="Content-Language" />
<meta content="text/html; charset=utf-8" http-equiv="Content-Type" />
<title>PSI Example HTML</title>
<style type="text/css">
.style1 {
    font-size: xx-large;
    text-align: center;
    font-family: Arial, Helvetica, sans-serif;
}
.style2 {
    color: #FF00FF;
}
.style3 {
    font-size: medium;
    text-align: center;
    font-family: Arial, Helvetica, sans-serif;
}
.style5 {
    font-size: medium;
    text-align: left;
    font-family: Arial, Helvetica, sans-serif;
}
</style>
</head>
<body>
<p class="style1">
    <span class="style2"><strong>Processes, Systems, and Information</strong></span></p>
<p class="style1"> </p>
<p class="style3"><em>Second Edition</em></p>
<p class="style3"> </p>
<p class="style5">Example html Document</p>
<p class="style5"> </p>
<p class="style5"> </p>
<p class="style5">Click <a href="http://www.PearsonHigherEd.com/kroenke">here</a>
for the textbook&#39;s Web site at Pearson Education.</p>
</body>
</html>
```

(a) Sample html Code Snippet

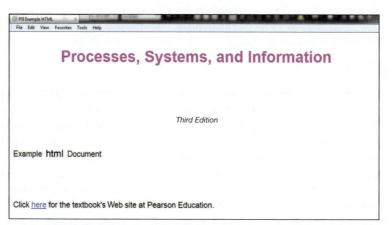

(b) Document Created from html Code in Figure 3-25(a)

Two important markup languages are html and xml. Snapchat and other social media sites use both html and xml.

Hypertext Markup Language (html) is the most common language for defining the structure and layout of Web pages. An html **tag** is a notation used to define a data element for display or other purposes. The following html is a typical heading tag:

```
<h2>Price of Item</h2>
```

Notice that tags are enclosed in < > (called *angle brackets*) and that they occur in pairs. The start of this tag is indicated by <h2>, and the end of the tag is indicated by </h2>. The words between the tags are the value of the tag. This html tag means to place the words "Price of Item" on a Web page in the style of a level-two heading. The creator of the Web page will define the style (font size, color, and so forth) for h2 headings and the other tags to be used.

Web pages include hyperlinks, which are pointers to other Web pages. A hyperlink contains the URL of the Web page to find when the user clicks the hyperlink. The URL can reference a page on the server that generated the page containing the hyperlink, or it can reference a page on another server.

Figure 3-8(a) shows a sample html document. The document has a heading that provides metadata about the page and a body that contains the content. The tag <h1> means to format the indicated text as a level-one heading. The tag <a> defines a hyperlink. This tag has an **attribute**, which is a variable used to provide properties about a tag. Not all tags have attributes, but many do. Each attribute has a standard name. The attribute for a hyperlink is href, and its value indicates which Web page is to be displayed when the user clicks the link. Here, the page is to be returned when the user clicks the hyperlink. Figure 3-8(b) shows this page as rendered by Internet Explorer.

HTML pages are often supported by **Cascading Style Sheets (CSS)**. A CSS defines the fonts and layout of all the elements on pages on a Web site so that the site has one consistent look and feel. For example, every <h2> value will be displayed the same way on every page. It is easier to write a CSS that governs all the various pages on a Web site than to write each font and indentation for every page.

XML (Extensible Markup Language) is a markup language like html but is machine readable and was designed to enable the exchange of structured data over the Web. An example XML page is shown in Figure 3-9. A tag in XML might be <customer_address>, which would tell the Web app reading the page the address of the customer.

SOA

One other method is commonly used on the Internet to help move data along. It is a design philosophy called **service-oriented architecture (SOA)**. First we define it, and then we give an example.

SOA provides a way for apps on a network to talk to each other. SOA apps use standard protocols to publish a menu of services that the application provides, the structure of the data that it expects to receive, the structure of the data that it will produce, and the ways in which services can be requested. The provider of a Web service, often a Web server, uses these standards to specify the work that it will perform and how it will provide it. Clients of that service use those standards to request and receive service.

An analogy might help. A house, a client in our analogy, needs services from a city, a Web server. The city provides water, electricity, sanitation, transportation, and other services to the house. The people in the house, the client apps in the SOA world, use lights, computers, toilets, and bathtubs. The people don't care how the city generates the clean water or electricity, they just know how to request it—they know how to turn on switches or rotate knobs, and they know what they will get in return. The designers of city services don't care if you want electricity delivered to an apartment, a mobile home, or a barn. Without SOA, the people in the house would have to contact each service provider and describe in some detail what they wish to receive. SOA helps automate these requests. Returning to our Snapchat example, your machine and the Snapchat servers use login and upload services designed to comply with SOA standards. You do not have to describe what a photo is nor how you want it stored.

```xml
<?xml version="1.0" encoding="utf-8" ?>
<customers>
 <customer>
   <first_name>Joe</first_name>
   <last_name>Howard</last_name>
   <customer_address>123 Elm</customer_address>
   <customer_city>Athens</customer_city>
   <customer_state>OH</customer_state>
 </customer>
 <customer>
   <first_name>Terry</first_name>
   <last_name>Jones</last_name>
   <customer_address>456 Oak</customer_address>
   <customer_city>Millwood</customer_city>
   <customer_state>OH</customer_state>
 </customer>
</customers>
```

FIGURE 3-9

XML page

Carriers

As your data moves across the Internet it moves between several large WANs operated by tele-communication providers. These carriers in the United States include AT&T, Verizon, Sprint, and Century. They form the Internet backbone and are called Tier 1 network providers. These providers earn revenue by selling services to ISPs, which connect to the Internet via these Tier 1 providers. In Figure 3-6 earlier, three blue Tier 1 WANs were shown.

Each of these large network providers freely shares its data with other Tier 1 providers. These exchanges are governed by **peering** agreements that specify how the data will move among providers.

One significant issue is that some Internet participants use a great deal of the bandwidth on these Tier 1 networks compared to the rest of us. In fact, Netflix uses about a third of all Internet traffic in North America between 9 p.m. and midnight. Some Tier 1 providers would like to cre-ate a high-traffic lane over the Internet for these content providers and charge them accordingly. Others favor a **net neutrality** approach where all data moving on the Internet is treated equally. Many governments worldwide are becoming involved in how these disputes are regulated and are beginning to favor a net neutral approach that regulates the Internet as a public good like electricity or water and less like a commercial venture.

Q3-3 ▶ How Does a Typical Web Server Move Data on a Network?

At this point, you know basic networking terms and have a high-level understanding of the types of networks and how data moves over these networks. To complete this chapter's high-level survey of network technology, you need to know a bit about the processing that occurs on a Web server.

When you log into Snapchat you are connected to one of many Snapchat Web servers as shown in Figure 3-10. Web servers are a key component in three-tier architecture. Almost all social media apps and e-commerce sites use the **three-tier architecture**, which is an arrange-ment of user computers and servers into three categories, or tiers. The user tier consists of computers, smartphones, and other devices that have browsers that request and process Web pages. The server tier is composed of computers that run Web servers and process applica-tion programs. The database tier consists of computers that run a database management system (DBMS) that processes requests to retrieve and store data. DBMS are explained more fully in Chapter 4, "Database Processing." Figure 3-10 shows only one computer at the database tier. Some sites have multicomputer database tiers as well.

When you enter *http://snapchat.com* in your browser, the browser sends a request that trav-els over the Internet to a computer in the server tier at Snapchat. That request is formatted and

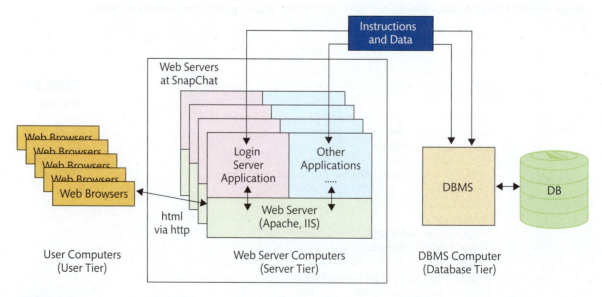

FIGURE 3-10

Three-Tier Architecture

processed according to the protocol rules of http. Notice that if you just type *Snapchat.com*, your browser will add the *http://* to signify that it is using http. In response to your request, a server-tier computer sends back a **Web page**, which is a document that is coded in one of the standard page markup languages such as html.

Web servers are software programs that run on a server-tier computer and that manage http traffic by sending and receiving Web pages to and from clients. A login server is an app program that runs on a server-tier computer. A login server receives requests from users via the Web server, takes some action, and returns a response to the users via the Web server. Typical login server functions are to obtain user names and passwords and compare them to credentials stored in the database. In Figure 3-10, the server-tier computers are running a Web server program, a login server app, and other apps having an unspecified purpose.

When you supply your user name and password and click submit, the login server sends your credentials to the DBMS and asks the DBMS to look through the database of accounts to determine if there is a match. If none is found the DBMS will reply to the login server that no match was found; if a match is found the login server will tell the Web server to send you your Snapchat home page.

To ensure acceptable performance, commercial Web sites usually are supported by several or even many Web server computers in a facility called a **Web farm** or server farm. Work is distributed among the computers in a Web farm so as to minimize customer delays. The coordination among multiple Web server computers is a fantastic dance, but, alas, we do not have space to tell that story here. Just imagine the coordination that must occur as you upload a photo, search for another user, or download images.

This concludes our overview of networks. We began with types of networks and their connections, then discussed how data moved over a network, and finished with how a Web server moves data at the server end. Most of the fundamentals have remained unchanged for the last several decades, except for the growth of cellular networks, XML, and SOA. Another recent development, cloud computing, deserves the entire second half of this chapter.

Q3-4 Why Is the Cloud the Future for Most Organizations?

Until 2010 or so, most organizations constructed and maintained their own computing infrastructure. Organizations purchased or leased hardware, installed it on their premises, and used it to support organizational email, Web sites, e-commerce sites, and in-house applications, such as accounting and operations systems. After about 2010, however, organizations began to move their computing infrastructure to the cloud, and it is likely that in the future all or nearly all computing infrastructure will be leased from the cloud. So, just what is the cloud, and why is it the future?

The Cloud

While it is called *the* cloud, there are many clouds. Amazon has the biggest cloud; Microsoft also offers a cloud, as do many other smaller vendors. We define the **cloud** as the *elastic* leasing of *pooled* computer resources over the *Internet*. The term *cloud* is used because most early diagrams of three-tier and other Internet-based systems used a cloud symbol to represent the Internet (see Figure 3-6 for an example), and organizations came to view their infrastructure as being "somewhere in the cloud."

Consider each of the italicized terms in the definition. The term **elastic**, which was first used this way by Amazon, means that the amount of resources leased can be increased or decreased dynamically, programmatically, in a short span of time and that organizations pay for just the resources that they use. Suppose a video game company is offering a hot new smartphone game tomorrow. It could plan to use its own servers to push the app out, but it expects about a 1,000-fold increase in traffic for the first week, and with that much traffic download speeds will be terrible. As a result, it decides to contract with its cloud vendor to add servers as demand dictates. Elastic means easily expandable.

The resources are **pooled** because many different organizations use the same physical hardware; they share that hardware. Cloud vendors dynamically allocate tasks to physical hardware as customer needs increase or decrease. The same servers that support the game company tomorrow are being leased today to a music company or a university. The important point here

FIGURE 3-11
2017 Cloud Market Share

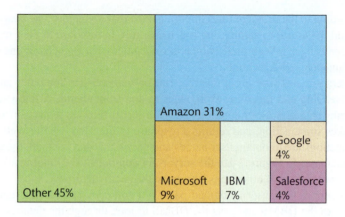

is that game company, the music company, and the university can benefit from **economies of scale**. According to this principle, the average cost of production decreases as the size of the operation increases. Cloud vendors can pass along the savings from economies of scale and reduce the cost of computing for everyone using the cloud.

Finally, the resources are accessed via **Internet protocols and standards**, which are additions to TCP/IP that enable cloud-hosting vendors to provide processing capabilities in flexible yet standardized ways. In the old days, if two companies wanted to share computing resources they would have to meet and iron out a thousand details about how the data would flow. The commonality of Internet protocols and SOA eliminates this.

Amazon, Google, Microsoft, and IBM offer cloud services, but the industry is dominated by Amazon and its Amazon Web Services (AWS), as shown in Figure 3-11. AWS generates more than $30 billion in revenue and holds more than 30 percent of the market share. Microsoft, IBM, and Google together own 20 percent of the market. Many expect that cloud services will soon become a leading source of revenue for them. Those are giant companies with billions in revenues, but the cloud is becoming their cash cow. The values are staggering. Recently, Snap announced that it was buying $3 billion worth of cloud services from Google and AWS over the next 5 years. To appreciate the size of this market, there are only 50 companies in the world larger than this $100 billion a year market.

The cloud market grew by a whopping 25 percent in 2016 and is expected to continue at that rate through 2020, a trend displayed in Figure 3-12. By some estimates, 85 percent of all data center traffic will be in the cloud by 2020.

Snapchat uses Google's cloud, your university is probably using Microsoft or Google's cloud for email, and Apple, Netflix, and Spotify use Amazon Web Services. A variety of business

FIGURE 3-12

Total Public Cloud Market
(Forrester)

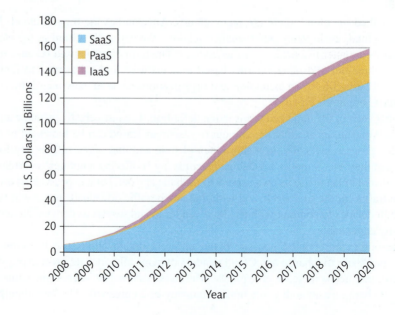

Microsoft—Office Online
Salesforce—CRM
Box—File storage
AWS—Variety
Google—G Suite
Concur—Expense management
JiRA—Service and ticket management
Slack—Collaboration
ADP—Payroll management

FIGURE 3-13

Top Business Cloud Apps

services are offered by cloud vendors as shown in Figure 3-13. Some of the more popular services are Microsoft Office Online, Google's Suite, storage, expense management, sales, and payroll.

Why Is the Cloud Preferred to In-House Hosting?

Figure 3-14 displays advantages of cloud-based and in-house hosting. As you can see, the positives are heavily tilted toward cloud-based computing. The cloud vendor Rackspace will lease you one medium server for as little as 1.5 cents per hour. You can obtain and access that server today, actually within a few minutes. Tomorrow, if you need thousands of servers, you can readily scale up to obtain them. Furthermore, you know the cost structure; although you might have a surprise with regard to how many customers want to access your Web site, you won't have any surprises as to how much it will cost.

Another positive is that you'll be receiving best-of-breed security and disaster recovery (discussed in Chapter 5). In addition, you need not worry that you're investing in technology that will soon be obsolete; the cloud vendor is taking that risk. All of this is possible because the cloud vendor is gaining economies of scale by selling to an entire industry, not just to you. The cloud also has personnel advantages. With in-house hosting, not only will you have to construct your own data center, you will also need to acquire and train the personnel to run it and then manage those personnel and your facility.

The primary advantage of in-house hosting is control of data. You know where your data—which may be a large part of your organization's value—is located. You know how many copies of your data there are or even if they are located in the same country as you are and the laws that apply to that data. You are not subject to changes in the vendor's management, policy, and prices. Finally, you know the security and disaster preparedness that is actually in place.

Cloud Advantages	In-House Advantages
Small capital requirements	Control of data
Known cost structure	No dependence on vendor
Responsive to fluctuations in demand	Visibility of security and disaster response
Strong security and disaster response	
No obsolescence	
Less cost due to economies of scale	
Less IT staff and personnel to acquire, train	

FIGURE 3-14

Comparison of Cloud and In-House Advantages

Why Now?

A skeptic responds to Figure 3-14 by saying, "If it's so great, why hasn't cloud-based hosting been used for years?" Why now?

In fact, cloud-based hosting (or a version of it under a different name) has been around since the 1960s. Long before the creation of the personal computer and networks, time-sharing vendors provided slices of computer time on a use-fee basis. However, the technology of that time, continuing up until the first decade of this century, did not favor the construction and use of enormous data centers.

Two factors have made cloud-based hosting advantageous today. First, processors, data communication, and data storage are so cheap as to be nearly free, as discussed in Chapter 1. At the scale of a Web farm of hundreds of thousands of servers, processing for an hour costs essentially nothing, as the 1.5-cent price per hour indicates. Because data communication is so cheap, getting the data to and from that processor is also nearly free. Second, advances in SOA and protocol adoption have made the cloud even more economical, transparent to the user, and convenient.

Outsourcing

Business decisions about using the cloud are similar to other business decisions about outsourcing. Outsourcing is the process of hiring another organization to perform a service. Typically, firms use outsourcing to reduce costs, gain expertise, or free management time. A business can outsource many activities such as customer support, accounting, graphic design, security, and IT. Snapchat, for example, might outsource the hiring of programmers, or its 24/7 customer support service. Outsourcing is also discussed in Extension 3 in the context of outsourcing the development of an IS.

In this question, we described the cloud and what makes it increasingly attractive. Next, we consider the options provided by cloud vendors.

Q3-5 What Are the Typical Cloud Options?

The cloud is not one size fits all. Customers choose among a number of options. Here we discuss the three main options that cloud vendors offer and conclude with a final option—a customer might want to make its own cloud.

Public Cloud Options

We can organize cloud-based service offerings into the three categories shown in Figure 3-15. An organization that provides **software as a service (SaaS)** provides not only hardware infrastructure but also an operating system and app programs on top of that hardware. For example, Salesforce.com provides programs for customer and sales tracking as a service. Similarly, Microsoft provides Office Online and OneDrive as a service. Exchange, Lync, and SharePoint apps are provided as a service "in the cloud."

The second category of cloud hosting is **platform as a service (PaaS)**, whereby vendors provide hosted computers, an operating system, and possibly a DBMS. Microsoft Windows Azure, for example, provides servers installed with Windows Server. Customers of Windows Azure then add their own apps on top of the hosted platform. Microsoft SQL Azure provides a host with Windows Server and SQL Server. Oracle On Demand provides a hosted server with Oracle Database. Google offers Google App Engine (GAE) as a Paas; Snap is using GAE to host its Snapchat app. Again, for PaaS, organizations add their own apps to the host.

FIGURE 3-15

Three Fundamental Cloud Types

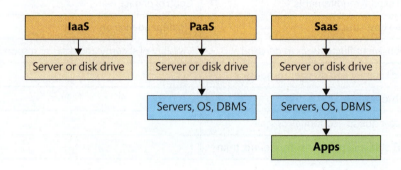

MIS InClass 3

Peanut Butter and Jelly

The purpose of this exercise is to help you gain a better understanding of process topics. In this exercise, you will make a list of activities required for the process of making a peanut butter and jelly sandwich.

To begin, write down on a piece of paper a sequential list of activities needed to make a peanut butter and jelly sandwich. Your instructor may choose to help the class develop a list of objects needed such as the jars of peanut butter and jelly, the knife, and the bread. Take 3 to 5 minutes to accomplish this step.

Call on one person in the class to read his or her list of activities. The teacher will follow each step. Discuss as a class or in small teams:

1. How accurate was the student's activity list? How accurate was your activity list?
2. What makes this apparently simple process challenging to write down?
3. How can a business improve its process of listing activities? If businesses struggle to articulate their activities, what things could be done to help make more accurate activity lists?
4. Below your own activity list, make a list of the assumptions you are making. Once complete, share your list and listen to the lists of assumptions other students recorded. Are you surprised how many assumptions are necessary?
5. Make a BPMN diagram of the Sandwich Making process. Assume two roles: a stationary assembler and a runner who gets the items from different spots in the kitchen.

6. If you operated a small business to make and sell 100 peanut butter and jelly sandwiches a day, would your process be structured or dynamic? What objectives would you specify? What IS might be helpful? For this IS, write down the procedure to use it.
7. Can your business scale up to produce 1,000 sandwiches a day? If it did, would it produce economies of scale, where the average cost of making a sandwich decreases as the size of the operation increases? The cloud is based on economies of scale; how are the cloud economies of scale similar and different to your operation?

Source: Hemeroskopion/Fotolia

The most basic cloud offering is **infrastructure as a service (IaaS)**, which is the cloud hosting of a bare server computer or disk drive. The Amazon AWS provides bare servers, and its Simple Storage Server provides, in essence, an unlimited, reliable disk drive in the cloud. Google's IAAS is Google Compute Engine, and Rackspace provides similar capabilities.

Organizations choose the cloud service they need. For example, in the chapter introduction, Juan is describing CBI's move to the cloud. Chuck's Bikes is planning on using a SaaS product like Salesforce for its customer-facing apps and other SaaS options for HR, payroll, and supply chain. It is also planning to run its SAP ERP system on a PaaS offering from AWS.

Private Cloud

Cloud-based hosting makes sense for most organizations. The only organizations or government agencies for which it may not make sense are those that are required by law or by industry standard practice to have physical control over their data. Such organizations might be forced to create and maintain their own hosting infrastructure. A financial institution, for example, might be legally required to maintain physical control over its data.

For these companies, an option is a private cloud. A **private cloud** is a cloud owned and operated by an organization for its own benefit. A private cloud, also called an on-premise cloud, is elastic and Internet based but not pooled with other organizations. Data and apps stay within the company's physical control. A large company, particularly in the finance and banking industry, might host a number of its apps in its own private cloud.

The cloud presents businesses with options. Our goal in this chapter was to help you understand network and cloud options so that you can participate in business decisions about their use. The Internet and the technologies that support it are constantly generating new opportunities, and it is valuable to understand the basics of how they work so that you can wisely make decisions that rely on them.

Ethics Guide

Showrooming: The Consequences

Showrooming occurs when someone visits a brick-and-mortar store to examine and evaluate products without the intention of buying at that store. Rather, once the consumer has decided on the most suitable product, he or she purchases that product elsewhere, usually online. Thus, if you visit a Best Buy store, check out the Windows Surface tablets, ask the sales personnel questions about the various alternatives, and then return home to purchase the one you like best from an online vendor, you are showrooming Best Buy merchandise.

In most cases, online vendors charge less than brick-and-mortar vendors because they save money on rent, employees, utilities, and other costs of operating a physical retail presence. If they choose, online vendors can pass those savings on to the purchaser, in the form of lower prices, free shipping, or both.

Online vendors have another advantage. While all brick-and-mortar stores must pay sales tax, unless an online vendor has a physical presence in your state, that vendor need not pay. You, as the purchaser of goods from out of state, are supposed to declare and pay state tax on your purchase, but few people do. Thus, the price charged by a brick-and-mortar store can be the same as the online vendor, but it can be cheaper to buy online if the cost of shipping is less than your state's sales tax. (This comparison is subject to recent changes in online taxation.)

To facilitate showrooming, Amazon.com developed a mobile native app called Price Check that is available for iOS and Android devices. Using mobile devices, consumers can scan the UPC product code, take a picture of a product, or say the name of a product, and Amazon.com will respond with its price as well as prices from many other online vendors.

DISCUSSION QUESTIONS

1. In your opinion, with regard to showrooming, are online vendors behaving unethically? Use both the categorical imperative (page 18) and utilitarianism (page 43) in your answer.
2. In your opinion, is Amazon.com behaving unethically by creating and disseminating the Price Check app? Use both the categorical imperative and utilitarianism in your answer.
3. In your opinion, are consumers behaving unethically when they showroom? Use both the categorical imperative and utilitarianism in your answer.
4. How would you advise senior managers of brick-and-mortar stores to respond to showrooming? How can brick-and-mortar stores compete?
5. Consider a consumer who elects not to pay state tax on online purchases from a vendor that need not pay that tax on his or her behalf:
   a. Is there an ethical responsibility to pay state tax? Again, consider both categorical imperative and utilitarianism perspectives.
   b. Suppose a consumer says, "Look, most of the state tax money just goes to bloated retirement programs anyway. All those old people aren't entitled to my money." Does this posture change your answer to question 5a? Why or why not?
   c. Suppose a consumer says, "I'm just one of millions who are doing this in our state. My piddly $50 really doesn't matter." Does this posture change your answer to question 5a? Why or why not?
   d. Suppose a consumer says, "I will do more for society in our state with my $50 than the state government ever will." Does this posture change your answer to question 5a? Why or why not?
6. Long-term, is showrooming good for an individual? Good for the economy? Both?

ACTIVE REVIEW

Q3-1 **What do business professionals need to know about networks and the Internet?**

Define *computer network*. Explain the differences among four basic types of networks. Explain the key distinction of a LAN. Describe the purpose of each component in Figure 3-2. List three ways of connecting a LAN or computer to the Internet; explain the nature of each. Describe the three wireless options: Bluetooth, Wi-Fi, and cellular. Explain the differences in the four generations of cellular networks.

Q3-2 **How does data move over a network?**

Define *protocol* and provide several examples. Explain the key difference between 802.3 and 802.11. Describe how packets and encapsulation enable data to move. Explain what an IP address is and its format. Describe how a domain name is related to an IP address. Describe html and explain how tags and attributes work. Explain the basic idea behind SOA. Describe how Tier 1 providers make revenue and explain a peering agreement.

Q3-3 **How does a typical Web server move data on a network?**

Define *three-tier architecture* and name and describe each tier. Explain the function of a Web page and a Web server. Describe the purpose of a Web farm. Explain the function of each tier in Figure 3-8 as a Web page is processed.

Q3-4 **Why is the cloud the future for most organizations?**

Define *cloud* and explain the three key terms in your definition. Using Figure 3-14 as a guide, compare and contrast cloud-based and in-house hosting. Explain three factors that make cloud computing possible today.

Q3-5 **What are the typical cloud options?**

Define *SaaS*, *PaaS*, and *IaaS*. Provide an example of each. For each, describe the requirements for when it would be the most appropriate option. Explain how a private cloud is different from a traditional cloud and which types of organizations it would appeal to.

KEY TERMS AND CONCEPTS

USING YOUR KNOWLEDGE

3-1. Suppose that you are Juan at CBI. List and describe three criteria you would use in helping CBI decide whether it should move a particular app to the cloud. Justify your criteria.
MyLab MIS

3-2. Suppose you manage a group of seven employees in a small business. Each of your employees wants to be connected to the Internet. Consider two alternatives:
MyLab MIS

Alternative A: Each employee has his or her own modem and connects individually to the Internet.

Alternative B: The employees' computers are connected using a LAN, and the network uses a single modem to connect.

a. Sketch the equipment and lines required for each alternative.

b. Explain the actions you need to take to create each alternative.

c. Which of these two alternatives do you recommend?

3-3. Net neutrality is an issue that continues to be challenging for the government. Do you favor net neutrality, or would you prefer a more commercial structure where content providers can be charged a premium to move their packets faster?

3-4. In Google search, type in "What is my IP address." Also, again using Google, discover your school's IP address.

3-5. Look up articles on the Internet about peering agreements. Describe two current peering issues faced by major networks.

3-6. In this chapter, we only briefly discussed TCP/IP, the Internet protocol suite. Read more about TCP/IP at Wikipedia using the term *Internet Protocol Suite*. Where and when did the Internet protocol suite begin? How long did the Internet use TCP/IP before the advent of the Web?

3-7. Read more about personal area networks and specify two products that you would buy, assuming you have the funds, and the reasons you would buy them.

3-8. Using Google, discover which large companies are using the cloud and the size of their contracts. Describe three of these large customers, their cloud vendor, and the size of the contract.

COLLABORATION EXERCISE 3

Collaborate with a group of fellow students to answer the following questions. For this exercise, do not meet face to face. Your task will be easier if you coordinate your work with SharePoint, Office 365, Google Docs, or equivalent collaboration tools. (See Chapter 10 for a discussion of collaboration tools and processes.) Your answers should reflect the thinking of the entire group, not just that of one or two individuals.

This exercise has two major parts. The first addresses installing a LAN and the second the use of wearable devices.

Suppose that you have been asked by your fraternity or sorority to look into improving the LAN in your house. Assume your house is approximately 6,000 square feet with about 25 active users of Internet services at one time. Also, assume your house uses a separate cable for its TV service.

Using Google, discover discussion boards where others have asked how to upgrade routers at fraternities and sororities. Read several of the posts and as many of the replies as you can.

3-9. List the attributes you want in a router. One is cost. What are three other important attributes to consider when buying a router? Specify the highest and lowest value for these attributes for use in your fraternity/sorority.

3-10. For you to advise your house on how to update its system, what are three specifics the decision-makers need to know before they hire someone? That is, based on your reading of the discussion boards, what are three topics most houses must decide before they can proceed?

A second topic: Personal area network (PAN) use. Also called wearables or wireless PAN (WPAN).

3-11. Using Google or other search engines, read about how athletes are using wearable devices. Describe four ways that athletes and coaches can use wearable devices to improve performance (for example, some soccer clubs use them to measure player workload, and baseball teams have used them to measure bat head speed and glove location).

3-12. Again using a search engine, discover how wearables can help students in the classroom. Describe four ways that students and teachers can use wearable devices to improve performance.

3-13. Finally, use a search engine to learn how wearables can be used by the elderly. Describe three ways that older individuals can use wearables in ways that improve their quality of living.

Case Study 3

McDonald's: New Options for that Burger

McDonald's is a giant international company, with 40,000 restaurants and 68 million customers in 120 countries. It is the world's largest hamburger fast food company. It thrives on providing the same quality food and service at a low cost worldwide. But McDonald's is in a box. After 25 consecutive years of increasing dividends, in 2014 quarterly sales fell for the first time in 17 years. At the end of 2015 there were fewer McDonald's in the United States than at the start of the year, the first time that has happened in 45 years. Labor costs are rising, tech-savvy customers are going elsewhere, and technology costs are eating McDonald's lunch. Increasingly McDonald's is looking to new technologies to help it compete. Three are robotics, mobile order app, and cloud computing.

With increases to minimum wages, McDonald's is investigating the use of robots to take orders, prepare food, and take payments. In an industry with strong rivals, McDonald's strategy of low cost and a focus on fast food requires it to use technology that can reduce cost. It currently is the second-largest private employer in the world with more than 1.9 million employees (Walmart is the largest). With that many employees, any cost saving that involves employees is very promising.

In the summer of 2016, a Phoenix, Arizona, McDonald's opened that was run entirely by robots. The claim is that the robots can run 50 times faster than a human crew. These McRobots have some other advantages—less error, better hygiene, fixed labor cost, they don't tire or feel stress and require fewer breaks. McDonald's intends to open 25,000 robot-run restaurants in the near future.

In addition to robots, McDonald's is also developing a mobile ordering and payment app. Starbucks and Domino's lead in the digitally derived sales area. Half of all Domino's pizzas are ordered via apps, and Starbucks recently passed 6 million orders a month on its mobile platform. Taco Bell has found that people order 20 percent more food when using an order app. When the Taco Bell customer arrives and clicks the "I'm Here" button on his or her phone, the drive-thru agent even knows the customer's name.

For McDonald's one goal of the order app is improved service, measured as a shorter wait time. A second goal is to increase the average size of the customer order. Down the road, the new app is expected to share data with a new McDonald's loyalty program. Further, if customers use mobile apps to order, in-store labor can be reduced, queues can be shorter, and food can be ready when customers arrive. The plan is to make food to customer order and store it in one of many small heated boxes immediately before the customer is to arrive. Then when the customer walks in, the smartphone app downloads the box location, and the Bluetooth device on the phone opens a box where their food has been kept. When the door opens, the Bluetooth connection automatically withdraws from the customer's financial institution. Fast food even faster.

A third technology that has attracted McDonald's attention is the cloud. McDonald's already partners with Amazon's AWS to host its existing corporate applications. It would like its mobile app to be completely hosted by AWS. McDonald's also plans to outsource the development of the app. By outsourcing the contract for the app, McDonald's can save in-house labor costs and leverage the expertise of software developers at the outsourcing firm. By hosting this app in the cloud, spikes in demand during meal times can be efficiently handled. A cloud option will also make it easier for customers to use the app anywhere in the world where they find a McDonald's.

McDonald's in the 1950s revolutionized the restaurant business with its production-line principles. It once again seeks to revolutionize the industry with new technologies.

Questions

3-14. Everyone does not have a smartphone. Should McDonald's delay its order app until a greater number of clients own a smartphone? Should it develop and use this technology outside of the United States first?

3-15. Some of the advantages of the cloud are mentioned. Are there other advantages of the cloud that will benefit McDonald's?

3-16. Read about Bluetooth on the Internet or in Extension 5. Why use a Bluetooth network? What are some advantages of Bluetooth?

3-17. Do you or your friends use the Starbucks' order app? If so, what makes it attractive?

3-18. Does McDonald's have a social responsibility to employ people rather than machines?

3-19. What are the advantages and disadvantages for McDonald's to outsource the development of the phone app?

3-20. What are other uses of IT at McDonald's that would help?

MyLab MIS

Go to **MyLab MIS.com** for Auto-graded writing questions as well as the following Assisted-graded writing questions:

3-21. Suppose you work for your university. They are considering using the cloud for their email services. Your job is to prepare a one-page document that highlights the advantages and disadvantages of moving email to the cloud. Use the Internet to research pros and cons and use the vocabulary of this chapter in your document.

3-22. Your grandparents are concerned about information security and realize they don't know the first thing about how the Internet works. Pick three important characteristics of the Internet and explain them in language your grandparents would understand.

Chapter 4

Database Processing

"Well, Mr. Schmidt, unfortunately our records show that you are indeed dead," said an embarrassed Lynda Carter, insurance claims processor at Wood Hospital. Most of her days are thunderously routine, so today's visit from a healthy-looking dead man made a welcome change of pace.

"Well, I don't think that's unfortunate. I think I'm glad not to be dead," replied an astonished John Schmidt.

Lynda continued, "You are the John Schmidt who lives on Gypsy Lane."

"Yes, that's me."

Peering at her computer screen Lynda finds John's most recent record. "Our records show you passed away about 6 months ago of a heart attack. That is odd, but it does happen from time to time. Sometimes our system kills patients by mistake."

"That's reassuring. I'm glad I'm not the first."

"Have you ever been admitted for a heart condition?"

"No, just for routine doctor appointments."

Lynda said, "When our system made you deceased, it removed all your insurance data too. So, all those unpaid bills your wife has received for outpatient care are because her insurance is through you and you're now dead."

John interjected, "Let's go back to the beginning…why does your system say I died 6 months ago when I wasn't even in the hospital?"

Lynda, after the long sequence of keyboard clickity clack, looks relieved. "I see what happened. Another Mr. Schmidt was admitted for heart problems, and he passed away. I think, yes, his admission ID number looks like your patient ID number, so someone mixed up the Schmidts. Both the admission number and patient number are eight-digit numbers, and somehow they got mixed up. Probably by the discharge office, which handles the updates to the system after someone dies."

More clickity clack and Lynda continued. "And yes, that Mr. Schmidt had no wife or children, so when our system dropped him and his insurance data, it did not ask for updates to spouse and children accounts. The system is pretty old—it was built when most family members were covered by one parent's insurance, usually the husband."

"So now what?" asked the living Schmidt.

After a discouragingly long pause, Lynda slowly responded, "I can't find your personal record Mr. Schmidt. I'm afraid you'll have to start over."

"Do I do that here? I didn't bring any documents with me today."

"It would help if you were sick; we could start a new patient billing and insurance entry. I only add new patients when they are sick or seeing a doctor. Healthy people dropping in to this office to start new accounts doesn't ever happen."

"Great. I have to be sick to be alive?"

"Exactly!"

"I'll come in next week when I see my doc for my annual and fill out all those insurance forms again."

"When you do we'll start the process of billing your insurance company for your wife's treatments. I'm sure that will make sense to them."

Q4-1. What is the purpose of a database?

Q4-2. What are the contents of a database?

Q4-3. What is a database management system (DBMS)?

Q4-4. What are the components of a database application?

Q4-5. How do data models facilitate database design?

Q4-6. How is a data model transformed into a database design?

Q4-7. Why are NoSQL and Big Data important?

Q4-8. How can the hospital improve its database?

PREVIEW

Clearly, the hospital has a database problem. But what is it, and how should the hospital fix it? We will address these questions at the end of this chapter, but for you to understand that explanation we first need to discuss important database fundamentals.

To begin, realize that businesses of all sizes organize their data records into collections called *databases*. At one extreme, small businesses use databases to keep track of customers; at the other extreme, huge corporations such as Google and Amazon use databases to support complex sales, marketing, and operations activities with millions of daily transactions. Hospitals like Wood Hospital are in between; they use databases as a crucial part of their operations but sometimes lack the trained and experienced staff to manage and support their databases. Behind the scenes, you touch databases every day when you use email, social media, Canvas, video games, music, banking, app stores, and texting services.

A decade ago, business professionals could leave data issues to technology professionals; not so today, and for several reasons. For one, some newer database systems are built to be self-service—they are intuitive and designed for use by professionals, not just technicians. Second, innovative organizations seek to become more data driven, meaning to more often use data to inform their decision making. Third, when fixing or improving business processes, new initiatives often require changes to the structure or processing of one or more databases. Fourth, when a new database is created, developers need the advice and assistance of business professionals to determine what should be in that new database. To do that, they will ask you many questions and may ask you to validate a blueprint called a data model. Fifth, data security is important to everyone in an organization, so everyone needs to know how data should be protected on its way into and out of a database. In this chapter, you can learn key ideas about databases and their supporting technology so that you can contribute in this environment.

This chapter discusses the what and the how of database processing. We begin with what: we describe the purpose of databases and then explain the important components of database systems. We then explain how data is moved into and out of a database before closing with a discussion of the process of creating a new database system. In Chapter 12, we again examine data, but there we focus on how it is analyzed and displayed; here we focus on how it gets in and out of a database.

FIGURE 4-1

List of Student Grades in a
Spreadsheet

	A	B	C	D	E	F	G	H
1	Student Name	Student Number	HW1	HW2	MidTerm	HW3	HW4	Final
2								
3	BAKER, ANDREA	1325	88	100	78			
4	FISCHER, MAYAN	3007	95	100	74			
5	LAU, SWEE	1644	75	90	90			
6	NELSON, STUART	2881	100	90	98			
7	ROGERS, SHELLY	8009	95	100	98			
8	TAM, JEFFREY	3559		100	88			
9	VALDEZ, MARIE	5265	80	90	85			
10	VERBERRA, ADAM	4867	70	90	92			
11								

| ◀ ▶ | **Student** | Sheet2 | Sheet3 | ⊕ |

Q4-1 ▶ What Is the Purpose of a Database?

The purpose of a database is to keep track of things. When most students learn that, they wonder why we need a special technology for such a simple task. Why not just use a list? If the list is long, put it into a spreadsheet. In fact, many professionals do keep track of things using spreadsheets. If the structure of the list is simple enough, there is no need to use database technology. The list of student grades in Figure 4-1, for example, works perfectly well in a spreadsheet.

Suppose, however, that the professor wants to track more than grades. Say that the professor wants to record email messages as well. Or perhaps the professor wants to record grades, email messages, and office visits. There is no place in Figure 4-1 to record that additional data. Of course, the professor could set up a separate spreadsheet for email messages and another one for office visits, but that awkward solution would be difficult to use because it does not provide all the data in one place.

Instead, the professor wants a form like that in Figure 4-2. With it, the professor can record student grades, emails, and office visits all in one place. A form like the one in Figure 4-2 is difficult, if not impossible, to produce from a spreadsheet. Such a form is easily produced, however, from a database.

The key distinction between Figures 4-1 and 4-2 is that the data in Figure 4-1 is about a single theme or concept. It is about student grades only. The data in Figure 4-2 has multiple themes; it shows student grades, student emails, and student office visits. We can make a general rule from these examples: Lists of data involving a single theme can be stored in a spreadsheet; lists that involve data with multiple themes require a database. We will say more about this general rule as this chapter proceeds.

FIGURE 4-2

Student Data in a Form, Data from a
Database

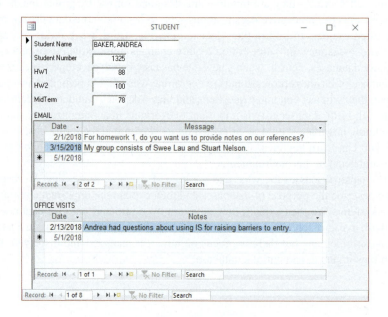

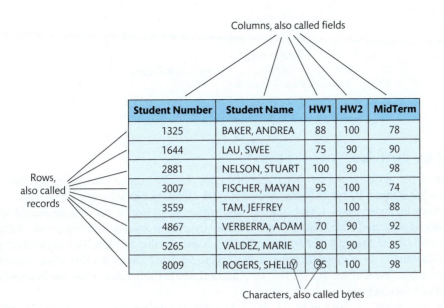

Columns, also called fields

Rows, also called records

Characters, also called bytes

FIGURE 4-3

Elements of the Student Table (also called a file)

Student Number	Student Name	HW1	HW2	MidTerm
1325	BAKER, ANDREA	88	100	78
1644	LAU, SWEE	75	90	90
2881	NELSON, STUART	100	90	98
3007	FISCHER, MAYAN	95	100	74
3559	TAM, JEFFREY		100	88
4867	VERBERRA, ADAM	70	90	92
5265	VALDEZ, MARIE	80	90	85
8009	ROGERS, SHELLY	95	100	98

Q4-2 What Are the Contents of a Database?

A **database** is a self-describing collection of integrated records. To understand the terms in this definition, you first need to understand the terms illustrated in Figure 4-3. As you learned in Extension 2, a **byte** is a character of data. In databases, bytes are grouped into **columns,** such as *Student Number* and *Student Name*. Columns are also called **fields.** Columns or fields, in turn, are grouped into **rows,** which are also called **records.** In Figure 4-3, the collection of data for all columns (*Student Number, Student Name, HW1, HW2,* and *MidTerm*) is called a *row* or a *record*. Finally, a group of similar rows or records is called a **table** or a **file.** From these definitions, you can see that there is a hierarchy of data elements, as shown in Figure 4-4.

It is tempting to continue this grouping process by saying that a database is a group of tables or files. This statement, although true, does not go far enough. As shown in Figure 4-5, a database is a collection of tables *plus* relationships among the rows in those tables, *plus* special data, called metadata, that describes the structure of the database. By the way, the cylindrical symbol labeled "database" in Figure 4-5 represents a computer disk drive. It is used in diagrams like this because databases are normally stored on disks.

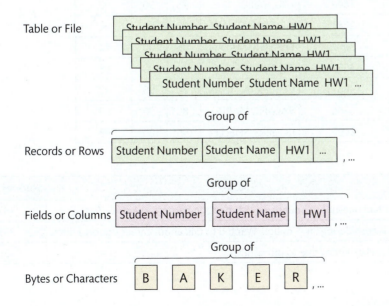

Table or File

Group of

Records or Rows | Student Number | Student Name | HW1 | ...

Group of

Fields or Columns | Student Number | Student Name | HW1 | , ...

Group of

Bytes or Characters | B | A | K | E | R | , ...

FIGURE 4-4

Hierarchy of Data Elements

FIGURE 4-5

Contents of a Database

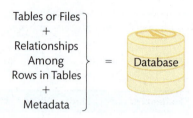

What Are Relationships Among Rows?

Consider the terms on the left-hand side of Figure 4-5. You know what tables are. To understand what is meant by *relationships among rows in tables*, examine Figure 4-6. It shows sample data from the three tables *Email*, *Student*, and *Office_Visit*. Notice the column named *Student Number* in the *Email* table. That column indicates the row in *Student* to which a row of *Email* is connected. In the first row of *Email*, the *Student Number* value is 1325. This indicates that this particular email was received from the student whose *Student Number* is 1325. If you examine the *Student* table, you will see that the row for Andrea Baker has this value. Thus, the first row of the *Email* table is related to Andrea Baker.

Now consider the last row of the *Office_Visit* table at the bottom of the figure. The value of *Student Number* in that row is 4867. This value indicates that the last row in *Office_Visit* belongs to Adam Verberra.

From these examples, you can see that values in one table relate the rows in that table to rows in a second table. Several special terms are used to express these ideas. A **key** (also called a **primary key**) is a column or group of columns that identifies a unique row in a table. *Student*

Email Table

EmailNum	Date	Message	Student Number
1	2/1/2018	For homework 1, do you want us to provide notes on our references?	1325
2	3/15/2018	My group consists of Swee Lau and Stuart Nelson.	1325
3	3/15/2018	Could you please assign me to a group?	1644

Student Table

Student Number	Student Name	HW1	HW2	MidTerm
1325	BAKER, ANDREA	88	100	78
1644	LAU, SWEE	75	90	90
2881	NELSON, STUART	100	90	98
3007	FISCHER, MAYAN	95	100	74
3559	TAM, JEFFREY		100	88
4867	VERBERRA, ADAM	70	90	92
5265	VALDEZ, MARIE	80	90	85
8009	ROGERS, SHELLY	95	100	98

Office_Visit Table

VisitID	Date	Notes	Student Number
2	2/13/2018	Andrea had questions about using IS for raising barriers to entry.	1325
3	2/17/2018	Jeffrey is considering an IS major. Wanted to talk about career opportunities.	3559
4	2/17/2018	Will miss class Friday due to job conflict.	4867

FIGURE 4-6

Examples of Relationships

Number is the key of the *Student* table. Given a value of *Student Number*, you can determine one and only one row in *Student*. Only one student has the number 1325, for example.

Every table must have a key. The key of the *Email* table is *EmailNum*, and the key of the *Office_Visit* table is *VisitID*. Sometimes more than one column is needed to form a key. In a table called *City*, for example, the key would consist of the combination of columns (*City, State*) because a given city name can appear in more than one state.

Student Number is not the key of the *Email* or the *Office_Visit* tables. We know that about *Email* because there are two rows in *Email* that have the *Student Number* value 1325. The value 1325 does not identify a unique row; therefore *Student Number* cannot be the key of *Email*. Nor is *Student Number* a key of *Office_Visit*, although you cannot tell that from the data in Figure 4-6. If you think about it, however, there is nothing to prevent a student from visiting a professor more than once. If that were to happen, there would be two rows in *Office_Visit* with the same value of *Student Number*. It just happens that no student has visited twice in the limited data in Figure 4-6.

In both *Email* and *Office_Visit*, *Student Number* is a key, but it is a key of a different table, namely *Student*. Hence, the column *Student Number* in the *Email* and *Office_Visit* tables is called a **foreign key**. This term is used because such columns are keys of a different (foreign) table than the one in which they reside.

Before we go on, databases that carry their data in the form of tables and that represent relationships using foreign keys are called **relational databases**. (The term *relational* is used because another, more formal name for a table like those we are discussing is **relation**.) In the past, there were databases that were not relational in format, but such databases have almost disappeared. However, new nonrelational databases are making a comeback for specialized applications, as we'll see later in Q6.[1]

Metadata

Recall the definition of database: A database is a self-describing collection of integrated records. The records are integrated because, as you just learned, rows can be tied together by their key/foreign key relationship. But what does *self-describing* mean?

It means that a database contains, within itself, a description of its contents. Think of a library. A library is a self-describing collection of books and other materials. It is self-describing because the library contains a catalog that describes the library's contents. The same idea also pertains to a database. Databases are self-describing because they contain not only data but also data about the data in the database.

Metadata are data that describe data. Figure 4-7 shows metadata for the *Email* table. The format of metadata depends on the software product that is processing the database. Figure 4-7 shows the metadata as they appear in Microsoft Access. Each row of the top part of this form

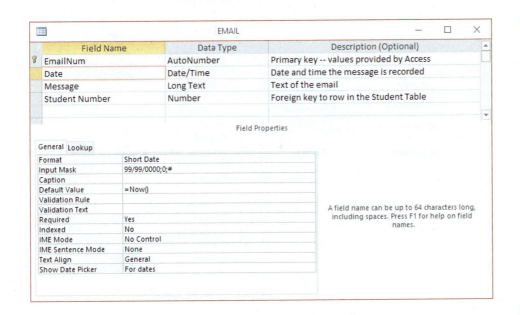

FIGURE 4-7

Metadata for Email Table

describes a column of the *Email* table. The columns of these descriptions are *Field Name, Data Type*, and *Description*. *Field Name* contains the name of the column, *Data Type* shows the type of data the column may hold, and *Description* contains notes that explain the source or use of the column. As you can see, there is one row of metadata for each of the four columns of the *Email* table: *EmailNum, Date, Message,* and *Student Number*.

The bottom part of this form provides more metadata, which Access calls *Field Properties*, for each column. In Figure 4-7, the focus is on the *Date* column (note the light rectangle drawn around the *Date* row). Because the focus is on *Date* in the top pane, the details in the bottom pane pertain to the *Date* column. The Field Properties describe formats, a default value for Access to supply when a new row is created, and the constraint that a value is required for this column. It is not important for you to remember these details. Instead, just understand that metadata are data about data and that such metadata are always a part of a database.

The presence of metadata makes databases much more useful. Because of metadata, no one needs to guess, remember, or even record what is in the database. To find out what a database contains, we just look at the metadata inside the database.

Q4-3 ▸ What Is a Database Management System (DBMS)?

Figure 4-8 shows the three major components of a **database application system**: a database, a DBMS, and one or more database applications. We have already described the contents of the database. We will next describe the DBMS and then, finally, discuss database applications.

Of course, as an information system, database application systems also have the other three components: hardware, people, and procedures. Because the purpose of this chapter is to discuss database technology, we will omit them from this discussion.

A **database management system (DBMS)** is a program used to create, process, and administer a database. As with operating systems, almost no organization develops its own DBMS. Instead, companies license DBMS products from vendors such as IBM, Microsoft, Oracle, and others. Popular DBMS products are **DB2** from IBM, **Access** and **SQL Server** from Microsoft, and **Oracle Database** from the Oracle Corporation. Another popular DBMS is **MySQL**, an open

FIGURE 4-8

Components of a Database Application System

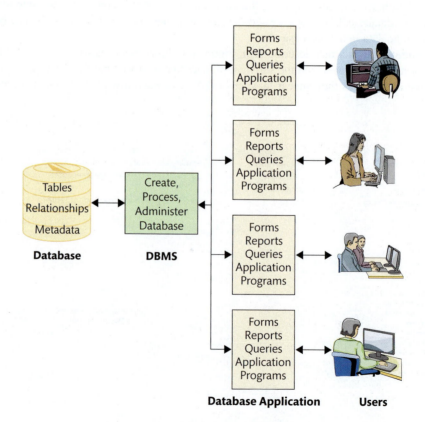

Database   **DBMS**

Database Application   **Users**

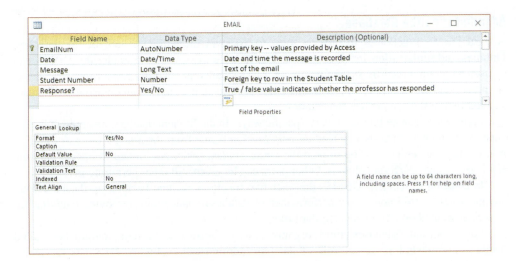

FIGURE 4-9

Adding a New Column to a Table
(Microsoft Access)

source DBMS product that is license-free for most applications.[2] Other DBMS products are available, but these five process the bulk of databases today.

Note that a DBMS and a database are two different things. For some reason, the trade press and even some books confuse the two. A DBMS is a software program; a database is a collection of tables of data, relationships, and metadata. The two are very different in nature.

Creating the Database and Its Structures

Database developers use the DBMS to create tables, relationships, and other structures in the database. The form in Figure 4-7 can be used to define a new table or to modify an existing one. To create a new table, the developer just fills the new table's metadata into the form.

To modify an existing table—say, to add a new column—the developer opens the metadata form for that table and adds a new row of metadata. For example, in Figure 4-9 the developer has added a new column called *Response?* This new column has the data type *Yes/No*, which means that the column can contain only one of two values—*Yes* or *No*. The professor will use this column to indicate whether he has responded to the student's email. A column can be removed by deleting its row in this table, though doing so will also delete its existing data.

Processing the Database

The second function of the DBMS is to process the database. Such processing can be quite complex, but, fundamentally, the DBMS provides four processing operations: *read, insert, modify*, or *delete* data. These operations are requested in different ways. From a form, when the user enters new or changed data, a computer program behind the form calls the DBMS to make the necessary database changes. From a Web application, a program on the client or on the server calls the DBMS to make the change.

Structured Query Language (SQL) (pronounced "see-quell") is an international standard language for processing a database. All five of the DBMS products mentioned earlier accept and process SQL statements. As an example, the following SQL statement inserts a new row into the *Student* table:

```
INSERT INTO Student
([Student Number], [Student Name], HW1, HW2, MidTerm)
VALUES
(1000, 'Franklin, Benjamin', 90, 95, 100);
```

As stated, statements like this one are issued "behind the scenes" by programs that process forms. Alternatively, they can be issued directly to the DBMS by an application program.

You do not need to understand or remember SQL language syntax. Instead, just realize that SQL is an international standard for processing a database. SQL can also be used to create databases and database structures. You will learn more about SQL if you take a database management class.

Administering the Database

A third DBMS function is to provide tools to assist in the administration of the database. **Database administration** involves a wide variety of activities. For example, the DBMS can be used to set up a security system involving user accounts, passwords, permissions, and limits for processing the database. To provide database security, a user must sign on using a valid user account before she can process the database.

Permissions can be limited in very specific ways. In the Student database example, it is possible to limit a particular user to reading only *Student Name* from the *Student* table. A different user could be given permission to read the entire *Student* table, but limited to update only the *HW1, HW2,* and *MidTerm* columns. Other users can be given still other permissions.

In addition to security, DBMS administrative functions include backing up database data, adding structures to improve the performance of database applications, removing data that are no longer wanted or needed, and similar tasks.

For important databases, most organizations dedicate one or more employees called database administrators, to the role of database administration, Figure 4-10 lists the major responsibilities of the DBA or the DBAs. You will learn more about this topic if you take a database management course.

Category	Database Administration Task	Description
Development	Create and staff DBA function	Size of DBA group depends on size and complexity of database. Groups range from one part-time person to small group.
	Form steering committee	Consists of representatives of all user groups. Forum for community-wide discussions and decisions.
	Specify requirements	Ensure that all appropriate user input is considered.
	Validate data model	Check data model for accuracy and completeness.
	Evaluate application design	Verify that all necessary forms, reports, queries, and applications are developed. Validate design and usability of application components.
Operation	Manage processing rights and responsibilities	Determine processing rights/restrictions on each table and column.
	Manage security	Add and delete users and user groups as necessary; ensure that security system works.
	Track problems and manage resolution	Develop system to record and manage resolution of problems.
	Monitor database performance	Provide expertise/solutions for performance improvements.
	Manage DBMS	Evaluate new features and functions.
Backup and Recovery	Monitor backup procedures	Verify that database backup procedures are followed.
	Conduct training	Ensure that users and operations personnel know and understand recovery procedures.
	Manage recovery	Manage recovery process.
Adaptation	Set up request tracking system	Develop system to record and prioritize requests for change.
	Manage configuration change	Manage impact of database structure changes on applications and users.

FIGURE 4-10

List of Database Administration Tasks

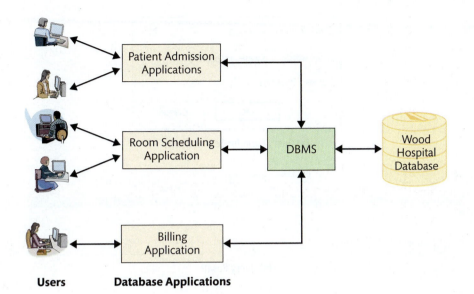

FIGURE 4-11

Three of Wood Hospital's Database Applications

Users   Database Applications

Q4-4 ▶ What Are the Components of a Database Application?

A database, all by itself, is not very useful. The tables in Figure 4-6 have all of the data the professor wants, but the format is unwieldy. The professor wants to see the data in a form like that in Figure 4-2 and also as a formatted report. Pure database data are valuable, but in raw form they are not pertinent or useful. In terms of information, it is difficult to conceive differences that make a difference among rows of data in tables.

A **database application** is a collection of forms, reports, queries, and application programs that use the DBMS to process a database. A database may have one or more applications, and each application may have one or more users. As stated, the database application(s), the DBMS, and the database comprise the database application system.

Figure 4-11 shows three applications used at Wood Hospital, the hospital described in the opening vignette. The first one is used to admit patients, the second schedules hospital rooms, and the third generates bills for patients and insurance companies. These applications have different purposes, features, and functions, but they all process the same database.

Forms, Reports, Queries, and Application Programs

Figure 4-2 shows a typical database application data entry **form.** Data entry forms are used to read, insert, modify, and delete data. **Reports** show data in a structured context. Some reports, like the one in Figure 4-12, also compute values as they present the data. An example is the computation of *Total Points* in Figure 4-12. If forms and reports are well designed, they allow users to readily identify *differences that make a difference*. Thus, they enable users to conceive information.

FIGURE 4-12

Example Report

Student Homework Progress with Emails			
Student Name	Student Number	HW1	HW2
BAKER, ANDREA	1325	88	100

	Email Date	Message
	3/15/2018	My group consists of Swee Lau and Stuart Nelson.
	2/1/2018	For homework 1, do you want us to provide notes on our references?

LAU, SWEE	1644	75	90

	Email Date	Message
	3/15/2018	Could you please assign me to a group?

FIGURE 4-13

Example Database Query

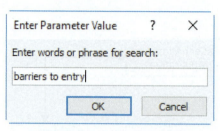

(a) Query Form for Search Result

(b) Query Result

But there's more. DBMS products provide comprehensive and robust features for querying database data. For example, suppose the professor who uses the Student database remembers that one of the students referred to the topic *barriers to entry* in an office visit, but cannot remember which student or when. If there are hundreds of students and visits recorded in the database, it will take some effort and time for the professor to search through all office visit records to find that event. The DBMS, however, can find any such record quickly. Figure 4-13(a) shows a **query** form in which the professor types in the keyword for which she is looking. Figure 4-13(b) shows the results of the query in the *Notes* field of the *Email* table.

Database Application Programs

Forms, reports, and queries work well for standard functions. However, most applications have unique requirements that a simple form, report, or query cannot meet. For example, at the hospital if a patient changes health insurance while a patient, how should the database record this change of billing? Should the database administratively "discharge" the patient when the first insurance plan is canceled and admit the patient when the second coverage begins or simply divide the cost to the two plans?

Application programs process logic that is specific to a given business need. In the Student database, an example application is one that assigns grades at the end of the term. If the professor grades on a curve, the application reads the breakpoints for each grade from a form and then processes each row in the *Student* table, allocating a grade based on the breakpoints and the total number of points earned.

Another important use of application programs is to enable database processing over the Internet. For this use, the application program serves as an intermediary between the Web server and the DBMS and database. The application program responds to events, such as when a user presses a submit button; it also reads, inserts, modifies, and deletes database data.

For example, Figure 4-14 shows four different database application programs running on a Web server computer. Users with browsers connect to the Web server via the Internet. The Web server directs user requests to the appropriate application program. Each program then processes the database via the DBMS.

Multi-User Processing

Figures 4-8, 4-11, and 4-14 show multiple users processing the database. Such **multi-user processing** is common, but it does pose unique problems that you, as a future manager, should know about. To understand the nature of those problems, consider the following scenario.

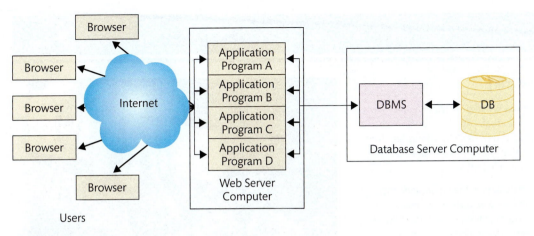

FIGURE 4-14
Applications Running on a Web Server

Suppose two of the users are Wood Hospital employees using the room scheduling application in Figure 4-11. For convenience, let's call them Andrea and Jeffrey. Assume that Andrea, an ER nurse, wants to admit a patient to the hospital and move him to an open hospital room. At the same time Jeffrey, a postoperation nurse, needs to move a patient from post-op to an open hospital room. Andrea reads the database to determine open rooms. While doing this, she invokes the room scheduling app when she types in her data entry form. The DBMS returns a row showing open rooms.

Meanwhile, just after Andrea accesses the database, Jeffrey does too, and his room scheduling app reads the database and shows him the same open rooms. Both nurses pick the first room. Clearly, there is a problem. Both patients have been assigned the same room.

This problem, known as the **lost update problem**, exemplifies one of the special characteristics of multi-user database processing. To prevent this problem, some type of locking must be used to coordinate the activities of users who know nothing about one another. Locking brings its own set of problems, however, and those problems must be addressed as well. We will not delve further into this topic here, however.

Realize from this example that converting a single-user database to a multi-user database requires more than simply connecting another computer. The logic of the underlying application processing needs to be adjusted as well. Be aware of possible data conflicts when you manage business activities that involve multi-user processing. If you find inaccurate results that seem not to have a cause, you may be experiencing multi-user data conflicts. Contact your IS department for assistance.

Enterprise DBMS Versus Personal DBMS

DBMS products fall into two broad categories. **Enterprise DBMS** products process large organizational and workgroup databases. These products support many, possibly thousands, of users and many different database applications. Such DBMS products support 24/7 operations and can manage databases that span dozens of different magnetic disks with hundreds of gigabytes or more of data. IBM's DB2, Microsoft's SQL Server, and Oracle's Oracle Database are examples of enterprise DBMS products.

Personal DBMS products are designed for smaller, simpler database applications. Such products are used for personal or small workgroup applications that involve fewer than 100 users—and normally fewer than 15. In fact, the great bulk of databases in this category have only a single user. The professor's Student database is an example of a database that is processed by a personal DBMS product.

In the past, there were many personal DBMS products—Paradox, dBase, R:base, and Fox-Pro. Microsoft put these products out of business when it developed Access and included it in the Microsoft Office suite. Today, about the only remaining personal DBMS is Microsoft Access.

MIS InClass 4

How Much Is a Database Worth?

The Firm, a highly successful health club in Minneapolis (*www.TheFirmMpls.com*) realizes more than 15,000 person-visits a month, an average of 500 visits per day. Neil Miyamoto, one of the two business partners, believes that The Firm's database is its single most important asset. According to Neil:

> Take away anything else—the building, the equipment, the inventory—anything else, and we'd be back in business 6 months or less. Take away our customer database, however, and we'd have to start all over. It would take us another 8 years to get back to where we are.
>
> Why is the database so crucial? It records everything the company's customers do.

If The Firm decides to offer an early morning kickboxing class featuring a particular trainer, it can use its database to offer that class to everyone who ever took an early morning class, a kickboxing class, or a class by that trainer. Customers receive targeted solicitations for offerings they care about and, maybe equally important, they don't receive solicitations for those they don't care about. Clearly, The Firm's database has value and, if it wanted to, The Firm could sell that data.

In this exercise, you and a group of your fellow students will be asked to consider the value of a database to organizations other than The Firm.

1. Many small business owners have found it financially advantageous to purchase their own building. As one owner remarked upon his retirement, "We did well with the business, but we made our real money by buying the building." Explain why this might be so.
2. To what extent does the dynamic you identified in your answer to item 1 pertain to databases? Do you think it likely that, in 2050, some small businesspeople will retire and make statements like, "We did well with the business, but we made our real money from the database we generated?" Why or why not? In what ways is real estate different from database data? Are these differences significant to your answer?
3. Suppose you had a national database of student data. Assume your database includes the name, email address,

Source: Image Source/Alamy.

university, grade level, and major for each student. Name five companies that would find that data valuable, and explain how they might use it. (For example, Pizza Hut could solicit orders from students during finals week.)

4. Describe a product or service that you could develop that would induce students to provide the data in item 3.
5. Considering your answers to items 1 through 4, identify two organizations in your community that could generate a database that would potentially be more valuable than the organization itself. Consider businesses, but also think about social organizations and government offices.

   For each organization, describe the content of the database and how you could entice customers or clients to provide that data. Also, explain why the data would be valuable and who might use it.
6. Prepare a 1-minute statement of what you have learned from this exercise that you could use in a job interview to illustrate your ability to innovate the use of technology in business.
7. Present your answers to items 1–6 to the rest of the class.

To avoid one point of confusion for you in the future, the separation of application programs and the DBMS shown in Figure 4-11 is true only for enterprise DBMS products. Microsoft Access includes features and functions for application processing along with the DBMS itself. For example, Access has a form generator and a report generator. Thus, as shown in Figure 4-15, Access is both a DBMS *and* an application development product.

FIGURE 4-15

Microsoft Access as Application Generator and DBMS

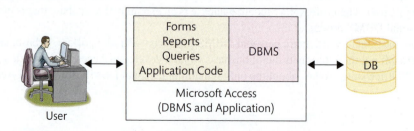

Q4-5 ▶ How Do Data Models Facilitate Database Design?

In Extension 3, we will describe the process for developing information systems in more detail. However, business professionals have such a critical role in the development of database applications that we need to anticipate part of that discussion here by introducing two topics: data modeling and database design.

Because the design of the database depends entirely on how users view their business environment, user involvement is critical for database development. Think about the Student database. What data should it contain? Possibilities are: *Students, Classes, Grades, Emails, Office_Visits, Majors, Advisers, Student_Organizations*—the list could go on and on. Further, how much detail should be included in each? Should the database include campus addresses? Home addresses? Billing addresses?

In fact, there are dozens of possibilities, and the database developers do not, and cannot, know what to include. They do know, however, that a database must include all the data necessary for the users to perform their jobs. Ideally, it contains that amount of data and no more. So, during database development, the developers must rely on the users to tell them what to include in the database.

Database structures can be complex, in some cases very complex. So, before building the database, the developers construct a logical representation of database data called a **data model.** This model describes the data and relationships that will be stored in the database; it is akin to a blueprint. Just as building architects create a blueprint before they start building, database developers create a data model before they start designing the database.

Figure 4-16 summarizes the database design process. Interviews with users lead to database requirements, which are summarized in a data model. Once the users have approved (validated) the data model, it is transformed into a database design. That design is then implemented into database structures. We will consider data modeling and database design briefly in the next two sections. Again, your goal should be to learn the process so that you can be an effective user representative for a development effort. Also, Figure 4-16 is just part of the systems development process; other requirements used to develop application programs and features are beyond the scope of this book.

What Is the Entity-Relationship Data Model?

The **entity-relationship (E-R) data model** is a tool for constructing data models. Developers use it to describe the content of a data model by defining the things (*entities*) that will be stored in the database and the *relationships* among those entities. A second, less popular tool for data modeling is the Unified Modeling Language (UML). We will not describe that tool here. However, if you learn how to interpret E-R models, with a bit of study you will be able to understand UML models as well.

Entities

An **entity** is something that the users want to track. Examples of entities are *Order, Customer, Salesperson,* and *Item.* Some entities represent a physical object, such as *Item* or *Salesperson;* others represent a logical construct or transaction, such as *Order* or *Contract.* For reasons

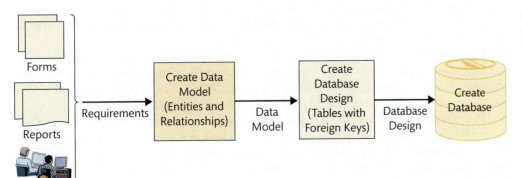

FIGURE 4-16

Database Design Process

FIGURE 4-17

Example Entities

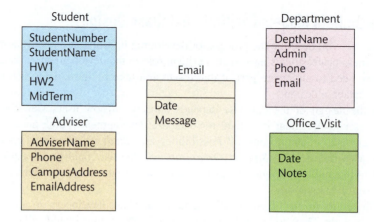

beyond this discussion, entity names are always singular. We use *Order*, not *Orders*; *Salesperson*, not *Salespersons*.

Entities have **attributes** that describe characteristics of the entity. Example attributes of *Order* are *OrderNumber, OrderDate, SubTotal, Tax, Total*, and so forth. Example attributes of *Salesperson* are *SalespersonName, Email, Phone*, and so forth. Entities also have an **identifier**, which is an attribute (or group of attributes) whose value is associated with one and only one entity instance. For example, *OrderNumber* is an identifier of *Order* because only one *Order* instance has a given value of *OrderNumber*. For the same reason, *CustomerNumber* is an identifier of *Customer*. If each member of the sales staff has a unique name, then *SalespersonName* is an identifier of *Salesperson*.

Before we continue, consider that last sentence. Is the salesperson's name unique among the sales staff? Both now and in the future? Who decides the answer to such a question? Only the users know whether this is true; the database developers cannot know. This example underlines why it is important for you to be able to interpret data models because only users like you will know for sure.

Figure 4-17 shows examples of entities for the Student database. Each entity is shown in a rectangle. The name of the entity is just above the rectangle, and the identifier is shown in a section at the top of the entity. Entity attributes are shown in the remainder of the rectangle. In Figure 4-17, the *Adviser* entity has an identifier called *AdviserName* and the attributes *Phone, CampusAddress*, and *EmailAddress*.

Observe that the entities *Email* and *Office_Visit* do not have an identifier. Unlike *Student* or *Adviser*, the users do not have an attribute that identifies a particular email. *Student Number* will not work because a student could send several emails. We *could* make one up. For example, we could say that the identifier of *Email* is *EmailNumber*, but if we do so we are not modeling how the users view their world. Instead, we are forcing something onto the users. Be aware of this possibility when you review data models about your business. Do not allow the database developers to create something in the data model that is not part of your business world.

Relationships

Entities have **relationships** to each other. An *Order*, for example, has a relationship to a *Customer* entity and also to a *Salesperson* entity. In the Student database, a *Student* has a relationship to an *Adviser*, and an *Adviser* has a relationship to a *Department*.

Figure 4-18 shows sample *Department, Adviser*, and *Student* entity instances and their relationships. For simplicity, this figure shows just the identifier of the entities and not the other attributes. For this sample data, *Accounting* has a relationship to three professors—Jones, Wu, and Lopez—and *Finance* has relationships to two professors—Smith and Greene.

The relationship between *Advisers* and *Students* is more complicated because in this example an adviser is allowed to advise many students and a student is allowed to have many advisers. Perhaps this happens because students can have multiple majors. In any case, note that Professor Jones advises students 100 and 400 and that student 100 is advised by both Professors Jones and Smith.

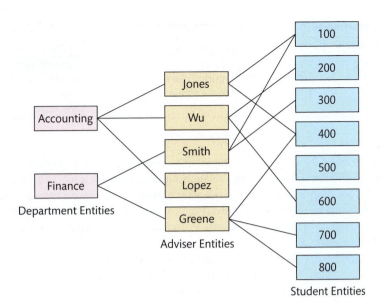

FIGURE 4-18

Example Entity Instances and
Relationships

Diagrams like the one in Figure 4-18 are too cumbersome for use in database design discussions. Instead, database designers use diagrams called **entity-relationship (E-R) diagrams**. Figure 4-19 shows an E-R diagram for the data in Figure 4-18. In this figure, all of the entity instances of one type are represented by a single rectangle. Thus, there are rectangles for the *Department*, *Adviser*, and *Student* entities. Attributes are shown as before in Figure 4-17.

Additionally, a line is used to represent a relationship between two entities. Notice the line between *Department* and *Adviser*, for example. The forked lines on the right side of that line signify that a department may have more than one adviser. The little lines, which are referred to as **crow's feet**, are shorthand for the multiple lines between *Department* and *Adviser* in Figure 4-18. Relationships like this one are called **1:N**, or **one-to-many relationships**, because one department can have many advisers but an adviser has at most one department.

Now examine the line between *Adviser* and *Student*. Notice the crow's feet that appear at each end of the line. This notation signifies that an adviser can be related to many students and that a student can be related to many advisers, which is the situation in Figure 4-18. Relationships like this one are called **N:M**, or **many-to-many relationships**, because one adviser can have many students and one student can have many advisers.

Students sometimes find the notation N:M confusing. Just interpret the *N* and *M* to mean that a variable number, greater than one, is allowed on each side of the relationship. Such a relationship is not written *N:N* because that notation would imply that there are the same number of entities on each side of the relationship, which is not necessarily true. *N:M* means that more than one entity is allowed on each side of the relationship and that the number of entities on each side can be different.

Figure 4-20 shows the same entities with different assumptions. Here advisers may advise in more than one department, but a student may have only one adviser, representing a policy that students may not have multiple majors.

Which, if either, of these versions is correct? Only the users know. These alternatives illustrate the kinds of questions you will need to answer when a database designer asks you to check a data model for correctness.

FIGURE 4-19

Entity Relationships, Version 1

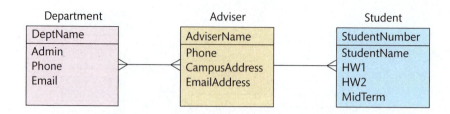

Figures 4-19 and 4-20 are typical examples of an entity-relationship diagram. Unfortunately, there are several different styles of entity-relationship diagrams. This one is called, not surprisingly, a **crow's-foot diagram.** You may learn other versions if you take a database management class. These diagrams were created in PowerPoint, which works fine for simple models. More complex models can be created in Microsoft Visio and other products that were purpose-built for creating E-R models.

The crow's-foot notation shows the maximum number of entities that can be involved in a relationship. Accordingly, they are called the relationship's **maximum cardinality**. Common examples of maximum cardinality are 1:N, N:M, and 1:1 (not shown).

Another important question is "What is the minimum number of entities required in the relationship?" Must an adviser have a student to advise, and must a student have an adviser? Constraints on minimum requirements are called **minimum cardinalities**.

Figure 4-21 presents a third version of this E-R diagram that shows both maximum and minimum cardinalities. The vertical bar on a line means that at least one entity of that type is required. The small oval means that the entity is optional; the relationship *need not* have an entity of that type.

Thus, in Figure 4-21 a department is not required to have a relationship to any adviser, but an adviser is required to belong to a department. Similarly, an adviser is not required to have a relationship to a student, but a student is required to have a relationship to an adviser. Note, also, that the maximum cardinalities in Figure 4-21 have been changed so that both are 1:N.

Is the model in Figure 4-21 a good one? It depends on the policy of the university. Again, only the users know for sure.

Q4-6 ▸ How Is a Data Model Transformed into a Database Design?

Database design is the process of converting a data model into tables, relationships, and data constraints. The database design team transforms entities into tables and expresses relationships by defining foreign keys. Database design is a complicated subject; as with data modeling, it occupies weeks in a database management class. In this section, however, we will introduce two important database design concepts: normalization and the representation of two kinds of relationships. The first concept is a foundation of database design, and the second will help you understand important design considerations.

Normalization

Normalization is the process of converting a poorly structured table into two or more well-structured tables. A table is such a simple construct that you may wonder how one could possibly be poorly structured. In truth, there are many ways that tables can be malformed—so many, in fact, that researchers have published hundreds of papers on this topic alone.

Consider the *Employee* table in Figure 4-22(a). It lists employee names, hire dates, email addresses, and the name and number of the department in which the employee works. This table

Employee

Name	HireDate	Email	DeptNo	DeptName
Jones	Feb 1, 2017	Jones@ourcompany.com	100	Accounting
Smith	Dec 3, 2015	Smith@ourcompany.com	200	Marketing
Chau	March 7, 2013	Chau@ourcompany.com	100	Accounting
Greene	July 17, 2011	Greene@ourcompany.com	100	Accounting

(a) Table Before Update

Employee

Name	HireDate	Email	DeptNo	DeptName
Jones	Feb 1, 2017	Jones@ourcompany.com	100	Accounting and Finance
Smith	Dec 3, 2015	Smith@ourcompany.com	200	Marketing
Chau	March 7, 2013	Chau@ourcompany.com	100	Accounting and Finance
Greene	July 17, 2011	Greene@ourcompany.com	100	Accounting

(b) Table with Incomplete Update

FIGURE 4-22
Table with Problematic Structure

seems innocent enough. But consider what happens when the Accounting department changes its name to Accounting and Finance. Because department names are duplicated in this table, every row that has a value of "Accounting" must be changed to "Accounting and Finance."

Data Integrity Problems

Suppose the Accounting name change is correctly made in two rows, but not in the third. The result is shown in Figure 4-22(b). This table has what is called a **data integrity problem,** which is the situation that exists when the database contains inconsistent data. Here two rows indicate that the name of Department 100 is "Accounting and Finance," and another row indicates that the name of Department 100 is "Accounting."

This problem is easy to spot in this small table. But consider a table like the *Customer* table in the Amazon database or the eBay database. Those databases may have hundreds of millions of rows. Once a table that large develops serious data integrity problems, months of labor will be required to remove them.

Data integrity problems are serious. A table that has data integrity problems will produce incorrect and inconsistent data. Users will lose confidence in their ability to conceive information from that data, and the system will develop a poor reputation. Information systems with poor reputations become heavy burdens to the organizations that use them.

Normalizing for Data Integrity

The data integrity problem can occur only if data are duplicated. Because of this, one easy way to eliminate the problem is to eliminate the duplicated data. We can do this by transforming the table in Figure 4-22 into two tables, as shown in Figure 4-23. Here the name of the department is stored just once; therefore no data inconsistencies can occur.

Of course, to produce an employee report that includes the department name, the two tables in Figure 4-23 will need to be joined back together. Because such joining of tables is common, DBMS products have been programmed to perform it efficiently, but it still requires work. From this example, you can see a trade-off in database design: Normalized tables eliminate data duplication, but they can be slower to process. Dealing with such trade-offs is an important consideration in database design.

The general goal of normalization is to construct tables such that every table has a *single* topic or theme. In good writing, every paragraph should have a single theme. This is true of databases as well; every table should have a single theme. The problem with the table in Figure 4-22 is that it has two independent themes: employees and departments. The way to correct the problem is to

FIGURE 4-23

Two Normalized Tables

Employee

Name	HireDate	Email	DeptNo
Jones	Feb 1, 2017	Jones@ourcompany.com	100
Smith	Dec 3, 2015	Smith@ourcompany.com	200
Chau	March 7, 2013	Chau@ourcompany.com	100
Greene	July 17, 2011	Greene@ourcompany.com	100

Department

DeptNo	DeptName
100	Accounting
200	Marketing
300	Information Systems

split the table into two tables, each with its own theme. In this case, we create an *Employee* table and a *Department* table, as shown in Figure 4-23.

As mentioned, there are dozens of ways that tables can be poorly formed. Database practitioners classify tables into various **normal forms**, which are classifications of tables according to the kinds of problems they have. Transforming a table into a normal form to remove duplicated data and other problems is called *normalizing* the table.[3] Thus, when you hear a database designer say, "Those tables are not normalized," she does not mean that the tables have irregular, not-normal data. Instead, she means that the tables have a format that could cause data integrity problems.

Summary of Normalization

As a future user of databases, you do not need to know the details of normalization. Instead, understand the general principle that every normalized (well-formed) table has one and only one theme. Further, tables that are not normalized are subject to data integrity problems.

Be aware, too, that normalization is just one criterion for evaluating database designs. Because normalized designs can be slower to process, database designers sometimes choose to accept nonnormalized tables. The best design depends on the users' processing requirements.

Representing Relationships

Figure 4-24 shows the steps involved in transforming a data model into a relational database design. First, the database designer creates a table for each entity. The identifier of the entity becomes the key of the table. Each attribute of the entity becomes a column of the table. Next, the resulting tables are normalized so that each table has a single theme.

For example, consider the E-R diagram in Figure 4-25(a). To create the database design, we construct a table for *Adviser* and a second table for *Student*, as shown in Figure 4-25(b). The key of the *Adviser* table is *AdviserName*, and the key of the *Student* table is *StudentNumber*.

FIGURE 4-24

Summary of Database Design
Process

- Represent each entity with a table
  - Entity identifier becomes table key
  - Entity attributes become table columns
- Normalize tables as necessary
- Represent relationships
  - Use foreign keys
  - Add additional tables for N:M relationships

FIGURE 4-25

Representing a 1:N Relationship

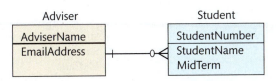

(a) 1:N Relationship Between Adviser and Student Entities

Adviser Table—Key is AdviserName

AdviserName	EmailAddress
Jones	Jones@myuniv.edu
Choi	Choi@myuniv.edu
Jackson	Jackson@myuniv.edu

Student Table—Key is StudentNumber

StudentNumber	StudentName	MidTerm
100	Lisa	90
200	Jennie	85
300	Jason	82
400	Terry	95

(b) Creating a Table for Each Entity

Adviser Table—Key is AdviserName

AdviserName	EmailAddress
Jones	Jones@myuniv.edu
Choi	Choi@myuniv.edu
Jackson	Jackson@myuniv.edu

Student—Key is StudentNumber

StudentNumber	StudentName	MidTerm	AdviserName
100	Lisa	90	Jackson
200	Jennie	85	Jackson
300	Jason	82	Choi
400	Terry	95	Jackson

Foreign Key Column Represents Relationship

(c) Using the *AdviserName* Foreign Key to Represent the 1:N Relationship

Further, the *EmailAddress* attribute of the *Adviser* entity becomes the *EmailAddress* column of the *Adviser* table, and the *StudentName* and *MidTerm* attributes of the *Student* entity become the *StudentName* and *MidTerm* columns of the *Student* table. These tables have a single theme and are already normalized.

The next task is to represent relationships. Advisor has a 1:N relationship to Student. Because we are using the relational model, we know that we must represent this relationship with a foreign key. The possibilities are: (1) place the foreign key *StudentNumber* in the *Adviser* table or (2) place the foreign key *AdviserName* in the *Student* table.

The correct choice is to place *AdviserName* in the *Student* table, as shown in Figure 4-25(c). To determine a student's adviser, we just look into the *AdviserName* column of that student's row. To determine the adviser's students, we search the *AdviserName* column in the *Student* table to determine which rows have that adviser's name. If a student changes advisers, we simply change the value in the *AdviserName* column. Changing *Jackson* to *Jones* in the first row, for example, will assign student 100 to Professor Jones.

FIGURE 4-26

Representing an N:M Relationship

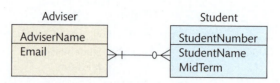

Adviser | Student

(a) N:M Relationship Between Adviser and Student

Adviser—Key is AdviserName

AdviserName	Email
Jones	Jones@myuniv.edu
Choi	Choi@myuniv.edu
Jackson	Jackson@myuniv.edu

No room to place second or third AdviserName

Student—Key is StudentNumber

StudentNumber	StudentName	MidTerm	AdviserName
100	Lisa	90	Jackson
200	Jennie	85	Jackson
300	Jason	82	Choi
400	Terry	95	Jackson

(b) Incorrect Representation of N:M Relationship

Adviser—Key is AdviserName

AdviserName	Email
Jones	Jones@myuniv.edu
Choi	Choi@myuniv.edu
Jackson	Jackson@myuniv.edu

Student—Key is StudentNumber

StudentNumber	StudentName	MidTerm
100	Lisa	90
200	Jennie	85
300	Jason	82
400	Terry	95

Adviser_Student_Intersection

AdviserName	StudentNumber
Jackson	100
Jackson	200
Choi	300
Jackson	400
Choi	100
Jones	100

Student 100 has three advisers

(c) Adviser_Student_Intersection Table Represents the N:M Relationship

For this data model, placing *StudentNumber* in *Adviser* would be incorrect. If we were to do that, we could assign only one student to an adviser. There is no place to assign a second student.

This strategy for placing foreign keys will not work for all relationships, however. Consider the data model in Figure 4-26(a); here, advisers and students have a many-to-many relationship. An adviser may have many students, and a student may have multiple advisers (for multiple majors).

The foreign key strategy we used for the 1:N data model will not work here. To see why, examine Figure 4-26(b). If student 100 has more than one adviser, there is no place to record second or subsequent advisers.

To represent an N:M relationship, we need to create a third table, as shown in Figure 4-26(c). The third table has two columns, *AdviserName* and *StudentNumber*. Each row of the table means that the given adviser advises the student with the given number.

What Is the User's Role in the Development of Databases?

As stated, a database is a model of how the users view their business world. This means that the users are the final judges as to what data the database should contain and how the records in that database should be related to one another.

The easiest time to change the database structure is during the data modeling stage. Changing a relationship from one-to-many to many-to-many in a data model is simply a matter of changing the 1:N notation to N:M. However, once the database has been constructed, loaded with data, and application forms, reports, queries, and application programs have been created, changing a one-to-many relationship to many-to-many means weeks of work.

You can glean some idea of why this might be true by contrasting Figure 4-25(c) with Figure 4-26(c). Suppose that instead of having just a few rows, each table has thousands of rows; in that case, transforming the database from one format to the other involves considerable work. Even worse, however, is that someone must change application components as well. For example, if students have at most one adviser, then a single text box can be used to enter *AdviserName*. If students can have multiple advisers, then a multiple-row table will need to be used to enter *AdviserName*, and a program will need to be written to store the values of *AdviserName* into the *Adviser_Student_Intersection* table. There are dozens of other consequences, consequences that will translate into wasted labor and wasted expense.

Thus, *user review of the data model is crucial.* When a database is developed for your use, you must carefully review the data model. If you do not understand any aspect of it, you should ask for clarification until you do. *Entities must contain all of the data you and your employees need to do your jobs, and relationships must accurately reflect your view of the business.* If the data model is wrong, the database will be designed incorrectly, and the applications will be difficult to use, if not worthless. Do not proceed unless the data model is accurate.

As a corollary, when asked to review a data model, take that review seriously. Devote the time necessary to perform a thorough review. Any mistakes you miss will come back to haunt you, and by then the cost of correction may be very high with regard to both time and expense. This brief introduction to data modeling shows why databases can be more difficult to develop than spreadsheets.

Q4-7 ▶ How Do NoSQL DBMS Differ from Relational DBMS?

Relational DBMS are the workhorse of the information systems industry today and likely will be for many years to come. As such, they are general-purpose tools. They will reliably store and process most organizational data. They remain the choice of organizations that process typical business data and that don't have the deep resources required to build a special-purpose DBMS to suit their unique needs.

Consider, however, the case of an organization like Twitter. Its database consists of billions of 140-character messages, millions of users, and millions of relationships about who is following whom. At least that was its data when it started. The structure of that data is simple, and Twitter doesn't need a product like Oracle that can process the 1,000 or more tables needed for a manufacturing database used by Boeing. Twitter simply does not need that representational power.

Similarly, Twitter's processing needs are different. If someone's tweet is lost, who cares? If the tweeter thinks the message important enough, he or she will tweet again. On the other hand, if you deposit $100,000 into your Vanguard account and your deposit is lost, you care quite a bit. Major relational DBMS products like Oracle, DB2, and SQL Server must go to great lengths to ensure that the processing of business transactions is complete, is consistently done, and is durable. (For more on this topic, search the Internet for the term *ACID*.) Twitter does not need all that processing power and does not want to pay for it in terms of increased processing and reduced throughput.

If Twitter were a $10 million a year in sales company, it would not have the capital to invest in developing an alternative to relational DBMS. However, it is a billion-dollar company, and it, along with organizations like Amazon, Google, Facebook, and others, decided to develop its own DBMS products, products that are suited to its own representational and processing needs.

Many of these high-performance, special-requirements DBMS were developed in the first decade of this century and have come to be known as **NoSQL databases.** As you might expect, it's a catchall category that includes many different types of DBMS. In fact, the name itself has no standard meaning; sometimes it means no processing of SQL at all; other times it means *Not only SQL*, meaning the DBMS will process both SQL and something else, where *something else* is not standard.

NoSQL DBMS are an emerging market. As of 2018, there are perhaps fewer than 10 relational DBMS products but probably more than 200 NoSQL products. Some NoSQL products process trivially simple data structures while others store and process complex documents. Some NoSQL products make no guarantee that updates will be consistent or durable, while others ensure that updates will be made eventually and will be durable at least a lot of the time. Some allow the designer to select the degree of consistency and durability that will be provided.

As a rule, NoSQL DBMS products require substantial software knowledge, considerable training, and developer patience with sometimes-cumbersome user interfaces. As of 2018, there is no standard, easily learned query language such as SQL.

Difficulty of use, need for high-level expertise, and the fact that few organizations can afford to convert their relational data to NoSQL format (of whatever flavor) mean that, for the foreseeable future, NoSQL databases are likely to be used only by wealthy organizations with unique database needs. They will most often be used for new databases that will not require conversion of existing relational data.

You will see additional applications for NoSQL DBMS products when we discuss Big Data in Chapter 12. Keep watching; there may be an important opportunity for you around the corner!

Q4-8 ▶ How Can the Hospital Improve Its Database?

Mr. Schmidt's problem at Wood Hospital was caused by four, and probably more, problems. First, no system should be designed with two different, identifying numbers that have the exact same format. Imagine the confusion in the world if social security numbers had the same format as telephone numbers [(800) 555-1212] or if nine-digit zip codes were written 555-55-5555 (the same format as social security numbers). The information system should have been designed with two different formats for admission number and patient number (if, indeed, two such numbers are necessary).

Second, it is exceedingly unlikely that any hospital deletes patient data upon a patient's death. Numerous medical practice and legal reasons require hospitals to maintain such records for many years. More likely here is that the patient's records were coded as deceased, and at that point, control and security measures prevented Ms. Carter from accessing those records. The remedy here is for a better process, procedures, and training to enable Ms. Carter to take more appropriate action when such an error occurs.

In addition, it is possible that the hospital's database is mis-designed. Consider the relationship between *Patient* and *Insurance Policy* shown in Figure 4-27. Notice that *Insurance Policy* is required to have a *Patient* record. That makes sense; the rule prevents policies from being created that do not relate to a patient. However, what happens when a patient record is deleted (or, more realistically, moved from one database to another)? Among other alternatives, the database can be designed so that (a) the deletion of any Patient that has an outstanding Insurance Policy record is to be prevented or (b) the deletion of a Patient record will cause the deletion of all

FIGURE 4-27

Wood Hospital Patient and Insurance Policy Entities

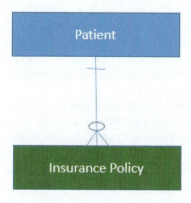

Insurance Policy records connected to that Patient. The hospital database should be designed for alternative a and not b.

Finally, according to Figure 4-27, the relationship between Patient and Insurance Policy is 1:N. This design is incorrect if multiple patients are covered by the same policy; it should be N:M and not 1:N.

Do not be misled by this example, which we study for educational purposes. An actual hospital patient database would have dozens (or more) of tables with dozens of relationships. The ERP systems that you will learn about later in this text might even have more than 1,000 tables in a hospital database. Patient and insurance policy data and rules for processing that data would likely be recorded in many of those tables. Your takeaway from this example is that the design or mis-design of databases and their applications have important consequences on the ability of users to do their jobs and on the satisfaction of the system's clientele.

Ethics Guide

Querying Inequality?

MaryAnn Baker works as a data analyst in human relations at a large, multinational corporation. As part of its compensation program, her company defines job categories and assigns salary ranges to each category. For example, the category M1 is used for first-line managers and is assigned the salary range of $75,000 to $95,000. Every job description is assigned to one of these categories, depending on the knowledge and skills required to do that job. Thus, the job titles Manager of Customer Support, Manager of Technical Writing, and Manager of Product Quality Assurance are all judged to involve about the same level of expertise and all are assigned to category M1.

One of MaryAnn's tasks is to analyze company salary data and determine how well actual salaries conform to established ranges. When discrepancies are noted, human relations managers meet to determine whether the discrepancy indicates a need to:

- Adjust the category's salary range;
- Move the job title to a different category;
- Define a new category; or
- Train the manager of the employee with the discrepancy on the use of salary ranges in setting employee compensation.

MaryAnn is an expert in creating database queries. Initially she used Microsoft Access to produce reports, but much of the salary data she needs resides in the organization's Oracle database. At first she would ask the IS Department to extract certain data and move it into Access, but over time she learned that it was faster to ask IS to move all employee data from the operational Oracle database into another Oracle database created just for HR data analysis. Although Oracle provides a graphical query interface like that in Access, she found it easier to compose complex queries directly in SQL, so she learned it and within a few months was a SQL expert.

"I never thought I'd be doing this," she said. "But it turns out to be quite fun, like solving a puzzle, and apparently I'm good at it."

One day, after a break, MaryAnn signed into her computer and happened to glance at the results of a query that she'd left running while she was gone. "That's odd," she thought, "all the people with Hispanic surnames have lower salaries than the others." She wasn't looking for that pattern; it just happened to jump out at her as she glanced at the screen.

As she examined the data, she began to wonder if she was seeing a coincidence or if there was a discriminatory pattern within the organization. Unfortunately for MaryAnn's purposes, the organization did not track employee race in its database, so she had no easy way of identifying employees of Hispanic heritage other than reading through the list of surnames. But, as a skilled problem solver, that didn't stop MaryAnn. She realized that many employees having Hispanic origins were born in certain cities in Texas, New Mexico, Arizona, and California. Of course, this wasn't true for all employees; many non-Hispanic employees were born in those cities, too, and many Hispanic employees were born in other cities. This data was still useful, however, because MaryAnn's sample queries revealed that the proportion of employees with Hispanic surnames who were also born in those cities was very high. "OK," she thought, "I'll use those cities as a rough surrogate."

Using birth city as a query criterion, MaryAnn created queries that determined employees who were born in the selected cities earned, on average, 23 percent less than those who were not. "Well, that could be because they work in lower-pay-grade jobs." After giving it a bit of thought, MaryAnn realized that she needed to examine wages and salaries within job categories. "Where," she wondered, "do people born in those cities fall in the ranges of their job categories?" So, she constructed an SQL query to determine where within a job category the compensation for people born in the selected cities fell. "Wow!" she said to herself, "almost 80 percent of the employees born in those cities fall into the bottom half of their salary range."

MaryAnn scheduled an appointment with her manager for the next day.

DISCUSSION QUESTIONS

When answering the following questions, suppose that you are MaryAnn:

1. Given these query results, do you have an ethical responsibility to do something? Consider both the categorical imperative (page 18) and the utilitarian (page 43) perspectives.
2. Given these query results, do you have a personal or social responsibility to do something?
3. What is your response if your manager says, "You don't know anything; it could be that starting salaries are lower in those cities. Forget about it."
4. What is your response if your manager says: "Don't be a trouble-maker; pushing this issue will hurt your career."
5. What is your response if your manager says: "Right. We already know that. Get back to the tasks that I've assigned you."
6. Suppose your manager gives you funding to follow up with a more accurate analysis and, indeed, there is a pattern of under-payment to people with Hispanic surnames. What should the organization do? For each choice below, indicate likely outcomes:
   a. Correct the imbalances immediately
   b. Gradually correct the imbalances at future pay raises
   c. Do nothing about the imbalances, but train managers not to discriminate in the future
   d. Do nothing
7. Suppose you hire a part-time person to help with the more accurate analysis, and that person is so outraged at the outcome that he quits and notifies newspapers in all the affected cities of the organization's discrimination.
   a. How should the organization respond?
   b. How should you respond?

ACTIVE REVIEW

Use this Active Review to verify that you understand the material in the chapter. You can read the entire chapter and then perform the tasks in this review, or you can read the text material for just one question and perform the tasks in this review for that question before moving on to the next one.

▶ Q4-1 What is the purpose of a database?

State the purpose of a database. Explain the circumstances in which a database is preferred to a spreadsheet. Describe the key difference between Figures 4-1 and 4-2.

▶ Q4-2 What are the contents of a database?

Define the term *database*. Explain the hierarchy of data and name three elements of a database. Define *metadata*. Using the example of *Student* and *Office_Visit* tables, show how relationships among rows are represented in a database. Define the terms *key, foreign key*, and *relational database*.

▶ Q4-3 What is a database management system (DBMS)?

Name the components of a database application system and sketch their relationship. Explain the acronym DBMS and name its functions. List five popular DBMS products. Explain the difference between a DBMS and a database. Summarize the functions of a DBMS. Define *SQL*. Describe the major functions of database administration.

▶ Q4-4 What are the components of a database application system?

Explain why a database, by itself, is not very useful to business users. Name and describe the components of a database application. Explain the need for application programs. For multi-user processing, describe one way in which one user's work can interfere with another's. Explain why multi-user database processing involves more than just connecting another computer to the network. Define two broad categories of DBMS and explain their differences.

▶ Q4-5 How do data models facilitate database design?

Explain why user involvement is critical during database development. Describe the function of a data model. Sketch the database development process. Define *E-R model, entity,*

relationship, attribute, and *identifier*. Give an example, other than one in this text, of an E-R diagram. Define *maximum cardinality* and *minimum cardinality*. Give an example of three maximum cardinalities and two minimum cardinalities. Explain the notation in Figures 4-18 and 4-19.

Describe the users' role in database development. Explain why it is easier and cheaper to change a data model than to change an existing database. Use the examples of Figures 4-25(c) and 4-26(c) in your answer. Describe two criteria for judging a data model. Explain why it is important to devote time to understanding a data model.

▶ Q4-6 How is a data model transformed into a database design?

Name the three components of a database design. Define *normalization* and explain why it is important. Define *data integrity problem* and describe its consequences. Give an example of a table from this chapter with data integrity problems and show how it can be normalized into two or more tables that do not have such problems. Describe two steps in transforming a data model into a database design. Using an example not in this chapter, show how 1:N and N:M relationships are represented in a relational database.

▶ Q4-7 How do NoSQL DBMS differ from relational DBMS?

Describe two reasons why organizations like Twitter and Google choose to develop their own, nonrelational DBMS products. Give two definitions for the acronym NoSQL and explain why it is a catchall. Explain why NoSQL DBMS products are unlikely to supplant relational DBMS products in the near term.

▶ Q4-8 How can the hospital improve its database?

List and explain four problems at Wood Hospital that led to the situation described in the opening vignette. Explain why this example is most likely too simple and describe what you can properly take away from it.

KEY TERMS AND CONCEPTS

Access 76
Attributes 84
Byte 73
Columns 73
Crow's feet 85
Crow's-foot diagram 86
Data integrity problem 87
Data model 83
Database 73
Database administration (DBA) 78
Database application 79
Database application system 76
Database management system
  (DBMS) 76
DB2 76
Enterprise DBMS 81
Entity 83

Entity-relationship (E-R) data
  model 83
Entity-relationship (E-R) diagrams 85
Fields 73
File 73
Foreign key 75
Form 79
Identifier 84
Key 74
Lost update problem 81
Many-to-many (N:M) relationships 85
Maximum cardinality 86
Metadata 75
Minimum cardinality 86
Multi-user processing 80
MySQL 76
Normal forms 88

Normalization 86
NoSQL database 91
Object-relational database 103
One-to-many (1:N) relationships 85
Oracle Database 76
Personal DBMS 81
Primary key 74
Query 80
Records 73
Relation 75
Relational databases 75
Relationships 84
Report 79
Rows 73
SQL Server 76
Structured Query Language (SQL) 77
Table 73

USING YOUR KNOWLEDGE

4-1. Draw an entity-relationship diagram that shows the relationships among a database, database applications, and users.
MyLab MIS

4-2. Consider the relationship between *Adviser* and *Student* in Figure 4-20. Explain what it means if the maximum cardinality of this relationship is:
MyLab MIS
  a. N:1
  b. 1:1
  c. 5:1
  d. 1:5

4-3. Identify possible entities in Figure 4-28. What attributes exist in each. What do you think are the identifiers of those entities.
MyLab MIS

4-4. Identify an needless duplication in the form in Figure 4-28 and explain why it is needless.

4-5. Identify possible entities in Figure 4-29. What attributes exist in each. What do you think are the identifiers of those entities.

FIGURE 4-28

Sample Data Entry Form

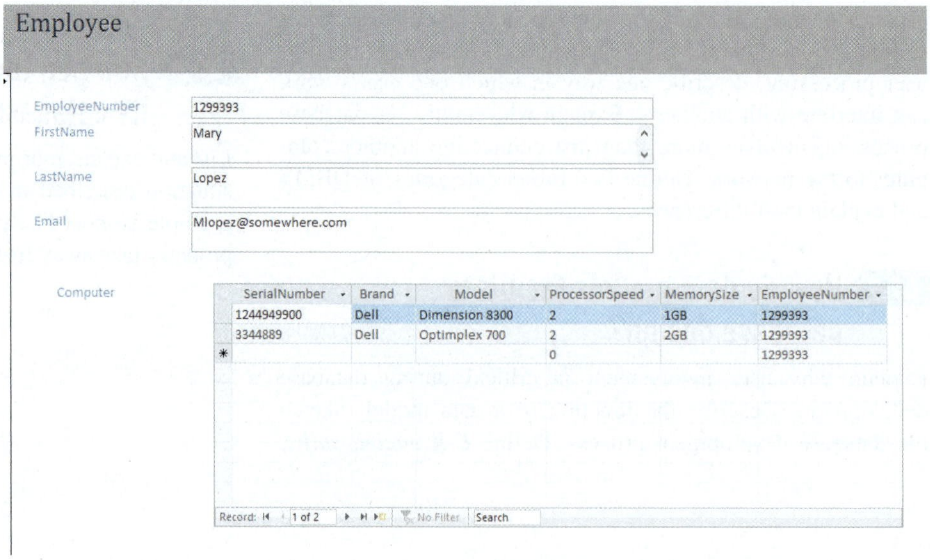

		Employee				
EmployeeNumber		1299393				
FirstName		Mary				
LastName		Lopez				
Email		Mlopez@somewhere.com				

Computer	SerialNumber	Brand	Model	ProcessorSpeed	MemorySize	EmployeeNumber
	1244949900	Dell	Dimension 8300	2	1GB	1299393
	3344889	Dell	Optimplex 700	2	2GB	1299393
	*			0		1299393

Record: I◄ ◄ 1 of 2 ► ►I ►⁕ No Filter Search

FIGURE 4-29

Second Sample Data Entry Form

Employee Class Attendance

EmployeeNumber   1299393

FirstName   Mary

LastName   Lopez

Email   Mlopez@somewhere.com

Class

CourseName	CourseDate	Instructor	Remarks
Presentation Skills I	3/17/2018	Johnson	Excellent presenter!
CRM Administrator	5/19/2018	Wu	Needs work on security administration
*			

Record: I◄ ◄ 1 of 2 ► ►I ►❑   No Filter   Search

4-6. Combine your answers to questions 4-3 and 4-4 and draw an entity-relationship diagram. Indicate both maximum and minimum cardinality and justify your answers.

4-7. The partial E-R diagram in Figure 4-30 is for a sales order. Assume there is only one *Salesperson* per *SalesOrder*.

   a. Specify the maximum cardinalities for each relationship. State your assumptions, if necessary.

   b. Specify the minimum cardinalities for each relationship. State your assumptions, if necessary.

4-8. Consider the report in Figure 4-12 in the context of information as a *difference that makes a difference*. What differences does the structure of this report show? Describe five ways this report could be changed that would make it easier for humans to conceive information. Name the criteria you used in suggesting these five changes.

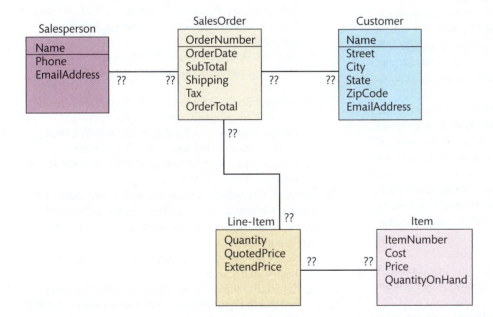

FIGURE 4-30

Partial E-R Diagram for Sales Order

COLLABORATION EXERCISE 4

Collaborate with a group of students to answer the following questions. For this exercise, do not meet face to face. Your task will be easier if you coordinate your work with SharePoint, Office 365, Google Docs, or equivalent collaboration tools. (See Chapter 10 for a discussion of collaboration tools and processes.) Your answers should reflect the thinking of the entire group, not just that of one or two individuals.

FIGURE 4-31

Sheet Music Spreadsheet

	A	B	C	D	E
1	Last Name	First Name	Email	Phone	Part
2	Ashley	Jane	JA@somewhere.com	703.555.1234	Soprano
3	Davidson	Kaye	KD@somewhere.com	703.555.2236	Soprano
4	Ching	Kam Hoong	KHC@overhere.com	703.555.2236	Soprano
5	Menstell	Lori Lee	LLM@somewhere.com	703.555.1237	Soprano
6	Corning	Sandra	SC2@overhere.com	703.555.1234	Soprano
7		B-minor mass	J.S. Bach	Soprano Copy 7	
8		Requiem	Mozart	Soprano Copy 17	
9		9th Symphony Chorus	Beethoven	Soprano Copy 9	
10	Wei	Guang	GW1@somewhere.com	703.555.9936	Soprano
11	Dixon	Eleanor	ED@thisplace.com	703.555.12379	Soprano
12		B-minor mass	J.S. Bach	Soprano Copy 11	
13	Duong	Linda	LD2@overhere.com	703.555.8736	Soprano
14		B-minor mass	J.S. Bach	Soprano Copy 7	
15		Requiem	J.S. Bach	Soprano Copy 19	
16	Lunden	Haley	HL@somewhere.com	703.555.0836	Soprano
17	Utran	Diem Thi	DTU@somewhere.com	703.555.1089	Soprano

The purpose of this exercise is to identify the limitations of spreadsheets and the advantages of databases.

Figure 4-31 shows a spreadsheet that is used to track the assignment of sheet music to a choir—it could be a church choir or school or community choir. The type of choir does not matter because the problem is universal. Sheet music is expensive, choir members need to be able to take sheet music away for practice at home, and not all of the music gets back to the inventory. (Sheet music can be purchased or rented, but either way lost music is an expense.)

Look closely at this data and you will see some data integrity problems—or at least some possible data integrity problems. For one, do Sandra Corning and Linda Duong really have the same copy of music checked out? Second, did Mozart and J. S. Bach both write a Requiem, or in row 15 should J. S. Bach actually be Mozart? Also, there is a problem with Eleanor Dixon's phone number; several phone numbers are the same as well, which seems suspicious.

Additionally, this spreadsheet is confusing and hard to use. The column labeled *First Name* includes both people names and the names of choruses. *Email* has both email addresses and composer names, and *Phone* has both phone numbers and copy identifiers. Furthermore, to record a checkout of music the user must first add a new row and then reenter the name of the work, the composer's name, and the copy to be checked out. Finally, consider what happens when the user wants to find all copies of a particular work: The user will have to examine the rows in each of four spreadsheets for the four voice parts.

In fact, a spreadsheet is ill-suited for this application. A database would be a far better tool, and situations like this are obvious candidates for innovation.

1. Analyze the spreadsheet shown in Figure 4-32 and list all of the problems that occur when trying to track the assignment of sheet music using this spreadsheet.

2. Figure 4-32(a) shows a two-table data model for the sheet-music-tracking problem.
   a. Select primary keys for the *ChoirMember* and *Work* tables. Justify your selection.

   b. This design does not eliminate the potential for data integrity problems that occur in the spreadsheet. Explain why not.
   c. Design a database for this data model. Specify primary key and foreign key columns.

3. Figure 4-32(b) shows a second alternative data model for the sheet-music-tracking problem. This alternative shows two variations on the *Work* table. In the second variation, an attribute named *WorkID* has been added to *Work_Version3*. This attribute is a primary key for the work; the DBMS will assign a unique value to *WorkID* when a new row is added to the *Work* table.
   a. Select primary keys for *ChoirMember, Work_Version2, Work_Version3*, and *Copy_Assignment*. Justify your selection.
   b. Does this design eliminate the potential for data integrity problems that occur in the spreadsheet? Why or why not?
   c. Design a database for the data model that uses *Work_Version2*. Specify key and foreign key columns.
   d. Design a database for the data model that uses *Work_Version3*. Specify key and foreign key columns.
   e. Is the design with *Work_Version2* better than the design for *Work_Version3*? Why or why not?

4. Figure 4-32(c) shows a third alternative data model for the sheet-music-tracking problem. In this data model, use either *Work_Version2* or *Work_Version3*, whichever you think is better.
   a. Select primary keys for each table in your data model. Justify your selection.
   b. Summarize the differences between this data model and that in Figure 4-32(b). Which data model is better? Why?
   c. Design a database for this data model. Specify key and foreign key columns.

5. Which of the three data models is the best? Justify your answer.

FIGURE 4-32
Three Data Model Alternatives

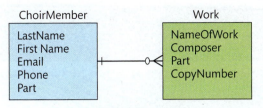

(a) Data Model Alternative 1

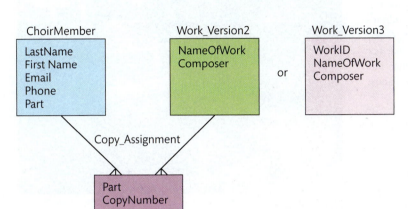

(b) Data Model Alternative 2

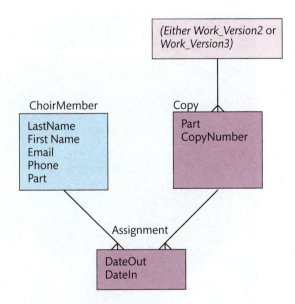

(c) Data Model Alternative 3

CASE STUDY 4

How about "A Clown's Database"

Dean Petrich is a certified piano tuner and technician who has been repairing and restoring pianos since 1973. He also has a career as Deano the Clown, a clown entertainer who performs children's parties in the Seattle, WA, metro area. (See Figure CS4-1, *http://deanotheclown.com/*). The schedule of his two businesses balance each other: He's busy as a clown in the late spring, summer, and fall, and during the rest of the year, he repairs and restores pianos.

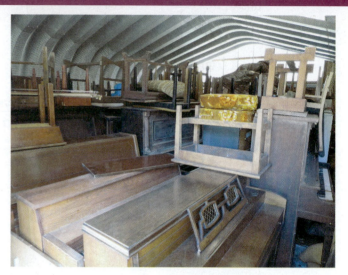

FIGURE CS4-2

FIGURE CS4-1

Over the past 20 years, the demand for pianos has dramatically declined. When a grandmother dies, the kids move out, or some other life change occurs, families have no further use for their piano, and when they find there is no market for it, they call Dean, who picks up that piano for a modest fee. For several years, Dean restored those pianos and either resold or rented them. Since the turn of the century, however, the decreasing demand for pianos has affected him as well, and over time, he's accumulated far too many pianos. Even discarding the worst of them, he has, today, nearly 100.

As you can imagine, 100 pianos occupy considerable storage. At first, Dean stored them in his workshop. When he ran out of room in his workshop, he built and stored them in a large metal shed (Figure CS4-2). When the shed overflowed with pianos, he moved them to plastic tents in a meadow on his property (Figure CS4-3). Unfortunately, the plastic tents are prone to rips and tears, and because Dean lives in the Pacific Northwest, many pianos have been ruined by rain, even when he covers them with plastic tarps inside the plastic tents.

FIGURE CS4-3

Two years ago, sinking in his steadily increasing piano inventory, Dean began to offer pianos for free. Not the very best pianos—those he hopes to sell—but he offers many quality pianos for free.

However, Dean has two problems. First, he doesn't know which pianos are best and where they are located in the shop, shed, or tents. Second, few people are unwilling to crawl over the tops of the pianos in the large shed and tents (through refuse of squirrels, rats, and mice) looking for their perfect piano.

To resolve this issue, Dean created a Microsoft Access database with only one table: Piano. To fill the database with data, Dean had to first take an inventory of all the pianos and record the data shown in the columns of Figure CS4-4.

As you know, a one-table database could just as easily have been stored in Excel, but Dean used Access because he wants to query his data in a variety of ways. He wants to know, for example, all the pianos located in a tent that have a sound quality of 4 or higher. And he wants to know which pianos have a sound quality of 1 or less so he can dispose of them. Further, customers have particular needs. One might, for example, want a Baldwin spinet (a type of piano); without a database he has no idea if he has one or where. Or when he needs a replacement key top, he might want to know the location of all the pianos in the workshop that have ivory keys and a sound quality of 2 or less, and so on.

Because of the dynamic nature of his needs, Dean uses the Access query facility. Figure CS4-5 shows an example query that returns all the pianos of a sound quality higher than 4 that are in a tent, and Figure CS4-6 shows the result of that query. Dean also suspects that the quality deteriorates faster in the tents than in the shed or the shop. To determine if this is the case, he created the report shown in Figure CS4-7.

Questions

4-9. Explain why a one-table database could be stored just as readily in Excel as in Access.

4-10. Justify the decision to use Access to store the piano database.

4-11. Examine the columns in Figure CS4-4. Name three characteristics of pianos that are not represented in this table.

    a. If you were a consultant advising Dean, what criteria should you and he use in deciding whether to include that additional data?

    b. Is this database a model of an inventory of pianos, or is it a model of Dean's model of an inventory of pianos? Explain the difference.

    c. How does your answer to question 3b influence your answer to question 3a?

FIGURE CS4-5

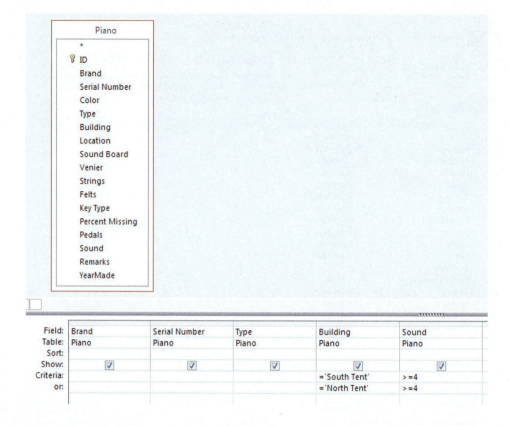

4-12. Suppose that, in addition to the data about pianos, Dean wants to store data about the manufacturer such as its address (or last known address), its years of operation, and general comments about that manufacturer.

   a. Design a Manufacturer table.

   b. Alter the design of the Piano table (Figure CS4-4) to represent the relationship between Piano and Manufacturer. State and justify any assumptions.

4-13. Using the data in Figure CS4-7, draw conclusions about the effect of location on piano sound quality. Justify your statements using this data.

4-14. Explain the statement "A database is an abstraction of some aspect of a business." Using this example, explain the ways that processing an abstraction is more effective than examining pianos. Explain the ways that processing an abstraction is more efficient that examining pianos. Generalize your observation to databases for business in general.

4-15. This database will soon become useless if it is not kept up-to-date. List procedures that Dean needs to create and follow to keep his database current.

4-16. Download a copy of this database from I don't know what this should be. Perhaps MyLab MIS is enough? and create queries to provide the following data:

   a. Sort the pianos from high quality to low.

   b. Sort the pianos from high quality to low and, within each quality, sort by building and then by location within that building.

MyLab MIS

FIGURE CS4-6

Brand	Serial Numb	Type	Building	Sound
Baldwin	70452	Spinet	South Tent	4
Esteu	20158	Upright	North Tent	4
H.G. Johnson	10749	Upright	North Tent	4
Winter ???	326493	Spinet	North Tent	4
Baldwin	637957	Spinet	North Tent	4
Briggs	80360	Upright	North Tent	4
Hobart Cable	77182	Upright	North Tent	4
Mehlin	28733	Upright	North Tent	4
Aeolian	182562	Spinet	North Tent	4
Farrand	27631	Upright	South Tent	4
Kurtzman	21398	Upright	South Tent	5
Mathushek	12963	Upright	South Tent	4

Piano Sound Quality by Building

Building	Sound Quality	Number Pianos
North Tent	1	1
North Tent	3	3
North Tent	4	8
Shed	0	10
Shed	1	1
Shed	2	7
Shed	3	13
Shed	4	12
Shop	0	2
Shop	1	2
Shop	3	5
Shop	4	2
South Tent	0	6
South Tent	2	3
South Tent	3	2
South Tent	4	3
South Tent	5	1

FIGURE CS4-7

c. List the pianos in the shed and sort the results by manufacturer.
d. List all the pianos with a type of "Spinet."
e. Count the pianos for each value of quality (ranging from 1 to 5).
f. Write a query to produce the report in Figure CS4-7.

CHAPTER RESOURCES

[1] Another type of database, the **object-relational database**, is rarely used in commercial applications. Search the Web if you are interested in learning more about object-relational databases.

[2] MySQL was supported by the MySQL company. In 2008, that company was acquired by Sun Microsystems, which was, in turn, acquired by Oracle later that year. Because MySQL is open source, Oracle does not own the source code, however.

[3] See David M. Kroenke, David J. Auer, Scott L. Vandenberg, and Robert C. Yoder. *Database Processing: Fundamentals, Design and Implementation* (15th ed.) (Upper Saddle River, NJ: Prentice-Hall, 2018), Chapter 3.

MyLab MIS

Go to **MyLab MIS.com** for Auto-graded writing questions as well as the following Assisted-graded writing questions:

4-17. Your name and student number are stored in a database by your university. In addition to fields like FirstName, Lastname and StudentNumber, what other fields comprise the database record with your name? The purpose of a database is store data for use by many different applications. Name at least 5 offices on the campus that have an app that might use the data in your student name record, for each describe the data about you needed for that app.

4-18. If you were a teacher would you keep data about the performance of students in your classes in database or in a spreadsheet? What are the advantages of each? What are the names of the tables and fields in a database that keeps track of student performance for a teacher.

Chapter 5

Information Systems Security

"I never got paid last month." You can hear the stress in Matt's voice.

Matt, an administrator at the Wood Hospital, was talking to Bethany, a security analyst at the hospital.

Bethany asked, "Have you contacted your bank? Did the money ever show up there?"

"Yes, I called the bank. That was the first thing I did. According to them, the money never made it to the account."

"OK," replied Bethany as she accessed an online report. "I can see our records now, and we did issue your bank your payment on the first."

Bethany added, "Do you remember logging in to your account at the end of last month and doing any work on your profile or your account?"

"No, I think the last thing I did on my account was change my password last month after I got that email from Dr. Smith telling all of us to update our passwords. It had something to do with converting to a new system or something."

Bethany was surprised, "That's odd. I don't remember that event. Could you find that email and send it to me?"

"Sure, here it is."

> Staff,
>
> Due to a recent change in our cloud provider, our IT staff has asked me to send everyone this request to change their login settings. We have chosen a new lower-cost provider to do our email account data storage, and they need to reactivate all email accounts.
>
> You can go to your Web email and reset your credentials, or you can click here.
>
> Thank you,
>
> Dr. Smith
> President, Wood Hospital

Matt said, "I clicked on the link at the end of the email, and I think it all went well from there."

"Matt, I think we have discovered the problem. That email was not from Dr. Smith. That was a phishing email. When you clicked on the link and changed your password, you were doing it on the hacker's server, not on ours. They then logged into your real account and reset your password to the new one, so when you later logged on to our server the new password worked. Then the day prior to payday they went into your account and changed the bank where your pay would be sent."

"Great. They're good, I guess."

"We've seen this attack done elsewhere; you're the first lucky contestant at our place."

"Can you get to the bank where they sent it and get it back?"

"No, I'm sure they closed that account after the first of the month. I suspect they used it to collect a number of paychecks that month, and then they set up a new one for the next month."

Q5-1. What is information systems security?

Q5-2. What are the most significant threats and potential losses they can cause?

Q5-3. How should you respond to security threats?

Q5-4. How should organizations respond to security threats?

Q5-5. How can technical and data safeguards protect against security threats?

Q5-6. How can human safeguards protect against security threats?

Q5-7. How should organizations respond to security incidents?

PSI BIG PICTURE

IS: An IS must be secured to be useful

Bethany continued, "Don't worry, you'll get paid—the hospital has insurance for this type of thing."

"That's a relief."

"Just be careful. Don't ever click on a link in an email asking you to reset anything. If Dr. Smith or we here want you to reset your password, we'll always tell you to go to the site. We won't give you a link."

"Thanks. Any other advice?"

"We tell folks to not use file-sharing networks, and don't spend any more time on a public Wi-Fi network than in a public restroom. They are both rather filthy."

"I'll keep that in mind."

PREVIEW

MyLab MIS

- Using Your Knowledge Questions 5-1, 5-2, 5-3
- Essay Questions 5-16, 5-17
- Excel and Access Application Questions 5-1, 5-2

Matt was concerned—and for good reason. Security failures can be expensive for both individuals and organizations. You only need read today's news to see why IS security is so important. Security failures at Sony, Target, Tinder, Home Depot, Snap, Verizon, Yahoo, and healthcare organizations as well as the U.S. federal government are becoming commonplace. Any organization for which you work is subject to the same security vulnerabilities and threats as these organizations are. As you will see, you have important roles to play in implementing safeguards to protect yourself and your organization.

This chapter closes the technical section of this textbook by applying your knowledge of networks, databases, hardware and software from earlier chapters to information security. This chapter aims to help you understand security so that you can help organizations make wise security choices as well as learn to follow good personal security practices. We begin the chapter in the first question by outlining the scope of the security challenge and a typical security scenario. In Q2 we discuss the major sources of threats and the losses they can inflict. Then in Q3 to Q6 we discuss how organizations respond to these threats, particularly how organizations use safeguards to reduce the security threat. We conclude by outlining how organizations should respond after an actual security incident.

The main theme is that security is a trade-off—more security often means more cost and less freedom for end users. By understanding the technical aspects of security, you will be able to help your organization make wise trade-offs.

Q5-1 ▸ What Is Information Systems Security?

Information systems security is the process of preventing unauthorized access to an IS or modification of its data. To be effective, information security must address unavoidable trade-offs. One trade-off is between risk and cost. **Risk** is simply the chance of loss; if the likelihood of a hack is greater than the chance of a virus, we would say the risk of a hack is greater than the risk of a virus. Reducing risk always costs, and the elimination of all risk would be exceptionally expensive if not impossible.

A second trade-off is between security and freedom. For example, your online bank does not give you the freedom to do anything you wish online; it restricts, it controls, the types and sizes of your transactions so that the security of your accounts can be ensured.

Our goal is to help you make good trade-offs to protect yourself and your organization. To do so, we first introduce all the things that can go wrong, the risks, and then in the second half of the chapter, we describe all the things that you and your organization can do to prevent and respond to those risks. Each of these security features is costly, and each restricts end user freedom.

We begin by addressing the scope of the security challenge. Quite simply, security is the single biggest challenge facing IS professionals today. By some estimates, a billion records are breached every year; attacks on prepaid debit cards netted hackers $5 million in a single month from only five cards. Criminals attack baby monitors, Twitter accounts, servers, moving cars, hospital patient records, video cameras, and DVRs. Furthermore, for every one crime that results in an arrest, there are likely 10 or even hundreds that go unreported or unsolved. The Director of the National Security Agency said recently that cybercrime is leading to the greatest transfer of wealth in human history and stated that the global cost of cybercrime may be approaching $1 trillion a year.[1]

Security is breached frequently, and there is no sign of such breaches slowing down. Further, nations like North Korea and others pose a whole new level of threat. In addition, natural disasters, though rare, also are a security breach and cost organizations millions. There is some good news: Companies that invest in safeguards have been shown to reduce the frequency and severity of their security losses.

To understand the nature of the security challenge, we begin with a description of the security threat/loss scenario and then discuss the sources of security threats.

The IS Security Threat/Loss Scenario

Figure 5-1 illustrates the major elements of the security problem that individuals and organizations confront today as well as the key terms of this chapter. A **threat** is a person or organization that seeks to obtain or alter data or other assets illegally, without the owner's permission and often without the owner's knowledge; in the opening vignette, the hackers were the threat.

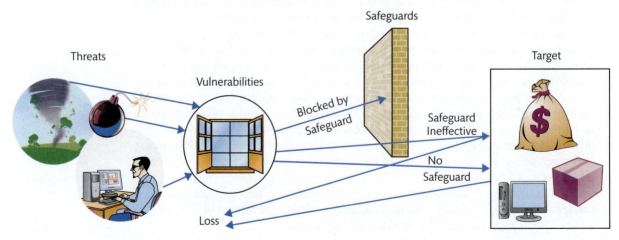

FIGURE 5-1

Threat/Loss Scenario

Threat/Target	Vulnerability	Safeguard	Result	Explanation
Xbox Live gamer wants your credit card data	You use your credit card to buy online	Buy only using https	No loss	Effective safeguard
	You send credit card data to friend in email	None	Loss of credit card data	No safeguard
Employee posts sensitive data to public Facebook group	Public access to not-secure group	Passwords Procedures Employee training	Loss of sensitive data	Ineffective safeguard

FIGURE 5-2
Examples of Threat/Loss

A **vulnerability** is a weakness in the IS that provides an opportunity for threats to gain access to individual or organizational assets. For example, when you buy something online, you provide your credit card data; when that data is transmitted over the Internet, it is vulnerable to threats. A **safeguard** is some measure that individuals or organizations take to block the threat from obtaining the asset. Notice in Figure 5-1 that safeguards are not always effective; some threats achieve their goal despite safeguards. Safeguards are a type of control; and like all controls, they limit behavior. They limit behavior of users, and hackers, in order to improve security. Finally, the **target** is the asset that is desired by the threat.

Figure 5-2 shows examples of threats/targets, vulnerabilities, safeguards, and results. In the first two rows, an Xbox gamer (the threat) wants your credit card data (the target) to buy more games using your account. As stated previously, when you provide your credit card data for an online transaction, that data is vulnerable to the threat as it travels over the Internet.

However, if, as shown in the first row of Figure 5-2, you conduct your transaction using https rather than http (discussed in Q5), you will be using an effective safeguard, and you will successfully counter the threat.

If, however, as described in the second row of Figure 5-2, you send your credit card data to a friend via email, you will, in most cases, have no safeguard at all. That data is open to any threat that happens to sniff your traffic on the Internet. In this case, you may soon be paying for hours and hours of Xbox games for a person you do not even know.

The bottom row of Figure 5-2 shows another situation. Here an employee at work obtains sensitive data and posts it on what he thinks is a work-only Facebook group. However, the employee errs and instead posts it to a public group. The target is the sensitive data, and the vulnerability is public access to the group. In this case, there are several safeguards that should have prevented this loss; the employee needed passwords to obtain the sensitive data and to join the private, work-only group. The employer has procedures that state employees are not to post confidential data to any public site, such as Facebook, but these procedures were either unknown or ignored. A third safeguard is the training that all employees are given. Because the employee ignores the procedures, though, all of those safeguards are ineffective and the data is exposed to the public.

Q5-2 What Are the Most Significant Threats and Potential Losses They Can Cause?

Figure 5-3 summarizes the two main sources of security threats and the three major types of losses they inflict. The type of threat is shown in the columns, and the type of loss is shown in the rows.

What Are the Types of Threats?

HUMAN ERROR/INTERNAL EMPLOYEES Human errors and mistakes include accidental or unintended problems caused by both employees and nonemployees. An example is an employee who misunderstands operating procedures and accidentally deletes customer records. Another example is an employee who, in the course of backing up a database, inadvertently installs an old database on top of the current one. This category also includes poorly written application

FIGURE 5-3

Security Threats and Losses

		Threat	
		Human Error **INTERNAL EMPLOYEES**	**Computer Crime** **EXTERNAL ATTACKERS**

Loss	**Data**	Inadvertent
		  Procedure problems
		  Social engineering
		Deliberate—sabotage
			Impersonation
			  Pretexting, phishing, spoofing
			Sniffing
			Malware
			Brute force
			Session hijacking
			XSS
			Hacking
			SQL injection

	Software	Procedure problems	Denial of service Overflow Usurpation Malware
	Hardware/ Infrastructure	Accidents	Theft Terrorism APT

programs and poorly designed procedures. Finally, human errors and mistakes include physical accidents such as spilling water on a server.

COMPUTER CRIME/EXTERNAL ATTACKS The second threat type is computer crime called *attacks*. This threat type includes hackers who break into a system as in the opening vignette as well as viruses and worms that infect computer systems.

What Are the Types of Loss?

The types of security losses can be grouped into three categories: data, software, and hardware/ infrastructure. A data loss is an unauthorized data disclosure or an incorrect data modification. A software loss typically is the loss of a service—an app no longer works or a server is taken offline. Hardware/infrastructure loss implies a physical compromise—a bulldozer cuts a conduit of cable, or a fire suppression sprinkler turns on and ruins a bank of servers. In the following sections, we explore the variety of errors and crimes that result in these three types of losses. As you will see, there are many ways to lose.

DATA A data loss occurs when a threat obtains data that is supposed to be protected—an unauthorized disclosure. It can occur by human error when someone releases data in violation of policy. One example is an employee who unknowingly or carelessly releases proprietary data to competitors or to the media. Incorrect data modification is a second type of data loss. Examples include incorrectly increasing a customer's discount or incorrectly modifying an employee's salary, earned days of vacation, or annual bonus. Other examples include placing incorrect information, such as incorrect price changes, on a company's Web site or company portal.

As shown in Figure 5-3 there are two types of human errors that lead to data loss: inadvertent and deliberate. One type of inadvertent error is a procedure problem. The popularity and efficacy of search engines have created a source for procedural errors that lead to inadvertent disclosure. Employees who place restricted data on Web sites that can be reached by search engines might mistakenly publish proprietary or restricted data over the Web.

Another inadvertent error is **social engineering**. It occurs when employees are manipulated into divulging data or bypassing security on behalf of others. These others are typically hackers or criminals, but employees are unaware of that. Instead, the employees may think they are helping someone reset a password, find a file, or meet a looming deadline.

A final human error that leads to data loss is from deliberate human action—sabotage. Disgruntled employees or those motivated by factors outside of the business can deliberately cause data loss. A disgruntled, terminated employee might walk off with corporate data or crucial equipment. One example of deliberate human action that leads to data disclosure is WikiLeaks, which is the subject of the case at the end of the chapter.

Computer crime and attacks, the second column in Figure 5-3, also lead to data loss. We begin the discussion of computer crimes with three types of impersonation—pretexting, phishing, and spoofing—before finishing this section with the other seven types of data attacks.

Pretexting occurs when someone deceives by pretending to be someone else. A common pretext involves a telephone caller who pretends to be from a credit card company and claims to be checking the validity of credit card numbers: "I'm checking your MasterCard number; it begins with 5491. Can you verify the rest of the number?" Thousands of MasterCard numbers start with 5491; the caller is attempting to steal a valid number.

Phishing is a similar technique for obtaining unauthorized data that uses pretexting via email. The **phisher** pretends to be a legitimate company or individual and sends an email requesting confidential data, such as account numbers, social security numbers, passwords, and so forth. The opening vignette is an example of a phishing attack.

Spoofing is another term for someone pretending to be someone else. If you pretend to be your professor, you are spoofing your professor. **IP spoofing** occurs when an intruder uses another site's IP address to masquerade as that other site. Email spoofing is a synonym for phishing.

Wireless access points can be spoofed by similar-sounding access points that then eavesdrop on an unsuspecting user who mistakes the **evil twin** access point for the legitimate one. For example, at your local Starbucks the legitimate access point may be labeled Starbucks. An attacker, in the parking lot of that Starbucks, can generate an access point and give it a name like Free Starbucks Wi-Fi. An unsuspecting user may connect to this evil twin access point and divulge all types of passwords and secure data. The same attack can occur within an organization when a malicious painting company gains access to your building and sets up an evil twin access point in the room it is painting.

Sniffing is a technique for intercepting computer communications. Computers on a LAN are always chatting with each other even without their human masters around. Each computer generates automated messages about its current activity, the address it is using for itself, and its need for software updates. These messages can be sniffed, and rogue machines, using similar messages, can be added to the network without being noticed. With wired networks, sniffing requires a physical connection to the network. With wireless networks, no such connection is required: Wardrivers simply take computers with wireless connections through an area and search for unprotected wireless networks.

Malware is a term used to describe a variety of software that damages or disables computers. It can be a virus, a worm, a Trojan horse, spyware, adware, or ransomware. A virus is a computer program that replicates itself. A worm is a virus that propagates using the Internet or other computer network. Trojan horses are viruses that masquerade as useful programs or files. Spyware programs are installed on the user's computer without the user's knowledge or permission. Adware is similar to spyware, but it watches user activity and produces pop-up ads. **Ransomware** blocks access to a computer until the victim pays money to the attacker. The WannaCry attack in 2017 used ransomware and affected 200,000 computers in 150 countries in all types of organizations.[2]

A **brute force** attack is a trial-and-error method used to obtain passwords or a personal identification number (PIN). The attacker uses automated software to create every possible combination of characters.

Hijacking, also called **session hijacking**, occurs when a hacker steals an encryption key that client is using to access a secure site and reuses that key to impersonate the legitimate user.

Cross-site scripting (XSS) is a technique used by criminals to infect target machines with malware. In a typical XSS attack, the criminal posts a reply to a discussion board but along with the plaintext reply adds malicious code invisible to the discussion board. Then, when you click on the criminal's reply to participate in the discussion, the criminal's plaintext reply and the malicious invisible code are downloaded to your machine. To prevent this attack, the discussion board must be designed to accept only text, and most are now configured that way. However, amateur sites or poorly managed discussion boards can still be a risk.

Other forms of computer crime include **hacking**, which is breaking into computers, servers, or networks to steal data such as customer lists, product inventory data, employee data, and other proprietary and confidential data. Not only are individual hackers a threat, so too are hacking groups like Anonymous and LuluSec.

A final criminal threat to data is a **SQL injection attack**, which is when an attacker enters a SQL statement into a form on a Web page in which a client is supposed to enter a name or other data. If the Web page is improperly designed, it will accept this code and make it part of a database command that it issues to its database. Improper data disclosure and data loss are possible consequences. A well-designed application will make such injections ineffective.

SOFTWARE Human errors are typically procedure problems—incorrect procedures or procedural mistakes. These problems can result in losses to software in the form of faulty service or denial of service. For example, human error can inadvertently shut down a Web server or corporate gateway router by starting a computationally intensive application. A poorly designed app that uses the operational DBMS can consume so many DBMS resources that order-entry transactions cannot get through.

Turning to the second column of Figure 5-3, computer criminals can launch a **denial-of-service (DoS)** attack in which a malicious hacker floods a Web server with millions of bogus service requests that so occupy the server that it cannot service legitimate requests. DoS attacks can also use insecure IoT devices as was used in the 2016 attack on Twitter, Facebook, and other major Internet sites. Attackers harnessed a bot army, a large number of simple insecure devices such as video cameras and DVRs, and used these simple devices to bombard Web servers with meaningless requests for service. Like a bus full of customers all ordering at once at a McDonald's, service slows down for everyone.

A second form of external attack is called an **overflow attack**. In an overflow attack the hacker presents malicious code to a computer's operating system or application that deliberately overflows the capability of the software. The overflowing code contains damaging instructions that are later executed.

Another type of criminal activity is **usurpation**. Usurpation is unauthorized control of some part of an IS. It occurs when criminals replace a legitimate user or software program with their own access or illegitimate software program to give the attacker unauthorized control of some part of the IS. Finally, criminal malware as discussed earlier can also disrupt software.

HARDWARE AND INFRASTRUCTURE At times, human accidents cause loss of hardware or infrastructure, the last loss type. Examples include physical accidents such as cars, trucks, or forklifts striking exposed technology in a warehouse and cleaning operations spilling liquids on hardware in an office building.

Theft and terrorist events also cause loss of infrastructure. A new threat, called an **Advanced Persistent Threat (APT)**, is a sophisticated, possibly long-running computer hack that is perpetrated by large, well-funded organizations such as governments. APTs are a means to engage in cyberwarfare and cyberespionage. APT1 in Shanghai is one example. In 2014 five individuals from APT1 were indicted for theft of intellectual property from 150 victims over a 7-year period.[3] Another APT named "Deep Panda" recently hacked the Anthem healthcare data center and obtained healthcare records of 80 million people.

Before concluding this section on threats and losses, we need to point out a third type of threat to data, software, and hardware/infrastructure not shown in Figure 5-3. This is the threat from natural events and disasters. This category includes fires, floods, hurricanes, earthquakes, tsunamis, avalanches, and other acts of nature. In addition to the losses due to the event itself, employees might inadvertently disclose or damage data during recovery from a natural disaster. During a recovery, everyone is so focused on restoring system capability that they might ignore normal security safeguards. A request such as "I need a copy of the customer database backup" will receive far less scrutiny during disaster recovery than at other times.

Challenges of Information Systems Security

There are indeed many threats, but threats are just one reason security is difficult. Information security is a challenge for other reasons as well—attackers don't have to follow rules; data was designed to be copied and shared easily, not bottled up in a fortress; Big Data and the Internet of Things are constantly creating new data and types of data that must be secured; and firms like to use the newest but often insecure technology to build their applications. Another challenge is that security depends on everyone in the organization using good security practices; security is only as strong as the weakest link, the least secure employee. Don't let that be you.

But perhaps the most challenging aspect of security is that businesses do not have the time to thoroughly test the security of their new systems before they are employed. To do so costs too much money and time. Understandably, most businesses have to operate on the principle "let's build this new money-making system, and if it works and we're still in business, we'll have the time and money to do security right." This attitude was evident in the previously mentioned DoS on the Internet in the fall of 2016 when cheap, insecure devices were hacked. The builders rushed to make those devices available for sale without making them adequately secure.

To respond to these threats and challenges, organizations employ safeguards. One safeguard is well-trained employees with good security habits. We discuss these personal habits next and organizational safeguards in later sections.

Q5-3 ▶ How Should You Respond to Security Threats?

Your personal IS security goal should be to find an effective trade-off between the risk of loss and the cost of safeguards. However, few individuals take security as seriously as they should, and most fail to implement even low-cost safeguards.

Figure 5-4 lists recommended personal security safeguards. The first safeguard is to take security seriously. You cannot see the attempts that are being made, right now, to compromise your computer. Even though you are unaware of these threats, they are present, as you just learned.

When your security is compromised, the first indication you receive will be bogus charges on your credit card or messages from friends complaining about the disgusting email they just received from your email account.

If you decide to take computer security seriously, the single most important safeguard you can implement is to create and use strong passwords.

In addition to using long, complex passwords, you should also use different passwords for different sites. That way, if one of your passwords is compromised, you do not lose control of all of your accounts. Make sure you use very strong passwords for important sites (like your bank's site) and do not reuse those passwords on less important sites (like your social media sites).

Never send passwords, credit card data, or any other valuable data in email or IM. As stated numerous times in this text, most email and messaging are not protected by encryption, and you should assume that anything you write in email or messaging could be posted on Facebook tomorrow.

Buy only from reputable online sites and use a secure https connection. If the vendor does not use https, don't use that online vendor.

Your browser automatically stores a history of your browsing activities and temporary files that contain sensitive data about where you've visited, what you've purchased, what your account names and passwords are, and so forth. It also creates **cookies**, which are small files that your browser stores on your computer when you visit Web sites. Cookies enable you to access Web sites without having to sign in every time, and they speed up processing of some sites. Unfortunately, some cookies also contain sensitive security data. The best safeguard is to remove your browsing history, temporary files, and cookies from your computer and to set your browser to disable history and cookies.

Create strong and multiple passwords.
Send no valuable data via email or messaging.
Use https to buy from trusted Web sites.
Clear browser history, temp files, and cookies.
Regularly update antivirus software.
Use caution when using public machines or hot spots.
Log out after high-value activities.
Do not use USB drives.
Use your smartphone securely.

FIGURE 5-4
Personal Security Safeguards

FIGURE 5-5
Personal Security Safeguards–
Smartphone Practices

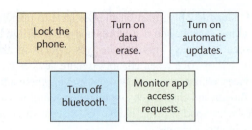

Removing and disabling cookies presents an excellent example of the trade-off between improved security and end user freedom. Your security will be substantially improved, but your computer will be more difficult to use. You decide, but make a conscious decision; do not let ignorance of the vulnerability of such data make the decision for you.

To finish our discussion of the personal security safeguards in Figure 5-4, regularly update your antivirus software. Do not use public computers or Wi-Fi networks such as the ones in hotels, coffee shops, Internet cafés, or airports for any communication you deem important. The malware running on these machines makes them as unsanitary. Public Wi-Fi is notoriously insecure, and you may be logged into an evil twin access point. Don't leave important Web sites open in your browser after you are finished; log out—don't simply close the window. Logging out eliminates cookies and other possible vulnerabilities of your browser. Don't use USB sticks. While they are convenient, you cannot easily see the malware they contain.

Finally, learn to use your smartphone securely. Good smartphone security practices are listed in Figure 5-5. Lock your phone and use advanced passcode features that require a fingerprint or six digits to gain access to the device. Also, turn on the data erase feature that will wipe your phone in the event of 20 straight incorrect logins, turn on automatic security updates, and turn off Bluetooth and Wi-Fi when not in use. Finally, be aware of access requests by apps running on your phone.

Having discussed appropriate personal security practices, in the remainder of the chapter we examine organizational information security practices.

Q5-4 ▶ How Should Organizations Respond to Security Threats?

In this question we examine how organizations respond to the threats discussed earlier. More specifically, we examine three critical security fundamentals: security policy, risk management, and defense in layers as shown in Figure 5-6. Then in Q4 to Q6 we discuss a fourth fundamental—safeguards—the preventative measures used by organizations to reduce IS security risk.

Considering the first security fundamental, senior management must establish a company-wide security policy that states the organization's posture regarding data that it gathers about its customers, suppliers, partners, and employees. At a minimum, the policy should stipulate:

- What sensitive data the organization will store?
- How it will process that data?
- Whether data will be shared with other organizations?
- How employees and others can obtain copies of data stored about them?
- How employees and others can request changes to inaccurate data?
- What employees can do with their own mobile devices at work?
- What non-business-related actions employees can take with employee-owned equipment?

Specific policy depends on whether the organization is governmental or nongovernmental, whether it is publically held or private, the organization's industry, the relationship of management to employees, and other factors. As a new hire, seek out your employer's security policy if it is not discussed with you in new employee training.

FIGURE 5-6
Three Organizational Security
Fundamentals

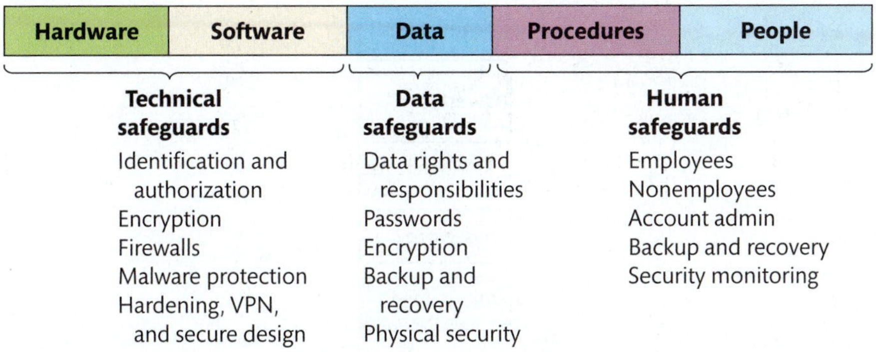

Hardware	Software	Data	Procedures	People

Technical safeguards	**Data safeguards**	**Human safeguards**
Identification and authorization	Data rights and responsibilities	Employees
Encryption	Passwords	Nonemployees
Firewalls	Encryption	Account admin
Malware protection	Backup and recovery	Backup and recovery
Hardening, VPN, and secure design	Physical security	Security monitoring

FIGURE 5-7

Security Safeguards as They Relate to the Five Components

The second security fundamental is to manage risk. Risk as defined earlier is the chance of loss. IT security experts identify and assess risks and work with senior management about how to manage these risks. Risk management, as shown in Figure 5-6, has four options. Risk can be accepted and budgeted for, and some risks can be avoided by not engaging in an activity. Management can also decide to transfer risk via insurance or outsourcing, and risks can be mitigated or reduced by safeguards. The second half of this chapter emphasizes this fourth response to risk, but it is important to point out that management can use these other options to address risk as well.

Before moving on, a note about cloud security: One way to transfer security risks is to use the cloud. The fundamentals of cloud options are discussed in Chapter 3. Increasingly security experts view the cloud as a secure option; most believe the cloud is more secure than in-house options. The cloud has several advantages. Cloud vendors use current technology, they can afford to hire leading security experts, they remove physical access to the data, they require customers to simplify and streamline procedures, and they have benefited from the most frequent and thorough security audits in the security business.

The third security fundamental is that defensive safeguards must be layered. No safeguard by itself is completely effective; there is no silver bullet, no simple solution. It can impede some attacks, but by itself it can stop few. As a result, there is no master list of safeguards, no list that would ensure complete protection. Therefore, management must rely on a security defense that is layered. One way to organize the layers is to select safeguards from each of the categories: technical, data, and human.

Keep in mind that safeguards are costly and often restrictive. As mentioned in the introduction, security is a trade-off between risk and cost. Safeguards can be expensive as they reduce work efficiency by making common tasks more difficult, adding labor expenses. Security is also a trade-off with freedom. Safeguards restrict freedoms by limiting what employees can do. An easy way to remember information systems safeguards is to arrange them according to the five components of an information system, as shown in Figure 5-7. Some of the safeguards involve computer hardware and software. Some involve data; others involve procedures and people. We will consider technical, data, and human safeguards in the next three questions.

Q5-5 How Can Technical and Data Safeguards Protect Against Security Threats?

Technical safeguards block threats from obtaining an asset by using the hardware and software components of an information system. Figure 5-8 lists primary technical safeguards. Consider each.

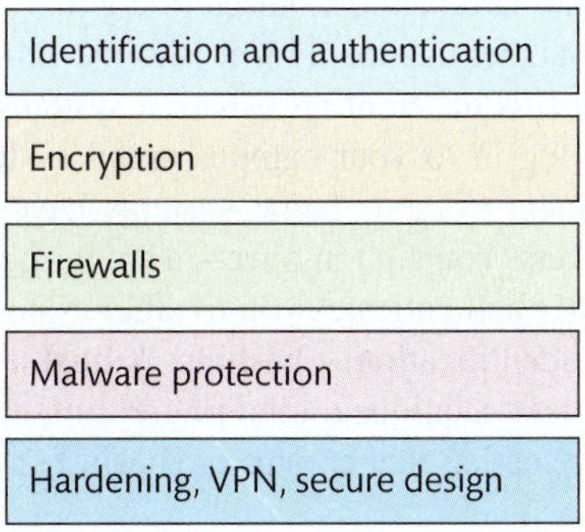

Identification and authentication
Encryption
Firewalls
Malware protection
Hardening, VPN, secure design

FIGURE 5-8

Technical Safeguards

FIGURE 5-9
Common Passwords

| 123456789 |
| qwerty |
| 111111 |
| password |
| 987654321 |

Identification and Authentication

Information systems today typically require users to sign in with a user name and password. The user name *identifies* the user (the process of identification), and the password *authenticates* that user (the process of authentication). The process of **authentication** verifies the credentials of the individual seeking access to a computer resource. The identification and authentication processes are supported by five technologies we discuss next: passwords, smart cards, biometrics, single sign on, and hashing.

Passwords have important weaknesses. In spite of repeated warnings, users often share their passwords, and many people choose ineffective, simple passwords. Because passwords are weak, they are a vulnerability. In fact, a 2014 Verizon report states, "Passwords, usernames, emails, credit/debit card and financial account information, and social security numbers are being comprised at a staggering rate, endangering the identity of customers nationwide."[4]

In addition to weak passwords, individuals often rely on common passwords. The five most common passwords are shown in Figure 5-9. According to *Money* magazine, the Twitter heist of 2016 was due to user passwords of *123456*. One type of attack on common passwords is brute force attack (mentioned earlier). A safeguard against a brute force attack is the use of **CAPTCHA**, a pseudo acronym for "Completely Automated Public Turing test to tell Computers and Humans Apart," which uses a simple challenge-response exercise to determine if the user is a human or a computer program such as a brute force attacker. Because of these problems, some organizations choose to use smart cards and biometric authentication in addition to passwords.

A **smart card** is a plastic card similar to a credit card. Unlike credit, debit, and ATM cards, which have a magnetic strip, smart cards have a microchip. The microchip, which holds far more data than a magnetic strip, is loaded with identifying data. Users of smart cards are required to enter a PIN to be authenticated.

Biometric authentication uses personal physical characteristics such as fingerprints, facial features, and retinal scans to authenticate users. Biometric authentication provides strong authentication, but the required equipment is expensive. Often, too, users resist biometric identification because they feel it is invasive. Note that authentication methods fall into three categories: what you know (password or PIN), what you have (smart card), and what you are (biometric).

To make authentication stronger, two actions may be required, a process often called two-factor authentication. In two-factor authentication, also called multifactor authentication, a password is used and a second authentication step is also required. This second step may be something the user has, something the user is (biometrics), or, with mobile devices, where the user is located. For example, a bank Web site may require a user to provide a code sent to the user by text message sent to the user from the bank; a second example is using a device carried by the user that generates a time-based code required to log in.

So far we have discussed authentication as if it is a one-time event, even if it requires two factors. However, when you access different information systems, often you have to log in several times. For example, you log in to your campus email system as well as your Canvas or Blackboard learning management system. Some systems have the capability to authenticate you to networks and other servers. You sign in once—a single sign-on (SSO)—and your laptop, smartphone, or app subsequently authenticates you to other systems.

A final technique used in identification is hashing. A **hash** is a scrambled series of characters generated from a string of text, a unique digital fingerprint used in identification procedures. A hash function is a one-way function that creates the hash. For example, when you enter your

PIN at an ATM, the ATM applies a hash function to your PIN to create a hash. This hash is compared to the stored value of your hash. A hash function is one-way; anyone who steals your digest cannot go backward (like a two-way function) and determine the right PIN to use that would generate your hash.

Before closing this section on identification and authentication, be aware that smartphones provide new opportunities to improve these processes. You spend so much time with your phone that it can vouch for you because it can easily ask you simple questions that only you can answer, for example, "Where were we yesterday at 3?" It can also easily identify your speech.

Encryption

Encryption is the process of transforming clear text into coded, unintelligible text for secure storage or communication. Commonly used methods are 3DES, RSA, and AES; search the Web for these terms if you want to know more about them.

A **key** is a number used to encrypt the data. It is called a *key* because it locks and unlocks a message, but it is a number used with an encryption algorithm and not a physical thing like the key to your apartment.

To encrypt a message, a computer program uses the encryption method with the key to convert a plaintext message into an encrypted message. The resulting coded message looks like gibberish.

Decoding (decrypting) a message is similar; a key is applied to the coded message to recover the original text. With **symmetric encryption**, the same key is used to encode and to decode. With **asymmetric encryption**, two keys are used; one key encodes the message, and the other key decodes the message. Symmetric encryption is simpler and much faster than asymmetric encryption.

A special version of asymmetric encryption, **public key/private key**, is used on the Internet. With this method, each site has a public key for encoding messages and a private key for decoding them. Before we explain how that works, consider the following analogy.

Suppose you send a friend an open combination lock (like you have on your gym locker). Suppose you are the only one who knows the combination to that lock. Now, suppose your friend puts something in a box and locks the lock. Now, neither your friend nor anyone else can open that box. The friend sends the locked box to you, and you apply the combination to open the box.

A public key is like the combination lock, and the private key is like the combination. Your friend uses the public key to code the message (lock the box), and you use the private key to decode the message (use the combination to open the lock). Now, suppose we have two generic computers, A and B. Suppose A wants to send an encrypted message to B. To do so, A sends B its public key (in our analogy, A sends B an open combination lock). Now B applies A's public key to the message and sends the resulting coded message back to A. At that point, neither B nor anyone other than A can decode that message. It is like the box with a locked combination lock. When A receives the coded message, A applies its private key (the combination in our analogy) to unlock or decrypt the message.

Again, public keys are like open combination locks. Computer A will send a lock to anyone who asks for one. But A never sends its private key (the combination) to anyone. Private keys stay private.

Most secure communication over the Internet uses a protocol called **https**. With https, data are encrypted using a protocol called the Secure Socket Layer (SSL), which is also known as Transport Layer Security (TLS). SSL/TLS uses a combination of public key/private key and symmetric encryption.

The basic idea is this: Symmetric encryption is fast and is preferred. But the two parties (say, you and a Web site) don't share a symmetric key. So, the two of you use asymmetric encryption to share the same symmetric key. Once you both have that key, you use symmetric encryption.

Figure 5-10 summarizes how SSL/TLS works when you communicate securely with a Web site:

1. Your computer obtains the public key of the Web site to which it will connect.
2. Your computer generates a key for symmetric encryption.

FIGURE 5-10

The Essence of https (SSL or TLS)

1. Your computer obtains public key of Web site.

Web Site Public Key

2. Your computer generates key for symmetric encryption.

3. Your computer encrypts symmetric key using Web site's public key.

Symmetric Key Encrypted Using Web Site's Public Key

4. Web site decodes your message using its private key. Obtains key for symmetric encryption.

Communications Using Symmetric Encryption

5. All communications between you and Web site use symmetric encryption.

You

Web Site

3. Your computer encodes that key using the Web site's public key. It sends the encrypted symmetric key to the Web site.
4. The Web site then decodes the symmetric key using its private key.
5. From that point forward, your computer and the Web site communicate using symmetric encryption.

Using this method, most of your secure communication uses the faster symmetric encryption. Once the symmetric encryption method kicks in, the asymmetric keys are discarded. By using the asymmetric keys only briefly, they are less likely to be discovered and copied.

Firewalls

A **firewall** is a computing device that prevents unauthorized access to parts of a network. A firewall can be a special use computer, or it can be an app on a general purpose computer or router. In essence, a firewall acts like a filter.

Firms often use multiple types of firewalls. A perimeter firewall is located between the organization's network and the public Internet as shown in Figure 5-11. In contrast, an internal

FIGURE 5-11

Perimeter Firewall

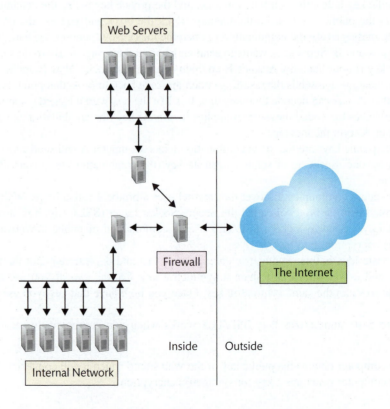

Web Servers

Firewall

The Internet

Inside   Outside

Internal Network

firewall is located within an organization's network and limits movement of data between sections of the network.

Firewalls must make decisions about which type of traffic to permit and which to restrict. Some firewalls base their decisions by inspecting each packet—evaluating its home, destination, contents, and other data in order to make the decision. These are called packet sniffers. Other firewalls can use more sophisticated rules and algorithms to evaluate the overall pattern of communication, the type of protocol being used, and other technical aspects to decide.

All organizations use firewalls. Most home routers include firewalls as do operating systems. As a future manager, if you have particular sites with which you do not want your employees to communicate, you can ask your IS department to enforce that limit via the firewall.

Malware Protection

The next technical safeguard in our list in Figure 5-8 concerns malware protection. Malware, as defined earlier, damages or disables computers.

Figure 5-12 lists some of the symptoms of malware. Sometimes these symptoms develop slowly over time as more malware components are installed. Should these symptoms occur on your computer, remove the spyware or adware using anti-malware programs.

Fortunately, it is possible to avoid most malware using the following malware safeguards:

1. **Install antivirus and antispyware programs on your computer.** Your IS department will have a list of recommended (perhaps required) programs for this purpose. If you choose a program for yourself, choose one from a reputable vendor. Check reviews of anti-malware software on the Web before purchasing.

2. **Set up your anti-malware programs to scan your computer frequently.** You should scan your computer at least once a week and possibly more often. When you detect malware code, use the anti-malware software to remove it. If the code cannot be removed, contact your IS department or anti-malware vendor.

3. **Update malware definitions.** Malware definitions—patterns that exist in malware code—should be downloaded frequently. Anti-malware vendors update these definitions continuously, and you should install these updates as they become available.

4. **Open email attachments only from known sources.** Also, even when opening attachments from known sources, do so with great care. With a properly configured firewall, email is the only outside-initiated traffic that can reach user computers. Most anti-malware programs check email attachments for malware code. However, all users should form the habit of *never* opening an email attachment from an unknown source.

5. **Promptly install software updates from legitimate sources.** Unfortunately, all programs are chock-full of security holes; vendors are fixing them as rapidly as they are discovered, but the practice is inexact. Install patches to the operating system and application programs promptly.

6. **Browse only in reputable Internet neighborhoods.** It is possible for some malware to install itself when you do nothing more than open a Web page. Don't go there!

7. **Don't use questionable discussion boards.** It is easy for hackers to install hidden malware on discussion board posts.

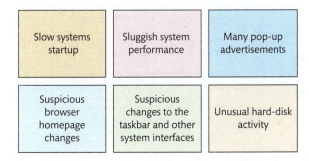

FIGURE 5-12
Spyware and Adware Symptoms

Hardening, VPN, and Secure Design

Another technical safeguard is hardening. Hardening is the process of reducing the vulnerabilities of a computer by restricting the functions and actions it is willing to perform. A security technician can lock down the number of features or functions the operating system or Web server will handle to only those needed for its intended work, making the computer less functional but more secure. Cloud vendors harden their servers and only permit a small number of well-vetted processes to run.

Still another technical safeguard is a **virtual private network**, or **VPN**. A VPN uses software or a dedicated computer to create a private network over the public Internet. This private network connects a client and server, enabling secure communication, a process also called tunneling.

A final technical safeguard is designing security into software, called secure design, a process of building in security as an app is developed. One example of good security in design is input validation. Web sites and applications are built to allow users to type in all sorts of inputs—from passwords to URLs to discussion board posts. A securely designed app would inspect all inputs for signs of an attack. This is input validation—testing all input fields from users. One type of input to reject is SQL code to prevent SQL injection attacks (mentioned earlier).

Q5-5 ▶ How Can Data Safeguards Protect Against Security Threats?

Data Safeguards

Data safeguards are outlined in Figure 5-13. One data safeguard is to define a specific data policy such as "We will not share identifying customer data with any other organization." Second, data administration and database administration(s) work together to specify user data rights and responsibilities. Third, those rights should be enforced by user accounts that are authenticated at least by passwords.

The organization should protect sensitive data by storing it in encrypted form. Such encryption uses one or more keys in ways similar to that described for data communication encryption.

One potential problem with stored data, however, is that the key might be lost or that disgruntled or terminated employees might destroy it. Because of this possibility, when data are encrypted, a trusted party should have a copy of the encryption key. This safety procedure is sometimes called **key escrow**.

Another data safeguard is to periodically create backup copies of database contents. The organization should store at least some of these backups off premises, possibly in a remote location. Additionally, IT personnel should periodically practice recovery to ensure that the backups are valid and that effective recovery procedures exist. Do not assume that just because a backup is made that the database is protected.

Physical security is another data safeguard. The computers that run the DBMS and all devices that store database data should reside in locked, controlled-access facilities. If not, they are subject not only to theft but also to damage. For better security, the organization should keep a log showing who entered the facility, when, and for what purpose. In the chapter-opening vignette, the locks on the computer labs are an example of physical security.

When organizations store databases in the cloud, all of the safeguards in Figure 5-13 should be part of the cloud service contract.

While these technical and data safeguards are essential, the most important safeguards wear shoes. Like most topics in this text, people play the most important role in security.

FIGURE 5-13

Data Safeguards

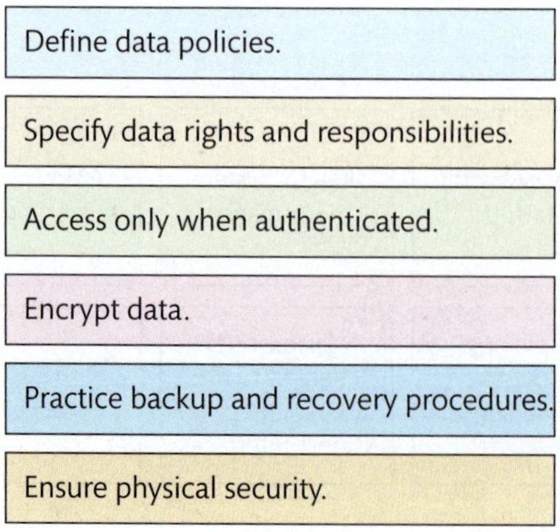

Define data policies.

Specify data rights and responsibilities.

Access only when authenticated.

Encrypt data.

Practice backup and recovery procedures.

Ensure physical security.

Q5-6 How Can Human Safeguards Protect Against Security Threats?

Human safeguards block threats from obtaining an asset by using the people and procedure components of information systems. In general, human safeguards result when authorized users follow appropriate procedures for system use and recovery. Restricting access to authorized users requires effective authentication methods and careful user account management. In addition, appropriate security procedures must be designed as part of every information system, and users should be trained on the importance and use of those procedures. In this section, we will consider the development of human safeguards for employees, nonemployees, account administration, backup and recovery, and security monitoring.

Human Safeguards for Employees

Figure 5-14 lists more specific security considerations for employees. Consider each.

TRUST BUT VERIFY If motivated and trained about security, employees can make the security task much easier. The most important security safeguard for employees is to be less trusting of others using the system. More specifically, they should employ the Russian proverb "trust but verify." Employees should seek to verify that the people or Web sites they are communicating with are actually who they claim to be. People spend years learning who to trust and how to verify in the real world but throw this skill out the window when communicating online.

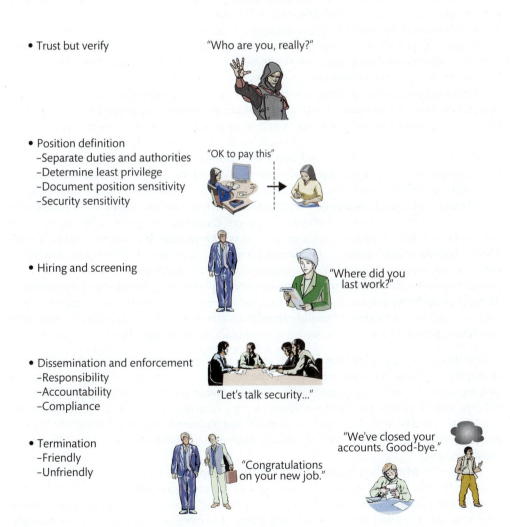

- Trust but verify

"Who are you, really?"

- Position definition
  - Separate duties and authorities
  - Determine least privilege
  - Document position sensitivity
  - Security sensitivity

"OK to pay this"

- Hiring and screening

"Where did you last work?"

- Dissemination and enforcement
  - Responsibility
  - Accountability
  - Compliance

"Let's talk security..."

- Termination
  - Friendly
  - Unfriendly

"Congratulations on your new job."

"We've closed your accounts. Good-bye."

- Enforce mobile device security policy

Use your own phone but be careful.

FIGURE 5-14

Human Safeguards for Employees

POSITION DEFINITIONS Effective human safeguards also include definitions of job tasks and responsibilities. In general, job descriptions should provide a separation of duties and authorities. For example, no single individual should be allowed to both approve expenses and write checks. Instead, one person should approve expenses, another pay them, and a third should account for the payment. Similarly, in inventory, no single person should be allowed to authorize an inventory withdrawal and also to remove the items from inventory. Given appropriate job descriptions, user accounts should be defined to give users the *least possible privilege* needed to perform their jobs.

Finally, security sensitivity should be made explicit and documented for each position. While some jobs such as employee compensation and proprietary marketing involve highly sensitive data, other positions require little access to sensitive data. Documenting position sensitivity enables security personnel to ensure the right data is available to the right employees.

HIRING AND SCREENING Security considerations should be part of the hiring process. Of course, if the position involves no sensitive data and no access to information systems, then screening for information systems security purposes will be minimal. When hiring for high-sensitivity positions, however, extensive interviews, references, and background investigations are appropriate. Note, too, that security screening applies not only to new employees but also to employees who are promoted into sensitive positions.

DISSEMINATION AND ENFORCEMENT Employees cannot be expected to follow security policies and procedures they do not know about. Therefore, employees need to be educated about the security policies, procedures, and responsibilities they will have.

Employee security training begins during new employee training with the explanation of general security policies and procedures. That general training must be amplified in accordance with the position's sensitivity and responsibilities. Promoted employees should receive security training that is appropriate to their new positions.

Enforcement consists of three interdependent factors: responsibility, accountability, and compliance. First, the company should clearly define the security *responsibilities* of each position. The design of the security program should be such that employees can be held *accountable* for security violations. Procedures should exist so that when critical data are lost, it is possible to determine how the loss occurred and who is accountable. Finally, the security program should encourage security *compliance*. Employee activities should regularly be monitored for compliance, and management should specify disciplinary action to be taken in light of noncompliance.

Management attitude is crucial—management needs to cultivate a culture of compliance. Culture starts with management behavior: Employee compliance is greater when management demonstrates, both in word and deed, a serious concern for security. If managers write passwords on staff bulletin boards, work on confidential documents on an unsecured wireless network, or ignore physical security procedures, then employee security attitudes and employee security compliance will suffer. Note, too, that effective security is a continuing management responsibility. Managers need to remind employees about security on a recurring basis, and perhaps the most effective reminders are stories of real-life security failures and their consequences. Stories, more than boring lists of do's and don'ts, have a bigger impact on the security behavior of employees.

TERMINATION Companies also must establish security policies and procedures for the termination of employees. Many employee terminations are friendly and occur as the result of promotion or retirement or when the employee resigns to take another position. Standard human resource policies should ensure that system administrators receive notification in advance of the employee's last day so they can remove accounts and passwords. The need to recover keys for encrypted data and any other special security requirements should be part of the employee's out-processing.

Unfriendly termination is more difficult because employees may be tempted to take malicious or harmful actions. In such a case, system administrators may need to remove user accounts and passwords prior to notifying the employee of his or her termination. Other actions may be needed to protect the company's data assets. A terminated sales employee, for example, may attempt to take the company's confidential customer and sales-prospect data for future use at another company.

The terminating employer should take steps to protect those data prior to the termination. The human resources department should be aware of the importance of giving IS administrators early notification of employee termination. No blanket policy exists; the information systems department must assess each case on an individual basis.

MOBILE DEVICE SECURITY Security must be applied to the increasing number of mobile devices used by employees. Security is worthless if employees carry sensitive data on mobile devices that are then lost, stolen, or hacked. A company must establish and enforce mobile device policy about where sensitive data can be stored or accessed, how sensitive data can be used on personal devices, and the use of VPNs on mobile devices.

Companies often allow employees to use their own personal mobile device to conduct company activities, a policy called **Bring Your Own Device (BYOD)**. BYOD can save money for the business as it avoids paying for devices, but it increases risk. This is a challenging issue— how best to balance the freedom employees enjoy using their own mobile devices for business work as well as the cost savings of BYOD with the additional security risks of mobile devices.

Human Safeguards for Nonemployee Personnel

Business requirements may necessitate opening information systems to nonemployee personnel—temporary personnel, vendors, partner personnel (employees of business partners), and the public. Although temporary personnel can be screened, to reduce costs the screening will be abbreviated from that for employees. In most cases, companies cannot screen either vendor or partner personnel. Of course, public users cannot be screened at all. Similar limitations pertain to security training and compliance testing.

In the case of temporary, vendor, and partner personnel, the contracts that govern the activity should call for security measures appropriate to the sensitivity of the data and the IS resources involved. Companies should require vendors and partners to perform appropriate screening and security training. The contract also should mention specific security responsibilities that are particular to the work to be performed. Companies should provide accounts and passwords with the least privilege and remove those accounts as soon as possible.

Finally, note that the business relationship with the public, and with some partners, differs from that with temporary personnel and vendors. The public and some partners use the information system to receive a benefit. Consequently, safeguards need to protect such users from internal company security problems. A disgruntled employee who maliciously changes prices on a Web site potentially damages both public users and business partners. As one IT manager put it, "Rather than protecting ourselves from them, we need to protect them from us."

Account Administration

The administration of user accounts, passwords (Figure 5-15), and help-desk policies is another important human safeguard. Account management concerns the creation of new user accounts, the modification of existing account permissions, and the removal of unneeded accounts. Information system administrators perform all of these tasks, but account users have the responsibility to notify the administrators of the need for these actions. As a future user, you can improve your relationship with IS personnel by providing early and timely notification of the need for account changes. It is particularly important to notify security administrators when an account or access to sensitive data is no longer necessary.

Backup and Recovery Procedures

Backup procedures concern the creation of backup data to be used in the event of failure. Whereas operations personnel have the responsibility for backing up system databases and other systems data, departmental personnel have the need to back up data on their own computers.

> I hereby acknowledge personal receipt of the system password(s) associated with the user IDs listed below. I understand that I am responsible for protecting the password(s), will comply with all applicable system security standards, and will not divulge my password(s) to any person. I further understand that I must report to the Information Systems Security Officer any problem I encounter in the use of the password(s) or when I have reason to believe that the private nature of my password(s) has been compromised.

FIGURE 5-15

Sample Account Acknowledgment Form

Systems analysts should develop procedures for system recovery. First, how will the department manage its affairs when a critical system is unavailable? Customers will want to order and manufacturing will want to remove items from inventory even though a critical information system is unavailable. How will the department respond? Once the system is returned to service, how will records of business activities during the outage be entered into the system? How will service be resumed? The system developers should ask and answer these questions and others like them and develop procedures accordingly.

Security Monitoring

Security monitoring is the last of the human safeguards we will consider. Important monitoring functions are activity log analyses, security testing, investigating and learning from security incidents, and performing security audits.

Many information system programs produce *activity logs*. Firewalls produce logs of their activities, including lists of all dropped packets, infiltration attempts, and unauthorized access attempts from within the firewall. DBMS products produce logs of successful and failed log-ins.

Web servers produce voluminous logs of Web activities. The operating systems in personal computers can produce logs of log-ins and firewall activities.

None of these logs add any value to an organization unless someone looks at them. Accordingly, an important security function is to analyze these logs for threat patterns, successful and unsuccessful attacks, and evidence of security vulnerabilities.

Security monitoring also requires that security analysts inventory hardware and software and compare settings on both to when the software or hardware was first activated. In this process called baselining, analysts look for unusual changes to hardware or software that might result in a new vulnerability. Today, most large organizations actively investigate their security vulnerabilities. When attacked or scanned, organizations then use free online tools, like DNSstuff, to determine who has attacked them. In fact many organizations create honeypots, which are false targets for hackers to attack. To the hacker the honeypot looks just like a typical target, but instead it contains a program to determine the hacker's IP address. If you are technically minded, detail-oriented, and curious, a career as a security specialist in this field is almost as exciting as it appears on *CSI*. To learn more, check out DNSstuff, Nessus, or Security AppScan.

One way companies monitor their security is with periodic security audits. A **security audit** is a systematic evaluation of security by assessing how well the security safeguards conform to established criteria. A security audit is conducted by external consultants or in-house security experts. Security, like quality, is an ongoing process. There is no final state when technical, data, or human safeguards are complete and security is achieved. Instead, companies must monitor security on a continuing basis.

Q5-7 ▶ How Should Organizations Respond to Security Incidents?

When safeguards fail and an incident occurs, organizations need to execute an incident response plan. If the incident is a serious one, the organization should execute its disaster recovery plan (DRP). Figure 5-16 lists the key attributes of disaster and incident response plans. First, every organization should have an incident response plan as part of the security program, and it should ensure employees know where to find it when an incident occurs. No organization should wait until some asset has been lost or compromised before deciding what to do. The plan should

FIGURE 5-16

Attributes of Successful Disaster and Incident Response Plans

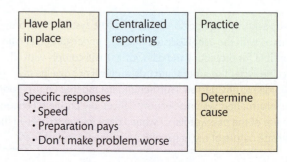

MIS InClass 5

Personal IS Security

Most of this chapter concerns security for organizations. This MIS InClass exercise is designed to help you generate your own personal list of security practices to use in your everyday life. A personal practice is an activity or procedure you follow that reduces IT security risk in your life.

Step 1: Each individual, using the chapter as a guide, writes down five personal practices.

Step 2: In teams, discuss each individual list of five practices. The output of this step is to generate a list of 10 practices.

Each team should post its list to either an online discussion forum or collaboration site so that the class can view every team's list.

Step 3: As a class generate a list of the most common 15 practices.

Step 4: Vote individually on the most important practices. Every student can vote for five practices. The output of this step is the top 10 list for the class.

Step 5: Commit to a time in 2 weeks when the teams will reassemble and discuss the top 10 list. The goal is for each student to do these good practices for 2 weeks and report to the team on which ones were maintained and which ones were not and why.

Step 6: At this future meeting generate a list for the class of the top five practices that should be maintained by students but that most students find hard to do.

include how employees are to respond to security problems, whom they should contact, the reports they should make, and steps they can take to reduce further loss.

The plan should provide centralized reporting of all security incidents. Such reporting will enable an organization to determine if it is under systematic attack or whether an incident is isolated. Centralized reporting also allows the organization to learn about security threats, take consistent actions in response, and apply specialized expertise to all security problems.

Finally, organizations should periodically practice incident response. Without such practice, personnel will be poorly informed on the response plan, and the plan itself may have flaws that only become apparent during a drill.

When an incident does occur, speed is of the essence. Viruses and worms can spread very quickly across an organization's networks, and a fast response will help mitigate the consequences. Because of the need for speed, preparation pays. The incident response plan should identify critical personnel and their off-hours contact information. These personnel should be trained on where to go and what to do when they get there. Without adequate preparation, there is substantial risk that the actions of well-meaning people will make the problem worse. Also, the rumor mill will be alive with all sorts of nutty ideas about what to do. A cadre of well-informed, trained personnel will serve to dampen such rumors.

After the initial response to the disaster or incident, **computer forensics** can help determine the cause of the event. The forensics investigation should also gather and preserve evidence for legal action.

This chapter included a wide variety of threats and safeguards. But keep the big picture in mind—security is about trade-offs—between security and cost and between security and freedom. Each of the security safeguards discussed in the second half of this chapter is expensive and reduces end user freedoms. Choices in these trade-offs made by management will affect your work. Be a part of the security solution for your organization by supporting the trade-offs—don't be part of the security problem.

Ethics Guide

Security Privacy

Some organizations have legal requirements to protect the customer data they collect and store, but the laws may be more limited than you think. The Gramm-Leach-Bliley (GLB) Act, passed by Congress in 1999, protects consumer financial data stored by financial institutions, which are defined as banks, securities firms, insurance companies, and organizations that provide financial advice, prepare tax returns, and provide similar financial services.

The Privacy Act of 1974 provides protections to individuals regarding records maintained by the U.S. government, and the privacy provisions of the Health Insurance Portability and Accountability Act (HIPAA) of 1996 give individuals the right to access their own health data created by doctors and other healthcare providers. HIPAA also sets rules and limits on who can read and receive your health information.

The law is stronger in other countries. In Australia, for example, the Privacy Principles of the Australian Privacy Act of 1988 govern not only government and healthcare data but also records maintained by businesses with revenues in excess of AU$3 million.

To understand the importance of the limitations, consider online retailers that routinely store customer credit card data. Do Dell, Amazon, the airlines, and other e-commerce businesses have a legal requirement to protect their customers' credit card data? Apparently not—at least not in the United States. The activities of such organizations are not governed by the GLB, the Privacy Act of 1974, or HIPAA.

Most consumers would say, however, that online retailers have an ethical requirement to protect a customer's credit card and other data, and most online retailers would agree. Or at least the retailers would agree that they have a strong business reason to protect that data. A substantial loss of credit card data by any large online retailer would have detrimental effects on both sales and brand reputation.

Data aggregators further complicate the risk to individuals because they develop a complete profile of households and individuals. And no federal law prohibits the U.S. government from buying information products from the data accumulators.

But let's bring the discussion closer to home. What requirements does your university have on the data it maintains about you? State law or university policy may govern those records, but no federal law does. Most universities consider it their responsibility to provide public access to graduation records. Anyone can determine when you graduated, your degree, and your major. (Keep this service in mind when you write your résumé.)

Most professors endeavor to publish grades by student number and not by name, and there may be a state law that requires that separation. But what about your work? What about the papers you write, the answers you give on exams? What about the emails you send to your professor? These data are not protected by federal law, and they are probably not protected by state law. If your professor chooses to cite your work in research, she will be subject to copyright law but not privacy law. What you write is no longer your personal data; it belongs to the academic community. You can ask your professor what she intends to do with your coursework, emails, and office conversations, but none of that data is protected by law.

The bottom line: Be careful with your personal data. Large, reputable organizations are likely to endorse ethical privacy policy and to have strong and effective safeguards to effectuate that policy, but individuals and small organizations might not. If in doubt, ask.

DISCUSSION QUESTIONS

1. Using the categorical imperative (page 18) and utilitarianism (page 43) perspectives, assess the privacy ethics of the online retailer, the data aggregator, governments, and your professor. State assumptions you need to support your assessment, if any.

2. When you order from an online retailer, the data you provide is not protected by U.S. privacy law. Does this fact cause you to reconsider setting up an account with a stored credit card number? What is the advantage of storing the credit card number? Do you think the advantage is worth the risk? Are you more willing to take the risk with some companies than with others? Why or why not?

3. Suppose you are the treasurer of a student club and you store records of club members' payments in a database. In the past, members have disputed payment amounts; therefore, when you receive a payment, you scan an image of the check or credit card invoice and store the scanned image in a database.

   One day, you are using your computer in a local wireless coffee shop and a malicious student breaks into your computer over the wireless network and steals the club database. You know nothing about this until the next day, when a club member complains that a popular student Web site has published the names, bank names, and bank account numbers for everyone who has given you a check.

   What liability do you have in this matter? Could you be classified as a financial institution because you are taking students' money? (You can find the GLB at *http://business.ftc.gov/privacy-and-security/gramm-leach-bliley-act.*) If so, what liability do you have? If not, do you have any other liability? Does the coffee shop have a liability?

4. Suppose you are asked to fill out a study questionnaire that requires you to enter identifying data as well as answers to personal questions. You hesitate to provide the data, but the top part of the questionnaire states, "All responses will be strictly confidential." So, you fill out the questionnaire.

Source: Max Krasnov/Shutterstock.

ACTIVE REVIEW

Use this Active Review to verify that you understand the material in the chapter.

Q5-1 ▸ What is information systems security?

Define *information systems security* and explain the major trade-offs that security must address. Describe the scope of the security challenge. Define *threat, vulnerability, safeguard,* and *target* and give an example of each. Give different examples for each of the three rows of Figure 5-2.

Q5-2 ▸ What are the most significant threats and potential losses they can cause?

List two types of threats and three types of security losses. Summarize each of the elements in the cells of Figure 5-3. Explain why information security is difficult.

Q5-3 ▸ How should you respond to security threats?

Explain each of the elements in Figure 5-4. Summarize the characteristics of a strong password. Define *cookie.* Explain why avoiding USB drives is a good idea. Describe several security practices for smartphones.

Q5-4 ▸ How should organizations respond to security threats?

Name and describe the three security fundamentals that senior management should address. Summarize the contents of a security policy. Explain what it means to manage risk. Describe the four options for risk. Discuss the security advantages of cloud vendors. Explain why safeguards should be layered.

Q5-5 ▸ How can technical and data safeguards protect against security threats?

Define *technical safeguard* and explain which of the five components are involved in such safeguards. Explain the use of identification and authentication and describe different authentication options. Describe a hash and how it contributes to authentication. Explain symmetric and asymmetric encryption and explain how they are used for SSL/TLS. Define *firewall.* Describe several malware safeguards. Explain how hardening, VPNs, and software design can contribute to security. Give examples of data safeguards.

Q5-6 ▸ How can human safeguards protect against security threats?

Name and describe the human safeguards for employees and nonemployee personnel. Summarize account administration safeguards. Describe backup and recovery options. Explain four security monitoring functions. Describe a security audit.

Q5-7 ▸ How should organizations respond to security incidents?

Summarize the actions that an organization should take when dealing with a security incident.

KEY TERMS AND CONCEPTS

Advanced Persistent Threat (APT)   110
Asymmetric encryption   115
Authentication   114
Biometric authentication   114
Bring your own device (BYOD)   121
Brute force   109
CAPTCHA   114
Computer forensics   123
Cookies   111
Cross-site scripting (XSS)   109
Denial-of-service (DoS)   110

Encryption   115
Evil twin   109
Firewall   116
Hacking   109
https   115
Hash   114
Human safeguards   119
Information systems security   106
IP spoofing   109
Key   115
Key escrow   118
Malware   109

Overflow attack   110
Phisher   109
Phishing   109
Pretexting   109
Public key/private key   115
Ransomware   109
Risk   106
Safeguard   107
Security audit   122
Session hijacking   109
Smart card   114
Sniffing   109

USING YOUR KNOWLEDGE

5-1. Reread the opening vignette regarding the hospital at the beginning of the chapter. What safeguards discussed in this chapter would reduce the risk of this type of attack in the future?
MyLab MIS

5-2. Describe three safeguards used at your university. How does each cost the university in reduced efficiency, and how does each reduce freedoms of end users?
MyLab MIS

5-3. Describe how your university should prepare for security incidents.
MyLab MIS

5-4. For two of your personal accounts, create a new strong password. List the two accounts here (e.g., Facebook) but not the password, of course.

5-5. Of the personal security safeguards listed in Figure 5-4, which three can you implement? How will these safeguards reduce your freedom?

5-6. Of the five smartphone practices listed in Figure 5-5, which two can you implement? How will these safeguards reduce your freedom?

5-7. For a computer lab at your school, create a list of safeguards that are in place and safeguards that are not used. Explain which of the safeguards that are not used should be implemented and why.

5-8. For one of the attacks shown in the cells in Figure 5-3, search the Internet. Find an example of how this attack was used. Describe that attack situation and provide three safeguards that would have helped.

COLLABORATION EXERCISE 5

Collaborate with a group of students to answer the following questions. Your task will be easier if you coordinate your work with SharePoint, Office 365, Google Docs, or equivalent collaboration tools. (See Chapter 10 for a discussion of collaboration tools and processes.) Your answers should reflect the thinking of the entire group, not just that of one or two individuals.

As mentioned in the chapter, one way companies monitor their security is with periodic security audits. A security audit is a systematic evaluation of the security by assessing how well the security safeguards conform to established criteria. A security audit is conducted by external consultants or in-house security experts.

Create an IT security audit list that could be used to conduct a security audit for an organization like your university or a mid-sized firm. Use the topics discussed in this chapter as well as Internet resources you find (e.g., Securityfocus.com, Cert.org, and mitre.org/work/cybersecurity.html). Organize this list into three to five major headings such as technical safeguards or policies, and create a list of at least 10 items from this chapter and five from Internet sources. One entry on your list might be about firewalls: "Does the firm update its firewall settings regularly?"

Each item in the audit should be fail-able, that is, an inspector using the audit list can clearly determine if the listed item is present or absent. Each item should also be specific and clear, not general or ambiguous.

CASE STUDY 5

WikiLeaks: One More Security Risk

In the spring of 2017 WikiLeaks published CIA internal documentation that seems to indicate that the CIA uses a variety of tools to "spy" on individuals such as malware, spyware, and viruses that can be installed on smart TVs, cars, and smartphones. Using these tools, the CIA could determine what individuals watch on their TVs, where they drive, and how they use their smartphones.

Founded in 2006 by Julian Assange, WikiLeaks is a self-described media organization with a stated goal of disseminating original documents from anonymous sources. Assange, now the editor in chief of WikiLeaks, founded it to counter what he calls secrecy-based, authoritarian conspiracy governments, one of which, in his view, is the U.S. government. His intent is not to let sunlight into the room as much as to change the room itself.

Assange was once a computer programmer and hacker in the late 1980s and '90s. The Australian Federal Police tapped his modem, discovered his hacking, and charged him with more than 30 counts of hacking and crimes. After paying restitution, he worked for Police Child Exploitation units and wrote books on security. More recently, after WikiLeaks revealed a number of classified documents and emails, he was called a terrorist by former Vice President Joe Biden, and others have considered his work illegal, while still others support him. In this supportive camp are a former Russian president, politicians in Europe and South America, and a number of activists and celebrities. In 2012, after sexual assault allegations in Sweden, Assange applied for political asylum at the Ecuadorian embassy in London, where he has resided since.

The WikiLeaks site began as a typical wiki—public readership and active posts that were subject to editing, much like Wikipedia. Very few of the early classified documents were redacted or heavily edited by WikiLeaks. These early documents reported on corruption in Kenya and military equipment expenditures in the Afghanistan War. Then, in 2010, WikiLeaks released a video called "Collateral Murder," gunsight footage from a Baghdad airstrike that killed Iraqi journalists. It portrayed a very specific political viewpoint and was not offered to inform like a typical wiki.

Later in 2010, WikiLeaks became front-page news when it released more than 700,000 documents including Iraqi war logs and diplomatic cables thought to be from a U.S. Army intelligence soldier named Bradley Manning (now Chelsea Manning). It also released files on the detention of prisoners in the Guantanamo Bay detention camp.

Most recently, WikiLeaks has adopted the practice of giving five news organizations—*Le Monde, El Pais, The Guardian, Der Spiegel*, and the *New York Times*—different sets of classified documents before they are released to the public. WikiLeaks relies on these newspapers to redact data in the documents that would be harmful to any particular individual.

WikiLeaks has also published a heavily encrypted "insurance" file that is 1.4 GB in size. Many speculate that these are the original unredacted documents, and Assange has asserted the password to this file will be released in the event of his death or destruction of WikiLeaks.

During the 2016 U.S. presidential election, WikiLeaks released emails and other documents from the U.S. Democratic National Committee (DNC) and from Hillary Clinton's campaign manager, causing lasting embarrassment. According to U.S. intelligence, these documents were hacked by Russian sources, but WikiLeaks denies that claim.

The impacts of WikiLeaks are significant. It is making intelligence gathering by governments more difficult, and much of what is eventually released by WikiLeaks violates personal privacy expectations. However, WikiLeaks believes free speech is the highest-order principle for any society and that government power that tends to limit true freedom should be the concern of all people seeking a truly democratic society.

5-9. What is the best aspect of WikiLeaks' work? The worst aspect?

5-10. How would the categorical imperative and utilitarianism viewpoints discussed in Ethical Guides in Chapters 1 and 2 view the work of WikiLeaks?

5-11. Will the actions of WikiLeaks result in more encryption? Is that a good outcome?

5-12. If you were a manager in the CIA or DNC, which safeguards in Figure 5-7 would you identify as needing to be more widely used?

5-13. Government agencies have a different threat than most business or nongovernmental organizations: employees dissatisfied with government policy. Think about your school, your local government, or a government agency: What sensitive data might a dissatisfied employee release?

5-14. Some have accused WikiLeaks of being biased—that it only releases documents that support its goals. Is this a valid criticism?

5-15. The last question in this chapter describes how organizations should respond to security incidents. Read about how the DNC and the CIA reacted to WikiLeaks' actions. How would you evaluate their reactions? What could they have done better?

CHAPTER RESOURCES

[1] NSA: Cybercrime is "the greatest transfer of wealth in history," July 10, 2012, accessed August 30, 2017, www.zdnet.com/article/nsa-cybercrime-is-the-greatest-transfer-of-wealth-in-history/.

[2] "Cyber-Attack: Europol Says It Was Unprecedented in Scale," *BBC News*, May 13, 2017, accessed May 13, 2017, http://www.bbc.com/news/world-europe-39907965.

[3] Mandiant, "APT1: Exposing One of China's Cyber Espionage Units," February 18, 2013, accessed June 15, 2017, http://intelreport.mandiant.com/Mandiant_Report.pdf.

[4] 2014 Data Breach Investigations Report, accessed June 15, 2017, www.verizonenterprise.com/resources/reports/rp_Verizon-DBIR-2014_en_xg.pdf.

MyLab MIS

Go to **MyLab MIS.com** for Auto-graded writing questions as well as the following Assisted-graded writing questions:

5-16. You have decided to open a security consulting business specializing in teaching senior citizens in nursing homes how to use the Internet safely. First, list five apps you think that generation would like to use. Second, list the top seven rules they should follow to protect themselves. Finally, what are the three most significant threats they face.

5-17. Write an effective phishing attack email designed to obtain personal data from your peers. After your phishing email include a note to the instructor explaining how your attack will work. For example, you may explain that once a student clicks on a link they will be taken to a Web site that will ask them for something.

Part 3

Structured Processes and Information Systems

Chapters 1 and 2 introduced the idea of business processes and their relationship to information systems. In Chapters 3, 4, and 5, we diverted from the process topic to discuss the fundamental technologies that you need to know to understand the relationship of processes and information systems in greater depth. With that background, we are now able to return to the topic of business processes. Although we will discuss processes in business, processes are common in every type of organization as well as in your everyday life—you have a process for starting a car, for doing laundry, and for uploading photos on social media.

Chapters 6 through 9 discuss structured processes and related information systems. Chapter 6 provides an overview of business processes and how they can be improved with information systems. Chapter 7 introduces ERP systems that support many business processes by consolidating all the data for the business in one large and complex database. The chapter also discusses SAP, a common ERP system, and describes the fundamentals of how it works.

Chapters 8 and 9 are "applied" chapters. They show how SAP is used in two representative business processes—procurement and sales. As processes that are fundamental to business and are widely used, these two processes, buying and selling, were chosen to demonstrate what is common to all processes and what might differ between processes.

Chapter 6

Using IS to Improve Processes

It is a hot and humid night, and Jake, a young hospital employee, is fighting off sleep when he is bolted to attention.

"*Help!* This man is dying!" comes a shout from the nearby ER waiting room.

Jake jumps from his desk and runs to the waiting room.

"He just fell over. I don't think he's breathing!" says an elderly woman in the waiting room.

Jake bends over the man to check his pulse and breathing, and both are faint. Just then several nurses and the ER doctor arrive. CPR is quickly started, and a nurse runs off to retrieve a defibrillator. Once stabilized, the patient is hurried off to the ER.

The next morning Jake is giving an account of the near-death experience to his boss.

"Jake, you're telling me he almost died in our ER waiting room!" Joe Smit, the general manager, is equal parts shocked, frustrated, and mad.

"It was close. If they didn't paddle him and wheel him into ER right away, I don't think Mr. Jones would be our patient today."

"I think I was told half the story. Give it to me from the top."

"About 7 last night, Mr. Jones drove himself to our ER and complained of vomiting and nausea like he's never had before. They took his vitals and his insurance info and told him to sit in the waiting room. I was over sitting next to Debbie at the info center. He was in the waiting room for like 20 minutes, and then someone yelled for help. Right after I got there, the ER folks rushed out and found him unconscious with almost no pulse. By the time the bed arrived he had stopped breathing. They paddled him right there and wheeled him into the ER. I think later they found out he had a reaction to some medicine and food combination."

"Why was he in the waiting room?"

"Apparently the ER was full."

"Wasn't the ER staffed for 10 beds last night?"

"I think that's right, but on the nights I work, it's not unusual for all of them to be in use at some point during the night."

"I guess we could fit a couple more stations in there, but I don't get it. When I was younger, I worked some shifts in there, and we never seemed to have all the beds in use."

"Yeah, boss, but the ER docs now tend to use them to treat patients that come in but can't afford to be admitted. I've been told that only about half the ER patients have insurance, so it costs the hospital more to admit them than to have them stay in the ER for a bit while they are treated."

"That doesn't seem like the best use of those beds, but I guess that makes some sense. If we want to keep people like Mr. Jones alive, either we make more ER beds or we admit more patients without insurance. Jake, fix this for me by morning," Joe said jokingly.

Q6-1. What are the important characteristics of processes in organizations?

Q6-2. What are examples of common business processes?

Q6-3. How can management improve processes?

Q6-4. How can information systems be used to improve processes?

Q6-5. How can process management principles improve processes?

Q6-6. How do process teams diagram process improvement?

Q6-7. How can an IS hinder a process?

PREVIEW

In this chapter, we examine more closely the subject of processes we defined in Chapter 2, with a special emphasis on process improvement. Processes have now become the fabric of organizations, the means by which people organize their work activities. By analyzing processes, businesses can better execute strategy, lower cost, and increase productivity. While strong processes are a key to business success, they are important to you, too—every manmade thing you see was assembled, shipped, stored, sold, paid, and accounted for with business processes.

But we start with an admission—processes are not exciting. No one makes a movie, sends a photo on Snapchat, or writes a best seller about an exciting process. It's the end product that makes the process worthwhile. Many IS professionals once took processes for granted. After all, computers were going to change everything—the new tricks, rapidly improving performance, and mind-numbing speeds would make the computers the star—not the processes they supported. Those days are over.

To help us explain why processes are so important, we'll use the processes in two organizations as recurring examples throughout this chapter. The first is the hospital described in the opening vignette. Hospitals execute a process every time a patient is admitted, tested, fed, treated, or moved. Hospitals also have many of the traditional processes of every business—they purchase things, maintain an inventory, and bill patients and insurance companies. Our second organization is a pizza shop like the one at many college unions, a restaurant that is part of a national pizza chain.

Supporting processes is the main task of IS. In the previous chapters, you learned what they *are* and their components; here you will learn what they *do* for business processes. Business process improvement is also mentioned briefly in Extension 3, Process Management and IS Development. There we discuss the general topic of business processes in a broad and general framework that would be common in a non-MIS textbook. Here in Chapter 6, we focus on how to improve business processes with IS in a way unique to this textbook. We surround this topic with an introduction to business processes in Q1 and Q2, which focus on the characteristics of processes. We also describe how processes can be improved by managers in Q3 and by process improvement experts in Q5. We conclude by examining how process teams diagram processes and how IS can hinder a process.

One day in the not too distant future, you'll be responsible for a process, and you will want to be able to improve it. Take time today to begin to master the vocabulary and key ideas of processes. The effectiveness of your process and your ability to improve it will depend, in part, on how well you can apply information systems to that process.

Q6-1 ▶ What Are the Important Characteristics of Processes in Organizations?

You can fill a library with books about the characteristics of business processes, and half that library would focus on how to improve them. There are thousands of ideas in these books; process improvement in business is a very big deal. Improving a process even just a little can make a big, big difference if an organization executes that process frequently. Consider processes that occur millions of times a day—finding a parking spot, ordering coffee, buying fast food, using a credit card, finding a Web site, logging into a computer, uploading a photo, or downloading music. In one of these common processes, if you can find a way to shave off as little as 6 seconds, you will save about 5 cents each time, or $50,000 each million times. With common processes, 6 seconds is worth $50,000. We want you to be able to find those 6 seconds.

Every organization would like to improve its processes. Throughout your business career, you will work with process improvement and IS professionals to improve processes. Even if you are an accounting, supply chain, or marketing student, you will soon be collaborating with other professionals to improve processes.

Let's review what we already know about processes. In Chapter 2, we defined a **business process** as a sequence of activities for accomplishing a function. We also defined **activity** as a task within a business process and **resources** as the items, such as people, computers, and data and document collections, necessary to accomplish an activity. **Actors** are resources who are either humans or computer hardware. Finally, a **role** is a subset of the activities in a business process that are performed by a particular actor.

Examples of Processes

In this chapter, we will apply process lessons to the hospital setting in the opening vignette and to a pizza shop, located in a student union on a college campus. At the college pizza shop, a manager, Mr. Pizzi, is trying to improve five processes. These five, shown in Figure 6-1, are Order, Assemble, Bake, Package, and Deliver.[1] For each of the five processes, activities, roles, resources, and actors can be specified. The five processes are accomplished by the Cashier, Chef, and Driver roles as shown. Further, each process can be broken down into activities. For example, the Assemble process has three main activities—Prepare Dough, Add Sauces, and Add Toppings. Within the Prepare Dough activity, Sarah, an actor, plays the role of Chef and uses resources such as a Recipe and Utensils.

Processes and their activities are both depicted by rectangles because in practice the terms are often used interchangeably. For example, the Add Sauces activity could also be considered a process with activities of its own such as Add Tomato Sauce and Sprinkle on Spices.

While the goal of this chapter is to understand how IS can improve processes, a good first step is to understand the characteristics of processes. Processes have a variety of characteristics— like animals in a zoo. Your interactions with the animals will go better if you treat them differently.

FIGURE 6-1

Five Processes, Resources, Actors, and Roles at the Pizza Shop

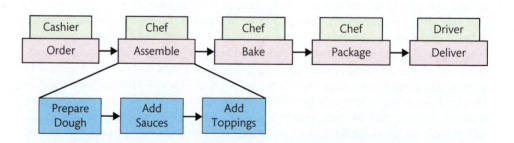

Assemble Process Activities	Resources	Role
Prepare Dough	People, Recipe, Utensils, etc.	Chef
Add Sauces	People, Measuring Cup, Scales, etc.	Chef
Add Toppings	People, Quantity of Toppings, Sequence List, etc.	Chef

FIGURE 6-2

Four Characteristics of Processes

Characteristic of Process	Categories of Process Characteristics
Stability of Flow	Structured Dynamic
Scope	Operational Managerial Strategic
Objectives	Effectiveness Efficiency
Location in Value Chain	Inbound Logistics Operations Outbound Logistics Sales and Marketing Service Technology Development Infrastructure

The same is true of processes. They have different characteristics, so to get the result you want, you need to be able to tell them apart by these characteristics. The four characteristics of processes are listed in Figure 6-2.

In Chapter 2, we described the first characteristic—the stability of the flow of process activities. Some processes are structured and others are dynamic. In a structured process, the activities typically follow a fixed predefined sequence; a good example is logging into your email account. Dynamic processes are more informal; the activity sequence is less fixed, like when you collaborate with classmates on a group project.

Here we add three more important characteristics of processes—their scope, objectives, and location in the value chain. We begin with the three categories of process scope: operational, managerial, and strategic, as shown in Figure 6-3.

Scope of Processes

Operational processes are commonplace, routine, everyday business processes. At the pizza shop, operational processes include ordering supplies, paying bills, and checking out customers. These may be executed hundreds or thousands of times a day across all the restaurants in the local franchise. The procedures, or instructions, for these processes are changed very infrequently. Typically there are more computerized actors in an operational process than in

Scope	Characteristics	Mix of Actors	Frequency of Occurrence	Examples	IS Supporting This Type of Process
Operational	Common, routine, day-to-day	More computers than other processes	High	Order supplies, pay bills, check out customers	Transaction Processing System (TPS)
Managerial	Allocation and use of resources	Mix	Medium	Assess seasonal promotions, plan and schedule cashiers	Management Information System (MIS)
Strategic	Broad-scope, organizational issues	More people than other processes	Low	Decide on new restaurant location, corporate budgeting	Executive Support System (ESS)

FIGURE 6-3

Scope of Processes

other types of processes. Finally, because many actors contribute to this process, changing operational processes is more difficult than changing other types of processes. Information systems that facilitate operational processes are sometimes called **transaction processing systems (TPS)**.

Managerial processes concern resource use. These processes include planning, assessing, and analyzing the resources used by the company in pursuit of its objectives. Managerial processes occur much less frequently and with many fewer computerized actors than operational processes. At the pizza franchise, these processes include assessing seasonal promotions, planning and scheduling cashiers, and determining which personnel to promote. Information systems that facilitate managerial processes are often referred to as **management information systems (MIS)**, which is a second meaning for the term MIS.

Strategic processes seek to resolve issues that have long-range impact on the organization. These processes have broad scope and affect most of the firm. Because judgment and a tolerance for ambiguity are important, there are typically more human actors than in operational or managerial processes. Examples of strategic processes at the pizza shop include deciding where to locate a new restaurant, corporate budgeting, and new product introduction. Information systems that support strategic processes are sometimes called **executive support systems (ESS)**.

Operational, managerial, and strategic processes are three levels of processes within the organization. Most of this book addresses processes within an organization, but many of the principles you learn about processes can also apply to inter-organizational processes. One example of this type of process is the supply chain in the auto industry—companies like Ford integrate their assembly process with the assembly process of their suppliers to make the entire process perform well.

Objectives of Processes

The operational—managerial—strategic distinction is an important way to classify a process. A third important characteristic is the type of objective, as shown in Figure 6-4. An **objective** is a desired goal an organization has decided to pursue. These objectives can be classified into two types: efficient and effective.

Efficiency means that a process creates more output with the same inputs or the same output with fewer inputs. To say this more formally, efficiency is a ratio of process outputs to inputs. One efficiency objective for the pizza-making process might be to go green and use less energy. This objective led management to buy better-insulated ovens for its new restaurant.

A second type of objective is **effectiveness.** An effective objective helps achieve an organizational strategy. One simple effectiveness objective is to sell better-tasting pizzas, and this objective led Mr. Pizzi to design the walk-in refrigerator that preserves the freshness of the ingredients until they are needed.

To summarize, an efficiency objective aims to conserve resources, whereas an effectiveness objective helps achieve a company strategy. A good way to remember the difference is that effectiveness is doing right things while efficiency is doing things right. As we will see shortly, objectives, unlike the other characteristics, are not mutually exclusive; processes can have effectiveness or efficiency objectives or both.

These two categories of process objectives—efficiency and effectiveness—can occur at any of the three levels of processes—operational, managerial, and strategic. That said, the most common combinations are operational processes with efficiency objectives and strategic processes with effectiveness objectives.

FIGURE 6-4

Types of Process Objectives

Objective Category	Definition	Example Process and Objective at Pizza Shop
Efficiency	Create more output with same input or same output with less input	Bake Process: Use less energy
Effectiveness	Achieve organizational strategy	Assemble Process: Better-tasting pizzas

Primary Activity	Description	Support Activity		
Inbound logistics	Receiving, storing, and disseminating inputs to products	Human resources	Technology development	Infrastructure
Operations	Transforming inputs into final products			
Outbound logistics	Collecting, storing, and physically distributing products to buyers			
Sales and marketing	Inducing buyers to purchase products and providing a means for them to do so			
Customer service	Assisting customers' use of products and thus maintaining and enhancing the products' value			

FIGURE 6-5
The Value Chain

Q6-2 ▶ What Are Examples of Common Business Processes?

So far, we have classified processes by their stability of flow (structured or dynamic), scope (strategic, managerial, and operational), and objectives (effectiveness and efficiency). A fourth characteristic of processes is their place within the value chain. Recall from Chapter 1 that a value chain is a series of value-adding activities.[2] As shown in Figure 6-5, a value chain is composed of five primary activities and several support activities. The primary activities are inbound logistics, operations, outbound logistics, sales and marketing, and customer service. The support activities include human resources, technology, and infrastructure. The supporting activities support each of the primary activities.

Figure 6-6 highlights a variety of processes in each of the primary activities and support activities. This overview of business processes will help you see the variety of processes at a typical firm within the context of the value chain—a framework that is common in business. You will learn more about these business processes and value chains in other business school courses. For now, use this review to become familiar with the variety of processes within a business and how the processes in your area of study integrate with processes outside of your area. One day soon you'll be helping to improve one of your processes, and it will be helpful to be aware of the other processes that are affected by changes to your process.

Value Chain Activity	Operational Process	Managerial Process	Strategic Processes
PRIMARY ACTIVITIES			
Inbound logistics	Procurement (Chapter 8)	Manage inventory	Evaluate potential suppliers
Operations	Assemble product (Appendix A)	Schedule maintenance	Open new restaurant
Outbound logistics	Sales (Chapter 9)	Award refund	Determine payment policy
Sales and marketing	Mail promotion	Evaluate promotional discounts	Launch new product
Service	Track orders	Evaluate complaint patterns	Evaluate outsourcing options
SUPPORT ACTIVITIES			
Human resources	Recruit employees	Plan future needs	Determine pay scales
Technology development	Test software	Estimate milestones	Evaluate acquisition options
Infrastructure	Quality assurance test	Generate financial statements	Decide to pursue a patent

FIGURE 6-6
Value Chain Activities and Process Examples

Processes in the Value Chain

INBOUND LOGISTICS PROCESSES **Inbound logistics processes** receive, store, and disseminate product input.[3] Processes in inbound logistics listed in Figure 6-6 include Procurement, Manage Inventory, and Evaluate Potential Suppliers. **Procurement** is an operational process that acquires goods and services. Procurement activities at the pizza shop include ordering ingredients and boxes as well as receiving and paying for those items. This Procurement process is the subject of Chapter 8. Inventory Management is a managerial process that uses past data to compute stocking levels, reorder levels, and reorder quantities in accordance with inventory policy. An example of a strategic inbound logistics process is the evaluation of potential suppliers. When the pizza shop orders ingredients, it uses only suppliers who were previously approved by the strategic process called Supplier Selection.

OPERATIONS PROCESSES Operations transform inputs into outputs; in some industries, this is called the Production process. Operations processes schedule the equipment, people, and facilities necessary to build or assemble a product or provide a service. Assembling and baking pizzas are two operational operations processes. An example of a management operations process is scheduling maintenance on the ovens. Strategic processes evaluate if the pizza company should open another restaurant or change its menu.

OUTBOUND LOGISTICS PROCESSES **Outbound logistics processes** collect, store, and distribute products to buyers. Outbound logistics processes concern the management of finished-goods inventory and the movement of goods from that inventory to the customer. Outbound logistics processes are especially prominent for nonmanufacturers, such as distributors, wholesalers, and retailers.

An operational outbound process is the **Sales process** that records the sales order, ships the product, and bills the customer. Other operational outbound logistics processes at the pizza shop include the Order, Package, and Deliver processes. A managerial outbound logistics process is Award a Refund. A strategic outbound logistics process is Determine Payment Policy, such as a process that decides if the shop will accept personal checks.

SALES AND MARKETING PROCESSES Sales and Marketing provide the means and incentives for customers to purchase a product or service. The primary objective of sales and marketing processes is to find prospects and transform them into customers by selling them something. The end of the Sales and Marketing process is the beginning of the Sales process mentioned earlier. When the pizza chain mails promotions to prospects, it is executing its operational Promotion process. Evaluate Promotional Discounts is a managerial marketing process. Examples of strategic marketing processes are Launch New Product or Hire New Marketing Firm.

SERVICE PROCESSES Providing after-sales support to enhance or maintain the value of a product is called **service**. Operational customer service processes include Track Orders, Customer Support, and Customer Support Training. Customers call customer service to ask questions about their order status, to query and report problems with their accounts, and to receive assistance with product use. When a customer calls the pizza shop about a late delivery, the store manager initiates a service process. This process records some of the key circumstances for later analysis and awards the customer a discount on a future purchase or the immediate delivery of another pizza. A management service process evaluates customer complaints to determine if there are patterns to the complaints such as day of the week or a particular delivery person. Evaluating Outsourcing Service Options is a strategic service process.

HUMAN RESOURCES PROCESSES **Human resources processes** assess the motivations and skills of employees; create job positions; investigate employee complaints; and staff, train, and evaluate personnel. Operational human resources processes recruit, compensate, and assess employee performance for the organization. In a small company such as the pizza shop, posting a job may be a simple process requiring one or two approvals. In a larger, more formal organization, posting a new job may involve multiple levels of approval requiring use of a tightly controlled and standardized process. Management processes address the development and training of the organization's workforce and planning for future needs. Strategic processes in HR determine pay scales, authorize types of incentives, and decide organizational structure.

TECHNOLOGY DEVELOPMENT PROCESSES **Technology development processes** include designing, developing, and testing technology in support of the primary activities. An operational technology development process tests whether newly developed software can handle tens of thousands of possible keystroke entries. A managerial technology development process is a milestone

Ask good questions about objectives.
Standardize structured processes and keep dynamic processes fluid.
Don't confuse process and IS.
Ensure processes work together.
Continually improve your own processes.

FIGURE 6-7

Insights from Applying Process Characteristics

development process that estimates time required for each step in a software development process. A strategic technology development process decides if a particular technology will be purchased or developed by the company.

INFRASTRUCTURE PROCESSES **Infrastructure processes** are essential supporting processes in the organization that enable day-to-day operations. These include processes in accounting, administration, quality assurance, and legal and financial areas. An operational process would be executing the quality assurance evaluation on product as it moves through a production line. An example of a managerial process is the production of financial statements, and a strategic process is determining if a patent should be obtained for a new product.

Applying Process Concepts and Characteristics

Having introduced four process characteristics, let's briefly examine how you might apply your budding process knowledge. While Figure 6-7 lists several ways to apply this knowledge to any process, here we show how to apply that knowledge to the processes at the new pizza shop.

ASK GOOD QUESTIONS ABOUT OBJECTIVES You can ask good questions about the objectives for the pizza shop's Delivery process—does the owner want pizzas to be delivered by car, which would be faster, or by foot, which would improve promotion? You can also ask if there are other objectives such as driver safety or keeping the pizza hot.

STANDARDIZE STRUCTURED PROCESSES AND KEEP DYNAMIC PROCESSES FLUID The pizza shop should try to standardize structured processes in the student union restaurant as soon as possible—processes like making pizzas and taking orders. However, you can suggest that dynamic processes such as dealing with unhappy student customers or finding new employees should remain flexible, as efforts to standardize the flow of their activities would not be helpful.

DON'T CONFUSE PROCESS AND IS The franchise owner currently uses one IS, the company's TPS, to support many of his operational processes such as taking orders from customers and procuring supplies and ingredients. If the manager in the student union decides to create a Tweet Discount process, he still must decide which IS will support it—should he use the existing TPS or create a new IS for this purpose? The key is that the new process is not an IS, but it may need IS support. By making processes and IS distinct, you can ask if a new process needs a new IS or if an existing IS can work.

ENSURE PROCESSES WORK TOGETHER The processes at the pizza shop must work well together. When Mr. Pizzi discusses one process, you can point out how that process needs to be in sync with the other processes. For example, when he designs a new Twitter Promotional process, you can point out that this promotional process must integrate with the Sales process—when a pizza is sold with a Twitter promotional discount, the student Twitter name and promotion code should be recorded during the Sales process.

CONTINUALLY IMPROVE YOUR OWN PROCESSES Learn and experiment with your own processes to improve them. Become that person who is comfortable trying new ways to do things. If you worked at a pizza shop, experiment with different customer greetings and suggest new ways to use mobile apps for customer payment.

So far we have investigated the four characteristics of business processes with the goal of describing them more completely and understanding their differences. With this knowledge, we can have a better chance of improving their performance, which is our next topic.

Q6-3 ▶ How Can Management Improve Processes?

Here and in the next two questions, we narrow the topic of process improvement into three categories. First, in this question we highlight how managers like the pizza shop owner can improve processes by specifying and communicating process objectives and measures. In the next question, we explore how IS can be applied to improve processes at both the pizza shop and a hospital; and in the third question, we conclude with how process management techniques can lead to process improvement.

To begin, recognize that the vital phrase **process improvement** means that a process better achieves its objectives based on its measures. Therefore, it is essential to first understand the concepts of objectives and measures and the responsibilities of managers to specify and communicate them.

Process Objectives

Every business process has one or more possible objectives. It is the job of the managers responsible for the process to specify the most appropriate objectives and convey those objectives to people who play roles in the process, as shown in Figure 6-8. When objectives are specified and clearly communicated, process participants better understand how the process can be improved.

Managers don't set objectives on their own; they collaborate. To collaborate effectively, they need to assemble the right individuals and then work with the team to generate potential objectives. At the pizza shop, Mr. Pizzi would like to improve the scheduling process. His own objective for the scheduling process would be to have fewer student employees working more hours as he believes that would improve the consistency of the food and reduce training needs. When he collaborates with his student employees, they suggest an objective should be more student input on the schedule. Management needs to collaborate effectively and not assume agreement on process objectives. Setting objectives is a team sport.

As mentioned earlier, process objectives can be classified as either efficient or effective. At the pizza shop, for example, the Sales process has two objectives. One objective is an efficiency objective—reduce the time needed to place an order by phone—and the other is an effectiveness objective—sell to freshmen. By clearly specifying an objective as either efficient or effective, objectives are less vague. Vague objectives, such as "have a great sales process" or "be good to our customers," are difficult to improve.

Often, a process will have unstated objectives, and managers should make these explicit. The Deliver process may not have stated objectives. To make the Deliver process work well, Mr. Pizzi should clearly state its objectives.

Finally, processes may have stated objectives that are inappropriate—not matched to strategy. If the strategic plan of the pizza shop is to target freshmen, but the only two Promotional process objectives are to promote multi-topping pizzas and salad orders, the Promotional process objectives are inappropriate for the stated strategy.

The pizza shop is a small organization, so Mr. Pizzi has firsthand knowledge of the processes and can directly communicate the objectives of the processes to those who execute them. In contrast, a manager responsible for a process in a large organization may be several layers of supervision removed from the people who execute them. As a result, process objectives may get muddled by layers of management. Managers in large firms must find a way to ensure objectives are well communicated to those executing them.

Process Measures and KPIs

Process owners must also specify and communicate measures for each objective. **Measures**, also called **metrics**, are quantities assigned to attributes. Measures are common inside and outside of process improvement. You have measures—your height, weight, GPA, and family size, to name just a few. In process improvement, the measures selected by managers to use to assess process performance are called **key performance indicators (KPIs)**.

FIGURE 6-8

Options for Improving Process Objectives

Classify objectives: either effective or efficient.

Make unstated assumptions explicit.

Match objectives to strategy.

Characteristic	Descriptive Terms for Characteristic
Reasonable	• Valid • Compelling
Accurate	• Exact • Precise
Consistent	• Reliable

FIGURE 6-9

Characteristics of Good KPIs

One possible KPI for the Deliver process is the elapsed time in minutes and seconds from leaving the store until arrival at the customer's location. Just as there are many possible objectives for each process, there are many possible ways to measure each objective—it is the manager's job to specify the best KPIs or, if necessary, to improve the choice of KPIs and communicate these measures to process participants.

Specifying KPIs can be difficult, as it requires a very thorough knowledge of the process. Even then, some objectives are challenging to quantify. Mr. Pizzi at the pizza shop wants to sell to freshmen so that these students become frequent customers over their time at the university. However, it is hard to know which customers are freshmen. As a result, the pizza shop decides to measure the number of deliveries to the dorms as an approximation. Freshmen are not the only dorm residents, but this may be the only measure that is available to the pizza shop that they can use as a KPI.

Although measuring dorm sales is clearly not a perfect KPI of freshmen sales, the pizza shop owner realizes that all measures and KPIs are imperfect to some degree. Einstein once said, "Not everything that can be counted counts, and not everything that counts can be counted." When considering measures, recognize they all have limitations and that the key business challenge is to select the best ones available and know their limits.

The best KPIs are reasonable, accurate, and consistent, as shown in Figure 6-9. A reasonable KPI is one that is valid and compelling. It is reasonable to approximate freshmen pizza orders with dorm orders. Accurate KPIs are exact and precise. An accurate measure is 26 pizzas; a less accurate one is "more than last week." To accurately assess an objective, it may be appropriate to have multiple KPIs. For example, to assess selling to freshmen, the pizza shop might also record the number of pizzas delivered to campus during the freshman orientation weekend. A final characteristic of a good measurement is consistency. Managers should develop KPIs of processes that are reliable, that is, the KPI returns the same value if the same situation reoccurs.

Finally, managers should avoid the common trap of falling in love with their favorite KPI. If Mr. Pizzi discovered the freshman orientation weekend KPI and it works for several years, he may not be willing to entertain new KPI suggestions even if they are more reasonable, accurate, or consistent. Managers should not marry KPIs they need to be able to move on when a better KPI option emerges.

Once managers specify and communicate the stated objectives and KPIs, the next step is to consider how to improve the process with IS. The results of the improvement will be apparent in the specified KPIs.

Q6-4 How Can Information Systems Be Used to Improve Processes?

Today, information systems are playing an increasingly important role in business processes. IS affect many processes, and because IS constantly change and improve, IS often provide new and promising options for improving all types of processes. An IS can improve a process in a number of ways; here we consider five ways, as shown in Figure 6-10.

Improve an Activity

One way to improve a process with IS is to improve one of the activities in the process. At the pizza shop, the Delivery process driving activity can be improved by adding a GPS or Waze app to each delivery vehicle that displays traffic updates. As a result, the KPI of the Delivery objective—delivery time—is improved. Another example is the Sales process. One activity, the Promotion activity, can be improved by using Twitter to identify and attract freshmen.

FIGURE 6-10

Options for Improving a Process with an IS

Improve an Activity
- Pizza Shop: Driving activity improved with GPS.
- Hospital: Prescription writing activity improved with medication checker.

Improve Data Flow Among Activities
- Pizza Shop: Display order process data on GPS in delivery process.
- Hospital: Prescription data electronically recorded and shared with pharmacy.

Improve Control of Activities
- Pizza Shop: Better control of order details.
- Hospital: Appointment no-shows reduced.

Use Automation
- Pizza Shop: Send scheduled tweets in tweet promotion process.
- Hospital: Phone answering system in office reception process.

Improve Procedures
- Pizza Shop: Payment procedure improved and payment process improves.
- Hospital: Office procedures rewritten to improve office processes.

To broaden our discussion, consider how IS can help improve healthcare service processes at the hospital described in the opening vignette. To show how an IS can improve an activity, consider the Write a Prescription process. When a doctor types a prescription on a tablet, software can compare that medicine to other medicines the patient is taking. If the new drug conflicts with any previously prescribed drug or interacts with the patient's allergies, a warning message is displayed.

Improve Data Flow Among Activities

Information systems can also improve a process by adding or improving the data flow between activities in the same or different processes. For example, consider the Web site used by the pizza shop for the Order process. The order data from the Order process can be used to improve the Delivery process if the order data flows to GPS displays in the delivery cars in real time. Using this data about upcoming deliveries, drivers can make better plans about when to stop for gas or when to wait for one more pizza to finish cooking before heading out on deliveries.

At the hospital, improving data flow can improve the process of filling a prescription. When the doctor writes a prescription, the prescription data can be sent to the local pharmacy so the prescription is ready when the patient arrives. The data, the prescription, flows from the Write a Prescription process to the Fill a Prescription process at the pharmacy. The data flows automatically rather than being hand-carried by the patient. Not only does the data flow reduce the waiting time in the Fill Prescription process, there are fewer errors about the prescription than when it is handwritten.

Improve Control of Activities

A third way that IS can improve a process is to improve the control of activities in the process. In general, **control** limits behavior. A process is like a river; controls are like dams and sidewalls that limit the behavior of the river. You have controls in your life that help you limit your own behavior, as shown in Figure 6-11. Your alarm clock limits your sleep, the cruise control on your car limits your speed, your phone password limits who can use your phone, your social media privacy controls limit who can see your posts, and your ATM PIN limits who can execute banking transactions. In Chapter 5 on security, we stated that safeguards are controls that reduce end user freedom. They reduce freedom because they limit the behavior of end users.

In the process world, controls help limit wide variations in activities so a process runs more consistently and smoothly. In other words, by limiting the behavior of the activities, control helps the process provide consistent results. Consider how a lack of control can lead to wide variations and even disaster—the absence of control has been blamed for the Enron, World-Comm, and Freddie Mac financial debacles. If you can suggest ways to improve control of a

Control	Reduces Variation in
Alarm clock	Wake-up time
Cruise control	Speed of the vehicle
Phone password	Who can use your phone
Social media privacy settings	Who can see your content
ATM PIN	Who can execute banking activities

FIGURE 6-11
Common Controls

business process, you'll be the life of the process party. For many processes, an information system is the most reliable way to improve control.

In business, managers spend a lot of time reacting to **exceptions**. Exceptions are unexpected or unwelcome outputs from a process that require an action—the parts don't arrive, the employee performs poorly, the budget is overspent. Controls can help reduce the frequency of these exceptions and the headaches they cause.

Controls at the pizza shop help make every pizza the same size, keep the oven at a consistent temperature, and allow only the manager to void sales on the cash register. An example of an IS control is the new computer for the in-restaurant Order process. Waiters and waitresses now type in orders on the new computer rather than on handwritten slips. One control on this process is that software checks for incomplete orders, and if the order is incomplete it is not sent to the kitchen. For example, if a waiter fails to enter three pizza toppings for a three-topping pizza or a dressing is not specified for a salad, the computer alerts the waiter to enter the missing data. The kitchen is not given the order until it is corrected by the waiter. This control helps reduce variation in delivery time and variations between what the customer ordered and what the customer is served.

At the hospital, one recurring problem is appointment no-shows. To exercise better control of these problem patients, the hospital now sends voice and text reminders of the appointment to the patient's cell phone. In addition, patient healthcare records have been converted to electronic records to improve control of the records and limit who can see them.

Use Automation

A fourth way that IS can improve a process is automation. **Automation** means that a computer does an activity or a part of an activity that was once done by a person. The computer can be either a robot or an artificial intelligence (AI) program. AI and robots are discussed in Extension 4. One classic example of this is the ATM that replaced some of the activities of the bank teller; another is e-commerce Web sites that do several activities of salespeople. A more recent automation example is the Google car. Google has developed and tested a driverless car, an automated vehicle designed to improve driving and reduce the number of accidents, as shown in Figure 6-12.

FIGURE 6-12
Automation Example—Google Driverless Car

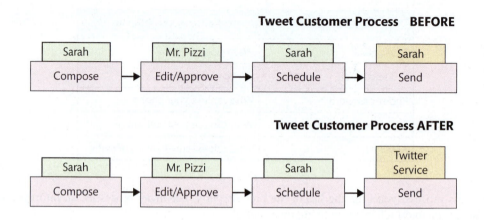

An example of using automation is the Tweet Customers process at the pizza shop, as shown in Figure 6-13. The top diagram shows the Tweet Customer process before automation. Each of these activities is currently done by a person. Sarah composes a list of 5 or 10 tweets and emails the list to Mr. Pizzi. He edits and approves the list and emails these back to Sarah, who then schedules the best time to send them. When each appointed time arrives, Sarah logs into Twitter and sends the tweet. One way to automate an activity is to use a Twitter service to automatically send the tweets at the scheduled times so that Sarah does not need to log in and send them herself; this process is shown in the bottom of Figure 6-13.

At the hospital, automation can improve a number of processes. Automation can spot fraudulent healthcare billing, making the hospital's billing process more efficient. Automated phone systems can connect callers with the correct office. Automated systems that monitor the health of patients can make the recuperation process more effective. The hospital can use service robots to move meals, equipment, and linens around the hospital to improve several patient care processes.

The decision to automate can be challenging. Clearly computers have many advantages—productivity, speed, quality, scale, consistency, and reduction of human injury. They don't go on vacation or leave early for a child's ball game, they are very consistent and easy to control, and they don't have birthdays to remember. Automation often improves control of an activity—the computer will do the activity exactly the same way every time—no variation. But people have their advantages, too—lower development cost, better security, less upfront costs, much greater flexibility and ability to make judgments in uncertainty. If a comparison of these advantages does not answer the question, "Should a person actor or computer actor do this activity?" then consider the amount of judgment required by the actor. Automated actors are more capable in low-judgment settings where well-known and repeatable activities are performed, like timing the inputs on an assembly line, holding an altitude for an airplane, or checking if every box has been completed on a form. But computers also break down unexpectedly and require maintenance; and while this may only be a nuisance for the pizza shop if it affects the tweeting of discounts, it can be a big deal if it shuts down the ovens. Humans, on the other hand, are uniquely able to deal with high-judgment activities that feature uncertainty or ambiguity like the diagnosis and treatment of illness; risk assessment; and human communication, interaction, and learning.

The decision to automate is even more vexing because the decision is never final. Unrelenting advances in technology will require that businesspeople continually reassess automation decisions. The decision to automate an activity may change as new technologies are developed or made more affordable.

Improve Procedures

Before we can discuss how the procedures of an IS can improve a process, it is important to be clear about how IS and processes are related to each other. In Chapter 2, we first introduced processes, IS, and their relationship. We explained that each process can rely on zero, one, or many IS and that an IS may support one or many processes. In Figure 6-14, we show one IS—your cell phone—supporting two Go To Movie processes.

As shown in Figure 6-14, a procedure anchors an IS to a process. Each application of an IS to a process has a unique procedure. For example, your smartphone supports both Go To Movies processes, but each process has its own procedure. When you execute the Movie With Friends

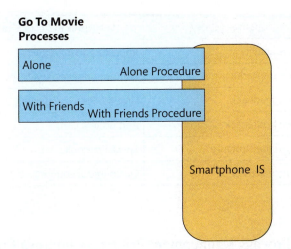

Go To Movie Processes

Alone

Alone Procedure

With Friends

With Friends Procedure

Smartphone IS

FIGURE 6-14

Two Go To Movies Processes and Smartphone IS

process, you use your phone to view trailers with your friends before you decide. Your procedure takes you to a movie app, then via some search magic to the trailer of the movie you are considering. When you execute the Movie Alone process, you use your phone only to see showtimes. One phone, two processes, two procedures.

That is nice to know. However, the real advantage of thinking about IS, processes, and procedures is to recognize that the procedure is often the weak link between a process and its IS. Someone new to Pinterest or Netflix needs to master the procedures before they can enjoy the outcomes of the process.

Improving a procedure can often lead to process improvement. For example, you might have a great phone but lousy Movie processes because you never learned how to search nearby theaters for showtimes or reviews. Your procedures are holding you back; fix those and your Movie process will get much better.

The pizza shop is in the same pickle. For several years, the university allowed local restaurants to use the student ID card as a charge card. Recently, Mr. Pizzi noticed that only a few pizzas were sold using the student ID card. To improve the Payment process, he asked some of his cashiers what was going on. It turns out they were not sure if they could execute the sale with the student ID card and did not know how to enter the student ID number on the cash register. Mr. Pizzi rewrote the Payment procedure with the help of one of his cashiers, they trained the other cashiers, and soon the Payment process was working better. The Payment process had a poorly understood procedure that was holding it back; once the procedure was improved, the Payment process performed better.

At the hospital, healthcare professionals had to use a new healthcare IT system to comply with the federal Affordable Care Act. However, when they switched over to the new IS, their office processes suffered. Hospital managers soon realized that the hospital's processes were still appropriate but that no one knew the procedures for the new IS.

Before we move on, recognize the hospital's problem is a common one—anytime an IS or a process changes, a procedure should change. Often, a new IS is purchased or a process is changed but the procedure is left unchanged. Procedures in business need to be constantly refined as technology changes and processes change. As you will find out in your career, keeping procedures current is easier said than done.

These examples show some of the possibilities for improving processes with information systems. The opportunities to use IS to improve processes will continue to grow as the price-performance ratio of computers continues to plummet, new technologies and ideas continue to enter the business world, and young professionals join the workforce who are more comfortable with technology than any previous generation. The most significant information system for improving business processes emerged over the past 15 years. These are multimillion-dollar ERP systems that are designed to improve a wide range of company processes. These ERP systems are described in Chapter 7.

Although information systems can have a big impact on process performance, there are other ways to achieve process improvement. An entire process management industry has emerged over the past 50 years. This movement acknowledges the role of IS in process improvement but has also developed a wide range of techniques and suggestions to improve processes that do not depend on an IS. We investigate these next.

Improvement Category	Examples in Pizza Shop
Improve activity	Improve parking activity
Remove unproductive resources	Remove unnecessary drivers
Improve feedback	Give Mr. Pizzi late delivery report
Remove bottleneck	Add waiters
Redesign the structure	Specialize cooks
Outsource activity	Outsource accounting activities

Q6-5 ▶ How Can Process Management Principles Improve Processes?

Process management experts have developed a number of process principles that can improve processes, as shown in Figure 6-15. Process management experts call these process improvement principles a number of names: systems engineering, workflow/WfMc, Business Process Modeling, Business Process Reengineering, Continuous Improvement, xMatrix, Kata, 5 Whys, Kaizen, and Six Sigma. A common goal of these principles is to create in an organization a culture of continuous improvement. From these various approaches we distill the six of the most common techniques shown in Figure 6-15.

While we have seen earlier that an IS can improve a process by improving an activity, the techniques here are ways to improve an activity that do not involve an IS. For example, the Pizza Delivery process can be enhanced by improving the parking activity of the drivers or using better-insulated pizza boxes. One common way to improve an activity is to add resources to it such as adding drivers to the Delivery process.

Another simple improvement is to remove unproductive resources from a process. For example, if drivers assigned to a particular pizza outlet are not busy, they could be trained to do other jobs so their time is more productive.

A third technique is to improve the feedback generated by the process. **Feedback** is the return of a part of the output of process to the input, as shown in Figure 6-16. In education, a grade on an assignment creates feedback about your studying activity, and this feedback might lead to changes in your studying activity that semester. In sports, a coach might use the feedback of how the team performed in the previous game as one of the inputs for the next game. The coach might remind the players that in the previous game the players learned to share the ball. Feedback closes the loop. At the pizza shop, the Delivery process should generate feedback to Mr. Pizzi on the number of orders delivered by each driver and the number of deliveries that are late. With richer feedback, process managers and participants can identify problems, suggest process improvements, and test potential solutions.

Another technique is to remove a process bottleneck. A **bottleneck** occurs when one activity reduces the performance of the overall process. In the pizza restaurant, a bottleneck occurs when too many customers are being served by one waiter. In a similar way, the elevator is often a bottleneck in the dorm during the move-in process. A process management expert would identify the bottleneck and propose that other employees do waiter activities on busy nights and that the university allow a longer move-in period to reduce spikes in elevator demand.

FIGURE 6-16

Process with Feedback

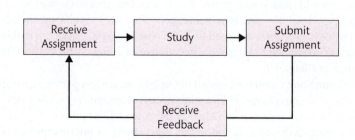

A business process can also be improved by redesigning it—by changing its structure. To change structure simply means to change the arrangement or roles of the activities of a process. An example of changing a structure can be seen in the Assemble Pizza process. Currently each chef rolls dough, adds toppings, then loads his or her own pizza in the oven and takes it out when it is finished. On hectic nights, a better structure to the process would be to specialize the jobs. That is, one chef rolls dough for all the pizzas, another adds ingredients, and a third moves pizzas in and out. This helps reduce delays, an objective of the Assemble process.

Another reason to redesign a process is to reduce **slack**, the time an activity is idle. In the pizza shop, if the waiters are busy with customers and food is ready, the process should be redesigned to allow the cook to bring the pizza to the table. This will reduce the slack in the serve pizza activity.

A final way to improve the process may be to outsource an activity—that is, have a supplier, customer, or business partner do one of the activities in the process. Customers seem willing to swipe their own credit cards, change their password, pump their gas, check out their groceries, make their travel arrangements, and check in at an airport. Customers should not be the only ones considered for outsourcing; other businesses should also be considered. For example, the pizza shop can outsource its accounting activities.

Whether it is using process management principles or other methods of improving processes listed in this chapter, most businesspeople can suggest ways to improve processes. The issue is whether it is worth the cost and if the improvements help the process better achieve the firm's strategy. For example, the pizza shop can always add more drivers or use Twitter to take orders, but managers must decide if these improvements are better than other choices that might be less expensive or time consuming and achieve the strategy better.

While this chapter is a good way to begin your process education, the most common approach to process improvement, particularly in the manufacturing industry, is called Six Sigma. **Six Sigma** seeks to improve process outputs by removing causes of defects and minimizing variability in the process. Each Six Sigma project follows a very structured sequence of steps with quantified financial measures. Six Sigma gets its name from its goal that 99.99966 percent of process outputs will be free from defects. Without such high quality processes, Six Sigma proponents argue we would be without electricity 10 minutes each week, 810 commercial airliners would crash every month, and 50 newborn babies would be dropped at birth by a doctor everyday.[4]

For you to be able to contribute in today's business environment, hone your ability to visualize and assess business processes. That is, once you isolate a particular process, determine its objectives, assess the quality of its KPIs, and determine if IS or process management principles can improve the process. To this end, this chapter is offered to help you be like Jake in the chapter vignette—to equip you with a series of questions you can ask to better understand a process and make suggestions for improvement.

Q6-6 How Do Process Teams Diagram Process Improvement?

Whether it is using our approach, Six Sigma, or another technique, process improvement at medium to large organizations always involves a team. Typically, the team includes the users who are the actors in the process, general managers responsible for the process, IT analysts, and business analysts. Unless the process is very simple like assembling or baking a pizza, diagramming a process is typically necessary in order for team members to understand the process and to identify activities that must be changed. It is necessary for the redesign team to understand how the current process works and what the intended process should look like. Diagrams of the current process are typically called **"as-is" diagrams**, and diagrams of suggested improvements are called **"ought-to-be" diagrams**. Diagrams can take many forms, but, as mentioned in Chapter 2, we will use the current gold standard, BPMN.

To better understand how a process improvement team might use BPMN diagramming, consider the ought-to-be Select New Supplier process for the pizza shop. This is the process the pizza franchise company wants to adopt. The company must find and select suppliers for fresh pizza items, cleaning supplies, uniform cleaning, office supplies, and waste removal. The objectives of this managerial process are to find good quality suppliers in a reasonable amount of time. The KPIs for these objectives are shown in Figure 6-17.

FIGURE 6-17

Objectives and Measures of the
Select New Supplier Process

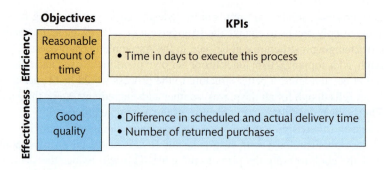

The Select New Supplier process is shown in Figure 6-18. It begins when the franchise communicates a request for proposal (RFP) to potential suppliers (the Request Proposal from Supplier activity). This activity, completed by the warehouse manager, finds potential suppliers, performs a cursory investigation of their products, and contacts the potential supplier's sales office. If the supplier responds positively, the next step is the Receive Proposal from Supplier activity. In this activity, a supplier provides address and contract data and a list of products the supplier expects to sell to the franchise if the supplier is approved. These application data and product data are inserted as new supplier data in a resource labeled Warehouse DB. Once this activity is complete, the warehouse manager evaluates the potential supplier's product list to determine items that may be appropriate. While this activity is happening, an accountant is also evaluating the supplier's credit policies in the Evaluate Supplier Credit Policies activity. The data

FIGURE 6-18

BPMN Diagram of the Select New
Supplier Process

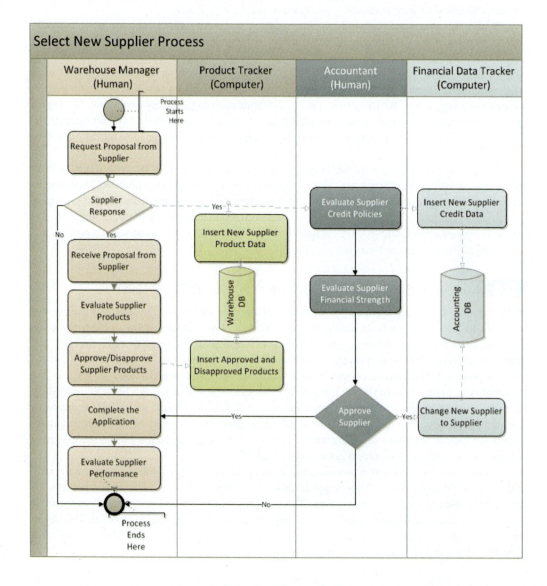

generated about the supplier's credit policies is stored in the Accounting DB. This data will be used later by the accounting department in payment processes. Accounting also collects other data on the supplier in order to reach an approve/disapprove supplier decision. This activity is called Evaluate Supplier Financial Strength. If the accountants approve the potential supplier, a Complete the Application activity is initiated that specifies the potential products to be ordered. Finally, after the first month, the final activity, Evaluate Supplier Performance, is accomplished. The franchise strives to determine quickly if a supplier is working out.

Our goal here is for you to see how process teams use formal tools like BPMN diagramming to depict process improvement. Extension 3 is a more complete explanation of the sequence of actions organizations use to improve a process; it is a process of process improvement.

Q6-7 How Can an IS Hinder a Process?

As we have seen, information systems usually support and improve processes. As we mentioned earlier, one way they do that is by improving the data flow between activities. However, IS are not always the process hero; sometimes they are the goat. If an IS prevents or restricts the flow, this can hinder a process. This situation is called an **information silo**—the data needed for a process activity is unavailable because it is stored in an isolated, separated information system. For example, if your tablet or phone is not synced to your iTunes account, your music is trapped in the iTunes silo. Let's consider a few business examples of silos, how silos can be corrected, and why they exist.

Notice that the objectives of the Select New Supplier process are to select suppliers that are good quality in a reasonable amount of time. The final activity in the Select New Supplier process is Evaluate New Supplier Performance. To evaluate the new supplier, an analyst must obtain data on the new supplier's deliveries to the pizza shops. One KPI of good quality is the timeliness of delivery—the difference in time between scheduled delivery and actual delivery. Unfortunately, the scheduled delivery times are stored in the franchise information system, but actual delivery times are stored in spreadsheets at the different shops. These spreadsheets are information silos. To make matters worse, the delivery time data is not in a consistent format at the different shops, making it even harder for the data to flow to the franchise.

One other example of information silos may be closer to home: your smartphone. You may have music, email, chat, contact, and other data on your smartphone that is not easily synced with similar programs on your laptop. If you wanted to improve your music listening process or your calendar update process, having two silos can be a hindrance.

Information silos not only plague business, they are common in healthcare and government settings as well. Hospitals are working on making the electronic healthcare records of their patients more accessible to other healthcare providers. U.S. government agencies are often accused of not sharing intelligence with each other. One fix to the information silo problem is to duplicate the data—make a copy of the data that is isolated and make it available to the process that needs it. However, when duplicated, the data can quickly become inconsistent when changes are made to only one set of data. The most complete fix to eliminate information silos is to store a single copy of data in a shared database and connect the business processes to that database. A single-copy database solution is a feature of the ERP systems that we will discuss in the next three chapters.

Why Information Silos Exist

Information silos at the pizza franchise are caused in part by the physical separation of the stores from the franchise headquarters. However, this information silo problem occurs even when all the data is under the same roof. For example, at the franchise office, one database stores data on restaurant sales while another database keeps track of the inventory and deliveries. In each database, the data are compiled at the end of the day and shared with the other database. This delay normally does not affect the franchise; however, several times a year sales are quite unusual and this delay leads to running out of items at the restaurants or unneeded deliveries. If the data were all in one system, these problems would be less likely to occur.

If the problems of information silos are so evident, why does this issue ever arise? Organizations store data in separate databases for several reasons. Given a choice, organizational departments prefer to control the data they use; they are, after all, the experts about the data. For example, accountants know more than anyone about how the accounting database should be

MIS InClass 6

Improving the Process of Making Paper Airplanes[5]

The purpose of this exercise is to demonstrate process concepts. In this exercise, students will form assembly lines to create paper airplanes. Each assembly line will have the same four activities, each called a Work Center (WC), as shown in Figure 6-19. Raw material is a stack of plain paper, finished goods are the folded airplanes, and WIP is Work In Progress, which is the output of the WC prior to the WIP.

One student is assigned to each of the four WCs in the assembly line. Student 1 (in WC 1) creates the first fold, as shown at the top of Figure 6-20. Student 2, at WC 2, folds the corners, also shown in Figure 6-20. The location and assembly instructions for Students 3 and 4 are also shown in Figure 6-20. In addition to the four students who fold the planes, seven other students observe, time, and record each assembly line as listed below using the three forms in Figure 6-21:

Observer 1: Use Form 1, record WC 1 task times.
Observer 2: Use Form 1, record WC 2 task times.
Observer 3: Use Form 1, record WC 3 task times.
Observer 4: Use Form 1, record WC 4 task times.
Observer 5: Use Form 2, record cycle time at the end of the line.
Observer 6: Use Form 3, record colored sheet throughput time.
Observer 7: Count WIP at the end of each run.

Each assembly line is run to construct 20 airplanes. Prior to beginning the process, each line will run a practice session of four or five planes. Then clear the line, start the clock, and make the 20 airplanes. Each WC continues to work until the 20th plane is finished, which means that more than 20 will be started as there will be WIP when the 20th is finished. About halfway through the run, the instructor will insert a colored piece of paper as raw material. Each student assembler works at his or her own pace. As workers build planes, they should work at a comfortable pace and not speed. This is not a contest for maximum output, but for quality.

After the first run is completed, make a second run of 20 planes with all the same roles. However, each student can work only when there is an airplane in his or her inbox (WIP) and no airplane in his or her outbox (WIP). Again, midway through the run, the instructor will insert a colored sheet of paper.

Source: dotshock/Shutterstock.

After the runs:

1. In teams, diagram the Assembly process using BPMN symbols such as roles, swimlanes, activities, and decisions. Name resources assigned to roles.
2. Use the ideas in this chapter to improve this Assembly process. Discuss the objectives of the assembly line. If you were in charge of an assembly line like this one, do you think your objective would be efficiency or effectiveness? Specify the KPIs used to monitor progress toward your objective(s).
3. Assume the WC folding is done by four machines. In that scenario, the second run uses different software than the first run. Does this new IS improve an activity, data flow, control, automation, or procedure?
4. Is any data in an information silo on the first or second runs?
5. Which KPI changed most significantly from the first to the second run? Did you anticipate this? Are other processes with other KPIs just as subject to change with a similar minor change in information?
6. Were there any controls on the assembly process? Could an IS improve the process by improving control? On which KPI(s) will this improvement appear?

FIGURE 6-19
Classroom Assembly Line Setup

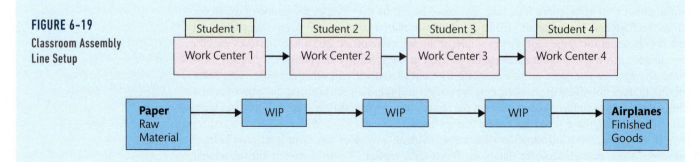

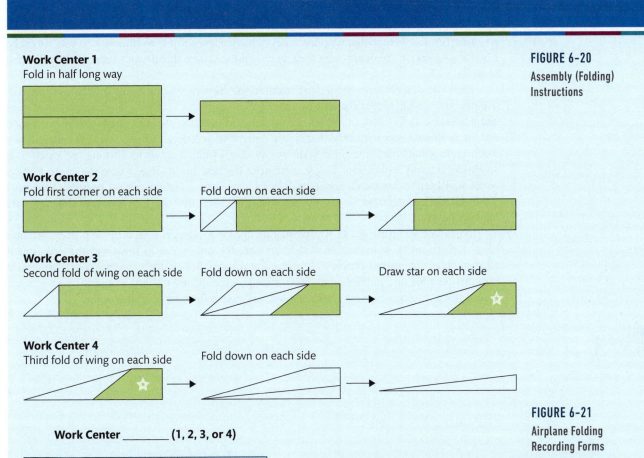

FIGURE 6-20

Assembly (Folding)
Instructions

Work Center 1
Fold in half long way

Work Center 2
Fold first corner on each side   Fold down on each side

Work Center 3
Second fold of wing on each side   Fold down on each side   Draw star on each side

Work Center 4
Third fold of wing on each side   Fold down on each side

FIGURE 6-21

Airplane Folding
Recording Forms

Work Center _____ (1, 2, 3, or 4)

Unit	Run 1 (seconds)	Run 2 (seconds)
1		
2		
3		
4		
5		
6		
7		
8		
9		
10		
11		
12		
13		
14		
15		
16		
17		
18		
19		
20		
Sum		
Average		

Form 1: Airplane manufacturing task time. Observers 1, 2, 3, and 4 use this form to record assembly times for each Work Center.

System	Throughput Time for 20 Sheets Run 1	Throughput Time for 20 Sheets Run 2
Start time		
Finish time		
Total time		

Form 2: Airplane manufacturing cycle time for 20 airplanes. Observer 5 uses this form to record start and finish time for entire run of 20 planes.

System	Throughput Time for Colored Sheets Run 1	Throughput Time for Colored Sheets Run 2
Start time		
Finish time		
Total time		

Form 3: Paper airplane manufacturing color sheet throughput time. Observer 6 uses this form to record start and finish time for colored sheet.

used, so it is natural for them to want to control how it is set up, what the data will look like, and how the database will be updated. Also, a department may have very different objectives than other departments in the firm. These objectives might be to minimize inventory or serve customers. A department system that supports a key objective, even if it is an information silo, might be a better solution for the department than an enterprise system that doesn't support that objective as well.

There are other reasons for a department to use its own system. Some processes use sensitive data that should not be shared with other processes such as tax data in accounting processes and healthcare claims data in the HR department. Also, a department system can be purchased and implemented more quickly than most enterprise solutions. Finally, departmental IS are much more affordable; enterprise systems can cost as much as 10 to 50 times as much as a single-department application. This is evident at the new pizza shop, where the student union outlet will keep its own data about student Twitter names. The process of tweeting discounts may well work at the other shops, but the cost of restructuring the TPS to record this new data may not be worth the cost.

In the past, a department IS was frequently chosen to support a department process because cross-department IS were rare. Just 20 years ago, the only game in town was the departmental system, as enterprise systems only existed in dreams. Today, the expectation is to minimize information silos and promote data flow among departments, not just in pizza franchises but across global enterprises. This is a theme we continue in the next several chapters.

Ethics Guide

The Ethics of Automation

This chapter is devoted to the idea that improving business processes is essential for organizational success. However, what about situations where improving the process comes at an ethical price? Here we focus on this ethical challenge by examining two contexts—employment and safety.

Earlier we described automation as the performance of an activity by a computer once done by a person. In Extension 4, we also discussed automation and defined AI as computers that think like us and robots as computers that act or move like us.

CONTEXT 1: EMPLOYMENT

Automation will affect employment—for every automated job, someone needs a new job or retraining. Automation in manufacturing jobs, banking, fast food, telemarketing, tax preparation, data entry, and insurance underwriters will lead to fewer jobs. In one telling example, in a McDonald's restaurant in Arizona, a small set of employees supervise a crew of robots.

In the Fast Food Industry

1. You are now CEO of McDonalds. If you use the categorical imperative to base your decision, would you favor more or less automation at your restaurants?
2. You again are the CEO, but now use utilitarianism. Does this change your answer to the first question? Why or why not?
3. As a fast food customer, would you be less inclined to go to a restaurant that uses robots?
4. Again, as a customer, would you be willing to buy products "made by people for people" if they come with a higher price?

In Society

Automation will also require societies and governments to make ethical decisions. Some politicians believe that as automation grows, displaced workers need compensation. They argue for a robot tax on companies—that for every robot they "employ," a tax should be levied on the employer to help compensate the people who lost their jobs. These politicians believe that an automated future can generate enough taxes to provide a guaranteed income for all citizens. In fact, in 2017 Finland began an experiment in universal basic income where all 2,000 participants receive $600 per month regardless of income, wealth, or employment status.

5. Should robot use by companies be taxed? If so, how should that tax be calculated—by robot, by robot work hour, by robot output value? Explain.
6. Using either the categorical imperative or utilitarianism, is universal basic income ethical? If so, is it appropriate? Why or why not?

CONTEXT 2: SAFETY

There are many ways that automating activities will affect public safety. Driverless cars, drones, pilotless airliners, automated police surveillance, and even robotic police and firefighters, to name a few.

Most experts agree that eventually all vehicles will be driven or flown without a human driver or pilot on board. How governments and societies get from here to there is full of ethical considerations.

1. How should the government outlaw human driving—when the safety record of driverless cars is better than human drivers? Or twice as safe? Does utilitarianism move this date sooner or later? Does the categorical imperative suggest moving this date sooner or later?
2. How should the transition take place? Should all roads be declared driverless after a specific date or just highways first? Or should all vehicles sold after a given date be driverless?
3. There are also ethical considerations about the programming of the automated drivers. For example, if a pedestrian walks in front of your vehicle, how violently should your automated driver avoid making contact? Should it be programmed to never make contact even if this threatens the lives of the occupants of the car? Does using utilitarianism or the categorical imperative for the basis of the programming give the pedestrian a better chance of surviving?
4. When do you expect to fly in an airliner without pilots on board? Specify a year. Assume each airline will have pilots flying the airplanes remotely supported by on-board automation.

Source: Tatiana Shepeleva/Shutterstock

ACTIVE REVIEW

Use this Active Review to verify that you understand the material in the chapter. You can read the entire chapter and then perform the tasks in this review, or you can read the text material for just one question and perform the tasks in this review for that question before moving on to the next one.

Q6-1 What are the important characteristics of processes in organizations?

Explain how a small change to a process can lead to a significant financial payoff. Define *business process* and the key terms that describe business processes: *activity, resource, role,* and *actor.* Name the term that can be fulfilled by either a human or computer. Explain the four characteristics of processes. List the three main categories of process scope, and explain how each one is different from the others. Give examples of processes in each of the categories. Define *efficiency* and *effectiveness.* What things are efficient and effective?

Q6-2 What are examples of common business processes?

Explain a process in each of the primary activities of the value chain. Specify if that process is operational, managerial, or strategic, and explain why you classified it that way. Explain the support activities. Describe a procurement process and a sales and marketing process. Describe how knowledge of process characteristics can be used.

Q6-3 How can management improve processes?

What does the term *process improvement* imply? Explain what managers of processes are responsible for. Describe ideal process objectives. Explain measures and KPIs and discuss why KPIs are difficult to develop. Give examples of reasonable, accurate, and consistent KPIs. What should managers avoid about KPIs?

Q6-4 How can information systems be used to improve processes?

Explain the five ways IS can be used to improve a particular process. Specify a process and explain how an IS can improve that process. Specify objectives and KPIs for the process. Give an example of a process where an activity can be improved using an IS. Describe how data flow can improve a process. Explain why control is important for a business process and their affect on exceptions. Describe an example of how IS can improve control in a process. Give an example where automation of an activity improved the process. What makes the decision to automate challenging? Explain the relationship between a process, an IS, and a procedure. Give an example of how a poorly executed procedure limits the performance of a process.

Q6-5 How can process management principles improve processes?

Explain the ways process management principles can improve a process. Describe feedback and why it is important. Explain two reasons to redesign a process. Give an example of each and explain the process objective that is improved. Explain slack and why it is important to process improvement. State the goal of Six Sigma.

Q6-6 How do process teams diagram process improvement?

Identify common participants in a process improvement team. Describe the two types of BPMN diagrams. Explain the new supplier process and its roles, resources, and activities.

Q6-7 How can an IS hinder a process?

Describe how IS configuration in a company can hamper a process and limit its improvement. Describe an information silo. Explain the impact of silos on process objectives. Explain the most common fix to the silo problem. Describe why departments like to control the systems they use. Explain why a department may legitimately seek to keep its data in multiple databases.

KEY TERMS AND CONCEPTS

Activity   132
Actor   132
As-is diagram   145
Automation   141
Bottleneck   144
Business process   132

Control   140
Effectiveness   134
Efficiency   134
Exceptions   141
Executive support system (ESS)   134
Feedback   144

Human resource processes   136
Inbound logistics processes   136
Information silo   147
Infrastructure processes   137
Key performance indicators
   (KPI)   138

USING YOUR KNOWLEDGE

6-1. For each of the following processes, suggest how an
MyLab MIS IS can improve the process. Specify if the improvement is due to improving an activity, improving data flow, improving control, implementing automation, or improving procedures.
  a. the process of selecting a job after college
  b. the process of planning and executing a wedding or a funeral
  c. the process of taking photos and uploading the photos to Facebook
  d. the process the pizza shop uses to buy supplies

6-2. For each process, specify an IS that supports the process
MyLab MIS and the first three steps of the procedure that links that IS to the process.

6-3. For each of these processes, suggest how they may be
MyLab MIS improved by non-IS means; that is, by management and by process management principles.

6-4. When you go to a restaurant, that restaurant must execute several operational processes. Apply the concepts in this chapter to several of these processes. These processes might include seating, ordering, cooking, delivering, and paying.

6-5. How can your college use IS to make its processes better? Can you think of ways to use new IS tools like smartphones and social media to make college processes better? Specify the objective and measure that these IS help improve. For two of these processes, describe the procedures. Does your college have information silos? Which departments keep data needed by processes outside the department?

6-6. When you order a meal at McDonald's, that data is stored in an enterprise IS to be used by various processes. Make a list of the McDonald's processes in which your Happy Meal purchase will appear. You may want to review the value chain processes discussed in Q2.

6-7. Apply the process improvement steps to improve studying for this class. Go to Studyblue.com and create an account. This site, like others, allows students to share flashcards with other students in the same course at the same school. It should help improve your studying process. To see how this IS can improve your studying process, first decide on objectives and KPIs for your studying process—perhaps one objective is to raise your grade to an A and the KPIs are scores on tests and quizzes. Then use the flashcards for several chapters while recording your KPIs. Afterward complete the following questions:
  a. Are the objectives of your studying process effectiveness or efficiency objectives?
  b. Which KPIs are most appropriate for your studying process? Are these KPIs reasonable, accurate, and consistent? If not, why not?
  c. In which of the five ways that IS improve a process is Studyblue improving your studying process? Explain.

6-8. Assume you are flying to a vacation resort. Create a BPMN diagram of the five to seven key activities in the process of getting your suitcase to your destination. Specify objectives and measures for this process.

6-9. Create a BPMN diagram for a patient to be admitted to an emergency room as described in the opening vignette. Assume the patient arrives conscious. The end of the admission process is the patient in a bed in the ER before seeing a nurse or doctor.

COLLABORATION EXERCISE 6

Collaborate with a group of students to answer the following questions. For this exercise, do not meet face to face. Your task will be easier if you coordinate your work with SharePoint, Office, Google Docs or equivalent collaboration tools. (See Chapter 10 for a discussion of collaboration tools and processes.) Your answers should reflect the thinking of the entire group, not just that of one or two individuals.

Congratulations. Your firm has won the contract to sell concessions at the new football stadium at Big State University. You sell a wide variety of candy, drinks, chips, and popcorn as well as alcoholic beverages. The university wants your firm to offer two types of concession stands: one stand for the general customer with a standard level of service and a stand with high-end service for exclusive use by elite customers who pay the university an extra fee for suites or make significant contributions. The fundamental process—order, dispense food items, calculate cost, receive payment is common to both.

You face a number of design issues with process implications.

1. The first issue is the number of concession stands. Just considering the standard level of service, make a list of the advantages and disadvantages of having fewer and having many stands. Make sure your list addresses the objectives you set for your standard service process—both efficiency and effectiveness objectives. Also, specify the KPIs you will use.

2. The second issue has to do with how a standard service stand operates. One option is to receive customers' orders, dispense items, calculate cost, and make payment with one employee. A second is to have several employees in several roles accomplish the activities. A third option is to have the customers serve themselves (no order or dispense activities) and pay an employee.

What are advantages and disadvantages of each of the three processes?

3. A third issue is configuration of the stand. One option is the one-station stand—all activities are done at one spot. In contrast, multiple stations have the customer ordering and employee dispensing at one stand and then moving to a checkout location to calculate and pay. Again, advantages and disadvantages?

4. Finally, how should a process work that serves the high-end customers? Again, start with objectives and KPIs. These customers have a longer-term financial connection to the university that presents new options for the calculate and pay options. Specifically, the university already has a debit or credit card account with these customers. Nominate three options you will present to the university for this group; at least one must involve using new technology. Think outside the box and make this group different.

CASE STUDY 6

Where Are Ü Now, Justin Bieber?

What do you make of Justin Bieber? Is he the immature, over-hyped pop sensation who can't dance, as his detractors claim? Or are you a Belieber and think he's a musical prodigy? Does something like "Where Are Ü Now" make your decision easier? And where are you on EDM—is it misery or is it inspired?

"Where Are Ü Now" is the result of collaboration between Bieber and Jack Ü—Skrillex and Diplo. Skrillex, born Sonny Moore, is a music producer, singer, and songwriter. He is credited with popularizing the dubstep sound in EDM. Diplo (Wesley Pentz) is a music producer and record executive based in LA. He has created dance beats for MIA, Usher, and others. "Where Are Ü Now" began as a piano ballad collaboration in the spring of 2014 between Justin Bieber and Jason "Poo Bear" Boyd. Later that summer, Skrillex and Diplo took an hour-and-a-half recording of it and synthesized the song we now know as "Where Are Ü Now" over a 4-month period. They reversed the order of verses in the Bieber/Poo Bear recording and added dance beats and new chords. They created a "dolphin," the music's most recognizable melody, and using electronic devices raised the pitch two octaves, distorted the sound, and added reverb. The song was released in February 2015 and received both critical acclaim and popularity—reaching the top 10 in eight countries as well as eighth on Billboard's Hot 100. It was selected as one of the top 10 songs of the year by a number of music critics.

"Where Are Ü Now" belongs to the music genre called EDM. EDM, a youth music movement that features percussive electronic music played by DJs at raves, festivals, and upscale clubs. First popular in Europe, its emergence in the United States has been attributed to Madonna's 1998 breakout "Ray of Light." In EDM, the DJ typically creates a series of tracks by transitioning from one to the other and emphasizes bass, tempo shifts, or "drops." EDM has been called crass, vulgar, and commercial, often at the same time. But its emphasis is to create something to dance to, not overly analyze.

EDM is particularly popular as a live event or gig. DJs play EDM for 4 hours or more at raves that attract much bigger crowds than traditional musical performances. Early DJs such as Deadmau5, David Guetta,

FIGURE 6-22

and Skrillex have become celebrities, and their performances at festivals like Electric Daisy Carnival and Ultra Music Festival can attract more than 250,000 attendees over a multiday period. Currently popular EDM DJs include Dimitri Vegas & Like Mike, Hardwell, and Martin Garrix. Popular artists and songwriters include Diplo, Above and Beyond, Flume, and Calvin Harris.

IS puts the *E* in EDM. Increasingly sophisticated software allows producers and creators to make new and unique sounds that they can weave into music. Skrillex and Diplo in "Where Are Ü Now" took Bieber's original slow ballad recording and first manipulated the vocals, added natural harmonies, mixed in a drum backbeat with unique drops, and experimented with all that before deciding on a final version. IS also plays an essential role in the expression of the music. DJs use technology to perform the music during performances and mix the sounds in artistic ways. Without IS there would be no EDM.

One way to view this new music is to say it is an IS that supports the process of creating and performing EDM. The creation of EDM begins with several iterations of composition and recording. Then these recordings are electronically mixed, altered, and recombined in many attempts. The final product is performed in front of key people including marketers and producers and then altered again, if necessary, before it is eventually released. Several processes—creating and performing—and one IS.

To see and hear about "Where Are Ü Now," including interviews with Bieber, Skrillex, and Diplo, watch the *NY Times* video at *www.nytimes.com/video/arts/music/100000003872410/bieber-diplo-and-skrillex-make-a-hit.html*.

6-10. Draw a simple EDM music creation process with five to eight activities.

6-11. Figure 6-15 lists several ways that process management principles can improve processes. Can any of these principles be used to improve this process of creating music?

6-12. Is music creation a structured or dynamic process? Why? How is IS to be used for that type of process (see Chapter 2)?

6-13. What are the objectives and KPIs of the EDM music creation process?

6-14. IS can improve a process in five ways. How can each of those five ways be used to improve the music creation process for EDM?

6-15. How can each of the five ways be used to improve the music performance process for EDM?

6-16. In Chapter 1, four employability skills were discussed. Which of these skills are being used by Skrillex and Duplo? Explain your answer.

CHAPTER RESOURCES

[1] "Manufacturing and Work Processes," University of Illinois, accessed September 18, 2013, www.ler.illinois.edu/sociotech/documents/590slides-lp-9-29-09.pdf.

[2] Warning: Porter uses the term *activities* to describe these categories. We use the term *activity* in our definition of a process as a series of activities.

[3] Definitions of value chain activities from Michael Porter, *Competitive Advantage* (New York: Simon and Schuster, 1998).

[4] H. James Harrington and Kenneth C. Lomax, *Performance Improvement Methods* (New York: McGraw-Hill, 2000), p. 57.

[5] Based on "A Classroom Exercise to Illustrate Lean Manufacturing Pull Concepts," by Peter J. Billington, in *Decision Sciences Journal of Innovative Education*, 2(1), 2004, pp. 71–77.

MyLab MIS

Go to **MyLab MIS.com** for Auto-graded writing questions as well as the following Assisted-graded writing questions:

6-17. Describe a process with at least three activities that college students accomplish everyday such as get ready for class, buy a meal, or accomplish a class assignment. Explain the activities, who accomplishes the activities, and if any information system (smartphone alarm, cash register, etc.) can help improve the process. Also, explain the goals of this process.

6-18. Describe a process you encounter frequently outside your role as a student. Describe its goal. Suggest a way to improve that process. Specify KPI(s) that should be used that will demonstrate that your improvement actually made the process better.

Chapter 7

Supporting Processes with ERP Systems

On a quiet morning at the corporate offices of CBI, Megan and Heidi are trying to hide their anxiety.

Heidi breaks the tension. "I haven't been this nervous since my wedding day. First morning since go live, and the world still seems to be spinning." Heidi is referring to the cutover an hour ago of the company's ERP system, its IT backbone. The transition was the culmination of years of planning and thousands of labor hours.

Megan replies, "Your wedding turned out OK, and so will this. It can't be as bad as that ERP disaster in Great Britain I read about yesterday. I think they pulled the plug after 10 years of problems."

Not to be outdone, Heidi says, "If we're going to list disasters, my favorite is the Hershey Chocolate one. They tried to cut over right before Halloween one year. Cost them millions and IT heads rolled on that fiasco."

"If you had to guess, where do you think we'll see our biggest problems?"

"Well…for the finance folks, this is only an upgrade to what they've been using, so the scale of that part is OK. I think our biggest issues will be in sales. We're adding supply chain and sales to the system this go-round, and I think our work with the supply chain people was better than the sales folks. I think supply chain understands how important this project is and what they will be able to do with it; the salespeople seemed to treat it like a burden. Working with them felt like pulling teeth."

As the phone rings, Megan and Heidi exchange a furtive glance.

"Maybe it's someone calling to say how great the system is," says Heidi.

"Doubt that," replies Megan.

Megan answers the call. "You said the truck driver called and can't find the warehouse?" To Heidi she says, "Heidi, look up the address of the warehouse for Miami Bikes in the new system."

"123 Main Street," replies Heidi.

"Where's the truck driver again…573 East Wooster?"

"That is the address of Miami Bike Sales. I think the driver went to the store and not the warehouse."

"We'll update the system and start looking for other address mistakes, thanks," says Megan and hangs up the phone.

"Didn't we ask during our configuration meetings…I guess there were just too many details at times, but holy cow, I hope we don't have all our trucks going to stores and not warehouses."

Q7-1. What problem does an ERP system solve?

Q7-2. What are the elements of an ERP system?

Q7-3. What are the benefits of an ERP system?

Q7-4. What are the challenges of implementing an ERP system?

Q7-5. What types of organizations use ERP?

Q7-6. Who are the major ERP vendors?

Q7-7. What makes SAP different from other ERP products?

PSI BIG PICTURE

PROCESS: ERP systems integrate processes

IS: ERP systems are one type of IS

Just then Mark walks in from Sales. "Got a call just now from Philly Bikes. They said they just received 12 of our water bottles but ordered 12 boxes that should have 10 water bottles each."

The phone rings again, sounding like a gunshot. "Megan, we've got a problem here," says Wally in the warehouse. "I can't buy the touring bikes from our best vendor in Houston. I can't find the vendor name in the system. Maybe somebody didn't load all the vendors into the system."

As the office heats up on day one, Megan is beginning to wonder if this is the start of a very sad case study in an ERP textbook or just normal problems that will quickly die down. She hopes her planning and knowledge of ERP were enough to save the day. At the same time she's nagged by doubts: Maybe we didn't train the salespeople well enough, maybe the bosses overhyped everything, and maybe we didn't ask the right questions.

PREVIEW

Heidi and Megan were nervous, and for good reason. Installing new capabilities and updating a piece of software as complex as an ERP system are significant challenges. An upgrade can take years to implement and cost millions of dollars. These systems also require an organization to make difficult changes in the way it does things. CBI must get this right to stay competitive in the industry, but with that reward comes the challenge of getting the upgrade to work.

In the previous chapter, we looked at business from a process perspective and examined how to make processes more efficient and effective. Here we discuss the same issue of IS and business process improvement but from the IS point of view. More specifically, we investigate how one type of IS, a large-scale ERP system like the one implemented at CBI, can improve processes across an entire organization and help the processes play well together. To do so, we will examine the components of an ERP system as well as the benefits and challenges of implementing an ERP system. With this foundation in the fundamentals of ERP systems, we will examine how two major processes—procurement and sales—are supported by ERP systems in Chapters 8 and 9. First we revisit the information silo problem from Chapter 6.

MyLab MIS

- Using Your Knowledge Questions 7-1, 7-2, 7-3
- Essay Questions 7-16, 7-17
- Excel and Access Application Questions 7-1, 7-2

▶Q7-1▶ What Problem Does an ERP System Solve?

To appreciate the popularity of ERP systems today, consider how businesses operated before they were introduced. Business functions and departments ran their own processes using their own information systems and databases. Information silos were everywhere. Recall from Chapter 6 that an information silo is isolated data stored in separated information systems. With information silos, the data needed by one process are stored in an information system designed and used in another process. Because information silos exist in isolation from one another, they create islands of automation that can reduce the performance of processes and make process integration difficult.

You may have experienced information silos in the healthcare industry. If you had any surgery, your medical records may exist in several locations—with your primary care doctor, surgeon, physical therapist, and insurance company. One goal of healthcare reform is to overcome these types of information silos. Image the time savings to you and the better care if all your records resided in one system.

In business, the silo problem is solved by ERP systems. **ERP systems** are very large enterprise IS that bring data together in a big database and help a company improve its processes.

This topic, ERP systems, may appear painfully technical, and you might be asking yourself, "Why study this?" While you don't need to know all the technical details, you will need to know how to use an ERP system. Like Microsoft Office, your company will need you to be good at it. In addition, you will collaborate with your company's technical staff to make your ERP system support your sales, supply chain, or accounting activities, so you need to know the vocabulary, the options, and the challenges of these systems. These systems are both costly and essential; your company needs well-educated users to help make these systems successful.

An ERP system is an IS designed to integrate processes by consolidating data. Early ERP systems emerged about 20 years ago as advances in network speeds and data storage enabled the development of a large, centralized, well-connected database that could span an entire company.

An ERP system is an IS with two key characteristics, as shown in Figure 7-1. First, as shown in the top of the figure, an ERP system creates a single database. By consolidating data, a company can avoid the problem of having multiple versions of the same thing—for example, storing data about a customer in two silos and not knowing which customer data is correct.

By having this single source of truth, this single database, the second key characteristic of ERP systems is made possible. ERP systems provide a set of industry-leading processes that are well integrated with each other as shown in the bottom of Figure 7-1. Process integration has

FIGURE 7-1

Two Characteristics of ERP Systems

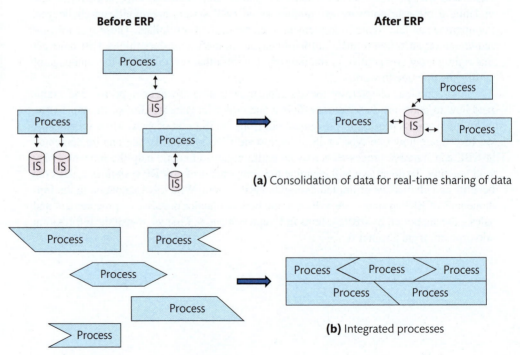

enormous benefit. ERP process integration allows the "left hand of the organization to know what the right hand is doing." For example, data from a new sale is immediately sent to the database and that new data updates the pace of production and the procurement of supplies.

You may already be using a type of ERP at your university: a learning management system. Two are Canvas and Blackboard. All the data—grades, discussion board posts, and email—are stored in one place to support a wide variety of processes including grading, course management, communication, student collaboration, and course scheduling.

ERP Implementation: Before and After Examples

To better understand the impact of an ERP system, we will examine processes in two organizations before and after an ERP system is implemented. The first organization is a university; the second is Chuck's Bikes.

In this section, we compare organizations before and after ERP implementation to provide a clear discussion of the benefits of an ERP system, not because firms are still deciding whether the benefits outweigh the risks. Today, almost all large firms have implemented an ERP system, at least in part. The challenges now involve updates and expansions, not the initial implementation.

EXAMPLE 1: SINGLE PROCESS—UNIVERSITY PURCHASING Compare a university's procurement process before and after implementing an ERP system, as shown in Figure 7-2. In the top half of the figure, each university department works with its own purchasing agent to buy goods and services from three different suppliers. In the bottom half, each department purchasing agent works through a centralized university purchasing agent who in turn buys from the three suppliers. By integrating all the purchasing activity in one central office, the school is better able to standardize its purchasing process, manage it more effectively, and gain bargaining power over suppliers.

Figure 7-2 shows the effect of an ERP system on the university. The effect of an ERP system on a department is shown in the BPMN diagram in Figure 7-3. The top half shows the activities before implementing an ERP system, and the bottom half shows the activities after implementation. Before implementation, each department's procurement process had three main

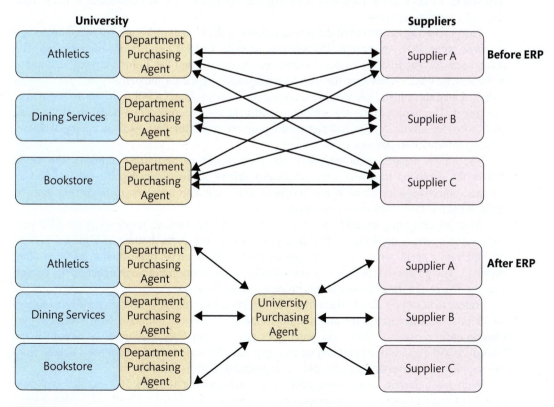

FIGURE 7-2

University Departments Procurement Before and After ERP

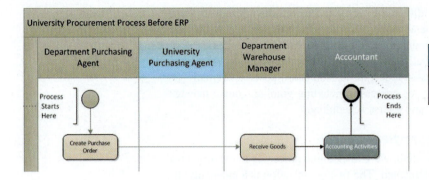

Before ERP Implementation

Objectives	KPIs
Use reliable suppliers	Not specified
Use boosters (unstated)	Not specified

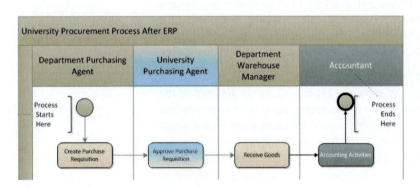

After ERP Implementation

Objectives	KPIs
Reduce cost	Cost

FIGURE 7-3

Impact of ERP System on Department

activities—Create Purchase Order, Receive Goods, and Accounting Activities. The process was initiated by an actor in the Department Purchasing Agent role. Every department at the university had a purchasing agent.

The purchasing agent started the process shown at the top left of Figure 7-3 by completing a purchase order (PO). An example PO might be an order for 500 T-shirts for summer camp. The second activity was Receive Goods. Goods were received when the T-shirts arrived on campus at the athletic warehouse where the warehouse manager signed for the delivery and put them on a shelf. Later, the athletic department accounting office would get a bill from the T-shirt maker and pay it. The purchases by the athletic department were recorded in a department database (not shown for simplicity). Each department on campus maintained its own purchasing database, creating information silos as a result.

The athletic department objectives for this process were to use reliable suppliers who would deliver the goods on time and were reasonably priced. The athletic department also had an unstated objective, which was to use suppliers who were also boosters of the athletic department. KPIs for these objectives were never specified.

After implementing the ERP system, a new procurement process provided by the ERP vendor is used by every department. This new process is shown in the bottom of Figure 7-3. Now the purchasing agent completes a purchase requisition. A purchase requisition is a PO awaiting approval. The purchase requisition is approved by a university purchasing agent as the second activity. The rest of the activities in this process remain the same.

Rather than storing data in department information silos, the new ERP process consolidates all the procurement data for the different departments in a central database. Now when the purchasing agent requests T-shirts, her order goes to a clothing vendor who already supplies the bookstore with thousands of clothing items every year. Because the university buys in bulk from this supplier, the university gets the athletic department T-shirts for less.

With the university purchasing office now orchestrating the process, specific and clear objectives and KPIs have been developed for the process and shared with all purchasing agents. The university's objective with the new process is efficiency—lowering cost as measured by comparing this month's expenditures to last year's during the same month.

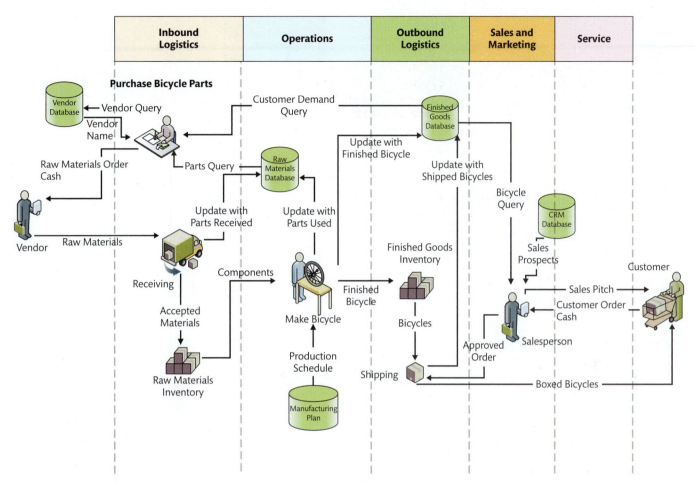

FIGURE 7-4

Pre-ERP Information Systems for Chuck's Bikes

Although it is helpful to understand how an ERP system can improve a single process such as procurement at the university, it is perhaps more important to understand how an ERP system can improve processes for an entire organization. To see these larger-scale impacts, we shift gears to Chuck's Bikes.

EXAMPLE 2: MANY PROCESSES—CHUCK'S BIKES Some of the main processes for CBI before ERP implementation are shown in Figure 7-4. This figure illustrates how many of CBI's processes work together, with the primary activities of the value chain across the top.

Notice the five databases shown as cylinders—Vendor, Raw Material, Manufacturing, Finished Goods, and CRM. CRM is customer relationship management; a CRM database keeps track of data about customers. These five databases are information silos, isolated from each other as they support different processes.

By not having data consolidated in one place, CBI faces difficulty when data need to be shared in real time. For example, if the sales department has the unexpected opportunity to sell 1,000 bicycles, the sales manager must know if the company can produce these bikes in time to meet the delivery date. Unfortunately, the sales manager does not have all the data she needs because the data are stored in isolated databases throughout the firm. She does not know the current data of finished bikes in the Finished Goods database or of bike parts in the Raw Materials database. With data scattered throughout the firm, the potential sale is in jeopardy.

Contrast this situation with the ERP system in Figure 7-5. Here all of CBI's processes are supported by an ERP system, and the data are consolidated into a centralized ERP database. When the sales manager gets the opportunity to sell 1,000 bicycles, the data that the sales manager needs to confirm the order is readily available in the ERP system. From her desk, the sales manager can see how many bikes are finished and ready to sell and how many bikes will be

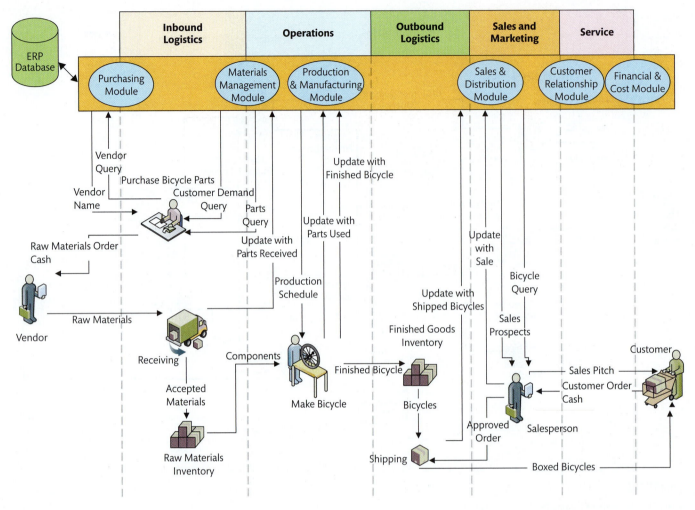

FIGURE 7-5
ERP System for Chuck's Bikes

produced in the coming days. Further, the ERP system can show the sales manager that if this current inventory is not quite enough, the company can double production next week but the cost of the bikes will go up 40 percent.

If the sales manager decides to proceed with the sale and production must double, the ERP system notifies managers in inbound logistics, operations, and outbound logistics with supply and production schedules. By consolidating the data in one place, the impact of the sale can be shared in real time with all affected processes.

As these two examples show, ERP systems consolidate data in one place, which makes it easier to share data. As a result, better process integration is achieved. While the single database and integrated processes are the big magic in ERP systems, the other components of the ERP IS also play a role in the success and failure of ERP systems. We consider these components and ERP processes next.

Q7-2 What Are the Elements of an ERP System?

To better understand the components of current ERP systems, consider their evolution. Current ERP systems are particularly strong in the areas in which they were first developed, such as manufacturing and supply processes.

Although the term *ERP* is relatively new, businesses have been using IS to support their processes for 50 years, well before the Internet. In the 1960s, a business could use a dedicated phone line, a computer card reader, and punch cards to send inventory orders to a supplier. By the 1970s, businesses began to buy their own mainframe computers, and manufacturing companies began to use software called **material requirements planning (MRP)** to efficiently manage inventory, production, and labor. As computing power became cheaper, **manufacturing resource planning (MRPII)** was developed that added financial tracking capabilities as well as the opportunity to schedule equipment and facilities.

The business environment continued to evolve with the advent of **just in time (JIT)** delivery. JIT integrates manufacturing and supply—manufacturing occurs just as raw materials arrive. To execute JIT, tight supplier relationships were needed. These relationships depended on unimpeded flows of data between partners. Just as this business need was emerging, Internet technologies globalized supply chains and customer markets in the 1990s.

Businesses began to see newly emerging ERP solutions as a comprehensive way to address their growing supply chain needs, ensure that the looming Y2K problem was solved, and overcome their information silo problem. A short time later, new federal laws such as the **Sarbanes-Oxley Act (SOX)** required companies to exercise greater control over their financial processes, and ERP systems addressed that new requirement. From this brief review, notice that businesses and IS coevolve; one makes progress and has an impact on the other, and vice versa.

As business changes, so must ERP systems. Today, for a product to be considered a true ERP product, it must include applications that integrate processes in the following business functions:[1]

- Supply chain management (SCM; procurement, sales order processing, inventory management, supplier management, and related activities)
- Manufacturing (manufacturing scheduling, capacity planning, quality control, bill of materials, and related activities)
- Customer relationship management (CRM; sales prospecting, customer management, marketing, customer support, call center support)
- Human resources (payroll, time and attendance, HR management, commission calculations, benefits administration, and related activities)
- Accounting (general ledger, accounts receivable, accounts payable, cash management, fixed-asset accounting)

Although ERP solutions can integrate these processes, frequently an organization will purchase and implement just parts of the total ERP package. For example, a defense contractor might rely on just SCM and manufacturing, and a university may only install the human resources and accounting functions. The most common partial implementations are CRM to support promotion, sales, and service processes or SCM to integrate supply chain processes and promote data sharing with supply chain partners.

The Five Components of an ERP IS: Software, Hardware, Data, Procedures, and People

As shown in the top left side of Figure 7-6, an ERP vendor provides a set of integrated processes as well as two of the five components of an IS—the software and an empty database. The product that an ERP vendor sells is not the same thing as a living, breathing ERP system used in a

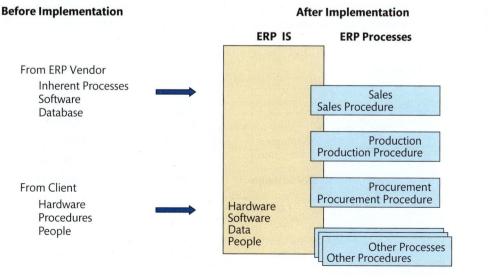

FIGURE 7-6

ERP IS and ERP Processes

company after implementation, which is shown on the right side of Figure 7-6. To implement the ERP system, a company installs the ERP product's software and database on the company's hardware, writes procedures, and trains its people to follow them, as shown in the bottom left side of Figure 7-6. Consider each component.

SOFTWARE ERP software typically resides on servers on client machines in the company although cloud implementations are becoming popular. The software can be customized to meet customer requirements without changing program code. This customization is called **configuration**.

This process of configuring the software is similar to the configuration you do with a new smartphone. Before you can use the phone, you must specify a carrier, a plan, email addresses, and a host of other requirements. You and your phone's salesperson collaborate to address each requirement.

In the same way, a company like CBI in the opening vignette will make more than 8,000 configuration decisions to customize the ERP system to its needs. These include decisions on the number of hours in the standard workweek, the holidays recognized by CBI, the hourly wages for different job categories, the wage adjustments for overtime and holiday work, the units of measure for water bottles, and spending limits for each department.

Of course, there are limits to how much configuration can be done. If a new ERP customer has requirements that cannot be met via configuration, then the customer either needs to adapt its business to what the software can do or write application code to meet its requirements. Writing new code to supplement an ERP system is called **customization**.

For example, CBI sponsors a competitive team of bike racers by providing specially made bicycles and equipment at various times throughout the year. CBI would like to account for this expense as a global marketing cost but could not configure the ERP system to record these unusual expenditures that way. In the end, CBI had to either write the code or hire another firm to write the code and add it to the ERP software. Code can be added to any ERP implementation using specific application languages such as Java.

DATA An ERP solution includes a gigantic but largely unpopulated database, a database design, and initial configuration data. It does not, of course, contain the company's actual operational data. Operational data are entered during development and use.

ERP systems rely on a DBMS to process and administer the ERP database. Chapter 4 distinguished between the DBMS that creates and maintains the database and the database itself. Figure 7-7 shows this relationship. Common DBMS products used by ERP systems include IBM DB2, Oracle Database, and Microsoft SQL Server. ERP software interacts with the DBMS to update data in the database.

In an ERP database, there are several different types of data. **Transactional data** are data related to events such as a purchase or a student enrollment. For CBI, examples of transactional data include purchases payments, deliveries, and payroll expenditures. **Master data**, also called reference data, are data used in the organization that don't change with every transaction. Master data includes supplier names and addresses, item names and units of measure, and employee data. ERP systems also designate **organizational data**, data about the company such as the location of its warehouses, the mailing addresses of the buildings, and the names it of its financial accounts.

FIGURE 7-7

ERP Software, DBMS, and Database

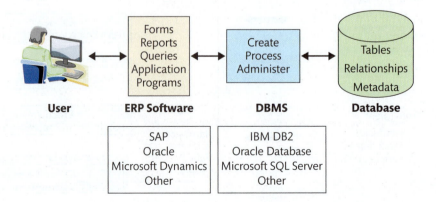

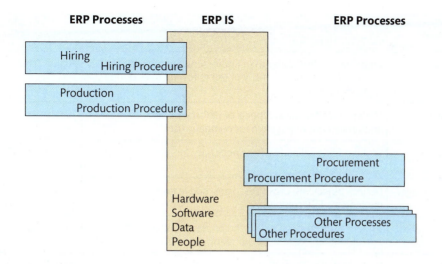

FIGURE 7-8

Example of ERP Processes, IS, and Procedures

HARDWARE Each ERP implementation requires a wide variety of hardware, including disk storage, servers, clients, printers, scanners, network devices, and cables. To determine the necessary levels for each of these hardware devices, an organization first estimates the number of users, the processes supported, and the volume of data for the intended system. With these estimates, hardware sizing can be accomplished.

As mentioned earlier, cloud computing is being an increasingly popular choice. With the cloud, ERP systems may be rented with a much lower upfront cost, and paid for by use.

PROCEDURES A procedure is a set of instructions for a person to follow when operating an IS. The relationship between ERP systems and processes is shown in Figure 7-8. On the left-hand side of the figure are two processes, Hiring and Production, that are linked to the ERP information system with procedures. Procurement and other processes are shown with their procedures on the right side.

Every ERP installation requires a firm to select ERP processes and then specify how those processes will be executed on the ERP software. These specifications and procedures are unique to the firm. For example, after CBI selects a Sales process, it must write a procedure for its employees to use when executing this process. These procedures tell the user which buttons to click and what text to enter into dialogue boxes like usernames and passwords.

Procedures not only specify instructions, they also are an important opportunity for organizations to improve control of a process. In the previous chapter, we defined control as limiting behavior; one example was the cruise control of a car and how it limits variation in the car's speed. A well-written procedure for a process can limit the behavior of people executing the process. By limiting behavior, procedures help processes provide consistent results. For example, a good Sales procedure would include specific instructions for what to do with missing data, what to do with customers without ID numbers, and how to handle expired customer accounts.

Crafting the procedure is the first step; training employees to use the procedure is the second step. Training employees how to interact with an ERP system can be a time-consuming and costly operation. To support this need, ERP vendors have developed extensive training classes and training curricula to enable users to learn the ERP system. ERP vendors typically conduct classes on site prior to, during, and after implementation. To reduce expenses, the vendors sometimes train the organization's users to become in-house trainers in training sessions called **train the trainer**. Even with this approach, the training bill is very large; a firm may budget a third of the total cost of the implementation on training and consulting fees.

PEOPLE The people involved with an ERP system fall into three general categories. *Users* are the employees of the firm implementing the system. IT analysts, also called *systems analysts*, are also employees. IT analysts have specialized training or education that enables them to support, maintain, and adapt the system after it has been implemented. Many analysts have a background or education in MIS or IT. In the opening vignette, Heidi and Megan are IT analysts at CBI. A third role is *consultant*. A consultant works for the ERP vendor or a different company, called a *third party*, and helps budget, plan, train, configure, and implement the system. These consultants may work at the implementing firm for a period before, during, and after the implementation.

Title	Job Description	Salary (in U.S. dollars)
Consultant	Employed by firm other than implementing company or ERP vendor, can perform any of the following roles during implementation	70,000–110,000
Systems analyst	Understands technical aspects of ERP; helps plan, configure, and implement ERP system for company use	70,000–90,000
Developer	Writes additional code where necessary for implementing ERP systems	76,000–92,000
Project manager	Defines objectives; organizes, plans, and leads team that implements ERP solution	80,000–120,000
Business analyst	Understands process aspects; helps plan, configure, and implement ERP system for company use	75,000–95,000
Architect	High-level planner of IS at an organization; ensures compatibility of technology and directs technology toward strategic goals	90,000–130,000
Trainer	Trains end users on how ERP system operates, explains their roles, and trains trainers	65,000–78,000

FIGURE 7-9
ERP Job Titles, Descriptions, and Salary Estimates

Although job titles and descriptions vary, a short list of the most common ERP positions is presented in Figure 7-9. Salary estimates are provided, although they vary widely by experience and location. Like an increasing number of IS jobs, success in these positions is based less on technical skill and more on process understanding and an ability to work with people. According to the Bureau of Labor Statistics, job opportunities in ERP and IS in general are expected to grow by nearly 25 percent from 2012 to 2022.[2]

Inherent Business Processes

As mentioned earlier, ERP systems are more than an IS. They also specify processes called **inherent processes** or **process blueprints**. An inherent process is an optimized business process designed by an ERP vendor to be used by client firms. For the client organization, some of the changes it must make from existing processes to inherent processes are minor and hardly noticed, but some changes can be significant. Organizations implementing an ERP system must either adapt to the predefined inherent processes or design new ones. In the latter case, the design of a new process may necessitate changes to software and database structures, all of which mean great expense!

We have already seen an example of an inherent process in Figure 7-3. That figure shows how the university adopted the ERP vendor's inherent procurement process. Another example is how Canvas' inherent grading process changed how professors record and share grades with students.

Implementing the ERP Components and Processes

Now that we've discussed the pieces of the ERP puzzle, let's see how a firm puts these components together to create a functioning ERP system. This system may be an in initial implementation or a significant upgrade. The steps necessary to put the pieces together is itself a process—a simplified version of this Implementation process is shown in Figure 7-10. First, the top managers of the company revisit their strategy so that the ERP system has clear goals. Next, they conduct a **gap analysis**, a study that highlights the differences between the business requirements that emerge from strategic planning and the capabilities of the ERP system. The Implementation team then develops processes it will use and configures the software. In the final steps, the company's

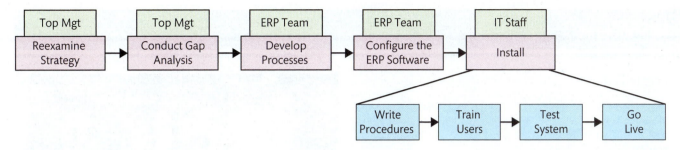

FIGURE 7-10

Implementation Process of an ERP System

IT staff writes procedures, trains the users, and tests the system. This final step culminates with a Go Live activity when cutover occurs, when the new ERP system replaces the previous system; CBI had reached this final activity in the opening vignette. This Implementation process can require a year to 18 months for a large firm. If implementation is successful, the organization can take advantage of benefits described in the next question.

Q7-3 What Are the Benefits of an ERP System?

An ERP system provides a number of benefits to the organization as a whole. These organizational benefits are listed in Figure 7-11. Notice that the two key characteristics of ERP systems—consolidating data for real-time sharing and inherent processes that integrate well—headline this list of benefits.

One benefit of an ERP system is that real-time data sharing allows managers to see trends as they occur and respond appropriately. For example, the purchasing office at the university can see up-to-the-minute totals for each department's purchases. As a result, if food prices rise significantly, the purchasing office can help dining services re-allocate funds from other dining services accounts or change upcoming orders. Similarly, if an academic department is approaching its enrollment limit on a class, the ERP system can notify the department chair.

A second benefit of an ERP system for the organization is converting its processes to the well-integrated, inherent, best-practice processes of the ERP vendor. For example, at the university, best practices are now a part of the university procurement process. These practices include buying in bulk, negotiating prices prior to purchase, and a centralized procurement requisition approval activity. Prior to implementing the ERP system, the separate university departments purchased individually and not in bulk, they had little opportunity to negotiate price, and if a delivery was late or poor quality, the department had little training or expertise in making things right.

A third benefit for the organization is that an effective ERP system can lead to better management as more managers have visibility to more data. For example, if the athletic director wants to check on the status of an order before meeting with a coach, that data is only seconds away. Similarly, the university purchasing department can easily total all the purchases from a particular vendor and renegotiate prices.

- Data sharing occurs in real time.
- Implements integrated are industry best processes.
- More managers see more data, leads to better oversight.
- The information silo problem is solved.
- Better integration with supply chain partners.
- Opportunity to create economies of scale after mergers.

FIGURE 7-11

Benefits of Using an ERP Solution

MIS InClass 7

Google Golf

ERP systems create enormous databases; as a result, being able to search a large database is becoming a vital but underrepresented skill. While Google's data is not an ERP database, it does provide a valuable setting in which to hone your search skills. Take a moment to search the Internet and read about Google search tips, and then use this new knowledge to play Google Golf in teams of two or three students.

Here's how the game is played and scored. Golf holes are questions, and for each question, your team's goal is to input the minimal number of keywords into the Google search bar so that the answer to the question appears early in the search result provided by Google—in one of the top three links. If you use five words and the answer appears in the top three links, your score on that hole is a 5. If you need to search three times, you score is the sum of all three search terms. Acronyms count as one word.

You will play the first nine holes and compare answers and scores with the class. As a class, determine the best search terms for each hole. After this discussion, collaborate with teammates to improve your searching. Then play the final nine holes, the questions for which come from the other teams in the class. All teams contribute to a class list of questions from which the instructor selects the final 9. Getting answers is easy; the game is designed to help you learn how to minimize your word use.

Place the number of words used in the search to the left and the answer to the question at the end on the right.

1. What was the undergraduate enrollment at your school in the fall of this academic year? _____

2. What is the value of 50 pesos in U.S. dollars today? _____
3. What is the meaning of the word *furtive*? _____
4. Show the most recent Twitter post of LeBron James. _____
5. Who spoke at Gettysburg before Lincoln gave his address? _____
6. Which college in California has the nickname *Anteater*? _____
7. What is the name of the closest movie house to the Empire State Building in New York City? _____
8. Where was the computer mouse invented? _____
9. What are the three states other than Massachusetts with a city named Boston in them? _____

To help managers spot trends and changes, ERP systems can provide managers with **dashboards**, which are easy to read, concise, up-to-the minute displays of process KPIs. Like a car dashboard displays speed, fuel, and oil readings, a process dashboard will show sales for today, output of a production machine, or a summary of expenditures for the current month. In today's era of Big Data, discussed in Chapter 12, ERP systems store data for later analysis: a potential gold mine of information.

Fourth, as was discussed earlier, another significant benefit of an ERP system is solving the information silo problem. This means that at the university, the different departments no longer create and maintain their own purchasing databases.

ERP systems make it easier to exchange data with supply chain partners. Sharing data throughout a supply chain can reduce costs and create efficiencies for every business in the chain. For this reason, some customers and suppliers will not want to do business with an organization that does not use an ERP system.

Finally, one benefit of an ERP system is that that it can create economies of scale. While this is helpful within a single organization, it is especially helpful after a merger or acquisition. By sharing data and common processes throughout the new combined firm, the organization can reduce cost and gain economies of scale by bringing all the transactions under one roof.

Clearly, the benefits of an ERP system are significant. However, these benefits are hard earned—the many challenges of implementing an ERP system are discussed next.

Year	Client	Costs	Vendor
2016	Miller Coors	$100 million, Indian contractor HCL could not deliver	SAP
2013	U.K. Healthcare	$18 billion, project terminated, failed to deliver	CSC
2013	Avon	$125 million project results in reps quitting, project halted	SAP
2012	U.S. Air Force	$1 billion cost, no system implemented	Oracle
2011	Montclair State University	$20 million cost overrun	Oracle
2011	Ingram Micro Australia	$22 million reduction in net income	SAP

FIGURE 7-12
ERP Implementation Failures

Q7-4 What Are the Challenges of Implementing an ERP System?

The process of converting an organization like the one shown in Figure 7-4 to an ERP-supported organization like that in Figure 7-5 is daunting and expensive. In the opening vignette, Heidi and Megan at CBI were understandably anxious about the pending ERP cutover. Some have called ERP implementation the corporate equivalent of a brain transplant or a 9-month root canal. If not done well, the losses are often very significant. For example, the U.S. Air Force recently pulled the plug on its 10-year ERP implementation, having already spent $1 billion. This epic failure is the subject of the case at the end of this chapter. Well-known firms like Kmart[3] and Hershey's[4] lost more than $100 million implementing ERP systems. In another debacle, the United Kingdom scrapped an ERP system designed to support electronic healthcare records after 10 years and $18 billion.[5] Other well-known recent failures are listed in Figure 7-12.

Here we describe the wide range of implementation challenges that fall into two general categories—decision making and people.

Decision-Making Challenges

Decision-making challenges that are common to ERP implementation are listed in Figure 7-13. Most implementations encounter each.

ERP VENDOR SELECTION One of the most challenging decisions for the client firm comes early: selecting the right ERP vendor. Client firms have unique needs, and ERP vendors have a variety of strengths and weaknesses. Picking the right vendor is an important challenge because it creates a long-term relationship between the firms; this relationship will have an impact on the effectiveness of the ERP system for the length of the contract.

GAP ANALYSIS Once the vendor is selected, a second challenge emerges. As mentioned earlier, the organization conducts a gap analysis to identify the differences between the business requirements that emerge from strategic planning and the capabilities of the chosen ERP system. The first difficult decision is deciding what the company would like the ERP system to do. A long list of "likes" will lead to a long list of gaps and a difficult implementation. The top leadership team should ensure that a focused, well-understood, short list of "likes" is adopted. The second decision is what to do about the gaps. The company can write custom code, look for a solution outside of ERP, or live with the gap for now.

- ERP vendor selection
- Gap analysis—decide on "like to dos" and what to do with gaps
- Configuration—identifiers, order sizes, BOM
- Data issues
- Cutover method

FIGURE 7-13
Implementation Decision Challenges

A related gap analysis decision is whether to integrate existing information systems with the new ERP system. Many existing IS will be replaced by the ERP system, but those that remain might need to integrate with it. For example, manufacturing firms in Brazil need to generate documents for every delivery truck to carry that show the delivery has permission from the state to use the highways. This is not a current feature of ERP systems, but the firm will need to figure out how to make the existing system that prints these documents compatible with the new ERP system. Making exiting IS compatible with new ERP is challenging, but the devil of implementation is in these details.

CONFIGURATION A third set of challenging decisions occurs during configuration. As mentioned earlier, firms may need to make as many as 8,000 configuration decisions. To make matters even more challenging, many of the most important decisions require a wide understanding of both the business and the ERP system. Earlier in this chapter, the configuration decisions about wages and holidays were introduced. Figure 7-14 lists a sample of the other kinds of configuration decisions implementation teams must make. For brevity here, we consider just the first three—item identifiers, order size, and bill of material—to give you a glimpse of the overall challenge.

One configuration decision is item identifiers. Does the company want to identify or track every item in an incoming and outgoing shipment, a bundle of items, or just the entire shipment itself? Further, does it want to track material as it is being assembled or only when it is finished?

Another set of issues is order size—the organization must specify the number of items in a standard order. In the opening vignette, Heidi and Megan discovered, too late, that water bottles come in boxes of 10 and are not sold individually.

A third detailed decision is the structure of the **bill of material (BOM)**. The BOM is like a recipe; it specifies the raw materials, quantities, and subassemblies needed to create a final product. Most large organizations have a wide variety of BOM structures in place for making their products. Deciding on one BOM standard can be challenging, particularly when the organization makes different types of products in different divisions.

For each of these configuration decisions, the implementation teams must first decide if any of the configuration choices offered by the ERP vendor are suitable. If not, the team must then weigh the advantages and disadvantages of using customized software. Configuring an ERP system is like an 8,000-question multiple-choice test, and on each question, the none-of-the-above answer—customization—is available.

DATA ISSUES Returning to the list of implementation decision challenges in Figure 7-13, a fourth set of decisions must be made about the data in the ERP system. One issue is the format of the data; for example, the sales department uses a five-digit customer ID, whereas the service department uses a four-digit number. In the past, each department maintained its own data and built processes on that numbering system. Committing to one number format can be a challenge and will make at least one department mad. Other data decisions include how duplications will be avoided and deciding who can enter and edit the data.

CUTOVER METHOD A fifth challenging set of decisions occurs during the transition, or cutover, from the current way of doing things to the new ERP system. These cutover decisions are common with any new IS and are discussed more in Extension 3; at this point, just recognize that cutover is like deciding which option to use to overcome an addiction. The addict or firm

FIGURE 7-14

A Sample of Configuration Decisions

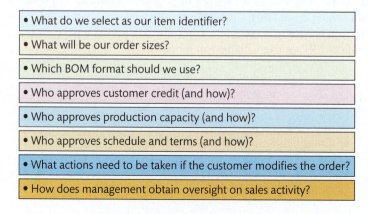

- What do we select as our item identifier?
- What will be our order sizes?
- Which BOM format should we use?
- Who approves customer credit (and how)?
- Who approves production capacity (and how)?
- Who approves schedule and terms (and how)?
- What actions need to be taken if the customer modifies the order?
- How does management obtain oversight on sales activity?

can go cold turkey and cutover all at once, it can do it gradually in a series of steps like rehab, or it can choose another option. The challenge for the addict or implementation team members like Heidi and Megan in the opening vignette is making good decisions under the stress of transition.

People Challenges

In addition to the challenge of making good decisions, the actions and attitudes of the people in the client organization can make implementation even more challenging. This challenge is aptly summarized by the saying, "All our problems wear shoes." Although this may overlook the technical ERP challenges, the saying wisely identifies the biggest challenge to successful implementation: people. Common people-related issues are listed in Figure 7-15. These challenges can be classified as top management, team, and individual.

MANAGEMENT MOVES ON PREMATURELY One common problem occurs when top management believes the hard part of the implementation process is the decision to implement. Managers believe that once that decision is made, they can move on. Instead, they need to stay involved and ensure implementation is monitored, resources are committed, good procedures are written, and thorough training is conducted.

MANAGEMENT OVERSELLS A second top management problem is overselling the vision of what the system will do. Often management can be blinded by the benefits of the promised system and not look carefully at the assumptions behind the promises. This can lead top management to buy more features than it needs or than the organization can implement successfully. Employees who may be more familiar with the assumptions and the necessary change can quickly become jaded when the "grand solution" runs into inevitable implementation problems. Expectation setting is hard. In most cases the expectations of top management and lowest-level employees are not consistent with each other, which creates surprises and frustration during cutover.

MANAGEMENT FAILS TO ANTICIPATE CULTURAL RESISTANCE An ERP implementation can change the culture of an organization. **Culture** is the day-to-day work habits and practices that workers take for granted. Culture is both difficult to see and difficult to change. When an ERP system is implemented, the way work is done is changed and the culture typically bites back. Changing the culture can lead to employee resistance as the change in work habits may threaten **self-efficacy**, which is a person's belief that he or she can be successful at his or her job.

MANAGEMENT HAS POOR PROJECT MANAGEMENT SKILLS ERP projects are very large, and many businesses struggle to find managers with the project management skills necessary to make these projects successful. If the project is poorly managed and runs long, the business is faced with a bad choice—rush to finish and make mistakes due to rushing or reduce training time and money and suffer from end users not being properly trained.

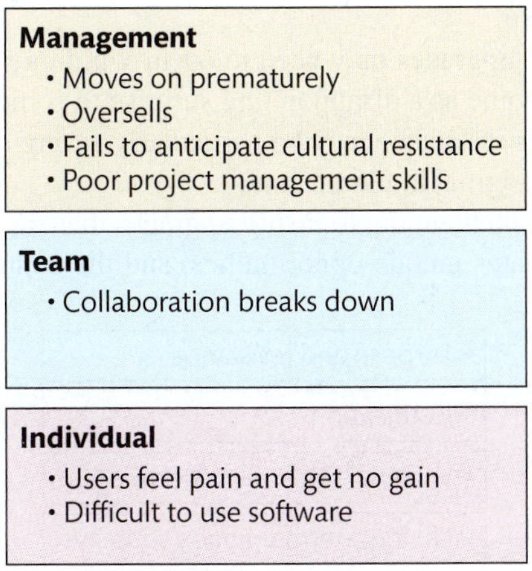

Management
- Moves on prematurely
- Oversells
- Fails to anticipate cultural resistance
- Poor project management skills

Team
- Collaboration breaks down

Individual
- Users feel pain and get no gain
- Difficult to use software

FIGURE 7-15
Implementation People Challenges

TEAM COLLABORATION BREAKS DOWN Implementing an ERP system requires extensive and effective collaboration; when collaboration breaks down, implementation suffers. Consultants from the vendor, IT analysts from the client firm, and end users all know things the others don't know; these missing bits of knowledge can only be learned by collaborating. For example, at CBI, one collaboration team includes Heidi, an ERP consultant, and a supply chain manager. If Heidi does not ask the group if customer warehouses and store addresses are different, the system will be configured as if there is only one address.

USERS FEEL PAIN AND GET NO GAIN As mentioned, implementation changes the work people do. However, the people whose work has changed often receive no benefit from the change; they get the pain but no gain. The benefits occur for the organization. For example, sales work doesn't get much easier at CBI after the ERP system is implemented, but the organization benefits by the change. As a result, employees may need to be given extra inducement to change to the new system. As one experienced change consultant said, "Nothing succeeds like praise or cash, especially cash." Straight-out pay for change is bribery, but contests with cash prizes among employees or groups can be very effective at inducing change.

DIFFICULT-TO-USE SOFTWARE A final challenge is how to get the firm's people to learn and use ERP software that is not particularly user-friendly. A common unfriendly ERP screen is shown later in Figure 7-21, and if you compare that screen with the user-friendly apps on your smartphone, you'll see the challenge in training end users. ERP screens are jargon filled, are difficult to correct, offer unhelpful help, and are hard to explain.

There are a lot of challenges when implementing an ERP system. Each one is not pass-fail; each one can take a toll in terms of cost, time, or system performance. We included this long discussion of challenges here to drive home one of the key lessons of this chapter. Implementing an ERP system or a significant upgrade is a very big deal for any organization. Fortunately, companies are getting better at this, and one reason may be that they have learned to anticipate some of these challenges, and now so have you.

ERP Upgrades

Today, many firms have survived an initial implementation and are executing a second or third upgrade to their original system. These upgrades frequently involve adding new functions to the system. Often, a company will first implement an ERP on a small scale in one division or function with the intent to expand later.

Aggressive client firms upgrade their ERP systems as frequently as every 2 or 3 years, while 5 to 6 years is more common for less aggressive firms. Often an upgrade is justified on a pending change of service from the ERP vendor or a significant increase in service support fees from the vendor. Companies also upgrade to leverage advances in information technology and to better integrate their processes.

Having survived an initial implementation, most firms have learned how to cope with many of the problems just discussed. However, the challenges described above return for a rematch during the upgrade phase, and although they rarely overcome the firm, they often force delays and cost overruns. Upgrades also have unique challenges compared to initial implementation; these are listed in Figure 7-16.

First, discussions about upgrades may need to occur within a year or two after the original implementation. This may come as a disappointing surprise to some in the organization, getting things off to a bad start. This resistance may be particularly strong if people believe the upgrade will be as disruptive as the original implementation.

Second, it may be more challenging to justify upgrades than an original implementation. An original implementation creates unique opportunities, and the contrast of the new ERP system

FIGURE 7-16
ERP Upgrade Challenges

- Surprise and resistance
- Justification
- Version lock from customization
- No long-term upgrade strategy

with the old non-ERP system is both stark and encouraging. With an upgrade, these opportunities and the contrast between new and newer are not so vivid.

A third problem with upgrades is sometimes referred to as version lock. **Version lock** occurs when a client firm has so customized ERP software that it has locked itself out of upgrading to new ERP software. When a firm customizes the ERP software, it is often incompatible with new ERP software versions. To understand version lock, recall that during implementation, the client firm may decide to write custom software to enable the system to do things unique to that client. Some organizations choose to customize heavily—they attempt to build into the ERP processes their unique way of doing things. However, when the ERP vendor upgrades their system to a new version, the new ERP software may not be compatible with the customization done by client firms. For firms that do little customization, an upgrade is relatively painless. In contrast, firms that customize extensively have essentially locked themselves into a particular version of ERP software, and upgrading is more difficult.

Finally, upgrades are challenging if the client firm has not developed a long-term strategy for ERP updates. This strategy should specify plans for upgrading different business functions and should allocate sufficient funds and manpower to ensure future upgrades are wisely conceived and executed. Despite these challenges, many ERP client firms overcome them and are able to use and upgrade ERP systems effectively. The characteristics of these client firms are considered next.

Q7-5 What Types of Organizations Use ERP?

ERP systems are used by many organizations. Use depends on many factors, two of which are examined next: the organization's industry and the organization's size.

ERP by Industry

The first major ERP customers were large manufacturers in the aerospace, automotive, industrial equipment, and other industries. In these industries, ERP use is widespread and typically very effective. Given success in manufacturing, it was natural for ERP vendors to go up the supply chain and sell ERP solutions to those industries that supplied the manufacturers: distributors, raw materials extractors and processors, and the petroleum industry. At the same time, health care was becoming more complex, and hospitals were changing from a service to a profit orientation and began to adopt ERP solutions.

Over time, ERP use spread to companies and organizations in other industries, such as those listed in Figure 7-17. Today, ERP systems are used by governments and utilities, in the retail industry, and in education. However, in industries where ERP use has been less extensive, implementation may not be as smooth.

ERP by Organization Size

ERP, as stated, was initially adopted by large manufacturing organizations that had complex process problems that needed ERP solutions. Those large organizations also had the resources and skilled personnel needed to accomplish and manage an ERP implementation. Over time, as ERP implementation improved, other smaller organizations were able to implement ERP. Today,

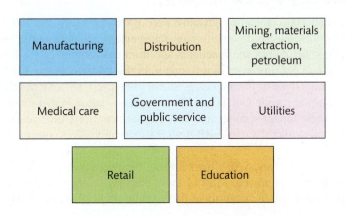

FIGURE 7-17
ERP by Industry

84 percent of organizations with between 100 and 1,000 employees have already implemented ERP.[6] ERP systems are now increasingly common in firms with yearly revenues as low as $5 million.

Value chains and basic business processes are not different in character between small and large organizations. To quote F. Scott Fitzgerald, "The rich are no different from you and me, they just have more money." The steps required to check credit, verify product availability, and approve terms are no different for order processing at Amazon.com than they are at Phil's Muffler Shop. An excellent sales process for a multimillion-dollar company is very helpful to midsize companies. They differ in scale, but not in character.

However, companies of different sizes have one very important difference that has a major impact on ERP: the availability of skilled business and IT analysts. Small organizations employ only one or two IT analysts who not only manage the ERP system but also manage the entire IS department. They are spread very thin and are often in over their heads during an ERP implementation. Smaller, simpler ERP solutions are common among these companies.

Midsize organizations may expand IT from one person to a small staff, but frequently this staff is isolated from senior-level management. Such isolation can create misunderstandings and distrust. Because of the expense, organizational disruption, and length of ERP projects, senior management must be committed to the ERP solution. When IT management is isolated, such commitment is difficult to obtain and may not be strong. This issue is problematic enough that many ERP consultants say the first step for these firms in an initial implementation or upgrade is to obtain deep senior-level commitment to the project.

Large organizations have a full IT staff that is headed by the chief information officer (CIO), a business and IT professional who sits on the executive board and is an active participant in organizational strategic planning. ERP implementation will be part of that strategic process and, when begun, will have the full backing of the entire executive group.

International Firms and ERP

One way that the needs of large organizations differ in character from those of small organizations is international presence. Most billion-dollar companies operate in many countries, and the ERP application programs must be available in many languages and currencies.

Once implemented, ERP brings huge benefits to multinational organizations. International ERP solutions are designed to work with multiple currencies, manage international transfers of goods in inventories, and work effectively with international supply chains. Even more important, ERP solutions provide a worldwide consolidation of financial statements on a timely basis. As a result, they can produce one set of financial reports, better analyze where costs could be saved, and identify where production can be optimized.

While it is advantageous for these international firms to consolidate all their operations within one large ERP implementation, called a **single instance**, some firms maintain **multiple instances**, or an ERP for each country, business unit, or region. For these firms, the advantages of one set of data, a single financial system, and worldwide process standards are outweighed by the cost of consolidating or the disparity among divisions.

Q7-6 ▶ Who Are the Major ERP Vendors?

Although more than 100 companies advertise ERP products, many are designed for one or two business functions: customer relationship management, manufacturing, supply chain, or accounting. At the other end of the functional spectrum are comprehensive ERP systems that support most of the major processes in a business. In this comprehensive ERP industry, three vendors have the lion's share of the market, as shown in Figure 7-18. SAP has the largest market share and longest history, while Oracle and Microsoft have trailed in that order for most of the previous decade. These top three companies are often labeled Tier 1 ERP vendors and comprise about half of the total market share for ERP. A wide variety of vendors compete for the other half of the market.

Over the last several years, SAP's market share has decreased slightly as smaller vendors and cloud offerings have improved. Most of these changes can be attributed to growth in the small-to-medium market and the maturity of ERP systems in large organizations.

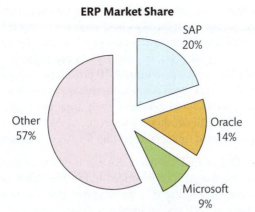

ERP Market Share

FIGURE 7-18
ERP Vendors and Market Share

Goals of Large ERP Vendors

Tier 1 vendors are trying to make their ERP systems simpler to use, more secure, and with cloud-based options as shown in Figure 7-19. They are also seeking to empower the end users to be their own data analyst. In the old days, an accountant seeking to analyze corporate data would need to work with an IT analyst who could interact with the software to get the needed data. Now, ERP vendors want to remove the need for the IT analyst by making the system easier to use to make it possible for the accountant to directly work with the ERP data.

These current goals are common for the large Tier 1 ERP vendors, as are many of the goals for their next version of ERP software. One next-generation goal is to improve the interface between ERP systems and IoT objects and 3D printers. Another is to improve connectivity between ERP system data and large external data sources. For example, Walgreens would like its ERP system to interface with weather forecast data in order to improve in-store supplies of necessities like bottled water when dangerous weather is forecasted. Finally, vendors are seeking to reduce manual key inputs by individuals and allow more automated data inputs to the system.

ERP Products

MICROSOFT DYNAMICS **Microsoft Dynamics** is composed of a variety of ERP products, all obtained via acquisition. Each product is particularly capable in different business functions. Compared with Oracle and SAP products, a Dynamics implementation is typically smaller in scale and functionality and, as a result, a bit less expensive and time consuming to implement. None of these products are well integrated with Microsoft Office, and none of them are integrated at all with Microsoft's development languages. In fact, Microsoft's ERP direction is difficult to determine. It seems to have four horses headed in different directions, and none of them are attached to the primary Microsoft coach.

ORACLE Oracle is an intensely competitive company with a deep base of technology and high-quality technical staff. Oracle developed some of its ERP products in-house and has

Current Goals

- Simple to use
- More secure
- Cloud based
- Support end user analysis

Next Generation Goals

- Improve interface with IoT, 3D
- Improve connectivity to Big Data sources
- More automated inputs

FIGURE 7-19
Goals of Large ERP Vendors

complemented those products with others obtained through its acquisition of PeopleSoft (high-quality HR products) and Siebel (high-quality CRM products). Oracle has pledged to continue to support these acquired ERP systems. Oracle also provides the glue that allows their different systems to interoperate. As a result, Oracle provides a more federated approach to ERP with independent, coordinated subsystems, than other ERP providers. Beginning with its first DBMS product release, Oracle has never been known to create easy-to-use products. It is known, however, for producing fully-featured products with superior performance. They are also expensive. Oracle CEO Larry Ellison owns 70 percent of NetSuite, a company that offers a cloud-based solution for integrated financial reporting for large, international organizations.

SAP   SAP is the gold standard of ERP products. SAP is used by midsized and large companies and offers the most extensive line of ERP products. In Q7, we elaborate more on SAP than the other ERP products because we will use it in the next two chapters to explain the procurement and sales processes and how an ERP system improves those processes.

OUTSIDE OF TIER 1   While the titans of Tier 1 duke it out trying to be everything to everybody, smaller firms are establishing a strong niche by offering industry-specific systems, solutions for particular business functions, or pay-as-you-go cloud services. While the functional breadth and opportunity for corporate-wide standardization of processes make Tier 1 vendors appealing to large firms, many midsize to small firms find smaller, more nimble, or cloud-based solutions less disruptive and lower risk. Keep your eye on one of the more popular choices: Salesforce.com, an industry leader in CRM cloud services.

We close this chapter with a more thorough look at SAP. While some of you will use the SAP tutorials at the end of Chapters 8 and 9 to practice with SAP software, it is helpful for all of you to better understand some background on the industry leader as well as some of the features of SAP software that are common to all ERP products.

Q7-7 ▸ What Makes SAP Different from Other ERP Products?

SAP is a product of **SAP AG**, a German firm. It is pronounced as three letters, "S-A-P," not as the word *sap*. The letters are an abbreviation for "Systems, Applications, Products," which in German is "*Systeme, Anwendungen, Produkte.*" Detractors humorously claim it might also stand for "Stop All Progress" or "Start And Pray," titles that hint at the challenges of using SAP and of its importance to the company.

Founded in 1972 by five former IBM employees, SAP AG has grown to become the third-largest software company in the world, with about 50,000 employees, 100,000 customers, and 10 million users in more than 100 countries. The core business of SAP AG is selling licenses or access to cloud access fees for software solutions and related services. In addition, it offers consulting, training, and other services for its software solutions. The stated goal of SAP software is to help companies make their business processes more efficient and agile. To do this, it relies on a database of more than 25,000 tables.

More than 80 percent of *Fortune* 500 companies use SAP, including Coke, Caterpillar, Exxon Mobile, Procter & Gamble, IBM, Marathon Oil, General Motors, Nike, and General Electric. To install SAP today, those companies might spend $100 million or more. Of this total cost, hardware may account for 20 to 25 percent, software 20 to 25 percent, and "human ware" (training, consulting, and implementation) 50 to 60 percent. Training, consulting, and implementation of SAP products has become a career for many in IT, and it is easy to see why—companies need technical people who understand the business and business processes and can make SAP work for them.

The prices mentioned above vary because getting SAP up and running in a company varies—in some cases the process can take years. One time-consuming process is answering the more than 8,000 configuration decisions mentioned earlier. To speed up the configuration process, SAP produces and sells **industry-specific platforms**. An industry-specific platform is like a suit before it is tailored; it is a preconfiguration platform that is appropriate for a particular industry, such as retail, manufacturing, or health care. All SAP implementations start with an SAP industry-specific platform and are further configured to a particular company with the configuration choices mentioned earlier. A second lengthy and expensive process is training employees of all levels how to use the system.

A common way to view SAP is as a collection of interconnected and interdependent modules, some of which are listed in Figure 7-20. A **module** is a distinct and logical grouping of processes. For example, SD, the Sales and Distribution module, is a collection of processes supervised by

FIGURE 7-20
SAP Modules

SAP Modules			
QM	Quality Management	PP*	Production Planning
FI	Financial Accounting	CO	Controlling
PM	Plant Maintenance	SD**	Sales and Distribution
PS	Project Systems	BI	Business Intelligence
HR	Human Resource	MM***	Materials Management

*PP includes operations and is the topic of Appendix A.
**SD includes sales processes, the topic of Chapter 9.
***MM includes procurement processes, the topic of Chapter 8.

the marketing department. These processes record customer data, sales data, and pricing data. Not every module is implemented in every installation of SAP. Companies that install SAP choose modules for their implementation and add modules when upgrading their system.

SAP Inputs and Outputs

An example SAP screen is shown in Figure 7-21. When the screen first loads, it is largely empty. On a screen like this, a purchasing agent, following CBI's procedure, enters a vendor number in the box numbered 1 and the material in box number 2. After clicking the check icon, marked as 3, SAP populates the screen as shown with data about the company, payment options, and pricing choices for the agent. The screen shown in Figure 7-21 is called the Create Purchase Order: Overview screen. When SAP is implemented and configured at a particular organization, this screen is made available only to approved purchasing agents in each department. Different roles in the organization give people access to different screens and different data; accountants would have access to their screens, warehouse people their screens, and so on. Although it is difficult to tell from this example, the purchasing agent does not have the option to permanently delete a purchase order once it has been saved. SAP is designed to preclude deleting saved records. This control makes auditing and supervision of the transactions more complete and reduces the risk of fraud. Other controls limit the data the salesperson can enter. For example, items sold must already be in inventory, ZIP codes must match cities, and delivery locations to a warehouse must be specified.

SAP Software

The most widely implemented version of SAP is called **R/3**. The R/3 program (where *R* means "real time") was the first truly integrated system that was able to support most of an organization's major operational processes. Built in the 1990s, the R/3 platform uses client-server

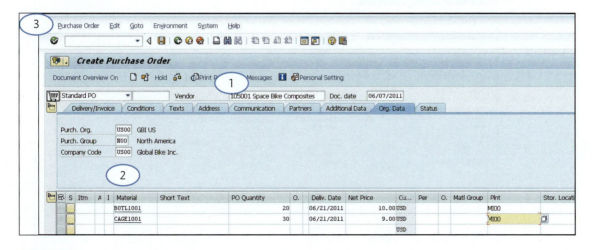

FIGURE 7-21

SAP Procurement Example Screen

architecture. It experienced runaway growth in the 1990s and was installed in 17,000 organizations. Ironically, this past success creates a problem today. SAP R/3 uses classic, native app, client-server architecture, rather than a browser-based approach that would be easier to use on a wide range of devices, such as smartphones and other thin clients.

Because of this large installed base, it has been difficult for SAP to update its core platform R/3. Asking its customers to change platforms is not reasonable unless the new system offers profound advantages. But SAP is offering customers a new system called S/4 Hana. S/4 Hana's two main advantages are an in-memory processor that runs much, much faster and the introduction of a new end user interface called Fiori. A Fiori screen is shown in Figure 7-22. It is obviously a much easier screen to use than the one shown in Figure 7-21, and can be tailored to each customer company. There are thousands of old R/3 screens that will need to eventually be replaced, a process that will take years.

SAP recognizes that the market for new large-scale ERP customers is rapidly shrinking as almost all large firms have adopted some form of ERP system. As a result, SAP has shifted its marketing and product focus from providing process efficiency for its customers to an emphasis on customer effectiveness goals. SAP believes that its customers can use company data stored in their ERP system to innovate and support competitive advantage. SAP wants its customers to view their ERP system as an ecosystem in which applications can grow fueled by ERP data. This represents a shift from selling efficiency to effectiveness. SAP expects many of these applications to be cloud based and offered by third parties.

Helping your future company, whether large or small, make wise use of ERP systems will be one of the challenges you will face during your business career. You will be hired initially into a department based on your experience and education, but all businesses want integrated processes. As a result, you will be asked to think about how your department's processes can be improved with the ERP system and how they can be integrated with other processes in the firm.

This will take some of the skills mentioned in Chapter 1: the ability to experiment, collaborate, think about systems, and use abstract reasoning. Employers seek new hires who have mastered some of the aspects of ERP systems. So take time to command the vocabulary in these next several chapters. Learn how the procurement and sales processes work in Chapters 8 and 9 and how an ERP system supports those processes. If you have access to SAP, accomplish the SAP exercises at the end of the next two chapters and, once complete, start over and deliberately make mistakes, try new things, and see how SAP acts. Learn beyond the book; later you'll be glad you did.

FIGURE 7-22

Fiori Screen of a Purchase Order

Source: ©2019. SAP SE or an affiliate company. All rights reserved. Used with permission of SAP SE or an SAP affiliate company.

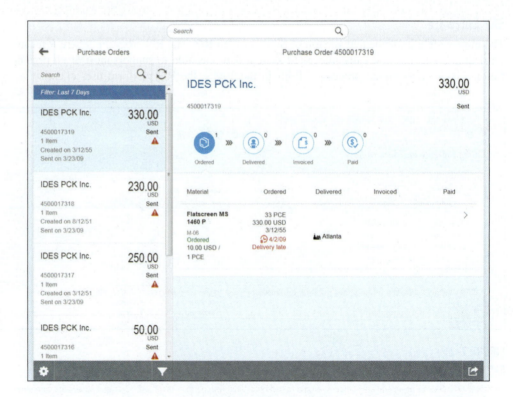

Ethics Guide

ERP Estimation

Todd Douglas Jones was the director of IT at a university when an ERP system was implemented. He was a big advocate of the ERP system because he had seen such systems work elsewhere and was convinced it would work well at the university.

Todd was charged with the task of determining the costs and benefits for the new system. After some preliminary research on the topic, he decided that cost should primarily be measured in the price of the product and the number of hours of training for the users of the system. Benefits will be determined by the reduction in operating costs.

In order to help the university's president and staff see that the benefits of purchasing and implementing an ERP solution outweighed the costs, Todd shaded the facts in order to make the ERP choice look more promising. Todd did a number of questionable things:

a. He researched 10 schools that had implemented a similar system. He could have used the cost and labor of all 10 schools as estimates for his school. However, in his opinion, three of the schools mismanaged the implementation, and he chose not to include those schools in his estimate, resulting in a lower cost estimate for his university.

b. He estimated that end-user training would be 750 hours, although he expected at least 1,000 hours would be needed. He planned to fund the other 250 hours from his IT training budget for next year.

c. To calculate cost savings, Todd used a different set of 10 schools than he used in item a. He believed that these 10 schools were closer in size to his own school and were more representative of his university, and they made the cost savings look better than the 10 other schools.

Six months after the very successful implementation, Todd was hailed as a visionary. The university is saving thousands of dollars a month. Seven months after the implementation, an auditor discovered the three questionable activities listed above.

You are Todd. Your boss knows what you did. You look into your own motivations and with a clear conscience you tell yourself: I did not tell a lie. I knew that the system would be a tremendous success, and if I did not help the boss come to see that, I would have let a great opportunity pass us by. I did what was best for the most people. I did not directly profit from this. If I were the boss, I would want my IT manager to help me reach the right conclusion, too. And look how it turned out—that alone shows I did the right thing.

DISCUSSION QUESTIONS

1. Was Todd ethical in his actions? Use both the categorical imperative (page 18) and utilitarianism (page 43) in your answer.
2. Of the actions taken by Todd, which one was the least ethical?
3. What would you do if you were Todd's boss? How does this change your management of Todd in the future?
4. What is the difference between inappropriate rationalization and justification?
5. How do you know when you are rationalizing inappropriately?
6. Do you agree with Todd's last statement? Does a good result always indicate a good process or a good decision?

Source: Orange Line Media/Shutterstock.

ACTIVE REVIEW

Use this Active Review to verify that you understand the material in the chapter. You can read the entire chapter and then perform the tasks in this review, or you can read the text material for just one question and perform the tasks in this review for that question before moving on to the next one.

Q7-1 What problem does an ERP system solve?

Explain how businesses used IS before ERP systems. Identify the problem solved by an enterprise system. Explain information silos. Describe the two key characteristics of ERP systems.

Q7-2 What are the elements of an ERP system?

Explain how businesses used computers for inventory purposes before the Internet. Explain the difference between MRP and MRPII. Explain how business and IS have coevolved. Name several of the business functions integrated by ERP. What is the difference between an ERP product and an implemented ERP system at a company? Describe configuration. Explain why a company might create a custom program for its ERP implementation. Describe the relationship between ERP systems and databases. Differentiate among the three types of ERP data. Explain the two ERP hardware issues. Describe how procedures can improve control of a process. Explain several ERP jobs. Describe inherent processes.

Q7-3 What are the benefits of an ERP system?

Explain why it is not accurate to say that ERP improves existing processes. Describe the advantages of the real-time data benefit of ERP systems. Explain how ERP benefits management. Describe the contents and purpose of a dashboard.

Q7-4 What are the challenges of implementing an ERP system?

Why is selecting the right ERP vendor an important decision? In a gap analysis, why should a company avoid creating a long list of things it would like the ERP system to do? Give several examples of the types of decisions a firm must make to configure an ERP system. Explain the general options the implementation team has for each decision. Explain the disadvantages of using custom software with ERP. What makes the transition, the cutover, from the old system to the new a challenge? Explain each of the people implementation challenges. Describe culture and why it is important to ERP implementation. What problems are unique to ERP upgrades?

Q7-5 What types of organizations use ERP?

Explain how the type of firm that uses ERP has changed over time. How can the size of the organization affect ERP success? What ERP needs are unique to large organizations? Describe the unique benefits of ERP systems for international firms.

Q7-6 Who are the major ERP vendors?

How do the Tier 1 ERP vendors differ? Name the three top vendors and explain how they are unique. Explain the common current and next-generation goals of the Tier 1 vendors. Identify the relative market share of each. Explain which ERP vendors serve small and midsized organizations and which serve large organizations.

Q7-7 What makes SAP different from other ERP products?

Describe SAP AG. Break down the expenses for implementing SAP. Define *module* and give examples of SAP modules. Explain how access to SAP screens can be controlled and how SAP limits or controls data inputs. How is SAP's S/4 Hana different from R/3? Describe how SAP is shifting its marketing and product focus.

KEY TERMS AND CONCEPTS

Bill of material (BOM)   170
Configuration   164
Culture   171
Customization   164
Dashboards   168
ERP systems   158
Gap analysis   166
Industry-specific platform   176
Inherent processes   166
Just in time (JIT)   163

Manufacturing resource planning
 (MRPII)   163
Master data   164
Material requirements planning
 (MRP)   163
Microsoft Dynamics   175
Module   176
Multiple instances   174
Organizational data   164
Process blueprints   166

R/3   177
SAP AG   176
Sarbanes-Oxley Act (SOX)   163
Self-efficacy   171
Single instance   174
Train the trainer   165
Transactional data   164
Version lock   173

USING YOUR KNOWLEDGE

7-1. *MyLab MIS* What would happen next fall if the freshman class is unexpectedly 20 percent larger than this year's class? Which campus organizations need to know that data early? Do you think your university has a way to share this data efficiently?

7-2. *MyLab MIS* An ERP can create a digital dashboard of important statistics and KPIs. What data would you like on your dashboard if you were the athletics director? Are they all measures of process objectives? What data would you like if you were the president of the university? Who else at the university could use a dashboard to do their work more effectively?

7-3. *MyLab MIS* What does this MIS class do differently than other classes? Maybe the assignments are a bit different, maybe the instructor does some things a little differently. What if a university instructional ERP system was invented that featured inherent processes that removed these unique elements? Would that make the school's teaching process more efficient and effective? How could you measure that improvement? Would it be worth it?

7-4. If your school adopts a new ERP-like system to improve class scheduling, procurement, and HR functions, which of the implementation people challenges in Figure 7-15 might be particularly hard in a university setting?

7-5. The athletics director buys sports equipment from a supplier with a well-implemented ERP. What advantages are there for your school to buy from a supplier with an ERP system? You might expect to see an advertising claim from that company like "We can

meet customer orders in 20 percent less time than the industry average." Create a list of two or three KPIs you would expect to hear from a supplier with an effective ERP system and two or three KPIs that an ERP system might not improve.

7-6. To have a successful ERP system, a sports equipment supplier will have made a variety of good configuration decisions. Give examples of what you think might be the company's item identifiers and order sizes. Also, who do you think approves customer credit and production capacity increases? What actions need to be taken if a customer modifies an order?

7-7. Assume that a sports equipment supplier chose SAP and is an equipment wholesaler that does not produce the equipment it sells to universities. As a wholesaler, which module in Figure 7-20 might the supplier not purchase from SAP?

7-8. Figure 7-4 shows the procurement process now used at the university and the objectives and KPIs used by the athletics department. If you worked as the purchasing agent for dining services, buying all the food served in campus dining halls, what would be the objectives and KPIs of your procurement process?

7-9. Investigate the free online classes offered by SAP. Go to *https://open.sap.com/courses*. Which class is the most interesting to you?

7-10. In the opening vignette, Megan and Heidi were facing cutover pressures. Based on the challenges listed in Figures 7-13 and 7-15, what are two things end users could do to help make the cutover activity less stressful?

COLLABORATION EXERCISE 7

Collaborate with a group of students to answer the following questions. The goal of this exercise is to examine a common business context: identifying data needed to improve a process. Your group of classmates is in charge of upgrading your university's Campus Visit process. Each year hundreds of prospective students and families come to campus and receive a tour. Your university wants to show off its high-tech capabilities and wants you to figure out how to make the visit process a high-tech demonstration. You are not fixing the tour for just one visit but for all the tours all year round.

As a team, accomplish the following steps.

Step 1: Identify the series of activities in your new Campus Visit process. With your team create a diagram that shows a series of activities you desire for the high-tech tours. Also be clear about the objectives and KPIs of the process.

Step 2: Specify data needed by each activity in the process. The data might not reside at the school; for example,

you may want visiting students to find current students who went to their high school by using Twitter or some other social media platform. The data may not yet be collected; for example, you might decide to ask visiting students their food preferences and reuse that data after the visit to send each student a gift card to an appropriate restaurant.

Step 3: Turn in a report on your proposed Campus Visit process. Include a diagram of the activities in the process as well as the objectives and KPIs for your process. For each activity in the process, specify the data you will need to execute that activity.

Our goal here is for you to see that important business processes, like the campus tour, require data from many sources. This data at your school might now reside in many information silos. An ERP-like system that would bring all the important data together would make creating your new process much easier.

CASE STUDY 7

U.S. Air Force ERP Bonfire

The U.S. Air Force operates a very large supply chain to support its flying operations. This logistics mission, composed of a workforce of more than 90,000 individuals, is managed by Materiel Command (AFMC). AFMC is responsible for the purchasing, tracking, and use of thousands of parts and millions of gallons of fuel at more than 150 installations worldwide. AFMC supports the Air Force, an organization with a yearly budget of about $165 billion with about 300,000 service members. This makes it about the size of General Motors or General Electric.

In 2003, Air Force leadership began to notice the marked improvement in logistics enjoyed by other large organizations when they adopted an ERP system. Two years later it launched the beginning of its own ERP implementation, a system grandly titled the Expeditionary Combat Support System (ECSS). The ECSS was to be an Oracle system designed to replace 240 outdated information systems used throughout the United States and overseas with a single ERP system. The proposed system would be about 30 times larger than any system ever built by the Department of Defense and 100 times larger than any in the Air Force. Not only would the supply chain become more efficient and better managed, the new ERP would help the Air Force comply with new regulations requiring federal agencies to produce auditable books by 2017.

Unfortunately the implementation of ECSS stumbled at nearly every step. The Air Force failed to specify achievable objectives for the system, justifying the system with simplistic statements about how many different computer systems would be integrated. Sadly, the number of information systems to be replaced grew from 240 initially to more than 900. Other self-inflected injuries

slowed progress. Air Force leaders did not execute a thorough gap analysis, too many leaders supervised the project, and no one seemed to specify the desired capabilities of the new ERP system. Finally, as the project lurched forward, far too much customization was built into the ERP system as Air Force managers insisted that the new ERP system needed to support existing processes rather than adopt the inherent processes offered by Oracle.

After numerous setbacks and several failed attempts to restart the program, in November 2012, the Air Force canceled the entire project after spending $1.03 billion. The Air Force concluded that the new system had provided no significant military capability.

Senate investigations revealed three main problem areas:

- *Cultural* resistance to change within the Air Force
- Lack of *leadership* to implement needed changes
- Inadequate mitigation of identified *risks* at the outset

Military culture makes changing processes difficult. Investigators found entrenched civil servants had a strong pride in how things are done, and military officers too quickly rotated between jobs. The AF had to change the way it purchased parts and how those parts flowed between bases in order to use the ERP system effectively, a disruptive change. They had to be willing to change their business processes, but no culture of business process improvement existed.

AF leadership failed. The leadership team had no prior experience with ERP systems, process change, or IT governance; they were in over their heads. As mentioned, the system was perhaps 100 times larger than any system the Air Force had successfully created. Couple that with six project managers and five assistant project managers over its lifespan, and it was clear that leadership had failed its responsibilities.

Many of the risk factors—cultural change, leadership, and project size and scope—were identified by AF leaders along the way, but these issues were never addressed. The culture did not change, the turnover in leadership never abated, and confronting other risk factors never happened. For example, one particular risk was identified early: project ownership. The risk was that no one or no office would accept responsibility long term. Unfortunately, all the positions on the project team were temporary positions, filled on a short-term basis. As a result, officials working on the project were motivated to achieve short-term goals so they could continue their careers elsewhere. Leadership had identified the risk but failed to address it.

While the Air Force had good reason to pull the plug on the project, the need for a system-wide ERP platform still exists. The Air Force has an antiquated and inefficient system of tracking its parts and inventories, and it will need to implement an ERP system at some point in the future.

Questions

7-11. What benefits was the Air Force seeking? Are they like those sought by CBI?

7-12. Are the challenges similar for the Air Force as with civilian ERP implementations? Which are unique to the military?

7-13. Figures 7-13 and 7-15 list decision-making challenges and people challenges. Which of these are evident in this case? List the top three challenges, and briefly explain what the Air Force should do differently next time.

7-14. Which activity in the implementation process was done well?

7-15. It's time to try again. The Air Force can't keep wasting money with its current inefficient legacy logistics system. You're about to brief top Air Force leaders. What three things would you tell them will be essential to avoid repeating a disastrous result?

CHAPTER RESOURCES

[1] "ERP101: The ERP Go To Guide," *ERPsoftware360*, accessed September 11, 2013, www.erpsoftware360.com/erp-101.htm.

[2] Bureau of Labor Statistics, "Computer and Information Technology Occupations," *United States Department of Labor,* accessed March 29, 2012, www.bls.gov/ooh/computer-and-information-technology/home.htm.

[3] C. Ndubisi Madu and K. Chu-hua, *ERP and Supply Chain Management* (Fairfield CT Inc., 2005), p. 20.

[4] "Blaming ERP," Andrew Osterland, *CFO Magazine*, January 1, 2000, www.cfo.com/article.cfm/2987370.

[5] "10 Biggest ERP Software Failures of 2011," *PCWorld,* accessed December 20, 2011, www.pcworld.com/article/246647/10_biggest_erp_software_failures_of_2011.html.

[6] Nick Castellina, "A Guide for Successful ERP Strategy in the Midmarket," *Aberdeen Group,* accessed September 11, 2013, http://public.dhe.ibm.com/common/ssi/ecm/en/sml12349usen/SML12349USEN.PDF.

MyLab MIS

Go to **MyLab MIS.com** for Auto-graded writing questions as well as the following Assisted-graded writing questions:

7-16. Hospitals also use ERP-like systems to consolidate data about patients for use in many processes. Describe what types of data would be maintained for each patient. Explain 3 processes this data would support and specify activities and goals for each process.

7-17. If a hospital expands an ERP-like system to include more processes and more data, which of the implementation people challenges in Figure 7-15 might be more difficult to overcome for the hospital than in a traditional business setting? Explain your answer.

Chapter 8

Supporting the Procurement Process with SAP

"Tell me, Wally, what was the hardest part of your job as a warehouse manager?" asks Jerry Green. The two are huddled around a small table in a warehouse at Chuck's Bikes, They are discussing Wally's pending retirement.

"It was probably dealing with people. Suppliers would only tell me half the story when my orders were going to be late, and our salespeople seem to think I should be able to read their minds," says Wally.

"Wally, you are one of a kind. We can't replace you, but we can be specific about the skills we need," Jerry replies. Jerry, the head of human resources at CBI, and Wally are tweaking a draft job description to hire Wally's replacement. "Wally, do you see anything we missed?"

"Nothing is missing. I just wish I was this person we are describing here. *Good with statistics, data, and ERP systems*. I was just good enough to get by, I hope we find someone who is this capable. I really did not act fast enough when the salespeople told us about those new e-bikes. They had to cancel sales for those bikes because I simply didn't get the little electrical motors here in time. Maybe if I had figured out that SAP thing faster it would have helped. But then again that thing is less user friendly than my cat."

"As you suggested, we added experience with SAP as a requirement to your job description."

"The only person who's not afraid of that system is that guy we just hired—Anthony. He seems to know stuff from his college classes about it. For the rest of us, that system is not easy to use. And I didn't realize when we put it in how much it would change my job."

"That's an understatement. I'm still getting used to it. Some days I wish I were the one retiring."

After they work on some details, Jerry thanks Wally for his help and sees him out. Later, Jerry and Wally's boss, Tim, discuss the job description.

"Wally was the best warehouse manager Chuck's Bikes has ever had," Tim says.

"But he's also one reason the new system doesn't run well," adds Jerry. "His skill set matches the job description from 15 years ago, but those skills are outdated now."

> **PSI BIG PICTURE**
>
> **PROCESS:** Procurement process: Order, Receive, and Pay
>
> **IS:** ERP can improve procurement

"Wally did mention that he thought this new description overemphasizes math and computer skills."

"I see his point. I think we should balance those with team skills and communication. The new position will require more communication with the other warehouses and departments here."

"I'll add those. But look at this description now. Doesn't it seem odd that someone we both think was terrific at one time couldn't win his own job today?"

"It does seem like a new day."

PREVIEW

> **MyLab MIS**
> - Using Your Knowledge Questions 8-1, 8-2, 8-3
> - Essay Questions 8-18, 8-19
> - Excel and Access Application Questions 8-1, 8-2

In this chapter, we look into the Procurement process that Wally supervised before and after the implementation of SAP. We are interested in how SAP made that process and other processes at his company better.

In the previous two chapters, we introduced processes and ERP systems. Here and in the next chapter, we show how the general ideas about processes and ERP systems can be applied to two common business processes. We will see how the benefits of ERP—consolidating the data and using inherent processes that integrate well—can improve the Procurement process. In Chapter 9, we examine the Sales process. As a business student, the better you understand how these fundamental processes work, the more valuable you will be.

We begin by considering how CBI accomplished procurement before implementing SAP. We then examine how SAP improved CBI's Procurement process. Although most of the chapter concerns the Procurement process, toward the end of the chapter we will broaden our discussion to other processes in CBI's supply chain. While the Procurement process can be improved with SAP, the positive impact on the group of procurement-related processes is even more significant.

Q8-1 ▶ What Are the Fundamentals of a Procurement Process?

Procurement is a vital process in a firm's supply chain. A **supply chain** is a network of people, organizations, resources, and processes that create and distribute a particular product from the delivery of raw materials at the supplier to final delivery to consumer. Supply chain is a common business major where students learn how to coordinate the flow of materials within and between organizations. Supply chain jobs include warehouse operations management, demand forecasting, logistics management, and material planning.

Within a supply chain, **procurement** is the process of obtaining goods and services such as raw materials, machine spare parts, and cafeteria services. Procurement is an operational process executed hundreds or thousands of times a day in a large organization. The three main procurement activities are Order, Receive, and Pay, as shown in Figure 8-1. These three activities are performed by actors in different departments and were briefly introduced in Chapter 7 with the example of procurement at a university.

Procurement is the most common organizational process. Every organization, from single employee startups to Walmart and from county to federal governments, relies on its Procurement process. For businesses that make products, procurement is a vital process as all the **raw material**, the basic material used in the manufacturing or primary production of goods, must first be procured. However, even firms that provide services depend on procurement. For example, hospitals need thousands of healthcare products, and universities need food, equipment, landscaping services, and mascots. Look around you. Every man-made thing you see passed through at least one procurement process, and that Camry driving down the street has parts that were procured by hundreds of suppliers, each with its own procurement process.

Even college students procure items: You order books and movies online, and you buy clothes and food. Everything you own you procured in some way. And, like procurement at an organization, your process has objectives—you do not want to buy inferior goods, and you do not want to waste time or money.

Many organizations have similar procurement objectives; the most common are saving time and money. According to some estimates, a well-managed procurement process can spend half as much as a poorly managed procurement process to acquire the same goods.[1] The state of Pennsylvania has saved $360 million a year by restructuring its procurement process; other states have saved 10 to 25 percent of their purchasing budgets.[2]

Other procurement effectiveness objectives include finding reliable, high-quality suppliers; maintaining good relationships with existing suppliers; and supporting other processes in the organization such as sales and operations. Procurement processes also seek to be efficient—to be less costly and to generate fewer failures, such as stockouts, errors, and products that need to be returned to suppliers.

In this chapter, we consider the portion of procurement that supports the inbound logistics process in the value chain. In this role, procurement obtains the raw material and semifinished goods needed for subsequent assembly in the production process of the operations activity in the value chain, as shown in Figure 8-2. Other value chain activities also develop and execute procurement processes to obtain things other than raw materials, such as legal services, machine parts, consulting, computer systems, facilities, and transportation services.

The activities in the Procurement process at CBI are shown in Figure 8-3. To better understand the activities in Figure 8-3, consider how CBI acquires tires for its bikes. The first activity is to find qualified suppliers who make tires. Once these firms have been identified as potential suppliers, CBI asks each supplier to specify the price it would charge for each type of tire and

FIGURE 8-1

Main Procurement Process Activities and Roles

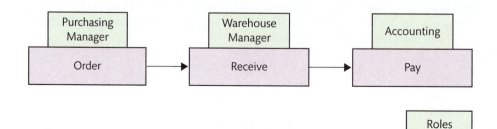

Primary Activity	Description	Process and Chapter
Inbound logistics	Receiving, storing, and disseminating inputs to products	Procurement, Chapter 8
Operations	Transforming inputs into final products	Production, Appendix A
Outbound logistics	Collecting, storing, and physically distributing products to buyers	
Sales and marketing	Inducing buyers to purchase products and providing the means for them to do so	Sales, Chapter 9
Customer service	Assisting customers' use of products and thus maintaining and enhancing the products' value	

FIGURE 8-2

Procurement Process within the Value Chain of CBI

order quantity. Using this price data, CBI creates a **purchase order (PO)**, a written document requesting delivery of a specified quantity of a product or service in return for payment. At CBI, the Purchase Order specifies a supplier, the tire part number, quantities of tires, and delivery dates. The tires are then received from the supplier in one of CBI's warehouses. Once the tires are received, CBI updates its Raw Materials Inventory database. Soon after, a bill arrives from the supplier and the supplier is paid. The procurement process is also called **procure-to-pay (P2P)** or the procure-to-pay cycle.

A final key aspect of the procurement process is the resource called inventory. CBI maintains two types of inventory, as shown in Figure 8-4. At the top of Figure 8-4, the Procurement process acquires raw materials, whereas the Production process, shown on the bottom, converts the raw materials into finished goods. **Raw materials inventory** stores components like bicycle tires and other goods procured from suppliers. These raw materials must be on hand for assembly operations to occur in the Production process. At CBI, raw materials inventory includes bike frames, wheels, and seats. **Finished goods inventory** is the completed products awaiting delivery to customers. At CBI, finished goods inventory is the assembled bikes and accessories.

The fundamentals of procurement are common to most organizations. To better understand the impact of SAP on procurement, we consider its use at CBI. We first examine how procurement worked before SAP was implemented, and then we will determine how SAP changed procurement processes at CBI. We make this before-and-after comparison to provide a clear discussion of types of procurement problems SAP can address. We don't want to give the impression that most firms are in the before stage, deciding whether the benefits

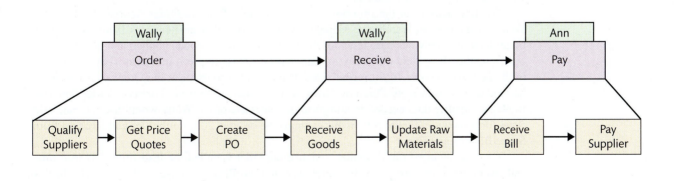

FIGURE 8-3

Main Procurement Process Activities, Subactivities, and Actors at CBI

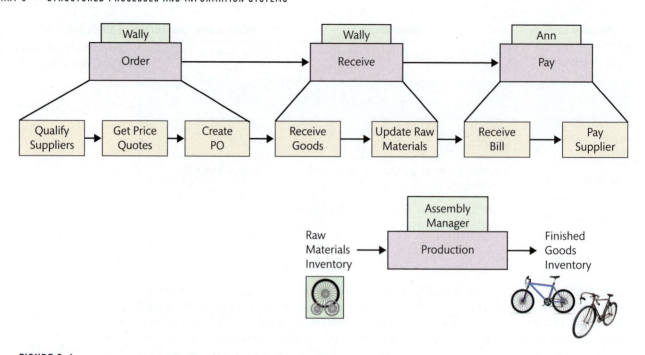

FIGURE 8-4

Main Procurement Process Activities, Subactivities, Production Process, and Inventories

outweigh the risks. Today, almost all large firms have implemented an ERP system, at least in part.

Q8-2 How Did the Procurement Process at CBI Work Before SAP?

Prior to the implementation of SAP at CBI, Wally was responsible for ordering and receiving raw materials. He issued orders when the raw materials inventory was low, stored parts when they arrived, kept track of where he put them, and planned and managed the people and equipment to accomplish those tasks. His objectives were to avoid running out of raw materials, to use reliable suppliers, and to stay within a budget. The KPIs for these objectives were number of stockouts, number of late deliveries, and price.

The Procurement process at CBI before SAP is shown in Figure 8-5. As shown, the process has six roles. Two of these, Warehouse Manager and Accountant, are performed by people; the other four are done by computers. As you will see, each of the computer roles uses its own database, creating four information silos.

The first activity in the process shown in Figure 8-5 is Pre-Order Actions. In this step, Wally, in his role as Warehouse Manager, would notice that an item was below its reorder point, look over previous purchases for the item to discover a good supplier, and determine his order quantity. He would often log into the Sales database to see if that item would be needed in the next few days to fulfill recent sales. If he decided to order at the Order decision node, he would start the Create Purchase Order activity and log into his Purchase Order database to obtain supplier data needed to complete the purchase order. Wally would use the purchase order form shown in Figure 8-6. In this example, he ordered 20 water bottles and 30 cages from Space Bike Composites.

The time required for a supplier to deliver an order is called the **lead time**. The lead time ends when the order arrives at the warehouse and the Receive Goods activity occurs. In this activity, a warehouse worker unpacks the box, counts the items, and updates the raw material inventory quantity in the Warehouse database. At the end of the day, Wally updates the Purchase Order database to reflect all the purchase orders that were received that day.

Several days later, an **invoice**, or itemized bill, is received from the supplier. The data on the invoice—the amount due and the purchase order number for that invoice—are entered

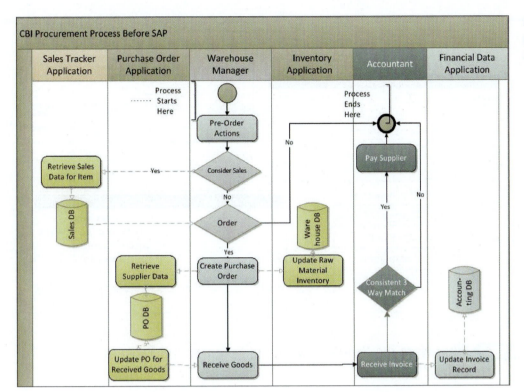

FIGURE 8-5

BPMN Diagram of Procurement
Process at CBI Before SAP

into the Accounting database. Before the accountants pay the bill, they make sure that the data on the invoice matches the data in the purchase order and the goods receipt an activity called a **three-way match**. Figure 8-7 shows a three-way match between the invoice, purchase order, and receipt for goods, with color coding for matching data. If the data in this three-way match are consistent, a payment is made and the payment data are posted to the Accounting database.

In the entire Procurement process at CBI, four databases are used—one in sales, two in the warehouse, and one in accounting. Each of these databases was constructed to serve the needs of different departments.

Because each department built its own information system, the inability of these systems to share data increasingly became a concern. These department information silos were not the only problem with CBI's procurement process, as we'll soon see.

FIGURE 8-6

Wally's Purchase Order
in Paper Form

FIGURE 8-7

Three-Way Match

Q8-3 ▸ What Were the Problems with the Procurement Process Before SAP?

The problems with the Procurement process before SAP were well known at CBI. They are listed in Figure 8-8. To be sure, there are many other problems with procurement, but these five are sufficient for our discussion.

Warehouse Problems

A key problem in the warehouse is that Wally was blind to sales price data. While Wally could see data on the bikes and accessories CBI sold the previous day, this data did not include price discounts; that data only existed in the sales information silo. He did not know if a sudden increase in sales of one bike was due to a deep price discount or whether the product was being bundled with something else that was selling well. The sudden increase might be due to these marketing campaigns, or it might be the first sign of a big spike in popularity for that bicycle. A big spike in e-bike demand was mentioned in the opening vignette. Wally did not have enough sales data to see that the spike in sales of e-bikes was the real deal; he mistakenly thought it was because the new bike was being sold at a very low price to the customer. As a result, Wally did not order enough raw materials to meet the sustained rise in customer orders for these e-bikes.

Accounting Problems

In accounting, Ann supervised the payment activities. Most of Ann's challenges occurred at the end of the Procurement process. One of her activities was to ensure that the three-way match was correct. When discrepancies occurred, the accounting department had to begin a costly and

FIGURE 8-8

Five Problems at CBI with Procurement Without SAP

Warehouse
• Warehouse manager doesn't have data on sales price discounts.

Accounting
• Three-way match discrepancies take time to correct.
• Accounting reports are not in real time.

Purchasing
• Purchasing agents not centralized; training and experience vary.
• Weak internal controls lead to limited scrutiny of purchases.

labor-intensive process that required several emails to the warehouse and the supplier to resolve. For example, if the warehouse miscounted or if the supplier shipped the wrong components, Ann would have to access various databases, compare results, and email suppliers to confirm the results of her inquiry.

The other accounting problem was that accounting reports always lagged; they were never up to the minute. Actually, they were never up to the day. This was a result of not sharing real-time accounting data throughout the organization. Instead, accounting reports were produced at the end of the month. It took the accountants several days to **roll up**, or compile and summarize, the accounting transactions into balance sheets and income statements. This was a problem because other firms that competed with CBI had begun to rely on ERP systems to produce real-time accounting reports. With more current data, managers at these other firms could notice problems sooner and respond to customers more quickly.

Purchasing Problems

CBI had no purchasing department, a fact that created numerous problems. First, the purchasing agents, like Wally, were scattered throughout the firm. As a result, they had diverse training, experience, and motivation, which in turn led to a variety of mistakes on the purchase orders. Further, they had little knowledge about what was happening in other parts of the organization. For example, CBI's repair shop had recently found several very good suppliers of bike parts that Wally in the warehouse would have used, too, but he was not aware of them. These suppliers would have granted CBI lower prices if both Wally and the repair shop combined their purchases. The old Procurement process at CBI required each of its purchasing agents to be meticulous record keepers. However, Wally and other purchasing agents sometimes forgot to transcribe data from the handwritten purchase order to the database, used wrong addresses for suppliers, or entered incorrect totals. Doing their primary jobs was their passion; the procurement paperwork was a much lower priority. Further, it was hard to train these dispersed purchasing agents because they were scattered throughout the organization and had great differences in training needs and expectations from their bosses.

A final problem with the old process was that the upper management at CBI was under pressure from the board of directors to exercise more control over financial processes. A lack of financial control was at the root of Enron and WorldCom's financial meltdowns, which led to new federal government financial requirements, such as the Sarbanes-Oxley Act. The Sarbanes-Oxley Act of 2002 imposed new regulations on how corporations govern themselves, requiring them to set higher standards for the control of their financial operations. Wally and his procurement colleagues could make costly mistakes, favor suppliers for the wrong reasons, or succumb to the temptation to procure items based on their own interests and not the firm's. By bringing all the purchasing to one office in the company, CBI could exercise much better oversight.

This improved oversight is an example of **internal control**. Internal controls systematically limit the actions and behaviors of employees, processes, and systems within the organization to safeguard assets and achieve objectives. These internal controls are an example of the control of activities first mentioned in Chapter 6. At CBI and elsewhere, ERP systems often dramatically improve internal controls.

To conclude, CBI, like many other companies, had evolved to the point where the problems of isolated processes and information silos could no longer be tolerated. CBI wanted a comprehensive and lasting solution to these problems and decided an ERP system was the most appropriate choice. Next we trace the steps taken by CBI to install its first ERP system.

Q8-4 ▶ How Does CBI Implement SAP?

The steps required for CBI to install an ERP system are called the Implementation process, briefly discussed in Chapter 7. While this process may have hundreds of activities, the most general are listed in Figure 8-9. The process begins with CBI examining and refocusing its strategy.

CBI began its Implementation process by using Porter's five forces model to determine the structure of its industry, as shown in Figure 8-10. CBI determined that the bike wholesale industry has strong rivalry and that customers have low switching costs. Because of low switching costs, a bike retailer could easily switch from one bike wholesaler to another.

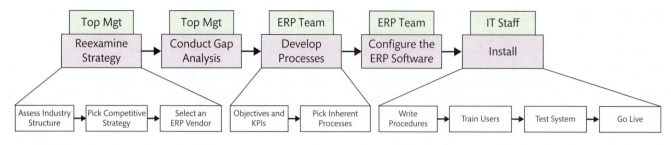

FIGURE 8-9

SAP Implementation Process at CBI

To survive and flourish in such an industry, CBI decided to pursue a competitive strategy that focused on high-end bikes and a differentiation strategy of responsiveness to retailers. This competitive strategy is shown in the bottom-right quadrant of Figure 8-11. The high-end bike industry segment includes very lightweight racing bikes and touring bikes with composite frames and sophisticated gear-shifting systems. Responsiveness means that orders from retailers are fulfilled rapidly; a retailer could order a wide range of products, and new hot-selling items would be available.

Next, CBI picked an ERP vendor. CBI top managers realized that most of their suppliers and customers used SAP and decided that SAP would be the best choice if they wanted to seamlessly fit into the supply chain of their business partners. Once SAP was selected, they spent several months on a gap analysis identifying where their process expectations and SAP capabilities differed. The most significant gap occurred in some promotions that CBI wanted to use with its newest customers. One example is that CBI wanted to give a price discount to new bike retailers who sold more than $250,000 worth of CBI products in the first 6 months.

Once the gap analysis was complete, CBI management crafted objectives and KPIs for each of CBI's processes. Wally participated on the team that created the objectives and KPIs for the Procurement process. This team decided on the two objectives shown in Figure 8-12.

Wally's team decided on one efficiency objective: reducing administrative time. It decided to measure this objective by tracking the average time spent to complete each of the most time-consuming activities: complete a PO, receive goods, and pay a supplier. On the effectiveness side, the team also decided on one objective: responsiveness to customers. To measure the responsiveness of procurement, the team picked average customer lead time; number of products to sell; and stockouts of new, hot-selling products such as the e-bike. The ultimate goal of the effectiveness objective was to have bikes ready to sell so CBI could quickly respond to shifting customer demand.

CBI then selected processes from the set of inherent processes that SAP had developed for companies in the material assembly industry and configured the software as described in

FIGURE 8-10

Determine Industry Structure with
Five Forces Model

	Cost	Differentiation
Industry-wide	Lowest cost across the industry	Better product/service across the industry
Focus	Lowest cost within an industry segment	Better product/service within an industry segment

(a) Competitive strategies

	Responsiveness	
High-End Bikes		**Competitive Strategy** High-end bikes Responsiveness to retailers

(b) Competitive strategy chosen by CBI of high-end bikes; customer responsiveness differentiation

Chapter 7. Then CBI wrote procedures for its employees on how to use SAP to execute these processes. For example, the procedure for one activity, Receive Goods, is shown in Figure 8-13. In this activity, Wally logs into SAP and inputs three data elements: the purchase order number, the item counts, and the location where these items will be stored in the warehouse. We will explain more about this activity in the next section. At this point, we want you to see that for each activity, CBI must write a procedure for its employees to use. In this example, the procedure has three simple steps. In Appendix 8A, you will accomplish many of the procedures for the activities in the procurement process at CBI.

Returning to our discussion of CBI, the company trained users, tested the system, and went live. This completed the Implementation process. Next we evaluate the impact of the new ERP system.

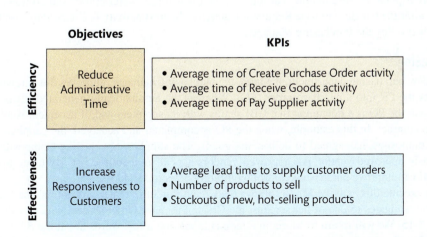

FIGURE 8-12
Objectives and KPIs for the New Procurement Process

FIGURE 8-13

Goods Receipt Procedure at CBI

Source: Copyright © SAP AG

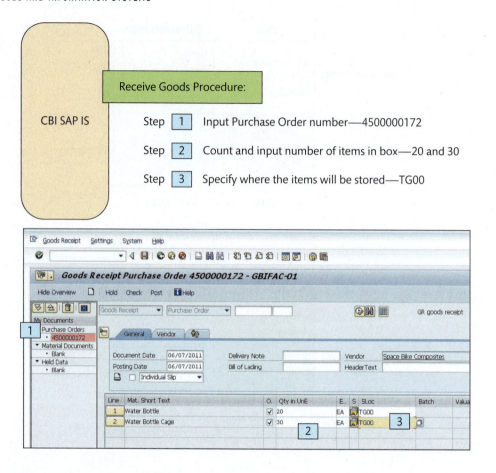

Q8-5 How Does the Procurement Process Work at CBI After SAP?

Let's fast-forward 2 years. CBI has now successfully completed the implementation process outlined above, and Wally, as first introduced in the opening vignette to this chapter, is approaching retirement. The SAP inherent Procurement process has replaced CBI's previous Procurement process. Although the new process has the same major activities—Order, Receive, and Pay—the Order activity has changed significantly.

Figure 8-14 shows a BPMN diagram of the new SAP-based Procurement process. The Order activity in the new Procurement process begins with the Create Purchase Requisition activity. A **purchase requisition (PR)** is an internal company document that issues a request for a purchase. This activity is automated at CBI; a computer is the actor, not a human. For example, a PR is automatically generated when the amount of raw material inventory goes below the reorder point. In the example that follows, the PR is for 20 water bottles and 30 water bottle cages. After the Create Purchase Requisition activity, the next activity is Create Purchase Order, which is done by the Purchasing Manager.

Purchasing

In the new purchasing department, if Maria, the purchasing manager, approves the purchase, she converts the PR into a purchase order (PO). Whereas the automatically-generated PR is a CBI document, the PO is a document that CBI shares with its suppliers and, if accepted, is a legally binding contract. In this example, when the PO is completed and accepted, the supplier, Space Bike Composites, has agreed to deliver the goods. The supplier, Space Bike Composites, is a previously approved vendor. All approved vendors appear on a **source list**. By using a source list, CBI can improve purchasing control by limiting potential vendors.

To execute this activity, Maria follows the Create Purchase Order procedure: She logs into SAP and navigates to one of her screens, the Create Purchase Order screen, which is shown in Figure 8-15. We will return to Maria in a moment, but first a few words about the SAP screens you will see here and in the next chapter. Tens of thousands of such screens exist in SAP R/3, so

FIGURE 8-14

Procurement Process at CBI
After SAP

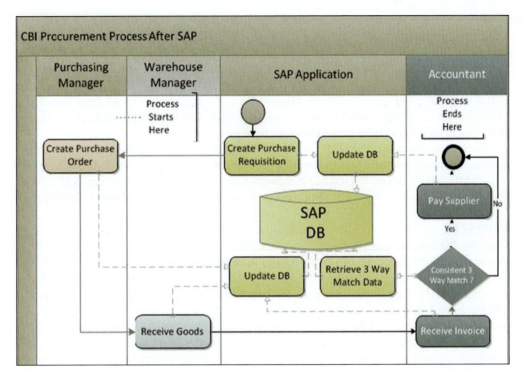

learning the particulars of a few of them is not of great value. Further, these screens are not easy to interpret, and you may be tempted to skip over them. We encourage you to spend some time studying them, learn the recurring features of an SAP screen, the data typed in by employees, and how the Procurement activity flows from one screen to the next. These skills will be useful for you no matter which ERP screens or processes you use. As mentioned in Chapter 7, S/4 Hana with Fiori screens will one day replace these R/3 screens. Until that happy day arrives, you will need to be capable with these difficult-to-interpret R/3 screens.

Every screen has a title. Here the Create Purchase Order title is shown on the top left. Immediately above the screen title is a drop-down menu (Purchase Order, Edit, GoTo, etc.) and a series of icons for navigating, saving, and getting help. Most of these menu items and icons are the same for almost all SAP screens. Below the title is a header section where Maria must input some data. We pick up her story again at this point.

FIGURE 8-15

Create Purchase Order Subactivity
Screen in SAP of Water Bottles and
Cages from Space Bike Composites

Source: ©2019. SAP SE or an affiliate
company. All rights reserved. Used with
permission of SAP SE or an SAP affiliate
company.

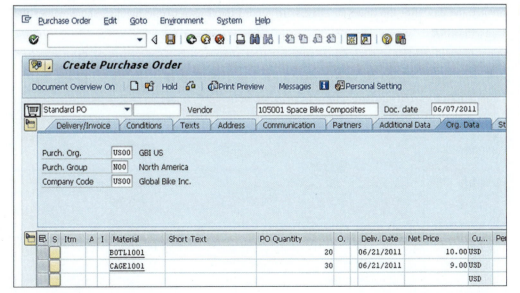

In this example, the header includes three identifying data items that Maria must input. The header's three boxes—Purch. Org., Purch. Group, and Company Code—are used to identify a particular CBI warehouse.[3] Other inputs would identify CBI's other divisions and warehouse locations. Below the header is the items section that allows Maria to specify for this PO the Material (bottles and cages), PO Quantity (20 and 30), Delivery Date (06/21/2018), Net Price (10.00 and 9.00), and Plant (MI00 for Miami). Each PO can have many of these item lines. Maria finishes the PO procedure by specifying Space Bike Composites (105001) as the vendor in the box in the center of the screen above the header section.

Once Maria saves this PO, SAP records the data in the database. At that point, Maria might move on to entering another PO or log out. After each PO is saved, SAP accomplishes several other tasks. SAP creates a unique PO number and displays this number on Maria's screen. SAP notifies Space Bike Composites via email, a Web service, or an electronic message of the PO details.

Warehouse

Once the PO is saved and transmitted to Space Bike Composites, the next activity at CBI is Receive Goods when the shipment arrives. The Receive Goods activity is shown in the Warehouse Manager swimlane in Figure 8-14; Wally plays the Warehouse Manager role. Let's move the clock forward 7 days from when the PO was sent. The bottles and cages have arrived in a box delivered to Wally's warehouse. On the outside of the box, Space Bike Composites has printed the PO number and the contents of the box. Wally notes the PO number, opens the box, and counts and inspects the contents. He then goes to his computer and executes the Receive Goods procedure. First, he logs into SAP and the Goods Receipt screen. This screen is shown in Figure 8-16, and it is the same screen shown earlier in Figure 8-13.

The title of this screen, near the top, is Goods Receipt Purchase Order. The header includes a Document Date of 06/07/2018, the Vendor (Space Bike Composites), and the purchase order Wally types in. He counts the quantity of bottles and cages in the box and discovers that 20 bottles and 30 cages were shipped. He moves to the item section and enters 20 and 30 for the quantities that arrived. For larger orders, several shipments may be required. Here, one PO has one goods receipt. His last input is TG00 as the storage location for these bottles and cages. He clicks Save and exits SAP.

Once Wally saves the goods receipt, SAP creates a document number for this particular goods receipt. In addition, it updates records in the Raw Material Inventory table in the database to reflect the addition of these new bottles and cages. Because CBI now owns the goods, SAP posts a debit to the raw materials inventory account. Finally, an entry is made in the PO record to show that a goods receipt occurred that corresponds to that PO.

Accounting

The next activity, Receive Invoice, occurs when Space Bike Composites sends CBI an invoice for the material. Ann, playing the role of Accountant as shown in Figure 8-14, receives the invoice the day after the material arrives. To record the arrival of the invoice, she executes the

FIGURE 8-16

Goods Receipt Subactivity Screen in SAP

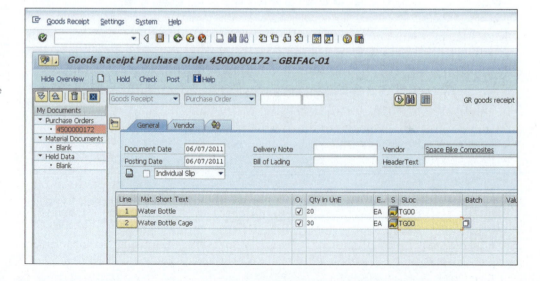

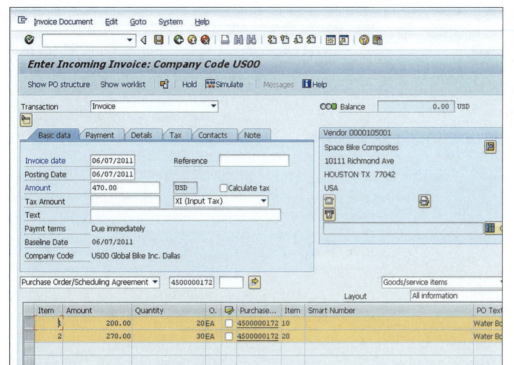

FIGURE 8-17
Receive Bill Subactivity Screen in SAP

Source: ©2019. SAP SE or an affiliate company. All rights reserved. Used with permission of SAP SE or an SAP affiliate company.

Enter Incoming Invoice procedure. She navigates to the Enter Incoming Invoice screen, shown in Figure 8-17. In the header section, she enters the date of the invoice (06/07/2018), the Amount ($470.00), and the Purchase Order number (4500000172). After she enters this data, the system finds other data about the PO and displays it on the screen. This data includes the vendor name and address and the two items that were ordered, each on its own row in the items section. When Ann saves this data, SAP records the invoice, displays a new document number for the invoice, and updates the accounting data records to reflect the arrival of the invoice.

The final activity, Pay Supplier, posts an outgoing payment to Space Bike Composites. This is the electronic equivalent of writing a check. Before she posts the payment, the process requires that Ann performs a three-way check. She compares the data on the PO, the goods receipt, and the invoice to make sure that all three agree on supplier name, PO number, items, quantities, and price. Ann opens the final SAP screen, Post Outgoing Payment, shown in Figure 8-18. Here she specifies the date of the payment (06/07/2018), the bank Account (100000), and the Amount (470.00). She also must specify an existing vendor in the Account box at the bottom of the screen (the vendor number for Space Bike Composites is 105001). She clicks the Process Open Items icon in the upper-left side of the screen and then saves the transaction. A document number is again created, and an accounting update is made to reflect the outgoing payment.

As you can see, each actor—Maria, Wally, and Ann—interacts with SAP using different screens, and CBI has created procedures for each activity.

The Benefits of SAP for the CBI Procurement Process

By using SAP, CBI enjoys two types of benefits, as shown in Figure 8-19 and 8-20. First, SAP solves each of CBI's five procurement problems discussed earlier, as shown in Figure 8-19. Second, SAP helps CBI achieve its two procurement objectives, also mentioned earlier, as shown in Figure 8-20.

The two key features of SAP first introduced in Chapter 7—a database that consolidates data for real-time sharing and inherent processes that integrate well—address each of CBI's five procurement problems. Consolidated, real-time data leads to fewer three-way match errors as input mistakes are reduced. The data are entered into only one database, and controls on inputs reduce input mistakes. For example, before SAP, Wally had to enter supplier data in both the PO database and the Inventory database. If he mistyped data in either system, that error would not be caught. Also, with real-time data, Ann in accounting has up-to-the minute accounting data

FIGURE 8-18
Pay Supplier Subactivity Screen in SAP

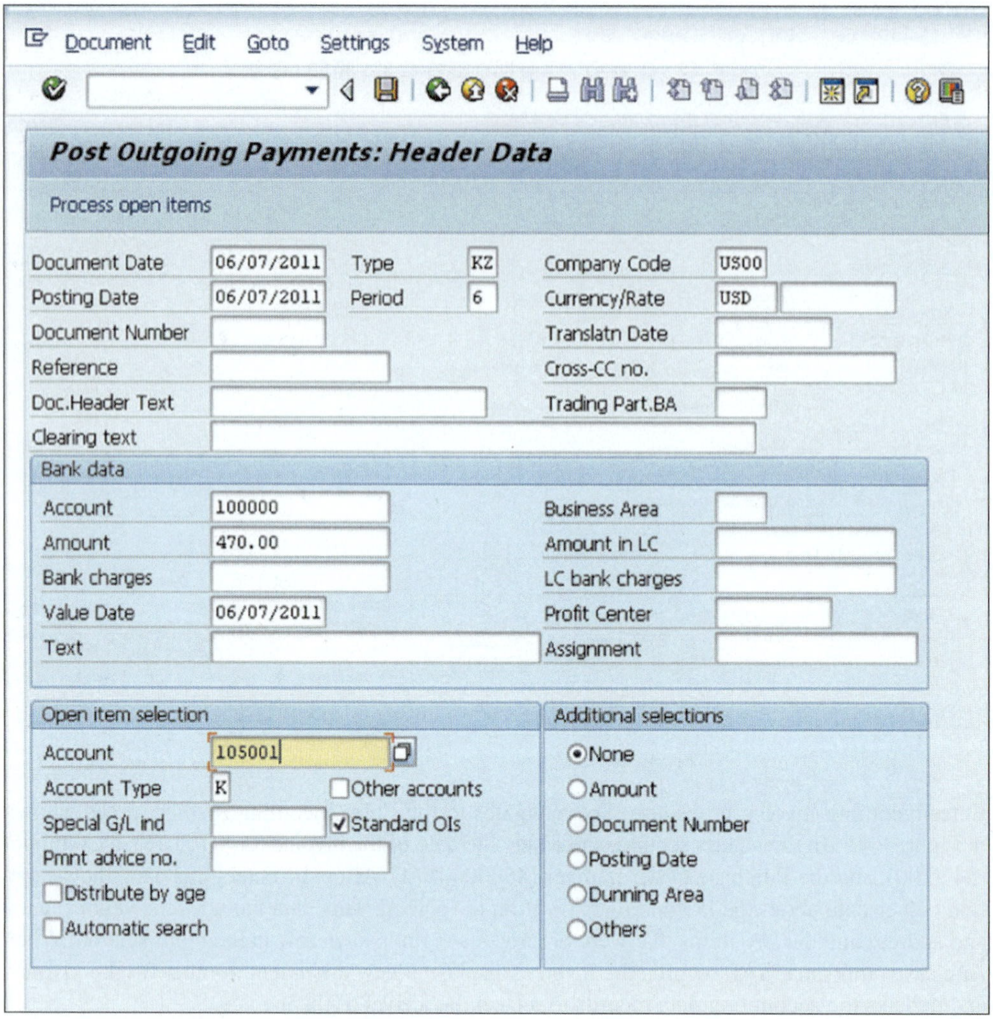

and does not have to wait until the end of the month to roll up the financial reports. Scrutiny of purchases is improved as real-time financial data is more informative to managers, who now request more financial reports and use them more frequently.

Also shown on Figure 8-19 is the impact of inherent processes that integrate on CBI's other two problems. Wally can see sales price discounts because the sales process and procurement

FIGURE 8-19
CBI Problems and SAP Solutions

Warehouse
- Warehouse manager doesn't have data on sales price discounts.
  Solution: Integrated inherent processes show warehouse price discounts.

Accounting
- Three-way match discrepancies take time to correct.
  Solution: Real-time data sharing limits errors.
- Accounting reports are not in real time.
  Solution: Real-time data sharing reduces roll-up time.

Purchasing
- Purchasing agents not centralized; training and experience vary.
  Solution: Integrated purchasing activity of ERP system.
- Weak internal controls lead to limited scrutiny of purchases.
  Solution: Real-time data sharing increases use of financial reports.

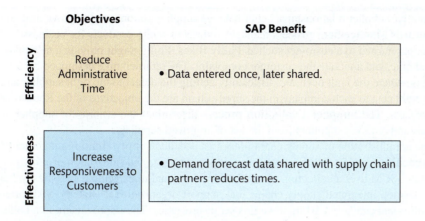

FIGURE 8-20
CBI Procurement Process Objectives and SAP Benefits

process are integrated. The lack of a centralized office is also overcome as SAP's inherent procurement process integrates all the procurement in CBI into one office, enabling more consistent training and motivation of purchasing agents.

As stated, CBI implemented SAP not only to overcome problems but also to pursue its particular strategy. This strategy and the Procurement process objectives that support it were listed earlier in Figure 8-12 and shown in Figure 8-20 with SAP's benefits.

With real-time data sharing, administrative time spent on procurement can be reduced. The Create PO, Receive Goods, and Pay Supplier activities are more efficient when data is entered once, then shared in later steps.

Consolidating data also helps CBI's Procurement process be more responsive to customer demands. CBI uses SAP to share sales and sales forecast data with its suppliers. As a result of having more data, forecasts by each supplier in the chain can be more accurate. The improved supply chain helps CBI reduce order lead times to its customers, increase product variety, and suffer fewer stockouts. Ideally, with this more responsive Procurement process, the e-bike fiasco will not recur.

Q8-6 ▶ How Can SAP Improve Supply Chain Processes at CBI?

To this point, for simplicity we have focused on one process: Procurement. However, no organization would implement an ERP system for just one process. The real payoff is evident only when a set of processes is examined. So we shift our focus from the single Procurement process and examine how SAP improves a collection of processes. We consider how SAP improves the set of processes related to procurement called Supply Chain processes.

Supply Chain Processes

Earlier we defined the supply chain as a network of people, organizations, resources, and processes that create and distribute a particular product from the delivery of raw materials at the supplier to final delivery to the consumer. Several processes in CBI's supply chain are listed in Figure 8-21. The **Supplier Relationship Management (SRM) process** automates, simplifies, and accelerates a variety of supply chain processes. Broader than the single Procurement process, SRM is a management process that helps companies reduce procurement costs, build

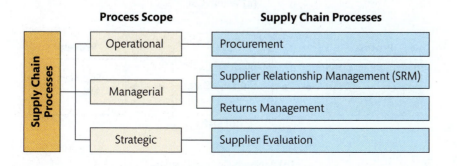

FIGURE 8-21
Sample of Supply Chain Processes

collaborative supplier relationships, better manage supplier options, and improve time to market. The **Returns Management process** manages returns of faulty products for businesses. At CBI, if a bike is returned to a customer such as Philly Bikes, Philly might provide a new bike, tag the returned bike, and annotate the customer complaint. The returned bike is shipped back to CBI to determine where the fault occurred. Efficiently getting the defect to the right supplier and charging the right cost to each company in the supply chain are the objectives of the Returns Management process. The **Supplier Evaluation process** determines the criteria for supplier selection and adds and removes suppliers from the list of approved suppliers.

The administration of supply chain processes is called **supply chain management (SCM)**. More specifically, SCM is the design, planning, execution, and integration of all supply chain processes.[5] SCM uses a collection of tools, techniques, and management activities to help businesses develop integrated supply chains that support organizational strategy. SAP offers SCM capabilities and can help CBI improve this set of processes. The improvement in a collection of processes can be attributed to data sharing between processes in real time and improving integration. Recall from Chapter 7 that the chief benefits of an ERP system are that it consolidates data in one place so the data can be shared and that it improves the integration of processes.

Improving Supply Chain Processes by Data Sharing

Supply chain processes are improved when processes share data. Figure 8-22 shows two examples where processes are improved by sharing data. **Data sharing** is the practice of distributing the same data to multiple processes. For example, data from the Returns Management process about defective bicycle parts should be shared with the Supplier Evaluation process to ensure that suppliers with high defect rates are removed from the list of approved suppliers.

Not only can data sharing help improve the supply processes at CBI, data sharing with CBI suppliers also can improve CBI's processes, as shown in the bottom of Figure 8-22. Before CBI and its suppliers shared data, CBI's raw material inventories were quite large. For example, CBI maintained a large quantity of tires and other raw materials to feed its production lines. In those days, procuring raw materials could take weeks, so running out of a raw material could shut down production for days. One reason that procurement was a slow process was that CBI's suppliers only produced raw materials when orders arrived. Today, CBI shares its sales data with its suppliers in real time. As a result, suppliers can anticipate CBI's orders and make raw materials in anticipation of orders, reducing lead time. By sharing more data and sharing this data rapidly, raw material inventory at CBI could shrink as suppliers become better informed about changes in CBI's sales, allowing them to be more responsive to CBI's orders. Inventories shrink and customer responsiveness improves as more and more data are shared.

FIGURE 8-22

Examples of Data Sharing Among Supply Chain Processes

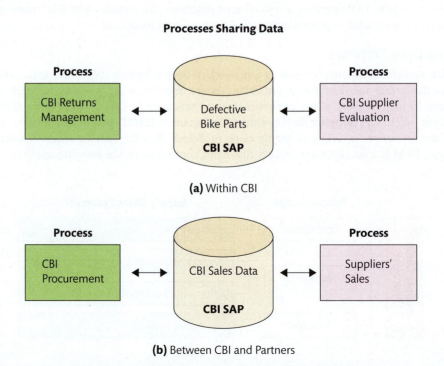

Processes Sharing Data

(a) Within CBI

(b) Between CBI and Partners

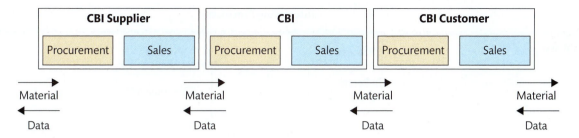

FIGURE 8-23
Procurement Processes, Material, and Data Flow in a Supply Chain

This link between CBI procurement and its supplier's sales process can be extended to all firms in a supply chain. Figure 8-23 shows a series of suppliers and the sales process of each supplier integrated with the procurement process of each customer. Also notice in this chain that as material moves from left to right, from suppliers to customers, data is shared from right to left. For example, the sales data to CBI's customers that are collected in the CBI ERP system are shared with CBI's suppliers, who share their sales data with their suppliers. In this way, the ERP system at CBI talks to the ERP systems of its suppliers. Overall, the more data moves, the more efficient the process becomes as less inventory is needed.

Sharing data not only reduces raw material inventory at CBI, it helps reduce the bullwhip effect in the supply chain. The **bullwhip effect** occurs when companies order more supplies than are needed due to a sudden change in demand. For example, if a spike in sales occurred in the old days, CBI would increase its orders to its suppliers. However, in the old days it might be several days after the initial spike for the order to arrive at the supplier. By this time, if sales keep up, CBI could be facing a critical shortage and its order would increase. This type of delay in ordering would also occur for CBI's supplier, the frame manufacturer. While the middle man, the frame maker, was waiting for parts from its supplier, CBI might increase its demand still more as it sees even stronger retailer demand and grow increasingly impatient. If the frame manufacturer was pressed by CBI and others it sells to, the frame manufacturer may raise its order to its suppliers, too. By the time upstream suppliers crank up supply for parts for the new bike frame, demand from customers may recede, leaving the frame manufacturer or CBI holding extra inventory that cannot be sold. This effect can be diminished by real-time sharing of sales order data among collaborating firms in the supply chain.

Improving Supply Chain Processes with Integration

The second characteristic of ERP, process integration, can improve the set of supply chain processes at CBI. Up to this point, we have not been specific about the notion of process integration. Integration, to be more precise, occurs when processes are mutually supportive; that is, when one process is done well, the objectives of another process are also achieved. You integrate your dating and studying processes when you study with your significant other. You integrate your shopping and your banking by doing both on one trip. Examples of integration among CBI supply processes are shown in Figure 8-24.

One example of process integration occurs at CBI between the Returns Management process and the Production process. One of the objectives of production is to reduce defective bikes. The Returns Management process collects data on defective returns from retailers of CBI bikes and accessories. The final step of the Returns Management process is to analyze how to improve the Production process to create fewer defects and thus fewer returns. When the Returns Management process is done well, an objective of the Production process is supported.

The benefits of SAP process integration can also be seen in CBI's supply chain. If retailer demand shifts suddenly, CBI and its suppliers can quickly shift production lines to meet the new demand. CBI and its suppliers rely on the SW Trucking Company to deliver raw materials. In the old days without process integration, SW Trucking had no excess capacity to support the extra shipping needed to move the bike parts from suppliers to CBI to retailers. SW Trucking was a bottleneck. A **bottleneck** occurs when a limited resource greatly reduces the output of an integrated series of activities or processes. SW Trucking decided to improve its Shipping process by keeping excess capacity available. As a result, the Production process at CBI was

FIGURE 8-24

Examples of Process Integration
Among Supply Chain Processes

Integrating Processes

Process

CBI Returns
Management

Improves →

Process

CBI Production

(a) Within CBI

Process

SWT Shipping

Improves →

Process

CBI Production

Process

SWT Shipping

Improves →

Process

CBI
Procurement

(b) Between CBI and Partners

improved because one of its objectives was being responsive to customer demand. Not only did this improve production at CBI, it also improved procurement because the additional shipping capacity meant that CBI's Procurement process could better achieve its objective of being more responsive to customers.

This discussion of the integration of processes also has an impact on how you approach your business education. Businesses want to hire individuals who not only understand the processes associated with their major but also understand how their processes interact with other processes in the business. As a result, if your academic major is sales and marketing, learn as much as you can about procurement and vice versa. If you are an accountant, learn about other processes. If you are studying operations and production, learn about supply chain processes, sales, and other processes. The drive to integrate processes rewards a jack-of-all trades and someone who is able to collaborate with coworkers from other processes.

Improving CBI Processes Beyond the Supply Chain

We have progressed from seeing how SAP can improve one procurement process to seeing how SAP can improve a set of processes in supply chain management. Many firms first use SAP to improve just one function of the business, such as the supply chain. Of course, there is one more level: multiple functions throughout a firm. Some firms like CBI use SAP to improve processes throughout the enterprise, as shown in Figure 8-25. The most common enterprise-wide approach is to use SAP in Accounting, Procurement, Production, and Sales.

FIGURE 8-25

Major Categories of Business
Process in Enterprise-wide Systems

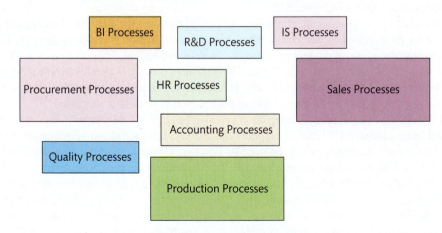

MIS InClass 8

The Bicycle Supply Game[6]

The purpose of this exercise is to better understand how supply chains are affected by information systems. In this game, the class will form supply chains and attempt to be the most efficient supplier.

The four links in each chain are retailer, distributor, wholesaler, and frame maker. The game is played for a period of 50 weeks. Each week each of the four teams in the supply chain orders bikes from its supplier and each team fulfills the orders from its customer. Pennies represent bicycles as the sole item in the supply chain, drinking cups are used to transport pennies between stations, and Post-it notes are used to make orders.

The objective is for each supplier in the chain to have the most efficient procurement process; that is, minimizing inventory and back orders.

Set up as many identical supply chains as needed, as shown in Figure 8-26. Notice that the supply chains are constructed with delays between the ordering of bicycles and their arrival. Each supplier is a team of one to three students. Each supplier records its orders, inventory, and backlog on a form like the one shown in Figure 8-27.

The retailers perform the same actions as the other groups, except their orders come from a stack of 3 × 5 cards that contain prerecorded orders that specify customer demand for the 50 weeks. Students are not to look at incoming orders, prerecorded orders, or supplies until that activity, and then they may look at only that week's order and supply.

Source: Peter Burian/Stock Connection Blue/Alamy.

Each week follows the same process with these five activities:

1. Receive inventory and advance the shipping delay.
2. Receive incoming orders and advance the order delay.
3. Fill the order.
4. Record inventory or backlog.
5. Place and record orders.

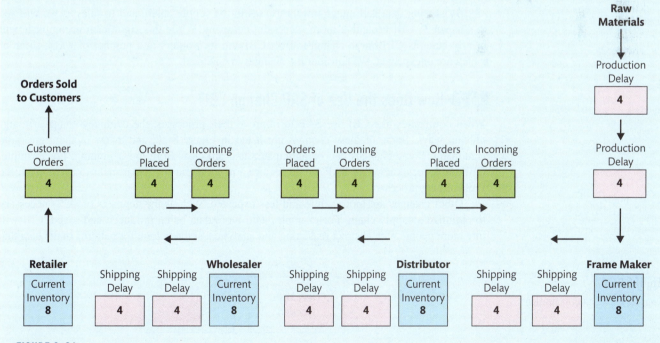

FIGURE 8-26
Supply Chain Game Setup

FIGURE 8-27

Supply Chain Game Record Form

Game Record

Position: _____   Team Member Names: _____

Week	Inventory	Backlog	Total Cost for Week
1.	4	0	$ 2.00
2.			
3.			
4.			
5.			

When the game is played, follow these activities as the instructor directs so that every team has accomplished each activity before any team moves on to the next. The game begins with a balanced condition in the supply chain; that is, every existing order is for four pennies, every delivery cup is filled with four pennies, and every supplier begins with eight pennies in inventory.

At the end of the game, each supplier calculates its overall costs.

Cost = .50 (inventory) + 1.00 (backlog)

A backlog occurs when an order is made that cannot be fulfilled. This backlog accumulates from week to week until it is paid off completely. The supplier with the lowest value is the winner.

At the end of the game, discuss the following:

1. Describe the order pattern from the customers to the retailer every week.
2. Why did the ordering pattern between the suppliers in the supply chain evolve the way it did?
3. What are the objectives and KPIs for each team's procurement process?
4. Where is the IS? What would more data allow? What data are most needed?
5. If you spent money on an IS to improve your procurement process, would it improve an activity, data flow, control, automation, or procedure?
6. Create a BPMN diagram of your team's weekly procurement process.

By sharing data and integrating processes in the supply chain, and in sales as we will see in Chapter 9, CBI became a more successful company. While this significant accomplishment clearly benefits CBI, these changes affect CBI and its workers in a number of ways, some of which are unexpected. We consider the changes to CBI next.

Q8-7 ▶ How Does the Use of SAP Change CBI?

When companies like CBI use SAP to improve their processes, the company changes in significant ways. Some of these changes are listed in Figure 8-28, and a few of them are quite significant. Some changes can be anticipated and are clear from the beginning. For example, CBI employees knew that SAP would require a new purchasing department to accomplish the Procurement process.

Other changes are more subtle and less expected, such as the new sets of skills necessary to optimize a supply chain. For example, with more data being produced and saved, CBI will hire more people with abstract reasoning and analytical skills to look for patterns in the data that

FIGURE 8-28

Impacts of SAP on Organizations

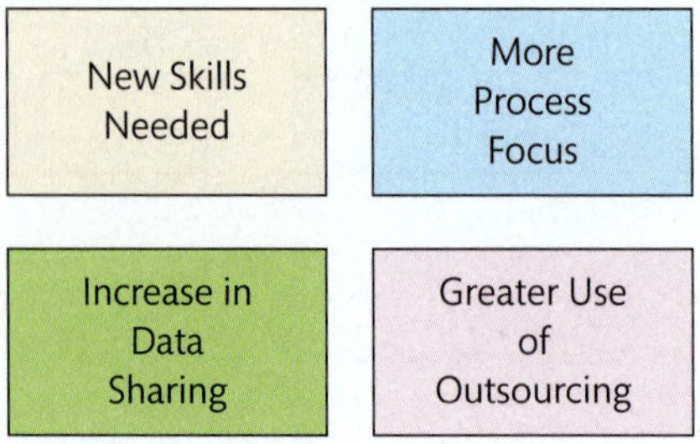

New Skills Needed

More Process Focus

Increase in Data Sharing

Greater Use of Outsourcing

will lead to new ways to improve processes. Wally recognized this hiring emphasis and his own limitations. Another change that can be expected is that CBI will become more process focused; that is, it will increasingly focus on the inputs and outputs of its processes to connect with partner firms. Pressures from suppliers and customers to share more and more data will lead CBI to be more open with company data than in the past. Finally, the adoption of SAP may lead CBI to use more outsourcing. Many firms outsource parts of their production to take advantage of other firms that can produce a subassembly or service cheaper than they can.

In the CBI warehouse, Wally has seen these organizational and technological changes in the past few years. One result is that CBI is doing less production of bicycles and is instead purchasing more finished bicycles. CBI believes this will help it reduce costs by shifting production to suppliers who can do the work at a lower cost. CBI is also lowering costs by using more full-truck shipments rather than partial loads. Because of these large shipments, storage of the finished goods is optimized across CBI's worldwide system and is not done locally. The inventory system dictates where each item is stored in the warehouse; in fact, at Wally's warehouse, the SAP system now dictates an item's location to the robot forklifts. Another recent change is that much more data are produced by the new system and shared with CBI customers and suppliers than was ever done in the past. This willingness to share inventory and pricing data gives CBI customers the opportunity to compare prices.

Finally, one more change is significant for Wally and the other warehouse managers at other locations. Before SAP, they were the ones who decided what was purchased. They would notice low raw material levels and then use their experience to decide if, when, and how many parts or bikes were ordered. Now, the system automatically tracks raw material inventory and generates purchase requisitions when reorder levels are reached.

Wally is fiction; you are not. Both of you face change, the only constant in business. Change is the only thing that will not change, and it will affect you throughout your career. Embrace it; become good at it. Becoming good at change requires practice, so practice by learning a new piece of software, making yourself learn with a new device, and volunteering for new jobs and responsibilities.

Q8-8 ▸ What New IS Will Affect the Procurement Process in 2028?

Before we wrap up this chapter, you should understand that SAP is just one IS that has an impact on procurement processes. Other IS, just now emerging, may have a significant impact on procurement over the next 10 years. The impact of these technologies will vary by company and industry, but these IS technologies, listed in Figure 8-29, will drive the next generation of Procurement process improvements.

AUGMENTED REALITY With **augmented reality (AR)**, computer data or graphics are overlaid onto the physical environment. An example of augmented reality is shown in Figure 8-30. AR was the magic behind Pokemon Go, demonstrating the potential of AR in the gaming industry. Its potential in the supply chain may be just as significant.

An early example of AR was Google Glass, which superimposes computer data on eyeglasses to augment what the user sees. While widespread use of AR glasses is still years away, they are already in use in some warehouses. Wearing these glasses, warehouse workers can see data about the location of a product they are looking to pick, the fastest route to the next item, the arrival date of the next shipment of a particular item, the weight of a container, and the best packing arrangement for a box. AR can also help a truck driver find the correct order

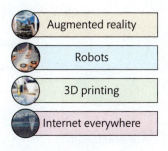

FIGURE 8-29
New IS That Will Impact Supply
Chain Processes by 2028

FIGURE 8-30
Augmented Reality

in a truck during the delivery activity. By augmenting reality with procurement data, companies can save time looking for items and make other procurement and supply chain activities more efficient.

ROBOTS Robots will have a very significant impact on the supply chain in the coming years. At warehouses, robotic forklifts move pallets of raw material inventory from inbound delivery trucks to storage locations and then to outbound trucks. Other, smaller robots are used in many Amazon fulfillment centers, shown in Figure 8-31. These robots move inventory during unloading, storage, and picking activities. The next robotic step is to use driverless trucks and drones to move inventory between warehouses and to consumers.

Clearly robots and drones are a key emerging technology for procurement and the supply chain. Their other uses are discussed in Extension 4, and using robots as automation is discussed in Chapter 6. Supply chains are an obvious application for robots as many of the tasks are structured activities on which robots excel.

3D PRINTING Three-dimensional (3D) printing technologies will also affect supply chain processes. With **3D printing**, also called *additive manufacturing*, objects are manufactured through the

FIGURE 8-31
Robots Moving Racks in Warehouse

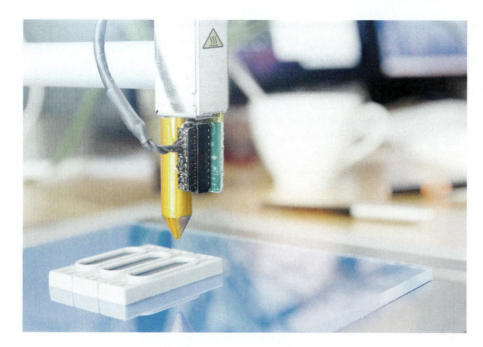

FIGURE 8-32
3D Printer

deposition of successive layers of material, as shown in Figure 8-32. Just as two-dimensional printers deposit ink in two dimensions, 3D printers deposit material in three dimensions, layering material in the third dimension as it dries. These devices will become more widely used in healthcare to print perfect-match dental work, joints, and hearing aids. In the supply chain domain, rather than rely on suppliers for all their raw materials, firms may choose to "print" some raw materials in house or use 3D printing to make manufacturing machine parts when they fail.

INTERNET EVERYWHERE Supply chains are more efficient when supplies and raw materials are connected to the Internet. Imagine the supply chain challenges with no Internet—no digital maps, no moving location data, and no network communication that provides updates and alerts of changes. These challenges exist in many parts of the world today—almost 4 billion people are not connected to the Internet. However, several major technology companies are expected to help remedy the lack of coverage in the next 10 years, and the impact on logistics will be significant. Google, Facebook, and SpaceX are making very large investments into technologies that will spread the Internet across the globe. From helium balloons, called Google Loons (shown in Figure 8-33)

FIGURE 8-33
Internet Everywhere with the Google Loon Project

to a low-orbit satellite network to high-altitude drones projects, this effort is lifting off drawing boards and will soon show viability. Supply chains and procurement processes will grow to all parts of the planet as worldwide Internet coverage becomes a reality.

These IS are affecting procurement now, and other, new IS technologies are on the way. As companies continue to pursue their strategies, new technologies will be absorbed into the companies' processes. SAP will choose to adapt its applications to some of these new technologies, but for the rest, organizations will need to develop their own patches of the new technology into SAP. The bottom line: SAP and other new IS can significantly improve the Procurement process, but they will need to work together.

Estimation Ethics

A **buy-in** occurs when a company agrees to produce a system or product for less money than it knows the project will require. An example at CBI would be if a consultant proposed $15,000 to provide some software code when good estimating techniques indicate it would take $35,000. The consultant will absorb the extra costs. The consultant would use the strategy if the contract opens up other business opportunities that are worth the $20,000 loss. Buy-ins always involve deceit. Most would agree that buying in and planning to stick the customer with the full cost later is wrong.

What about in-house projects? Do the ethics change if an in-house coding team is doing the work? If team members know there is only $15,000 in the budget, should they start the project if they believe that its true cost is $35,000? If they do start, at some point senior management will either have to admit a mistake and cancel the project with a loss or find the additional $20,000. Project sponsors can state all sorts of reasons for such buy-ins: for example, "I know the company needs this system. If management doesn't realize it and fund it appropriately, then we'll just force its hand."

Other buy-ins are more subtle. Suppose you are a project manager of an exciting new project that is possibly a career-maker for you. You are incredibly busy, working 6 days a week and long hours each day. Your team has developed an estimate of $50,000 for the project. A little voice in the back of your mind says that maybe not all costs for every aspect of the project are included in that estimate. You mean to follow up on that thought, but more pressing matters in your schedule take precedence. Soon you find yourself in front of management, presenting the $50,000 estimate. You probably should have found the time to investigate the estimate, but you didn't. Is there an ethical issue here?

Or suppose you approach a more senior manager with your dilemma. "I think there may be other costs, but I know that $50,000 is all we've got. What should I do?" Suppose the senior manager says something like "Well, let's go forward. You don't know of anything else, and we can always find more budget elsewhere if we have to." How do you respond?

DISCUSSION QUESTIONS

1. Assess the ethics of buying in on a cost-and-materials project from the perspective of both the categorical imperative (page 18) and utilitarianism (page 43).
2. Suppose you learn through the grapevine that your opponents in a competitive bid are buying in on a contract. Does this change your answer to question 1?
3. Suppose you are a project manager who is preparing a request for a proposal of a systems development project. What can you do to prevent buy-ins?
4. Assess the ethics of buying in on an in-house project from the perspective of the categorical imperative and utilitarianism. Are there circumstances that will change your ethical assessment? If so, state what they are and why they change your thinking.
5. Suppose you ask a senior manager for advice as described in the guide. Does the manager's response absolve you of ethical responsibility? Suppose you ask the manager and then do not follow her guidance. What problems could result?
6. Explain how you can buy in on schedule as well as costs.

ACTIVE REVIEW

Use this Active Review to verify that you understand the material in the chapter. You can read the entire chapter and then perform the tasks in this review, or you can read the text material for just one question and perform the tasks in this review for that question before moving on to the next one.

Q8-1 ▶ What are the fundamentals of a Procurement process?

Define *procurement* and explain its three main activities. Explain possible objectives for a procurement process. Name the value chain activity in which the Procurement process, as addressed in this chapter, operates. Explain the common subactivities in the Procurement process. Explain how raw material and finished goods inventories differ.

Q8-2 ▶ How did the Procurement process at CBI work before SAP?

Explain the Procurement process at CBI before SAP. Describe the Pre-Order Actions activity, particularly with regard to the Sales database. Describe which data are stored in the four different databases. Explain what an invoice is, who sends it, and what happens when it arrives. Describe which data must match for a three-way match.

Q8-3 ▶ What were the problems with the Procurement process before SAP?

Explain the problems at CBI in the warehouse, in accounting, and in purchasing prior to the implementation of SAP. Explain how not having price data affects the Procurement process. Describe why a company might want to restrict purchasing to just one department and not scatter it throughout the organization. Explain what the Sarbanes-Oxley Act requires and how ERP systems address that requirement.

Q8-4 ▶ How does CBI implement SAP?

Describe the activities in CBI's ERP Implementation process. Explain the competitive strategy chosen by CBI. Describe why CBI selected SAP as its ERP vendor. Describe a gap analysis. Explain the objectives and KPIs selected by CBI for the Procurement process.

Q8-5 ▶ How does the Procurement process work at CBI after SAP?

Describe the Procurement process after the implementation of SAP. Explain the difference between a purchase requisition and a purchase order. Explain the three roles in the new Procurement process and the name of the CBI employee who plays each role. Describe the main sections of an SAP screen. Explain the actions that automatically occur after a purchase order is saved and after a goods receipt is saved. Describe how the new Procurement process with SAP overcomes CBI procurement problems and achieves procurement objectives.

Q8-6 ▶ How can SAP improve supply chain processes at CBI?

Describe the processes of Supplier Relationship Management, Returns Management, and Supplier Evaluation. Define *supply chain management (SCM)* and explain the benefits of effective SCM. Explain how data sharing and process integration can improve the family of supply chain processes. Explain the bullwhip effect and bottlenecks and explain how they occur. Also describe how ERP systems can alleviate these situations. Explain how process integration impacts business education. What other domains of a business outside of supply and sales are common to enterprise-wide ERP implementations?

Q8-7 ▶ How does the use of SAP change CBI?

Explain some of the new skills needed at CBI after SAP is implemented. Describe why CBI is becoming more process-focused after implementing SAP. How does the adoption of SAP lead CBI to share more data with suppliers and customers? Explain the advantages of outsourcing. Explain some of the changes at CBI due to SAP. Explain how Wally accomplished his Procurement process before SAP. Describe some of the actions Wally took to support a smooth transition to SAP. Describe how Wally's job changed.

Q8-8 ▶ What new IS will affect the Procurement process in 2028?

Explain AR and how it might be used to support the procurement process. How will robots affect procurement? What is another name for 3D printing, and how can 3D printing improve procurement? Balloons are proposed to help deliver Internet everywhere; describe two other methods.

KEY TERMS AND CONCEPTS

3D printing   206
Augmented reality (AR)   205
Bottleneck   201
Bullwhip effect   201
Buy-in   209
Data sharing   200
Finished goods inventory   187
Internal control   191
Invoice   188

Lead time   188
Procure-to-pay (P2P)   187
Procurement   186
Purchase order (PO)   187
Purchase requisition (PR)   194
Raw material   186
Raw materials inventory   187
Returns Management process   200
Roll up   191

Source list   194
Supplier Evaluation process   200
Supplier Relationship Management (SRM) process   199
Supply chain   186
Supply chain management (SCM)   200
Three-way match   189

USING YOUR KNOWLEDGE

8-1. Two supply chain processes introduced in this chapter are Returns Management and Supplier Evaluation.
MyLab MIS
  a. Create a BPMN diagram of each of these processes.
  b. Specify efficiency and effectiveness objectives for each process and identify KPIs appropriate for CBI.
  c. What new information system technologies could be used by CBI to improve these processes, as specified by your KPIs in part b? Can AR, RFID, or 3D printing be used to improve these processes?

8-2. Which of the four nonroutine cognitive skills identified in Chapter 1 (i.e., abstract reasoning, systems thinking, collaboration, and experimentation) did you use to answer the previous question?
MyLab MIS

8-3. Which of the four skills in Exercise 8-2 would be most important for Wally's replacement?
MyLab MIS

8-4. The Procurement process in this chapter is an inbound logistics operational process. Name two other operational processes at CBI. Describe two inbound logistics managerial processes and two strategic processes.

8-5. If a warehouse worker opens a box and the contents are broken, those items will be returned to the supplier. Add this activity to the BPMN diagram of the Procurement process (Figure 8-14).

8-6. For the Procurement process after SAP implementation, what are the triggers for each activity to start? For example, what event or action (trigger) initiates the Create PO activity?

8-7. What kinds of errors can Wally, Maria, and Ann make that are not captured by SAP? One example is that Wally might count 20 bottles and 30 cages but mistakenly enter 20 cages and 30 bottles. Describe a particularly harmful mistake that each can make and how the process could be changed to prevent that error.

8-8. How does a pizza shop's Procurement process differ from CBI's? What do you believe is the corporate strategy of your favorite pizza franchise? What are the objectives and KPIs of its Procurement process to support this strategy?

8-9. 3D printing has many benefits for businesses. Suggest three products that CBI might print instead of procure with traditional means and three that your university might print. Which procurement objectives does 3D printing support?

8-10. Robots are already having a significant impact on the Procurement process. In which supply chain process will drones first be used, and why?

COLLABORATION EXERCISE 8

Collaborate with a group of students to answer the following questions. For this exercise, do not meet face to face. Your task will be easier if you coordinate your work with SharePoint, Office 365, Google Docs, or equivalent collaboration tools. (See Chapter 10 for a discussion of collaboration tools and processes.) Your answers should reflect the thinking of the entire group, not just that of one or two individuals.

In Chapter 7, a university implemented an SAP system. One of the changes is that most purchases must now be approved by a new university purchasing office. The athletics director is

concerned that centralizing the purchasing at the university will impose difficulties on the athletics department.

1. Figure 8-8 lists problems with the Procurement process at CBI. Which of these would apply to the university? Which would not? What are some procurement problems that might be unique to an athletics department?

2. Figure 8-12 lists objectives and KPIs that the managers at CBI determined for the Procurement process. What objectives and KPIs would you suggest for the

university? What objectives and KPIs would you expect the athletics director to suggest (do not use the objectives and KPIs from Chapter 7)?

3. Figure 8-28 lists the impacts of SAP on an organization. Which of these impacts would affect the athletics department?

4. For the four IS listed in Figure 8-29, explain how each could be used by the university; be specific about which process each will support.

5. Chapter 1 explained four nonroutine cognitive skills: abstract reasoning, systems thinking, collaboration, and experimentation. Explain how implementing the new Procurement process at CBI will require each of these skills from the members of the SAP implementation team.

ACTIVE CASE 8

SAP Procurement Tutorial

A tutorial for a Procurement process using SAP is located in the appendix to this chapter. That tutorial leads the student through a Procurement process that orders, receives, and pays for 20 bicycle water bottles and 30 water bottle cages. Once the tutorial is complete, students should answer the following questions.

Questions

8-11. Describe your first impressions of SAP.

8-12. What types of skills are necessary to use this system?

8-13. Create a screen capture of an SAP screen. Underneath the image, provide an answer to each of the following questions:
   a. In which of the activities does this screen occur?
   b. What is the name of this screen?
   c. What is the name of the screen that precedes it? What screen comes after it?
   d. Which actor accomplishes this activity?
   e. Describe an error that this actor may do on this screen that SAP will prevent.

8-14. Make an informal diagram of the four main actors: Supplier (Composite Bikes), Purchasing (Maria), Warehouse (Wally), and Accounting (Ann). Draw arrows that show

the data that flows among the actors during this process. Number the arrows and include on each arrow what data are included in the message.

8-15. Using the same four main actors as in question 8-14, this time show with the arrows how the material (the water bottles and cages) moves.

8-16. One concern of a business is fraud. One fraud technique is to create suppliers who are not suppliers but are coconspirators. The conspirator inside the business accepts invoices for nonexistent deliveries. For this fraud scheme to work, who at CBI has to take part? How can SAP processes decrease the chance of this type of fraud?

8-17. Select any of the main activities or subactivities in the Procurement process.
   a. What event triggers this activity?
   b. What activity follows this activity?
   c. For one data entry item for this activity, describe what would happen in the rest of the process if that entry was erroneous.
   d. For one data entry item for this activity, describe what limits (controls) you would put in place on the data to prevent the type of error described in item c.

CHAPTER RESOURCES

[1] "Supply Management Transformation," Axiom Capital Services, accessed September 27, 2013, http://axicap.com/general_and_administrative_services.html.

[2] David Yarkin, "Saving States the Sam's Club Way," *New York Times,* February 28, 2011, p. A23.

[3] Note that the figures refer to Global Bike Inc. (GBI), not CBI. CBI is used in this textbook; GBI is the dataset provided by SAP to all University Alliance members.

[5] Association for Operations Management, *APICS Dictionary*, 13th ed. (Chicago: 2011).

[6] See the "MIT Beer Game" in Chapter 3 of Peter Senge's *The Fifth Discipline: The Art and Practice of the Learning Organization,* rev. ed. (New York: Random House, 2006). Also see Wikipedia, "Beer Distribution Game," http://en.wikipedia.org/wiki/MIT_Beer_Game.

MyLab MIS

Go to **MyLab MIS.com** for Auto-graded writing questions as well as the following Assisted-graded writing questions:

8-18. Several new IS are described in the final question of the chapter. Pick two of these technologies and explain how each could improve university procurement. Specify objectives and KPI for the university Procurement process.

8-19. Your university has decided to improve not only procurement, but their collection of supply chain processes by data sharing and improving integration. Describe one other supply chain process and explain how your university can improve both that process and the procurement process by data sharing; then explain another supply chain process and explain how your university can improve both with improved integration.

APPENDIX 8—SAP PROCUREMENT TUTORIAL

This tutorial follows the Procurement process shown in Figure 8A-1. The top of Figure 8A-1 appears in Chapter 8 as Figure 8-3. This top figure shows the three main Procurement activities—Order, Receive, and Pay—and their subactivities (Qualify Suppliers, etc.). At the bottom of Figure 8A-1, we have added the six SAP screens that are completed during the Procurement process. This tutorial directs you through the procedures for completing each screen. These six screens were chosen to keep this tutorial simple. To further simplify the process, we begin with screen 3, Create Purchase Order. As shown in Figure 8A-1, you will play the roles of Wally and Ann.

FIGURE 8A-1

Procurement Process and SAP Screens

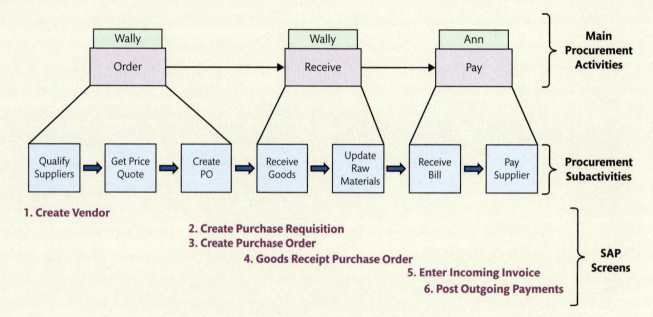

Main Procurement Activities

Procurement Subactivities

1. **Create Vendor**

2. **Create Purchase Requisition**
3. **Create Purchase Order**
4. **Goods Receipt Purchase Order**
5. **Enter Incoming Invoice**
6. **Post Outgoing Payments**

SAP Screens

Navigate to the SAP Welcome screen (Figure 8A-2).

FIGURE 8A-2

Welcome Screen

Source: Copyright © SAP AG.

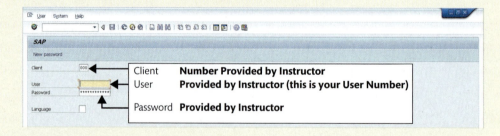

First Exercise

In this first exercise, we will purchase 20 water bottles and 30 water bottle cages from an existing vendor called Space Bike Composites. The bottles cost $10.00 and the cages $9.00. While our company in this tutorial is Global Bike Inc., our actors—Wally and Ann—and our Procurement process are from Chuck's Bikes.[1] The three digits at the end of your User ID will be used throughout this tutorial. For example, if your User ID is GBI-123, then 123 is your User Number. In this tutorial, 001 is used as the User Number.

[1] All tutorials in this text use SAP GBI Intro to ERP (SCC).

1. Create Vendor

Skipped—does not apply to this first exercise; it is introduced later.

2. Create Purchase Requisition

Skipped—does not apply to this first exercise; it is introduced later.

3. Create Purchase Order

A purchase order, when received and accepted by a vendor, creates a legally binding contract between two parties. As a warehouse manager like Wally, the first screen to complete is the Create Purchase Order Screen. From the SAP Easy Access screen (Figure 8A-3), navigate to the Create Purchase Order screen by selecting:

Logistics > Materials Management > Purchasing > Purchase Order > Create > Vendor/Supplying Plant Known

FIGURE 8A-3

SAP Easy Access Screen

Source: Copyright © SAP AG.

After selecting the desired vendor type, the Create Purchase Order screen will appear (Figure 8A-4).

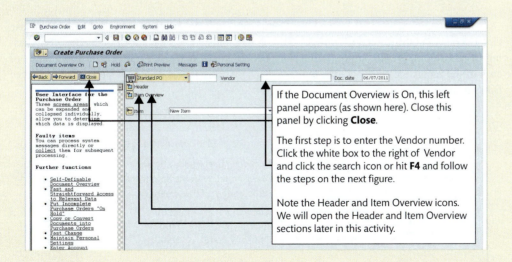

FIGURE 8A-4

Create Purchase Order Screen

Source: Copyright © SAP AG.

The next screen is the Vendor Search screen (Figure 8A-5). We need to find the vendor number for Space Bike Composites to complete the Purchase Order. While Wally might have this number memorized, we want to search in order to demonstrate how searching is done within SAP. Please note that where 001 appears in Figure 8A-5, you will type in your User Number.

FIGURE 8A-5

Vendor Search Screen

Source: Copyright © SAP AG.

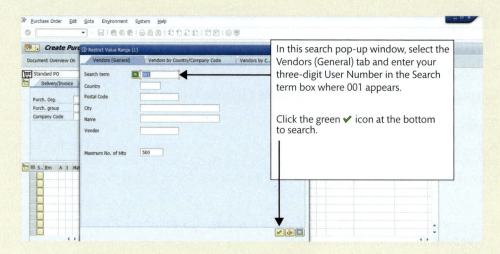

The Vendor List screen (Figure 8A-6) now loads.

FIGURE 8A-6

Vendor List Screen

Source: Copyright © SAP AG.

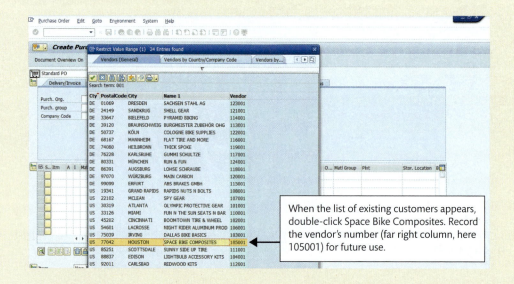

After double-clicking on Space Bike Composites, the system returns to the Create Purchase Order screen. On this screen (Figure 8A-7), you will enter three inputs for Purch. Org. (Purchasing Organization), Purch. Group (Purchasing Group), and Company Code. The last two digits of each of the inputs are zeros, not the letter "O." These three inputs specify which office at Global Bikes is making the order.

FIGURE 8A-7

Create Purchase Order with Vendor Screen

Source: Copyright © SAP AG.

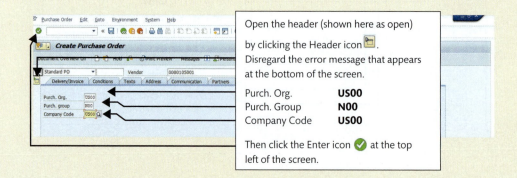

After clicking Enter, the system loads more data on the screen. Next, we will enter data about the Material (the water bottles and cages) we are purchasing (Figures 8A-8 through 8A-11).

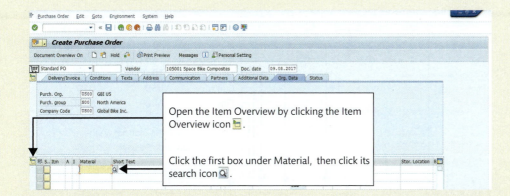

FIGURE 8A-8

Create Purchase Order with Item Overview On Screen

Source: Copyright © SAP AG.

This will load the Material Search screen (Figure 8A-9) that will help us find the Material numbers we need for the Purchase Order.

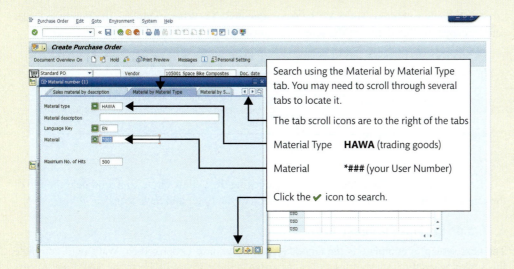

FIGURE 8A-9

Material Search Screen

Source: Copyright © SAP AG.

HAWA is the code used by SAP to identify trading goods. The next screen (Figure 8A-10) will show the trading goods you can order.

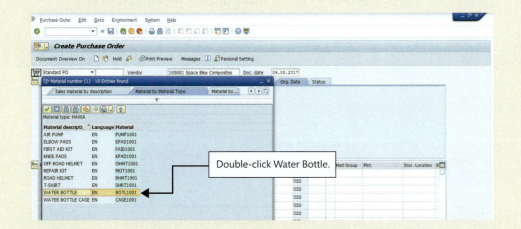

FIGURE 8A-10

Material List Screen

Source: Copyright © SAP AG.

When you return to the Create Purchase Order screen after selecting Water Bottle, complete the following inputs (as shown in Figure 8A-11). Then to complete the second line, you can search for *Water Bottle Cages* or simply type in *Cage1###* (where ### is your User Number). On the following screen (Figure 8A-11), you will enter a date (for the delivery date). To enter date data, use the convenient Search button located to the right of the date input box. Also note, the plant (Plnt on the screen) is MI00, not M100.

FIGURE 8A-11

Create Purchase Order with Material Screen

Source: Copyright © SAP AG.

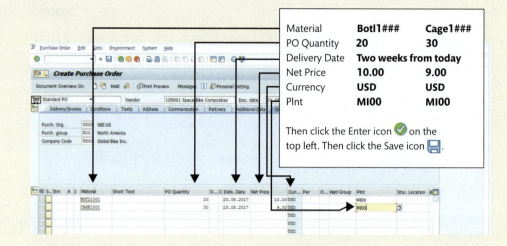

Click the Save button. The SAP database now updates. When complete, the Purchase Order screen reappears; the bottom of the screen is shown in Figure 8A-12.

FIGURE 8A-12

Purchase Order Number Screen

Source: Copyright © SAP AG.

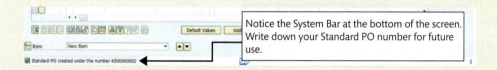

Return to the SAP Easy Access menu by clicking the yellow circle Exit icon near the top of the screen. This icon is located on the same ribbon as the Enter and Save icons.

4. Goods Receipt Purchase Order

The next screen to complete is the Goods Receipt Purchase Order screen. Wally will complete this screen when the water bottles and cages arrive at the warehouse. From the SAP Easy Access screen, navigate to the Goods Receipt Purchase Order screen by selecting:

> *Logistics > Materials Management > Inventory Management > Goods Movement > Goods Receipt > For Purchase Order > GR for Purchase Order (MIGO)*

A goods receipt is recognition that the goods ordered in the PO have arrived. Once the goods receipt has been created, inventory for these items is increased and accounts payable is increased (Figure 8A-13).

FIGURE 8A-13

Goods Receipt Screen

Source: Copyright © SAP AG.

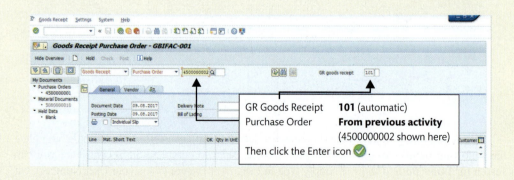

The system loads data from the PO, as shown in Figure 8A-14.

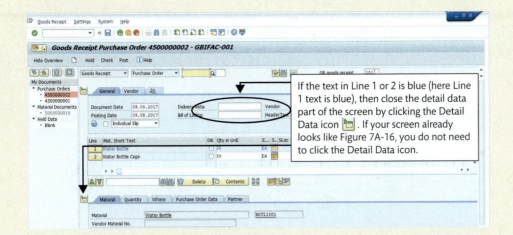

FIGURE 8A-14

Goods Receipt with Detail On Screen

Source: Copyright © SAP AG.

By closing the detail data part of the screen, your screen will look like Figure 8A-15. The reason the Water Bottle line was grayed out in 8A-14 is that the Detail Data section was open at the bottom of the screen. Notice in 8A-15 that the Detail Data section is closed.

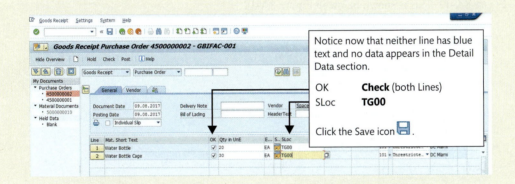

FIGURE 8A-15

Goods Receipt with Detail Off Screen

Source: Copyright © SAP AG.

By checking OK, you are verifying that 20 water bottles and 30 cages were delivered as shown in Figure 8A-15. If not, you would not check OK and would instead enter the quantity that did arrive. Figure 8A-15 shows this column header as O. instead of O.K., which can be shown by adjusting the column width. When the Goods Receipt screen is complete and saved, a Material document is created (Figure 8A-16).

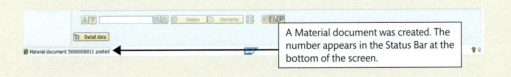

FIGURE 8A-16

Goods Receipt Material Document Screen

Source: Copyright © SAP AG.

Return to the SAP Easy Access menu by clicking the Exit icon.

5. Enter Incoming Invoice

An accountant, like Ann, would complete the final two screens in this tutorial: Enter Incoming Invoice and Post Outgoing Payments. From the SAP Easy Access screen, navigate to the Enter Incoming Invoice screen by selecting:

Logistics > Materials Management > Logistics Invoice Verification > Document Entry > Enter Invoice

Shortly after the goods arrived, the vendor has sent us a bill for $470.00 for the bottles and cages, and here we record this bill in our system (Figure 8A-17). Note, in Figure 8A-17 that the Tax Amount is entered via a drop-down box, which is the rightmost input box for Tax Amount.

FIGURE 8A-17

Enter Incoming Invoice Screen

Source: Copyright © SAP AG.

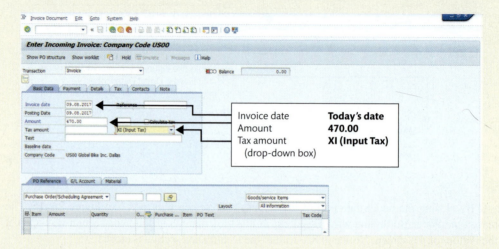

We also enter our PO number, which was generated earlier in this process at the bottom of Figure 8A-12. This is shown below in Figure 8A-18.

FIGURE 8A-18

Enter Incoming Invoice with PO Number Screen

Source: Copyright © SAP AG.

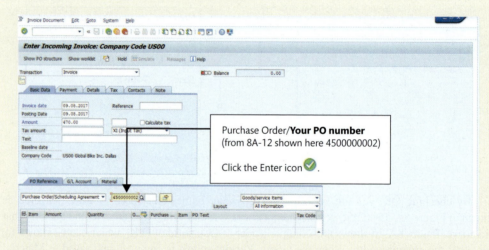

The system loads vendor data and displays the updated Enter Incoming Invoice screen (Figure 8A-19).

FIGURE 8A-19

Enter Incoming Invoice Final Screen

Source: Copyright © SAP AG.

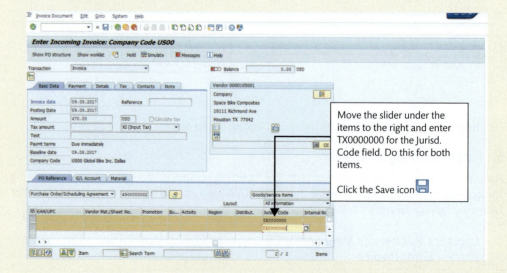

If there are no errors, a document number is produced on the bottom of the next screen (Figure 8A-20).

FIGURE 8A-20

Enter Incoming Invoice Document Number Screen

Source: Copyright © SAP AG.

Return to the SAP Easy Access menu by clicking the Exit icon.

6. Post Outgoing Payments

The final screen gets completed when you or Ann pays the vendor. This payment may be made immediately upon receipt of the invoice or shortly thereafter. From the SAP Easy Access screen, navigate to the Post Outgoing Payments screen by selecting:

Accounting > Financial Accounting > Accounts Payable > Document Entry > Outgoing Payment > Post

In this activity, we record our payment to the vendor for $470.00 (Figure 8A-21). A journal entry is made to decrease accounts payable.

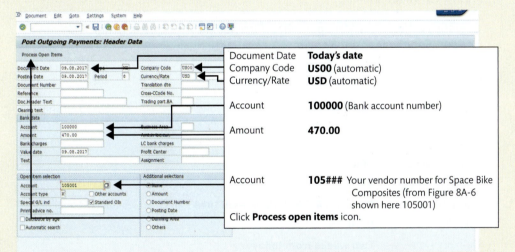

FIGURE 8A-21

Post Outgoing Payments Screen

Source: Copyright © SAP AG.

If you have to search for your vendor number in the bottom Account text box, select the Vendors (General) tab in the search pop-up window and use your three-digit User Number as the search term. Once you click on Process open items, the Post Outgoing Payments Process open items screen appears (Figure 8A-22).

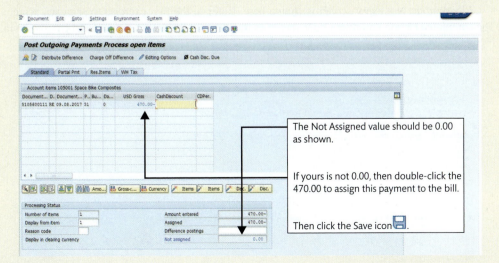

FIGURE 8A-22

Post Outgoing Payments Final Screen

Source: Copyright © SAP AG.

The SAP database is again updated and the Post Payment Document Number screen (Figure 8A-23) appears.

FIGURE 8A-23

Post Outgoing Payments Document Number Screen

Source: Copyright © SAP AG.

☑ Document 1500000001 was posted in company code US00   ◄—   *Again the system creates a unique document number at the bottom.*

Record the document number that once again appears on the Status bar. Return to the SAP Easy Access screen by clicking the Exit icon. This will generate a pop-up window that is misleading. There is no data to be lost at this point, so click Yes.

You have finished the first exercise.

You Try It 1

Purchase the following three materials from a different vendor—Rapids Nuts N Bolts:

5	Air Pumps	$14.00 each
10	Elbow Pads	$37.50 each
15	First Aid Kits	$20.00 each

Request delivery in 2 weeks. Use Miami for the plant. The total amount is $745.00.

3. Create Purchase Order

Logistics > Materials Management > Purchasing > Purchase Order > Create > Vendor/Supplying Plant Known

Data needed:

Vendor	**108###** (Your Rapids Nuts N Bolts vendor number based on your User Number)
Purch. Org.	**US00**
Purch. Group	**N00**
Company Code	**US00**
Material	**PUMP1###, EPAD1###, FAID1###** (These are Trading Goods)
Quantity	**5, 10, 15**
Delivery Date	**Two weeks from today**
Net Price	**14.00, 37.50, 20.00**
Currency	**USD**
Plnt	**MI00**

Please note: Not every screen is shown here. Refer to the first exercise to see each screen. The completed Create Purchase Order screen as it appears at the *end* of Figure 8A-11 is shown in Figure 8A-24.

FIGURE 8A-24

Completed Create Purchase Order

Source: Copyright © SAP AG.

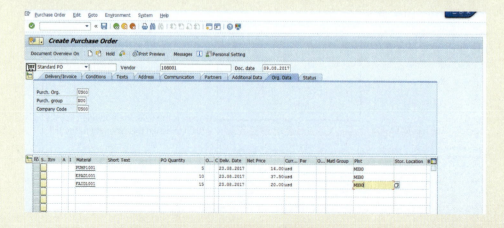

Click the Enter, then the Save icon. Record the PO number at the bottom of the screen. Return to the SAP Easy Access menu by clicking the Exit icon.

4. Goods Receipt Purchase Order

Logistics > Materials Management > Inventory Management > Goods Movement > Goods Receipt > For Purchase Order > GR for Purchase Order (MIGO)

Data needed:

Gr Goods Receipt	**101**
Purchase Order	**From previous screen** (4500000019 shown here)
Click on Enter	
OK	**Three check marks**
SLoc	**TG00** (Trading Goods)

The completed Goods Receipt Purchase Order screen is shown in Figure 8A-25.

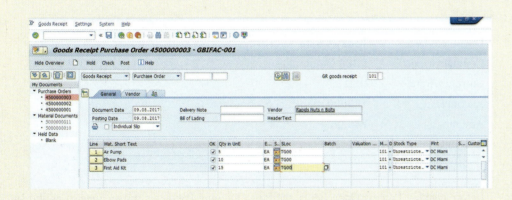

FIGURE 8A-25
Goods Receipt Final Screen
Source: Copyright © SAP AG.

Click the Save icon. Return to the SAP Easy Access menu by clicking the Exit icon.

5. Enter Incoming Invoice

Logistics > Materials Management > Logistics Invoice Verification > Document Entry > Enter Invoice

Data needed:

Invoice Date	**Today's date**
Amount	**745.00**
Tax Amount	**XI (Input Tax)**
Purchase Order	**Your PO number** (4500000003 shown here)

Once these four items have been entered and the Enter icon has been clicked, the Enter Incoming Invoice screen will appear, as shown in Figure 8A-26. Then pull the slider under the items to the right and enter TX0000000 for Jurisd. Code. Then click on Save. If done correctly, the Balance box in the upper right-hand corner should indicate 0.00.

FIGURE 8A-26

Enter Incoming Invoice Final Screen

Source: Copyright © SAP AG.

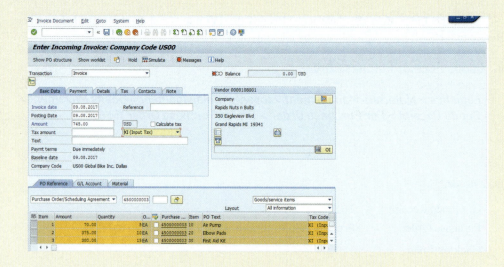

Return to the SAP Easy Access menu by clicking the Exit icon.

6. Post Outgoing Payments

Accounting > Financial Accounting > Accounts Payable > Document Entry > Outgoing Payment > Post

Data needed:

Document Date	**Today's date**
Company Code	**US00** (automatic)
Currency/Rate	**USD** (automatic)
Account	**100000** (Bank account number)
Amount	**745.00**
Account	**108###** (Rapids Nuts N Bolts vendor number based on your User Number)

Before clicking Process Open Items, the Post Outgoing Payments screen appears as shown in Figure 8A-27:

FIGURE 8A-27

Post Outgoing Payments Header Screen

Source: Copyright © SAP AG.

After clicking Process Open Items, the screen appears as shown in Figure 8A-28. If correct, the Not Assigned at the bottom-right corner will be 0.00. Then click the Save icon.

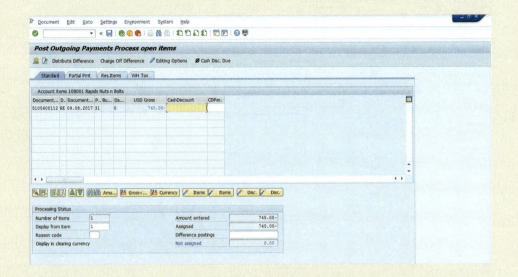

FIGURE 8A-28

Post Outgoing Payments Final Screen

Source: Copyright © SAP AG.

You are now finished with You Try It 1. Return to the SAP Easy Access menu by clicking the Exit icon.

You Try It 2

In screen 1 of You Try It 2, you will create a new vendor called Bike Parts. Then, in screen 2, Creating a Purchase Requisition, you will request a price quote for 10 repair kits. In screen 3, you will once again create a PO; however, this time the PO is based on the purchase requisition you created in screen 2.

1. Create Vendor

Logistics > Materials Management > Purchasing > Master Data > Vendor > Central > Create

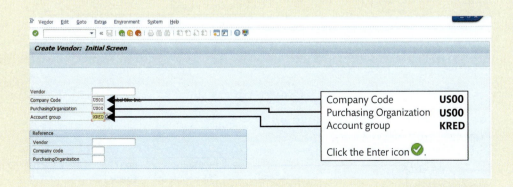

FIGURE 8A-29

Create Vendor Initial Screen

Source: Copyright © SAP AG.

FIGURE 8A-30

Create Vendor Address Screen

Source: Copyright © SAP AG.

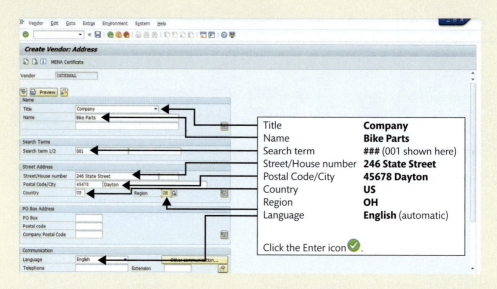

FIGURE 8A-31

Create Vendor Tax Screen

Source: Copyright © SAP AG.

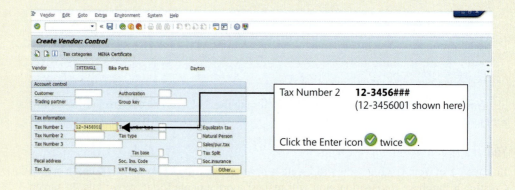

FIGURE 8A-32

Create Vendor Accounting Screen

Source: Copyright © SAP AG.

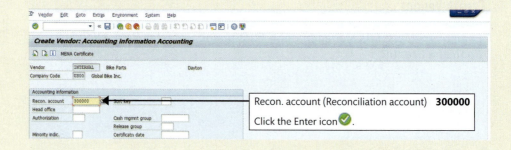

FIGURE 8A-33

Create Vendor Payment Screen

Source: Copyright © SAP AG.

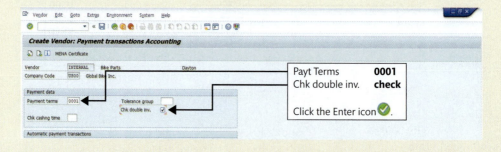

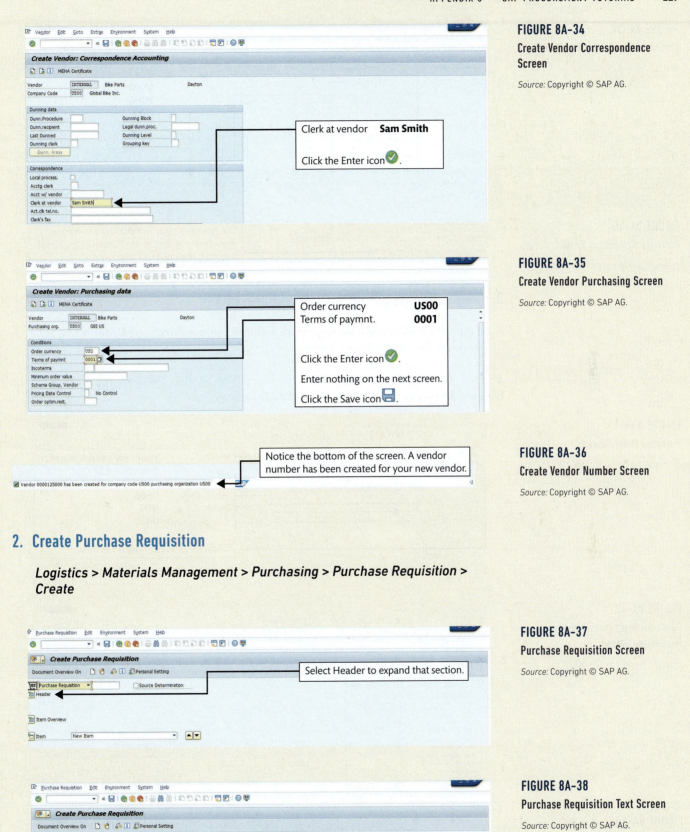

FIGURE 8A-34
Create Vendor Correspondence Screen
Source: Copyright © SAP AG.

FIGURE 8A-35
Create Vendor Purchasing Screen
Source: Copyright © SAP AG.

FIGURE 8A-36
Create Vendor Number Screen
Source: Copyright © SAP AG.

2. Create Purchase Requisition

Logistics > Materials Management > Purchasing > Purchase Requisition > Create

FIGURE 8A-37
Purchase Requisition Screen
Source: Copyright © SAP AG.

FIGURE 8A-38
Purchase Requisition Text Screen
Source: Copyright © SAP AG.

FIGURE 8A-39

Purchase Requisition Item Screen

Source: Copyright © SAP AG.

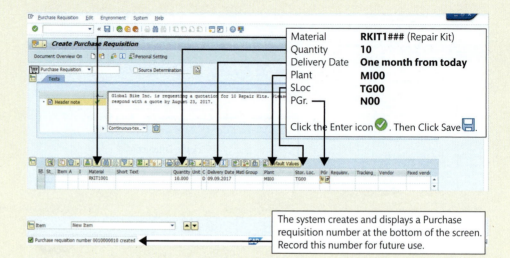

		RKIT1### (Repair Kit)
Material	**RKIT1###** (Repair Kit)	
Quantity	**10**	
Delivery Date	**One month from today**	
Plant	**MI00**	
SLoc	**TG00**	
PGr.	**N00**	

Click the Enter icon ✅. Then Click Save 💾.

FIGURE 8A-40

Purchase Requisition Number Screen

Source: Copyright © SAP AG.

The system creates and displays a Purchase requisition number at the bottom of the screen. Record this number for future use.

3. Create Purchase Order (now from Requisition)

Logistics > Materials Management > Purchasing > Purchase Order > Create > Vendor/Supplying Plant Known

Screen 3 was completed in the first exercise and in You Try It 1. This time you are creating the PO from the purchase requisition you created in screen 2.

FIGURE 8A-41

Purchase Order Screen

Source: Copyright © SAP AG.

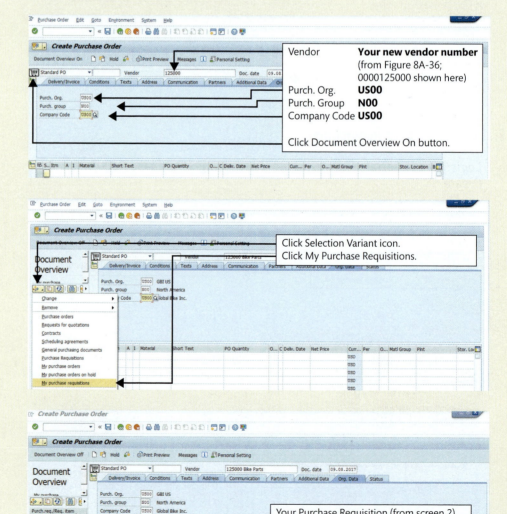

Vendor	**Your new vendor number** (from Figure 8A-36; 0000125000 shown here)
Purch. Org.	**US00**
Purch. Group	**N00**
Company Code	**US00**

Click Document Overview On button.

FIGURE 8A-42

Purchase Order from Purchase Requisition Screen

Source: Copyright © SAP AG.

Click Selection Variant icon.
Click My Purchase Requisitions.

FIGURE 8A-43

Purchase Order from Purchase Requisition Selection Screen

Source: Copyright © SAP AG.

Your Purchase Requisition (from screen 2) should be displayed (10000010 shown here).

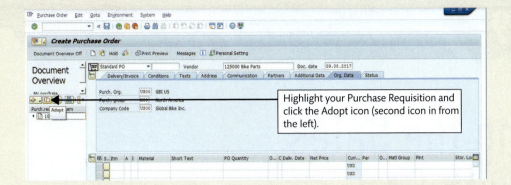

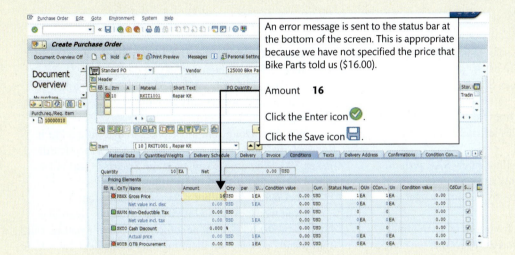

You have finished You Try It 2.

Chapter 9

Supporting the Sales Process with SAP

"Our best client! And we lost the sale!" Sue, CBI's top salesperson, is having one of *those* days.

"Nothing you could have done, Sue. You can't sell bikes that we don't have."

"But, Doug, why, why, why does this keep happening? Don't they know we're losing sales left and right? And now Heartland, our biggest customer!"

"I guess this won't happen with the new SAP system. It will give us up-to-the-minute inventory figures."

"I hope CBI is still in business by the time we get the system."

Sue later hears the full story from Ann in accounting.

"Ann, when I looked at my screen, I saw that we had 55 of the new e-bikes they wanted, and I only needed 50 for the sale."

"Yeah, it did show that. But what it didn't show is that Doug had sold 10 of them earlier that day."

"So, when I thought we had 55, which is what the computer showed, we actually had 45?"

"Right."

"But, Ann, Doug sold those bikes to that little outfit in Kansas City. Those guys make three orders a year. Heartland makes 300. Why are we selling to the Smurfs? Couldn't we cancel their order instead of Heartland's?"

"That makes sense, but we've never done that."

"Even worse, Ann, and it kills me to say it, Heartland didn't want the bikes until next month. Couldn't we order the frames and parts and put them together in the next 2 weeks or so? We've done that before to save sales."

"Wouldn't work. Space Bike Composites is our only supplier of that frame, and they were completely sold out."

"Why wasn't the sales department told?"

"We thought another supplier was going to come through with the frame, but that was a dead end."

Sue is now really frustrated. "We've got to find a way to keep the sales reps in the loop. We're going to lose Heartland if I have to cancel more orders."

"I agree, but how? There are hundreds of items we sell and hundreds of suppliers, and the suppliers have suppliers. Would sales reps read hundreds of emails about possible problems?"

"Fine. That doesn't do anything about Heartland, though . . . or my commission check."

Q9-1. What are the fundamentals of a Sales process?

Q9-2. How did the Sales process at CBI work before SAP?

Q9-3. What were the problems with the Sales process before SAP?

Q9-4. How does CBI implement SAP?

Q9-5. How does the Sales process work at CBI after SAP?

Q9-6. How can SAP improve CRM processes at CBI?

Q9-7. How does e-commerce improve processes in an industry?

Q9-8. What new IS will affect the Sales process in 2028?

PSI BIG PICTURE

PROCESS: Sales process: Sell, Ship, and Pay

IS: ERP can improve sales

PREVIEW

In this chapter, we examine sales—more specifically, the Sales process at Chuck's Bikes Inc. before and after the implementation of SAP. To accomplish this, we will examine the same questions we used in Chapter 8 when we discussed the Procurement process. It is not a coincidence that our approach here is the same as in Chapter 8. One of the most valuable aspects of a process perspective is that its lessons are reusable—once its lessons are learned, many of those lessons can be applied to other business processes.

We begin by examining the Sales process at CBI before SAP and learning how SAP ultimately improved it. We conclude the chapter by considering other processes that involve customers and how SAP and IS can be used to improve them. As with the procurement discussion, it is easy to get lost in the details. Keep in mind that sales is the most vital process in a business, and the ERP system plays a key role.

MyLab MIS

- Using Your Knowledge Questions 9-1, 9-2, 9-3
- Essay Questions 9-16, 9-17
- Excel and Access Application Questions 9-1, 9-2

Q9-1 ▶ What Are the Fundamentals of a Sales Process?

Sales is the lifeblood of every business. Look at the book in front of you. If it's printed, the printing company had to buy ink, glue, paper, printing machines, office space, advertising, and computers to run the operation. If you are reading on an electronic device, someone sold the hardware maker the software, components, and all the items that fit inside the device. The Sales process is so common it is almost always taken for granted, so take a moment and count the number of sales you've been a part of today or this week. Did you ever think of the Sales process behind any of them?

The Sales process is part of marketing. According to the American Marketing Association, **marketing** is the activity, set of institutions, and processes for creating, communicating, delivering, and exchanging offerings that have value for customers, clients, partners, and society at large. Within marketing, **customer relationship management (CRM)** is the management of

FIGURE 9-1

Marketing and Supply Chain Components

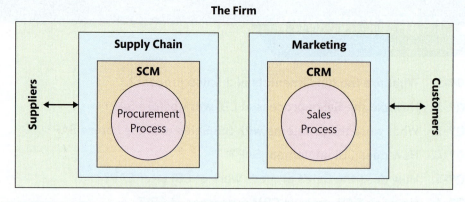

Supply Chain	Broad Academic Area In Business—Resources, People, Relationships, Processes, and Data	Marketing
Supply Chain Management (SCM)	Management of Processes, Data	Customer Relationship Management (CRM)
Procurement Process	Exemplar Process for Chapter	Sales Process

customer-facing customer facing processes and data such as the Sales process. As shown in Figure 9-1, the relationship of the Sales process, CRM, and marketing is similar to the relationship of the Procurement process, SCM, and supply chain discussed in Chapter 8.

To explain how ERP can help CBI sales we first consider the fundamental elements of any sale. The business definition of a **sale** is an exchange of goods or services for money. More precisely, a sale is revenue from delivery of merchandise or a service where payment may be made in cash or other compensation. The Sales process is an operational process with three main activities—Sell, Ship, and Payment—as shown in Figure 9-2.

The sales activities—Sell, Ship, and Payment—are accomplished by actors playing the roles of Sales Agent, Warehouse Manager, and Accountant. The Sales process is located within the value chain in the sales and marketing primary activity shown in Figure 9-3.

For a business, sales is one of the most important processes. Without sales, no one gets paid and buildings go dark. Although sales is a complex and difficult process, it is also governed by one simple overriding principle: Satisfy the customer. Peter Drucker, one of the fathers of modern management theory, once said that there are no results that matter inside the company; the only result that matters is a satisfied customer.[1]

The online sale of flowers provides a good overview of the Sales process. Online florists use effective sales processes to build long-term, mutually beneficial relationships with customers. For example, when you send flowers to your mother for her birthday and include a birthday greeting, the flower company keeps track of this transaction and will send you a reminder email or text a few days before her next birthday. If you regularly send flowers to a particular person

FIGURE 9-2

Main Sales Process Activities and Roles

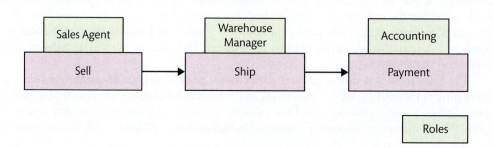

Primary Activity	Description	Process and Chapter
Inbound logistics	Receiving, storing, and disseminating inputs to products	Procurement, Chapter 8
Operations	Transforming inputs into final products	Production, Appendix A
Outbound logistics	Collecting, storing, and physically distributing products to buyers	
Sales and marketing	Inducing buyers to purchase products and providing the means for them to do so	Sales, Chapter 9
Customer service	Assisting customers' use of products thus maintaining and enhancing the products' value	

FIGURE 9-3

Sales Process Within the Value Chain of CBI

and then lapse, the company may again send a reminder: "It's been 2 months since you last sent Debbie flowers." The florist may also suggest a particular arrangement or offer you a discounted price to retain you as a frequent customer.

The florist would like to retain good customers, as acquiring new customers can cost 5 to 10 times as much as retaining existing ones. To retain customers, the florist needs to know things about its customers, like buying preferences, important dates, and how to address its customers—does Daniel Smith prefer to be called Mr. Smith, Dr. Smith, Dan, Danny, or Daniel? The more the company knows about its customers and their needs, the greater the likelihood it will keep that customer satisfied.

While understanding customers is key to making a sale, the sales process is key to delivering on the sale. To begin our discussion of the Sales process, consider the Sales process at CBI in the chapter-opening scenario. Figure 9-4 shows the main sales activities and subactivities. The first subactivity is to create a sales order that specifies that Heartland wants 50 bikes in 1 month. Later, on the planned shipping date, Wally, the warehouse manager, ensures that the bicycles are picked, packed in a box, and shipped to Heartland. Soon after, Ann sends Heartland an invoice, and when its payment arrives, she posts the payment to the CBI bank account. The sales process is also called **order-to-cash (O2C)** or the order-to-cash cycle.

We make two simplifications to the Sales process in this chapter. First, we address sales from one business to another rather than from a business to its consumers. These **business-to-business (B2B)** sales are much more common than **business-to-consumer (B2C)** sales like the florist example given earlier. This is because each B2C sale typically requires many B2B sales to acquire and assemble the product before it can be sold to a customer. A second simplification is that this chapter primarily addresses the sale of products, not services.

To better understand the impact of SAP on sales, we consider its use at CBI. We first investigate how sales worked before SAP was implemented. As mentioned in the previous chapter,

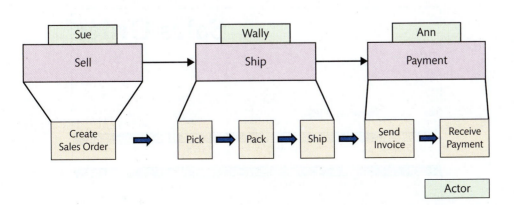

FIGURE 9-4

Main Sales Process Activities, Subactivities, and Actors at CBI

FIGURE 9-5

BPMN Diagram of Sales Process at CBI Before SAP

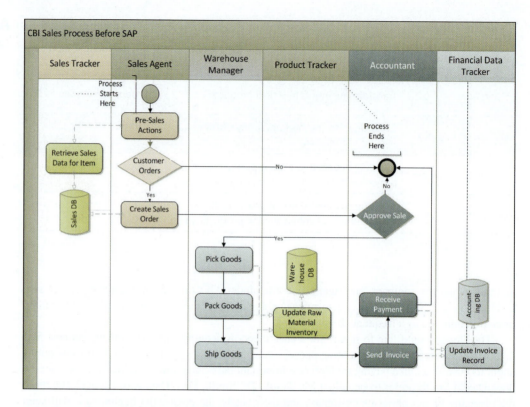

we make this before-and-after comparison to provide a educational discussion of types of sales problems SAP can address. Firms are not in the before stage, deciding whether the benefits outweigh the risks. Today, almost all large and even medium-sized firms have implemented a CRM component of an ERP system, at least in part.

Q9-2 How Did the Sales Process at CBI Work Before SAP?

To understand why Sue's sale was canceled, consider the Sales process for CBI before SAP shown in Figure 9-5. This process had six roles, three performed by human actors—Sue, Wally, and Ann—and three by computer. Each computer actor was served by its own database, creating three information silos.

The first activity in Figure 9-5 is Pre-Sales Actions. In this activity, Sue and other sales reps contacted customers, gave price quotes, verified that products were available, checked on special terms, and confirmed delivery options. A price quote, or more formally a **quotation**, is a binding agreement to sell a product at a specific price to a customer on a specific date. If the customer decided to order, the next activity is Create Sales Order. An example of a sales order (SO) is shown in Figure 9-6. On the example shown, Sue sold Heartland Bike 50 Stream bikes at $300 each for a total price of $15,000.

FIGURE 9-6

Sue's Sales Order in Paper Form

Sales Order

CBI   7/11/18

To: Heartland Bike

Salesperson	Job	F.O.B Point	Delivery Date	Due Date
Sue Clark		Midpoint	7/11/18	

Qty	Item #	Description	Unit Price	Line Total
50.00	TXTR1001	Stream N3	$ 300.00	$ 15,000.00

As shown in Figure 9-5, once complete, the SO was sent to accounting for approval. To approve the SO, Ann in accounting got price data from the Sales database, customer data from the Accounting database, and inventory data from the Warehouse database. She also saw what was sold and approved earlier in the day. These data flows to Ann are not shown in Figure 9-5 for sake of simplicity. For existing customers, Ann used data in the Accounting database to determine the history of payments by the customer—Heartland, in this case—before approving the sale. If this sale was for a new customer, there would be no customer data in the Accounting database, and Ann would add the new customer to that database and determine the risk of selling to this customer.

During this activity, Ann also accessed data in the Warehouse database to make sure there was sufficient inventory to sell. If there was not enough inventory, the sale is usually disapproved. However, as in the case of Sue's sale to Heartland, if the delivery for the sale could be delayed, Ann would call the warehouse to ask if future deliveries could be expected that would replenish the inventory in time.

If approved by accounting, the SO was passed onto the warehouse where Wally and his staff would collect (or "pick"), pack, and ship the bicycles on the correct day, as shown in Figure 9-5. Once the bikes were shipped by the warehouse, Wally sent a notice to accounting that the goods had been shipped so that accounting could send Heartland the invoice. The final activity, Receive Payment, occurred when Heartland sent a payment to CBI for the sale.

This process rejected Sue's sale for two reasons. When Sue made the sale, her sales database indicated the inventory at the beginning of the day—55 Stream bikes. However, 10 of those bikes were sold to a little retailer in Kansas City before Sue's sale to Heartland. When the SO of 50 bikes arrived at accounting, there were only 45 Streams available to sell. As mentioned in the opening vignette, Ann in accounting will coordinate to get an additional shipment of bike frames if the delivery of the sale provides enough time. However, in this case, Ann discovers that the supplier had sold out of the frame.

As you can see, the Sales process at CBI, like the Sales process at most organizations prior to an ERP system, involved several different people in several different departments. For the process to work well, these people needed to be able to share data and integrate their activities. CBI struggled on both accounts, as we discuss next.

Q9-3 What Were the Problems with the Sales Process Before SAP?

The pre-SAP Sales process at CBI was plagued with problems, five of which are summarized in Figure 9-7. These were just some of the problems that Sue had to deal with before SAP was implemented.

Sales Problems

Salespeople want to have the authority and data available to offer a **real-time price discount** a discount offered to a particular customer based on current market and customer factors. For example, in the before SAP process, if a customer considered doubling the size of an order but needed a price discount to close the deal, Sue would have to request a price discount from the

---

Sales
- No opportunity for real-time price discounting.
- Inaccurate data on products available for sale.

Warehouse
- No communication to Sales on significant changes to future inventory.

Accounting
- Wasted time spent on invoice and other errors.
- New customer delays.

FIGURE 9-7
Problems at CBI with Sales Before SAP

sales manager and contact the customer later. To be effective in today's competitive environment, salespeople needed to be able to offer real-time price discounting—offering discounts during a sales call.

A second problem in sales at CBI was that Sue did not have accurate data on bikes available for sale. At CBI, inventory data were sent to the salespeople during the overnight hours. When CBI opened in the morning, the salespeople knew which bikes and accessories were available in the warehouse that day. At times, as in the opening scenario, this led to the sale of too many bicycles, as salespeople only knew how many bikes and accessories were available at the beginning of the day. As a result, salespeople promised bikes and delivery dates to customers that could not be met. This overselling was particularly common when new or popular items like the e-bike were selling fast.

Warehouse Problems

The most significant problem for Wally was that he could not easily communicate inventory forecasts to the sales force. For example, he knew that the e-bike frame supplier had sold CBI the last of its inventory, but he had no way to communicate this. He knew this would be useful for salespeople, but the old system did not offer any way to communicate big changes in future inventory.

Accounting Problems

Things are not much better in accounting. Ann supervises a staff of very careful accountants who made the occasional data entry and arithmetic errors. Some problems were unique to the Accounting role. Her office occasionally received payments from customers with incorrect or missing invoices. The staff may also credited the wrong account or make other update errors. These infrequent errors took hours to sort out and damaged customer relations.

Delays also occurred in checking the credit of new customers. When a salesperson made a sale to a new customer, he or she inputted the customer data and told the accounting department that a credit check was needed. When accounting received a sales request for a new customer, an accountant entered the new customer data into the Accounting database before the new customer approval process could begin. In this old system, the customer data had to be entered by two different departments, delaying the process and introducing the opportunity for more input errors.

These problems cost CBI sales and customers over the years. As industry competition increased, CBI had to change or it would go out of business. CBI believed that SAP would help correct these Sales process deficiencies. Next we outline the steps CBI executed to implement their ERP system.

Q9-4 ▶ How Does CBI Implement SAP?

Before CBI committed to an SAP solution, it was intrigued by an offer from **Salesforce**, the leading vendor of cloud-based CRM systems. Salesforce specializes in the CRM piece of the ERP puzzle. It offers easy-to-use software and a streamlined implementation process that enables customers to quickly get up and running. While CBI liked Salesforce for these reasons, it selected SAP to better integrate with its suppliers and not simply focus on the customer side.

SAP not only helped CBI overcome its problems listed in the previous question but also helped achieve strategy. In the previous chapter, we discussed the implementation of the SAP system at CBI. In this chapter, we discuss how that implementation affected marketing in general and sales in particular.

To implement SAP successfully, top management reexamined CBI's strategy and committed to a competitive strategy that focused on a particular industry segment—high-end bikes—and a differentiation on responsiveness to retailers. CBI then selected the SAP Sales process most appropriate for this strategy. Sales managers decided on one efficiency objective and two effectiveness objectives, which are shown in Figure 9-8.

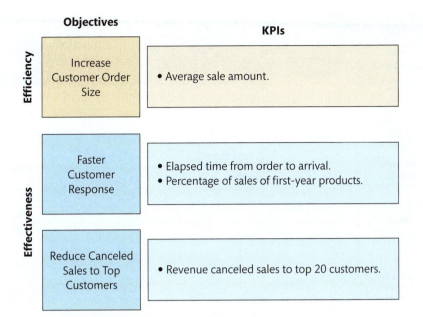

FIGURE 9-8

Objectives and KPIs for the New Sales Process

CBI believed that one way to be more efficient in sales is to encourage the sales force to make larger individual sales. Every sale takes time and delivery costs, so less frequent but larger sales increase efficiency. As a result, CBI decided an efficiency objective should be larger sales, as measured by the average sale amount.

The first effectiveness objective—faster customer response—will be measured by customer lead time—the time from creation of a sales order to the arrival of ordered products. A second KPI will be the percentage of sales of first-year products. CBI offers new bikes and accessories based on customer input. If these new products are being purchased by retailers, this is a sign that CBI is responding well to customer requests. A second effectiveness objective is to reduce lost revenue from canceled sales to their best customers. CBI wants to maintain the right to cancel lower-revenue sales when they conflict with higher-revenue sales.

Based on these three objectives, CBI selected a sales process from SAP's inherent processes that would best support these objectives. They then organized teams of ERP analysts to configure the system and develop procedures appropriate for CBI employees to use and trained their employees to complete the implementation process.

Q9-5 ▶ How Does the Sales Process Work at CBI After SAP?

Now consider the situation 2 years later. CBI has implemented the SAP system, and employees know how to use it. Figure 9-9 shows the SAP inherent Sales process implemented at CBI. Notice that after SAP only four actors are needed, as shown by the four swimlanes. Before SAP, as indicated earlier in the chapter in Figure 9-5, six actors were needed.

Sales

The new Sales process features the same three actors as the previous Sales process—Sue, Wally, and Ann. However, the three computer actors are reduced to the single SAP system that tracks all the sales data. For comparative purposes, we will trace the same Sales process as before. This is the sale of 50 Stream bikes to Heartland when only 45 are available.

The Pre-Sales Actions activity is the same as before with three exceptions. The inventory and price data are now current. Sue can see that 55 bikes are available and that 10 of the 55 have been sold. She can see that the 10 bikes have not been shipped and that her customer will have priority. In addition, Sue has access to real-time price discounts to enable her to offer Heartland additional pricing options. Finally, Sue can see long-term inventory availability; in this case, she can see that Wally has indicated no future inventory of Streams.

FIGURE 9-9

Sales Process at CBI After SAP

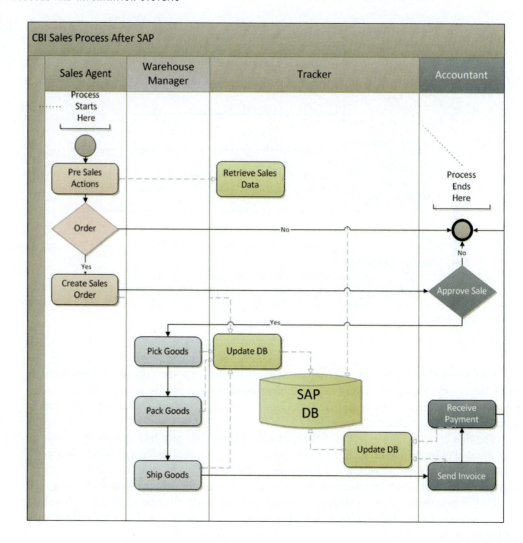

As we pick up Sue's story, she has just made the sale and is sitting down in her office to input the sales data into SAP in the Create Sales Order activity. She initiates the Create Sales Order procedure by logging into SAP. Her Sales Order screen looks like Figure 9-10.

The Sales Order screen has many of the same features as the Procurement process screens in Chapter 8. The title, at the top left in this case, is Create Standard Order: Overview. In the header section, Sue enters Heartland's customer number (25056), the date of the transaction (PO date of 06/20/2017), and the transaction number (PO Number 05432). The PO date for Heartland is the sales date for CBI—the date the sale was made. Once Sue enters these three data elements, SAP retrieves the customer's name and address. In the detail section at the bottom of the screen, Sue inputs the material number for Stream bikes (TXTR1001) and the number ordered (50). Sue then saves the data and enters another sale or exits the system.

Once Sue saves the SO, SAP creates a SO number and updates the inventory table in the database to reflect the sale of 50 Streams. In addition, a new SO record is created that will subsequently be updated when the warehouse picks, packs, and ships the bikes.

In addition to updating data, several other automatic actions are triggered. First, an **availability check** is conducted—SAP determines if the promised delivery quantity can be met by the promised delivery date. This is also called Available to Promise. Second, a message is sent to the accounting department to approve or disapprove the sale. A third action updates the assembly schedule for CBI. SAP recognizes that the warehouse only has 45 Stream bikes and attempts to acquire from suppliers the additional bike frames and parts to assemble. When automated responses in the supply chain indicate no opportunity to acquire these frames, Ann in accounting receives a message. She sees Sue's pending sale to a preferred customer, the

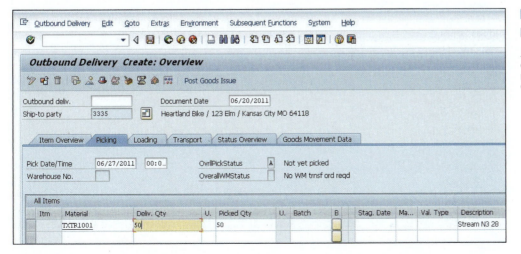

45 bikes in inventory, and the 10 bikes sold earlier that day to another customer. Because Heartland is a preferred customer, Ann is able to cancel the sale of 10 bikes and move 5 of these bikes to Heartland.

Warehouse

Once this sale is approved, SAP sends a message to Wally in the warehouse to ship the bikes on the scheduled date. On the appointed day, Wally removes the bikes from finished goods inventory, packs them into a crate, and places the crate in the truck loading bay. Once the bikes are picked and packed, Wally logs into SAP. After he enters the SO number, he sees the Outbound Delivery screen shown in Figure 9-11. He confirms that the data provided by SAP in the header

and detail sections are correct. If he did not pick the entire quantity specified in the sale, 50 in this case, he would overwrite the defaulted value of 50 that appears in the Deliv. Qty column. Once he saves this data, the inventory table is updated and the sales record is edited to reflect that the Stream bikes have now been picked and packed.

The Ship Goods activity occurs when the delivery truck leaves the warehouse with the shipment. Again, Wally navigates to the Outbound Delivery screen. Because this sales order has been picked and packed, the screen is now labeled Change Outbound Delivery, as shown in Figure 9-12. Wally executes the procedure by selecting the Post Goods Issue button near the middle of the screen. **Posting** means that legal ownership of the material has changed. The bikes are no longer owned by CBI; they are now the property of Heartland. Posting in this example occurs when the bikes are shipped.

Accounting

After Wally has posted the goods issue and the bicycles have changed ownership, Ann in accounting receives a message that she can bill Heartland for the 50 Streams. She logs into SAP and begins the Send Invoice procedure with the Maintain Billing Due List screen that is shown in Figure 9-13. She enters Heartland's number in the Sold-To Party field (25056) and selects the

Billing document Edit Goto Settings System Help

Maintain Billing Due List

⊕DisplayBillList   DisplayVariants

Billing Data

Billing Date from		to	06/20/2011
Billing Type		to	
SD Document		to	

Selection	Default Data	Batch and Update

Organizat. Data

Sales Organization	UE00		
Distribution channel		to	
Division		to	
Shipping point		to	

Customer Data

Sold-To Party	25056	to	
Destination country		to	
Sort Criterion		to	

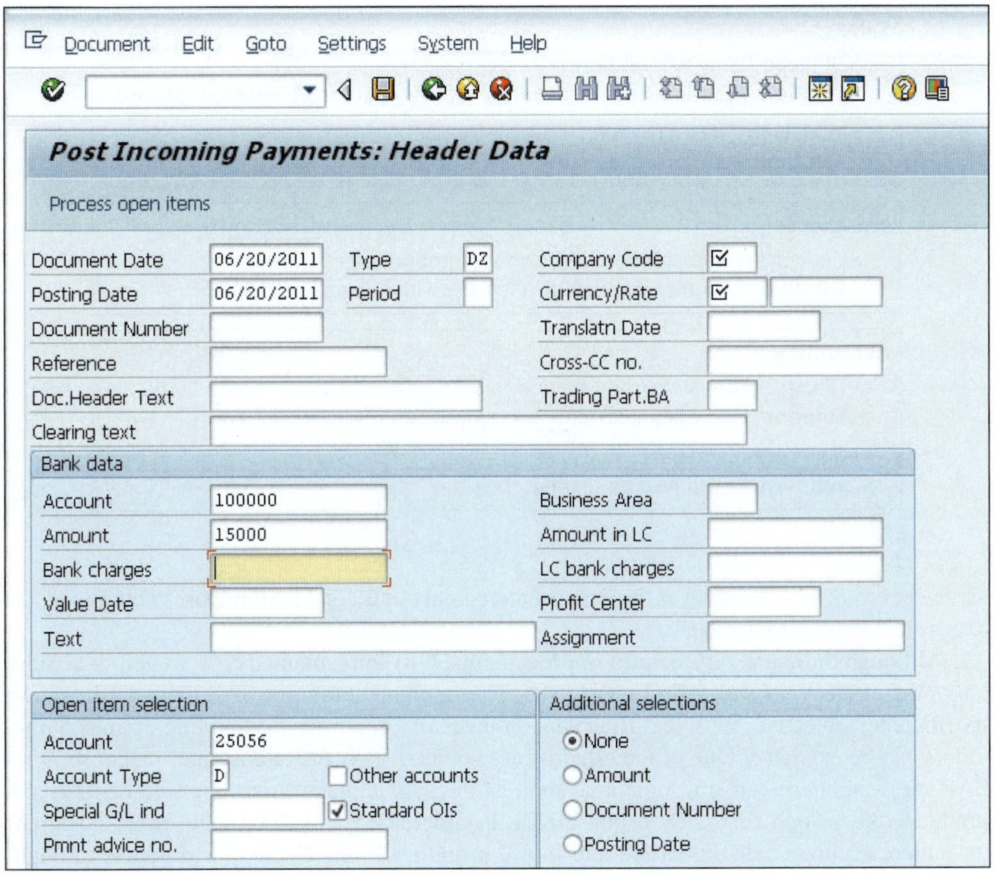

FIGURE 9-14

Receive Payment Subactivity Post Incoming Payments Screen in SAP

Source: ©2019. SAP SE or an affiliate company. All rights reserved. Used with permission of SAP SE or an SAP affiliate company.

DisplayBillList icon near the top of the screen. On the following screen (not shown), Ann selects from a list of sales orders to Heartland, adds the sales order for the 50 Stream bikes, and clicks the Save icon.

This action triggers SAP to send a bill, called an invoice, to Heartland Bike for the 50 bikes. A week later, Ann in accounting receives payment for the 50 Streams.

To accomplish the Receive Payment activity in Figure 9-9, Sue navigates to the Post Incoming Payments screen shown in Figure 9-14. Here she specifies that Heartland, with Account number 25056, has paid $15,000 and that the money has been placed in Account number 100000. Once Ann saves the documents, SAP updates the sales record and makes the appropriate accounting entries.

The Benefits of SAP for the CBI Sales Process

By implementing SAP, CBI enjoys two types of benefits. First, SAP solves each of the five Sales process problems discussed earlier, as shown Figure 9-15. Second, SAP helps CBI achieve its sales objectives, also mentioned earlier, as shown in Figure 9-16.

The data sharing aspect of SAP knocks out problems 3 and 5. The warehouse and sales office no longer maintain information silos. As a result, sales has accurate, current data on what's in the warehouse inventory. Further, with data sharing, the checking of credit for new customers is faster because the accounting department does not retype this data into its own database. Instead, new customer data gets entered once by the salesperson and the process of checking credit kicks off immediately.

The integrated processes of SAP address problems 1, 2, and 4 in Figure 9-15. First, the SAP inherent Sales process includes a real-time price discounting feature. Second, due to the integration of sales, procurement, and production processes, salespeople can check future inventory availability and make informed commitments to customers about upcoming sales. Finally, there

FIGURE 9-15

CBI Sales Process Problems and SAP Benefits

Sales
- No opportunity for real-time price discounting.
  Solution: Real-time price discounting activity a part of SAP inherent process.
- Inaccurate data on products available for sale.
  Solution: Real-time data sharing.

Warehouse
- Limited communication to Sales on inventory changes.
  Solution: Inventory forecasts sent to sales with integration of SAP processes.

Accounting
- Time spent on invoice and other errors.
  Solution: Inherent processes enforce input controls to reduce errors.
- New customer delays.
  Solution: Real-time data sharing.

are fewer errors in accounting as the data is entered only once, and SAP imposes controls on the data as it is typed into the database.

Although these are very helpful improvements, CBI implemented SAP to help it achieve a specific strategy, as shown in Figure 9-16. The implementation of SAP helps CBI achieve its efficiency objective. With real-time data on inventory and price discounting options, larger orders can be expected. One of the effectiveness objectives is faster customer response. With SAP, the warehouse can ship orders as soon as the sale is made. Also, the sale of first-year products, the second customer response KPI, has increased with SAP. With SAP, sales reps have more accurate data on current and future inventory levels of the new products throughout the supply chain. Prior to SAP, these new products would not appear as inventory in the Warehouse database for potential sale until the day they arrived. Now, sales reps can see when these new products will be available and have accurate data on pending sales of these new items.

The second effectiveness objective of reducing canceled sales to the best customers is also achieved. The SAP inherent process allows the accounting department to give priority to its better customers when products are limited.

Having considered the benefits of SAP on the Sales process, we now broaden our consideration of the impact of SAP on CRM processes.

FIGURE 9-16

CBI Sales Process Objectives and SAP Solutions

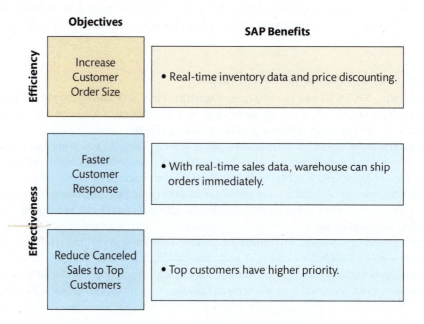

Objectives

SAP Benefits

Efficiency

Increase Customer Order Size
- Real-time inventory data and price discounting.

Effectiveness

Faster Customer Response
- With real-time sales data, warehouse can ship orders immediately.

Reduce Canceled Sales to Top Customers
- Top customers have higher priority.

MIS InClass 9

Building a Model

The purpose of this exercise is to participate in a process that satisfies an external customer. In this exercise, student teams will build replicas of a model that is hidden from their sight.

Before class, the instructor, the external customer, constructed a model that is now hidden from view. The goal of the student team is to build a model identical to that one. The model is concealed in the hallway immediately outside the classroom. The class is divided into teams, and each person on the team is assigned one of four roles. Each team is composed of between four and six students with the following roles:

- **Looker:** The looker looks at the instructor's model and remains in the hallway. The looker cannot write anything down. The looker explains to the messenger how to assemble the model.
- **Messenger:** The messenger listens to the looker's description. The messenger relays these verbal instructions to the builders in the room. The messenger cannot look at either the instructor's model or the team's model as it is being assembled.
- **Feedbacker:** The feedbacker can look at the instructor's model and the team's model. The feedbacker can say only "yes" or "no" to questions asked by any other team member.
- **Builders:** The rest of the team is made up of builders. Builders construct the replica of the instructor's model. They acquire the pieces from a supplier who supplies all the teams.

The game begins with the lookers in the hallway each giving their messenger an initial set of instructions. Play the game until the last team has built the replica.

After the game, discuss the following:

1. Do the roles in the game correspond to business roles?
2. Describe your team's building process and its objectives. Construct a BPMN diagram of your team's building process. Use the looker–messenger exchange as the first activity and assembling pieces as the last activity.

Source: Andresr/Shutterstock.

3. How did your process evolve from the first iteration of the process to the last? How did you learn to use the feedbacker? If the feedbacker is considered a simple IS, how does this IS lead to process improvement?
4. Vocabulary is necessary for effective communication. Did the looker, messenger, and builders use the same vocabulary to describe the building pieces?
5. How well is data shared in the building process?
6. There is no (computer) IS in this game. If your team had some money to spend on an IS, what would you buy? In Chapter 6, we discussed five ways an IS can improve a process. For the IS you purchase, which of these five best describes how your IS will improve your process?
7. After spending money on an IS, which player's job would change? What is the relationship between a new IS and job change in general?
8. With the process used at the end of the game, how much time would it take to construct the next model?

Q9-6 ▶ How Can SAP Improve CRM Processes at CBI?

The Sales process is just one of many CRM processes that SAP can support. These processes are listed in Figure 9-17. The Promotion process is designed to increase sales, stimulate demand, or improve product availability over a predetermined limited time. The Sales process, defined earlier, is the exchange of goods or services for money. The Service process, first defined in Chapter 6, provides after-sales support to enhance or maintain the value of a product.

Just as supply chain processes were improved with data sharing and integration, so too are CRM processes. Recall from Chapter 7 that the chief benefits of an ERP system is that it consolidates data in one place so the data can be shared, and that it improves the integration of processes.

Improving CRM Processes by Data Sharing

CRM processes improve when processes share data. To see how this works, consider your process of returning merchandise to a retailer. It is easier for you to return your merchandise if you have a receipt. If this receipt was emailed to you, it may be easier to find than a printed receipt.

FIGURE 9-17

Sample of CRM Processes

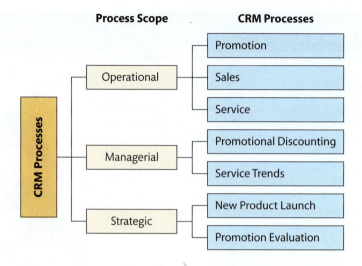

By using electronic receipts, your retailer's Sales process has made your Returns process easier. Rather than issue paper receipts, which are more costly and more frequently lost, many retailers are sharing receipt data with customers electronically by sending an email or a message to a customer's smartphone. Not only does this reduce sales costs, an objective of the retailer's Sales process, it also improves the customer's Returns process because customers can find their receipts more frequently.

Examples of improving processes by data sharing at CBI are shown in Figure 9-18. Both sales and service are improved when they share customer data. By having access to customer sales data, CBI service is improved. For example, when a customer calls for service about a problem with a particular shipment, the service agent at CBI knows the sales data for that shipment and all shipments to that customer. By having the sales data, the agent is better informed about the customer's situation. Likewise, the Sales process is improved with customer service call data. A sales representative can review service data from a customer before initiating a sales call. That way the sales representative can offer the customer products that were not the subject of a service call.

By sharing data, the Sales process of CBI and the Procurement processes of its customer retailers can be improved. For example, CBI sells to many small outlets. These small retailers do not have the resources to collect data on market trends, but CBI does. CBI can share its market

FIGURE 9-18

Examples of Data Sharing Among
CRM Processes

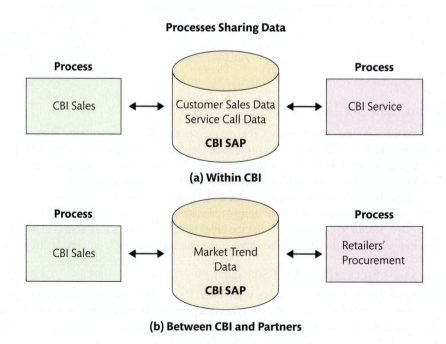

Integrating Processes

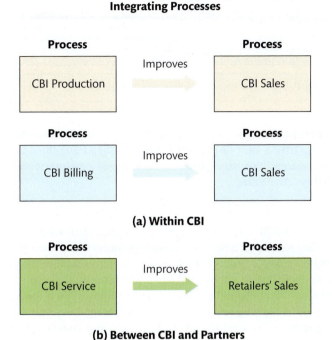

(a) Within CBI

(b) Between CBI and Partners

FIGURE 9-19

Examples of Process Integration
Among CRM Processes

trend data with retailers, who can then make better procurement decisions about what bikes to buy from CBI. Both firms win when CBI's Sales process and the small retailer's Procurement process share this market trend data because they both sell more bikes.

Improving CRM Processes with Integration

The second way to improve the collection of CRM processes is to increase their integration, or their synergy. Process synergy occurs when processes are mutually supportive—when one process is done well, then the objectives of another process are supported. Synergy between sales and procurement is evident in your personal life. Amazon recognizes the synergy between its Sales process and your personal Procurement process. When people want to buy something, they want to do it quickly. Therefore, it can be said that people have a Procurement process objective of not wasting time. Amazon has found that online sales revenue increases 1 percent for every one-tenth of a second decrease in load time.[2] As a result, it makes download time an objective of its Sales process, and this mutually supports your personal Procurement process.

Examples of increasing synergy at CBI are shown in Figure 9-19. At CBI, the Production process can support the objectives of the Sales process. If the Production process times are consistent, the assembly of bikes is on time and the delivery of a sale is rarely late. As a result, customers are satisfied and opportunities for future sales are improved. The objective of the Sales process, repeat customers, is supported by the Production process.

A second example of process synergy is the support of the Sales process by the Billing process. When an accountant at CBI is contacted by a customer or the accountant contacts a customer to clarify a bill, the Billing process requires the accountant to share current pricing of products with the customer. More specifically, the accountant shares prices on products if the new price is better than the price on the bill, which, in turn, leads to future sales.

To improve process synergy with retailers, CBI can use its Service process to support the Sales processes of its customer retailers. For example, when a defective bike is returned to CBI from one of its retailers, the CBI Service process uses overnight shipping to give the retailer a new bike within 24 hours. As a result, the retailer's Sales process is improved because each of CBI's retailers can promise customers 24-hour replacements.

In both this chapter and the previous one, we have seen that, with SAP, CBI can share data and integrate processes with its suppliers and customers. While we have been quick to sing the virtues of this closer arrangement, there is also a curse. ERP systems are a difficult and expensive necessity to keep up with the competition. In today's tech-savvy environment, customers

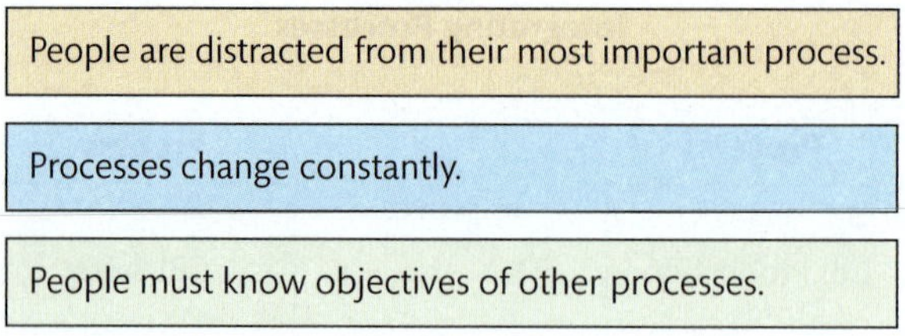

FIGURE 9-20

Challenges of Improving a Group of Processes

People are distracted from their most important process.

Processes change constantly.

People must know objectives of other processes.

have high technical expectations of sellers. Retailers like Heartland only want to purchase from bike wholesalers who have a state-of-the-art ERP system supporting their sales and service. For CBI and other wholesalers, this expectation curse increases pressure to spend and spend and spend to keep ERP systems current.

Challenges

Although it is clear that SAP can help improve the collection of CRM processes, improving CRM processes or any set of processes also presents challenges, as shown in Figure 9-20.

First, focusing on a single process is easier than trying to achieve the objectives of many processes at one time. Trying to improve all the CRM processes can be seen as a distraction by sales representatives who believe the sales process deserves all their focus. These representatives may see their job as building relationships with customers. They may view time spent with technology or time spent on sales-related processes as time they could use to improve these vital relationships.

A second challenge is that all of the processes are in a state of change. Processes change, as we have mentioned in earlier chapters, due to changes in technology, strategy, people, and products. Keeping all these processes working well together while they all change is difficult.

Finally, achieving the objectives of a set of processes can only happen when businesspeople understand other parts of the business. To make all the CRM processes work well, salespeople need to know their firm's Service processes and how payments are processed in accounting. By the way, this challenge is an opportunity for you. To help make processes work at your future firm, learn as much as you can about different functions in business so you can make your processes work well with other processes within the firm.

To summarize, improving the group of CRM processes requires data sharing and integrating processes. This can be a challenge, but SAP is an ally in this fight, and there are other IS that help processes work well together. Next, we consider IS that help processes in multiple firms work well together.

Before we close this question, a word of perspective: If you begin your career in business, keep in mind that enterprises run on revenue, and all revenue begins as a sale. Regardless of your role in the company, learn about how your product or service is sold and support that process; the sales process is the most essential one in the firm. Our goal in this chapter was to help you better understand how an ERP system like SAP plays a vital role in it.

Q9-7 ▶ How Does E-commerce Improve Processes in an Industry?

In the past two chapters, we have discussed buying and selling between CBI and its partners and how SAP can make processes better for both. However, ERP systems are not the only way to improve processes between organizations. Another approach is e-commerce. E-commerce not only supports buying and selling in a supply chain, it also supports selling to the final customer, people like you and me. Before we close this chapter, it will be helpful to you in the future if we consider some key aspects of e-commerce.

Formally, **e-commerce** is a multi-firm process of buying and selling goods and services using Internet technologies. While popular B2C e-commerce is accomplished via the Web at places like Amazon and Apple, much of B2B e-commerce uses private networks and company- or industry-specific software.

CBI participates in B2B e-commerce as shown in Figure 9-21. Starting on the left end of Figure 9-21, composites, which are raw materials for bike frames, are created by Carbon Fibers, Inc. The composites are sold to a frame manufacturer, Southern Frames, who makes the bicycle frames. The frames are sold to a frame wholesaler, Space Bike Composites in this scenario,

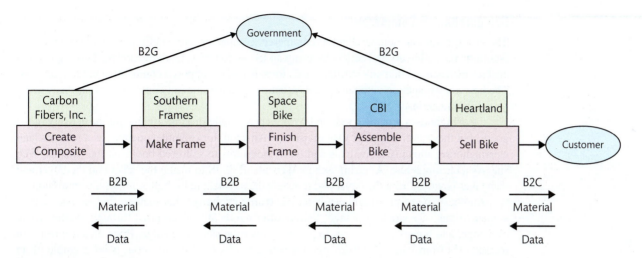

FIGURE 9-21

E-commerce in Bike Supply Chain

where the frames are finished. CBI assembles the bikes and sells the finished product to retailers such as Heartland who, in turn, sell to a final customer.

As defined earlier, e-commerce consists of both a multi-firm buying and selling process and the internet-based IS that supports it. ERP systems can support e-commerce, as do IS that support fund transfers, inventory management, and transaction processing systems. These systems are often referred to as **interorganizational IS**, which are IS used by more than one firm.

Figure 9-22 lists categories of companies that participate in e-commerce. The U.S. Census Bureau, which publishes statistics on e-commerce activity, defines **merchant companies** as those that own the goods they sell. They buy goods and resell them. It defines **nonmerchant companies** as those that arrange for the purchase and sale of goods without ever owning or taking title to those goods. With regard to services, merchant companies sell services that they provide; nonmerchant companies sell services provided by others. Of course, a company can be both a merchant and nonmerchant company.

E-Commerce Merchant Companies

The three main types of merchant companies are those that sell directly to consumers, those that sell to companies, and those that sell to government. Each uses slightly different IS in the course of doing business. B2C e-commerce concerns sales between a supplier and a retail customer (the consumer). IS that support the Sales process of B2C companies are typically **Web storefronts** that customers use to enter and manage their orders. Amazon, REI.com, and LLBean.com are examples of companies that use Web storefronts.

B2B e-commerce refers to sales between companies. As Figure 9-21 shows, raw materials suppliers and other firms use interorganizational IS like ERP systems to integrate B2B supply chains. **B2G**, or **business-to-government** merchants, sell to governmental organizations. In Figure 9-21, the composite raw material supplier and the bike retailer might sell their products to government agencies.

Merchant Companies

- Business-to-consumer (B2C)
- Business-to-business (B2B)
- Business-to-government (B2G)

Nonmerchant Companies

- Auctions
- Clearinghouses
- Exchanges

FIGURE 9-22

E-commerce Merchant and Nonmerchant List

Nonmerchant E-Commerce

The most common nonmerchant e-commerce companies are auctions and clearinghouses. **Auctions** match buyers and sellers by using an IS version of a standard auction. This application enables the auction company to offer goods for sale and to support a competitive bidding process. The best-known auction company is eBay, but many other auction companies exist; many serve particular industries.

Clearinghouses provide goods and services at a stated price and arrange for the delivery of the goods, but they never take title. One division of Amazon, for example, operates as a nonmerchant clearinghouse, allowing individuals and used bookstores to sell used books on the Amazon Web site. As a clearinghouse, Amazon uses its Web site as an IS to match the seller and the buyer and then takes payment from the buyer and transfers the payment to the seller, minus a commission.

Another type of clearinghouse is an **electronic exchange** that matches buyers and sellers, similar to that of a stock exchange. Sellers offer goods at a given price through the electronic exchange, and buyers make offers to purchase over the same exchange. Price matches result in transactions from which the exchange takes a commission. Priceline.com is an example of an exchange used by consumers.

How Does E-Commerce Improve Market Efficiency?

E-commerce, both the processes and interorganizational IS that support them, improves market efficiency in a number of different ways, as shown in Figure 9-23. For one, e-commerce leads to **disintermediation**, which is the elimination of middle layers of distributors and suppliers. You can buy a bicycle from a typical "brick-and-mortar" retailer like Heartland, or you can use CBI's Web site and purchase the bike directly from CBI. If you take the latter route, you eliminate the retailer. The product is shipped directly from CBI's finished goods inventory to you. You eliminate the retailer's inventory-carrying costs, and you eliminate shipping overhead and handling activity. Because the retailer and associated inventories have become unnecessary waste, disintermediation increases market efficiency.

E-commerce also improves the flow of price data. As a consumer, you can go to any number of Web sites that offer product price comparisons. You can search for the bike you want and sort the results by price and vendor reputation. You can find vendors that avoid your state sales tax or that omit or reduce shipping charges. The improved distribution of data about price and terms enables you to pay the lowest possible cost and serves ultimately to remove inefficient vendors. The market as a whole becomes more efficient.

A third way e-commerce improves market efficiency is sharing customer marketing data. Two examples of improved consumer data sharing come from Google: AdWords and Analytics.

Google pioneered search advertising with its AdWords software. AdWords is Google's popular pay-per-click advertising product. With AdWords, companies pay a predetermined price for particular search words. For example, Oracle might agree to pay $2 for the words *software* and

FIGURE 9-23
Three Ways E-commerce Improves Market Efficiency

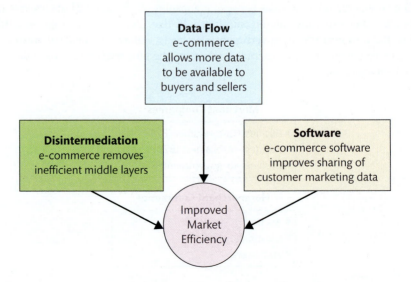

business. When a customer uses Google to search for those terms, Google will display a link to Oracle's Web site. If the user clicks that link (and *only* if the user clicks that link), Google charges Oracle $2. Oracle pays nothing if the user does not click.

Customer data sharing is also improved with free Google Analytics software that enables the Web site owner to collect Web traffic data. This data includes where the customer came from (from a search engine, another site, and so on), where the customer visited in the site, and the conversion rate, which is the ratio of the number of customers who eventually purchased divided by the number who visited. Analysts can examine this type of data and make changes to the site with the objective of increasing sales. Installed on more than a half million of the most popular Web sites, Google Analytics improves market efficiencies by improving the collection and sharing of customer data.

⯈ Q9-8 ⯈ What New IS Will Affect the Sales Process in 2028?

SAP and e-commerce will continue to have a significant impact on Sales processes for years to come. However, other IS that are just now emerging may also help improve the Sales process. These IS, shown in Figure 9-24, include blockchain, social CRM, Dash Buttons, darknet, and smartphone payment.

BLOCKCHAIN You will soon have a diploma. That diploma is valuable because not everyone has one. Unfortunately, LinkedIn has found that many professionals add degrees to their resume from schools they never attended. This reduces the value of all degrees. Turns out this copycat problem occurs all the time in property records, intellectual property, supply chains, and financial transactions. So how can we change things so we can ensure records like digital products and college degrees are valid? In a word, blockchain.

Keeping track of records has always been done by governments, banks, and institutions, in a role called a trusted third party. **Blockchain**, as shown in Figure 9-25, overcomes the need for a trusted third party and verifies records by maintaining data on a distributed database that is public and difficult to hack. This database, also called a ledger, records transactions and uses cryptography to make unapproved changes to the database virtually impossible. The result is a database of verified transactions, a verified ledger, available to all.

In simplified language, here's how blockchain works with Bitcoin, the popular cryptocurrency. If you want to use Bitcoin to buy an e-textbook from Bob's Bookstore, both you and Bob's need a Bitcoin wallet, a digital record of Bitcoin assets that hides the identity of its owner from the public. Your wallet nominates a transaction to the blockchain network that two bitcoins should be transferred from it to another wallet specified by Bob's. The Bitcoin network of nodes checks to see that the wallet you presented has two coins to give up and Bob's wallet can receive them. If so, your transaction gets a timestamp, joins other concurrent transactions, and is formed into a block. This block is lightly encrypted and shared to the network. Special nodes on the network, called miners, notice the new block and set about to break the light encryption. This decryption takes a while, and it's impossible to know which of the miners will be first to break it. But once one does, it shares its solution with the other miners; if they find the solution accurate, the new block becomes trusted by all nodes, and your transaction is complete. The clever miner that broke the encryption first also receives a small Bitcoin reward. In the end, no one knows you or Bob or what the coins were used for, only that two valid bitcoins changed wallets at a particular time.

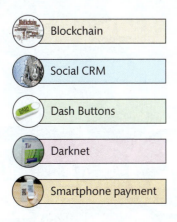

FIGURE 9-24
New IS That Will Impact Supply Chain Processes by 2028

FIGURE 9-25
Blockchain

A great benefit of the digital age is that copies of a document or file can be made and shared. A million of us can get a copy of our favorite recording. For many digital products, easy copy is wonderful; for many others, it destroys value such as your diploma, digital currency you may own, keys to an apartment on Airbnb, and an invoice. In every one of these cases, the nagging question is the same. Is this the only copy? For example, I'm a manufacturer, and I'd like to sell an invoice I have from a customer for $1 million due in 6 months to a bank that will pay me $950,000 today. The bank has a valid question: Is this a valid invoice, or are there five copies of this same invoice, and what trusted third party can I call to find out?

With its unique ability to validate transactions and maintain anonymity, blockchain technology will have a significant impact on sales by 2028. Blockchain may play a very valuable role in financial transactions, and as a result, some ERP vendors anticipate that blockchain apps will emerge that will validate data that flows between firms.

SOCIAL CRM As mentioned previously, one way customer processes are improved is by data sharing. **Social CRM** is an information system that helps a company collect customer data from social media and share it among its CRM processes, as shown in Figure 9-26.

Businesses use social media to offer many different customer touch points, and customers interact with business by their use of those touch points. Social CRM data is collected through interactions on Facebook, Twitter, Snapchat, Pinterest, blogs, discussion lists, frequently asked questions, sites for user reviews, and other social media. Social CRM systems collect and distribute this data to a variety of CRM processes.

FIGURE 9-26
Social CRM

FIGURE 9-27
Dash Button

DASH BUTTONS Amazon has introduced Dash Buttons, shortcuts to efficiently reorder common products. When you shop at Amazon, it will create a Dash Button on your Amazon home page so when you click on it, the item is shipped. Physical buttons, as shown in Figure 9-27, are also available to post around the home, and with one physical click on this Wi-Fi–connected button, the item is ordered. Not only have buttons increased sales, data collected from Dash Buttons helps Amazon better model the shelf life of different products in a variety of homes. Buttons may not last until 2028, but they represent a first wave of one-touch or highly automated home sales.

DARKNET The darknet is a network underneath the Internet, or surface web, that you commonly use. The darknet is part of the **deep web**, the extended Internet with addresses that are not indexed by search engines such as academic resources, members-only Web sites, dynamic pages that are created when users visit a site, government agencies and records, and corporate internal networks. This deep web is estimated to be 100 times larger than the surface web.

The **darknet** is intentionally hidden and inaccessible from traditional search engines. To access the darknet, you need a special browser, such as the Tor browser shown in Figure 9-28. This browser is designed to find and connect to sites with darknet extensions like .onion and to keep the user anonymous. The darknet is very helpful for political dissent but just as useful for sales of drugs, stolen credit cards, human trafficking, and copyrighted material. The notorious Silk Road site is an example of a site on the darknet.

SMARTPHONE PAYMENT Customers are increasingly using their smartphones to make purchases. It is already common for customers at Starbucks to use their phone to buy coffee and other products. To do so, customers first purchase a QR code online for their phone from Starbucks. Then, when they visit a Starbucks, they display the QR code on their phone and allow the cashier

FIGURE 9-28
Darknet

FIGURE 9-29
Smartphone Payment

to scan it. Coffee is not the only thing people are buying with smartphones. In Shanghai, China, customers use their phones to shop for groceries at subway stations. On posters in the subway, a grocery chain displays images of products along with a QR code for each item, as shown in Figure 9-29. Shoppers scan the QR code on their smartphones to register a purchase, and the groceries are delivered to their home of record later that day. While smartphone payments are already becoming common, by 2028 some experts believe these types of payments will dominate consumer sales and may also increasingly include digital currencies like Bitcoin.

Process Integration and You in 2028

While technology will help businesses integrate sales processes, so too will you. One of the goals of this textbook is to help you become comfortable with processes and begin to see how they can work together. We first explained processes and then discussed how a set of processes work together in a supply chain and in CRM within one firm. We also applied integration concepts to processes between firms. Our goal all along was to get to the following conclusion: *Processes must work well together.*

In every job you will have, in every company large and small, you will play a role in many processes. If you are an accountant, your accounting classes will prepare you well to do those roles; if you are in sales like Sue, your marketing courses will get you ready for your role as a salesperson. But in every job and in every role you play, you will be more effective if you keep in mind the big picture that processes must work well together.

In Chapter 1, we suggested that four skills will be valuable to you in your career: abstract reasoning, systems thinking, collaboration, and experimentation. Recall from that chapter that a systems thinker is one who understands how the inputs and outputs of processes relate. Here we can express that in a more specific way. A systems thinker is a process thinker. A good systems thinker considers how the change in one process output affects other processes.

Where there are business processes, there is likely to be an ERP system. Whether you are an accounting, supply chain, marketing, or finance student, chances are that you will work with SAP or another ERP system on your very first job after college. As an accountant, you will post payments and configure SAP to allow different payment schedules and to create automatic price discounts. As a salesperson, you may record every customer interaction in your CRM module, post and edit sales, and invent new reports that will help your company identify new trends and opportunities. These activities will affect other processes outside your office. You and your employer will be pleased if, by the time you start, you have mastered some aspects of SAP so you can anticipate these impacts. So take this time to master the vocabulary in these chapters. Learn how to navigate to different screens and to move around within the screens. Think about processes and how ERP systems change and improve processes. If you can, do the tutorials in the appendix, make mistakes, start over—learn beyond the book.

Ethics Guide

Are My Ethics for Sale?

Suppose you are a salesperson at CBI. Your boss says that it has been a bad quarter for all of the salespeople. It's so bad, in fact, that the vice president of sales has authorized a 20 percent discount on new orders. The only stipulation is that customers must take delivery prior to the end of the quarter so that accounting can book the order. "Start dialing for dollars," she says, "and get what you can. Be creative."

Using CBI's CRM system, you identify your top customers and present the discount offer to them. The first customer balks at increasing her inventory: "I just don't think we can sell that much."

"Well," you respond, "how about if we agree to take back any inventory you don't sell next quarter?" (By doing this, you increase your current sales and commission, and you also help your company make its quarterly sales projections. The additional product is likely to be returned next quarter, but you think, "Hey, that's then, and this is now.")

"OK," she says, "but I want you to stipulate the return option on the purchase order."

You know that you cannot write that on the purchase order because accounting won't book all of the order if you do. So you tell her that you'll send her an email with that stipulation. She increases her order, and accounting books the full amount.

With another customer, you try a second strategy. Instead of offering the discount, you offer the product at full price, but agree to pay a 20 percent credit in the next quarter. That way you can book the full price now. You pitch this offer as follows: "Our marketing department analyzed past sales using our fancy new system, and we know that increasing advertising will cause additional sales. So, if you order more product now, next quarter we'll give you 20 percent of the order back to pay for advertising."

In truth, you doubt the customer will spend the money on advertising. Instead, they'll just take the credit and sit on a bigger inventory. That will kill your sales to it next quarter, but you'll solve that problem then.

Even with these additional orders, you're still under quota. In desperation, you decide to sell product to a fictitious company that you say is owned by your brother-in-law. You set up a new account, and when accounting calls your brother-in-law for a credit check, he cooperates with your scheme. You then sell $40,000 of product to the fictitious company and ship the product to your brother-in-law's garage. Accounting books the revenue in the quarter, and you have finally made quota. A week into the next quarter, your brother-in-law returns the merchandise.

Meanwhile, unknown to you, CBI's SAP system is scheduling bike assemblies. The assembly schedule reflects the sales from your activities (and those of the other salespeople) and finds a sharp increase in product demand. Accordingly, it generates a schedule that calls for substantial assembly increases and schedules workers for the assemblies. The production system, in turn, schedules the material requirements with the inventory application, which increases raw materials purchases to meet the increased production schedule.

DISCUSSION QUESTIONS

1. Considering the email you write that agrees to take the product back:
   a. Is your action ethical according to the categorical imperative (page 18) perspective?
   b. Is your action ethical according to the utilitarianism perspective (page 43)?
   c. If that email comes to light later, what do you think your boss will say?
2. Regarding your offer of the "advertising" discount:
   a. Is your action ethical according to the categorical imperative perspective?
   b. Is your action ethical according to the utilitarianism perspective?
   c. What effect does that discount have on your company's balance sheet?
3. Regarding your shipping to the fictitious company:
   a. Is your action ethical according to the categorical imperative perspective?
   b. Is your action ethical according to the utilitarianism perspective?
   c. Is your action legal?
4. Describe the effect of your activities on next quarter's inventories.

Source: privilege/Shutterstock

253

ACTIVE REVIEW

Use this Active Review to verify that you understand the material in the chapter. You can read the entire chapter and then perform the tasks in this review, or you can read the text material for just one question and perform the tasks in this review for that question before moving on to the next one.

Q9-1 ▶ What are the fundamentals of a Sales process?

Describe the relationship between the sales process, CRM and marketing. Define *sale* and explain the activities and subactivities in the Sales process. Explain the overriding principle of sales. Locate the Sales process within the value chain.

Q9-2 ▶ How did the Sales process at CBI work before SAP?

Explain the major activities in the Sales process at CBI before SAP and identify the actor who accomplishes each activity and what data are used. Explain how the Sales process is different at CBI for new customers. Identify the two reasons that Sue's sale was disapproved.

Q9-3 ▶ What were the problems with the Sales process before SAP?

Explain the problems in the Sales process at CBI for sales, the warehouse, and accounting.

Q9-4 ▶ How does CBI implement SAP?

Explain the advantages of Salesforce CRM. State CBI's competitive strategy. Describe the efficiency objective and its KPI. Identify the two effectiveness objectives and the KPIs used to assess each one.

Q9-5 ▶ How does the Sales process work at CBI after SAP?

How is the Pre-Sales Action activity different after SAP is implemented? Explain the major activities in the Sales process after SAP. Specify what data each actor supplies for each activity and what SAP does once each actor saves the data on his or her screen. Describe how the new Sales process with SAP overcomes CBI sales problems and achieves sales objectives.

Q9-6 ▶ How can SAP improve CRM processes at CBI?

Explain how data sharing and process integration can improve the set of CRM processes. Why is trying to improve a family of processes like CRM processes a challenge?

Q9-7 ▶ How does e-commerce improve processes in an industry?

Define *e-commerce*. Describe an interorganizational IS. How do merchant and nonmerchant companies differ? Explain the three types of nonmerchant companies. Describe how e-commerce can improve market efficiency. Explain how Google AdWords and Analytics support e-commerce.

Q9-8 ▶ What new IS will affect the Sales process in 2028?

Describe how blockchain works and the role of the miner. Explain the benefits of using blockchain. Describe the data used in social CRM. Explain the benefits to Amazon of the Dash Button. Describe the deep web and the darknet. Explain how a QR code and smartphone can be used to make a sale payment. Explain how process integration impacts your business future.

KEY TERMS AND CONCEPTS

Auction   248
Availability check   238
Blockchain   249
Business-to-business (B2B)   233
Business-to-consumer (B2C)   233
Business-to-government (B2G)   247
Clearinghouse   248
Customer relationship management
   (CRM)   231

Darknet   251
Deep web   251
Disintermediation   248
E-commerce   246
Electronic exchange   248
Interorganizational IS   247
Marketing   231
Merchant company   247
Nonmerchant company   247

Order to cash (O2C)   233
Posting   240
Quotation   234
Real-time price discount   235
Sale   232
Salesforce   236
Social CRM   250
Web storefront   247

USING YOUR KNOWLEDGE

9-1. *MyLab MIS* This chapter introduced the Service process and the Promotion process:
   a. Diagram each process with a BPMN.
   b. For each process, specify efficiency and effectiveness objectives and KPIs appropriate for CBI.
   c. What new IS technologies could CBI use to improve these processes, as specified by your KPI in item b?

9-2. *MyLab MIS* Which of the four nonroutine cognitive skills discussed in Chapter 1 (abstract reasoning, systems thinking, collaboration, or experimentation) did you use to accomplish question 9-1?

9-3. *MyLab MIS* Even after SAP is implemented, input errors can still be made. What kinds of errors can Wally, Sue, and Ann still make? Describe a particularly harmful mistake that each can make and how the process could be changed to prevent that error.

9-4. Think of a company from which you buy a product or service. Specify when and where you share data with that company. Do you believe the company does a good job collecting data from these encounters?

9-5. Think of another company from which you have purchased a product and been disappointed. Identify the

CRM process that may be at fault. Specify how that process could be improved.

9-6. Using the example of a fast food restaurant or coffee shop, identify three processes that must integrate well for the outlet to run smoothly. Specify what data the processes must share or which processes can support the objectives of other processes. Give an example of how the processes not integrating well would be apparent to you as a customer.

9-7. This chapter focused on product sales, but service sales processes are also useful to investigate. Consider the outpatient surgery process at a local hospital.
   a. Diagram the outpatient surgery process using BPMN.
   b. What other processes at the hospital would a patient be a part of when he or she receives outpatient surgery services?
   c. What data should be exchanged among the processes, and how can process synergy with these processes be achieved?

9-8. Blockchain will have a significant impact on the sales process. List three objectives with one KPI each that might be in use for different sales processes that blockchain will improve.

COLLABORATION EXERCISE 9

Collaborate with a group of students to answer. For this exercise, do not meet face to face. Your task will be easier if you coordinate your work with SharePoint, Office 365, Google Docs or equivalent collaboration tools. (See Chapter 10 for a discussion of collaboration tools and processes.) Your answers should reflect the thinking of the entire group, not just that of one or two individuals.

Groupon offers a "Daily Deal" through its Web site, www.groupon.com. Groupon originated in Chicago in 2008 and quickly spread to other cities in North America and then around the world. Groupon offers a Daily Deal in each of its geographic areas each day. If a specified minimum number of

customers accept the deal, the deal becomes available to everyone who signed up. The coupon for each deal is made available to participating customers the day following its announcement. If the minimum number of customers is not met, the deal is canceled for all.

For example, a popular health spa may offer through Groupon a $50 savings on a $125 weekend pass. If the minimum number of customers was set at 500 and, for purposes of this example, 800 accept the offer, then the 800 are notified that "The deal is on." Groupon charges each customer's credit card for $75. Groupon stores customers' credit card data so that customers can accept and participate in deals with minimal fuss.

By charging the credit cards for each customer, Groupon receives cash up front. The next day, each of the 800 customers who purchased the Groupon can log into Groupon, navigate to his or her list of Groupons, and print the $125 voucher. Customers take the voucher to the spa and redeem it on arrival.

Participating firms, such as the spa, do not pay Groupon up front. Groupon takes a percentage of the $75 for each customer and pays the spa the rest. Visit Groupon at www.groupon.com to read more about its CRM processes.

As a team, complete the following:

1. Create a process diagram in BPMN to show Groupon's Sales process.
2. Create a process diagram in BPMN for the spa that shows activities from contacting Groupon for the first time through the end of the spa's promotion.

3. What are the objectives of the processes in Questions 1 and 2? Label each as either an effective or efficient objective.
4. What KPI should both firms use to assess accomplishment of the objectives identified in step 3?
5. Describe how Groupon's IS supports this process.
6. Groupon's Procurement process integrates with the spa's Sales process. How is this integration accomplished?
7. Groupon's Sales process integrates with a customer's Procurement process. How is this integration accomplished?
8. Which of the IS listed in Figure 9-24 could Groupon use to improve its Promotion or Sales process? Explain how they would use the new IS.

ACTIVE CASE 9

SAP Sales Tutorial

A tutorial for the Sales process using SAP is included in the appendix to this chapter, Appendix 9. The tutorial leads the student through a Sales process that sells five bicycles to a customer called Philly Bikes. Once the tutorial is complete, students should answer the following questions.

Questions

9-9. If you completed the case study/tutorial in Chapter 8, how is the Sales process in SAP similar to the Procurement process in SAP? In what important ways are they different?

9-10. Create a screen capture of an SAP screen. Underneath the image, provide an answer to each of the following questions:
   a. In which of the activities does this screen occur?
   b. What is the name of the screen?
   c. What is the name of the screen that precedes it? What screen comes after it?
   d. What actor accomplishes this activity?
   e. Describe an error that this actor could make on this screen that SAP will prevent.

9-11. Make an informal diagram of the four main actors: the Customer (Philly Bikes), Sales (Sue), the Warehouse (Wally), and Accounting (Ann). Draw arrows that show the data that flows between each of the actors during

this process. Number the arrows and include on each arrow what data are included in the message.

9-12. Using the same four main actors, this time show with the arrows how the material (the bikes) moves.

9-13. One concern of a business is fraud. One fraud technique is to create customers who are not customers but who are coconspirators. The conspirator inside the business credits the account of the coconspirator for payments that were never actually received. For this fraud scheme to work, who at CBI has to take part? How can SAP processes decrease the chance of this type of fraud?

9-14. Select any of the main activities or subactivities in the Sales process and:
   a. Specify what event triggers this activity to occur.
   b. Identify what activity follows this activity.
   c. For one data entry item, describe what would happen in the rest of the process if that entry was erroneous.
   d. For one data entry item, describe what limits (controls) you would put in place on the data to prevent the type of error described in item c.

9-15. Having completed one or both tutorials, make two suggestions about how:
   a. SAP could make its software easier to use.
   b. the tutorial(s) could be improved to help new students learn about processes and SAP.

CHAPTER RESOURCES

[1] Peter Drucker, "Infoliteracy," *Forbes*, August 29, 1994, S104.

[2] Jolie O'Dell, "Why Web Sites Are Slow and Why Speed Really Matters," *Mashable*, accessed April 5, 2011, http://mashable.com/2011/04/06/site-speed/.

MyLab MIS

Go to **MyLab MIS.com** for Auto-graded writing questions as well as the following Assisted-graded writing questions:

9-16. Upon graduation you enter the workforce; in a way, this is your university's Sales process. What are the goals of this process from the university's point of view, what are good KPI, and which of the new technologies described in the last section of the chapter can your university use to improve its "Sales" process.

9-17. Salesforce is the leading vendor in cloud based CRM. Research Salesforce on the Internet. What features make Salesforce so attractive to companies? What features make it less attractive to companies than SAP or Oracle systems?

APPENDIX 9—SAP SALES TUTORIAL

This tutorial follows the Sales process shown in Figure 9A-1. The top of this diagram appears in Chapter 9 as Figure 9-4. This top figure shows the three main Sales activities—Sell, Ship, and Payment—and their subactivities (Create Sales Order, etc.). At the bottom of Figure 9A-1, we have added the eight SAP screens that are completed during the Sales process. This tutorial directs you through the procedures for completing each screen. These eight screens were chosen to keep this tutorial simple. To further simplify the process, we begin with screen 3, Create Standard Order.

FIGURE 9A-1

Sales Process and
SAP Screens

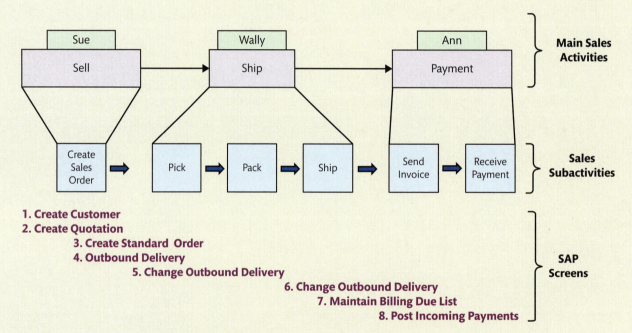

First Exercise

In this first exercise, we will sell five black Deluxe Touring bicycles to Philly Bikes. While our company in this tutorial is Global Bike, Inc., our actors—Sue, Wally, and Ann—and our Sales process are from Chuck's Bikes. Log in using data provided by your instructor (see Figure 8A-2).

1. Create Customer

Skipped—does not apply to this first exercise. It is introduced later.

2. Create Quotation

Skipped—does not apply to this first exercise. It is introduced later.

3. Create Standard Order

This first activity, creating a sales order, is accomplished by a salesperson. At CBI, this is Sue. From the SAP Easy Access screen (Figure 9A-2), navigate to the Sales Order screen by selecting:

Logistics > Sales and Distribution > Sales > Order > Create

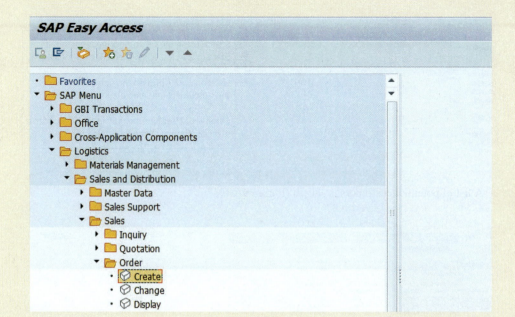

FIGURE 9A-2

SAP Easy Access Screen

Source: Copyright © SAP AG.

When you double-click Create, the next screen to appear is the Create Sales Order: Initial screen (Figure 9A-3). On this screen (Figure 9A-3), you will enter OR (Standard Order), UE00 (US East), WH (Wholesale), and BI (Bicycles). As in the tutorial in Chapter 7, the last two digits in Sales Organization in Figure 9A-3 are zeros, not the letter "O."

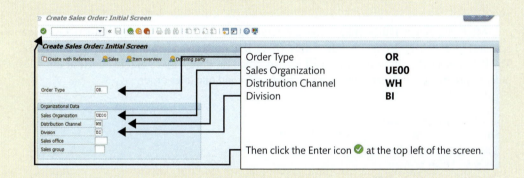

FIGURE 9A-3

Create Sales Order: Initial Screen

Source: Copyright © SAP AG.

The next screen to appear is the Create Standard Order: Overview screen (Figure 9A-4). This is the same screen Sue completed in Figure 9-9.

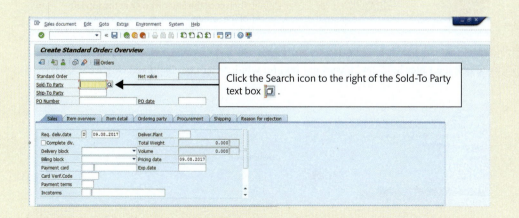

FIGURE 9A-4

Create Standard Order: Overview Screen

Source: Copyright © SAP AG.

This will produce the pop-up search window shown in Figure 9A-5.

FIGURE 9A-5

Customer Search Screen

Source: Copyright © SAP AG.

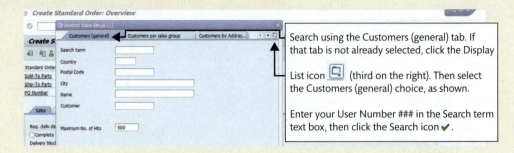

A list of potential customers is shown (Figure 9A-6).

FIGURE 9A-6

Customer List Screen

Source: Copyright © SAP AG.

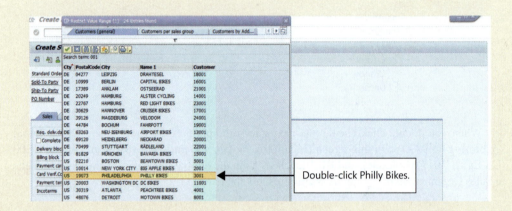

After you select Philly Bikes, you are returned to the Create Standard Order: Overview screen (Figure 9A-7). Notice that the Philly Bikes ID number appears in the Sold-To Party box. The PO number (65430 in this exercise) was specified by Philly Bikes and included in the sales order to provide the link between their purchase order and our sales order.

FIGURE 9A-7

Create Standard Order: Overview Screen, with Philly Bikes ID Number and PO Number

Source: Copyright © SAP AG.

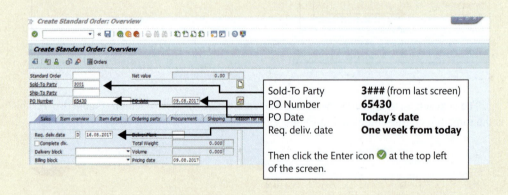

Click the Enter icon, and a warning pop-up window will be displayed (Figure 9A-8).

FIGURE 9A-8

Pop-up Warning Screen, Change in Invoice Date

Source: Copyright © SAP AG.

Click the Enter icon to continue. The system retrieves data about the Philly Bikes customer and displays an updated Create Standard Order: Overview screen (Figure 9A-9).

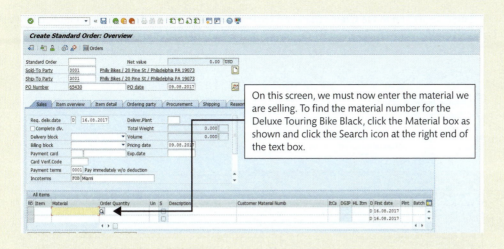

FIGURE 9A-9

Create Standard Order: Overview Screen, with Philly Bikes Customer Info

Source: Copyright © SAP AG.

On this screen, we must now enter the material we are selling. To find the material number for the Deluxe Touring Bike Black, click the Material box as shown and click the Search icon at the right end of the text box.

This will load the material search pop-up screen (Figure 9A-10).

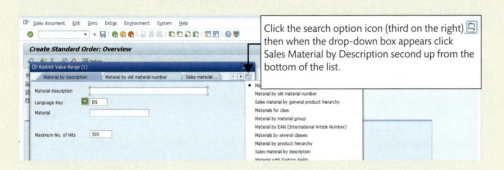

FIGURE 9A-10

Material by Description Search Screen

Source: Copyright © SAP AG.

Click the search option icon (third on the right) then when the drop-down box appears click Sales Material by Description second up from the bottom of the list.

This will reload a new search pop-up screen (Figure 9A-11). Search for Material as shown in Figure 9A-11.

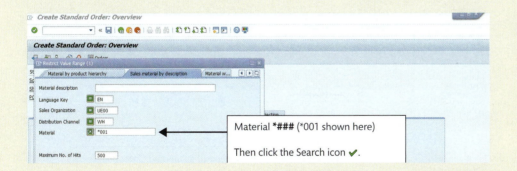

FIGURE 9A-11

Sales Material by Description Search Screen

Source: Copyright © SAP AG.

Material *### (*001 shown here)

Then click the Search icon ✔.

This will show you the sales material you can sell (Figure 9A-12). Find and select Deluxe Touring Bike (Black).

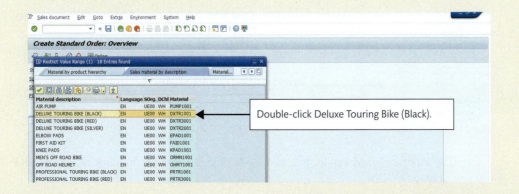

FIGURE 9A-12

Material List Screen

Source: Copyright © SAP AG.

Double-click Deluxe Touring Bike (Black).

This returns you to the Create Standard Order: Overview screen. The material number for the Deluxe Touring Bike (Black) is now displayed in the Material column (Figure 9A-13).

FIGURE 9A-13

Create Standard Order: Overview Screen, with Material Number Displayed

Source: Copyright © SAP AG.

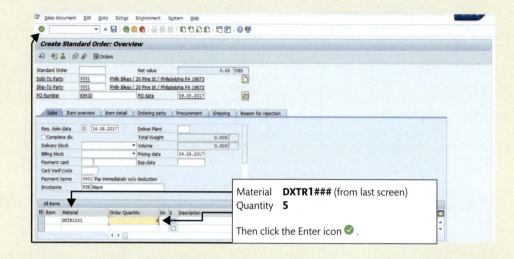

The system will check availability and retrieve Item Number, Total Weight, Net Value, and other data to complete your sales order, as shown in Figure 9A-14.

FIGURE 9A-14

Create Standard Order: Overview Screen, with Item Description Added

Source: Copyright © SAP AG.

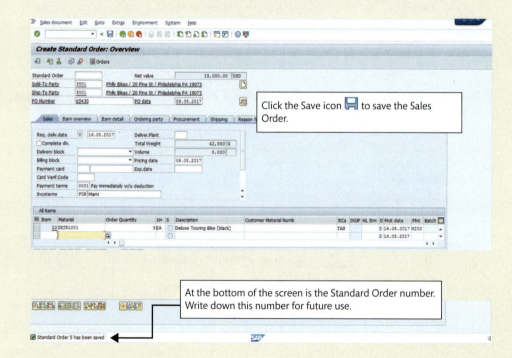

FIGURE 9A-15

Standard Order Number Screen

Source: Copyright © SAP AG.

The sales order is now complete. To return to the SAP Easy Access Screen, click on the exit icon as shown in Figure 9A-16.

FIGURE 9A-16

Toolbar Screen

Source: Copyright © SAP AG.

The Easy Access Screen can be returned to its original structure by clicking on the SAP Menu icon (Figure 9A-17).

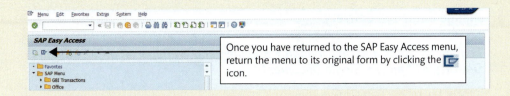

FIGURE 9A-17

Easy Access Screen

Source: Copyright © SAP AG.

4. Outbound Delivery

To initiate the series of warehouse activities—Pick, Pack, and Ship—we must first create an Outbound Delivery. This is the second and last step accomplished by a salesperson. From the SAP Easy Access screen, navigate to the Create Outbound Delivery with Order Reference screen by selecting:

Logistics > Sales and Distribution > Shipping and Transportation > Outbound Delivery > Create > Single Document > With Reference to Sales Order

When the Create Outbound Delivery with Order Reference screen appears (Figure 9A-18), the Order number should automatically load, and it should correspond to the number you just created in the Sales Order activity. Note that our Shipping point is our Miami plant, and the second digit is the letter "I," not the number 1. Also, the sales order number is not your User Number.

FIGURE 9A-18

Create Outbound Delivery with Order Reference Screen

Source: Copyright © SAP AG.

The Outbound Delivery Create: Overview screen is displayed containing the data from the sales order (Figure 9A-19).

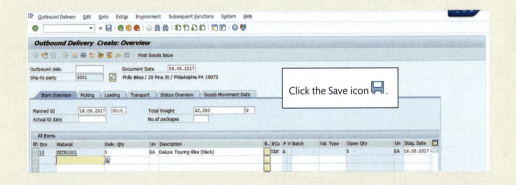

FIGURE 9A-19

Outbound Delivery Create: Overview Screen

Source: Copyright © SAP AG.

By saving the document, the SAP system ensures that the material is available and can meet the specified delivery date. The SAP system assigns a unique number to this delivery document and displays it at the lower-left corner of the Status bar (Figure 9A-20).

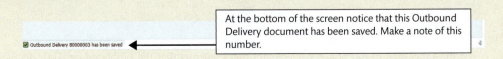

FIGURE 9A-20

Outbound Delivery Document Number

Source: Copyright © SAP AG.

Return to the SAP Easy Access screen by clicking the Exit icon.

5. Change Outbound Delivery

Logistics > Sales and Distribution > Shipping and Transportation > Outbound Delivery > Change > Single Document

When a sales order is picked, the material is moved from its storage location to the packing area. This picking activity, as well as the next two activities, packing and shipping, are accomplished by the warehouse manager. At CBI, this is Wally. To do this, we must change the delivery document. The first screen in this activity is the Change Outbound Delivery screen (Figure 9A-21).

FIGURE 9A-21

Change Outbound Delivery Screen

Source: Copyright © SAP AG.

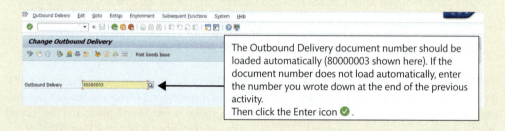

The Outbound Delivery document number should be loaded automatically (80000003 shown here). If the document number does not load automatically, enter the number you wrote down at the end of the previous activity.
Then click the Enter icon ✅ .

The Outbound Delivery Change: Overview screen will appear (it is very similar to the Outbound Delivery Create: Overview screen in the previous activity). Notice in the item detail section that the Item Overview tab has been selected (Figure 9A-22).

FIGURE 9A-22

Outbound Delivery Change: Overview Screen, Item Overview Tab

Source: Copyright © SAP AG.

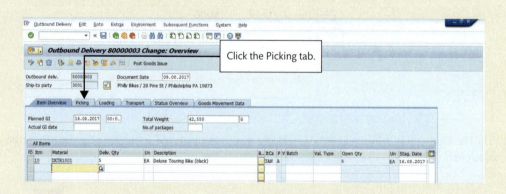

Click the Picking tab.

Add the SLoc (Storage Location) and Picked Qty (Picked Quantity) as shown in Figure 9A-23. On this screen, SLoc may appear as a very narrow column with its visible heading shortened as "S…"

FIGURE 9A-23

Outbound Delivery Change: Overview Screen, Picking Tab

Source: Copyright © SAP AG.

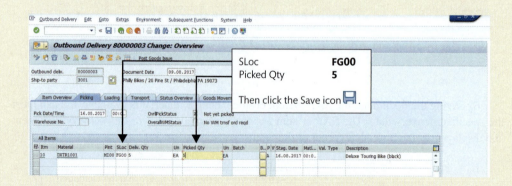

| SLoc | FG00 |
| Picked Qty | 5 |

Then click the Save icon 💾 .

Again, a message in the Status bar appears that confirms that the outbound delivery document is saved. It will be the same document number you created in Figure 9A-20. Return to the SAP Easy Access screen by clicking the Exit icon.

6. Change Outbound Delivery

Logistics > Sales and Distribution > Shipping and Transportation > Outbound Delivery > Change > Single Document

After the picking activity, Wally accomplishes the packing activity. No SAP screens are required for packing. Posting, also called shipping, occurs next. When posting occurs, possession of the material transfers from Global Bike to Philly Bikes, and inventory at Global Bike is reduced. Legal ownership of the material also changes hands. The first screen that appears in this activity, Change Outbound Delivery (Figure 9A-24), is the same as the first and last screen in the previous activity (Figure 9A-21).

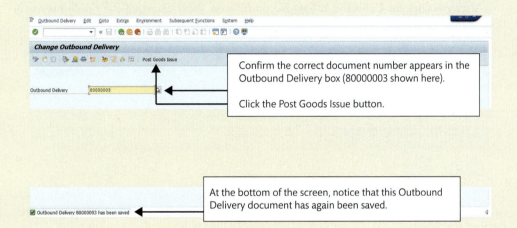

FIGURE 9A-24

Change Outbound Delivery Screen

Source: Copyright © SAP AG.

Confirm the correct document number appears in the Outbound Delivery box (80000003 shown here).

Click the Post Goods Issue button.

At the bottom of the screen, notice that this Outbound Delivery document has again been saved.

FIGURE 9A-25

Change Outbound Delivery Screen, Saved Confirmation

Source: Copyright © SAP AG.

Return to the SAP Easy Access screen by clicking the Exit icon.

7. Maintain Billing Due List

Logistics > Sales and Distribution > Billing > Billing Document > Process Billing Due List

This activity creates an invoice for the bikes that have been shipped. This invoice is sent to the customer. Sending the invoice and receiving payment are activities accomplished by an accountant. At CBI, this is accomplished by Ann. The first screen is the Maintain Billing Due List screen (Figure 9A-26).

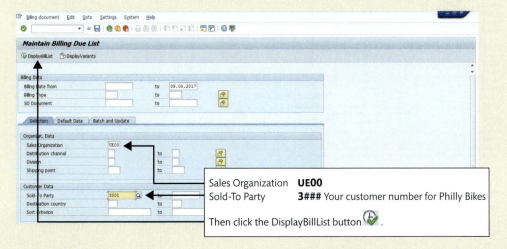

FIGURE 9A-26

Maintain Billing Due List Screen

Source: Copyright © SAP AG.

Sales Organization **UE00**
Sold-To Party **3###** Your customer number for Philly Bikes

Then click the DisplayBillList button.

The bill list will be displayed with the new bill highlighted, as shown in Figure 9A-27. Click the Collective Billing Document button.

FIGURE 9A-27

Maintain Billing Due List Screen, Bill List Displayed with New Bill Highlighted

Source: Copyright © SAP AG.

After you click the Collective Billing Document icon, the background color of this row will disappear, as shown in Figure 9A-28. An invoice has now been created.

FIGURE 9A-28

Maintain Billing Due List Screen, Bill List Displayed without Background Color

Source: Copyright © SAP AG.

The Maintain Billing Due List screen is now complete. Because this data is automatically saved, you do not need to click Enter or Save. Return to the SAP Easy Access screen by clicking the Exit icon twice.

8. Post Incoming Payments

Accounting > Financial Accounting > Accountants Receivable > Document Entry > Incoming Payments

In the previous activity we sent Philly Bikes a bill. It has now sent us a $15,000 payment. In this activity we record receipt of that payment. The first screen is the Post Incoming Payments: Header Data screen (Figure 9A-29).

FIGURE 9A-29

Post Incoming Payments: Header Data Screen

Source: Copyright © SAP AG.

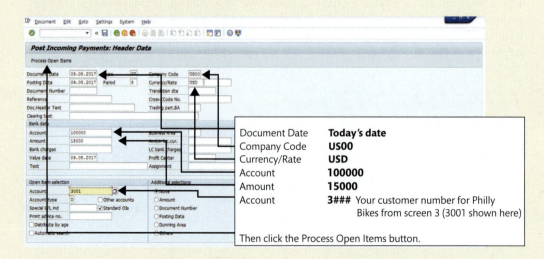

The Post Incoming Payments Process Open Items Screen will appear, as shown in Figure 9A-30.

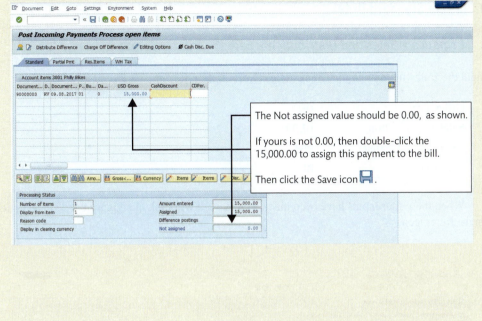

FIGURE 9A-30

Post Incoming Payments Process Open Items Screen, Standard Tab

Source: Copyright © SAP AG.

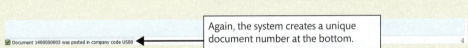

FIGURE 9A-31

Payment Document Screen

Source: Copyright © SAP AG.

Return to the SAP Easy Access screen by clicking the Exit icon. This will generate a pop-up window that is misleading (Figure 9A-32). There is no data to be lost at this point, so click Yes. You are finished with the first exercise.

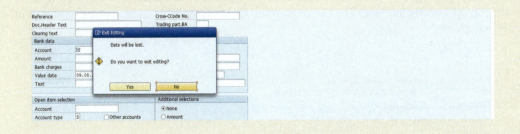

FIGURE 9A-32

Data Lost Pop-up Warning Screen

Source: Copyright © SAP AG.

You Try It 1

You will sell 10 Professional Touring Black Bikes to Philly Bikes. All the data necessary is included for each screen.

This is PO 65431, the PO date is today, and the requested delivery date is 1 week from today. Ship the order a week from today. Use Miami as the shipping point. The total price is $32,000.

<u>Please note</u>: Not every screen is shown here. Refer to the first exercise to see each screen.

3. Create Standard Order

Logistics > Sales and Distribution > Sales > Order > Create

Input the following data in the Create Sales Order: Initial Screen.

Order Type	**OR**
Sales Organization	**UE00**
Distribution Channel	**WH**
Division	**BI**

When these four inputs have been made, your screen will look like Figure 9A-33. Then click on the Enter icon.

FIGURE 9A-33

Create Sales Order Screen

Source: Copyright © SAP AG.

Enter the next four items on the Create Standard Order: Overview screen.

Sold-To Party	**3###** (3001 shown here)
PO Number	**65431**
PO date	**Today's date**
Req. delv.date	**One week from today**

After entering these four data items, click the Enter icon and then click the Enter icon on the pop-up warning message. The Create Standard Order: Overview screen appears, as shown in Figure 9A-34.

FIGURE 9A-34

Create Standard Order Screen

Source: Copyright © SAP AG.

Enter the material data:

Material	**PRTR1###**
Order Quantity	**10**

After entering these two data items, click the Enter icon and then the Save icon.

4. Outbound Delivery

Logistics > Sales and Distribution > Shipping and Transportation > Outbound Delivery > Create > Single Document > With Reference to Sales Order

Enter the following data, click Enter, then save the document and record the Outbound Delivery document number.

Shipping point	**MI00**
Selection date	**One week from today**
Order	**Your sales order number** (automatic, from the previous step)

5. Change Outbound Delivery

Logistics > Sales and Distribution > Shipping and Transportation > Outbound Delivery > Change > Single Document

Click on Enter. Input the following data in the Outbound Delivery Change: Overview screen. Remember to click on the Picking tab first.

SLoc	**FG00**
Picked Qty	**10**

After you have made these two inputs, your screen will look like Figure 9A-35. Save the document.

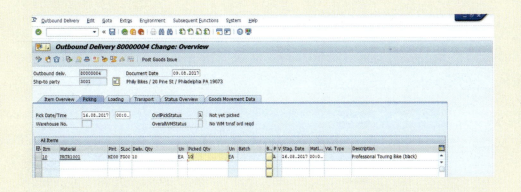

FIGURE 9A-35
Outbound Delivery Change Screen

Source: Copyright © SAP AG.

6. Change Outbound Delivery

Logistics > Sales and Distribution > Shipping and Transportation > Outbound Delivery > Change > Single Document

Click the Post Goods Issue button after confirming that the document number is correct.

7. Maintain Billing Due List

Logistics > Sales and Distribution > Billing > Billing Document >
Process Billing Due List

Input the following data in the Maintain Billing Due List:

Sales Organization	**UE00**
Sold-To Party	**3###** Your customer number for Philly Bikes

After clicking the DisplayBillList button and the Collective Billing Document button, the Maintain Billing Due List screen appears, as shown in Figure 9A-36.

FIGURE 9A-36

Maintain Billing Due List Screen

Source: Copyright © SAP AG.

8. Post Incoming Payments

Accounting > Financial Accounting > Accountants Receivable >
Document Entry > Incoming Payments

Enter the following data in the Post Incoming Payments: Header Data screen. Your screen should look like Figure 9A-37.

Document Date	**Today's date**
Company Code	**US00**
Currency/Rate	**USD**
Account	**100000**
Amount	**32000**
Account	**3###** (3001 shown here)

FIGURE 9A-37

Post Incoming Payments Screen

Source: Copyright © SAP AG.

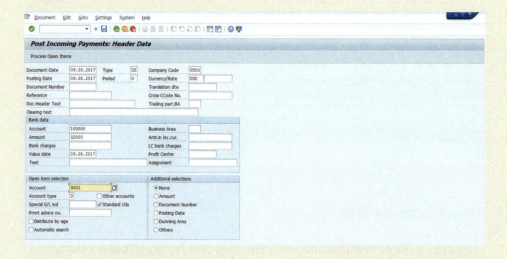

After clicking the Process Open Items button, the Post Incoming Payments Process Open Items screen will appear, as shown in Figure 9A-38.

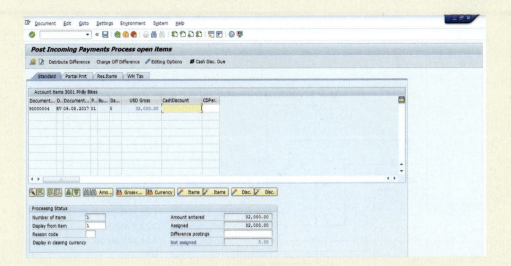

FIGURE 9A-38
Post Incoming Payments Process Open Items Screen

Source: Copyright © SAP AG.

Click on Save.

You Try It 2

Sell three Deluxe Touring Black Bikes to a new customer—Cycle Works—and give it a price quote. The Cycle Works data can be found on the following New Customer screens (Figures 9A-39 through 9A-45).

1. Create Customer

Logistics > Sales and Distribution > Master Data > Business Partner > Customer > Create > Complete

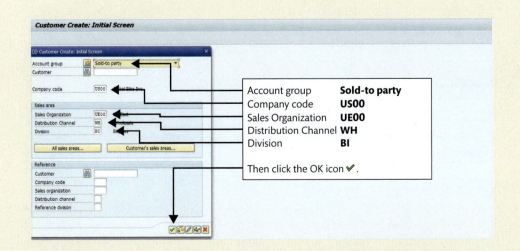

FIGURE 9A-39
Customer Create: Initial Screen

Source: Copyright © SAP AG.

FIGURE 9A-40

Create Customer: General Data Screen

Source: Copyright © SAP AG.

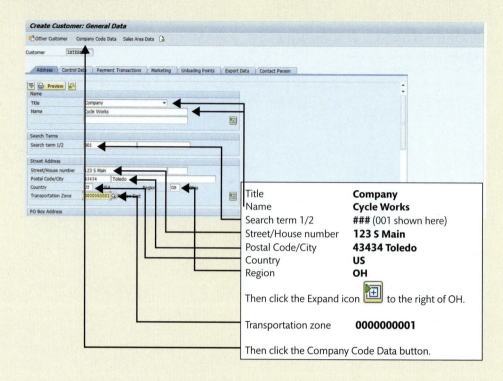

FIGURE 9A-41

Create Customer: Company Code Data Screen, Account Management Tab

Source: Copyright © SAP AG.

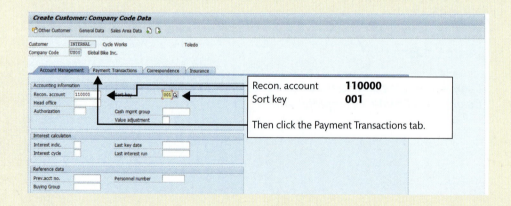

FIGURE 9A-42

Create Customer: Company Code Data Screen, Payment Transactions Tab

Source: Copyright © SAP AG.

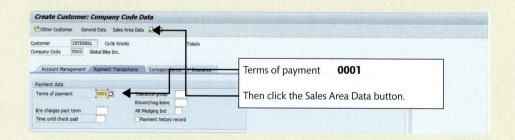

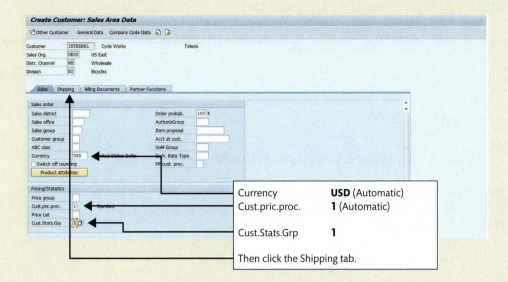

FIGURE 9A-43
Create Customer: Sales Area Data Screen, Sales Tab
Source: Copyright © SAP AG.

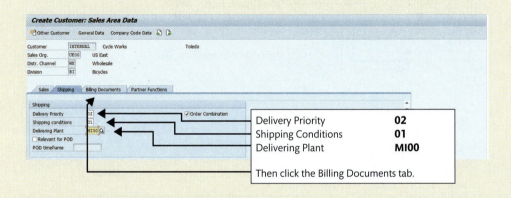

FIGURE 9A-44
Create Customer: Sales Area Data Screen, Shipping Tab
Source: Copyright © SAP AG.

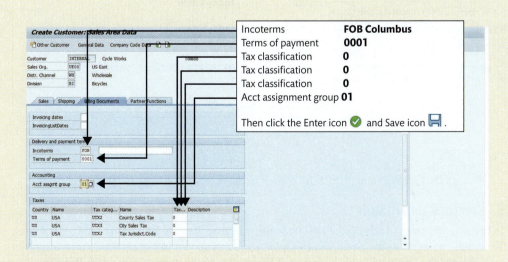

FIGURE 9A-45
Create Customer: Sales Area Data Screen, Billing Documents Tab
Source: Copyright © SAP AG.

A new customer is created (Figure 9A-46).

FIGURE 9A-46

Create Customer Number Screen

Source: Copyright © SAP AG.

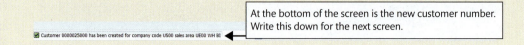

At the bottom of the screen is the new customer number. Write this down for the next screen.

2. Price Quotation

Logistics > Sales and Distribution > Sales > Quotation > Create

Cycle Works, our new customer, has asked for a price quote on Deluxe Black Bikes (Figures 9A-47 and 9A-48). You will create a sales order to sell these bikes to Cycle Works as shown in Figure 9A-49.

FIGURE 9A-47

Create Quotation: Initial Screen

Source: Copyright © SAP AG.

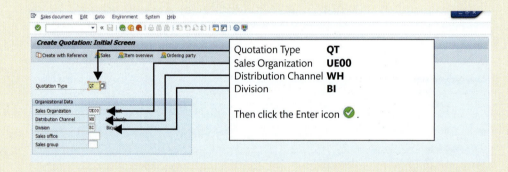

Quotation Type	**QT**
Sales Organization	**UE00**
Distribution Channel	**WH**
Division	**BI**

Then click the Enter icon ✅ .

FIGURE 9A-48

Create Quotation: Overview Screen

Source: Copyright © SAP AG.

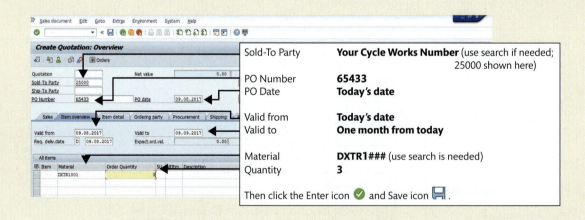

Sold-To Party	**Your Cycle Works Number** (use search if needed; 25000 shown here)
PO Number	**65433**
PO Date	**Today's date**
Valid from	**Today's date**
Valid to	**One month from today**
Material	**DXTR1###** (use search is needed)
Quantity	**3**

Then click the Enter icon ✅ and Save icon 💾 .

Record the Quotation number at the bottom of the screen.

3. Create Standard Order

In this activity, create a sales order to sell the three Deluxe Touring Black Bikes to Cycle Works. To do this, navigate to the Create Sales Order screen as shown in Figure 9A-2; then after you have entered the four data fields as shown in Figure 9A-49, click on "Create with Reference"—see Figure 9A-49. Enter your Quot. number from screen 2: Price Quotation. On the Create

Standard Order: Overview screen, the PO is 65433, the PO date is today, and Req. Deliv. Date is a week from today. Follow this order through to screen 8. Then in screen 8, record a payment from Cycle Works for $9,000. All the other data is the same as in the first exercise.

FIGURE 9A-49
Create with Reference
Sales Order Screen

Source: Copyright © SAP AG.

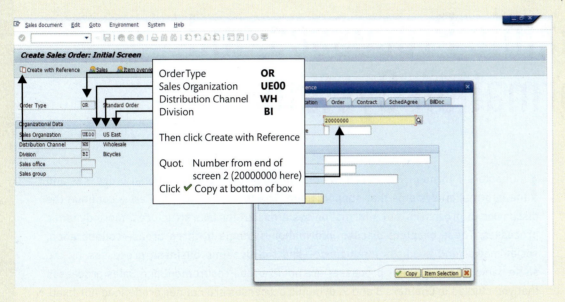

Part 4

Dynamic Processes and Information Systems

In Chapters 6 through 9 of Part 3, we discussed structured, operational processes and the information systems that support them. The three chapters in Part 4 continue the discussion of processes and information systems, but for less structured, more dynamic processes. These chapters discuss information systems in three areas—collaboration, social media, and business intelligence—and the dynamic business processes by the same name. These dynamic processes are not like the Procurement and Sales processes that you studied in Chapters 8 and 9; dynamic processes are neither predefined nor fixed. That does not mean, however, that they are unstructured. Dynamic processes have a structure, but their structure is often created on the fly, the activities are fluid and frequently changed and intermingled with other processes, and they often include a lot of backtracking and repetition. You execute a dynamic process when you and your friends collaborate about where to go out to eat—topics are made up on the fly and change rapidly, and you backtrack and start over when someone vetoes a choice or a time.

Dynamic processes such as collaboration, social media, and business intelligence are not typically an end unto themselves. Instead, they are executed to support other business processes. You and your friends collaborate about where to go out to eat; the goal is going, not just collaborating. In these chapters, we will examine how the three dynamic processes support business processes such as project management, promotion, and decision making.

Although specifying objectives and measures is as important to dynamic processes as it is to structured operational processes, dynamic processes typically have fewer well-accepted objectives and measures. Objectives are not as well accepted because they also tend to be dynamic, changing as actors, outputs, and situations change. Further, while dynamic processes have activities in which particular objectives are achieved, the means by which those objectives are achieved vary widely. A final difference with structured processes is that dynamic processes are typically not diagrammed using techniques such as BPMN. As you will see, when we do use such techniques, the activities become very high level and generic, such as "analyze data."

To help you organize your thinking about the three dynamic processes and the business processes they support, each of the three chapters follows a similar outline. First, we address the process—collaboration, social media, or business intelligence—and then

Dynamic Process	Objectives	Key Activities	Example IS	Business Processes Containing Activities
Collaboration **Chapter 10**	Successful output Growth in team capability Meaningful and satisfying experience	Communication Iteration	SharePoint Google Drive E-mail	Project Management Workflow
Social Media **Chapter 11**	For people—belonging For businesses—support strategy For app providers—market share	Create content Share content	Facebook Twitter LinkedIn	Promotion Customer Service
Business Intelligence **Chapter 12**	Inform to assess Inform to predict	Acquire Analyze Publish	Excel SAP Business Objects Tableau	Decision Making Next Best Offer Counterterrorism

FIGURE 10-1
Three Dynamic Processes of Part 4

we explain the information systems that support the activities of the process. We conclude by examining how IS support these activities in actual business processes. A summary of the chapter topics is shown in Figure 10-1.

Before we begin, keep in mind that the title of each chapter—collaboration, social media, and BI—can apply to both the processes and the IS that support them. In this text, we make them distinct to better understand them. However, realize that people often confuse a process with the IS that supports it, so don't be surprised when they don't distinguish between the two.

Chapter 10

Collaboration and IS

Because of recent changes in healthcare law and insurance, market conditions favor large medical organizations. Consequently, many hospital systems have acquired small and medium-sized medical practices and integrated them into the larger system. Wood Hospital is no exception; in the past year, it acquired seven separate medical practices.

Integrating these separate businesses has been challenging; one of the biggest headaches has been patient billing. Melissa Huser, manager of patient billing at Wood Hospital, thought it would be useful to bring all the new billing managers together in a series of meetings to develop standardized billing processes, procedures, and data coding. After six such meetings, the group has finished its work.

Several committee members stop to speak with Melissa at the end of the last meeting.

"Melissa, I was wrong." Gerri Swanson, billing manager of one of the recently acquired practices, says rather sheepishly.

"What do you mean, Gerri?"

"When I got your email telling me to come to these meetings, I just dreaded it. For one, it's hard for me to get here during rush hour, but also, well, you know how some meetings can just drag on and not get anything done? Well, we got a lot done. And it's going to help me."

"Me, too!" John Abramson, another member of the committee, jumps into their conversation. "All these treatment and billing codes are so complex, and as a small group, I'm the only one who deals with them in our practice. I really learned a lot from everyone else."

"Melissa, I didn't just want to compliment you," continued Gerri. "Much as I hate to admit it, I think we need to keep this going."

"Why so?" Melissa asks this question, but she's been thinking the same thing.

"Because we know there is going to be change, and lots of it, for the foreseeable future. And why should each of our groups fight those battles alone?" John nods as Gerri says this.

"OK. I agree," Melissa responds, pleased as she can be. This is exactly the outcome she'd been hoping for. "But what about the traffic and the time away from your offices?"

"Well, why don't we set up some kind of Web site to share documents? And do some, maybe all, of these meetings online? Using Skype or something like that?" Gerri's been thinking about this while she drives to the meetings.

"And I'd like to have some kind of message board where we post thoughts, rumors, fears, and so on, and comment on them." John does billing only part time, and

Q10-1. What is collaboration, and why is it important to business?

Q10-2. What are the objectives of the collaboration process?

Q10-3. What are the key components of a collaboration IS?

Q10-4. How can collaboration IS support the communicating activity?

Q10-5. How can collaboration IS support the iterating activity?

Q10-6. How can collaboration IS support business processes?

Q10-7. Which collaboration IS is right for your team?

Q10-8. 2028?

PSI BIG PICTURE

PROCESS: Collaboration process: Communicate and Iterate

IS: Collaboration IS can improve processes

he doesn't have as much time to keep up with changes as some of the others do. He'd like to know what they think is coming down the line.

"Yeah, great. And what about a task list? So we could see who's working on what and maybe post our own tasks … pass things around the committee?" Gerri's super organized, and she wants to know who's doing what and when.

"These seem like great ideas. I'm sure it could be done. But how?" Melissa asks.

But how? That's what you'll learn in this chapter.

PREVIEW

The billing staff at Wood Hospital have a problem. They know that they want to work together and share ideas, tasks, and documents. They also know that technology can help them. But they don't know how. This chapter will show you what they (and you!) can do to harness technology for collaboration. First, we discuss the dynamic collaboration process and the information systems used in collaboration. Next, we discuss how collaboration information systems support specific collaboration activities, and then we discuss how collaboration IS support collaboration activities in actual business processes.

You are already familiar with some collaboration IS—texting, Skype, and FaceTime. The point of this chapter is for you to understand how those and other tools are used to support collaboration activities in actual business processes. This understanding is practical and useful, and you can apply it as soon as tonight. Many of your classes require collaboration of some sort, and you will improve the quality of your work if you apply this knowledge to your collaboration.

MyLab MIS

- Using Your Knowledge Questions 10-1, 10-2, 10-3
- Essay Questions 10-12, 10-13
- Excel and Access Application Questions 10-1, 10-2

Q10-1 What Is Collaboration, and Why Is It Important to Business?

Business is collaboration—it's a social activity, a team sport. Collaborating teams accomplish work that creates value for customers; it is the glue that holds an organization together.[1] Absent the glue, the business struggles. At Wood Hospital, not only the billing staff but everyone in the hospital does their work using collaborative processes.

While collaboration has always been important, it is becoming increasingly essential as strategies, processes, products, and services become more complex. The more complicated the work, the more collaboration is needed to take action. For example, look at how systems that bring data to your dorm room have changed over time. The business of delivering high-speed Internet is much more complicated than delivering telephone services a few years ago. When you encounter problems with your Internet service, the person that troubleshoots your problem will need to collaborate much more often than the phone tech of yesteryear.

While collaboration is now more common, its payoffs can be quite uncommon. In the airline industry just 20 years ago, the captain on the flight deck was the king (most captains were male), the copilot and flight engineer were expected to kept quiet or risk losing their jobs, and flight attendants kept their distance. Collaboration meant getting coffee for the captain. Today, the flight deck is much more collaborative, not just about the flight, but about passenger concerns, too. According to Captain Sullenberger, who safely landed his crippled Airbus in the Hudson River, this better collaboration has led to a remarkable decrease in airline accidents over the past 20 years. Adopting many of the same collaborating ideas, healthcare teams of doctors, nurses, and other professionals are becoming much more collaborative about patient diagnoses and treatments. The result has been a noticeable decline in treatment errors. However, you don't have to fly or volunteer for surgery to see effective teams. As mentioned in Chapter 1, effective collaboration is an increasingly common business skill.

As collaboration has grown over the years, so too has the technology that supports collaborative work. In your grandparents' day, communication was done using letter, phone, and office visits. Those technologies were augmented in the 1980s and 1990s with fax and email and more recently by texting, conference calls, and videoconferencing. Today, products such as Google Drive and Office 365 provide a wide array of tools to support collaborative work. By the time you land your first job, there will surely be other new technologies to use.

While you will read important concepts and terms in this chapter, the best learning will occur when you apply these lessons to your own teams to improve your collaboration skills. You already collaborate and use collaboration IS, but as you read, ask yourself what you do well and not so well and if you can use these ideas to improve your collaborations. Use these ideas on teams for academic assignments and on teams outside of class. Not only will your collaboration skills improve, but you will be ready for interviewers who will ask questions like "Why you think of yourself as a team player?" or "Can you tell me about a time when your needed to manage a challenging team dynamic?" and "What could you have done to be more effective?"

To get started, we need to first distinguish between the terms *cooperation* and *collaboration*. **Cooperation** is a process where a group of people work together, all doing essentially the same type of work, to accomplish a job. A group of four painters, each painting a different wall in the same room, are working cooperatively. Similarly, a group of checkers at the grocery store or clerks at the post office are working cooperatively to service customers. A cooperative team can accomplish a given task faster than an individual working alone, but the cooperative result is usually not better in quality than the result of someone working alone.

The Two Key Activities of Collaboration

In this text, we define **collaboration** as a dynamic process: a group of people working together to achieve common objectives *via communication and iteration*. One person will produce something, say the draft of a document, and communicate that draft to a second person, who will review that draft and communicate feedback. Given the feedback, the original author or someone else will then revise the first draft to produce a second. The work proceeds in a series of stages, or *iterations*, in which something is produced, members create feedback, and then another version is produced. Using iteration and communication, the group's result can be better than what any single individual can produce alone. This is possible because different group members provide different perspectives. "Oh, I never thought of it that way" is a typical signal of collaboration success.

Many, perhaps most, student groups rely on cooperation rather than collaboration. Given an assignment, a group of five students will break it up into five pieces, work to accomplish their pieces independently, and then merge their independent work for grading by the professor. Such a process will enable the project to be completed more quickly, with less work by any single individual, but it will not be better than the result obtained if the students were to work alone.

In contrast, when students work collaboratively, they set forth an initial idea or work product, communicate feedback to one another on those ideas or products, and then revise in accordance with feedback. Such a process can produce a result far superior to that produced by any student working alone.

Importance of Effective Critical Feedback

One key aspect of team communication is feedback—for collaboration to be successful, members must provide and receive *critical* feedback. A group in which everyone is too polite to say anything critical cannot collaborate. As Darwin John, the world's first chief information officer (CIO), once said, "If two of you have the exact same idea, then we have no need for one of you." On the other hand, a group that is so critical and negative that members come to distrust, even hate, one another cannot effectively collaborate, either. For most groups, success is achieved between these extremes.

To underline this point, consider the research of Ditkoff, Allen, Moore, and Pollard. They surveyed 108 business professionals to determine the qualities, attitudes, and skills that make a good collaborator.[2] Figure 10-2 lists the most and least important characteristics reported in the survey.

Twelve Most Important Characteristics for an Effective Collaborator
1. Is enthusiastic about the subject of our collaboration.
2. Is open-minded and curious.
3. Speaks his or her mind even if it's an unpopular viewpoint.
4. Gets back to me and others in a timely way.
5. Is willing to enter into difficult conversations.
6. Is a perceptive listener.
7. Is skillful at giving/receiving negative feedback.
8. Is willing to put forward unpopular ideas.
9. Is self-managing and requires "low maintenance."
10. Is known for following through on commitments.
11. Is willing to dig into the topic with zeal.
12. Thinks differently than I do/brings different perspectives.

Nine Least Important Characteristics for an Effective Collaborator
31. Is well organized.
32. Is someone I immediately liked. The chemistry is good.
33. Has already earned my trust.
34. Has experience as a collaborator.
35. Is a skilled and persuasive presenter.
36. Is gregarious and dynamic.
37. Is someone I knew beforehand.
38. Has an established reputation in field of our collaboration.
39. Is an experienced businessperson.

FIGURE 10-2
Importance of Collaboration Characteristics

Most students are surprised to learn that five of the top 12 characteristics involve disagreement (highlighted in blue in Figure 10-2). Most students believe that "we should all get along" and more or less have the same ideas and opinions about team matters. Although it is important for the team to be social enough to work together, this research indicates that it is also important for team members to have different ideas and opinions and to express them to each other.

When we think about collaboration as an iterative process in which team members give and receive feedback, these results are not surprising. During collaboration, team members learn from each other, and it is difficult to learn if no one is willing to express different, or even unpopular, ideas. The respondents also seem to be saying, "You can be negative, as long as you care about what we're doing." These collaboration skills do not come naturally to people who have been taught to "play well with others," but that may be why they were so highly ranked in the survey.

The characteristics rated *not relevant* are also revealing. Experience as a collaborator or in business does not seem to matter. Being popular also is not important. A big surprise, however, is that being well organized was rated 31st out of 39 characteristics. Perhaps collaboration itself is not a very well-organized process?

Guidelines for Giving and Receiving Critical Feedback

Giving and receiving critical feedback is the single most important collaboration skill. So, before we discuss the role that information systems can play in collaboration, study the guidelines for giving and receiving critical feedback shown in Figure 10-3.

Many students have found that when they first form a collaborative group, it's useful to begin with a discussion of critical feedback guidelines like those in Figure 10-3. Begin with this list, and then, using feedback and iteration, develop your own list. Of course, if a group member does not follow the agreed-upon guidelines, someone will have to provide critical feedback to that effect as well.

Warning!

If you are like most undergraduate business students, especially freshmen or sophomores, your life experience is keeping you from appreciating the value of collaboration. So far, almost everyone you know has the same experiences as you and thinks like you. Your friends and associates have the same educational background, scored more or less the same on standardized tests, and have the same orientation toward success. Most of the time, your teams have included others who are similar in age, experience, and education. So, why should you collaborate instead of just cooperating? You may feel that everyone in your group thinks the same way anyway.

FIGURE 10-3

Guidelines for Giving and Receiving Critical Feedback

Guideline	Example
Be specific.	"I was confused until I got to Section 2" rather than "The whole thing is a disorganized mess."
Offer suggestions.	"Consider moving Section 2 to the beginning of the document."
Avoid personal comments.	Never: "Only an idiot would miss that point . . . or write that document."
Strive for balance.	"I thought Section 2 was particularly good. What do you think about moving it to the start of the document?"
Question your emotions.	"Why do I feel so angry about the comment he just made? What's going on? Is my anger helping me?"
Do not dominate.	If there are five members of the group, unless you have special expertise, you are entitled to just 20 percent of the words/time.
Demonstrate a commitment to the group.	"I know this is painful, but if we can make these changes our result will be so much better." or "Ouch. I really didn't want to have to redo that section, but if you all think it's important, I'll do it."

In your effort to get the project done, your group asks, "What does the professor want and what's the easiest, fastest way to get it to her?" instead of "How can we complete this project with the highest quality possible?"

Consider this thought experiment. Your company is planning to build a new facility that is critical for the success of a new product line and will create 300 new jobs. The county government won't issue a building permit because the site is prone to landslides. Your engineers believe your design overcomes that hazard, but your CFO is concerned about possible litigation in the event there is a problem. Your corporate counsel is investigating the best way to overcome the county's objections while limiting liability. Meanwhile, a local environmental group is protesting your site because it believes it is too close to an eagle's nest. Your public relations director is meeting with this local group every week.

Do you proceed with the project?

To decide, you create a working team of the chief engineer, the chief financial officer (CFO), your legal counsel, and the PR director. These people vary widely in age, education and expertise, life experience, and values. In fact, the only thing they have in common is that they are paid by your company. Now compare this group to your student group. Although the business group will participate collaboratively in ways that are far different from your experience as a student, the groups may be more alike than you think. Although you may initially believe that other students think like you, that may be an illusion based on not knowing them well. Each student will bring a unique perspective to the group, which will become more evident as you get to know the group members.

While underappreciated by most young people, collaboration is both common and essential to every organization. To help you get ready to be productive in that environment, we start by considering the types of objectives collaborating teams pursue.

Q10-2 What Are the Objectives of the Collaboration Process?

Like most business processes, the key to understanding collaboration is to understand its objectives. As mentioned in Chapter 2, dynamic processes typically emphasize effectiveness more than efficiency. Here we outline three effectiveness objectives while recognizing that collaboration also has an underlying efficiency objective: to meet time and cost limits.

J. Richard Hackman studied teamwork for many years, and his book *Leading Teams* contains many useful concepts and tips for future managers.[3] According to Hackman, there are three general objectives for collaboration, as shown in Figure 10-4.

Product Objective: Successful Output

The output of collaboration is the deliverable—a homework assignment for a student team, a budget plan or new product for a business team. Most students are primarily concerned with this first objective, making a successful deliverable. Whatever the intended output is, the first objective is "Did we do it?"

Team Objective: Growth in Team Capability

The other two objectives are process, not output, objectives—they address how well the team worked together, not the product they delivered. These can be surprising to many students, probably because most student teams are short-lived. But, in business, where teams often last months or years, it makes sense to ask, "Did the team get better?" If you're a football fan, you've undoubtedly heard your college's coach say, "We really improved as the season progressed." Football teams last only a season. If the team is permanent, say a team of customer support

Effectiveness
Product objective—Successful output
Team objective—Growth in team capability
Individual objective—Meaningful and satisfying experience
Efficiency
Time and cost

FIGURE 10-4
Collaboration Process Objectives

personnel, the benefits of team growth are even greater. Over time, as the team gets better, it becomes more efficient; thus, over time the team provides more service for a given cost or the same service for less cost.

How does a team get better? For one, it develops better work processes. Activities are combined or eliminated. Communication is improved so that "the left hand knows what the right hand is doing," or needs, or can provide. Teams also get better as individuals improve at their tasks. Part of that improvement is the learning curve; as someone does something over and over, he or she gets better at it. But team members also teach task skills, give knowledge to one another, and provide perspectives that other team members need.

Individual Objective: Meaningful and Satisfying Experience

The third objective of Hackman's definition of team success is that team members have a meaningful and satisfying experience. Of course, the nature of team goals is a major factor in making work meaningful. But few of us have the opportunity to develop a life-saving cancer vaccine or safely land a stricken airliner in the Hudson River. For most of us, it's a matter of making the product, creating the shipment, accounting for the payment, or finding the prospects, and so on.

So, in that world, what makes work meaningful? Hackman cites numerous studies in his book, and one common thread is that the work is perceived as meaningful by the team. Keeping prices up to date in the product database may not be the most exciting work, but if that task is perceived by the team as important, it will become meaningful.

Furthermore, if an individual's work is not only perceived as important, but the person doing that work is also given credit for it, then the experience will be perceived as meaningful. So, recognition for work well done is vitally important for a meaningful work experience.

Another aspect of team satisfaction is camaraderie. Business professionals, just like students, are energized when they have the feeling that they are part of a group; each person is doing his or her own job and combining efforts to achieve something worthwhile that is better than any could have done alone.

As mentioned earlier in the text, dynamic processes tend to have less well-accepted objectives than structured processes. If you asked team members, "What is the objective of the team—a successful outcome, growth of capability, or a satisfying experience?" you will likely hear a different answer from every team member. Not only do objectives vary by team member, they also vary over the course of the life of the team; at different points in time, different objectives have higher priority. So a word to the wise—don't expect everyone on the team to be on the same page or to have the same objectives.

Now that we have explained the collaboration process and its objectives, we turn to the main focus of this chapter—the role of collaboration information systems in supporting business processes. Figure 10-5 depicts the relationship between collaboration IS, collaboration process

FIGURE 10-5

Collaboration IS Components and Business Processes

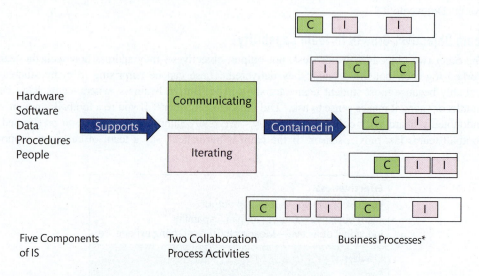

Five Components of IS

Two Collaboration Process Activities

Business Processes*

* White space represents other activities in the business process

activities, and business processes. Starting on the left, the five components of a collaboration IS are discussed next in Q10-3. Then the two collaboration activities—communicating and iterating—are described in Q10-4 and Q10-5. Finally, in Q10-6 we will describe how collaboration IS support the collaboration activities contained in business processes. Reading left to right, collaboration IS support collaboration activities that are contained in business processes. For simplicity, we display business processes as a rectangle, a display more suited for structured processes; in reality, these dynamic processes defy conventional diagramming.

Q10-3 ▶ What Are the Key Components of a Collaboration IS?

Some collaboration systems used in business are familiar to you from use in your personal life such as Skype and FaceTime. To better understand these systems and other systems used in businesses, let's consider their five components.

As you would expect, a **collaboration information system** is an information system that supports collaboration. Given our discussion in Q10-1, this means that the system needs to support iteration and communication among team members. As information systems, collaboration systems have the five components of every information system: hardware, software, data, procedures, and people. The distinguishing attributes of a collaboration IS are listed in Figure 10-6. Our goal here is to help you understand how collaboration systems are different from other IS like ERP or social media systems so you can employ them wisely.

The Five Components of a Collaboration IS

HARDWARE Concerning hardware, most collaboration systems are hosted on organizational servers or in the cloud, which you read about in Chapter 3. We will ignore that component in the discussion in this chapter. Just know that the tools you're using and the data you're sharing are supported by computer hardware somewhere. While servers are in the cloud, users interact with the collaboration system with client devices. These devices can be mobile platforms, laptops, or even traditional phones.

SOFTWARE Collaboration software programs are applications like email or text messaging that support collaborative activities. Throughout this chapter we will discuss a variety of collaboration software such as email, Google Drive, Microsoft SharePoint, and others. Figure 10-7 lists the most popular business collaboration software. This list is long because there is a wide range of combinations of people, work products, meeting schedules, and business contexts. For example, a two-member team editing a video for an online tutorial will need a different set of collaboration software programs than a 100-member team iterating plans for an ERP upgrade. The key for you as a student is to practice with many of these apps so you can learn their strengths and weaknesses and use them effectively when the time comes.

DATA Collaboration involves two types of data. **Project data** is data that is part of the collaboration's work product. For example, for a team that is designing a new product, design documents are examples of project data. A document that describes a recommended solution is project data for a problem-solving project. **Project metadata** is data that is used to manage the project. Schedules, tasks, budgets, and other managerial data are examples of project metadata. Another example of project metadata is the version number of a document. If Alice, Bruce, and

Five Components of IS	Collaboration IS
Hardware	Cloud for servers; various devices for clients
Software	Wide variety: email, Google+, Google Drive, Microsoft SharePoint
Data	Project data and project metadata
Procedures	Necessary but often implicit or assumed
People	People vary on time and place for collaboration People vary on ability to use IS and in motivation

FIGURE 10-6
Five Components of Collaboration IS

FIGURE 10-7

Examples of Collaboration
Information Systems

Collaboration Software
Email
Google+ Hangouts
FaceTime
GotoMeeting
SurveyMonkey
Mind Meister
Prezi
Yammer
SharePoint
Wikis
Google Drive and Docs

Charlie iterate a document, each version of the document is stored; with the document, one piece of metadata—the version number—is also stored.

PROCEDURES Procedures specify standards, policies, and techniques for conducting the team's collaboration activities using the technology. An example is the procedure for reviewing documents or other work products online. To reduce confusion and increase control, the team might establish a procedure that specifies who will review documents and in what sequence. Rules about who can do what to which data are also codified in procedures. Procedures for collaboration systems are often implicit. No one follows a procedure to read email, nor should they; it's simple. However, teams need to figure out the procedure to share documents, store meeting notes, update the team task list, and perform other activities. Teams are often careless about procedures—team members often assume others will use the same procedure they do. As a result, unless you raise the issue, you can expect that procedures will be followed differently by different people.

PEOPLE The final component of a collaboration system is, of course, people. We discussed the importance of the ability to give and receive critical communication in Q10-1. But people affect the collaboration IS in a couple of other ways, too. Will the participants collaborate for multiple projects? If so, a more complex system might be selected than if this is a one-time project for these participants. Also, will collaboration occur during face-to-face meetings or over a period of time when the participants will not be together? Another issue is whether the participants are co-located or are in different geographic locations. Finally, team members vary in their ability and motivation to use collaboration software. Some people know many of the procedures necessary to use the software, but most people have only mastered the simplest procedures.

Key Attributes of Collaboration IS

Collaboration IS have a number of important features that distinguish them from other IS. One fundamental feature is that there is a wide variety of *software* from which to choose. This variety is driven by the wide assortment of *people*, work products, team schedules, and business settings. As a result, the key to successful use of collaboration IS is choosing the right software based on the objectives and the people. *Procedures* are often used carelessly, and people differ on ability and motivation to use collaborative tools.

The components of a collaboration IS are important to understand, but it is more important to see how they collectively support the collaboration activities of teams. Next, we explore how they support the communication activity; then, in the following question, we see how they support iteration.

Q10-4 ▶ How Can Collaboration IS Support the Communicating Activity?

Information systems support the communicating activity. As we will see, there are three general types of communication, and different collaboration IS are well suited to support each. These three types are based on how and where people on the team communicate, as shown in Figure 10-8.

FIGURE 10-8

Three Types of Communication and Collaboration IS

Synchronous		Asynchronous
Shared calendars Invitation and attendance		
Single location	Multiple locations	Single or multiple locations
Office applications such as Word and PowerPoint	Conference calls Webinars Multiparty text chat Microsoft Web Apps Videoconferencing	Email Discussion forums Team surveys Microsoft OneDrive Google Drive Microsoft SharePoint

Virtual meetings

Synchronous communication occurs when all team members meet at the same time, such as with conference calls or face-to-face (F2F) meetings. **Asynchronous communication** occurs when team members do not meet at the same time. Employees who work different shifts at the same location or team members who work in different time zones around the world must meet asynchronously.

Most student teams attempt to meet F2F, at least at first. Arranging such meetings is always difficult, however, because student schedules and responsibilities differ. If you are going to arrange such meetings, consider creating an online group calendar in which team members post their availability week by week. Also, use the meeting facilities in Microsoft Outlook to issue invitations and gather RSVPs. If you don't have Outlook, use an Internet site such as Evite (*www.evite.com*) for this purpose.

For most F2F meetings, you need little; the standard Office applications or their freeware lookalikes, such as Open Office, will suffice. However, research indicates that F2F meetings can benefit from shared, online workspaces, such as the whiteboard shown in Figure 10-9.[4] Using a whiteboard, team members can type, write, and draw simultaneously, which enables more ideas to be proposed in a given period of time than when team members must wait in sequence to express ideas verbally. If you have access to such a whiteboard, try it in your F2F meetings to see if it works for your team.

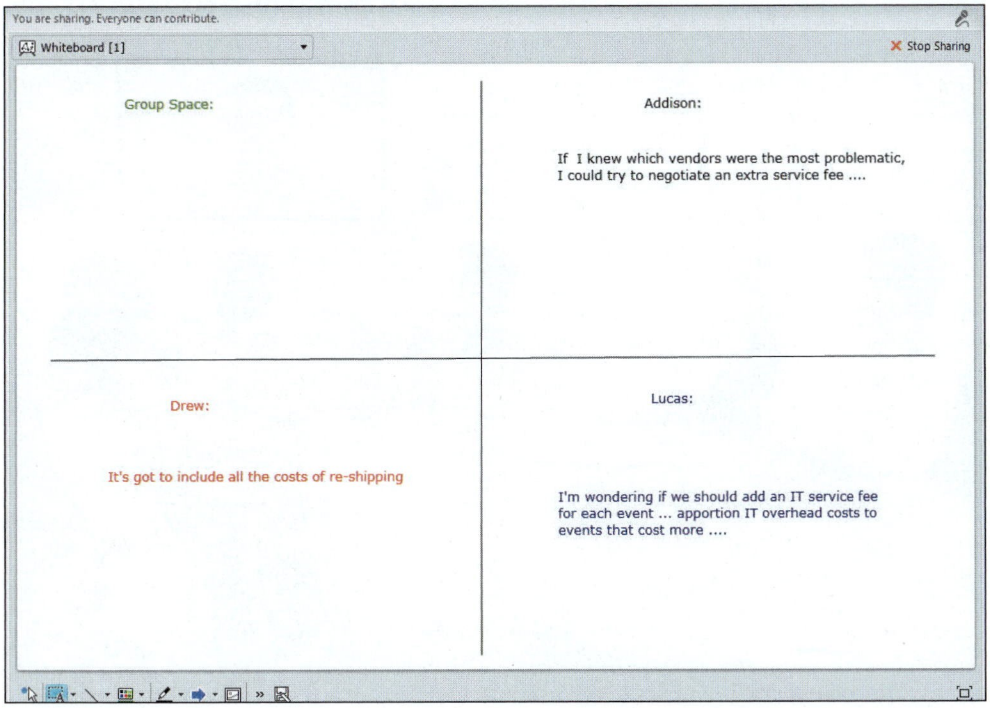

FIGURE 10-9

Whiteboard Example

However, *given today's communication technology, students can forgo the hassle of scheduling a F2F meeting in most circumstances* by using a virtual meeting instead. **Virtual meetings** are meetings in which participants do not meet in the same place and possibly not at the same time. F2F meetings are often too difficult to arrange and seldom worth the trouble when a virtual meeting will produce the same results with fewer scheduling problems.

If your virtual meeting is synchronous (all meet at the same time), you can use conference calls, multiparty text chat, screen sharing, webinars, or videoconferencing. Some students find it weird to use text chat for school projects, but why not? You can attend meetings wherever you are without using your voice. Google Text supports multiparty text chat, as does Microsoft Skype for Business Google or Bing *multiparty text chat* to find other, similar products.

Screen-sharing applications enable virtual meeting members to view the same whiteboard, application, or other display. Figure 10-9 shows an example whiteboard for a business meeting. This whiteboard allows multiple people to contribute simultaneously. To organize the simultaneous conversation, the whiteboard real estate is divided among the members of the group as shown. Some groups save their whiteboards as minutes of the meeting.

A **webinar** is a virtual meeting in which attendees view one of the attendees' computer screens for a more formal and organized presentation. WebEx (*www.webex.com*) is a popular commercial webinar application used in virtual sales presentations.

If everyone on your team has a camera on his or her computer, you can also do **videoconferencing**, like that shown in Figure 10-10. **Microsoft Skype** is one such product. FaceTime works, too, and you can find others on the Internet. Videoconferencing is more intrusive than text chat; you have to comb your hair, but it does have a more personal touch.

In some classes and situations, synchronous meetings, even virtual ones, are impossible to arrange. You just cannot get everyone together at the same time. In this circumstance, when the team must meet asynchronously, most students try to communicate via email. The problem with email is that there is too much freedom. Not everyone will participate because it is easy to hide from email. (Did Wally, in the opening scenario, really not get Sue's email?) Discussion threads become disorganized and disconnected. After the fact, it is difficult to find particular emails, comments, or attachments.

Discussion forums are an alternative. Here one group member posts an entry, perhaps an idea, a comment, or a question, and other group members respond. Figure 10-11 shows an example. Such forums are better than email because it is harder for the discussion to get off track. Still, however, it remains easy for some team members not to participate.

FIGURE 10-10

Videoconferencing Example

Source: Tom Merton/Getty Images

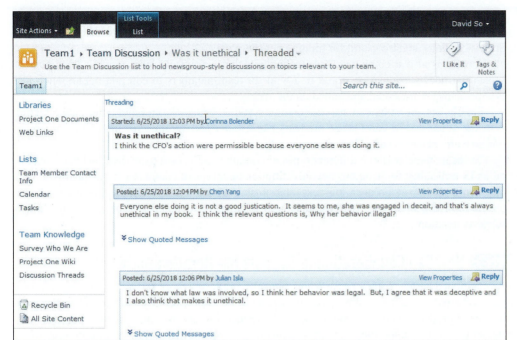

FIGURE 10-11
Discussion Forum Example

Team surveys are another form of communication technology. With these, one team member creates a list of questions and other team members respond. Surveys are an effective way to obtain team opinions; they are generally easy to complete, so most team members will participate. Also, it is easy to determine who has not yet responded. Figure 10-12 shows the results of one team survey. SurveyMonkey (*www.surveymonkey.com*) is one common survey application program. You can find others on the Internet.

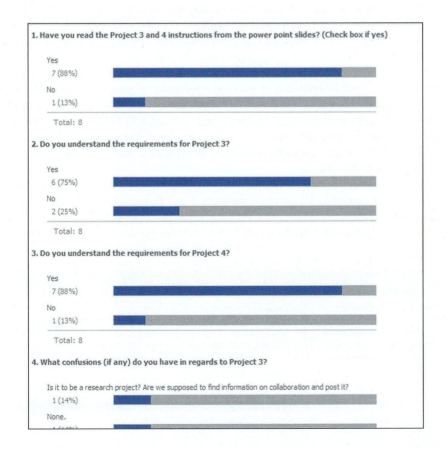

FIGURE 10-12
Survey Report Example

Video and audio recordings are also useful for asynchronous communication. Key presentations or discussions can be recorded and played back for team members at their convenience. Such recordings are also useful for training new employees.

A wiki is also a communication technology that a team can use. A work document or supporting documents can be stored in a wiki for team members to edit and iterate much like Wikipedia pages are stored and edited on the Web.

Finally, collaboration can also use texting systems. Unlike Twitter and other public texting systems, organizations can license products like Chatter and Yammer for internal communication so team members can collaborate privately.

To recap, there are three different types of communication on a team, and each has collaboration IS well suited for it. Teams not only differ on their type of communication but also on how they iterate their work product, our next topic. Just as a collaboration IS should be chosen based on which of the three types of communication it supports, it should also be chosen for how it supports iteration.

Q10-5 ▶ How Can Collaboration IS Support the Iterating Activity?

As mentioned earlier, collaborative teams typically produce a work product—a diagram, a new process, a budget, a healthcare record of a patient, or even a healthy patient. When the team iterates, it produces a new version of the work product. But not only does the work product iterate, so too do the supporting documents, illustrations, spreadsheets, PowerPoint presentations, video, and other data. Figure 10-13 lists three options of content iteration management: no iteration control, iteration management, and iteration control. Next, we consider each and the IS that support each option.

No Iteration Control

The most primitive way to iterate content is via email attachments. However, email attachments have numerous problems. For one, there is always the danger that someone does not receive an email, does not notice it in his or her inbox, or does not bother to save the attachments. Then, too, if three users obtain the same document as an email attachment, each changes it, and each sends back the changed document via email, different, incompatible versions of that document will be floating around. So, although email is simple, easy, and readily available, it will not suffice for collaborations in which there are many document versions or for which there is a desire for content control.

Another way to iterate content is to place it on a shared **file server**, which is simply a computer that stores files just like the disk in your local computer. If your team has access to a file server, you can put documents on the server and others can download them, make changes, and upload them back onto the server using ftp (discussed in Chapter 3). Storing documents on servers is better than using email attachments because documents have a single storage location. They are not scattered in different team members' email boxes. Team members have a known location for finding documents.

However, without any additional control it is possible for team members to interfere with one another's work. For example, suppose team members A and B download a document and edit it, but without knowing about the other's edits. Person A stores his version back on the server and then person B stores her version back on the server. In this scenario, person A's changes will be lost.

FIGURE 10-13

Collaboration Tools for Iterating Content

Alternatives for Iterating Content		
No Iteration Control	Iteration Management	Iteration Control
Email with attachments Shared files on a server	Google Drive Microsoft OneDrive	Microsoft SharePoint

Increasing degree of content control

Furthermore, without any iteration control it will be impossible to know who changed the document and when. Neither person A nor person B will know whose version of the document is on the server. To avoid such problems, some form of iteration management is recommended.

Iteration Management

Systems that provide **iteration management** track changes to documents and provide features and functions to accommodate concurrent work. The means by which this is done depends on the particular system used. In this section, we consider two systems that you should consider for your team's work: Google Drive and Microsoft OneDrive.

GOOGLE DRIVE **Google Drive** is a free thin-client application for sharing documents, presentations, spreadsheets, drawings, and other data. Google Drive is continually evolving; by the time you read this, Google may have added additional file types or changed the system from what is described here. In addition to what is described here, Google Drive includes a host of applications for special purpose use. Because those applications don't relate directly to collaboration, we won't consider them here.

You can create a Google document in several ways. An easy way is to go to *www.google .com/docs/about*. From this screen, select the type of document you want to create. For example, if you select *Docs* and click Go to *Google Docs*, Google will display the screen shown in Figure 10-14. Select a template, and you're up and running with a text document. You can also create worksheets, slides, and forms from the main menu. From that point on, you can create, upload, process, save, and share documents, spreadsheets, presentations, and other content. You can also save most of those documents to PDF and Microsoft Office formats, such as Word, Excel, and PowerPoint.

With Google Drive, you can make documents available to others by entering their email addresses or Gmail accounts. Those users are notified in an email that the document exists and are given a link by which they can access it.

Documents are stored on a Google server. Users can access the documents from Google and simultaneously see and edit documents. In the background, Google merges the users' activities into a single document. You are notified that another user is editing a document at the same time you are. Google tracks document revisions, with brief summaries of changes made.

MICROSOFT ONEDRIVE **Microsoft OneDrive** is Microsoft's answer to Google Drive. It provides the ability to store and share Office documents and other files and offers free storage. Additionally, OneDrive includes license-free Web application versions of Word, Excel, PowerPoint, and OneNote that are called **Office Web Apps**. These applications run in the browser and are quite easy to use. These programs have less functionality than desktop Office programs, but they are free and readily accessed on the Web.

In addition to Office Web Apps, the desktop Office applications are tightly integrated with OneDrive. You can open and save documents directly from and to OneDrive from inside Microsoft Office products.

To set up OneDrive, you need a Microsoft account, which used to be called a Windows Live ID. If you have either a Hotmail or MSN email account, that account is your Microsoft account. If you do not have a Hotmail or MSN email account, you can create a Microsoft account with some other email account, or you can create a new Hotmail account, which is free.

FIGURE 10-14

Creating a New Document on Google Drive

FIGURE 10-15
Creating a New Document with
OneDrive

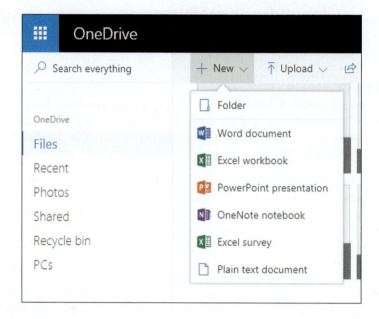

Once you have a Microsoft account, go to *www.onedrive.com* and sign in. You will be allocated cloud storage. You can create file folders and files and use either Office or Office Web Apps as well. Figure 10-15 shows creating a new OneDrive document.

Similar to Google accounts, you can share folders with others by entering their Microsoft account or their email account. Users who have a Microsoft account can view and edit documents; users who do not have a Microsoft account can only view documents.

Only one user at a time can open OneDrive documents for editing. If you attempt to open a document that someone else is editing, you'll receive an error message. As you can open the document in read-only mode, you can have your changes merged with the document when it is available or you can simply be notified when the document is available.

Both Google Drive and Microsoft OneDrive are free and very easy to use. They are both far superior to exchanging documents via email or via a file server. If you are not using one of these two products, you should be. Go to *http://drive.google.com* or *www.onedrive.com* and check them out. You will find easy-to-understand demos if you need additional instruction.

Iteration Control

Iteration management systems improve the tracking of iterated content and potentially eliminate problems caused by concurrent document access. They do not, however, provide **iteration control**, the technique that occurs when the collaboration tool limits, and sometimes even directs, user activity. Iteration control provides one or more of the following options:

- User activity limited by permissions
- Document checkout
- Version histories

PERMISSION-LIMITED ACTIVITY With most iteration control tools, each team member is given an account with a set of permissions. Then shared documents are placed into shared directories, sometimes called **libraries**. For example, on a shared site with four libraries, a particular user might be given read-only permission for library 1; read and edit permission for library 2; read, edit, and delete permission for library 3; and no permission even to see library 4. Wikipedia and other wikis also use permission limits; if a contributor has a history of disruptive edits to Wikipedia, that contributor can be restricted from editing pages in the future.

DOCUMENT CHECKOUT With iteration control applications, document directories can be set up so that users are required to check out documents before they can modify them. When a document is checked out, no other user can obtain it for the purpose of editing it. Once the document has been checked in, other users can obtain it for editing.

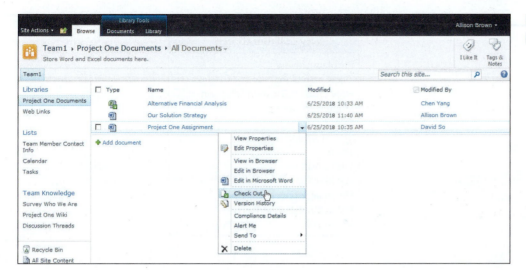

FIGURE 10-16

Document Checkout

Figure 10-16 shows a screen for a user of Microsoft SharePoint. The user, Allison Brown (shown in the upper right-hand corner of the screen), is checking out a document named Project One Assignment. Once she has it checked out, she can edit it and return it to this library. While she has the document checked out, no other user will be able to edit it, and her changes will not be visible to others.

VERSION HISTORY Because collaboration involves feedback and iteration, it is inevitable that dozens, or even hundreds, of documents will be created. Imagine, for example, the number of versions of a design document for the Boeing 787. In some cases, collaboration team members attempt to keep track of versions by appending suffixes to file names. The result for a student project is a file name like *Project1_lt_kl_092911_most_ recent_draft.docx* or something similar. Not only are such names ugly and awkward, no team member can tell whether this is the most current version.

Collaboration tools that provide iteration control have the data to readily provide histories on behalf of the users. When a document is changed (or checked in), the collaboration tool records the name of the author and the date and time the document is stored. Users also have the option of recording notes about their version.

While most of this question examined the three types of iteration control of text documents, the iteration needs of other work products are also supported. Whatever the product, teams should select collaboration software based on the type of iteration control they need as well as the type of communication they will use, as discussed in the previous question.

Q10-6 How Can Collaboration IS Support Business Processes?

Having described the two activities in the generic collaboration process and how collaboration IS support these activities, we now consider how collaboration IS support actual business processes. There are a great number of business processes that rely on collaboration activities, as shown in Figure 10-17. In fact, virtually all important business processes depend on some collaboration. To demonstrate the usefulness of collaboration IS, we investigate two processes: Project Management and Workflow.

The Project Management Process

One common business process that contains collaboration activities is project management. **Project management** is the process of applying principles and techniques for planning, organizing, and monitoring temporary endeavors. It is a rich and complicated subject, with many theories and methods and techniques. To illustrate how they are supported by collaboration IS, here we will just touch on the basics of project management.

Projects are formed to create or produce something; as a result, they have a defined beginning and end. The desired outcome might be a marketing plan, the design of a new factory or a

FIGURE 10-17

Business Processes Supported by Collaboration IS

Business Processes Supported by Collaboration IS
Problem solving
Decision making
New product/location selection
Strategic planning
Sales
Brainstorming
Training
Promotion
Health care
Financial services
Project management
Workflow

new product, or an annual audit. Project teams may include two or three individuals or as many as a few hundred. Project management activities vary widely, but most include setting milestones, keeping track of progress, and allocating funds.

Project team members communicate incessantly about the tasks they have completed, the next milestones, and problems they are encountering that may create havoc with the schedule. The type of communication they use is a mixture of F2F and virtual meetings, and they also use both synchronous and asynchronous communication. They produce and iterate a variety of work products such as their chart of milestones and flowchart of pending activities as well as budgetary documents. These products typically use iteration management controls, but other teamwork products such as meeting agendas and email correspondence may iterate without much control.

Project teams use a variety of collaboration information systems discussed in this chapter for their communication and iteration activities. Larger projects will often also use special project management software such as Microsoft Project and Oracle Primavera. This type of software is particularly helpful in organizing the flow of team activities and managing lists of tasks. A flowchart example using Microsoft Project showing team milestones is shown in Figure 10-18.

FIGURE 10-18

Microsoft Project Milestones Example

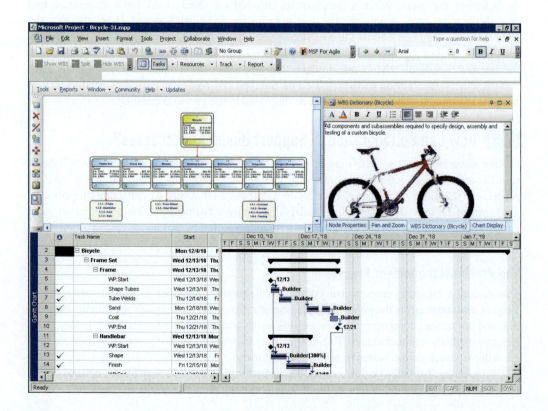

Project management software also supports communication among team members. Email and text can be sent from within the software, and permissions to view or edit flowcharts and task list are tightly controlled and previous versions automatically archived.

The Workflow Process

The **Workflow** process is a sequence of activities by which original content is created and subsequently acted upon by others within the organization. A workflow could help solve the billing problems at Wood Hospital discussed in the opening vignette. Standard billing procedures could be developed by the collaborative team and implemented in a system such as SharePoint. Such workflows would enable those with expertise in particular kinds of medical billing to share their knowledge with other billing personnel. Another workflow example is a process used by a company to ensure its employees have been briefed on new security procedures. In this company, every year employees are required to hear a security update from their supervisor. The director of IT in charge of this workflow must notify all 411 supervisors in the organization of the update and record when training occurs. In each of these examples, a workflow is executed—initial content is first created, then the content is acted on by a number of people in the organization. Unlike simple collaboration described earlier, a workflow often includes actors outside a team.

SharePoint offers a better way to communicate and exercise iteration control over work documents. SharePoint supports a workflow by automating many of the activities. It helps automate activities involving documents, lists, and other types of content in a workflow. SharePoint ships with several built-in workflows; we will illustrate one of them here. In addition, business analysts can create custom workflows using a graphical interface in SharePoint Designer.[5]

To illustrate a simple workflow, suppose that Jerry wants just two people to review all résumés of job applicants that are submitted to a particular SharePoint **document library**, which is a named collection of documents in SharePoint. Whenever a document is added to the document library, it should be reviewed first by Joseph Schumpeter and then by Adam Smith. Such an arrangement is called a **sequential workflow** because the review activities occur in sequence. In a **parallel workflow**, the reviews would occur simultaneously. Numerous other types of workflows are possible, but we will not consider them here.

Figure 10-19 illustrates this workflow. When a document creator submits a document to a particular SharePoint library (labeled *Data Repository* in Figure 10-19), SharePoint starts a workflow. It sends an email announcing the start of the workflow to Jerry as well as an email to Joseph Schumpeter telling him that he has been requested to review the document.

Schumpeter reviews the document (he will need to obtain it from the data repository, but this arrow has been omitted from Figure 10-19 for clarity). After he has made his review, he will store his comments on the task and mark it as completed. At that point, SharePoint sends an email to the next reviewer, Adam Smith. After Smith has completed his review, he stores his comments in the Tasks list and marks his task as completed. At this point, SharePoint sends a Workflow Completed email to Jerry.

By automating some of the activities, SharePoint has helped coordinate the asynchronous communication. SharePoint also provides iteration control by limiting the activity of Joseph and Adam to a particular sequence, and it keeps a version history of the resume evaluation form. By using SharePoint rather than email, administrative costs are reduced as Jerry and his staff spend less time coordinating and following up on the status of each resume. And the process is more reliable—for each applicant, both reviewers get the same time and reminders.

Supporting New Processes with Collaboration IS

Before finishing this topic of organizational processes and collaboration IS, we need to point out that collaboration IS not only support the existing business processes listed earlier, they also allow new processes to emerge. Collaboration IS have helped enable new online training processes, knowledge storage processes, and find-an-expert processes. Online training supported by collaboration systems are rapidly growing. Larger versions are known as massive open online courses (MOOCs), which are offered by Coursera, Udacity, and others. Knowledge storage processes use collaboration IS such as wikis to store company knowledge much like Wikipedia stores common knowledge. Finally, collaboration systems can enable a new find-an-expert process. This process is designed to collect and share expertise within a firm. For example, when

FIGURE 10-19

Gather Feedback Workflow

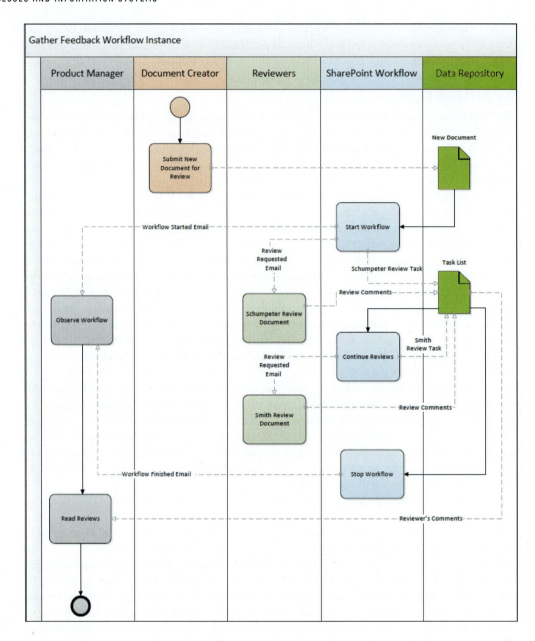

software engineers join a company like Microsoft, they input their areas of knowledge in a series of "Ask Me About" screens, where they can indicate expertise on SQL Server or SharePoint or fluency in Greek. Later, when someone at Microsoft needs to find a Greek-speaking SharePoint expert to help on a project for a company in Greece, the collaboration system helps with the process of finding the right people.

Q10-7 ▶ Which Collaboration IS Is Right for Your Team?

Earlier we mentioned that half the battle is picking the right collaboration IS for the team. In this question, we will define and set up your evaluation of three sets of collaboration tools. Most business courses involve a team project; why not use what you've learned in this chapter to pick a collaboration IS that will make teamwork easier and help you achieve a better product?

Three Sets of Collaboration Tools

Figure 10-20 summarizes three different sets of collaboration tools that you might use.

THE MINIMAL COLLABORATION TOOL SET The first, the Minimal set, has the minimum possible set of tools and is shown in the second column of Figure 10-20. With this set, you should be able to

	Minimal	**Good**	**Comprehensive**
Communication	Email; multiparty text, group chat	Facetime	Microsoft Skype
Content Sharing	Email or file server	Google Drive	SharePoint
Task Management	Word or Excel files	Google Calendar	SharePoint lists integrated with email
Nice-to-Have Features		Discussion boards, surveys, wikis, blogs, and share pictures/videos from third-party tools	Built-in discussion boards, surveys, wikis, blogs, and picture/video sharing
Cost	Free	Free	$10/month per user Or Free
Ease of Use (time to learn)	None	1 hour	3 hours
Value to Future Business Professional	None	Limited	Great
Limitations	All text, no voice or video; no tool integration	Tools not integrated, must learn to use several products; cannot share documents live	Cost, learning curve required

FIGURE 10-20

Collaboration Tool Sets

collaborate with your team, though you will get little support from the software. In particular, you will need to manage concurrent access by setting up procedures and agreements to ensure that one user's work doesn't conflict with another's. Your collaboration will be with text only; you will not have access to audio or video, so you cannot hear or see your collaborators. You also will not be able to view documents or whiteboards during your meeting. This set is probably close to what you're already doing.

THE GOOD COLLABORATION TOOL SET The third column of Figure 10-20 shows a more sophisticated set of collaboration tools. With it, you will have the ability to conduct multiparty audio and video virtual meetings; and you will also have support for concurrent access to document, spreadsheet, and presentation files. You will not be able to support surveys, wikis, and blogs and share pictures and videos with this set. If you want any of them, you will need to search the Internet to find suitable tools.

THE COMPREHENSIVE COLLABORATION TOOL SET The third set of collaboration tools is shown in the last column of Figure 10-20. This IS is provided by a professional version of Microsoft Office 365 that includes Skype for Business, SharePoint, Exchange, and Office applications. Office 365 is provided as a service over the Internet. Skype for Business is a communications application that provides IM, audio and video conferencing, and shared whitespaces as well as shared desktops and shared applications. This set is the best of these three because it has a full set of features, including iteration management and control and online meetings with sharing as just described. Furthermore, this set is integrated: SharePoint alerts can send emails via the Microsoft email server Exchange when tasks or other lists and libraries change. You can click on users' names in emails or in SharePoint, and Office 365 will automatically start a Skype text, audio, or video conversation with that user if he or she is currently available. All text messages that you send via Skype are automatically recorded and stored in your email folder.

Choosing the Set for Your Team

Which set should you choose for your team? Unless your university has already standardized on professional Office 365, you will have to pay for it. You can obtain a 30-day free trial, and if your team can finish its work in that amount of time, you might choose to do so. Otherwise, your

FIGURE 10-21
Power Curve

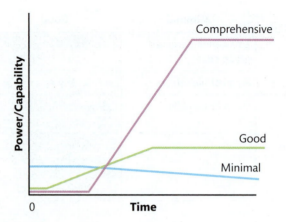

team will need to pay a minimum of $10 per month per user. So, if cost is the only factor, you can rule out professional Office 365.[6]

Even if you can afford the most comprehensive set of tools, you may not want to use it. As noted in the Ease of Use row of Figure 10-20, most team members will need to invest around 3 hours to understand the basic SharePoint features. Less time, on the order of an hour, will be required to learn the Good toolset, and you most likely already know how to use the Minimal set.

When evaluating learning time, consider Figure 10-21. This diagram is a product **power curve**, which is a graph that shows the relationship of the power (the utility that one gains from a software product) as a function of the time using that product. A flat line means you are investing time without any increase in power. The ideal power curve starts at some value at time zero and has no flat spots.

The Minimal product set gives you some power at time zero because you already know how to use it. However, as you use it over time, your project will gain complexity and the problems of controlling concurrent access will actually cause power to decrease. The Good set has a short flat spot as you get to know it. However, your power then increases over time until you reach the most capability your team can do with it. The Comprehensive set has a longer flat spot in the beginning because it will take longer to learn. However, because it has such a rich collaboration feature set, you will be able to gain considerable collaborative power, and the maximum capability is much greater than the Good set.

Finally, consider the Value row in Figure 10-20. The Minimal set has no value to you as a future professional and contributes nothing to your professional competitive advantage. The Good set has some limited value; there are organizations that use Google Drive and Skype. However, the Comprehensive toolset has the potential to give you a considerable competitive advantage, particularly because SharePoint skills are highly valued in industry. You can use knowledge of SharePoint to demonstrate the currency of your knowledge in job interviews.

So, which is the right set for your team? It's up to you. See Exercise 10-2 on page 303.

Don't Forget Procedures and People!

One last and very important point: Most of this chapter focuses on collaboration software. Regarding the other four components of a collaboration IS—you need not worry about hardware, at least not for the Good or Comprehensive sets, because those tools are hosted on hardware in the cloud. The data component is up to you; it will be your content as well as your metadata for project management and for demonstrating that your team practiced iteration and feedback.

As you evaluate alternatives, however, you need to think seriously about the procedure and people components. How are team members going to use these tools? Your team needs to have agreement on tools usage, even if you do not formally document procedures. As noted, such procedures are especially necessary for controlling concurrent access in the Minimal system. You need to have agreement not only on how to use these tools but also on what happens when teammates don't use these tools. What will you do, for example, if teammates persist in emailing documents instead of using Google Drive or SharePoint?

MIS InClass 10

In this exercise, you and your teammates will develop a prioritized list of items needed to survive a lunar landing gone wrong. (The instructor can obtain the NASA-approved list by using Google to find the NASA exercise "Survival on the Moon"; you could find the answers there too, but don't peek). The scenario is bleak: You and your team are 200 miles from a rendezvous point after your ship crashed on the moon. You have the 15 items listed in the chart below to take with you.

You realize your survival depends on reaching the outpost, finding a way to protect yourself until someone can reach you, or meeting a rescue party somewhere between your landing site and the outpost. It can be extremely cold at night and hot during the day. The Moon has basically no atmosphere or magnetosphere to protect you from space radiation. The gravity on the Moon is only one-sixth that of Earth's. Most of the surface of the Moon is made up of craters.

First rank these items by yourself, marking a *1* next to the most important item through a *15* next to the least in the rightmost ranking column.

Then, re-rank your list after you discuss your thoughts with your team. All members of the team will have identical rankings.

Finally, after the team has an initial list of items 1–15, force yourselves to iterate that list twice. Find one object and move it higher or lower on the list; do this twice. Place this ranking in the column "Your team iterated ranking."

Correct Answer	Your team iterated ranking	Your team ranking	Your individual ranking	Item and description
_____	_____	_____	_____	**1. Life raft** a self-inflatable floatation device
_____	_____	_____	_____	**2. Two 45.5-kilogram (100-pound) tanks of oxygen** pressurized tanks of oxygen
_____	_____	_____	_____	**3. Lights with solar-powered rechargeable batteries** portable lights powered by solar batteries
_____	_____	_____	_____	**4. Signal mirror** a handheld mirror
_____	_____	_____	_____	**5. 38 liters (10 gallons) of water** a container of water
_____	_____	_____	_____	**6. First aid kit** basic first aid kit with pain meds and medicine for infection
_____	_____	_____	_____	**7. Food concentrate** dehydrated food to which water is added
_____	_____	_____	_____	**8. Magnetic compass** a tool that uses a magnetic field to determine direction
_____	_____	_____	_____	**9. Solar-powered radio receiver-transmitter** a communication tool powered by the Sun
_____	_____	_____	_____	**10. Map of the Moon's surface** a map showing the Moon's terrain
_____	_____	_____	_____	**11. Parachute** a large piece of silk cloth
_____	_____	_____	_____	**12. Box of matches** wooden sticks with sulfur-treated heads
_____	_____	_____	_____	**13. One case of dehydrated milk** a good food concentrate
_____	_____	_____	_____	**14. 50 feet of nylon rope** useful to scale cliffs and to tie injured people together
_____	_____	_____	_____	**15. Portable heating unit** helpful to stay warm
_____	_____	_____	_____	**TOTAL**

(Continued)

After the final list is revealed, calculate your overall score in each column. To do this write down the deviation of your ranking from the final list ranking for each cell. For example if you had a 7 in the Parachute cell, and the correct answer was 5, write down a 2 for this cell. Your score in each column is the sum of these deviations for each cell.

1. Were you more accurate after collaboration with teammates or before. If your score was better before, does this mean that you should have been more assertive, candid, or critical? Was there enough feedback on the team? Did someone else on your team have a better score individually than your team? If so, what does that suggest about you?

2. Was your team list improved after the iteration cycle? In retrospect, did anyone suggest something that was ignored and then revealed to be better by the approved list? Why was it ignored?

3. How would you assess trust on your team?

4. Collaboration objectives, as shown in Figure 10-4, include individual, team, and product objectives as well as efficiency goals. Which of these objectives were achieved, which were not, and why?

5. If you had to do this exercise using a collaboration IS from the list shown in Figure 10-20, which IS would you use, and why?

Q10-8 ▶ 2028?

So, how will we collaborate in 2028? Where will the current trends in collaboration systems take us? One thing is clear—businesses are creating products and services that are more and more complicated and will require greater collaboration than ever. We believe the most important developments in the next decade will be the impact of collaboration on F2F meetings, the rise of more mobile collaboration platforms, the blending of collaboration and social media, and the integration of AI and robotic systems into collaborative networks.

Clearly, free data communications and data storage will make collaboration systems cheaper and easier to use. One consequence is that by 2028, F2F meetings will be rare. F2F meetings require everyone to be in the same place at the same time, and both of those *sames* can be problematic. When employees work in different locations, bringing them together is expensive in travel cost and time. Employees standing in line in airport security or waiting in their cars in traffic are hardly productive. And bringing everyone together is unfriendly to the environment.

Even when employees work at the same location, they may have schedule conflicts or they may not work at that location at the same time. And unless employees are providing an in-person service, such as physical training or surgery or construction, why do they need to work in the same location?

Further, by 2028 collaboration systems will greatly ease international business. If teams meet virtually most of the time and if it doesn't matter where team members are located, then projects can involve the best, or perhaps the most affordable, workers worldwide. Further, work can follow the sun. Workers in the United States can submit documents for feedback by team members in Asia. The Asian workers can contribute their feedback during their normal workday and pass the documents along to European team members for review during *their* normal workday. All the reviewed work will be available to the U.S. workers when their next day begins.

We can also expect that use of mobile collaboration will increase. New collaboration software for tablets and smartphones will take advantage of better networks and increased sophistication by end users. Mobile collaboration tools will help sales reps on the road with clients, home healthcare providers with patients, and maintenance workers with remote machine problems.

We also expect continued blurring of the distinction between collaboration and social media. When you contribute to a firm's social media application, you are collaborating with employees at that firm. Both you and the firm prosper in some fashion. It seems inevitable that both collaboration and social media use will grow and overlap.

Finally, the next 10 years will likely see an increase in collaboration between humans and machines. Both AI and robotic systems are likely to become collaborative agents. Most likely, collaboration systems will consist of a blend of humans and machines. Collaboration systems of pure machines will require that machines be able to learn from and iterate on one another's work. It seems unlikely that such a level of machine learning will occur by 2028, but then again, who knows?

This possibility brings up the issue of trust. How do we know that the collaborative agent is what he or she claims to be? That issue, which is addressed in the Ethics Guide, will increase in importance as nonhuman agents participate in collaborative systems.

Ethics Guide

Virtual Ethics?

The term *virtual* means something that appears to exist but does not exist in fact. A virtual private network (VPN) is a computer network that appears to be private but in fact operates on a public network. The term *virtual meeting* describes a meeting in which everyone is present, but via an information system and not face to face.

However, and it is a big however, "Is everyone present?" Is the person who signed on as Adam truly Adam? Or is it someone else? Or is it Adam with a staff of seven people, all of whom are anonymous to the rest of the group? Consider a team composed of Allison, Abby, and Amy. What if none of them was really involved? What if, in fact, those contributions were really made by Betty, Betsy, and Beatrice, but none of them knew the others were spoofing (pretending to be someone they are not)?

Suppose you run a consulting company and you want to send less experienced consultants out on jobs. During an initial meeting (held electronically, using text chat) with a potential client, you tell the client that he is meeting with Carl, a new and inexperienced employee. But the meeting actually includes Carl and Cathy, your most experienced and senior consultant. During the meeting, all of the remarks attributed to Carl were actually made by Cathy. The client is most impressed with what it thinks are Carl's perceptive comments about its situation and agrees to hire Carl, even though he is inexperienced. You keep using Cathy this way, spoofing several of your young associates to get jobs for them. You justify this by saying, "Well, if they get into trouble, we'll send Cathy out to fix the problem."

Or suppose you have an archrival, Danny. You and Danny compete for a future promotion, and you just cannot stand the idea of him moving ahead of you. So you set up a sequence of virtual meetings, but you never invite Danny. Then, just before a crucial meeting, one that involves senior members of your organization, you invite Danny to be your silent helper. You tell him you do not have the authority to invite him, but you want him to have a chance to express his thoughts. So you attend the meeting and you incorporate Danny's thinking into your chat comments. People think you are the sole author of those ideas and are impressed. Danny's work is never attributed to him.

Consider another possibility. Suppose Earl is an independent consultant who has been hired to write a blog. Earl, who is very busy, hires Erin to write the blog for him. Earl bills his time for $110 an hour and pays Erin $45, keeping the difference. And he has free time for more paid work. Earl reviews her work, but he does none of it himself. The client never knows that it's Erin, not Earl, who writes the blog.

Or let's bring it closer to home. Suppose you take online tests as part of your class. What keeps you from taking the test with your brother, who happens to work for Google as a product manager for Google Drive? Suppose you take the test by yourself, but you believe others are taking their tests with silent helpers. Given that belief, are you justified in finding your own helper? What do you think? Are your ethics virtual?

DISCUSSION QUESTIONS

1. Is it *illegal* to spoof someone? Does it matter whether you have that person's permission to spoof them?
2. Is it *ethical* to spoof someone? Does it matter whether you have that person's permission? Consider both the categorical imperative (page 18) and utilitarianism (page 43) in your response to this question and the remaining questions.
3. Under what circumstances do you believe it is ethical to spoof someone?
4. Consider the virtual meeting of Allison, Abby, and Amy (but Amy is actually not at the meeting; Beatrice is pretending to be Amy because Amy is taking her kid to a doctor's appointment). What are the consequences to the organization of such a meeting? What happens when Abby meets Amy in the hallway and Abby asks, "What did you think of our meeting?" Who has the knowledge of the meeting? Who knows that they have that knowledge?
5. Considering Cathy's spoofing of young associates. What is different between text chat and a speaker phone? Haven't we always had these problems, except Cathy was passing notes and making comments while the phone was muted? What behavior should you follow when talking with someone who is on a speaker phone? How does the videoconferencing capability of products like Skype change this situation?
6. Is it ethical to take credit for Danny's thinking? Suppose you are later heavily criticized for the quality of Danny's ideas that you appropriated. Do you disclaim them? How?
7. Is it cheating to have a helper on an online test? Are you justified if everyone else is doing it? What control is possible for online tests? Should such tests be used at all?

Source: Trinacria Photo/Shutterstock.

ACTIVE REVIEW

Use this Active Review to verify that you understand the material in the chapter. You can read the entire chapter and then perform the tasks in this review, or you can read the text material for just one question and perform the tasks in this review for that question before moving on to the next one.

▶ Q10-1 ◀ What is collaboration, and why is it important to business?

Explain why collaboration is increasingly important in business. Distinguish between cooperative and collaborative teams and give an example of each. Explain the importance of communication and iteration. What aspect of team communication is essential to collaboration? List critical collaboration skills. Explain why undergraduate business students undervalue collaboration.

▶ Q10-2 ◀ What are the objectives of the collaboration process?

Describe how the objectives of a dynamic process differ from a structured process. Explain the three effectiveness objectives and the efficiency objective of the typical collaboration process. Describe how collaboration IS support collaboration activities and business processes.

▶ Q10-3 ◀ What are the key components of a collaboration IS?

Describe the client and server hardware in a collaboration IS. Explain the variety of collaboration software. Describe the two types of collaboration IS data and give an example of each. Explain why collaboration IS procedures are often unstated. Describe the important attributes of the people using collaboration IS.

▶ Q10-4 ◀ How can collaboration IS support the communicating activity?

Describe the three types of communication and give an example. Explain the types of collaboration technology designed to support the communication of teams.

▶ Q10-5 ◀ How can collaboration IS support the iterating activity?

Explain the three options for iterating content. For each option, describe a collaboration technology that can support the iteration activity of teams. Explain iteration control and describe three options of iteration control.

▶ Q10-6 ◀ How can collaboration IS support business processes?

Describe the Project Management process and specify its common activities. What collaboration IS are available to support the Project Management process? Describe the Workflow process and explain what makes the iteration of a Workflow process different from the iteration of the typical collaborative team.

▶ Q10-7 ◀ Which collaboration IS is right for your team?

Describe the three collaboration tool sets. Explain the differences among them. Summarize the criteria for choosing the right set for your team. Explain the meaning of the power curve and discuss the power curve for each of the three alternatives. Describe different ways that people can limit collaboration.

▶ Q10-8 ◀ 2028?

Which type of team communication will be less frequent in the future? Describe the impact of mobile technology and social media on collaboration. In what ways might collaboration include actors other than humans.

KEY TERMS AND CONCEPTS

Asynchronous communication 287
Collaboration 280
Collaboration information system 285
Cooperation 280
Discussion forums 288
Document library 295
File server 290
Google Drive 291
Iteration control 292

Iteration management 291
Libraries 292
Microsoft Skype 288
Microsoft OneDrive 291
Office Web Apps 291
Parallel workflow 295
Power curve 298
Project data 285
Project management 293

Project metadata 285
Screen-sharing applications 288
Sequential workflow 295
Synchronous communication 287
Team surveys 289
Videoconferencing 288
Virtual meetings 288
Webinar 288
Workflow 295

USING YOUR KNOWLEDGE

10-1. Reread about 2028 in Q10-8. Do you agree with the conclusions? Why or why not? If F2F meetings become rare, what impacts do you see on the travel industry?

MyLab MIS

10-2. Choose one of the three alternatives described in Q10-7 for use by your collaborative team. To do so, answer the following questions (if possible, answer these questions with your team):

MyLab MIS

    a. List your team's collaboration requirements. Break them into mandatory and nice-to-have categories.

    b. Create a list of criteria for selecting collaboration tools and creating a collaboration IS. Start with the items in the first column of Figure 10-20, but add, modify, or delete items depending on your answer to question 10-2a.

    c. Score the three alternatives in Q10-7 against your requirements and your criteria. If you wish, change any of the elements of those three alternatives to create a fourth alternative. Score it as well.

    d. Based on your answer to question 10-2c, select a collaboration tool set. Explain your selection.

    e. Given your answer to question 10-2d, how will you construct your collaboration IS? Specifically, what procedures will you need to develop and how will your team members obtain training? Will you need to have any special jobs or roles for your team members? If so, describe them.

10-3. Reflect on your experience working on teams in previous classes as well as on collaborative teams in other settings, such as a campus committee. To what extent was your team collaborative? Did it involve communication and iteration? If so, how? Was critical feedback provided? How did you use collaborative information systems, if at all? If you did not use collaborative information systems, describe how you think such systems might have improved your work methods and results. If you did use collaborative information systems, explain how you could improve on that use, given the knowledge you have gained from this chapter.

MyLab MIS

10-4. Think back over your past week. When did you use either of the collaboration activities of communication and iteration outside of an academic setting? What process was your team engaged in? What were your team's objectives? Would any of the IS tools discussed in this chapter have made your process more effective?

10-5. This exercise requires you to experiment with Google Drive. You will need two Google accounts to complete this exercise. If you have two different email addresses, then set up two Google accounts using those addresses. Otherwise, use your school email address and set up a Google Gmail account. A Gmail account will automatically give you a Google account.

    a. Using Microsoft Word, write a memo to yourself. In the memo, explain the nature of the communication collaboration driver. Go to *http://drive.google.com* and sign in with one of your Google accounts. Upload your memo using Google Drive. Save your uploaded document and share your document with the email in your second Google account. Sign out of your first Google account. (If you have access to two computers situated close to each other, use both of them for this exercise. You will see more of the Google Drive functionality by using two computers. If you have two computers, do not sign out of your Google account. Perform step b and all actions

for the second account on that second computer. If you are using two computers, ignore the instructions in the following steps to sign out of the Google accounts.)

    b. Open a new window in your browser. Access *http://drive.google.com* from that second window and sign in using your second Google account. Open the document that you shared in step a.

    c. Change the memo by adding a brief description of the content-management driver. Save the document from your second account. If you are using just one computer, sign out from your second account.

    d. Sign in on your first account. Open the most recent version of the memo and add a description of the role of version histories. Save the document. (If you are using two computers, notice how Google warns you that another user is editing the document at the same time. Click Refresh to see what happens.) If you are using just one computer, sign out from your first account.

    e. Sign in on your second account. Reopen the shared document. From the File menu, save the document as a Word document. Describe how Google processed the changes to your document.

10-6. This exercise requires you to experiment with Microsoft OneDrive. You will need two Microsoft accounts to complete this exercise. The easiest way to do it is to work with a classmate. If that is not possible, set up two Microsoft accounts using two different Hotmail addresses.

    a. Go to *www.onedrive.com* and sign in with one of your accounts. Create a memo about collaboration tools using the Word Web App. Save your memo. Share your document with the email in your second Microsoft account. Sign out of your first account. (If you have access to two computers situated close to each other, use both of them for this exercise. If you have two computers, do not sign out of your Microsoft account. Perform step b and all actions for the second account on that second computer. If you are using two computers, ignore the instructions in the following steps to sign out of the Microsoft accounts.)

    b. Open a new window in your browser. Access *www.onedrive.com* from that second window and sign in using your second Microsoft account. Open the document that you shared in step a.

    c. Change the memo by adding a brief description of content management. Do not save the document yet. If you are using just one computer, sign out from your second account.

    d. Sign in on your first account. Attempt to open the memo and note what occurs. Sign out of your first account and sign back in with your second account. Save the document. Now, sign out of your second account and sign back in with the first account. Now attempt to open the memo. (If you are using two computers, perform these same actions on the two different computers.)

    e. Sign in on your second account. Reopen the shared document. From the File menu, save the document as a Word document. Describe how Microsoft OneDrive processed the changes to your document.

COLLABORATION EXERCISE 10

Collaborate with a group of students to answer. Kata are structured activities you practice deliberately so that their pattern becomes a habit. Some process improvement experts use kata to learn to see and respond to common process problems in a consistent and structured way. This structured way includes the following steps:

1. Get the direction or challenge	(Plan 1)	get from leaders of firm, not a target
2. Grasp the current situation	(Plan 2)	identify obstacles
3. Establish your next target	(Plan 3)	be specific about date and measures
4. Conduct experiments to get to target	(Execute 1)	learn from this step for next cycle

For example, a restaurant in a college town seeks to double the number of college students it serves (1-challenge). The managers and staff collaborate on identifying the obstacles that have prevented the restaurant from attaining this level in the past and the choices and opportunities they currently have available to increase student customer totals (2-grasp). Their first target is to raise the total 25 percent by the end of the month (3-target). They decide the first experiment is to double the number of coupons they offer (4-experiment). At the end of the month, they determine the results of this first experiment, discuss additional possible experiments, and select the next experiment. The activities 2, 3, and 4 repeat until the challenge is attained.

1. Collaboration is clearly essential to kata. But what exactly is iterated, the thing that is produced by the team that generates feedback?
2. What type of process is kata: structured or dynamic?
3. What collaboration IS can be used to support this process for the restaurant?
4. Practice kata. As a team, number 20 sheets of paper, turn them upside down, and shuffle them. When time begins, turn the sheets over one by one and make a pile of the same papers in numerical order. Your challenge is to do this task in less than 20 seconds. After you have completed the exercise answer the questions below.
   a. What was your first target?
   b. How many iterations did this take?
   c. Your experiment activity is iterated several times. When you collaborated on selecting an experiment, how was the feedback your team created? Did your collaboration have elements of Figure 10-2? Was your collaboration frank and candid, and did it include careful criticism?
   d. Did trust develop among team members? Why or why not?
   e. Did your team achieve the effectiveness and efficiency collaboration objectives shown in Figure 10-4?

CASE STUDY 10

Miracle on Hudson

Collaboration is essential to businesses of all types. Collaboration among professionals is also key in high-risk settings such as firefighting, healthcare, and aviation. In aviation, pilots are taught and trained to be excellent collaborators. Pilots collaborate with each other, with other members of the flight crew, with ground controllers, and with company support personnel. Pilots wear a lot of hats and participate on a number of teams every day. One reason collaboration is key is that airlines have long realized how essential teamwork is during emergencies. No recent in-flight emergency has received greater scrutiny than the flight that landed in the Hudson, and no flight in recent time demonstrated the value of collaboration as well.

Most of us have heard the story about the "Miracle on the Hudson," the landing of an Airbus 320 on the Hudson River in January 2009. The highly experienced crew, Chesley "Sully" Sullenberger, and his first officer Jeffrey Skiles safely piloted their aircraft to a landing after hitting a flock of Canadian geese only 90 seconds into their flight. With no thrust from either engine, the crew glided the aircraft to land on the river. Their work, the contributions of the flight attendants, and the quick work of

water rescue personnel helped save the lives of all 155 people on board.

While a dual engine failure is exceptionally unfortunate, the crew had several things working to its advantage. Both pilots were very experienced aviators; Captain Sullenberger was particularly well versed in aviation safety issues, and he had flown gliders earlier in his life. The sky was clear, allowing them to maneuver the aircraft using visual references and make quick and accurate visual estimations about how far the aircraft could fly. The quick response by tugboat and water ferry crews was also significant and cannot be overlooked.

Some might argue that an airplane with a fully automated flight deck, an AI system robotically moving all the controls, would have also survived. Presumably such an autopilot would immediately turn back to the departure airport. Simulations indicate an A320 could have made it back to the airport if an immediate turn was executed. Interestingly omitted from this debate about using AI and robotics to fly the plane is the question "What if the bird strike had simply occurred 30 seconds later?" The plane would have traveled several miles further away from the airport, and the runway could have been out of range even with an immediate turn back. With no landing runway available, would the autopilot "know" a water landing on the Hudson would be survivable? How can an AI system improvise? Looking back over the past 40 years of aviation, there are several remarkable improvisations by quick-thinking pilots.

The Miracle on the Hudson also highlights the value of excellent collaboration. Crew members could quickly analyze the situation, rule out options, maneuver the aircraft, coordinate with traffic controllers on the radio, warn the passengers, and execute a lengthy dual engine failure checklist. They developed a plan that began as "turn back to the airport," communicated it with their flight team, and improved it (iterated it) as more facts became known. The initial plan of turning back generated feedback that the runway was too far away. The next plan, to land at another airport, was also soon updated as no airports were within range. Crew members effectively communicated with each other and ground controllers several plans that generated lifesaving feedback.

Improving collaboration on the flight deck of airlines has been the goal of the aviation industry for almost 40 years. The industry was rocked in the 1960s and '70s by instances of crew members noticing an unsafe situation but failing to assertively present solutions. You can read about pilot error accidents such as the 747 accident in Tenerife in 1977 and the 737 takeoff accident on the Potomac River in 1982.

Because of these and many other pilot error accidents, the industry developed and taught aviation crews the principles of Crew Resource Management (CRM) to improve collaboration, leadership, and decision making in the cockpit. A key aspect of CRM is that pilots must be assertive, state concerns clearly to other team members, propose a solution, and listen to feedback. The program has been so successful that many other domains with highly trained professionals are adapting it for their teams, such as surgical units, firefighters, ship crews, paramedics, equipment maintenance operations, and even tandem canoe crews. The good news is that in the past 40 years the rate of pilot error mishaps and lack of communication errors has dropped dramatically. Captain Sullenberger and his crew are just one example of the value of improving crew collaboration.

10-7. What was iterated on this short flight? What is typically iterated on a routine flight?

10-8. How can feedback on a flight deck be encouraged? If you were a captain or a first officer, what things could you say to your partner that would foster feedback?

10-9. You don't often face disasters driving a car. However, even routine communication among occupants of a car about plans and choices often goes wrong. How can you practice better communication and feedback about driving intentions?

10-10. IT collaboration systems that link ground controllers and pilots are remarkably antiquated—just radio transmissions like the 1960s. Describe an ideal flight deck collaboration system: what would it look like and its features.

10-11. Think back to a team you have been on that exhibited poor collaboration. Was feedback given and ignored, or was feedback lacking? How can you avoid poor collaboration on a student team?

CHAPTER RESOURCES

[1] J. Richard Hackman and A. C. Edmondson, "Groups as Agents of Change," in *Handbook of Organizational Development*, edited by T. Cummings (Thousand Oaks, CA: Sage Publications, 2007), p. 217.

[2] Mitch Ditkoff, Tim Moore, Carolyn Allen, and Dave Pollard, "The Ideal Collaborative Team," Idea Champions, accessed July 5, 2013, www.ideachampions.com/downloads/collaborationresults.pdf.

[3] J. Richard Hackman, *Leading Teams: Setting the Stage for Great Performances* (Boston: Harvard Business Press, 2002).

[4] Wouter van Diggelen, *Changing Face-to-Face Communication: Collaborative Tools to Support Small-Group Discussions in the Classroom* (Groningen: University of Groningen, 2011).

[5] For more information about workflows and the Windows Workflow Foundation, see Mark J. Collins, *Office 2010 Workflow* (New York: Apress, 2010).

[6] To sign up for Office 365, go to http://office.microsoft.com/en-us/.

MyLab MIS

Go to **MyLab MIS.com** for Auto-graded writing questions as well as the following Assisted-graded writing questions:

10-12. Figure 10-4 depicts three effectiveness objectives of the collaboration process. Describe a team you have been a member of where two of the three objectives were met, but not the third. What could the team have done to meet this third objective?

10-13. Group messaging apps such as WhatsApp and WeChat as well as texting are often used to support collaboration. Explain how these types of apps support the two activities in the collaboration process. Describe the iteration controls available on these apps.

Chapter 11

Social Media and IS

"My wife is giving birth in the hallway at Wood Hospital!!!" ☹☹

Joe Smit, the director of patient services at Wood Hospital, is reading the tweet out loud to Jake.

He continues, "No way! Tell me this didn't happen! We really had someone in labor in the hallway?"

Jake replies, "Well, it was only the first three hours of labor. She had the baby about 15 minutes ago in a regular room."

"Oh, that's a relief."

"There were quite a few follow-on tweets the husband made. I can read them to you if you like," replies Jake.

"Thanks, no. Why did he go on and on?"

"I think he expected us to be listening and respond at some point. They also had a brief Facebook Live stream. But I think you have the idea."

"They livestreamed her labor pains? Maybe it's like Yogi Berra used to say—nobody goes there anymore. It's too crowded. Stuff like this happens every day on Facebook, so maybe no one will notice."

"Could be, boss, but I don't think that's a good plan."

"Can we delete these posts?"

"No, they're out there."

"So let's tell our side of the story! And do we have an our side of this stupidity?"

"We can claim that others were using the rooms for giving birth and this lady wasn't as far along as they were, but I think we'll lose that argument. We'll look defiant and like we don't care."

"So what do we do?"

"The key is winning back trust. So let's get the hospital CEO to record a heartfelt apology, give that couple a year of vitamins or something, and make some posts with that in mind."

Jake continues, "In the future, we can set it up so that when Wood Hospital is mentioned in a tweet, the patient service office gets an immediate notification, and they can learn to deal with responses. What we need is a consistent procedure so the right people get notified and they have preapproved options for responses."

While Joe is thinking that idea over, Jake presses on.

"We could also use social media to communicate some positive things, to get our good stories out—curing kids with cancer, opening a new treatment option, treating the poor, that sort of thing. It's what we do, and it's also good for morale for our employees. Everyone likes to be reminded they're in the helping business."

"Jake, go find some other hospital employees who understand this social media thing and start putting together a plan."

Q11-1. What is social media, and why is it important to business?

Q11-2. What are the objectives of the social media process?

Q11-3. What are the key components of a social media IS?

Q11-4. How do social media IS support social media activities?

Q11-5. How can social media IS support business processes?

Q11-6. How can social media IS support the process of building social capital?

Q11-7. How do businesses manage the risks of social media?

Q11-8. How can IS similar to social media support business processes?

Q11-9. What is the sharing economy?

Q11-10. 2028?

PREVIEW

Social media is both a blessing and curse to businesses like the hospital. It provides a wonderful opportunity for communicating with customers, but that communication can be challenging. What's more, the challenges of social media keep changing.

There is an old saying in the new field of IT—technique follows technology. It means that when a new technology appears on the scene, it takes a while for people to figure out the right technique for its use. New technology is always mesmerizing, and so it is with these new social media technologies. The technology is here—cheap storage and the bandwidth to livestream everything—but the technique to apply it to business is still a work in progress.

To us, the right technique is to apply enduring principles. In this chapter, we focus on the principles you have seen throughout the book: the five components of an IS, process activities, and how an IS supports business processes. We also believe that a key principle behind business use of social media is trust, a theme that will run throughout the chapter.

Just as we did in earlier chapters where we demonstrated the impact of SAP on processes such as procurement and sales, here we suggest ways to use social media information systems to make business processes better. Our approach is similar to Chapter 10—we first examine the components of a social media IS, then the activities of social media, and finally how social media IS support social media activities in actual business processes. We close the chapter with a brief description of several newer social technologies—Reddit, WhatsApp, Uber and Airbnb—and what businesses can learn from them. But we begin with the topic of social media—and its importance to business.

Q11-1 What Is Social Media, and Why Is It Important to Business?

With the arrival of Facebook and Twitter at the end of the last decade, the term *social media* was coined. **Social media** are Web apps that support the creation and sharing of user-generated content. **User-generated content** is publically available content created by end users. A **social media information system** supports the two activities in the social media process: creating and sharing user-generated content.

The social media process begins when a user creates content by posting on Instagram, tweeting, uploading a photo on Pinterest, updating a LinkedIn résumé, or participating in another creative act. This content is then collected and shared with other users by a social media application provider such as Instagram, Facebook, or YouTube.

While this two-step process is quite simple, people still buzz about it and proclaim "This changes everything!" With social media, the reality has lived up to the hype: social media is fundamentally changing the way people #communicate. It's hard to ignore 1.5 billion Facebook users; 200 million resumes on LinkedIn; and 700 million Twitter users, 4 billion YouTube videos, 10 billion Snapchat video views daily, and 18,000 Reddit votes every minute.

When this textbook was written, livestreaming, the growth of Instagram and Reddit, and fake news were changing the social media landscape. Each year this list of changes will be different as someone learns the technique to apply blockchain, virtual reality, artificial intelligence, or some other technology to social media.

As social media use continues to grow and change, the opportunities for organizations to use these technologies to improve their processes grow as well. For example, American Express is tweeting product discounts to valued customers to improve their customer service process, and the FBI used social media to help find the Boston Marathon bombers. And although social media comes with some quirky risks, as in the opening vignette, most businesses are wisely jumping on board, as highlighted in Figure 11-1. *Forbes'* pithy advice is spot on: "Social media is a must for any business."[1]

To engage their customers on social media, businesses depend on social media application providers. The most popular providers are listed in Figure 11-2. While the list contains the usual suspects, notice the wide variety of apps and the popularity of non-English-speaking apps. Also notice the number of apps that enable users to create and share images such as Tumblr, Tinder, Snapchat, Pinterest, and Instagram.

While you may have personal experience using many of the apps in Figure 11-2, in this chapter we focus on the business use of social media. We begin our discussion of social media in the next question where we consider the objectives of the social media process. As a future businessperson, think about how businesses can use an app rather than your personal like or dislike of it. When you take your first job after graduation, you may be asked how your new firm might use social media to support their processes. To be ready, practice with the different social media apps while you are in school and use this chapter to learn how businesses can leverage social media to their advantage.

FIGURE 11-1

Social Media Industry Trends

Source: https://wearesocial.com/special-reports/digital-in-2017; www.business2community.com/social-media/47-superb-social-media-marketing-stats-facts-01431126#2H74tvY8SHiyUG90.99-global-overview; www.pewinternet.org/fact-sheet/social-media/

- 2.8 billion people are active social media users, growing 20 percent annually.
- 1 million new active uses a day.
- 96 percent of small business owners use social media marketing.
- 92 percent agree with the statement "Social media marketing is important for my business."
- More young people use social media for discovery than search.
- 71 percent with a good social media service experience share it with others.
- 4 million businesses pay for advertising on Facebook.
- Social media is expected to grow to 25 percent of marketing budget by 2020.
- 78 percent of people who complain via Twitter expect a response within 1 hour.

FIGURE 11-2
Most Popular Social Media Apps
(according to Wikipedia)

App Provider	Description	Registered Users as of 2017
Facebook	General, video, blogs, apps	1,300,000,000
Twitter	General, microblogging, RSS	650,000,000
Qzone	General, Chinese	480,000,000
Sina Weibo	General, Chinese, microblogging	300,000,000
Instagram	Photo and video sharing	300,000,000
Habbo	General, teen oriented	270,000,000
VK	General, music, search in Russian	250,000,000
Tumblr	Multimedia microblogging	230,000,000
LinkedIn	Business and professional networking	200,000,000

Q11-2 ▶ What Are the Objectives of the Social Media Process?

For any business to use social media successfully, its managers need to understand the objectives of the social media process. However, like other dynamic processes, the social media process has few well-accepted objectives. For example, people use social media to communicate, share, support, and entertain while the objectives of a business may be to boost sales or respond to customer complaints.

To make things a bit more challenging, social media has a unique wrinkle; unlike all the other processes in this book, the social media process is not controlled by the business. Businesses must share control of the social media process with other participants—the app providers like Facebook and Twitter, and the users. Because businesses don't control it, they do not get to change it or determine its objectives. This lack of exclusive control can be unsettling for control freaks; for others it makes the game much more interesting.

Businesses, app providers, and users all play different roles in the social media process, and they all have their own objectives. These objectives are shown in Figure 11-3 and include both effectiveness objectives and efficiency objectives. While at times these objectives can align, at times they are in conflict.

Effectiveness Objectives

First, we will examine the effectiveness objectives for each of the three participants—the users, businesses, and app providers. These effectiveness objectives reflect the needs or goals of each participant.

Effectiveness
Users—Belonging, Communication
Businesses—Support strategy
App Providers—Market share, Revenue

Efficiency
Time and cost

FIGURE 11-3
Social Media Participants and Social
Media Process Objectives

USERS   Joining communities is a deep-seated emotional need for users, and this need is reflected in the first objective: belonging. Belonging to communities greater than oneself fosters a positive self-esteem. In the past, communities were based on family relationships or geographic location—everyone in the village formed a community. While belonging is an old objective, what's new with social media communities is the breathtaking variety of opportunities to belong to communities and the ease of joining them. In addition to belonging, users also appreciate the opportunity to express themselves and communicate. Humans are a particularly communicative animal, and social media feeds that need.

BUSINESSES   The primary objective for a business is to use social media to support strategy. For example, a business that differentiates on service uses social media to improve service; a low-cost leader uses social media to reduce expenses and improve efficiencies. These general strategies provide more specific objectives such as gain feedback from customers, build trust and brand identity, generate loyalty and authority, learn about potential hires, develop sales leads, and evaluate new products.

To achieve these different objectives, businesses use social media both internally with their employees and externally with their customers. While most of this chapter is devoted to external use, a brief note on internal use is helpful. When businesses employ social media internally to facilitate cooperative work, it is called **Enterprise 2.0**. For example, Red Robin used Yammer, an internal Twitter-like app, to give a voice to its 26,000 employees. As a result, when the restaurant launched an ill-conceived burger, Yammer comments from employees helped fix the recipe, and the chain introduced a fix within 4 months, a significant improvement on the traditional 12 to 18 months.

APP PROVIDERS   Most app providers seek either market share or revenue. Early on, most providers focus on growing the market share of their new app, but as the app reaches puberty, the objective shifts to revenue and the nagging question "How are we going to make money with this thing?" Many app providers fail to make the transition from market share to revenue.

Efficiency Objectives

Users, businesses, and app providers usually share a common efficiency objective: operate within time and cost constraints. While the objective is the same, it leads to different goals. Users want free apps that take little time to master. Businesses seek to limit their labor costs, and app providers use this objective to constrain their development costs.

Now that we have explained social media and its varied objectives, we turn to the main focus of this chapter: how social media information systems support business processes. Figure 11-4 depicts the relationship between social media IS, social media activities, and business processes. Starting on the left, the five components of a social media IS are discussed next in Q11-3. Then the

FIGURE 11-4

Social Media IS Components and Business Processes

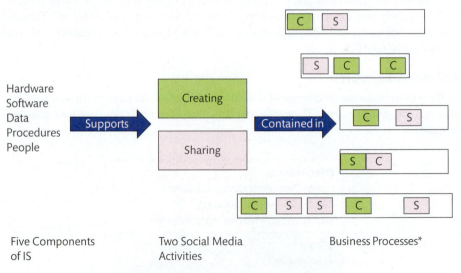

Five Components of IS

Two Social Media Activities

Business Processes*

*White space represents other activities in the business process

two social media activities—creating and sharing—are described in Q11-4. Finally, in Q11-5 we describe how social media IS support the social media activities contained in business processes. As in Chapter 10, we display in Figure 11-4 those business processes as a rectangle, as a structured process would look; in reality, these dynamic processes defy conventional diagramming.

Q11-3 What Are the Key Components of a Social Media IS?

In common use, the term *social media* can refer to apps, the use of the apps, or the industry. This ambiguity of terms is fairly common. When you use the term *social media*, try to be clear about whether you are referring to a process, an IS, or just software.

As mentioned earlier, a social media IS supports the creation and sharing of user-generated content. This definition means that the Twitter or Instagram apps on your smartphone are not social media IS by themselves, they are just the technology: the hardware and software. As businesspeople, we think the other components of an IS are also important—the data, procedures, and people.

After we have presented the five components of a social media IS, we will summarize the highlights before discussing how they are used in social media activities.

The Five Components of a Social Media IS

The key elements of the five components are shown in Figure 11-5. Let's consider each.

HARDWARE The hardware employed by users and app providers is different. Users interact with social media on mobile devices, laptops, and desktop systems. On the server end, most social media application providers use elastic servers in the cloud.

One important consideration of hardware is the size of the screen, as users increasingly rely on small-screen smartphones, there is much less space for advertising. However, in recent years revenues from smartphone advertisements have been strong, overcoming early concerns that small-screen advertising would be ineffective. Businesses love the opportunity to advertise to customers on the move, so ad revenue is a key source of funding for many social media application providers.

SOFTWARE For users, social media apps are free, fun to use, immediately rewarding, and frequently changed. Most of the features on social media apps are offered to the user at no cost, although advanced features may have a fee. The software is also updated frequently, sometimes with little notification to users. App providers expect users to experiment with the updated app to figure it out. For a business using social media, the attributes of free, fun, and frequently changed also hold true. However, unlike other software the business uses, it has little input on the features of the software. In some cases, like Facebook applications, businesses create their own applications and interface those applications with the social media site. App providers develop and operate their own custom, proprietary social media apps. Finally, app providers provide businesses data analysis software to analyze social media data. Businesses can also obtain social media analysis software from other sources such as Klout, Cyfe, or Quintly.

Many social media application providers use a NoSQL database management system to process their data, although traditional relational DBMS products are used as well.

Five Components of IS	Social Media IS
Hardware	Cloud for servers; various devices, increasingly mobile for clients
Software	Free, fun, frequently changed, wide variety, and businesses have little input
Data	Content and connection data are both valuable
Procedures	Informal for users, governed by social media policy for businesses
People	Freedom for users, users seek belonging and communication opportunities, and business users should follow established social media policies

FIGURE 11-5

Five Components of a Social Media IS

DATA Social media data falls into two categories: content and connections. **Content data** is user-generated content and the responses to that content contributed by other users. You provide the content data for your Instagram account, and your friends provide response content when they make comments, tag you, or otherwise publish on your site. Content data also includes metadata such as the location of a photo, its date and time, and copyright data. Increasingly, content data is composed of video, and most apps support creating and sharing video content.

Connection data is data about relationships. On Facebook, for example, the relationships to your friends are connection data. The fact that you've liked particular organizations is also connection data. Connection data differentiates social media IS from other Web apps. Both Web sites and social media sites present user and responder content, but only social media applications store and process connection data. Connection data is a clunky term; most social media sites use a related term, **social graph**, which is a mapping that depicts the relationships among connected people.

One unique feature of social media data is tags. A **tag** is a keyword or term given to a piece of data by its creator. A tag or hashtag makes it easier to search for that term or keyword. A **hashtag** is a user-created tag that adds the prefix # to a word. Hashtags are one type of tag, but names of people and Likes in Facebook photos, keywords in YouTube videos, names of Pinterest members in a pin description, and hyperlinks in wikis are also tags. Tags are metadata that highlight user-defined topics, making them easier for search engines to find. Tags also help classify and categorize content. A term for this emergent classification is **folksonomy**—a content structure that has emerged from the processing of many user inputs. The most popular folksonomy is Reddit.

Businesses are interested in data that measure the impact of social media on their customers. Marketers have developed two categories of measures, as shown in Figure 11-6. Passive measures focus on the size of audience. These types of measures include followers, views, visits, or traffic counts. Active engagement considers actions of the audience such as time on a Web site, clicks on a link, retweets, shares, comments, and ratings.

PROCEDURES When you upload a photo to Snapchat, retweet, or pin a photo on Pinterest, you are executing a procedure. Social media procedures are typically simple, informal, evolving, and socially oriented. You do what your friends do. When friends learn how to do something new and interesting, you copy them. Software is designed to be easy to learn and use, so the procedures are simple to follow.

While informality makes using social media easy, it also can lead to unintended consequences for the user. The most troubling examples concern user privacy. Many people have learned not to post pictures of themselves in front of their house numbers on the same publicly accessible site on which they're describing their new high-definition television. Many others, alas, have not.

For businesses using social media, procedures cannot be so informal and simple. Before initiating a social media presence, organizations must develop procedures for users to create content, manage user responses, and extract value from content. For an example of the latter, setting up a social media IS to gather data on product problems is a wasted expense unless procedures exist to extract knowledge from that social media data. Organizations also need to develop procedures to manage objectionable content as described in the opening vignette and in Q11-7.

PEOPLE Users of social media do what they want to do depending on their objectives and their personalities. They behave in certain ways and observe the consequences. This may or may not lead them to change their behavior.

FIGURE 11-6

Social Media Process Measures

Passive
- Followers
- Views
- Visits
- Traffic

Active
- Time on site
- Clicks
- Retweets
- Shares
- Comments
- Ratings

For businesses using social media, this freedom of behavior for users is both exciting and unnerving. Businesses depend on users to experiment with social media—to be willing to click here and there and write their first product reviews. However, this experimentation can also be hard to limit after the cat gets out of the bag.

While businesses exert little control over users, they can control their employees who represent the company on social media sites. The employees who speak for an organization should be trained on both social media IS user procedures as well as on the organization's social media policy. Selecting these employees raises some interesting questions: What makes for a good tweeter? What makes for an effective wall writer? What type of person should be hired for such jobs? What education should he or she have? How does one evaluate candidates for such positions, and what measures can be used?

Key Attributes of a Social Media IS

Social media IS have a number of important distinguishing features. First, the client *hardware* for social media is increasingly mobile devices. Second, social media apps are designed for personal use, not business use. As a result, organizations have little input on the *hardware* or *software* features, nor do they control much of the *data*; businesses are guests at the party. Third, the relationship data among the participants is key: if you post an image of the company's product on your wall or tweet about good service, the key for an organization is your relationships, your connection data—how many of your friends are reached. Finally, the social media phenomenon is based on the need for *people* to belong and communicate. This is the engine driving this train, and if an organization is successful with social media, it is because it piggybacks on this force.

While it is helpful to understand the components of a social media IS, it is also important to see how these components work together to support social media activities. Next, we explore how these components support the creation and sharing activities.

Q11-4 ▶ How Do Social Media IS Support Social Media Activities?

Social media information systems support the two social media activities: creating and sharing. Here we focus exclusively on the aspects of creating and sharing that affect business use. These dimensions are listed in Figure 11-7.

Creating

The first issue regarding content creation is that while users create content without any incentive from a business, they often create more when they are rewarded. Rewards vary from icons and status symbols to privileged placement, gifts, or entries in sweepstakes. Businesses need to understand reward system opportunities if they want to encourage users to create and disseminate content about the business.

Creating
User-created content
  Learn to reward customers.
  Listen on a variety of platforms used by customers.
  Be alert for unpredictable viral content.
  Make content creating convenient for customers.
Business-created content
  Focus on customers' needs more than the features of the product.
  Use a variety of accounts to have a variety of voices on key apps.

Sharing
Learn how your customers search.
Use apps that measure the impact of your content, your buzz.
Look for opportunity in new interactive content.

FIGURE 11-7

Business Aspects of Creating and Sharing

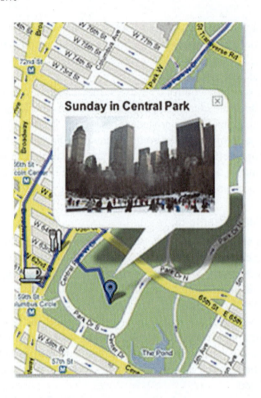

Users create a wide variety of content that may be of interest to a business; they create tweets, posts, Likes, reviews, resumes, photos, images, and geolocation data. They can also create **mashup** content—content that combines data from two or more web services, as shown in Figure 11-8. For a business, this variety means that users are talking about their products or services on a wide variety of social media apps. To hear what their customers are saying, businesses must also listen on a wide variety of social media apps.

While most content is routine, occasionally it erupts and goes **viral**—becoming extremely popular in a short time. For example, in 2016 Airbnb created a #livethere video campaign on Facebook and Instagram that quickly resulted in 11 million views. Viral content could be very good news for a business if the content shows the business in a positive light. However, viral content can also be risky—Starbucks wanted to give free iced coffee to friends and family members of its employees, but when the announcement went viral, it had to pull the plug on the offer. Bottom line—the impact of a viral event on a business is difficult to predict.

Finally, businesses should strive to make content creation convenient. When a customer buys a bicycle online from CBI, the CBI Web site should provide a simple process for the user to copy a photo of the new bike to post it on Facebook, Instagram, or Pinterest or a link to a page with a photo for Twitter. Businesses should support their customers' willingness to create content about them.

Having discussed customer-created content, let's turn to business-created content on social media. When businesses create content, their goal should be a closer connection with their customers. As a result, their content should be less about their products and services and more often about their customers. One social media guideline is for a business to discuss its own products and services with fewer than 10 percent of its content. Instead, businesses should post content about how their product plays a positive role in society, the social causes or volunteer activities of the business, interesting information for customers to use to solve their problems, attractive or humorous images, heart-warming stories about their customers, or thoughtful responses to their questions.

To better connect with customers, a business might consider having a variety of accounts on the same platform. For example, a college may use several Twitter accounts, one for school officials to post content in a formal and structured style and another for designated students to connect with prospective students in a less formal way. For example, these designated students may be tour guides who meet prospective students during campus tours and encourage them to stay in touch via social media. In the end, the goal for the college is for the prospective student to connect to several people on the campus.

Sharing

For businesses, the trick to understanding sharing is to learn how their customers search. Searching is essential to social media apps because all successful apps have an enormous database of content to share. One reason these apps became successful was that users could quickly learn how to search to find their friends' photos and their favorite talking cat videos. Twitter's easy-to-use search function allows users to find particular tweets in the torrent of the twitterverse. For a business to be successful in social media, it must learn how searching is done—it needs to learn how its customers search for tweets, how its customers use hashtags and expressions, and how its customers find content by geographic location. If a business understands search, it can improve the likelihood that the content it creates will be found by the customers it seeks. Search is a powerful user procedure and a must for businesses to master.

When businesses create content, they are particularly interested in impact—the buzz it creates when it is shared. Impact grows if their tweets are retweeted, if their Likes lead to other Likes, or if their help-wanted ads in LinkedIn are widely shared. A number of third-party apps such as Klout, Hootsuite, and Buffer help businesses measure the impact of their social media content.

Finally, businesses should be aware of new forms of content that can be shared on social media. Recently, Microsoft made it possible for users to create a document, spreadsheet, or presentation and share that content with others on social platforms. For example, a user can make a spreadsheet and embed it on his blog where visitors can see it and interact with it. A visitor can change the values in spreadsheet's cells and see how those changes ripple through the spreadsheet while still on the blog. Other software companies are also making it easy for their users to create content and share it in interactive form. Figure 11-9 shows how this is done with a YouTube video. To embed this video on a blog or on Tumblr, a user simply copies the html code in the red box. Businesses should look for opportunities to take advantage of these new forms of interactive sharing.

FIGURE 11-9

Html Code to Embed a YouTube Video on Another Platform

Source: http://www.youtube.com/watch?v=zncqb-n3zMo, accessed 8/20/2013

In Q11-4 we wanted to call your attention to the business aspects of social media activities. We continue this business focus by considering in Q11-5 how social media IS support business processes.

Q11-5 ▶ How Can Social Media IS Support Business Processes?

A number of essential business processes rely on social media, including collaboration, project management, promotion, product design, knowledge management, medical care, sales lead management, hiring, and others, as shown in Figure 11-10. And for good reason; more than 90 percent of large companies using social media have reported at least one measurable business benefit. Here we present a sample of the processes and some of the techniques they are using with social media technology. While the specific examples in this question will soon become out-of-date, the principles about how social media supports business processes are enduring. And note how frequently the principle that social media can build trust occurs.

The Promotion Process

Perhaps the most common way that social media helps business is by supporting the promotion process. **Promotion** is the process of sharing data about a product or service with the objective to improve awareness and sales. Traditionally, businesses executed promotion via well-crafted messages from the business to a broad customer base; however, with social media, promotion now includes sending informal messages and messages among customers in narrow customer groups.

Social media supports the promotion process by helping businesses find their customers, their target audience. Social media providers have access to potential customers' data and can offer businesses a targeted audience; Facebook knows about your interests, the items you have searched for, and advertisements you click on. As a result, businesses can buy advertising wisely and find their audience. Social media providers can also help a business target promotions by providing measures such as **click-through rates**, the number of clicks on an ad divided by the number of times the ad is displayed; and **conversion rate**, the percentage of users who take a desired action such as making an order. With these measures, a business can understand how many potential customers are attracted by their different advertisements and adapt their promotions accordingly.

Social media promotions involving consumers have two important characteristics. One is the network effect: If a network of consumers is buzzing about a product, the network itself draws an even bigger crowd because nothing draws a crowd like a crowd. The second important aspect of consumer promotion is trust. Consumers trust their friends much more than they do businesses. One recent study found that more than 80 percent of consumers trusted the recommendation of friends while less than 40 percent trusted online promotions.[2] Further, almost 60 percent of consumers ages 18 to 29 were more influenced by comments on social media than by either TV or Internet advertising. Sites that provide customer reviews such as Amazon, Angie's List, and TripAdvisor are growing. Yelp users input more than 90 million reviews a month, and more than 90 percent of consumers read online reviews before purchasing.

FIGURE 11-10

Business Processes Supported by Social Media IS

Business Processes Supported by Social Media IS
Promotion
Customer service
Crowdsourcing
Knowledge management
Hiring
Innovation
Product development
Financing
Project management
Sales

Process	Example	Objectives	Possible KPIs
Promotion	NASA *Deadpool*	Engagement Reach	Followers Views Visits Clicks Retweets Shares
Customer Service	Hospitals Xbox	Faster callback More communication	Time to callback Number of contacts
Hiring	UPS Home Depot	Hire quality Save time, cost	Retention after hire Length of search Cost of advertisement
Crowdsourcing	Frito-Lay Coach shoes	Easy for user to use Quality and quantity of inputs	Time required for input Number of ideas accepted

FIGURE 11-11

Example Promotion Process Objectives and Measures

Figure 11-11 includes the objectives and possible KPIs for a promotion process. Notice in the examples that follow the variety of products promoted, the techniques used by the business, and how the results of the promotions were measured.

- Stride Gum funded a YouTube video of Matt Harding dancing around the world in 42 different countries. At the end of this upbeat video, a Stride Gum announcement appears identifying Stride Gum as the video's sponsor. The Dancing Matt video was viewed 33 million times in its first 2 years. The promotion is credited with increasing sales by 8 percent and moving Stride Gum to fifth in the sugarless gum industry.
- NASA sent astronaut Mark Kelly to the space station for a year in space. To promote the event, NASA used the hashtag #AYearInSpace. Kelly communicated with millions of followers on earth by tweeting, posting, and uploading content to Instagram, YouTube, and Snapchat. He streamed on Facebook Live and hosted an AMA session on Reddit.
- The movie *Deadpool* was heavily promoted on social media. The first tweet, a year prior to the movie, was retweeted 55,000 times and received 52,000 likes.[3] Its Twitter handle had nearly 450,000 followers before the movie was released, fueled by actor Ryan Reynolds' personal involvement.
- Social media can also be used to promote social causes. The site Change.org allows visitors to promote causes and petitions and collect "signatures." Businesses can use social media to promote social issues; when this results in profit for the business, this process is called **cause marketing**.

The Customer Service Process

A second common process supported by social media is the customer service process. **Customer service** is the series of activities before, during, or after a sale with the goal of increasing customer satisfaction. Social media provides many new options for businesses to improve customer service. Figure 11-11 includes the variety of objectives for the customer service process as well as some of its possible KPIs. Notice in the examples that follow the variety of organizations, their techniques, and types of services that social media can support. Customer expectations for good service are high—nearly 80 percent of customers who tweet about a bad service experience expect a reply within an hour. And 67 percent of consumers have used social media for service requests.

- A key service that Amazon provides its customers is a set of product reviews. In order to provide reviews for new products, Amazon asks its most trusted reviewers to create a review before the product is made available for public purchase. These trusted reviewers, called Vine Voices, are selected based on the quality and usefulness of their existing reviews as determined by other Amazon customers.

- Software developers often volunteer their time to assist other developers and answer questions. Microsoft's Most Valuable Professional network and SAP's developer network are two examples.
- Hospitals help families share medical updates of patients with family and invited friends. One example is a social media platform called CarePages; another is CaringBridge. Both allow families to create free private pages on which they post patient updates and read encouraging posts from friends.
- Local and state government agencies use social media to coordinate garbage pickup, to share updates on wildfire and flood locations, and to post school closure data.
- Xbox not only has 22 million fans on Facebook, but its "Elite Tweet Fleet" service earned it recognition as one of the most responsive brands on Twitter. Using Twitter, it responds to rapid-fire, live gamer issues, and its Facebook team has one of the fastest average first response times in any industry. Not only does this service help to build strong relationships with its customers, it also reduces the number of live service calls, a much more expensive customer service method.

The Hiring Process

A third business process that is supported by social media is the hiring or recruitment process. The hiring process typically involves a series of activities—planning, attracting, selecting, and appointing. The effectiveness objective of the process is to hire high quality employees while also achieving efficiency goals such as reducing time and cost. Figure 11-11 includes example hiring process objectives and possible KPIs. More than 94 percent businesses use LinkedIn to recruit, and 80 percent of job seekers use social media to find jobs.[4] LinkedIn also allows firms to consider passive candidates who might not be looking for a job but are the perfect fit.

Social media supports not only attracting good candidates but also selecting among them. Many firms inspect social media posts of job candidates and often find posts that reflect negatively on the candidate—typically those involving discussion of sex, drugs, alcohol, profanity, or guns. While legal restrictions limit what data employers can use to evaluate candidates, negative impressions about a candidate on social media can be hard to overcome.

Notice in the examples that follow that social media supports the hiring process by enabling both candidates and firms to learn about each other in ways not supported by other means. When you begin to look for job opportunities after graduation, use social media to your advantage.

UPS uses its Facebook page to highlight its positive social actions and provides contact data for potential hires with these posts. It also seeks to respond in near real time to these job inquiries.

Home Depot uses its Facebook page to respond to questions individuals post about the status of their applications. This creates a transparent two-way communication that encourages others to apply for jobs at Home Depot.

Atlantic Business Technologies uses Twitter to get followers to retweet job postings. The company realizes that a job announcement from a friend is much more likely to engage an applicant than a job announcement directly from the company.

Marriott, through its careers page on Facebook, posts job openings, event images, and live hiring discussions. Marriott uses current employees to respond to many inquires from applicants in order to create a more personal interaction. Its Facebook page has more than a million followers.

Many companies use an Instagram page to improve hiring and recruiting. Starbucks Jobs, InsideZappos, and Verizon Careers are just three examples of large firms using Instagram to help match job openings to interested candidates.[5]

Supporting New Processes with Social Media IS

In the examples in the previous section, we examined how social media IS could improve existing processes. However, social media can also support the emergence of new processes within the organization. Businesses have used social media to create a number of new processes. Here we will highlight one: crowdsourcing.

Crowdsourcing is outsourcing a task to a large number of users. One example is Netflix, which created a competition to build a better algorithm for recommending the next movie for a customer. Another example was how the FBI used crowdsoucing to solicit inputs to find the Boston Marathon bombers. Traditionally, the outsourced task has been product design or redesign, but

FIGURE 11-12
Social Media Promotion Keys to Success

Connect to leaders in the community

Stay involved—have a plan to update promotion daily

Motivate early consumers to contribute

Develop a reward mechanism for prosumers

Do not underestimate time required

now social media crowdsourcing is used in variety of ways, as shown in Figure 11-11 and in the examples below.

- Frito-Lay created a Facebook app that allowed followers to create a new flavor combination for a Lay's chip. The campaign featured celebrity spokespeople and carried a $1 million reward to the top suggestion. In all, 3.8 million flavors were submitted, 2.2 million Facebook fans were added, and sales grew 12 percent during the campaign, more than twice the historical average.[6]
- Coach Shoes invited participants to upload selfies on Instagram with the hashtag #CoachFromAbove. Winners were featured on the homepage gallery of Coach, and no cash was awarded. The campaign raised the online conversion rate 6 percent and the average order amount 2 percent.
- Kickstarter.com provides tools for entrepreneurs to raise funds for new projects, disaster relief, and software development.
- You can raise funds for a new car using the Dodge Dart Registry. Select the options for your new ride on the Dart Web site, and share a link to the site with family and friends and ask them to sponsor a part of the car.

Tips for Conducting Social Media Promotions

As we close this section on how social media can improve business processes, we wanted to return to the Promotion process to offer a few practical words of advice when using social media for promotion. While still in school, these tips may help you promote your service, club, or volunteer activities that use social media.

Creating a successful promotional campaign on social media can be a challenge. Early studies of successful campaigns suggest that there are five keys to success, as shown in Figure 11-12. First, find and connect to leaders in the community. Follow them on Twitter, Like them, connect with them on LinkedIn, and a number of them will connect to you in return. As a result, when you tweet or post, your message has a greater chance to reach more of your targeted audience. Second, stay involved. Create a plan about how the promotion will be updated, and stay active with the promotion by including new content daily. Third, motivate your early consumers to contribute to the promotion. These early supporters might be willing to make a positive post, write a good review, or retweet your Twitter messages. Rely on their natural desire to belong and to communicate. Fourth, develop a reward mechanism to give status to contributors. You might award icons to screen names that are frequent posters or give them access to people or services at your upcoming event. Reward systems help convert customers into **prosumers**—those who promote for you. Finally, do not underestimate the time required. Promotions can be very time consuming. Often people say that social media is "free," and while the incremental cost in hardware, software, and data for promotions may be near zero, it can take a surprising amount of time and money for people to learn and execute the procedures.

Q11-6 How Can Social Media IS Support the Process of Building Social Capital?

In the previous question, we considered how social media IS can support business processes. Here we consider one more process—the process of building social capital. Karl Marx defined **capital** as the investment of resources for future profit. Business literature defines three types

MIS InClass 11

Using Twitter to Support the Class Discussion Process

Prior to class, your instructor will decide on a unique hashtag to use for this exercise. During class, use your Twitter account and create tweets that include this hashtag. Make sure your privacy setting is not turned on. Tweets can include observations about class ideas or questions about the day's topic. At the end of the class, you will discuss the tweets.

If you do not have a Twitter account, obtain one at the beginning of class.

As an alternative, rather than send tweets to the public twittersphere, you can use Twitter's direct message feature to send private tweets to a class Twitter account. To use this approach, your instructor must first create the class Twitter account. Prior to sending a direct message to that account, each student must be followed by the class account. The teacher can log in and display the direct messages at the end of class.

At the end of the class, discuss the following:

1. How well does Twitter support the class discussion process?
2. What are the objectives and measures of the class discussion process?

Source: Christin Gilbert / age fotostock / SuperStock

3. What other educational processes can Twitter support? What are the objectives of these processes, and how does Twitter help achieve them?
4. Can in-class use of Twitter be used to integrate educational processes? These processes might include student assessment, student collaboration, technology use, and class discussion.

---

of capital. **Traditional capital** refers to investments into resources such as factories, machines, manufacturing equipment, and the like. **Human capital** is the investment in human knowledge and skills for future profit. By taking this class, you are investing in your own human capital. You are investing your money and time to obtain knowledge that you hope will differentiate you from other workers and ultimately give you a wage premium in the workforce.

Social capital is the investment in social relations with the expectation of returns in the marketplace.[7] When you attend a business function for the purpose of meeting people and reinforcing relationships, you are investing in your social capital. Similarly, when you join LinkedIn or contribute to Facebook, you are (or can be) investing in your social capital. Businesses invest in social capital for many reasons, and your contributions to your firm's social capital will be valued.

Building social capital is a process supported by social media IS. The social capital process is executed by people on behalf of their organizations, but it also pays dividends to the participating individuals. Most successful social capital processes share three objectives:[8]

1. Increase the number of relationships in a social network
2. Increase the strength of those relationships
3. Connect to those with more resources

As you build social capital, consider these three objectives and how social media IS can help you achieve those objectives. You gain social capital by adding more friends and by strengthening the relationships you have with existing friends. Further, you gain more social capital by adding friends and strengthening relationships with people who control resources that are important to you. Such calculations may seem cold, impersonal, and possibly even phony. When applied to the recreational use of social networking, they may be. But when you use social networking for professional purposes, keep in mind that social capital flows both ways. Professionals in other organizations seek out relationships with you as investments in their social capital.

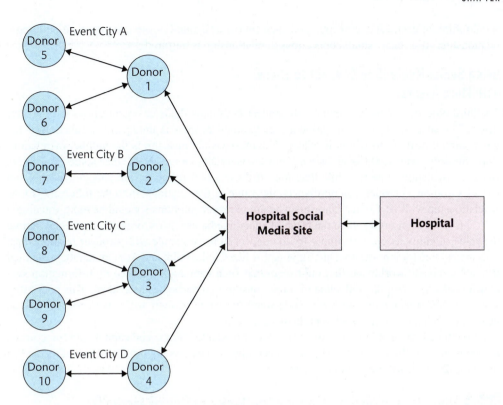

FIGURE 11-13

Social Media Increasing Number of Relationships

Using Social Media IS to Increase the Number of Relationships

Figure 11-13 shows the relationships of the Wood Hospital described in the opening vignette and its social media site. In this example, the hospital is using its social media site to promote its yearly fund-raising events in four different communities near the hospital: City A to City D. The hospital wants to attract more potential donors to these events with the overall objectives of raising funds and growing the donor base.

This diagram indicates how the hospital's relationship with four current donors can potentially lead to more donors. Donors 1–4 in this example have a direct relationship with the hospital social media site and have attended these events in the past. If the hospital can find a way to induce the four donors to form a relationship with the events, they might spread the word of these events to their friends, donors 5–10, who might spread the word to their friends. If successful, the number of donors with a relationship to the hospital will increase rapidly.

Such relationship sales have been going on by word of mouth for centuries; what is new here is the use of social media IS to more rapidly increase relationships than in the past; social media in this context has been called "world of mouth" and "word of mouth on steroids."[9]

Using Social Media IS to Increase the Strength of Relationships

To an organization, the **strength of a relationship** is the likelihood that the entity (person or other organization) in the relationship will do something that benefits the organization. An organization has a strong relationship with you if you buy its products, write positive reviews about it, post pictures of your use of its products, and so on. Strong relationships are built on trust.

In his autobiography, Benjamin Franklin provided a key insight.[10] He said that if you want to strengthen your relationship with someone in power, ask him or her to do you a favor. Before he invented the public library, he would ask powerful strangers to lend him their expensive books. In that same sense, organizations have learned that they can strengthen their relationships with you by asking you to do them a favor. When you provide that favor, it strengthens your relationship with the organization. Trust is established.

Each interaction strengthens relationships and hence increases social capital. The more you interact with a company, the stronger your commitment and trust. Businesses using social media should think of each Like, each pin, and each follow as a small positive step toward building a relationship. After many small connections, a relationship is nurtured.

Using Social Media IS to Connect to Those with More Assets

The third objective of social capital is to connect with individuals or organizations with greater assets. The success of an organization's social capital process is thus partly a function of the social capital of those to whom it relates. The most visible measure is the number of relationships. Someone with 1,000 loyal Twitter followers is usually more valuable than someone with 10. But the calculation is more subtle than that; if those 1,000 followers are college students and the organization's product is adult diapers, the value of the relationship to the followers is low. A relationship with 10 Twitter followers who are in retirement homes would be more valuable.

This discussion brings us to the brink of social media use. Most organizations today ignore the value of entity assets and simply try to connect to more people with stronger relationships. This area is ripe for innovation. Data aggregators like ChoicePoint and Acxiom maintain detailed data about people worldwide. It would seem that such data could be used by information systems to calculate the potential value of a relationship to a particular individual. This possibility would enable organizations to better understand the value of their social networks as well as guide their behavior with regard to particular individuals.

Stay tuned; there are many ways to use social media to build social capital, and some ideas, maybe yours, will be very successful. However, like all business opportunities, social media has its risks. We discuss these challenges next.

Q11-7 How Do Businesses Manage the Risks of Social Media?

Recently Dave Carroll, a singer and guitarist for a small touring band, was traveling from Chicago to Omaha, Nebraska, with his band. Having just boarded their United flight, they glanced out the window and saw to their horror that the ground crew loading the plane seemed to be playing catch with their instruments. When they arrived at their destination, Dave's $2,500 Taylor guitar was in pieces. After trying to resolve the claim for months, Dave wrote and recorded his biggest hit—*United Breaks Guitars*, a humorous ballad that went viral on YouTube. After 500,000 views in 3 days, United contacted Dave to see how it could make things right.[11]

United has learned the hard way that social media has changed the way businesses communicate with their customers. This new type of communication comes with risks. In this question, we will consider management risks, risks from employee communication, and risks from user-generated content.

Management Risks

The most significant management risks are:

- Underestimation of labor costs
- Absence of dependable return on investment
- Customer privacy
- Dependence on social media application provider

One of the management challenges with social media applications is that their labor requirements are difficult to estimate. As with any new technology, few guidelines are available to estimate the time required to use them effectively.

Another challenge is to create useful measures of costs and benefits. The most traditional method of measuring costs and benefits is **return on investment (ROI)**, which is the amount earned by an investment as a percentage. For example, if a $200 investment returned $50, the ROI would be 50/200, or 25 percent.

The returns on investment for a social media venture are typically hard to establish in financial measures. While there are plenty of social media measures and KPIs such as Likes, retweets, and comments that are easy to assess, the relationship of these measures and financial measures, while generally accepted, is often unclear, imprecise, or inconsistent. Just how much is a retweet or a sharing of a job posting worth to corporate revenue? Not only is this relationship between social media measures and financial measures difficult over the short term, it gets even murkier over the long haul. Perhaps successful social media use by a business builds trust over time that eventually leads to increased sales, but measuring the accumulation of small changes in trust due to effective use of social media is difficult. Perhaps the social media team learned lessons that can be used on upcoming projects—like how to estimate labor costs and mange such projects—but once again, these are hard to measure financially. For these reasons, it is not surprising that fewer than 15 percent of marketing executives say they have proved the impact of social media on overall company performance.[12] The benefits of social media are hard to quantify financially.

Another set of problems with social media are associated with customer privacy. **Privacy** is commonly defined as controlling how one's personal information is acquired and analyzed. If privacy is threatened, then the trust necessary for social media is at risk.

One problem is inadvertently violating a customer's privacy. Another problem is that many customers are naïve about privacy—they do not realize that if they did not buy the social media product, they are the product. This naiveté combined with a business desire to improve their processes using social media creates the perfect privacy storm. In fact, every time a business improves its customer-facing processes with social media data, the price is less privacy for the consumer. For example, if a hospital wants to improve collaboration among patients with a similar disease, this can only happen if the participants give up private data about their health. Businesses built on social media and businesses using this media must anticipate privacy concerns by users and privacy laws by governments that will restrict the use of social media data.

Although it is possible for organizations to develop their own social media capability, many organizations use social media application providers such as Facebook and Twitter. Those organizations are vulnerable to the success and policies of Facebook, Twitter, and others. For example, if fake news erodes trust in social media platforms, that reduction in trust affects businesses that use those platforms as well. The risk for businesses relying on these platforms has been compared to building on rented property.

Employee Communication Risks

It seems like just about every week a professional athlete tweets something embarrassing. Sports franchises understand the marketing value of allowing their athletes to tweet to their fans, but this often turns into a public relations nightmare when the athlete communicates inappropriately.

The key to limiting employee risk for that sports franchise or any organization is to develop and publicize a **social media policy**, which is a statement that delineates employees' rights and responsibilities. The social media policy is a welcome opportunity for the business to inject some control or limits on behavior in a medium that provides the business few controls. You can find an index to 100 different policies at the Social Media Today Web site.[13] A short list of the attributes of a good social media policy is shown in Figure 11-14.

In general, policies need to emphasize truth and honesty. As an experienced and wise business professional once said, "Nothing is more serviceable than the truth." It may not be convenient, but it is serviceable long term. Second, social media contributors and their employers should be transparent and above board. If you make a mistake, don't cover it up; instead, correct it, apologize, and make amends. Eric Qualman calls this being "flawsome." His point is that companies make mistakes but can use social media to show customers their true colors.

Disclose	Be timely—specify a response time goal. Be transparent—use your real name and employer. Be truthful—point out if you have a vested interest. Be yourself—stick to your expertise and write what you know.
Protect	Don't tell secrets. Don't slam the competition. Don't overshare.
Use Common Sense	Add value—make your contribution worthwhile. Keep it cool—don't inflame or respond to every criticism. Be flawsome—be upfront and quick with corrections.

FIGURE 11-14
Social Media IS Policy Attributes

A third aspect of the policy is to specify a target metric for responding to customer complaints—how long on average will customers have to wait before they get a response. Customer expectations about social media response times are rapidly rising. More than half of Twitter users expect a response within an hour of tweeting about a customer service issue, while more than half of Facebook users expect a 24-hour response.[14] Policies must meet customer expectations.

User-Generated Content Risks

User-generated content is the essence of social media relationships. As with any relationship, however, this content can be inappropriate or excessively negative in tone or otherwise problematic. The hospital in the opening vignette was confronted by very unfavorable tweets and livestreaming. Organizations need to determine how they will deal with such content before engaging in social media.

The major sources of user content problems are:

- Junk and crackpot contributions
- Erroneous contributions
- Unfavorable reviews
- Mutinous movements

Crackpots may use the site as a way of expressing passionately held views about unrelated topics, such as UFOs, government cover-ups, weird conspiracy theories, and so forth. Because of the possibility of such content, employees of the hosting business must regularly monitor the site and remove objectionable material immediately.

Less dramatic than crackpots are erroneous contributions, false statements made about a business. As you know from your own experience on social media, many comments on social media are incorrect. However, differentiating the innocent error that should be ignored from the more serious errors requires judgment and experience with the platform and the audience.

Unfavorable reviews are another risk. Research indicates that customers are sophisticated enough to know that few, if any, products are perfect. Most customers want to know the disadvantages of a product before purchasing it so they can determine if those disadvantages are important for their application. Customers expect both positive and negative comments; it is better to be perceived as honest and genuine than as old-fashioned and a hype machine. However, if every review is bad, if the product is rated 1 star out of 5, then the company is using social media to needlessly publish its problems. In this case, some action must be taken, as described next. An example of an unfavorable review was portrayed in the opening vignette.

A **mutinous movement** is an extension of bad reviews where prosumers revolt and use an organization's site in damaging ways. An example of a mutinous movement would be if a dissatisfied hospital patient attempts to hijack the hospital's Facebook page to build support to build another hospital.

The first task in managing social media is to know the sources of potential problems and monitor sites for problematic content. Once such content is found, however, organizations must have a plan for creating the organization's response. We consider those options next.

Responding to User Content Problems

Social media campaigns are like parties. While the party is ongoing, the host must know what to do with inappropriate behavior by a guest. The reaction needs to be swift but appropriate for the act and for the audience. The same applies to social media campaigns. What will it do with problematic content? Three possibilities are:

- Leave it
- Respond to it
- Delete it

If the problematic content represents reasonable criticism of the organization's products or services, the best response may be to leave it where it is. Such criticism indicates that the site is not just a shill for the organization but contains legitimate user content. Such criticism also serves as a free source of product reviews, which can be useful for the product development process.

A second response is to respond to the problematic content. This response is, however, dangerous. If the response could be construed, in any way, as patronizing or insulting to the content contributor, the response can enrage the user community and generate a strong backlash. Also, if the response appears defensive, it can become a strong public relations negative.

In most cases, responses are best reserved for when the problematic content has caused the organization to do something positive as a result. For example, if the hospital in the opening vignette changed procedures to ensure all expectant mothers with labor pains get admitted and placed in a room immediately, it can respond with a story about its new procedures. If a reasonable, nondefensive response generates continued and unreasonable content from that same source, it is best for the organization to do nothing. "Never wrestle with a pig; you'll get dirty and the pig will enjoy it." Instead, allow the community to constrain the user. It will.

Deleting content should be reserved for contributions that are inappropriate because they are contributed by crackpots, because they have nothing to do with the site, or because they contain obscene or otherwise inappropriate content. However, deleting legitimate negative comments can result in a strong user backlash. As Jake mentioned in the opening scenario, deleting Facebook contributions often appears arrogant and heavy-handed.

To wrap this up, most of the risks of using social media involve people: managers, employees, and customers. Because people use an IS by following procedures, procedures are essential in managing risk. While businesses have little impact on the social media procedures that their customers use, they can develop procedures for their own people that will guard customer privacy, guide employees' use, and govern user content issues. In the opening vignette, Jake and the hospital were operating without a procedure to respond to the inflammatory tweet. What do you think they should do? Regardless of your answer, the hospital needs procedures to follow.

Q11-8 ▶ How Can IS Similar to Social Media Support Business Processes?

Several IS, similar to social media, are also important enablers of business processes. These IS—Reddit and group messaging apps like WhatsApp and WeChat—have the same two activities as social media—create and share—but are not always considered to be social media. These two IS and their impact on business processes are described next.

Reddit is a very popular social news Web site built on crowdpolling and anonymous posting. Reddit calls itself the front page of the Internet. Registered and most often anonymous users create content and share it in on the site organized in topics called subreddits. Once content is posted on a subreddit, crowdpolling enables other users to vote it up or down, and based on these votes, the post is moved up or down in prominence and location.

Started in 2005, the site boomed in 2015, and by 2017 it was ranked in the top seven worldwide by Alexa with more than 1.5 billion sessions per month. Subreddits support a variety of discussions on almost a million topics. Many users are drawn to Reddit's ability to break news as anonymous submitters are less cautious than a traditional news source. Another popular aspect is that the site contains many helpful professional opinions about a wide variety of subjects.

Businesses and products can be promoted on Reddit but only by authentic users. Representatives of a company should absolutely avoid the temptation to promote a product on behalf of the company. Instead, if promotion is the goal, a business should encourage fans to create subedits and encourage their fans to post. Many popular TV shows, video games, entertainment companies, and sports teams have benefited from fan-based subreddit sites. In addition, businesses can promote sales through specific deals or contests on subreddits. Businesses can also support their promotions by purchasing Reddit ads that can be very specially tailored to the passionate individuals that participate in targeted subreddits.

Sales and promotion are not the only processes supported. Reddit can also help customer service. For example, the Xbox 360 subreddit helps direct users seeking help to the right online locations at Microsoft, and it provides a constantly updated list of helpful links. Firms can listen on Reddit pages to monitor talk about their product, read complaints, and respond to mentions. A CEO can host an Ask Me Anything (AMA) event, and an HR department can post job openings in appropriate subreddits by skills or location.

WhatsApp is the world's most popular smartphone social messaging app. This easy-to-use cross-platform app offers users the opportunity to make phone calls, share video and text messages, display their location to others in a group, and share documents and images on an encrypted platform. Similar features are available on other popular group messaging apps such as WeChat and Facebook Messenger.

Businesses can support a number of processes using social messaging apps. They can post a how-to video, a list of frequently asked questions, live video help, and real-time assistance to support customer service. They can create a customer group for use at a later time to share promotions, live feeds of special guests, musical events, demos of products, and giveaways to support promotions. Some businesses allow customers to schedule appointments, be notified of delays, contact support, notify police, find buses, and book tables at restaurants. Businesses need to avoid overt self-promotion and spam or abuse of their customer groups.

Q11-9 ▸ What Is the Sharing Economy?

To conclude our chapter, we consider a different type of social technology: the technology offered by firms in the sharing economy, such as Uber and Airbnb. Unlike social media app providers or Reddit and WhatsApp—all of which allow users to create and share messages—these companies and others in the sharing economy allow users to create and share assets or services.

Recently the value of Uber passed $50 billion and Airbnb passed $30 billion. And yet Uber owns no cars, Airbnb (described in the Case at the end of this chapter) no properties. How can they be so valuable? To many they seem to be nothing more than Web sites. To begin to answer these questions, here we describe this new industry and what these new companies depend on for success.

Uber and Airbnb are two of the best-known companies of the sharing economy. The **sharing economy** describes firms that enable peer-to-peer exchanges via online communities, where individuals can rent assets or obtain services offered by others. Other firms include eBay, Zipcar, Kickstarter, and others as shown in Figure 11-15. These companies are like social media providers—they connect peers who create profiles and share resources. Companies in the sharing economy dominate the list of **unicorns**—startup companies valued in excess of $1 billion.

Sharing economy firms enable **collaborative consumption**, mutual access to products and services rather than individual and exclusive ownership. The underlying premise of collaborative consumption is the underuse of resources—the average car is unused 92 percent of the time. Another reason it works is flexibility and control; participants exercise control over their own time and resources—if they want to be an Uber driver on their way home from work today, they can opt in or opt out on a whim. When collaborative consumption works, the result can be much more demand for a product or service—Uber and Lyft changed the demand for taxi rides in San Francisco from 130 million rides a year to more than 500 million.

Sharing economy firms provide participants the online IS that enables and supports the peer-to-peer transaction process. This transaction differs from industry to industry, but successful firms develop a state-of-the-art IS that is easy to use and easy to access. The IS enables both buyer and seller to trust the transaction. Trust is essential because switching costs are typically low in the sharing economy. Finally, in addition to an IS and trust, success also depends on access to resources in demand. Uber must be connected to high volumes of riders and drivers to be successful.

Trust grows with reliability, confidence, and belief. To gain trust, sharing economy firms depend on their information systems. The IS must enable parties to gather data on both the service being shared and the other party. Often the data on the other party includes photos, details about the customer, and ratings. Having a strongly positive rating is important as it leads to gaining the other party's trust. This concern for ratings also leads to better behaviors—Uber drivers are courteous, Airbnb travelers hang up towels. The trust in these situations is particularly vital for younger users, a generation that is inclined to trust individuals more than institutions and

FIGURE 11-15

Sharing Economy Firms and Characteristics

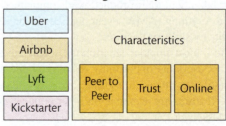

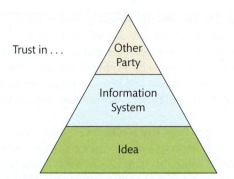

FIGURE 11-16
Three Levels of Trust

government. To enable this trust to grow, firms in the sharing economy need to be transparent, inclusive, and decentralized. Older users, on the other hand, learned to trust centralized, top-down, and licensed organizations.

This trust in the other party is actually the third and final level of trust as shown in Figure 11-16. First, each party must trust the idea such as ride sharing and also trust in the IS that enables it. Think about it yourself—what would it take for you to take a trust leap and sign up for Uber or Airbnb or any other service you have not previously used? First you would have to trust that this idea can work—perhaps reasoning that if it works for millions, it will work for you. Second you will have to trust the IS—the ratings are valid, the system is secure, the other party's data is accurate.

While trust is key to success, upcoming legal decisions will also affect success for these firms. Like other disruptive technology firms, Uber and Airbnb are facing a variety of legal challenges that will affect all sharing firms. Consider a few: Should Uber drivers be provided the legal protections of employees rather than independent contractors? Should Airbnb property owners be allowed to kick out long-term low-income occupants in favor of short-term customers, reducing the supply and increasing prices of affordable housing? Should neighborhood associations be able to limit short-term renters because they do not get involved in local communities or participate in neighborhood watch programs and other community-building activities? Should Uber and Airbnb do more to reduce discrimination by providers against minority participants? Legal rulings are emerging in many countries that seek to provide a compromise between the interests of owners, renters, and neighborhood groups. These rulings and subsequent legislation will have a significant impact on the growth of the sharing economy.

As of now, sharing economy firms comprise a very small percentages of revenue in a limited number of industries, but some estimate the sharing economy will grow from $20 billion in 2017 to $335 billion by 2025.[15] It will be interesting to see if Uber and Airbnb become giants like Microsoft, Apple, Amazon, Google, and Facebook—companies that learned to use a new technology. Or will they die as once-promising teens like AOL, Gateway, Betamax, Napster, Iridium, Sirius XM, Atari, Yik Yak, and Compaq? Those companies, once the darlings of the tech world, could not sustain a promising start or were crushed by legal challenges.

Businesses you will work for during your career will be asking questions about these new social technologies. Will they last? Do their techniques apply to our business? Can we use them to enable our processes? Businesses also ask questions about their own social media use. They still tinker with their technique. The better you understand these new technologies and social media, the more helpful your advice will be. You will be beginning your career in interesting and dynamic times. Your generation was the first to use the sharing economy and social media for personal use, so you have first-hand experience with them and the trust on which they depend. You will be instrumental in helping firms discover good techniques for these technologies to enhance their processes.

▶Q11-10▶ 2028?

Social media and the sharing economy are still changing, making forecasts difficult. However, one issue—privacy—will continue to affect social media and the sharing economy. Earlier in the chapter, we explained that privacy has always been challenge, but in 2028 privacy on social media will much different. The key difference will be that in the next 10 years, businesses will be able to employ much more powerful data analysis tools on social media data. Tools will be developed to mine video, voice, and image data that in the past were difficult to analyze. As data analysis tools advance, companies will be able to use data from different sources, so your online activity recorded by one company will be more frequently sold to other companies. The result—more accurate predictions and better understanding of your behavior and more conflicts with privacy.

While privacy will continue to evolve in the coming years, so too will you. By 2028 you will be much older, with assets to protect and perhaps a different outlook on the privacy needed to protect assets. Social media will have changed, and a new, younger generation will be driving its changes. What is important for you to realize is that you will be out-of-date and unable to have first-hand experience with that social technology. You will be like 30-year-olds now. Anticipate your own obsolescence, and learn to listen to the next generation explain its new social technology if you want to help your business communicate with its customers.

Ethics Guide

Ethics, Social Marketing, and Stretching the Truth

No one expects you to publish your ugliest picture on Instagram, but how far should you go to create a positive impression? If your hips and legs are not your best features, is it unethical to stand behind your sexy car in your photo? If you've been to one event with someone very popular in your crowd, is it unethical to publish photos that imply you meet as an everyday occurrence? Surely there is no obligation to publish pictures of yourself at boring events with unpopular people just to balance the scale for those photos in which you appear unrealistically attractive and overly popular.

As long as all of this occurs on an Instagram or Facebook account that you use for personal relationships, well, what goes around comes around. But in the following questions, consider the ethics of questionable social networking postings in the business arena.

DISCUSSION QUESTIONS

1. Suppose that a river rafting company starts a group on a social networking site for promoting rafting trips. Graham, a 15-year-old high school student who wants to be more grown-up than he is, posts a picture of a handsome 22-year-old male as a picture of himself. He also writes witty and clever comments on the site and claims to play the guitar and be an accomplished masseuse. Suppose someone decided to go on the rafting trip in part because of Graham's postings and was disappointed with the truth about Graham.
   a. Are Graham's actions ethical? Consider both the categorical imperative (page 18) and utilitarianism (page 43) perspectives.
   b. According to either ethical perspective, does the rafting company have an ethical responsibility to refund that person's fees?
2. Suppose you own and manage the rafting company in question 1.
   a. Is it unethical for you to encourage your employees to write positive reviews about your company? Use both the categorical imperative and utilitarianism perspectives.
   b. Does your assessment change if you ask your employees to use an email address other than the one they have at work? Use both the categorical imperative and utilitarianism perspectives.
3. Again, suppose you own and manage the rafting company and that you pay your employees a bonus for every client they bring to a rafting trip. Without specifying any particular technique, you encourage your employees to be creative in how they obtain clients. One employee invites his Facebook friends to a party at which he will show photos of prior rafting trips. On the way

to the party, one of the friends has an automobile accident and dies. His spouse sues your company.
   a. Should your company be held accountable?
   b. Does it matter if you knew about the presentation? Would it matter if you had not encouraged your employees to be creative?
4. Suppose your rafting company has a Web site for customer reviews. In spite of your best efforts at camp cleanliness, on one trip (out of dozens), your staff accidentally served contaminated food and everyone became ill with food poisoning. One of those clients from that trip writes a poor review because of that experience. Is it ethical for you to delete that review from your site? Again, consider both the categorical and utilitarianism perspectives.
5. Instead of being the owner, suppose you were at one time employed by this rafting company and you were, undeservedly you think, terminated. To get even, you use Facebook to spread rumors to your friends (many of whom are river guides) about the safety of the company's trips.
   a. Are your actions legal?
   b. Are your actions ethical? Consider both the categorical imperative and utilitarianism perspectives.
   c. Do you see any ethical distinctions between this situation and that in question 4?
6. Based on your answers in questions 1–5, formulate ethical principles for using social media for business purposes. Formulate ethical principles for creating or using user-generated content for business purposes.

Source: Rich Legg/iStockphoto.com

ACTIVE REVIEW

Use this Active Review to verify that you understand the material in the chapter. You can read the entire chapter and then perform the tasks in this review, or you can read the text material for just one question and perform the tasks in this review for that question before moving on to the next one.

Q11-1 ▶ What is social media, and why is it important to business?

Explain user-generated content and give an example. Describe the two activities of the social media process. Provide an example of how a business has used social media.

Q11-2 ▶ What are the objectives of the social media process?

Describe the unique wrinkle of social media. Explain the two objectives of users in the social media process. Describe the objectives of businesses and app providers. Explain Enterprise 2.0 and give an example. Describe the efficiency objective for social media.

Q11-3 ▶ What are the key components of a social media IS?

Describe the impact of the increasing use of mobile social media on advertising. Explain several of the key characteristics of social media software. Distinguish between content and connection data and give an example of each. Describe the result of informal social media procedures. Explain the characteristic of people that is both exciting and unnerving for businesses.

Q11-4 ▶ How do social media IS support social media activities?

Explain the concept of viral and why it is important to business. Describe the general rule about how often a business should describe its own products. Explain why understanding how customers search is useful for a business.

Q11-5 ▶ How can social media IS support business processes?

Give several examples of business processes supported by social media IS. Describe the promotion process, including its objectives. Explain the two important characteristics of social media promotions that involve customers. Define click-through and conversion rate and compare the two. Describe the customer service and hiring processes and their objectives. Explain crowdsourcing and how businesses apply it. Describe several tips for running a successful social media promotion.

Q11-6 ▶ How can social media IS support the process of building social capital?

Explain capital and describe the three types of capital. Explain the possible benefits of social capital for business. Identify and explain the three objectives of the process of building social capital. Provide an example of how social media supports each of these three objectives.

Q11-7 ▶ How do businesses manage the risks of social media?

Explain several of the management risks of using social media. Describe the attributes of a good social media policy. Explain the sources of user content problems and the options for businesses in responding to user content problems.

Q11-8 ▶ How can IS similar to social media support business processes?

Describe Reddit and how it uses crowdpolling. Explain subreddits. Describe how businesses can use Reddit to support the Promotion and Customer Service processes. Explain the features of WhatsApp. Describe how businesses can use WhatsApp.

Q11-9 ▶ What is the sharing economy?

Explain how the firms in the sharing economy are similar to and different from social media app providers. List and describe the key characteristics of the sharing economy. Explain collaborative consumption and its relationship to the sharing economy. Describe trust and how it has changed in the sharing economy. Explain each of the three levels of trust. Explain challenges facing firms in the sharing economy.

Q11-10 ▶ 2028?

Define *privacy* and explain how it is threatened by social media. Describe how the balance between social media and privacy will change in the next 10 years. Explain how your relationship to social media will change over the next 10 years.

KEY TERMS AND CONCEPTS

Capital   319
Cause marketing   317
Click-through rate   316
Collaborative consumption   326
Connection data   312
Content data   312
Conversion rate   316
Customer service   317
Crowdsourcing   318
Enterprise 2.0   310
Folksonomy   312

Hashtag   312
Human capital   320
Mashup   314
Mutinous movement   324
Privacy   323
Promotion   316
Prosumer   319
Reddit   325
Return on investment (ROI)   322
Sharing economy   326
Social capital   320

Social graph   312
Social media   308
Social media information system   308
Social media policy   323
Strength of a relationship   321
Tag   312
Traditional capital   320
Unicorn   326
User-generated content   308
Viral   314

USING YOUR KNOWLEDGE

11-1. Visit Zillow at *www.zillow.com*. Enter the address of
someone's home (your parents' perhaps) and obtain an
appraisal of it. Check out the appraised values of the
neighbors' homes. Do you think this site violates anyone's privacy? Why or why not? Find and describe features that demonstrate that this is a social media app.
Explain why this site might be considered a threat by
traditional real estate companies. How might real estate
agents use this site to market their services? How can
real estate brokers (those who own agencies) use this
site to their advantage?

11-2. Suppose you are in charge of designing the university
golf course's Facebook page. Describe three features
that the golf course could put on its page (e.g., a link
to tee time reservations). Explain what process would
be improved at the golf course with each new feature
and specify a measure you would use to assess this
improvement.

11-3. Go to the *Wall Street Journal* Web page titled "What
They Know." Read two recent articles. Describe three
things from those readings that surprised you. Also
write three bulleted statements for a company you
specify to follow based on what you read.

11-4. Go to Wikipedia. Read the "About Wikipedia" page and
the "Collaborative Writing" page. Make a diagram that
shows the process of creating and updating a Wikipedia
page. Is page creation and editing a process with an
effectiveness goal or efficiency goal? What measures
could be used to assess improvement in the process?

11-5. Search the Web using the words *Google My Maps* and
follow the links to learn how to make your own maps.
Then create a map of your own. Does My Maps have
all the features of a social media app?

11-6. Visit Airbnb and create a profile. Find two listings for
your favorite vacation location. Explain how features
and prices listed compare to hotels in the same location.

11-7. On Instagram, find three examples of firms using that
outlet to support their hiring process. Do the same with
Reddit, Facebook, and Twitter. For each, describe the
best use of that source by a company to support its
hiring process.

11-8. Assess your own stock of social capital. What activities
around campus would help you increase your social
capital? What social media apps could you use to
increase your social capital?

11-9. Become a prosumer. Find a cause or group on Instagram
that you believe in and contribute in ways that you do
not typically contribute. Does the organization value
your help in an encouraging way? If you were in
charge of the site, how would you reward prosumers?

11-10. Join LinkedIn if you have not done so already. Start a
résumé and connect to people you know. Investigate
job opportunities in your area of study. Locate organizations and research a few as you would if you had an
upcoming job interview. Find graduates of your school
in your speciality and ask them to connect with you.
Use LinkedIn before your job interview by reading the
résumés of people in your specialty.

MyLab MIS (for 11-1, 11-2, 11-3)

COLLABORATION EXERCISE 11

Collaborate with a group of fellow students to answer the following questions. For this exercise, do not meet face to face.
Your task will be easier if you coordinate your work with
SharePoint, Office 365, Google Docs or equivalent collaboration tools. (See Chapter 10 for a discussion of collaboration

tools and processes.) Your answers should reflect the thinking
of the entire group, not just that of one or two individuals.

With a group of classmates, propose and carry out a small
marketing promotional initiative for an organization using
social media. The organization may be a business, nonprofit,

university program, student activity group, or other suitable entity. Run the promotion for several weeks.

Your criteria for success include usefulness to the client (i.e., how successful it is), thoroughness, and professionalism. To better understand how to promote your product or service, consult any introductory marketing textbook or online resource and search for *promotion* or *social media promotion*. You should also reread the keys to success for a social media campaign at the end of Q11-5 in this chapter before you begin. To better understand social media promotions, you might visit Mashable (*www.mashable.com*), a leading online social media site, or Technorati (*http://technorati.com*) to search the blogosphere for guidance on social media use.

To begin, your team should discuss and specify:

1. Your target audience (you may have more than one)
2. The benefit offered by your product/service
3. The objective and KPIs of your promotional activity (e.g., provide information, increase demand, differentiate, etc.)
4. Your initial design, message(s), or content
5. How overall success will be measured

At the end of your promotion, present to the class your plan, your experiences during the promotion, and what you would do differently next time.

CASE STUDY 11

Airbnb

In early 2007, Brian Chesky and Joe Gebbia came up with an idea. They lived in a busy city with lots of visitors and tourists, so they decided to rent short-term living quarters to visitors. Visitors often could not find accommodations using traditional methods. They decided to try it out using their own apartment in San Francisco, and their hopes were quickly confirmed. They launched Airbedandbreakfast.com during the summer of 2008. Within a year they employed 15 full-time staff. By 2011 they celebrated passing 1 million bookings, and the next year they passed 10 million. They quickly expanded to Germany, England, Ireland, Australia, and Asian markets. By 2016 Airbnb's market cap was $20 billion, a higher value than Marriott and Wyndham.[16]

Airbnb connects hosts and those looking for lodging. Hosts list their properties—anything from a single room to a castle to a yacht. Listing is free, and hosts determine if they want to rent for a night, a week, or a month at a time as well as how much to charge. Guests search for accommodations using filters for price, room, size, neighborhood, and amenities. Searching requires no account, but to book a room guests need a profile.

Once guests find a property they wish to reserve, they click "Book It." Airbnb fees range from 6 to 12 percent. Hosts can turn down reservations and can view some aspects of the potential guest's profile. Hosts have 24 hours to respond to reservation requests. Hosts are rewarded for early and positive responses by the Airbnb search algorithm that displays the property of positively reviewed hosts higher than other hosts. Once a request is accepted, Airbnb processes the payment and provides the host with the guest's phone number and email address. Payment is held by Airbnb until the reservation begins. Methods of payment include major credit cards, PayPal, and Google Wallet.

One key aspect of Airbnb is a reputation system designed to build trust and reliability. Renters can use the system to read about hosts before making a reservation, and hosts can read about renters before confirming the reservation. To improve the informativeness of the system, guests now must provide three types of ID—phone number, ID photo, and Facebook/LinkedIn/Google account.

Recently, Airbnb has been criticized that its hosts deny reservations to guests with names that suggest the guest is a minority.[17]

In the past several years, a number of Airbnb reservations-gone-bad stories have become viral. As early as 2011, the *Wall Street Journal* recorded a rental disaster where the guests broke into locked cabinets, stole money, and vandalized the apartment. Other stories of horrible renters included meth parties, orgies, and destructive celebrations. Airbnb was slow to respond at first but now offers secondary insurance to hosts, calling it a host guarantee.

Recently other criticisms of Airbnb have emerged. Fellow apartment owners and residents complain that overnight Airbnb guests devalue their property. Subletting rooms may also be a breach of tenancy. Others complain that Airbnb disrupts the hospitality industry. Some cities, notably Quebec, Berlin, and San Francisco, outlawed or restricted the subletting practice, but San Francisco later passed an "Airbnb law" reinstituting it as long as hosts register with the city, carry insurance, and pay the 14 percent hotel tax.

Airbnb continues to evolve. Airbnb has added collaborative wish lists to enable groups of travelers planning a trip to collaborate during the booking process. Business booking will allow travel managers to reserve rooms for others in the business, and guest reviews submitted by renters allows both renters and the reserving party, when they are not the same, to both build reputation points.

Questions

11-11. Which sharing economy goods and services have you used? What were your first impressions?

11-12. Using BPMN or another technique, diagram the reservation process at Airbnb.

11-13. Which characteristics of an IS build trust, and which characteristics destroy it?

11-14. Visit the Airbnb site. Read about how to list a property as a new host. How would you suggest Airbnb improve this creation activity?

11-15. What are the risks for hosts, guests, and Airbnb? Can IS reduce these?

CHAPTER RESOURCES

[1] Jessica Bosari, "The Developing Role of Social Media in the Modern Business World," *Forbes,* last modified August 8, 2012, www.forbes.com/sites/moneywisewomen/2012/08/08/the-developing-role-of-social-media-in-the-modern-business-world/.

[2] *Nielsen Global Survey of Trust in Advertising 2015*, accessed July 6, 2017, www.nielsen.com/content/dam/nielsenglobal/apac/docs/reports/2015/nielsen-global-trust-in-advertising-report-september-2015.pdf.

[3] "When Social Media Campaigns Flat-Out Work: What to Learn from Deadpool and Burberry," accessed September 4, 2017, www.socialmediatoday.com/social-networks/when-social-media-campaigns-flat-out-work-what-learn-deadpool-and-burberry.

[4] "17 Interesting LinkedIn Job Statistics May 2017," accessed September 4, 2017, http://expandedramblings.com/index.php/linkedin-job-statistics/.

[5] "5 Companies that have nailed social media for recruiting," accessed September 4, 2017, www.tintup.com/blog/5-companies-that-have-nailed-social-media-for-recruiting/.

[6] "How Lay's Got Its Chips To Taste Like Chicken And Waffles," accessed September 4, 2017, www.fastcompany.com/1682425/how-lays-got-its-chips-to-taste-like-chicken-and-waffles.

[7] Nan Lin, *Social Capital: The Theory of Social Structure and Action* (Cambridge, UK: Cambridge University Press, 2002), Location 310 of the Kindle Edition.

[8] Henk Flap, "Social Capital in the Reproduction of Inequality," *Comparative Sociology of Family, Health, and Education,* Vol. 20 (1991), pp. 6179–6202.

[9] Erik Qualman, *Socialnomics: How Social Media Transforms the Way We Live and Do Business* (Hoboken, NJ: Wiley, 2009).

[10] Founding father of the United States. Author of *Poor Richard's Almanac.* Successful businessman; owner of a chain of print shops. Discoverer of groundbreaking principles in the theory of electricity. Inventor of bifocals, the potbelly stove, the lightning rod, and much more. Founder of the public library and the postal service. Darling of the French court and salons and, now, contributor to social network theory!

[11] "Singer's Revenge on United: A Hit Song," *UPI.com,* last modified July 9, 2009, www.upi.com/Odd_News/2009/07/09/Singers-revenge-on-United-A-hit-song/UPI-79301247160917/.

[12] The CMO Survey, February 2017 pdf available from https://cmosurvey.org/results/february-2017/. Accessed September 4, 2017.

[13] "Social Media Employee Policy Examples from Over 100 Organizations," *Social Media Today,* last modified July 3, 2010, http://socialmediatoday.com/ralphpaglia/141903/social-media-employee-policy-examples-over-100-companies-and-organizations.

[14] Lisa Wirthman, "Taking Care of Business: Social Media Will Transform Customer Service," *Forbes,* last modified April 10, 2013, www.forbes.com/sites/capitalonespark/2013/04/10/taking-care-of-business-social-media-will-transform-customer-service/.

[15] "The Current and Future State of the Sharing Economy." Brookings India No 032017 pdf available from https://www.brookings.edu/wp-content/uploads/2016/12/sharingeconomy_032017final.pdf. Accessed September 4, 2017.

[16] "The Pros and Cons of Using Airbnb." By Jean Folger March 3, 2016. Accessed September 4, 2017.

[17] "Airbnb CEO Chesky vows site overhaul with racism in mind." Marco della Cava, USA TODAY Published June 8, 2016. Accessed September 4, 2017.

MyLab MIS

Go to **MyLab MIS.com** for Auto-graded writing questions as well as the following Assisted-graded writing questions:

11-16. Evaluate university or hospital use of social media. Identify which processes are being supported and identify at least one objective of that process. Describe 3 examples of how social media can improve a university or hospital process. How should the university or hospital respond to user content problems?

11-17. Critically evaluate your own stock of Social Capital. Compare your Social Capital to other students you know well. Describe two things that these other students do well.

Chapter 12

Business Intelligence and IS

In a windowless office deep inside the corporate office of CBI, Ann, the manager of the accounting department, and Cody, an IT analyst, are looking intently at a monitor. Cody is showing Ann data about the CBI network traffic.

"Ann, we use this program to determine which computers are downloading music and video files," explains Cody.

Ann is curious: "What do we do when people abuse our system?"

"We let them know. Usually that takes care of it. But not with your man Shawn. We sent him our standard 'Don't abuse our system' emails, but nothing changed. Maybe it's time you do the supervisor thing and chat with him."

"Is he downloading illegally, or is it from iTunes or YouTube?"

"We don't look that closely. In either case, it slows our network."

Ann, not sure she likes where the conversation is headed, attempts to change the subject. "What else?"

With a mischievous glint, Cody shows Ann a screen that displays a line with each employee name and columns for popular applications like Facebook, Google, and Outlook. "We collect data on millions of packets of Internet traffic flowing in and out of CBI every day, and we sort them by IP address. This screen shows the IP address of each employee, their names, and how often they use each application."

As Ann struggles to find a measured response, Cody rambles on, "We track how often employees log in to Facebook. We also track when employees log into and out of the company network and what types of apps they use—email, video, the new ERP system. When they access email through our servers. Those kinds of things."

"I don't remember being told that someone is recording my keystrokes!"

"I thought HR put out a policy letter. A lot of companies are doing it. HR says this will help them someday determine who is productive and who is not."

"So if I don't send and receive email at night or on weekends someone is recording that? Do we have any reliable measures, or are we just guessing what the numbers might mean? Maybe people are using texting to get their job done faster than if they used email?"

"Hey that's a good point, I hadn't thought of that. I know Fred purchased like a terabyte of data from SPYIT to compare how people use our network to how employees at other companies use their networks. They have some pretty sophisticated statistics. I can't wait to see that data. I wish I knew how it works."

Undeterred by Ann's concerns, Cody carries on. "We've got other software that shows us how fast truck drivers are driving, how many insurance claims each employee makes, and when they swipe into and out of our buildings. It's a whole new game!"

Ann sighs. "But if we are going to be Big Brother and watch what everyone's doing, Big Brother has a lot to learn."

```
      ┌─────────────────────────────────────┐
      │   CHAPTER OVERVIEW                   │
      └─────────────────────────────────────┘
```

CHAPTER OVERVIEW

Q12-1. What is business intelligence, and why is it important to business?

Q12-2. What are the objectives of the BI process?

Q12-3. What are the key components of a business intelligence IS?

Q12-4. How do BI information systems support BI activities?

Q12-5. How can BI information systems support business processes?

Q12-6. What is a Big Data BI system, and how is it used?

Q12-7. How do businesses manage the risks of business intelligence?

Q12-8. How does SAP do BI?

Q12-9. 2028?

PSI BIG PICTURE

PROCESS: BI process: Acquire, Analyze, and Publish

IS: BI IS can improve processes

INFORMATION: BI IS help individuals inform themselves

PREVIEW

The Sales and Procurement operational processes described in Chapters 8 and 9 generate significant amounts of data. In addition, the dynamic processes associated with collaboration and social media in Chapters 10 and 11 can also spin off mountains of data. But these are just a few of the many processes generating data in an organization. Cody and Ann are examining another source of data—millions of packets of network traffic. All this data includes useful patterns, relationships, and insights, but it is hidden, like a needle in a haystack. Finding these useful patterns is the goal of business intelligence. In many ways, this chapter culminates our study of management information systems. In earlier chapters, we discussed technology and processes so we knew the *why* of analysis; here at the end we investigate *how* that analysis is done. This chapter considers business intelligence and the information systems that support it.

As a future business professional, your ability to analyze data will be a critical skill. According to Jim Goodnight, founder of SAS, "If you want to be successful in business, make sure you have some understanding of analytics and when to use them. People who can use analytics—such as data mining and forecasting—to turn raw data into better business decisions have never been in greater demand. With all the talk of "Big Data," organizations across industries need people who understand how to use analytics to make sense of it all. I encourage this year's graduates to learn about how and when analytics can support their decisions."[1]

In this chapter, we investigate how companies like CBI use BI systems to support their processes. Our approach is similar to the previous two chapters—we first examine the five components of a BI system, then the activities of BI, and finally the business processes that rely on BI. But we begin with BI—its importance to business and its objectives.

MyLab MIS

- Using Your Knowledge Questions 12-1, 12-2, 12-3
- Essay Questions 12-16, 12-17
- Excel and Access Application Questions 12-1, 12-2

FIGURE 12-1
Five Sources of Data Growth

Health Care
Financial Machine Scientific
Communication

Q12-1 What Is Business Intelligence, and Why Is It Important to Business?

The quantity of data flooding the world is mind numbing. Every day Facebook processes more than 500 terabytes of data and Google 24,000 terabytes. According to Google CEO Eric Schmidt, every week we create as much data as we did from the dawn of civilization to 2003.[2] YouTube grows by a terabyte every 4 minutes; the CERN Hadron particle accelerator generates 1,000 terabytes of data a second.[3] Consider the big picture: In 2009 there was about .8 ZB of data, in 2011 1.8 ZB, and estimates for 2019 are for 35 ZB of data.

While these numbers are growing at rates that are hard to fathom, the main sources of data remain the same. These five sources of data are shown in Figure 12-1. The first source is financial—data from the billions of financial transactions that occur every day. Second, data is being generated by scientific advances such as mapping the human genome and global climate. A third source is our communications—every tweet, post, click, Like, email, comment, photo and search. Fourth, healthcare services like blood tests, MRIs, and hospital visits generate billions of records a day. But the fifth source of data may make the first four seem almost insignificant. There will soon be trillions of data-generating devices on the planet with us; hundreds of billions of mobile devices, and sensors are already here, and they will soon join forces with generations of new devices. These devices will power the growth of data for many years to come.

As the amount of data has grown, so too has its stature in the world of business. Spending on the analysis of business data has tripled in the past 16 years. As *The Wall Street Journal* concluded, this is the "Next Big Thing."[4] Hundreds of articles appear yearly in well-respected business outlets that call for businesses to be **data driven**—to rely on evidence and data rather than intuition or personal experience when making business decisions.

While many of us look for patterns some of the time, some will look for patterns most of the time. These data sleuths, these BI analysts, have a unique blend of statistical training and intense curiosity. This career field may find you, as McKinsey estimates the U.S. economy alone may have 250,000 vacant data analysis jobs by 2024.[5] The job is sometimes referred to as *data scientist* and was hyped by *Harvard Business Review* as the sexiest job in the 21st century. Data scientists will be needed in business and we discuss mostly business examples in this chapter, but data scientists will also work in healthcare, science, sports, law enforcement, and government organizations. Not only will BI analysts be needed, there is a need for 1.5 million managers who can work alongside them and turn insights from data into improved business processes.

Business intelligence is a process of acquiring, analyzing, and publishing data with an objective of discovering or revealing patterns in data that will inform a businessperson. This process is depicted in Figure 12-2. A **business intelligence system** is an information system

FIGURE 12-2

Main BI Process Activities and Roles

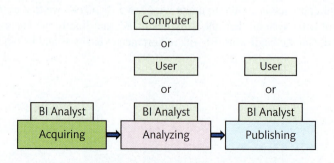

Company	Industry	Process	Objective
Target	Retail	Promote to new customers	Improve assessment of pregnancy
Netflix	Movie rental	Movie recommendation	Better prediction of next movie

FIGURE 12-3
Examples of BI

that supports these three business intelligence activities. Often, databases in BI systems are quite large and are called Big Data applications; however, BI has long been employed on more routine-sized datasets. In this chapter, we first explain these more common, smaller BI systems and later explore how Big Data BI systems differ.

Examples of BI

BI systems are only valuable because they support business processes. BI systems support business processes just like Facebook supports your processes. Facebook has acquired data that you can analyze to improve your personal processes. You improve your personal processes when you use Facebook data to find out (a nerd might say analyze) what is happening with friends, discover revealing patterns in relationships among people, notice trends in people's lives, and predict how some dramas will unfold. In a similar fashion, you analyze Google's data to find Web sites and map locations and uncover trending topics. In much the same way, businesses analyze data to improve their processes—consider the BI examples listed in Figure 12-3.

Marketers at Target realized that the key to gaining new customers is to get them in the store when their family situation changes.[6] Target had learned that shopping habits get ingrained; family members shop for the same items at the same stores until they experience a significant change in situation. These situation changes are things like having a baby, getting a new job, or moving to a new city. These events upset ingrained buying patterns and allow the merchant a rare opportunity to get customers in the door. Seizing on this, Target developed a statistical analysis that could accurately assess when a potential customer became pregnant. Target would then mail the expectant mother discounts and coupons for vitamins, maternity clothing, and baby furniture.

Netflix, sitting on a billion customer movie reviews, used BI to improve its Movie Recommendation process. Netflix uses movie attributes such as MPAA rating, star value, genre, and special effects to predict which movies you will like based on the value of these attributes in movies you have chosen in the past. If Netflix is better than its competitors at the Movie Recommendation process, you will probably rent more from Netflix than from its competitors. Why would you go to another cable or Web-based movie service if it cannot help you sift through thousands of movie choices and predict the ones you might like as successfully as Netflix?

While these are current examples of BI, also called *business analytics, predictive analytics, data science,* or simply *analytics,* businesses have been searching for patterns in data for a very long time. The term analytics dates back to the ninth century. BI systems used to analyze business data first became popular in the 1970s and were then called **decision support systems (DSS)**. A DSS is an information system used in support of decision making. It is still a term you may hear today when the supported process is decision making. We consider DSS to be a subset of BI.

To wrap this up, the business world is increasingly awash in data, and BI systems are growing in their capacity to help businesses identify important patterns in that data. To prepare you for a career that will frequently rely on BI, we start this chapter by considering the objectives of the BI process.

Q12-2 ▶ What Are the Objectives of the BI Process?

Like any process, the key to understanding the process is to understand its objectives. As shown in Figure 12-4, the objective of the BI process is to inform—an effectiveness objective—while staying within time and cost constraints—an efficiency objective.

The objective of most all Business Intelligence processes is to inform someone in the business. For example, a businessperson may be assessing a particular pattern or relationship, such

FIGURE 12-4

BI Process Objectives

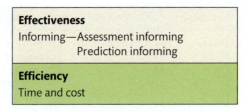

as looking to see if sales are increasing or decreasing. In contrast, the BI process may also be used to browse data with a more undirected purpose such as asking "How are we doing?" or "What is new?"

Informing is a rather general term, so more often we use the specific terms **assessment** and **prediction**. Assessment, in business, means to be informed about current conditions, while prediction is to be informed about the likelihood of future events. Using previous examples, Cody and Ann at CBI are attempting to assess if the company's network is being misused, Target is trying to assess who is pregnant, and Netflix wants to predict the likelihood that you will enjoy the next movie. Assessment typically asks questions such as, "What action is needed?" "What is the problem?" "Where is the item?" or "Who is doing what?" With prediction, the questions become "What is the next best thing that can happen?" "What if we change this?" "What will happen next?" and "What are the chances they will react in a certain way?"

BI processes also pursue an efficiency objective: time and cost constraints. For example, Target specified a time and budget for its staff to develop its pregnancy prediction algorithm. While it may seem obvious that time and cost objectives should be met, usually they are not even well specified. It is difficult to nail down goals for time and cost because many BI projects are one-offs, unique projects not attempted before. One-offs are more difficult to assign specific cost and time goals than recurring events because there is no precedence to guide cost and time goals. Therefore, BI efficiency objectives often shift depending on progress toward the end result. For example, we can imagine a one-off BI project for Target—build a model to predict when a potential new customer is moving into an area close to one of its stores. The BI team may discover after 3 months and $300,000 that it has made limited but promising progress; if team members are given more time, they think they could double the accuracy of the model. Then after 6 more months and more cash, they claim that if they could buy a new dataset they are sure to have an even more useable model. And on it goes.

Now that we have explained business intelligence objectives, we turn to the main emphasis of this chapter: how BI information systems support business processes. Figure 12-5 depicts the relationship between BI IS, business intelligence activities, and business processes. Starting on the left, the five components of a BI IS are discussed next in Q12-3. Then the three BI

FIGURE 12-5

BI IS Components and Business Processes

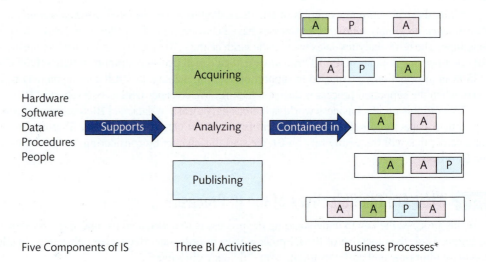

Five Components of IS   Three BI Activities   Business Processes*

* White space represents other activities in the business process.

activities—acquiring, analyzing, and publishing—are described in Q12-4. Finally, in Q12-5 we describe how BI IS support BI activities in actual business processes. As in Chapters 10 and 11, we display in Figure 12-5 those business processes as a rectangle, as a structured process would look; in reality, these dynamic processes can't be accurately represented using conventional diagramming.

Q12-3 ▶ What Are the Key Components of a Business Intelligence IS?

As we have done in the previous two chapters, here we review the components of the information system. We expect that you will be better able to use these BI systems if you can see how they are different from other IS.

The Five Components of a BI Information System

Like any other successful information system, each of the five components of a BI system shown in Figure 12-6 must be individually effective for the system to be effective.

HARDWARE The key piece of hardware in a BI system is a BI server. A BI server is used by an analyst to analyze the data and produce the output. A BI server can deliver output in a variety of formats such as .docx, .xlsx, PDF, XML, dashboards, and many others. For example, at Netflix the BI server can push the results of the movie recommendation algorithm to a laptop or any mobile device. A BI server can also control access so that only authorized people can interact with different data elements or see published outputs.

One of the key features of a BI system is that it needs to grow as the database grows; it needs to be scalable. To achieve scalability, BI servers are modular; that is, servers can be added easily as the system grows. This need for scalability makes cloud computing attractive, as one of the cloud's best features is the ability to expand services.

SOFTWARE A variety of BI software supports each of the three activities in the BI process: acquiring, analyzing, and publishing. While some software products such as Excel can support several of the activities, very few support each of the steps. SAP, Oracle, and Microsoft offer a comprehensive suite of BI software products that support each of the activities for medium to large organizations.

In recent years as BI software has become easier to use, end users are doing more of the analyzing and publishing activities without the assistance of BI analysts. When users do BI analysis by themselves, it is called **self-service BI**. In addition to being easy to use, BI software needs to be compatible with other software because there are many different types of data to acquire, statistical analyses to run, and types of output to publish.

DATA Data can be collected for a BI system in two ways. First, the data may come from an **operational database** that contains the data from the operational processes in a company. Second, data may come from other sources that are then combined with operational process data. In either case, once the data are collected, they are prepared and stored in a **data warehouse**, a repository for the organization's BI data. BI data are kept in a data warehouse because a data warehouse is specially designed to make sorting and retrieving large volumes of data efficient.

Five Components of IS	Business Intelligence IS
Hardware	Servers must be scalable, can provide control options, are often cloud based
Software	Differs by activity; analyze and publish software increasingly easier to use
Data	From operational sources and from external sources; data stored in a data warehouse
Procedures	Acquire activity requires technical training; analyze and publish activities increasingly designed for self service BI
People	Informing differences based on differences in knowledge, education, and experience; differences promote collaboration

FIGURE 12-6

Five Components of BI Information Systems

Operational databases, in contrast, are designed to make data inputs and updates efficient. In the BI world, operational databases are often referred to as **OLTP (online transactional processing)** systems, while the data warehouse is called **OLAP (online analytical processing)**.

PROCEDURES BI users and analysts follow a wide variety of procedures to acquire, analyze, and publish data. These methods of interaction depend on the activity and the analyst's knowledge and experience. For example, most of the procedures for acquiring and loading data into the warehouse are highly technical and require considerable training. While these "back end" structured procedures are always done by BI analysts, "front end" activities such as analysis and publishing are increasingly accomplished by trained end users following simple and intuitive procedures. In general, these front end BI procedures tend to be flexible and interactive, supporting users engaged in dynamic, nonroutine work.

PEOPLE There is no BI, no informing, without people. Two organizations could have very similar data, hardware, software, and procedures, but with different people, they can have vastly different results. One key difference is the knowledge people bring to the informing activity. If a rocket scientist and a high school student visit a vast public library looking for insights about recent advances in propulsion, the rocket scientist will quickly become more informed than the student. While we do not expect that college will make you a rocket scientist about every business topic, the conclusion is fairly clear—the business knowledge you develop at school will significantly affect your ability to use BI to be informed on the job; learn now to inform later.

There are two distinct types of people that use a BI system: end users and BI analysts. In the story at the beginning of the chapter, Ann is an example of a user and Cody is an analyst. Users interact with the output to find patterns in the data; BI systems are designed to help them become informed. Analysts often assist in this process by creating useful output and developing sound procedures for users to follow. However, analysts typically do not possess the business knowledge about the user's subject and must rely on the user for good questions to ask the data. The key is for users and analysts to collaborate effectively.

Key Attributes of BI Information Systems

The key aspects of BI systems include systems that are scalable. Typically, analysis begins with a small set of data, and if the analysis looks promising, the data is expanded. This need to scale makes cloud options particularly appealing. Second, BI software is increasingly easy to use, creating the opportunity for more self-service BI. Third, most BI applications depend on a data warehouse, so businesses must learn to acquire and store data in a different way from their traditional transactional database. Finally, informing is limited by user knowledge and collaboration skills.

▶ Q12-4 ▶ How Do BI Information Systems Support BI Activities?

Business intelligence information systems support the three primary BI activities shown in Figure 12-7: acquiring, analyzing, and publishing data. Here we examine each with particular emphasis on the two types of analyzing called reporting and data mining.

FIGURE 12-7

Outline of Discussion of BI Activities

| **Acquiring** |
| Four Sub-activities: |
| Obtain data |
| Cleanse data |
| Organize and relate data |
| Catalog data |
| **Analyzing** |
| Two Types: |
| Reporting—examples: RFM, OLAP |
| Data mining—examples: regression, MBA |
| **Publishing** |
| Topics: |
| Visualizations |
| Digital dashboard |

Acquiring

The first step, acquiring data, means gaining access to data, extracting it, and putting it into a data warehouse. Although it is possible to analyze data in a transactional database, this course is not usually recommended. If the BI analyst makes an error, that error could cause a serious disruption in the company's operations. Also, operational data is structured for fast and reliable transaction processing. It is seldom structured in a way that readily supports BI analysis. Finally, BI analyses can require considerable processing; placing BI applications on operational servers can dramatically reduce system performance.

For these reasons, most organizations extract operational data for BI processing. For a small organization, the extraction may be as simple as a few SQL statements in Access. Larger organizations, however, typically create and staff a group of people who manage and run the data warehouse.

For firms with extensive ERP systems in place, a wide variety of operational data is already conveniently consolidated and can be extracted to a data warehouse for analysis with a well-established set of procedures. The value of an ERP system is not only to integrate processes but to create a gold mine of data for later refinement and analysis. SAP calls data in an ERP a system of record and the data analyzed by BI tools the system of intelligence.

There are four sub-activities that comprise the Acquiring activity:

- Obtain data
- Cleanse data
- Organize and relate data
- Catalog data

Analysts obtain data for a data warehouse from several sources, as shown in Figure 12-8. Programs read production and other data and extract, clean, and prepare that data for BI analysis,

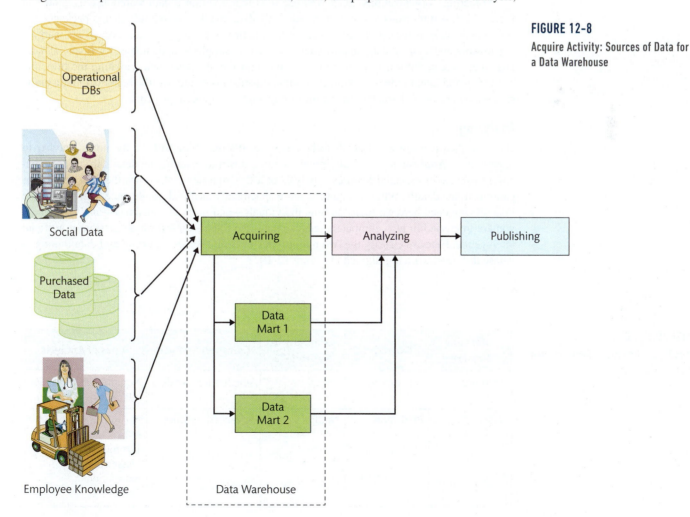

FIGURE 12-8

Acquire Activity: Sources of Data for a Data Warehouse

FIGURE 12-9
Purchased Data

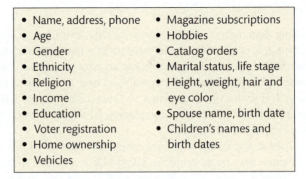

- Name, address, phone
- Age
- Gender
- Ethnicity
- Religion
- Income
- Education
- Voter registration
- Home ownership
- Vehicles
- Magazine subscriptions
- Hobbies
- Catalog orders
- Marital status, life stage
- Height, weight, hair and eye color
- Spouse name, birth date
- Children's names and birth dates

the second BI activity. The prepared data are stored in a data warehouse using a data warehouse DBMS, which can be different from the organization's operational DBMS. For example, an organization might use Oracle for its operational database but use SQL Server for its data warehouse. Cleaning, organizing, and cataloging data can take considerable time and effort, but if not done well the analysis activity becomes an exercise in garbage in, garbage out.

As shown in Figure 12-8, data warehouses include data that are purchased from outside sources. The purchase of data about other companies is not unusual or particularly disconcerting from a privacy standpoint. However, companies might choose to buy personal consumer data (e.g., marital status) from data vendors such as Acxiom Corporation. Figure 12-9 lists some of the consumer data that can be readily purchased. An amazing (and, from a privacy standpoint, frightening) amount of data is available.

Sometimes organizations create and use data marts within a data warehouse as shown in Figure 12-8. A **data mart** is a subset of read-only data in a data warehouse that is packaged for subsequent analysis for a particular client within the firm. CBI might create several data marts— one to store and analyze data on customers, another on suppliers, and another for financial data. Data marts create information silos that are not connected to other data, violating the principle of sharing and integrating data. However, some organizations find that the benefits of data marts such as lower cost and greater client control outweigh this general principle.

Analyzing

Once the data is acquired, it needs to be analyzed. It's one thing to have the notes, another to make music. **Analysis** methodically breaks a thing down to examine its details in order to discover or reveal its essential features. Analysis of a BI database breaks down the data to look for patterns in the details. While computers, more specifically artificial intelligence, can play a role in analyzing data, here we focus on how individuals—end users and analysts—analyze data. If you are interested in how computers analyze data, see Extension 4 for a discussion of artificial intelligence. Here we classify the two major types of BI analysis—reporting and data mining— whose differences are highlighted in Figure 12-10.

FIGURE 12-10

Two Types of Analysis: Reporting and Data Mining

Informing Version	Objective	Company in Figure 12-3	Common Analysis	Types of Analysis
Reporting	Assessment	Target	Simple sums, totals	Noninteractive—RFM Interactive—OLAP
Data mining	Prediction	Netflix	Advanced statistics	Regression MBA Text mining Classification Association Clustering

REPORTING **Reporting** applies simple operations to reveal patterns in the data. The analysis of the data is modest: Data are sorted and grouped, and simple totals and averages are calculated using operations such as sorting, grouping, and summing. The objective of the Reporting process is most often better assessment.

Reporting applications use four basic operations:

- Sorting
- Filtering
- Grouping
- Calculating

None of these operations is particularly sophisticated; they can all be accomplished using SQL and basic HTML or a simple report-writing tool. At times a single operation is the analysis activity; at other times these operations are combined like ingredients in a recipe to create a particular form of analysis for the end user. To whet your appetite, here we present two popular dishes—an RFM analysis and an OLAP slice and dice.

RFM Analysis **RFM** is used to analyze and rank customers according to their purchasing patterns. RFM considers how *recently* (R) a customer has ordered, how *frequently* (F) a customer ordered, and how much *money* (M) the customer has spent. The objective is to assess who the best customers are. For example, Best Buy found that 7 percent of its customers were responsible for 43 percent of its sales.[7]

To produce an RFM score as shown in Figure 12-11, the RFM reporting tool first sorts customer purchase records by the date of their most recent (R) purchase. In a common form of this analysis, the tool then divides the customers into five groups and gives customers in each group a score of 1 to 5. The 20 percent of the customers having the most recent orders are given an R score of 1, the 20 percent of the customers having the next most recent orders are given an R score of 2, and so forth, down to the last 20 percent, who are given an R score of 5.

The tool then re-sorts the customers on the basis of how frequently they order. The 20 percent of the customers who order most frequently are given an F score of 1, the next 20 percent of most frequently ordering customers are given a score of 2, and so forth, down to the least frequently ordering customers, who are given an F score of 5.

Finally, the tool sorts the customers again according to the amount spent on their orders. The 20 percent who have ordered the most expensive items are given an M score of 1, the next 20 percent are given an M score of 2, and so forth, down to the 20 percent who spend the least, who are given an M score of 5.

OLAP Slice and Dice **Slicing and dicing** uses the same basic analysis operations of sorting, grouping, filtering, and calculating, but, as the name implies, the operation is typically repeated. This analysis allows the user to execute these operations interactively; that is, the user or analyst can experiment with one operation, assess the output, and then go back and reanalyze the data. While it is a common way to analyze data, it also is frequently used by analysts to explore a new set of data. An initial exploration of data is always a good first step, as data doesn't talk to strangers.

Slicing and dicing is also referred to as OLAP cube slicing and dicing because the data that is sliced and diced is stored in an OLAP database structure called an info cube. Figure 12-12a

FIGURE 12-11

Example of RFM Analysis from CBI

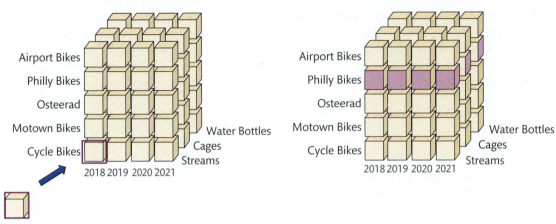

Revenue = $2344.56
for Cycle Bikes sales of Streams in 2018

(a) OLAP cube of three dimensions
with revenue measure

(b) OLAP cube sliced by Philly Bikes

FIGURE 12-12
OLAP Slice

shows a CBI info cube with three dimensions—customers, products, and year—and one measure—revenue. A **dimension** is a characteristic or attribute, and a **measure** is a data item of interest that can be summed, averaged, or otherwise processed. At CBI there are other dimensions such as division, warehouse, and salesperson that are available for OLAP analysis, but including all of them in a graphic is not possible in a 3D world.

Slicing removes one dimension. Figure 12-12b shows how the customer Philly Bikes is selected, sliced out in red. A slice is like a filter, filtering out the other customers.

Dicing is similar to slicing except instead of a single row or column being sliced off, a smaller cube is sliced off. As shown in Figure 12-13 the original cube is diced to leave only 2 years—2019 and 2020—one customer—Airport Bikes—and all three products. The analyst here is investigating just a portion of the original data.

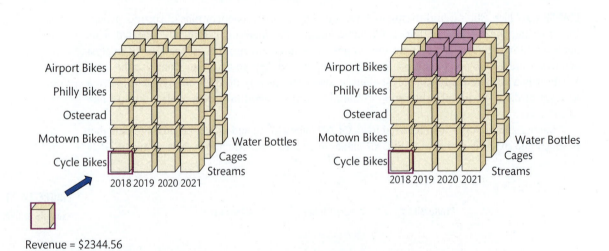

Revenue = $2344.56
for Cycle Bikes sales of Streams in 2018

(a) OLAP cube of three dimensions
with revenue measure

(b) OLAP cube diced showing
Airport Bikes for 2019–2020
for all three products

FIGURE 12-13
OLAP Dice

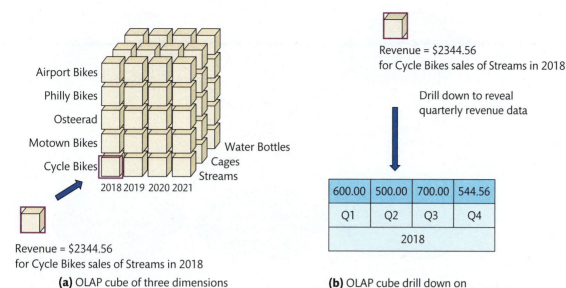

(a) OLAP cube of three dimensions with revenue measure

(b) OLAP cube drill down on Streams sold to Cycle Bikes in 2018 by quarter

FIGURE 12-14

OLAP Drill Down

Slicing and dicing have two lesser-known siblings (ignored because their names don't rhyme)—drill down and roll up. When a **drill down** operation is done, one cube in the larger cube is isolated and its data analyzed. Figure 12-14a shows the original cube, then one small cube—Cycle Bikes sales of Streams in 2018—is expanded in Figure 12-14b to reveal the revenue by quarter for Cycle Bikes sales of Streams in 2018. A roll up operation is the opposite of drill down—details are combined as in the grouping operation.

You can practice slicing and dicing while you are a student. Microsoft bundles an extension in Excel called PowerPivot that allows you to slice and dice large amounts of spreadsheet data. With PowerPivot, a self-service, easy-to-use analysis tool, you can sort, group, filter, and calculate. Figure 12-15 shows a PowerPivot analysis of CBI data—it shows the yearly revenue grouped by quarter for five CBI customers. Also, notice the small drop-down boxes Customer Name and Quarter. An end user can click on these buttons and slice the data further, perhaps selecting just one of the customers or two of the quarters. On the right side of the figure is the

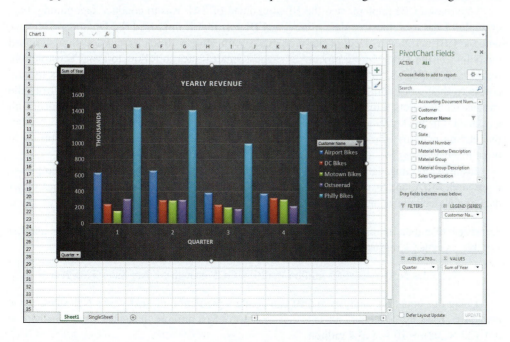

FIGURE 12-15

Excel PowerPivot Example of CBI Revenue by Quarter

FIGURE 12-16
Convergent Disciplines
for Data Mining

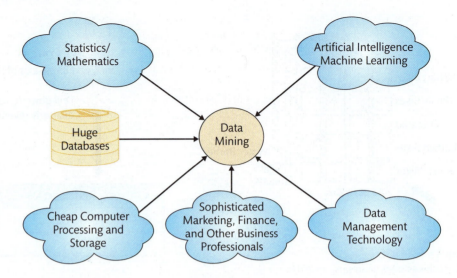

PowerPivot list of data fields to use in the analysis and an area in the bottom where an analyst can drag and drop these fields to create the chart. In addition to practicing with PowerPivot, you can practice analysis using SAP Lumira in Tutorial 12A.

DATA MINING **Data mining** has the same activities as the Reporting activity. However, in data mining the statistics used are much more sophisticated and complex and the objective is better *prediction*. Prediction is fundamental, as life is lived by looking forward based on the understanding gained from looking backward. Data mining seeks to not only predict a particular event, it more often predicts the likelihood of various outcomes. For example, the data mining used by Netflix generates predictions about the likelihood that a customer will enjoy the recommended movie. Another example of the data mining activity predicts products that tend to be purchased together. At Amazon, when a customer selects one product, data mining algorithms activate and display products that other customers purchased along with that product.

Data mining analysis has been applied to a wide variety of data. Online dating sites use data mining to predict compatible partners, cybersecurity applications look for digital signs to anticipate hacking, social media data mining predicts new customers for businesses, and Google Search uses data mining to predict links that will satisfy your search.

As shown in Figure 12-16, data mining resulted from a convergence of disciplines. Data mining emerged from statistics and mathematics and from artificial intelligence and machine-learning fields in computer science.

One reason CBI implemented the BI component of SAP was to conduct data mining. One example of the usefulness of data mining at CBI was that it improved the Outbound Delivery process. CBI outfitted its fleet of delivery trucks with sensors to track truck location and used the output of the Data Mining process to suggest smart routes to follow to avoid construction, traffic, and stoplights. In another application, CBI partnered with its retail customers to gain access to their sales data. The Data Mining process consolidates this customer data from the various retail outlets into a single data warehouse. Once combined, the data are mined with advanced statistical techniques to spot unusual buying patterns across the industry. These predictive buying patterns help CBI salespeople adjust future delivery dates and delivery options in order to save money for both the retailer and CBI.

Just like reporting, data mining has a variety of techniques. Here we present three examples—regression, MBA, and text mining—to give you a better idea of how data mining is done. Other data mining techniques include classification, association, and clustering.

Regression One data mining analysis, which measures the effect of a set of variables on another variable, is called a **regression analysis**. A sample result for the bike company is:

$$\text{Net Sales Next Year} = \$3 \text{ million} + (20 \times \text{GDP growth}) + \text{Net Sales This Year}$$

Using this equation, analysts at CBI can create a prediction of next year's Net Sales. If the economy grows by 2 percent and sales this year were $10 million, then sales next year will be $3 + (20 \times .02) + 10 = \$13.4$ million.

As you will learn in your statistics classes, considerable skill is required to interpret the quality of such a model. The regression tool will create an equation, such as the one shown. Whether that equation is a good predictor of future Net Sales depends on statistical factors, such as *t* values, confidence intervals, and related statistical techniques. Another common example of regression is to predict if a student will remain at a university. Retention is important to schools, and they use a regression model to identify which variables. such as GPA, class availability, and distance from home, are most predictive.

MBA Market Basket Analysis   At CBI, Sue is well known as the best salesperson at **cross-selling** her customers, or selling her customers items in addition to those they request. Any of CBI's sales associates can fill a customer's order, but Sue is especially good at predicting which products a customer may also buy. She explains how she does it.

"It's simple," she says. "I just ask myself what is the next product they would want to buy. If a small bike shop starts to buy our more expensive touring bikes, I realize that their customers will soon want our more expensive bike tire pumps and handlebar tape."

A **market basket analysis (MBA)**, a type of association analysis, predicts cross-selling opportunities. A market basket analysis shows the products that customers tend to buy together. For more details on MBA, see Application Exercise 12-2.

Text Mining   The term **text mining** refers to the analytical technique that extracts insights from unstructured data sources, typically textual documents. Rather than the numerical and structured data analyzed by regression, MBA, and other data mining analysis methods, text mining data comes from PDF files, email, XML files, Word documents, and text excerpts. Text mining is commonly used in medical, law, biology, and customer service applications and is also being used to identify deception in email used by phishers. Automated text mining using artificial intelligence can read drafts of job postings to reveal subtle biases.

Another use of text mining in business is to generate a sentiment analysis, a measure of the voice of the customer or voice of the market. **Sentiment analysis** classifies opinions about a business, product, or service, typically as either positive or negative. A customer sentiment analysis classifies textual data opinions of a large group of customers. For example, a vendor supplies CBI with a market sentiment analysis score about retail biking products. Recently, CBI has noticed that sentiment toward electronic-assisted biking is growing. Sentiment analysis is also used to assess the marketing impact of commercials during NFL broadcasts by analyzing text comments and their frequency on social media.

SUPERVISED AND UNSUPERVISED DATA MINING ANALYSIS   Data mining analysis can be categorized as unsupervised and supervised. With **unsupervised data mining**, analysts do not create a model or hypothesis before running the analysis. Instead, they apply the data mining software to the data and observe the results. With this method, analysts create hypotheses *after the analysis* in order to explain the patterns found. Another term for unsupervised analysis is *data-driven analysis*. An example of unsupervised data mining is displayed in the opening vignette. Cody and Ann did not create a model that would assess misuse of the network; they jumped into the data without a hypothesis and are attempting to explain misuse after they analyze the data. MBA is also an example of unsupervised data mining. With **supervised data mining**, analysts develop a model *prior to the analysis* and apply statistical analyses to the data to estimate parameters of the model. Regression analysis is an example of supervised data mining. Supervised data mining is also called a top-down technique as the analyst "on top" imposes a particular model on the data. Unsupervised data mining is bottom up as the data tells the analyst which relationships in the data exist.

Publishing

In the previous discussion, we illustrated the power and utility of reporting and data mining analysis. But for BI to be actionable, for it to inform, it must be published to the right user at the right time. In the Publishing activity, the results of the analysis activity are presented. A wide variety of presentations can be published, from simple text to charts and tables to more complex visualizations. Publishing options also include a variety of media. Some output is printed on paper; other output is generated in formats such as PDF files that can be printed or viewed electronically. Output can also be delivered to computer screens and smartphones.

FIGURE 12-17

Electoral Map Visualization

Source: Chris Howard (http://www.SaltwaterWitch.com) based on U.S. census data and the 2012 election maps created by Mark Newman (http://www.personal.umich.edu/~mejn).

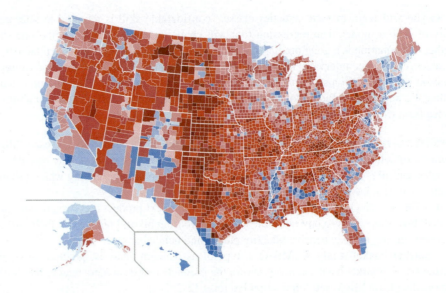

A **visualization,** or simply viz, is an image or diagram that communicates a data pattern in a highly readable format. One classic viz is an electoral map that uses color to show the party of the candidate leading in the poll. An example is Figure 12-17, which shows counties and the concentration of Democrat and Republican voters. Other recent, well-known examples of visualizations include infographics and stock market displays that show rising stocks in one color and declining stocks in another. Increasingly, data analysts create vizes for end users to filter the data, drill down on it, or interact with it in some other way. These interactive visualizations are also called dynamic visualizations to contrast them with static visualizations that cannot be changed by the end user. These advances in interactivity promote end user self-service and make it easier for users to inform themselves. Another important viz distinction is push or pull. A push viz is created by an analyst and sent to an end user, while a pull viz uses data that is selected by the end user.

A very popular software choice for interactive visualizations is Tableau; a Tableau viz is shown in Figure 12-18.[8] That visualization shows 12 of Chuck Bike's customers over a period of 8 years. Each line is color-coded and displays the revenue from sales for that company. A user can click on a company line to drill down and see more details. On the right, notice the Customer Name filter, which allows the user to display only selected companies. Tableau has also recently

FIGURE 12-18

Example Tableau Visualization

Source: www.tableausoftware.com/public/gallery/taleof100

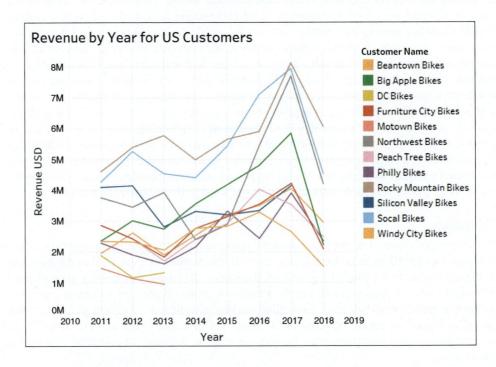

provided users the option to share their output by providing a clip of html code for a blog or Web site, much like YouTube provides a bit of code to embed a video on other sites. Using this feature, you can publish a viz about your fantasy sports team and post it on a blog where your friends could click on it and re-analyze the data and publish their own output. When you update your data on the Tableau server, all your friends' visualizations are updated.

One type of visualization is a digital **dashboard**, or simply dashboard, which is a viz customized for a particular user. Users of these services can define content they want—say, a local weather forecast, a list of stock prices, or a list of news sources—and the vendor constructs the display output customized for each user. Figure 12-19 shows an example of an SAP-generated dashboard. Dashboards are frequently used to monitor business processes and indicate abnormal conditions with clear signs such as red lights or gauges.

Q12-5 ▶ How Can BI Information Systems Support Business Processes?

Having considered the activities of a generic BI process and how BI information systems support these activities, here we consider specific business processes that rely on business intelligence IS. At the beginning of the chapter we gave two examples of processes that use BI systems: Target's New Customer Promotion process and Netflix's Movie Recommendation process. Here we expand on that list. Figure 12-20 lists a variety of the business processes supported by BI systems.

Business Processes Supported by BI IS	
Decision making	Site location
Machine maintenance	Customer service
Next best offer	Vendor selection
Online sales	Promotion
Cybersecurity	Branding
Project management	Product design
Healthcare and services	Fraud detection
Athlete assessment	Communication
Knowledge management	Transportation
Insurance	

FIGURE 12-20

Business Processes Supported by Business Intelligence IS

Process	Example	Objective	Predict or Assess	Data Acquired
Decision Making	Google Instant Search	Faster, more accurate	Predict	Google's index of sites, keywords
Machine Maintenance	Jet engine	Few fails, better efficiency	Predict	Engine speeds, sounds, composition of oil
NBO	Tesco	Increase redemption rates	Predict	Customer history, preferences, context
Online Sales	B2C site	Better conversion rate	Predict	Clicks, views, transactions

FIGURE 12-21

Example Processes Supported by BI Information Systems

Supporting Existing Processes with BI Information Systems

To provide insight about the value of BI for business processes, we chose four of the processes in Figure 12-20 to present in more detail; these are shown in Figure 12-21. As you read, please notice the variety of processes supported by BI and the benefits that can result. While the goals of these processes differ, BI support should result in higher achievement of these goals or achieving the goals at a lower cost.

DECISION MAKING The **Decision Making process** is the selection of a choice among available options and can be done individually or in a group. It is one of the most frequently occurring processes in organizations. BI systems support the Decision Making process by acquiring data and providing analysis and publication software. As mentioned earlier, when businesses rely on data rather than intuition or personal experience, the decision-making process is said to be data driven. One way to see the impact of BI on decision making is to examine the impact of Google Search on your decision making. Google has acquired one of the largest databases ever created—links and keywords for billions of pages, stored in a database called an **index**. As you type keywords into the Google search box, the search string is analyzed and compared to the index and suggested terms are published for your decision. By using one of the autocomplete suggestions, you save an average of 2.5 seconds per search, which amounts to a worldwide savings of 11 hours per second every second. What's more, the search is very accurate—using Google's predicted terms, you more often find what you seek.

MACHINE MAINTENANCE Machines break. In some industries, the failure of a machine can be fatal, such as jet engines, nuclear power cooling systems, generators for hospitals, and marine engines. In other industries, machine failures are less dramatic but often very costly. Companies that rely on these high-reliability machines acquire, analyze, and publish data that helps them predict machine failures and run efficiently. Jet engines are a good example. Every time a commercial jet lands, terabytes of data are downloaded from sensors, gauges, and sound recordings as well as from tests of engine oil. One airline, Southwest, acquires 200 petabytes of data every day. Analyzing this data allows airlines to make very accurate predictions of engine failure so that preventative repairs can be made. Analysis of jet engine data has led to remarkable reductions in engine failures over the past several decades. Analysis also helps airlines determine optimal engine power settings so that fuel consumption can be minimized. Southwest saves more than $100 million a year on fuel by analyzing engine data. At your future work, machine maintenance may not save lives, but data from your machines will be acquired and analyzed to operate the machines safely and at peak efficiency.

NEXT BEST OFFER (NBO) The **NBO process** is a targeted offer or proposed action for customers based on the data patterns in the customer's history and preferences, context, and attributes of the product or service.[9] The objective is to more accurately predict the percentage of customers who will accept the offer. An accurate prediction is essential. If you are too generous, too many customers accept and you lose money; if you are not generous enough, customers don't accept and you're stuck holding extra inventory. Businesses made NBOs for years before BI, but with BI, companies can more accurately predict the rate that offers will be accepted. For example, the UK retailer Tesco improved its NBO process by integrating BI data it had acquired about customer preferences. The result was redemption rates by its customers from 8 to 14 percent, which is four to seven times higher than traditional NBOs.

ONLINE SALES Retailers can improve their Online Sales process with BI. A key activity of the Online Sales process is acquiring customer data. This data might include which browser the visitor is using, the visitor's IP address, and whether the user eventually purchased from the site. Before BI, B2C businesses had to write their own code to acquire and analyze this type of data. Enter Google Analytics, mentioned in Chapter 9. Google Analytics is a powerful BI software for Web site owners to store and analyze site traffic data. This data includes the data mentioned earlier as well as where the customer came from (e.g., from a search engine or another site), the type of device being used, where the customer visited in the site, and the **conversion rate**, which is the ratio of the number of customers who eventually purchased divided by the number who visited. BI salespeople can analyze this type of data and predict useful changes to the site to increase conversion rates. One analysis technique is **A/B testing**, also called split testing. Using this technique, site developers build two identical pages, say two shopping cart pages. Page A shows a navigation menu across the top, whereas on Page B the same menu is on the left border of the screen. When visitors come to the site, they are randomly given either A or B, and the conversion rate for the two pages is analyzed to determine the better page.

Supporting New Processes with BI Information Systems

As was our habit in previous chapters, we also examine new processes supported by BI information systems. These are processes that could not exist without modern BI. One example is the Player Assessment process for professional athletes, as depicted in the movie *Moneyball*. There are many examples of new processes. Here we consider two, as shown in Figure 12-22.

AIRPLANE ETA ESTIMATION Airplane arrival time predictions are very important to airlines. Airlines need to be able to predict an accurate arrival time at the gate—if they get surprised by an early arrival, the plane sits there at the gate with hundreds of frustrated prisoners; if it is later than expected, the ground crew wastes time waiting for it and the airline cannot use that gate. In the old days, the process of estimating ETA was based on pilot estimates—pilots would use the airplane's radio and call in their estimated arrival time at the gate. Now PASSUR Aerospace provides a service called RightETA. PASSUR acquired data from years of airplane arrivals to each runway at all the major airports, including GPS location data, weather, winds, ground traffic congestion, and other magic ingredients. Analyzing the data, it continually creates an incredibly accurate prediction of an arrival time based on the current location of a plane. The savings is estimated to be several million dollars per year at major airports.

PREDICTION MARKETS Google experiments a lot. Some experiments turn out great; others—like Google Glass, Wave, and Google+—are dogs. To better forecast which experiments and projects deserve continued investment, Google experimented with something else—a prediction market to evaluate experiments. A prediction market is like a stock market, but rather than shares of stock, participants buy and sell the outcomes of future events such as experiments with tech projects, predictions of sales growth, or actions by competitors. Prediction markets outside of

New Process	Example	Objective	Predict or Assess	Data Acquired
Airplane ETA Estimation	Airlines	More accurate arrival time	Predict	Prior arrivals GPS
Prediction Market	Google	Improve investment decisions	Predict	Outcomes, Google dollar prices
Energy Conservation	Homes	Increase conservation	Assess	Electrical use

FIGURE 12-22

Examples of New Processes Supported by BI Information Systems

Google forecast election results by allowing participants to wager on candidates. At Google, employees use Google dollars in a prediction market to buy and sell different outcomes for Google Cars and other experiments. Outcomes that can be purchased range from an unprofitable invention to a billion-dollar profit, with several choices in between. If the Google dollar price of an experiment falls, Google knows that many of its tech-savvy employees are wagering that this project is heading for a bad outcome. Google is wagering on wagers being right.

ENERGY CONSERVATION Public utilities are also using BI to help homeowners reduce energy consumption. In Dubuque, Iowa, 1,200 households volunteered for a pilot project sponsored by the city and its BI partner IBM. IBM designed energy meters that are placed on dishwashers, hair dryers, water heaters, and other devices in the house to show the energy cost for each device in real time. In the past, residents were given data on energy use only at the end of the month. Now the data is continuously published, and with better intelligence homeowners can reduce energy use and help Dubuque become a more sustainable city.

In this question, we wanted to highlight the central role of BI in a variety of business processes. We intentionally picked processes that use BI in new or particularly clever ways. When you work in an organization, you'll see other less flashy but helpful ways that BI supports processes.

Q12-6 ▶ What Is a Big Data BI System, and How Is It Used?

Earlier, we hinted that the size of databases that businesses are acquiring and analyzing is growing. In nearly all industries in the U.S. economy, companies with more than 1,000 employees are sitting on 200 terabytes of data.[10] Applying BI activities to large datasets is called Big Data, a $5 billion-a-year industry that is expected to exceed $200 billion by 2020.[11] Business is not the only source of growth for Big Data BI, as governments also use it to spot tax evasion and fight terrorism, healthcare agencies use it to better understand diseases, and scientists use it to analyze the human genome. Here we examine the characteristics of Big Data information systems, their techniques, and the business processes they support.

Big Data is a term used to describe data collections that are characterized by huge *volume*, rapid *velocity*, and great *variety*:

- Big Data datasets are typically hundreds of terabytes in size, and usually larger.
- Big Data is generated rapidly or accessed rapidly.
- Big Data has structured data, free-form text, log files, and possibly graphics, audio, and video.

Volume refers to the size of the database, often a petabyte or larger in size. The size of Big Data systems can be mind numbing—terabytes and petabytes. To appreciate the enormity of these sizes, consider these quantities in seconds, mega seconds, and tera seconds. A mega second, or 1,000,000 seconds, is 11 days. A giga second would be 32 years, a tera second 32,000 years, and a petasec 32 million years.

The velocity of the data is the rate at which the data is created or accessed. For Google's Search to be useful, the search terms entered by a user must be applied to the data warehouse very quickly, and the auto-generated response must also be rapid. Credit card companies seek to improve their ability to detect unusual card use on the spot. In medicine, smart scalpels allow real-time analysis of cancer cells so surgeons can ensure that all the cancerous cells are removed during an operation.

Finally, the variety of data addresses the diversity of the data. For example, in many large datasets it is common to define dates in different formats, to have different rules about missing data values, and to include free-form text and audio, video, and graphic data as well. This type of data is called unstructured data.

Compared to routine-size databases, Big Data IS differ not only in data but software too. BI software in Big Data applications often must divide the data and processing steps into many smaller tasks and assign those tasks to different servers. As a result, BI software must be adept at balancing the load it places on the hardware.

A little history on Big Data. About 15 years ago, Amazon determined that relational database technology wouldn't meet its needs, and it developed a nonrelational data store called Dynamo. Meanwhile, for many of the same reasons, Google developed a nonrelational data store called Bigtable. Facebook took concepts from both of the systems and developed a third nonrelational data store call Cassandra, the first-large scale NoSQL application. Other vendors have since

Technology	Primary Component of IS	Key Attribute
NoSQL	Database	Nonrelational database
MapReduce	Software	Many processors
Hadoop	Software	Ecosystem supports other technologies
In-memory	Hardware	Massive RAM

FIGURE 12-23
Big Data Solutions

developed other techniques that help address the challenges of Big Data. Here we group them into four categories as shown in Figure 12-23—NoSQL databases, MapReduce, Hadoop, and in-memory systems—and describe each of them next.

NoSQL Databases

As described in Chapter 4, a **NoSQL database** is a nonrelational database designed to support very high processing rates on relatively simple and unstructured data that is replicated across many servers. These databases are faster and more scalable than relational DBMS, but because they spread data over many servers, they have data redundancy, have fewer controls, and require programming skills. NoSQL is not the best term as the key difference is the structure of the database that has nothing to do with SQL; NotRelationalDatabases would have been better, but the cake has been baked.

MapReduce

Because Big Data is so large, it cannot be processed using traditional techniques. **MapReduce** is a software technique for analyzing large amounts of data on thousands of computers working in parallel. The basic idea is that a batch of data is broken into pieces and thousands of independent processors search these pieces for something of interest. That process is referred to as the *Map* phase. For example, in Figure 12-24 a search log of millions of words is being analyzed so that each word and the frequency of that word can be listed. The search log is divided into

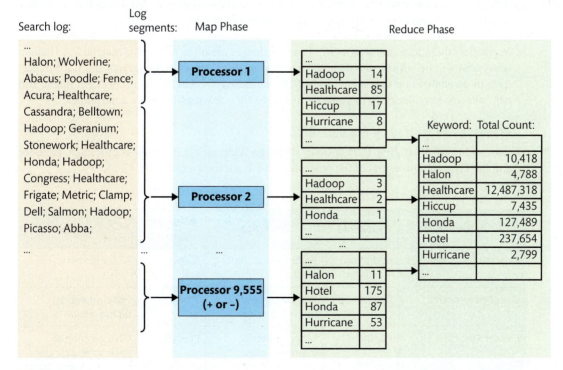

FIGURE 12-24
MapReduce

10,000 segments, and each segment is mapped out to one server to search for and count words. Figure 12-24 shows just a small portion of the data; here you can see a portion of the keywords that begin with *H*. As the processors finish, the MapReduce software combines the results in the *Reduce* phase. The result is a list of all the terms and the count of each. The process is considerably more complex than described here, but this is the gist of the idea.

Hadoop

Hadoop is scalable open source software framework supported by the Apache Foundation[12] that stores and analyzes Big Data on distributed computers. A Hadoop system stores data on many servers using the Hadoop Distributed File System (HDFS), data is typically in unstructured NoSQL databases, and MapReduce is often used. Hadoop is typically installed as an ecosystem and not as a single application. A Hadoop implementation includes the HDFS, hardware, job tracker, query writers, Web tools, and programming languages unique to Hadoop.

A common analogy for a Hadoop system is a data lake. A company builds a dam—a Hadoop cluster—and allows the water—the data—to flow in. Then users begin to use the data in a variety of ways, like water on a lake is used to drink, recreate, and generate power. Unlike a data warehouse where all the water is cleaned and then bottled, the water in the lake, which is vastly larger than the water in bottles, is not cleaned until it is time to drink it, as it might be used for other purposes that do not require the same treatment. Amazon and other large cloud vendors use Hadoop to power their cloud services. A lake in the cloud.

SAP HANA and In-Memory Database Systems

While Hadoop distributes data on a large number of servers, **SAP HANA** addresses the Big Data challenge by storing and analyzing data in a single computer system. Traditional database systems as well as Hadoop keep data in secondary storage and must access it to process it. However, these trips to and from secondary storage slow down database operations. SAP built HANA to eliminate these trips and keeps the entire database in memory. HANA is both the RAM to store and retrieve data and the software development platform to write applications for the system. HANA can be used with structured relational databases or with unstructured NoSQL databases. HANA is designed not only to support BI but also to store data from SAP ERP implementations. Vendors other than SAP are beginning to provide their own in-memory data systems. Oracle offers a similar in-memory database system called TimesTen, and other smaller vendors are also beginning to offer in-memory systems.

In practice, these four solutions to Big Data challenges are often mixed and matched. A Hadoop ecosystem will be built to distribute the data and analysis across many servers and use MapReduce to do analysis on data stored in NoSQL databases. Or this Hadoop ecosystem might also add an in-memory device to increase performance for a few data-intensive applications.

Processes Supported by Big Data BI IS

Like traditional BI IS, Big Data systems support a wide variety of business processes. Here we will briefly examine several of the processes, which are shown in Figure 12-25.

FIGURE 12-25

Business Processes Supported by Big Data BI

Processes	Example	Objective	Predict or Assess	Data Acquired
Continuous Auditing	Audit firm	Reduce fraud, faster audits	Assess	All transactions
Counterterrorism	Government	Accurately predict terror behavior	Predict	Government data on individuals
Cancer Treatment	Health	More successful treatment plan	Predict	DNA genome of patients and cancers
Urban Services	Barcelona	Improve safety, reduce emissions	Assess	Vehicle and traffic sensors and lights

CONTINUOUS AUDITING The **Auditing process** is the official, unbiased examination of an organization's financial accounts. Traditionally, to execute an audit, the audit team would select a sample of financial transactions over a recent period of time and examine these transactions for unusual activity. With Big Data, this process no longer needs to sample a subset of transactions; it can examine every transaction. Not only can all the transactions be evaluated, the audit can happen in real time as the transactions are occurring, not at the end of a month or year. If discrepancies are occurring, a real-time assessment can identify them. In addition, with Big Data the analysis can be much more sophisticated; the number and variety of unusual patterns that can be evaluated are much greater than before.

COUNTERTERRORISM Most of the examples here are about business organizations, but government agencies also have processes that are supported by BI. Government agencies use BI like business organizations to bill citizens (taxation), analyze cyber security, predict revenues and costs, improve service, and quicken response. Governments also have unique processes that Big Data systems support such as law enforcement, polling, and counterterrorism. Counterterrorism processes supported by Big Data technologies help connect data in information silos hoarded by different government agencies. Also, text mining of Web sites linked to terror cells can provide early warning. The result is a faster and more complete analysis of data to spot patterns that predict possible terrorist activity.

CANCER TREATMENT Big Data can improve the treatment of some forms of cancer.[13] With Big Data, a patient who has recently been diagnosed with cancer can undergo DNA testing, and the patient's DNA data and cancer cell genome data can be collected and analyzed. This data can then be compared to the data from other patients who were previously diagnosed with a similar type of cancer. If near matches are found, successful treatment sequences can be used for the new patient. This will help doctors prescribe better treatments for their patients. Not only can the treatment process be improved, but treatment can be started earlier; the process of creating a genetic map of a patient used to take 2 days, but now with Big Data systems it can be done in 20 minutes.

URBAN SERVICES Cities and municipalities throughout the world provide urban services such as public transportation, traffic control, and waste management. Many cities are using advances in Big Data to provide services that improve transportation safety and reduce vehicle emissions. The city of Barcelona, Spain, had, at one time, the distinction of having the world's worst transportation grid. Like most cities, nearly 30 percent of this traffic was simply looking for a parking place. The city hired Cisco to install recording devices around the city to measure vehicle and pedestrian traffic, smart traffic lights to react to current traffic, parking sensors in the pavement to identify open parking locations, and trash container sensors to measure trash levels. Using this data, garbage trucks only empty full containers, open parking spots are quickly found, bus routes carry 30 percent more passengers, and drivers have access to real-time traffic patterns throughout the city. The city has reduced traffic by 20 percent and increased revenue by $50 million a year by selling parking location data. Even lampposts have sensors that turn on the LED lights only when traffic is near, saving the city $40 million a year. Barcelona uses business intelligence to be one of the world's smartest cities.

Big Data is here to stay as more and more businesses learn how to use it to enhance their processes. We can also expect that today's Big Data will be tomorrow's Routine Data and tomorrow's Big Data will be hundreds and thousands of times larger. But while the size of the data will continue to grow, the fundamental lesson remains the same: information systems improve business processes. Size does not change the fundamental lesson, nor does it change the fundamental challenges; we describe these next.

Q12-7 How Do Businesses Manage the Risks of Business Intelligence?

Although the discussion in this chapter may have helped clarify the benefits of using a BI system, some of its problems may not be easy to see. Each of the BI components can have problems, and here we focus on the two most challenging: problems with data and problems with people.

FIGURE 12-26

Common Data Problems in BI

1. Dirty and Missing Values

ID	Last Name	Street	Zip Code	Cell Number
101	Smith	123 Elm	80840	419-398-9876
102	Jones	34	80840	(654)8769876
103	Baez	65 Ash	80865	(543) 543-9321
104	Baez	65 Ash	80865	(543) 543-9321

Duplicated data   Missing values   Different formats

2. Data not Integrated Information Silos
3. Wrong Granularity

Data Problems

Unfortunately, most operational and purchased data have problems that inhibit their usefulness for business intelligence. Figure 12-26 lists the major problem categories.

DIRTY DATA AND MISSING VALUES Problematic data are termed **dirty data**. Examples are a value of *B* for customer gender or *213* for customer age. More examples are shown in Figure 12-26. These values can be problematic for BI purposes. In addition, purchased data often contain *missing* elements. Most data vendors state the percentage of missing values for each attribute in the data they sell. An organization buys such data because for some uses, some data are better than no data at all. This is especially true for data items whose values are difficult to obtain, such as the number of adults in a household, household income, dwelling type, and the education of the primary income earner. For BI applications, though, a few missing or erroneous data points can be worse than no data at all because they bias the analysis.

DATA NOT INTEGRATED—INFORMATION SILOS Another problem is nonintegrated data. A particular BI analysis might require data from an ERP system, an e-commerce system, and a social networking application. Analysts might want to integrate that organizational data with purchased consumer data.

FIGURE 12-27

Integrating BI Data

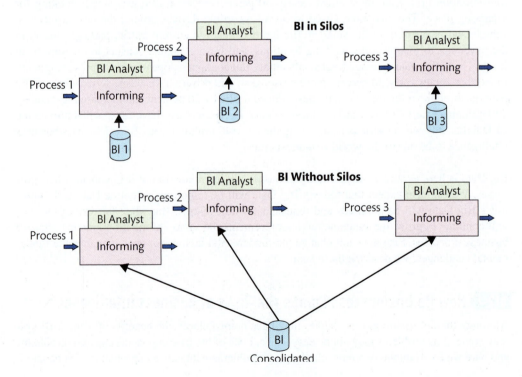

Such a data collection will likely have relationships that are not represented in primary key/foreign key relationships. It is the function of personnel in the data warehouse to integrate such data somehow.

Nonintegrated data may also be the result of information silos within the organization. As shown in Figure 12-27, one silo may have BI data for Process 1, and another silo may have BI data for Process 2. With this situation, BI analysts and users must learn to use many different databases in order to do analysis. By consolidating BI data in one location, as shown at the bottom of Figure 12-27, each BI process can be more efficient.

WRONG GRANULARITY Finally, data can also have the wrong **granularity**. Granularity is the level of detail of the data, and it can be too fine or too coarse. For the former, suppose we want to analyze the placement of graphics and controls on an order entry Web page. It is possible to capture the customers' clicking behavior in what is termed **clickstream data**. In the middle of the clickstream are data for clicks on the news, email, instant chat, and weather. Although all of that data may be useful for a study of consumer computer behavior, it will be overwhelming if all we want to know is how customers respond to an ad located differently on the screen. To proceed, the data analysts must throw away millions and millions of clicks. Data can also be too coarse. For example, a file of order totals cannot be used for a market basket analysis. For a market basket analysis, we need to know which items were purchased with which others. In general, it is better to have too fine a granularity than too coarse. If the granularity is too fine, the data can be made coarser by summing and grouping. If the granularity is too coarse, however, there is no way to separate the data into constituent parts.

People Problems

People problems fall into three categories: users, analysts, and leaders, as shown in Figure 12-28. Each group of people present unique challenges.

USERS User resistance is a common malady of all information systems, and BI is no exception. Users resist a BI system for a number of reasons—it may change their job, require knowledge the user does not have, or distract them from their primary work. A second problem is that an impressive visualization can be like putting lipstick on a pig; users may be entranced by the sophistication of the viz without realizing the underlying data is fairly meaningless.

A third type of user problem is that users may underestimate the cost of producing a BI report. It is difficult to identify accurately all the costs associated with a BI project. As a result, one or two users may consume too much of the BI analyst's time. They may believe that a particular dashboard or analysis is essential but may change their mind if accurate cost data were available.

Problems can also creep in when users do not understand the statistical operations done in the analysis activity. Some mistakes are unintentional and reflect a lack of understanding the data or the statistics and the assumptions behind them. But some mistakes may be intentional as users and analysts try to bend the analysis to support their conclusion. They decide before the analysis what the statistics should say, and they torture the data until it says what they want to hear.

Users
• Resistance
• Sophisticated viz may hide meaningless results
• Underestimate cost of reports
• Unintentional and intentional mistakes

Analysts
• No stopping point
• Asking wrong questions
• Not involving users
• Too much trust in analysis, not skeptical
• Biases in analysis

Leaders
• Failing to specify scope
• Inadequate funding
• Limited statistical understanding
• Overselling results

FIGURE 12-28

BI People Problems: Users, Analysts, and Leaders

MIS InClass 12

I Know That, I Think

Set a lower and an upper bound for each of the following 10 questions. For example, if the question was "What is the age of President Obama?" you might think the answer is about 45, so you would set a lower bound of 40 and an upper bound of 50. Make your lower and upper bounds reasonable estimates, but make sure they are wide enough so you get 9 of the 10 questions correct. You are not allowed to use any help on this exercise. Once you have answered these questions, your instructor will tell you the correct answers.

	Lower Bound	Upper Bound	Question
1.	___	___	What is the height of the Empire State Building?
2.	___	___	In what year was former President Reagan born?
3.	___	___	What is the length of the longest overland tunnel in the world?
4.	___	___	What is the current national circulation of *The Wall Street Journal*?
5.	___	___	What is the population of Australia?
6.	___	___	What is the distance between Atlanta and Dallas?
7.	___	___	How many books are in the Library of Congress?
8.	___	___	How many countries are there in the world?
9.	___	___	How many steps does the Washington Monument have?
10.	___	___	What year did Julius Caesar die?

Source: Sergejs Rahunoks/Fotolia

As a class, discuss the following questions:

1. Why did you set your boundaries where you did?
2. What does your score on this exercise suggest?
3. Which Informing process (Reporting or Data Mining) would have improved your answers?

ANALYSTS   BI analysts also contribute their own share of problems. Analysts have a hard time saying, "Enough." Many BI projects have no obvious or convenient stopping point. Rather, the analyst might think, "Just one more week of experimenting with this data or one more run with this new model, and I'll have it." While engaged on the project, it is very hard to know if the project will turn out to be a resource black hole or an informational holy grail.

Another problem with BI systems is asking the wrong questions. Clearly some of the questions being asked at CBI in the opening scenario about worker productivity are not good questions. Oftentimes, the poor questions are due to a lack of understanding of the process by the analyst. While poor questions lead to poor results, every BI success involves valuable questions. A wise person once said that questions are more important than answers. You will be rewarded in the future for asking good questions, so please take every opportunity to practice that skill while you are still in school.

A third problem occurs if analysts do not sufficiently collaborate with end users to find out what the end users need or to understand their exact problems. The analysts rush to analysis—their favorite work—and do not listen closely to the users.

A fourth problem common with analysts, and even end users, is too much trust in the validity of the data or analysis. Just as the explosion of news sources has led to "fake news," "fake analysis" is becoming more frequent with the explosion of analysis, and both require a dose of skepticism. Good skepticism is about determining not if an analysis is true or false but whether its assumptions are reasonable. Every analysis depends on assumptions that are often ignored. Good analysts and end users must not forget to question assumptions. They should ask questions like "Why was this KPI used?," "What other measures are available?," "Why does this measure mean that?," "Why does this measure mean we should do that?," and "What other reasonable explanations are there?" Learn to be skeptical; not all assumptions are valid.

Finally, analysts, and again end users, have analytical biases that can lead to problems. These analytical biases are not biases about race or sports teams but biases that affect reasoning, even the reasoning of experts. Biases have been identified by research on behavioral decision making, biases that affect us when we examine data. One bias is overconfidence—we are more confident in our judgment than we should be. Another is availability—we think certain results will occur more often than they actually do if it is easier to remember that event. A third is belief perseverance—we inordinately persist in earlier beliefs even if valid data is presented to us to change our minds. The overconfidence bias is demonstrated in the MIS InClass exercise. We are all biased, but some of us know it.

LEADERS The last group of people we consider here are the leaders of the organization. Leaders may not provide adequate objectives to BI projects, they may inadequately fund them, and they may not adequately staff them. Another problem is that they may not understand the statistics used in the analysis or the assumptions that the analyst had to make, causing the leaders to misinterpret or overstate the results. Leaders can also contribute to BI pushback by overselling the potential of a BI system. BI will not often transform a business with a shocking finding. More often, BI confirms intuition and leads to steady improvements in processes, such as packing trucks more efficiently, rescheduling robot forklifts, and tweaking pricing algorithms.

To conclude, most of the risks of BI systems can be attributed to either data or people. While most of this chapter identified the virtues of using BI, knowing the risks may be more valuable to you. Being able to help your future business identify sources of difficulty will be greatly appreciated.

Q12-8 ▶ How Does SAP Do BI?

A wide variety of vendors provide software that supports BI activities. The major vendors with apps supporting all three BI activities are shown in the top of Figure 12-29; vendors that support just the analysis and presentation activities are shown in the bottom.

As shown in Figure 12-29, SAP provides IS that support all three activities. They group these products into reporting and data mining applications. The SAP reporting applications are Crystal Reports and Web Intelligence, while its data mining app is Lumira. Lumira is used in the tutorial in Appendix 12A. Like all ERP systems, SAP consolidates operational data in an OLTP database. Data from the OLTP or from other sources can be extracted and placed into the SAP OLAP database, which SAP calls a data warehouse, or Business Warehouse (BW). Once in the warehouse, the data is formed into information cubes like the one shown in Figure 12-12.

A company that implements SAP can also choose to write program code to accomplish specific BI tasks that SAP does not provide. Approximately 95 percent of this program code is devoted to creating company-specific BI reports.

SAP and the other ERP vendors also make it possible to analyze data with software from other companies. One common method is to download data from SAP data warehouses into an Excel file and then use Excel to analyze the data. We provide data from CBI for analysis in Excel in Application Exercise 8-1 at the end of the textbook.

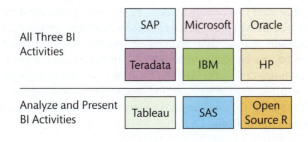

All Three BI Activities	SAP	Microsoft	Oracle
	Teradata	IBM	HP
Analyze and Present BI Activities	Tableau	SAS	Open Source R

FIGURE 12-29

Major BI Vendors and Products

If Ann at CBI wants to analyze the financial transactions in the SAP database, she has three general options. As just mentioned, she can learn to download data to Excel and conduct the analysis herself. She could also analyze the data using Lumira, or she could request from Cody and the IT department a specific report or dashboard that summarizes the data that she specifies.

Q12-9 2028?

BI use will continue to expand as display technologies improve and Big Data matures. We believe four changes will affect this growth: mobile BI, easier-to-use analysis software for unstructured data, the Internet of Things, and privacy.

Mobile BI

One change that will affect BI is the trend in business toward mobile devices. BI was born in the era of laptop and desktop machines. As mobile devices improve in output sophistication and computing power, BI will increasingly be done on smartphones and other mobile devices. For example, smartphones equipped with a cheap hardware device can evaluate blood samples in field clinics. That device can conduct sophisticated statistical analysis of the blood and provide users interactive diagnostic tools if the blood sample has anomalies. BI will increasingly move out of the office.

Mobile devices such as smartphones, tablets, watches, and other wearables will also create enormous volumes of location-based data (LBD) for businesses and governments to acquire and analyze. We defined LBD in Extension 5 as spatially referenced data, where an object or person is located on a map or reference system. Acquiring and analyzing this flood of new data presents many opportunities. For example, by evaluating the key terms of a text message and the location data of a smartphone used to send it, BI researchers are already able to pinpoint flu outbreaks, the movement of political ideas, the loneliness of individuals, and the eating habits of users.[14] LBD from participating shoppers at Walmart stores across the country help suppliers see how often shoppers stop and consider their products displayed on Walmart shelves. LBD will not only come from smartphones and devices we carry, it will come from the emerging widespread use of drones. Drones will provide businesses and governments new opportunities to acquire and analyze data on vehicle traffic, weather patterns, and agricultural production.

Easier-to-Use Analysis Software for Unstructured Data

One the three Vs in Big Data is variety; one reason Big Data is growing is the data being stored and analyzed is not just structured data such as words and numbers but also unstructured data from video, image, and relational data. Currently the methods, techniques, and procedures for acquiring and analyzing unstructured data are new, expensive, and limited to only highly technically trained analysts. As this unstructured data world matures, more and more traditional end users will be able to analyze and present results from unstructured data.

Internet of Things

The emerging Internet of Things will also have a big impact on BI by 2028. **Internet of Things** is a vision of everyday objects connected to the Internet and interacting with other devices, applications, and services, many of which without requiring human input. Devices will include home appliances, heart implants, microchips in farm animals, DNA sensors, vehicles, wearable healthcare monitors, keys, waste receptacles, parking spaces, and store shelves. Some estimate the number of connected devices will exceed 50 billion objects by 2020. Many of these "things" will use **radio-frequency identification (RFID)** technology, tags as small as a grain of rice on the object that broadcast data to receivers that can display and record the data.

One example of why BI will grow with IoT is the potential to improve processes. Both individuals and machines will analyze data. Automated systems will reduce energy costs of home appliances such as lights, air conditioners, washers, hair dryers, and ovens by reducing energy use, during peak cost times during the day. On a larger scale, for a city's public transportation system, devices in vehicles, smartphones, traffic lights, and parking spaces will share data so that human drivers analyzing the data can make better decisions and traffic lights can continuously adjust to changing traffic flows.

An example of a significant business commitment to IoT is GE's Industrial Internet, whose goal is to supply smart, connected devices to industries including medical care, energy production, aviation, railroads, and manufacturing. Microsoft has added 30,000 devices to its campus in Washington to monitor energy use and improve security, reducing energy costs 6 to 10 percent a year. Imagine the energy savings to your university if every room had a device that would control lighting, heating, and cooling for every minute of every day. Connected smart devices will simply make things better.

Privacy

We defined privacy in Chapter 11 as controlling how one's personal data is acquired and analyzed. In Chapter 11, we discussed privacy and social media conflicts; with BI, we can see that privacy concerns extend beyond social media and may affect many business processes that use customer data. In the opening vignette, CBI's Ann and Cody were snooping on network traffic use by other employees without informing them of their actions. As BI grows and improves, it will better predict human behavior, particularly when it can exploit personal data.

Earlier we discussed the benefits of BI for Target's New Customer process. However, after about a year of success for this program, a man in Minneapolis walked into a Target store and complained to the manager that his high school daughter got Target coupons for baby clothes and cribs. According to the father, his daughter was not pregnant and he did not appreciate Target's invasion of her privacy. The manager expressed regret at the obvious oversight. A few days later, the man called back and apologized. His daughter was, in fact, pregnant. Many people do not want organizations to know more about their behavior and their likes and dislikes than their parents and their friends.

Colleges collect data to try to reduce the number of dropouts. To help more students stay enrolled, schools are tempted to increase their use of personal data about students. They know that loneliness, social isolation, disconnectedness, and a lack of belonging are factors that lead to leaving school early, and these behaviors can be analyzed and predicted. In the interest of helping you and your classmates stay in school, your university may ask to monitor your use of social media—not the specific messages, just the frequency and variety of the messages and the friends you send them to. Today most students object to such monitoring on privacy grounds, but if such monitoring can be shown to lead to improved mental health or decreased violence, will future college students have the same concern for privacy?

These types of incidents will more frequently occur as BI improves and analysis of personal data becomes more accurate and widespread. Progress and compromise between BI and privacy will likely not be universally consistent; different counties will likely have different requirements and laws. For example, the European Union recently passed the **General Data Protection Regulation (GDPR)**, which regulates the business use of personal data in the EU. The BI–privacy conflict will intensify on many different battlegrounds.

Ethics Guide

Unseen Cyberazzi

A **data broker** or data aggregator is a company that acquires and purchases consumer and other data from public records, retailers, Internet cookie vendors, social media trackers, and other sources and uses it to create business intelligence that it sells to companies and the government.

So, what does it do with all this data? If you buy pizza online on Friday nights, but only if you can get a substantial discount, a data broker (or the broker's customer) knows to send you a discount pizza coupon Friday morning. If you use a customer loyalty card at your local grocery store and regularly buy, say, large bags of potato chips, the data broker or its customer will send you coupons for more potato chips or for a second snack product that is frequently purchased by potato chip consumers.

Of even greater concern, however, is the unknown processing of such data. What business intelligence techniques are employed by these companies? What are the accuracy and reliability of those techniques? If the data broker errs in predicting that you'll buy a pizza on Friday night, who cares? But if the data broker errs in predicting that you're a terrorist, it matters.

DISCUSSION QUESTIONS

1. Using business intelligence applied to consumer purchasing data for targeted marketing seems innocuous enough. However, is it? Using both the categorical imperative (page 43) and utilitarianism (page 18) perspectives, assess the ethics of the following:
   a. Some people, whether from genetic factors, habit, lack of education, or other factors, are prone to over-eating junk food. By focusing junk food sales offers at this market segment, data brokers or their customers are promoting obesity. Is their behavior ethical?
   b. Data brokers claim they can reliably infer ethnicity from consumer behavior data. Suppose they also determine that one ethnic group is more likely to attend college than others. Accordingly, they focus the marketing for college-prep materials, scholarships, and university admissions applications on this ethnic group. Over time, that group will be guided into positive (assuming you believe college is positive) decisions that other groups will not. Is this behavior different from ethnic profiling? Is it ethical?
2. If all of your behavior is ethical, then, according to the categorical imperative, you are willing to have your life story published on Facebook. Thus, you needn't be concerned about the data and business intelligence created about you. However, consider the following:
   a. Suppose, as the most junior member of a club, you are required to purchase beer for your club's bi-monthly beer fest. To obtain a substantial discount from the vendor, you use your customer loyalty card for these purchases. A data aggregator obtains your purchase history and classifies you as a heavy drinker. Unknown to you, the data aggregator informs your medical insurance company of its classification. Your insurance premiums increase and you never know why. Using either the categorical imperative or utilitarianism, is there an ethical problem here?
   b. Do you think something should be done to reduce the likelihood of situations like that in question a? If so, what?
   c. Suppose you have a personal medical problem that you wish to keep private. Your condition requires you to purchase a particular set of off-the-shelf products from the pharmacy at your grocery store. A data aggregator observes your purchasing pattern, infers your problem, and sends you coupons and other promotional products that clearly identify your condition. Against your strongest wishes, your roommates become aware of your medical problem. Using either the categorical imperative or utilitarianism, is there an ethical problem here?
   d. Do you think something should be done to reduce the likelihood of situations like that in question c? If so, what?
3. Assume lawmakers will soon write legislation to limit the behavior of aggregators. Specify two actions the law should prohibit, and identify the positive and negative consequences of each of the two.

Source: Sergey Nivens/Shutterstock

ACTIVE REVIEW

Use this Active Review to verify that you understand the material in the chapter. You can read the entire chapter and then perform the tasks in this review, or you can read the text material for just one question and perform the tasks in this review for that question before moving on to the next one.

Q12-1 What is business intelligence, and why is it important to business?

Describe the quantity of data in today's business environment and its five major sources. Explain the Business Intelligence process and its major activities. Describe how Target and Netflix are using BI.

Q12-2 What are the objectives of the BI process?

Describe the general effectiveness objective of the BI process and the two specific objectives. Explain the efficiency objective of the BI process.

Q12-3 What are the key components of a business intelligence IS?

Explain the functions of a BI server and its key feature. Describe how BI software has recently changed. Explain what is stored in a data warehouse and the difference between an OLTP and OLAP database. Describe how the procedures for the Acquiring activity differ from the Analyze and Publish activities. Explain how informing depends on people, and describe the two types of people that use a BI system.

Q12-4 How do BI information systems support BI activities?

Explain why operational data is typically not used for BI. Describe the sources of data in a data warehouse. Describe a data mart and explain why it might be used. Explain how the two types of analysis—reporting and data mining—differ. Describe the types of operations that are done with data in reporting. Explain the two examples of reporting. Describe in your own words slicing, dicing, drill down, and rollup. Explain regression, MBA analysis, and text mining and provide an example. Define *publishing* and *digital dashboards* and explain how dashboards are used with business processes.

Q12-5 How can BI information systems support business processes?

Explain KPIs and give an example. Name several business processes supported by BI information systems. Describe how the Google search engine supports your Decision Making process. Explain how machine maintenance can be improved with BI. Describe the objective of the NBO process. Explain how Google Analytics supports the Online Sales process. Describe the three new processes supported by BI information systems.

Q12-6 What is a Big Data BI system, and how is it used?

Name the three ways that Big Data systems differ from routine data systems. Explain briefly the history of Big Data systems. Describe how NoSQL MapReduce, Hadoop, and In-Memory handle large datasets. Explain how several processes are supported by Big Data BI systems and include several new processes.

Q12-7 How do businesses manage the risks of business intelligence?

Describe the problems of dirty data and data with missing elements. Explain how nonintegrated data leads to problems. Define granularity and how granularity can be incorrect for BI use. Name the four BI problems associated with end users and give an example. Describe the types of problems attributed to BI analysts. Explain how top management in an organization can create BI problems.

Q12-8 How does SAP do BI?

Describe two BI applications available with SAP. Explain the major use of SAP program code. Describe the three options for users to analyze SAP data.

Q12-9 2028?

Name and describe the three factors that will affect BI growth in the next 10 years. Explain how mobile apps will affect BI. Give an example of unstructured data in BI. Describe the Internet of Things and the devices it includes. Define *privacy* and explain how it will affect BI.

KEY TERMS AND CONCEPTS

A/B testing   351
Analysis   342
Assessment   338
Auditing process   355
Big Data   352
Business intelligence   336
Business intelligence system   336
Clickstream data   357
Conversion rate   351
Cross-selling   347
Dashboard   349
Data broker   362
Data driven   336
Data mart   342
Data mining   346
Data warehouse   339
Decision Making process   350

Decision support systems (DSS)   337
Dimension   344
Dirty data   356
Drill down   345
General Data Protection Regulation
   (GDPR)   361
Granularity   357
Hadoop   354
Index   350
Internet of Things   360
MapReduce   353
Market basket analysis (MBA)   347
Measure   344
Next Best Offer (NBO) process   350
NoSQL database   353
Online analytical processing
   (OLAP)   340

Online transactional processing
   (OLTP)   340
Operational database   339
Prediction   338
Radio-frequency identification
   (RFID)   360
Regression analysis   346
Reporting   343
RFM   343
SAP HANA   354
Self-service BI   339
Sentiment analysis   347
Slicing and dicing   343
Supervised data mining   347
Text mining   347
Unsupervised data mining   347
Visualization   348

USING YOUR KNOWLEDGE

12-1. Reread the two examples at the beginning of the chapter
MyLab MIS   that involved Target and Netflix. Specify the process
that BI improves at each firm and a second process that
BI could support. Explain the measures you would use
to demonstrate how the BI example would improve the
effectiveness or efficiency of the process.

12-2. Create a BPMN diagram of a Managerial process that
MyLab MIS   can be supported by the Informing process. As in question 12-1, specify objectives and measures for that
Managerial process and explain how the Informing
process will improve those measures.

12-3. Reflect on the differences between reporting and data
MyLab MIS   mining. What are their similarities and differences?
How do their costs differ? What benefits does each
offer? How would an organization choose between
these two?

12-4. Go to Tableau.com and inspect example visualizations
made with Tableau. In your opinion, what are three
features or attributes of a good visualization?

12-5. You are the director of student activities at your university. Recently, some students have charged that your
department misallocates its resources. They claim the
allocation is based on outdated student preferences.
Funds are given to activities that few students find
attractive, and insufficient funds are allocated to new
activities in which students do want to participate.
Describe how you could use reporting and/or data
mining to assess this claim.

12-6. In this chapter, we say that questions are more important than answers. Look at Figures 12-12, 12-13, and

12-14 and write down questions you have that might
reveal patterns in the data shown in these figures.

12-7. Reread the opening scenario. CBI owns the computers, and workers should be productive with their time,
but how did you react to the story? Do you think that
CBI should know how employees use the network?
Is it ethical to snoop on employee behavior? Assume
that CBI wants to collect data on network misuse.
Suggest measures that CBI could use to assess
network misuse.

12-8. The following sayings about data and information
are often used in business to convey an important
idea. As you read these, select three and write down
how they could be used to convey an idea from this
chapter:

> "If you want a green suit, turn on a green light."
> "You don't fatten the pig by weighing it."
> "Not everything that counts can be counted, and not
> everything that can be counted counts."
> "Statistics are no substitute for judgment . . . and
> vice versa."
> "Without data, you're just another person with an
> opinion."
> "It ain't so much the things we know that get us in
> trouble, it's the things we know that just ain't so."

12-9. Go to Google Trends (*www.google.com/trends*) and
enter the terms *Big Data, BigData, NoSQL, MapReduce,
Hadoop,* and *in-memory systems* to see how their popularity has grown recently.

COLLABORATION EXERCISE 12

Collaborate with a group of students to answer the following questions. For this exercise do not meet face to face. Your task will be easier if you coordinate your work with SharePoint, Office 365, Google Docs or equivalent collaboration tools. (See Chapter 10 for a discussion of collaboration tools and processes.) Your answers should reflect the thinking of the entire group, not just that of one or two individuals.

Mary Keeling owns and operates Carbon Creek Gardens, a retailer of trees, garden plants, perennial and annual flowers, and bulbs. "The Gardens," as her customers call it, also sells bags of soil, fertilizer, small garden tools, and garden sculptures.

Mary started the business 16 years ago when she bought a section of land that, because of water drainage, was unsuited for residential development. With hard work and perseverance, Mary has created a warm and inviting environment with a unique and carefully selected inventory of plants. The Gardens has become a favorite nursery for serious gardeners in her community.

"The problem," she says, "is that I've grown so large, I've lost track of my customers. The other day, I ran into Tootsie Swan at the grocery store, and I realized I hadn't seen her in ages. I said something like, 'Hi, Tootsie, I haven't seen you for a while,' and that statement unleashed an angry torrent from her. It turns out that she'd been in over a year ago and had wanted to return a plant. One of my part-time employees waited on her and had apparently insulted her, or at least didn't give her the service she wanted. So, she decided not to come back to The Gardens.

"Tootsie was one of my best customers. I'd lost her, and I didn't even know it! That really frustrates me. Is it inevitable that as I get bigger, I lose track of my customers? I don't think so.

"Somehow, I have to find out when regular customers aren't coming around. Had I known Tootsie had stopped shopping with us, I'd have called her to see what was going on. I need customers like her. I've got all sorts of data in my sales database. It seems like the insight I need is in there, but how do I get it out?" In this exercise, you will apply the knowledge of this chapter to Mary Keeling's problem.

1. Mary wants to know when she's lost a customer. One way to help her would be to produce a report, say in PDF format, showing the top 50 customers from the prior year. Mary could print that report or place it on a private section of her Web site so that she can download it from wherever she happens to be.

   Periodically—say, once a week—Mary could request a report that shows the top buyers for that week. That report could also be in PDF format, or it could just be produced onscreen. Mary could compare the two reports to determine who is missing. If she wonders whether a customer such as Tootsie has been ordering, she could request a query report on Tootsie's activities. Describe the advantages and disadvantages of this solution.

2. Describe the best possible application of an OLAP tool at Carbon Creek. Can it be used to solve the lost customer problem? Why or why not? What is the best way, if any, for Mary to use OLAP at Carbon Creek? If none, explain why.

3. Describe the best possible application of RFM analysis at Carbon Creek. Can it be used to solve the lost customer problem? Why or why not? What is the best way, if any, for Mary to use RFM at Carbon Creek? If none, explain why.

4. Describe the best possible application of text mining at Carbon Creek. Can it be used to solve the lost customer problem? Why or why not? What is the best way, if any, for Mary to use text mining at Carbon Creek? If none, explain why.

5. For questions 2 to 4, describe one PowerPivot chart that Mary should create to help her. Specify the variable on each axis and the measures displayed.

6. Which of the analysis options in this exercise will provide Mary the best value? If you owned Carbon Creek Gardens and were going to implement just one of these analysis options, which would you choose? Why?

CASE STUDY 12

Pizza and Big Data

A California newspaper has a data dilemma. To understand both sides of the dilemma, we provide a little history with names changed to protect privacy. In 2013, Sarah Smith was brutally raped outside Corleone's Pizzeria in Bakersfield. As would be expected, the local newspaper, the *Bakersfield Examiner*, ran a number of stories about the event over the next 6 months as investigators worked on the crime and charged the suspect and a court

convicted him. In virtually every story, the name of the pizzeria and the name of the alleged criminal were frequently mentioned.

Now, five years later, Corleone's Pizzeria has asked the newspaper to remove the pizzeria's name from the articles about the incident that are still available on the newspaper's Web site. Michael Corleone, the owner, has realized that when his restaurant is Googled, the top three returns have headlines about the rape, not the restaurant. He claims this is unfair to his restaurant that had no responsibility for the crime. The rape, not the restaurant, appears in search results for the restaurant because many other newspapers and Web articles about the crime link to the *Examiner*'s reports that include the name of the pizzeria.

Ryan Jones, the editor of the newspaper, is concerned about the impact of removing the location data. The rape did in fact occur very near that restaurant. If he removes the name, and another rape occurs and investigators find that the location was a factor—perhaps the lighting is poor or the neighborhood is dangerous—he will regret removing the location and the warning about potential danger contained in the location data. He also feels he is committed to being a source of facts for the public record. Now and in the future, many reporters and criminal experts will want to read the details of the investigation, perhaps sparking new insights about other crimes.

Further, if he decides to remove this information, does he remove all stories about the rape or just the location? What about all the other crime locations his paper has chronicled? Does he remove them after a period? Or does he make some other rule—perhaps based on the severity of the crime? He also considers just removing the restaurant name but leaving the address. All these ideas conjure up challenges in his mind about how to be fair to everyone. Also, what about the criminals? Every time a criminal's name is Googled, should their crimes be shown? Forever? In addition to concerns about businesses, maybe criminals have a right to be forgotten at some point.

The dilemma for the newspaper persists. Remove the name and significantly help the individual restaurant; keep the restaurant name and help society in a minor way. Is fact accuracy more important than how that fact is used by the public? What would you do as the paper editor? As BI tools allow the paper editor as well as the rest of us to record more and more data and the power to sift through it, these new questions arise.

The editor is also the owner of a radio station. During a recent fire, his reporter described a major road near the fire as being open, even though the reporter knew the local fire department declared it closed to vehicle traffic. The reporter wanted residents near the road to know that it was in fact available for evacuation, but the fire department wanted exclusive use of the road to move firefighters and equipment; as it turns out, the department's ability to fight the fire was reduced due to the traffic caused by the radio station's report. The state's firefighting agencies contacted the station owner and requested that the station in the future only report the official road closures. Just as in the pizzeria dilemma, Mr. Jones faces a data issue—is accuracy of data more important than how it is used?

12-10. What policy would you make if you were the editor/owner in each of the two situations?
   a. Explain why you chose that policy.
   b. Specify both the positive and negative outcomes of your choices.

12-11. Describe a policy that would cover other similar situations.

12-12. Who else acquires, analyzes, or publishes public data like this? Do they also need to make new rules?

12-13. Do customers have a right to be forgotten at some point? How would you write that policy for a supermarket that collects customer data in a loyalty program and for a pharmacy?

12-14. Healthcare agencies also struggle with this data dilemma. Describe two scenarios in which a patient's healthcare data could lead to a conflict between personal interests and the interests of the public.

12-15. Apply the two ethical principles used in the text—the categorical imperative and utilitarianism. For each scenario, apply both principles and explain what Mr. Jones should do based on each principle.

CHAPTER RESOURCES

[1] Eve Tahmincioglu, "CEO Advice for Grads: Travel, Learn, Follow Your Passion," *Today Money,* last modified June 5, 2012, www.today.com/money/ceo-advice-grads-travel-learn-follow-your-passion-813915.

[2] Eric Schmidt quoted in Klint Finley, "Was Eric Schmidt Wrong About the Historical Scale of the Internet?," *ReadWrite,* last modified February 7, 2011, http://readwrite.com/2011/02/07/are-we-really-creating-as-much#awesm=~obSZrnBnJCJKOy.

[3] Andrew McAfee and Erik Brynjolfsson, "Big Data: The Management Revolution," *Harvard Business Review,* last modified October 2012, http://hbr.org/2012/10/big-data-the-management-revolution; Thomas H. Davenport, Paul Barth, and Randy Bean, "How Big Data Is Different," *MIT Sloan Management Review* Fall 2012, http://sloanreview.mit.edu/article/how-big-data-is-different/; and Josh Constine, "How Big Is Facebook's Data? 2.5 Billion Pieces of Content and 500+ Terabytes Ingested Every Day," *Techcrunch,* August 22, 2012 http://techcrunch.com/2012/08/22/how-big-is-facebooks-data-2-5-billion-pieces-of-content-and-500-terabytes-ingested-every-day/.

[4] *The Wall Street Journal Online,* http://online.wsj.com/article/SB10001424127887323751104578147311334491922.html, accessed October 10, 2013.

[5] www.mckinsey.com/business-functions/mckinsey-analytics/our-insights/the-age-of-analytics-competing-in-a-data-driven-world.

[6] Charles Duhigg, "How Companies Learn Your Secrets," *The New York Times,* last modified February 16, 2012, www.nytimes.com/2012/02/19/magazine/shopping-habits.html?_r=2&hp=&pagewanted=all&.

[7] Dave Rich and Jeanne G. Harris, "Why Predictive Analytics Is a Game-Changer," *Forbes,* last modified April 1, 2010, www.forbes.com/2010/04/01/analytics-best-buy-technology-data-companies-10-accenture.html.

[8] Visit and interact with this viz at *http://blogs.wsj.com/venturecapital/2009/08/25/how-long-does-it-take-to-build-a-technology-empire/*.

[9] Thomas Davenport, *Enterprise Analytics* (New York: FT Press, 2013).

[10] James Manyika et al., "Big Data: The Next Frontier for Innovation, Competition, and Productivity," *McKinsey Global Institute,* last modified May 2011, www.mckinsey.com/mgi/publications/big_data/index.asp.

[11] www.informationweek.com/big-data/big-data-analytics-market-to-hit-$203-billion-in-2020-/d/d-id/1327092.

[12] A nonprofit corporation that supports open source software projects, originally those for the Apache Web server, but today for a large number of additional major software projects.

[13] Derek Klobucher, "Big Data Can Save Lives—If Culture and Strategy Let It," *Forbes,* last modified February 21, 2013, www.forbes.com/sites/sap/2013/02/21/big-data-can-save-lives-if-culture-and-strategy-let-it/.

[14] Robert Hotz, "The Really Smart Phone," *Wall Street Journal,* April 23, 2011.

MyLab MIS

Go to **MyLab MIS.com** for Auto-graded writing questions as well as the following Assisted-graded writing questions:

12-16. Using Figure 12-18, the Example Tableau Visualization, explain your answers to the following: Is this an example of reporting or data mining, give an example of a data problem that may exist in this database, and a people problem.

12-17. Go to https://trends.google.com and enter a variety of search terms in the Explore Topics box. What business processes could be supported by this BI and which process objectives could be improved? Is this BI an example of reporting or data mining, explain your answer.

APPENDIX 12—SAP BUSINESS INTELLIGENCE TUTORIAL

This tutorial allows you to practice analyzing a large dataset using one of SAP's BI applications. This application, Lumira, is designed for non-IS professionals to analyze a dataset and publish interactive graphical visualizations. While it supports advanced data mining techniques, this introductory tutorial will use its simple reporting operations such as sort, filter, group, calculate, and graph.

This tutorial is not a process tutorial like the tutorials after Chapters 8 and 9. Instead, it shows how to do several of the operations, and then it asks you to use those operations to answer a set of questions.

The example we will use is a very large dataset of sales transactions from the Global Bike Company. Your instructor will provide you with this dataset, which is an Excel file with tens of thousands of transactions.[1] These transaction records include measures such as revenue and quantity as well as dimensions such as year, customer name, and country. Analysts use this data to analyze trends in revenue by year, to calculate sales of each material, and to obtain answers to other questions.

1. Obtain a free Lumira account

Go to http://saplumira.com/try-it-free/ and create a free account.

2. Upload your Excel data

Click on Try with Samples in the blue box at the bottom left, and the screen in Figure 12A-1 will appear.

FIGURE 12A-1

First Screen

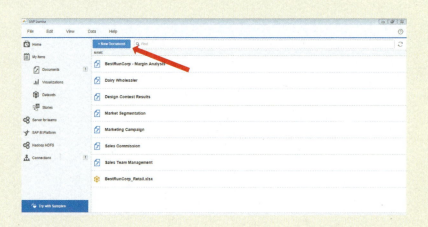

Click on +New Document in the top part of the screen as indicated by the red arrow in Figure 12A-1; then from the Select a Source Menu, click on Microsoft Excel and Next. Find the GBI_Dataset.xlsx file provided by your instructor and select it. Figure 12A-2 will appear. Make sure you click on "Set first row as column names" as indicated by the red arrow in Figure 12A-2. Then click on Create.

[1]This file is GBI_Dataset.xlsx. Instructors can obtain this file from the SAP University Alliance BI Workspace.

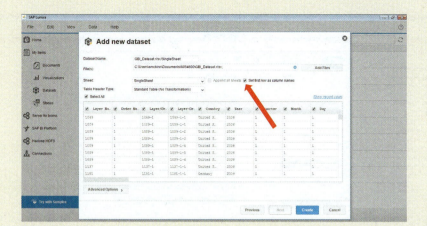

FIGURE 12A-2
Loading Data

3. Create your first visualization

When Lumira has loaded your data, the Visualize screen in Figure 12A-3 will appear. There are six areas highlighted:

1. Measures
2. Dimensions
3. Graph Option
4. Current Graph X Axis Variable
5. Current Graph Y Axis Variable
6. Current Graph

FIGURE 12A-3
Lumira Features

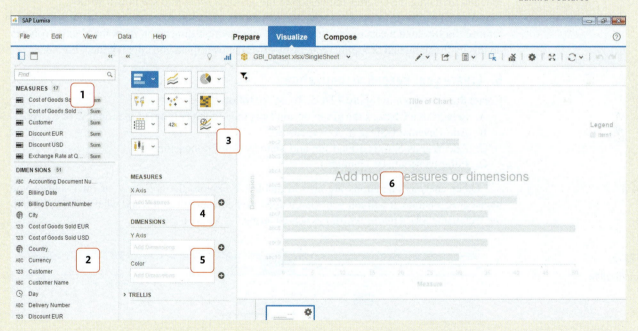

Area 1 lists measures available to the analyst to select. A measure is data that can be summed, averaged, or processed. Dimensions, which are characteristics or attributes such as Country and Year, are shown in Area 2. Area 3 offers a number of graphing options; the default is the bar chart. Areas 4 and 5, currently empty, allow the analyst to specify the data for the x- and y-axis of the current viz, which is shown in Area 6.

Create your first visualization as shown in Figure 12A-4. First drag the Year dimension (identified by the bottom red arrow) to the Y Axis box, and then drag the Revenue USD measure (top red arrow) to the X Axis box.

FIGURE 12A-4

First Visualization

4. Explore other features

Other options are available and are marked on Figure 12A-4. (1) Use the Filter option (above to the left of the main viz) to select just a subset of the data to view, for example, just the years 2010 and 2012. (2) A second common activity is to analyze multiple measures. To add the Unit Cost of Goods Sold USD as a second measure, drag it from the measures list and place it with Revenue USD in the X Axis box. (3) You can also sort the data so the tallest bar chart is on the top. The sort icon looks like a column graph with 123 bars. (4) The trellis option (below Legend Color) allows you to see more data; first expand the Trellis box by clicking on the arrow to its left, and then drag the Quarter dimension to the Trellis Row box to see how it works.

   We will use these features to create the second visualization. Before we begin the second viz, remove the Revenue measure from the X Axis and the Year dimension from the Y axis. You can do this by dragging and dropping them or by hovering over them and clicking the x button.

5. Create your second visualization

Create the viz shown in Figure 12A-5. To do so, follow these steps.

    A. Select Area Chart as the graph option (it is the second column in the top row of charts).

    B. Add Revenue USD as Y Axis measure.

    C. Add Year as X Axis dimension and State as Color dimension.

    D. Filter by Month 01 (January).

   Other analysis operations are also available, so explore the app on your own—when you mouse over a button, it will tell you what it does. To learn about Lumira and what it can do, search the Web using *SAP Lumira tutorial* as search terms.

FIGURE 12A-5

Second Visualization

6. Analysis

To practice with the simple operations explained above, answer the following questions. The first 5 answers are shown so you can check your work:

1. Graph Revenue USD (Y-axis), Year (X-axis). Which year has lowest revenue?
2. How much revenue (in USD) was received in 2006?
3. How much revenue was received from the lowest customer?
4. Filter by Year 2010. How much revenue was received from the lowest customer in 2010?
5. How much revenue was received from the lowest customer in the US in 2010?
6. Which quarter has lowest EUR revenue?
7. Which month has greatest quantity for Beantown Bikes?
8. Place Revenue (USD) in Y axis, Month in X axis, and Material Master Description in Legend. Which material generated more revenue in March than February (of the eight top-selling materials)?
9. How much revenue USD has been created by each of the two Divisions (AS and BI)?
10. Which year had the highest cost of goods sold USD?
11. There are four Sales Org Descriptions—US East and West and Germany North and South. Which has the highest and which has the lowest quantity?
12. For the year 2012, what is the revenue EUR in Germany North?
13. Using Material Master, which material has the greatest revenue USD?
14. Make a bubble chart with Price, Quantity, and Revenue as Measures and Year as the Dimension. What do you notice?
15. Make a heat map and then a tree map of revenue and month. Which do you prefer?

2013
$48,211,692.67
Motown Bikes $3,573,742
Ostseerad $250,347.77
Beantown Bikes $2,835,075

For more practice, write questions for other students and try to answer theirs.

For graphing practice, create a graph and then show a fellow student; try to make the graph the other student shows you.

Information Systems Careers

Have you thought about a career in IS? You might be surprised at the types of jobs in IS, that your talents match those jobs, and the opportunities presented by starting your career in IS. Here we try to make the case that you should consider it by describing the factors in the economy that are creating demand for IS graduates, the skills required for IS-related jobs, the types of jobs available for IS graduates, and the best aspects of IS jobs.

Before we start, two important clarifications: First, in the business world, most jobs for IS graduates are labeled "IT jobs." Few professionals are called IS professionals; instead they are more often called IT professionals. As a result, many students don't realize the great variety of IT jobs that are waiting for IS graduates. Second, many students believe all IT jobs require lots of programming or other highly technical skills. **Computer science graduates** are skilled programmers who take many highly technical classes. On the other hand, IS graduates are business school graduates who apply collaboration skills and business knowledge to technical challenges. More specifically, **IS graduates**:

> work with business partners to understand processes and requirements in order to design solutions that solve practical day-to-day problems and increasingly lead digital innovation. They then coordinate with computer scientists and engineers to build and implement the solutions and platforms.

IS programs do not emphasize programming skills. The other main difference between a computer science and IS education is that IS programs require many non-IS business school courses so that IS graduates can collaborate effectively with sales, accounting, and supply chain professionals. Computer science programs require many computer science courses so that graduates can master technical challenges.

Computer science and IS are both **STEM** (science, technology, engineering, and math) programs. Graduates of both types of programs are needed in businesses.

QE1-1 ▸ What Is the Employment Environment Like for IS Graduates?

In the current information economy, the role of IT is growing. As a result, job prospects for IS graduates are very bright. Use of new technologies such as social media, Big Data, AI, VR, 3D printing, the Internet of Things, drones, driverless cars, the cloud, and large-scale ERP systems grows year over year. While these new technologies are creating demand for IS graduates, growth is also the result of cheaper data storage, low-cost cloud options, increasing mobile use, and unprecedented security challenges. In addition to these technical drivers, other business factors are driving up demand for IS graduates. Many firms are increasing their in-house IT staff due to dissatisfaction with outsourcing and offshoring solutions, many IT professionals hired during the Y2K boom are approaching retirement, and many firms have not hired sufficiently during the past decade and are now hiring at a high rate to make up for lost time. All these factors have created a very promising employment situation for IT professionals, as shown in Figure CE1-1. That figure displays the Bureau of Labor Statistics forecast of a 12 percent growth in computer-related jobs.

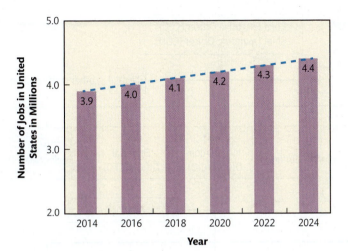

A final consideration in the IT employment environment is the role of international students. Many IS and computer science graduates are not U.S. citizens. The U.S. government grants visas to only a subset of these students. As a result, as many as 20 percent of current students in IS or computer science programs may not be able to take jobs in the United States.

In this promising job environment, IS graduates with appropriate skills will succeed. To have success in this career field, graduates will need to demonstrate the four employability skills introduced in Chapter 1: abstract reasoning, systems thinking, collaboration, and ability to experiment. These skills and examples of their application in an IT job are listed in Figure CE1-2.

QE1-2 ▶ What Are the Duties and Titles of IT Jobs?

Having outlined the general employment situation and some of the general skills needed in an IT job, let's be more specific about the duties and job titles an IS graduate will encounter. To examine the job opportunities for IS graduates consider the typical organization depicted in Figure CE1-3.

Figure CE1-3 shows typical top-level reporting relationships. As you will learn in your management classes, organizational structure varies depending on the organization's size, culture, competitive environment, industry, and other factors. Larger organizations with independent divisions will have a group of senior executives such as those shown here for each division. Smaller companies may combine some of these departments. Consider the structure in Figure CE1-3 as typical.

Abstract Reasoning
• An IS systems analyst creates a model of what end users want a new IS to deliver.

Systems Thinking
• A security analyst evaluates how the firm's data will enter and exit the cloud.

Collaboration
• A data analyst communicates with users to get the right data into and out of a database.

Ability to Experiment
• A web developer makes several pages to see which one customers use most effectively.

FIGURE CE1-2
Four Employability Skills and IS Tasks

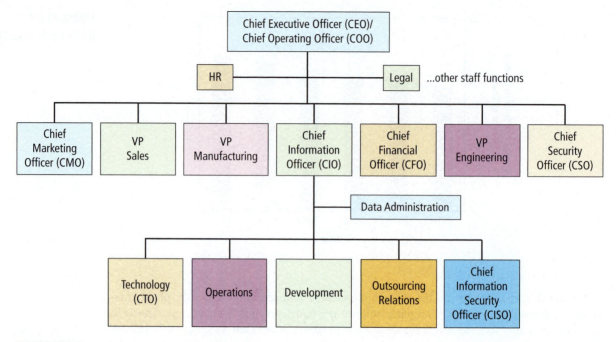

FIGURE CE1-3

Typical Senior-Level Reporting Relationships[1]

The title of the principal manager of the IS department varies from organization to organization. A common title is **chief information officer,** or **CIO.** Other common titles are *vice president of information services, director of information services*, and, less commonly, *director of computer services*. The CIO manages the IS department, communicates with the firm's executive team on IT issues, and is a member of an executive group.

In Figure CE1-3, the CIO, like other senior executives, reports to the *chief executive officer* (CEO), though sometimes these executives report to the *chief operating officer* (COO), who, in turn, reports to the CEO. In some companies, the CIO reports to the *chief financial officer* (CFO). That reporting arrangement might make sense if the primary information systems support only accounting and finance activities. In organizations such as manufacturing that operate significant non-accounting information systems, the arrangement shown in Figure CE1-3 is more common and effective.

The structure of the IS department also varies among organizations. Figure CE1-3 shows a typical IS department with five groups and a data administration staff function. Most IS departments include a *Technology* office that investigates new information systems technologies and determines how the organization can benefit from them. For example, today many organizations are investigating voice recognition, robotics, and cloud opportunities and planning how they can use them to better accomplish their goals and objectives. An individual called the **chief technology officer,** or **CTO,** often heads the technology group. The CTO evaluates new technologies, new ideas, and new capabilities and identifies those that are most relevant to the organization. The CTO's job requires deep knowledge of information technology and the ability to envision and innovate applications for the organization.

The next group in Figure CE1-3, *Operations,* manages the computing infrastructure, including individual computers, in-house server farms, networks, and communications media. This group includes system and network administrators. As you will learn, an important function for this group is to monitor the user experience and respond to user problems.

The third group in the IS department in Figure CE1-3 is *Development.* This group manages the process of creating new information systems as well as maintaining existing ones. The size and structure of the development group depend on whether programs are developed in-house. If not, this department will be staffed primarily by business and systems analysts who work with users, operations, and vendors to acquire and install licensed software and to set up the system components around that software. If the organization develops programs in-house, this department will include programmers, test engineers, technical writers, and other development personnel.

The fourth IS department group in Figure CE1-3 is *Outsourcing Relations*. This group exists in organizations that have negotiated outsourcing agreements with other companies to provide equipment, applications, or other services.

The final department group in Figure CE1-3 is *IS Security*. This group is typically led by the **chief information security officer**, or **CISO**. The CISO designs and leads the organization's information security program while managing IS security personnel. The information security program protects the security of information systems and ensures the confidentiality of company data while also making the secure data available to the appropriate end users.

Figure CE1-3 also includes a *Data Administration* staff function. The purpose of this group is to protect data and information assets by establishing data standards and data management practices and policies.

There are many variations on the structure of the IS department shown in Figure CE1-3. In larger organizations, the operations group may itself consist of several different departments. Sometimes, there is a separate group for business intelligence.

QE1-3 ▶ What IS-Related Job Positions Exist?

Having considered the top IT jobs in organizations and how the IS department is organized in a typical large firm, let's now consider the specific jobs that IS graduates perform during their careers. Figure CE1-4 summarizes the major job positions. The median annual wage of computer-related jobs in 2015 was $81,400 compared to the national average of $36,200.

Many of the positions in Figure CE1-4 have a wide salary range. Lower salaries are for professionals with limited experience or for those who work in smaller companies or on small projects. The higher salaries are for those with deep knowledge and experience who work for large companies on large projects. Do not expect to begin your career at the high end of these ranges.

Several of the jobs listed in Figure CE1-4 are general job titles that combine the more specific job titles you may encounter. Some of these more specific job titles include mobile app developer, help desk, social media analyst, and data center manager.

Typically, small to mid-sized firms combine several of the positions listed in Figure CE1-4 into jobs that span several responsibilities. These positions can be quite interesting as these workers are challenged by a wide variety of tasks throughout the workday. These mid-sized to smaller firms employ as many IS graduates as large firms. Finally, a number of these small to mid-sized firms offer unique IT jobs based on their product or service such as consulting, auditing, forensics, and health care.

Many of the jobs listed here are held by professionals who have obtained certifications. A **certification** is a designation earned by an individual that assures the individual can perform a particular job or task. Common certifications for IT jobs include MCSE, CISSP, CCSP, and TERP10. One benefit of obtaining a certificate is that it often raises pay, according to some estimates about 7 percent on average.

If you are interested in reading more about these opportunities, there are several ways to begin. You can visit LinkedIn.com and search for IT professionals using the job titles listed in Figure CE1-4. You can also visit IS career Web pages hosted by the Association of Information Systems or SAP as shown in Figure CE1-5. Other good sites to visit are hosted by Computerjobs, the federal government, and Monster.com. You might also ask your instructor for more options.

A final suggestion: For many jobs, knowledge of a business specialty can add to your marketability. If you have the time, a dual major in college can be an excellent choice. Popular and successful dual majors with IS are accounting, marketing, management, supply chain, or analytics.

Title	Responsibilities	Knowledge and Skills Required	U.S. Salary Range 2017
Business Analyst	Work with business leaders and planners to develop processes and systems that implement strategy and goals.	Knowledge of planning, strategy, process management, and technology. Strong interpersonal and communication skills needed.	$50,000–$100,000
Systems or IT Analyst	Work with users to determine system requirements, design and develop job descriptions and test plans.	Strong collaborative skills and knowledge of both business and technology. Adaptable.	$43,000–$98,000
Security Analyst	Plan and execute security measures to safeguard networks and computers.	Communication skills, tolerance for unexpected, thorough knowledge of attacks and defenses.	$42,000–$101,000
Programmer	Design and write computer programs.	Logical thinking and design skills, knowledge of programming language(s).	$36,000–$99,000
Technical Writer	Write program documentation, help text, procedures, job descriptions, training materials.	Quick learner, clear writing skills, high verbal communication skills.	$37,000–$88,000
Tech Support Engineer	Assist users with tech problems, conduct training.	Computer product knowledge, patience, collaboration skills.	$40,000–$92,000
Network Administrator	Monitor, maintain, fix, and tune computer networks.	Diagnostic skills, knowledge of network technologies.	$37,000–$78,000
IT Consultant	Varied: programming, texting, database design, network, project management, security, risk, social media, planning.	Quick learner, entrepreneurial attitude, collaboration skills, works well under pressure. Particular knowledge depends on work.	$42,000–$131,000
Technical Salesperson	Sell software, network, communications, and consulting services.	Quick learner, knowledge of products, sales skills.	$37,000–$92,000
IT Project Manager	Initiate, manage, monitor, plan, and close down projects.	Management and collaboration skills, technology knowledge, highly organized.	$53,000–$131,000
IT Manager	Supervise technical workers, implement IT strategies.	Collaboration and supervisory skills, critical thinking.	$47,000–$133,000
Database Administrator	Design, develop, implement, and secure databases.	Diplomatic skills, database technology knowledge.	$39,000–$108,000
Data Administrator	Ensure data accuracy, create automated data flows, enforce data standards throughout business.	Strong business knowledge, database technical knowledge.	$30,000–$63,000
Business Intelligence Analyst	Collaborate with users on projects to analyze and publish data.	Analytical, database, and visualization skills. Collaboration with users.	$46,000–$98,000
Data Scientist	Store, analyze, and interpret large datasets. Create end user visualizations.	Strong statistics, collaboration, and database skills.	$64,000–$139,000
Chief Information Security Officer (CISO)	Design and lead IS security program; protect the organization's information systems and data. Manage IS security personnel.	Deep knowledge of threats, safeguards, and trends. Excellent communication and diplomacy skills.	$47,000–$221,000
Chief Technology Officer (CTO)	Advise CIO and business managers on emerging technologies.	Quick learner, good communication skills. Deep business and IT knowledge. Innovative.	$87,000–$258,000
Chief Information Officer (CIO)	Manage IS department, communicate with executive team on IT issues. Member of executive group.	Outstanding management skills, knowledge of business and technology, collaboration, good judgment, unflappable.	$92,000–$270,000

FIGURE CE1-4

Job Positions for IS graduates

Descriptions of IT Careers

AIS
• aisnet.org/?AFutureinIS or isjobindex.com/

SAP
• www.sap.com/careers/index.html#

ComputerJobs
• www.computerjobs.com/us/en/IT-Jobs/

Government
• www.bls.gov/ooh/computer-and-information-technology/mobile/home.htm

Monster
• www.monster.com/jobs/q-it-jobs.aspx

Job Search Web Sites

Dice.com	CareerBuilder.com
ComputerJobs.com	Monster.com

FIGURE CE1-5
Descriptions for IS Careers and Job Search Web Sites

QE1-4 ▶ What Do IT Professionals Like About Their Jobs?

In the previous question, we outlined the variety of different types of jobs in IT. Despite this wide variety, several characteristics of the field are frequently mentioned when professionals are asked what they like about their jobs. A list of these characteristics is shown in Figure CE1-6. Many professionals enjoy the challenging and changing work, that they get to work with people and not just computers, that they can be employed by a wide variety of businesses and organizations during their careers, and that they often can work from home or start their own business. They also report that they enjoy the wide variety of roles they play from business focused to technology focused and everywhere in between. IT professionals enjoy the opportunity to create solutions to problems and help the business maximize opportunity—becoming at times the office superhero. They like the opportunity to have a direct impact throughout the business from setting and achieving company strategy to making each business function hum.

In addition to these appealing aspects of the job, IT professionals also are paid well right out of college as shown in Figure CE1-7. Salaries for graduates are approximately 17 percent higher than other business graduates at both the undergraduate and graduate level. Not only are yearly salaries high, signing bonuses are becoming more common. In a recent survey, the average reported signing bonus was $6,500 for undergraduates and $10,500 for master's graduates. While salaries and bonuses are encouraging, so too are employment rates for graduates. IS graduates were placed in jobs at a higher rate than other business school graduates. Eighty-nine percent of IS undergraduates were employed within 6 months of graduation compared with 80 percent of business school graduates and 94 percent of master's graduates were placed compared with 65 percent of business master's graduates.

Challenging work

Interesting people

Variety of work

Work from home

Solve important problems

Impact on business

FIGURE CE1-6
Best Aspect of IT Jobs

FIGURE CE1-7

Average Initial Salaries in 2015

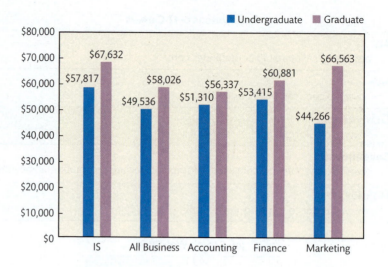

In closing, we believe the IS career field is an excellent choice. Here we wanted to share with you our passion for it by describing the factors in the economy that are providing positive job prospects for IS graduates, the skills required for IS-related jobs, the types of jobs available for IS graduates, and the appealing aspects of IT jobs. However, the main message we want to give you is simple. Firms need you. Career opportunities are plentiful. We think the field of IT is fascinating and will offer you a constant and rewarding challenge. As you study this topic during the semester we hope you consider a future in IT.

ACTIVE REVIEW

Use this active review to verify that you understand the ideas and concepts in this extension.

QE1-1 What is the employment environment like for IS graduates?

Name several new technologies that are contributing to IT job growth. Name other technological factors leading to IT job growth. Name several business factors that are increasing the demand for IT professionals. Describe each of the four critical skills, and provide an example of this skill in an IT job.

QE1-2 What are the duties and titles of IT Jobs?

Explain the factors that affect organizational structure. Describe the role of the CIO and the reporting relationships of the CIO. Explain the primary function and the responsibilities of each of the five groups within a typical IS department. Describe the data administration staff function. Explain the roles of CISO, CTO, and CIO and the differences in their responsibilities.

QE1-3 What IS–related job positions exist?

Explain the factors that affect salaries. Describe how IT jobs with small to mid-sized firms differ from IT jobs in large organizations. Explain certification, and name several IT-related certifications.

QE1-4 What do IT professionals like about their jobs?

Describe the best aspects of IT-related jobs. Summarize how salaries and employment rates of IS graduates differ from other business school disciplines.

KEY TERMS

Certification   375
Chief information officer
   (CIO)   374

Chief information security officer
   (CISO)   375
Chief technology officer (CTO)   374

Computer science graduates   372
IS graduates   372
STEM   372

USING YOUR KNOWLEDGE

E1-1. Visit the Bureau of Labor Statistics page that introduces IS careers (www.bls.gov/ooh/computer-and-information-technology/home.htm). Click on three different job titles listed in the Occupation column. Explore each of these three by selecting various tabs at the top of the page such as "What They Do," "Work Environment," and "How to Become One." Write a short description that describes:
   a. the occupation.
   b. the best aspects of the job (in your opinion).
   c. the education needed for the job.
   d. important qualities for the job.

E1-2. For an IS occupation you found in question 1 above, describe how each of the four critical employability skills in Figure CE1-2 would be used by a professional in that occupation.

E1-3. Use Google to discover more about the three C-level jobs introduced in this extension—chief information officer (CIO), chief technology officer (CTO), and chief information security officer (CISO). Explain which of these three jobs would be the best match for your skill set. Also use LinkedIn to find graduates of your institution who have these job titles. Describe the jobs they did before they became CIO, CTO, or CISO.

E1-4. Go to Monster.com and search for jobs listed near you in one of the job titles listed in Figure CE1-4. Search for three different job titles and for each:
   a. describe the job.
   b. explain the responsibilities and requirements.
   c. list related jobs. (Monster displays a list of related jobs on the right side of the screen for each job listing.)

E1-5. Examine Figure CE1-6, which lists the best aspects of IT jobs. Having read about IT jobs in the other questions above, do you think there are other aspects of IT jobs that should be listed in Figure CE1-6? Based on your own career goals, list the best aspects of IT jobs from most to least appealing to you.

EXTENSION RESOURCES

[1] Often, the department we are calling the IS department is known in organizations as the *IT* department. That name is a misnomer, however, because the IT department manages systems as well as technology. If you hear the term *IT department* in industry, don't assume that the scope of that department is limited to technology.

Hardware and Software

You will use computers every day of your life. That is the good news. The bad news is that computer hardware and software will continue to change and evolve as they have in the past. In order to get the most out of your time using them, understanding the basics of hardware and software is a must. A good grasp of hardware and software will also help you be productive at your first job. Finally, a good hardware and software foundation will help you understand changes in them and how businesses can turn those changes into opportunities.

Here we stitch together the two main topics—hardware and software—and in each, we address the most essential terms. Some terms you will know already, some will be new, and some you have always heard but never quite understood.

QE2-1 How Do the Main Components of Computer Hardware Work?

In Chapter 2, hardware is defined as the physical components of a computer. These components include input, output, storage, and the processor as shown in Figure CE2-1. At the end of each of these topics, we introduce newer technologies that might turn out to be disruptive. In the following question, we address the various types of hardware such as smartphone and laptops as well as their capacities to store and process data.

A wide variety of input, output, and storage devices move data into and out of computers. While it is common to think about individuals using these devices to create input and use output from computers, most input and output from computers are the output and input of other computers.

FIGURE CE2-1

Hardware Input, Processor, Output, and Storage

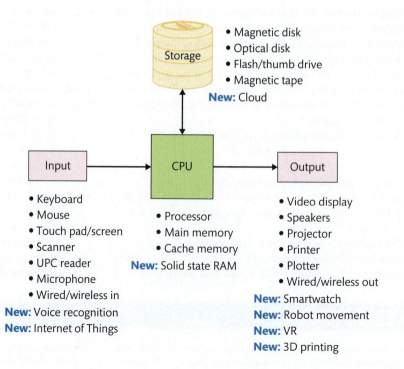

Storage
- Magnetic disk
- Optical disk
- Flash/thumb drive
- Magnetic tape

New: Cloud

Input
- Keyboard
- Mouse
- Touch pad/screen
- Scanner
- UPC reader
- Microphone
- Wired/wireless in

New: Voice recognition
New: Internet of Things

CPU
- Processor
- Main memory
- Cache memory

New: Solid state RAM

Output
- Video display
- Speakers
- Projector
- Printer
- Plotter
- Wired/wireless out

New: Smartwatch
New: Robot movement
New: VR
New: 3D printing

INPUT Input devices enter and input data and commands to a processor. Examples include keyboard, mouse, touch pad, screen, pointers, and game controllers. More recently, microphones using voice recognition software for voice inputs have become common as have motion-sensing devices common for video games and tilt/accelerators in phones. Other input devices such as bar code scanners, optical readers, digital cameras and webcams, point of sale devices, and smart card readers are automated and send commands to a processor without actions by individuals. Automated input devices will soon greatly expand when the **Internet of Things (IoT)**, everyday objects connected to the Internet, arrives.

OUTPUT Output devices allow users to see or hear the output of processors, or they form the input to other computing devices. They include computer or smartphone screens, printers or plotters, audio players or book readers. New forms of output include wearables like smartwatches, robotic movements, virtual reality (VR), and 3D printers. 3D printers, also called additive manufacturing, create physical 3D objects from digital files in an additive process of laying down successive thin layers of material.

STORAGE Secondary storage devices store data for long-term reuse. They are nonvolatile, meaning they are not erased when the power is removed. Examples include hard disks, CDs, DVDs, external drives, and solid-state drives such as USB drives. Secondary storage can be available on the local machine, on a shared drive, or in the cloud. This type of storage is called secondary storage, as primary storage is part of the processor, which is discussed next. Many experts believe cloud storage will soon make storage on a local machine obsolete.

CPU Every computer has a **central processing unit (CPU)**, the electronic circuits that execute the instructions specified in software. It is sometimes called "the brain" of the computer. Although the design of the CPU has nothing in common with the anatomy of a human brain, this description is helpful because the CPU does have the "smarts" of the machine. The CPU and other components of the processor are shown in Figure CE2-2.

The CPU selects instructions, processes them, performs arithmetic and logical comparisons, and stores results of operations in memory. Some computers have two or more CPUs. A computer with two CPUs is called a **dual-processor** computer. Quad-processor computers have four CPUs. Some high-end computers have 16 or more CPUs.

CPUs vary in speed, function, and cost. Hardware vendors such as Intel, Advanced Micro-Devices, and National Semiconductor continually improve CPU speed and capabilities while reducing CPU costs (as discussed under Moore's Law in Chapter 1). Whether you or your department needs the latest, greatest CPU depends on the nature of your work.

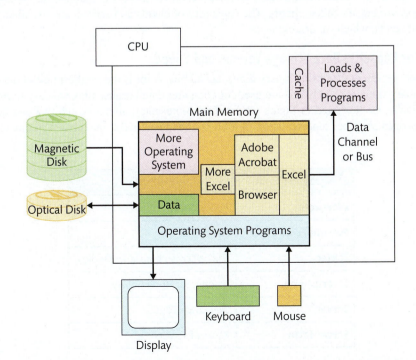

FIGURE CE2-2
CPU

The CPU works in conjunction with two types of memory: main and cache. **Main memory** is a temporary storage location that is directly accessible to the CPU. The CPU reads data and instructions from memory, and it stores results of computations in main memory. Main memory is sometimes called **RAM** for "random access memory." It is called random as any byte in memory can be accessed without touching bytes before or after it. The CPU also works with cache memory—a high-speed memory location a CPU can use even more quickly than RAM. A motherboard connects the CPU and RAM and other components and input and output devices. One recent change is the size of RAM on extremely high-performing computers. SAP offers almost 2 terabytes of RAM with a device called HANA, calling it in-memory processing.

One last comment: Main memory is volatile, meaning its contents are lost when power is off. If you suddenly lose power, the contents of unsaved memory—say, documents that have been altered—will be lost. Therefore, get into the habit of frequently (every few minutes or so) saving documents or files that you are changing.

QE2-2 ▶ What Are the Types of Computer Hardware and Their Capacities?

Hardware consists of electronic components and related gadgetry that input, process, output, and store data. Hardware today comes in a variety of types; we discuss that first and then explain hardware capacity—size and speed.

Types of Hardware

Figure CE2-3 lists the basic types of hardware. **Wearables** are small electronic devices worn on the body. The most common examples include headsets, glasses, and wristbands. **Personal computers** (PC) are classic computing devices designed for use by a single individual; they include desktops and laptops. An example of a modern PC is the MacBook Pro. Apple brought **tablets**, a mobile computer with a touchscreen display, to prominence with the iPad. Tablets are now offered by other manufactures such as Microsoft's Surface, Google's Pixel, and Samsung's Galaxy. Smartphones are cell phones with processing capability. The iPhone is a good example. Today, because it's hard to find a cell phone that isn't smart, people often just call them phones.

A **server** is a computer that is designed to support processing from many remote computers and users. You can think of a server as a PC on steroids; a typical example is the Dell PowerEdge server. Finally, a **server farm** is a collection of, typically, thousands of servers. Server farms are often placed in large truck trailers that hold 5,000 servers or more. PCs, tablets, and smartphones that access servers are called **clients**. The capacities of clients and servers are specified according to data units, which we discuss next.

Computer Capacity: Data Storage Volume and Speed

Computers represent data using binary digits, called bits. A **bit** is the smallest unit of data with a single binary value of 0 or 1. Bits are used for computer data because they are easy to represent electronically, as illustrated in Figure CE2-4. One representation is a switch that can be either closed or open. Another representation of a bit is a magnetic field; magnetism in one direction

FIGURE CE2-3

Types of Hardware

Hardware Type	Example
Wearable	Apple Watch, Fitbit
Personal computer	Apple Mac Pro
Tablet	iPad, Microsoft Surface, Kindle
Smartphone	iPhone, Samsung Galaxy
Server	Dell PowerEdge
Server farm	Racks of servers

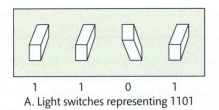

1 1 0 1
A. Light switches representing 1101

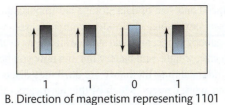

1 1 0 1
B. Direction of magnetism representing 1101

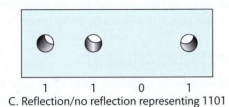

1 1 0 1
C. Reflection/no reflection representing 1101

FIGURE CE2-4
Representations of Bits

represents a zero, and magnetism in the opposite direction represents a one. For optical media, small pits are burned onto the surface of the disk so that they will reflect light. In a given spot, a reflection means a one; no reflection means a zero.

COMPUTER STORAGE VOLUME Bits are grouped into 8-bit chunks called **bytes**. For character data, such as the letters in a person's name, one character will fit into one byte. Thus, when you read a specification that a computing device has 100 million bytes of memory, you know that the device can hold up to 100 million characters. Bytes are used to measure sizes of noncharacter data as well. Someone might say, for example, that a given picture is 100,000 bytes in size. This statement means the length of the bit string that represents the picture is 100,000 bytes.

The specifications for the size of main memory, secondary storage, and other devices are expressed in bytes. Figure CE2-5 shows the set of abbreviations that are used to represent data storage capacity. A kilobyte, abbreviated *K*, is a collection of 1,024 bytes. A megabyte, or MB, is 1,024 kilobytes. A gigabyte, or GB, is 1,024 megabytes, and on it goes. Sometimes you will see these definitions simplified as 1K equals 1,000 bytes, 1MB equals 1,000K, and so on. Such simplifications are incorrect, but they do ease the math.

Computer storage capacities are specified according to the amount of data they can contain. Thus, a 500GB disk can contain up to 500GB of data and programs. There is some overhead, so it is not quite 500GB, but it's close enough.

COMPUTER SPEED You can order computers with CPUs of different speeds. CPU speed is expressed in cycles called *hertz*. In 2017, a slow personal computer has a speed of 2.5 Gigahertz. A fast personal computer has a speed of 4+ Gigahertz with quad processors. As predicted by Moore's Law, CPU speeds continually increase.

Additionally, CPUs today are classified as 32-bit or 64-bit. Without delving into the particulars, a 32-bit is less capable and cheaper than a 64-bit CPU. The latter can address more main memory; you need a 64-bit processor to effectively utilize memory. Most CPUs built after 2016 are 64-bit.

Term	Definition	Abbreviation
Byte	Number of bits to represent one character	
Kilobyte	1,024 bytes	K
Megabyte	1,024K = 1,048,576 bytes	MB
Gigabyte	1,024MB = 1,073,741,824 bytes	GB
Terabyte	1,024GB = 1,099,511,627,776 bytes	TB
Petabyte	1,024TB = 1,125,899,906,842,624 bytes	PB
Exabyte	1,024PB = 1,152,921,504,606,846,976 bytes	EB

FIGURE CE2-5

Important Storage-Capacity Terminology

Speed and size of data storage are important characteristics of computer hardware. When you buy your next tablet or desktop computer, you will read about processor speeds, now in 2.4 to 2.7 Gigahertz range, and data storage size, now available as 256GB or 512GB. You will also evaluate screen size, weight, and battery life, but now you better understand processor speed and storage size.

Understanding the hardware attributes discussed in these first two questions will be helpful for your work careers. Much of this hardware—the tablet, smartphone, and cloud—did not exist 10 years ago, but businesses quickly learned to use it well. Look for other disruptive changes in hardware in the next 10 years and help your business and the people you work with learn to use it. Change is opportunity, and change will also occur in the software domain that we discuss next.

QE2-3 ▶ What Is Operating System Software?

In Chapter 2, we defined software as the organized instructions used by a computer to accomplish tasks. Software can be classified as operating systems or as applications that run on the operating system. In this question, we examine operating systems for various types of computers and in the next question application software.

Every computer has an **operating system (OS)**, which is a program that controls that computer's resources. Some of the functions of an operating system are to read and write data, allocate main memory, perform memory-swapping, start and stop programs, respond to error conditions, and facilitate backup and recovery. In addition, the operating system creates and manages the user interface, including the display, keyboard, mouse, and other devices.

Although the operating system makes the computer usable, it does little application-specific work. If you want to check the weather or access a database, you need apps such as an iPad weather app or Oracle's customer relationship management (CRM) software. Both client and server computers need an operating system, though they need not be the same.

What Are the Major Operating Systems?

The major operating systems are listed in Figure CE2-6. Consider each.

FIGURE CE2-6

Major Operating Systems

Operating System	Used By	Remarks
Nonmobile Client		
Windows	PC	Most widely used in business, currently Windows 10
macOS	Mac PC	Easiest to use
Unix	Workstation	Used by science/engineering, difficult to use
Linux	Everything	Open source version of Unix, used on many hardware types

Operating System	Used By	Remarks
Mobile Client		
Android	Samsung, Google	Most widely used in business
iOS	iPhone, iPad	Shares features with macOS
Windows 10	Surface Pro	Microsoft attempt to unify OS across hardware types

Operating System	Used By	Remarks
Server		
Windows Server	Servers	Businesses with commitment to Microsoft products
Unix	Servers	Fading from use, replaced by Linux
Linux	Servers	Most popular, pushed by IBM

NONMOBILE CLIENT OPERATING SYSTEMS Nonmobile client operating systems are used on personal computers. The most popular is **Microsoft Windows**. Some version of Windows resides on more than 80 percent of the world's desktops, and if we consider just business users, the figure is more than 90 percent. The most recent client version of Windows is Windows 10.

Apple Computer, Inc. developed its own operating system for the Mac, MacOS, now called **macOS**. Apple touts its OS as the world's most advanced client operating system, and until Windows 8, it was. Now macOS and Windows 10 compete neck and neck for that title. Recently Apple has made it possible to run Windows on the Mac, so both operating systems work on a Mac. Some analysts also believe that Apple is shifting its priorities toward its more lucrative iPhone product and away from Macs.

Unix is an operating system that was developed at Bell Labs in the 1970s and supports scientific and engineering communities. Unix is generally regarded as being more difficult to use than either Windows or Mac and is seldom used in business.

Linux is a version of Unix that was developed by the open source community (discussed on page 387 later in this extension). This community is a loosely coupled group of programmers who mostly volunteer their time to contribute code to develop and maintain Linux. The open source community owns Linux, and there is no fee to use it. Linux can run on client computers, but usually only when budget is of paramount concern. Linux is the most popular server OS.

MOBILE CLIENT OPERATING SYSTEMS Figure CE2-6 also lists the three principal mobile operating systems. **iOS** is the operating system used on the iPod Touch, iPhone, and iPad. **Android** is a mobile operating system licensed by Google. Android powers Samsung and Google phones as well as tablets manufactured by Samsung, Google, Sony, and Dell. **Windows 10 mobile** is Microsoft's attempt to unify OS across both mobile and nonmobile platforms.

Most industry observers would agree that Apple has led the way, with both the macOS and the iOS, in creating easy-to-use interfaces. Certainly, many innovative ideas have first appeared in a Mac or iSomething and then later been added, in one form or another, to Android or Windows. It seems clear that touch-based interfaces are the future for all client devices.

SERVER OPERATING SYSTEMS The last three rows of Figure CE2-6 show the three most popular server operating systems. **Windows Server** is a version of Windows that has been specially designed and configured for server use. It has much more stringent and restrictive security procedures than other versions of Windows and is popular on servers in organizations that have made a strong commitment to Microsoft.

Unix can also be used on servers, but it is gradually being replaced by Linux. Linux is frequently used on servers by organizations that want, for whatever reason, to avoid a server commitment to Microsoft. IBM is the primary proponent of Linux and in the past has used it as a means to compete against Microsoft. Although IBM does not own Linux, IBM has developed many business systems solutions that use Linux. By using Linux, neither IBM nor its customers have to pay a license fee to Microsoft.

Before closing the section on operating systems, consider a related type of software called utility software. **Utility software** helps optimize and configure the computer and provide additional functionality for the OS. Computer manufacturers load some utility software at the factory; consumers can add utilities afterward also. Utilities support the computer's infrastructure rather than apps that support the user. Examples of utility software include antivirus, screen saver, encryption, uninstall, and compression software.

▶ QE2-4 What Are the Types of Software Apps, and How Do Organizations Obtain Them?

App software performs a service or function. Some apps are general purpose, such as Microsoft Excel or Word. Other apps provide specific functions. QuickBooks, for example, is an app that provides general ledger and other accounting functions, and FaceTime provides video call functions on an iPhone. We begin by describing categories of apps and then describe sources for them as shown in Figure CE2-7. Also shown in that figure are the six valid combinations of software type and source.

FIGURE CE2-7

Software Sources, Types, and
Six Valid Combinations

Categories of Apps	Sources of Apps			
	Off the Shelf	Off the Shelf & Customized	Custom Developed	Open Source
Horizontal app	✔			✔
Vertical app	✔	✔		✔
One-of-a-kind			✔	

Valid Combination ✔

Categories of Apps

Horizontal-market apps provide capabilities common across all organizations and industries. Word processors, graphics programs, spreadsheets, email, and texting are all horizontal-market apps. Examples include Microsoft Word, Excel, PowerPoint, and Adobe's Acrobat. They are purchased off the shelf and are not typically customized.

Vertical-market apps serve the needs of a specific industry. Examples of such programs are those used by dental offices to schedule appointments and bill patients, those used by auto mechanics to keep track of customer data and customers' automobile repairs, and those used by parts warehouses to track inventory, purchases, and sales. Vertical apps usually can be altered or customized. Typically, the company that sold the app will provide such services or offer referrals to qualified consultants who can provide this service.

One-of-a-kind apps are developed for a specific, unique need. The IRS develops such software, for example, because it has needs that no other organization has.

Sources of Apps

Having described the three types of apps that comprise rows in Figure CE2-7, consider the four sources of apps that make up the columns of that figure.

The first three sources of apps can be acquired in exactly the same ways that you can buy a new suit. The quickest and least risky option is to buy your suit off the rack. With this method, you get your suit immediately, and you know exactly what it will cost. You may not, however, get a good fit. Alternately, you can buy your suit off the rack and have it altered. This will take more time, it may cost more, and there's some possibility that the alteration will result in a poor fit. Most likely, however, an altered suit will fit better than an off-the-rack one.

Finally, you can hire a tailor to make a custom suit. In this case, you will have to describe what you want, be available for multiple fittings, and be willing to pay considerably more. Although there is an excellent chance of a great fit, there is also the possibility of a disaster. Still, if you want a yellow and orange polka-dot silk suit with a hissing rattlesnake on the back, tailor-made is the only way to go. You can buy software in exactly the same ways: **off-the-shelf software**, **off-the-shelf with alterations** software, or tailor-made. Tailor-made software is called **custom-developed software**.

Organizations develop custom apps themselves or hire a development vendor. Like buying the yellow and orange polka-dot suit, such development is done in situations in which the needs of the organization are so unique that no horizontal or vertical apps are available. By developing custom software, the organization can tailor its app to fit its requirements.

Custom development is difficult and risky. Staffing and managing teams of software developers is challenging. Managing software projects can be daunting. Many organizations have embarked on app development projects only to find that the projects take twice as long—or longer—to finish as planned. Cost overruns of 200 and 300 percent are not uncommon. We will discuss such risks further in the systems development extension.

Every app needs to be adapted to changing needs and changing technologies. The adaptation costs of horizontal and vertical software are amortized over all of the users of that software, perhaps thousands or millions of customers. For custom-developed software, however, the using organization must pay all of the adaptation costs itself. Over time, this cost burden is heavy. Because of the risk and expense, custom development is the last-choice alternative and is used only when there is no other option.

When you acquire an app from the first three sources shown in Figure CE2-7, you are not actually buying that program. Instead, you are buying a license to use that app. For example, when you buy a Windows license, Microsoft is selling you the right to use Windows. Microsoft continues to own the Windows program. Large organizations do not buy a license for each computer user. Instead, they negotiate a **site license**, which is a flat fee that authorizes the company to install the product (operating system or app) on all of that company's computers or on all of the computers at a specific site. The fourth source of apps, open source, no company can sell you a license to use. We describe open source next.

Open Source

The term *open source* means that the source code of the program is available to the public. In a closed source project—say, Microsoft Office—the source code is highly protected and only available to trusted employees and carefully vetted contractors. With open source, anyone can obtain the source code from the open source project's Web site. Programmers alter or add to this code depending on their interests and goals. In most cases, programmers can incorporate code they find into their own projects. Open source succeeds because of collaboration. A programmer examines the source code and identifies a need or project that seems interesting. He or she then creates a new feature, redesigns or reprograms an existing feature, or fixes a known problem. That code is then sent to others in the open source project who evaluate the quality and merits of the work and add it to the product, if appropriate.

In an open source project there is a lot of give and take; there are many cycles of iteration and feedback. Because of this iteration, a well-managed project with strong peer reviews can result in very high-quality code, like that in Linux.

The Internet proved to be a great asset for open source, and many open source projects became successful, including:

- LibreOffice (a Microsoft Office package)
- Firefox (a browser)
- MySQL (a DBMS, see Chapter 4)
- Apache (a Web server)
- Hadoop (a Big Data technology, see Chapters 4 and 12)
- Android (a mobile device operating system)

So, is open source viable? The answer depends on the individual company or business and its needs. Open source has certainly become legitimate. According to *The Economist,* "It is now generally accepted that the future will involve a blend of both proprietary and open source software."[1] During your career, open source will likely take a greater and greater role in software. However, whether open source works for a particular situation depends on the requirements and constraints of that situation. The code used to create open source apps, as well as closed source apps, is called source code. **Source code** is computer code that is written and understood by humans. Figure CE2-8 shows a portion of computer code that supports an animation on an Android phone. Source code is compiled into machine code that is processed by a computer. **Machine code** is, in general, not understandable by humans and cannot be modified. When you access the phone app, the machine code version of the program in Figure CE2-8 runs on your computer. We do not show machine code in a figure because it would look like this:

11010010100101111110011101111001000111000001111110111011111100111...

Open source is clearly a way for firms to save money. Virtualization, our next software topic also saves firms money.

```
/// <summary>
/// Allows the page to draw itself.
/// </summary>
private void OnDraw(object sender, GameTimerEventArgs e)
{
    SharedGraphicsDeviceManager.Current.GraphicsDevice.Clear(Color.CornflowerBlue);

    SharedGraphicsDeviceManager.Current.GraphicsDevice.Clear(Color.Black);

    // Render the Silverlight controls using the UIElementRenderer.
    elementRenderer.Render();

    // Draw the sprite
    spriteBatch.Begin();

    // Draw the rectangle in its new position
    for (int i = 0; i < 3; i++)
    {
        spriteBatch.Draw(texture[i], bikeSpritePosition[i], Color.White);
    }

    // Using the texture from the UIElementRenderer,

    // draw the Silverlight controls to the screen.
    spriteBatch.Draw(elementRenderer.Texture, Vector2.Zero, Color.White);

    spriteBatch.End();
}
```

FIGURE CE2-8
Source Code Sample

QE2-5 ▸ What Is Virtualization?

Virtualization is the process by which one computer hosts the appearance of many computers. One operating system, called the host operating system, runs one or more operating systems as apps. Those hosted operating systems are called **virtual machines (vm)**. Each virtual machine has disk space and other resources allocated to it. The host operating system controls the activities of the virtual machines it hosts to prevent them from interfering with one another. With virtualization, each vm is able to operate exactly the same as it would if it were operating in a stand-alone, nonvirtual environment.

Three types of virtualization exist:

- PC virtualization
- Server virtualization
- Desktop virtualization

With **PC virtualization**, a personal computer, such as a desktop or laptop, hosts several different operating systems. Say a user needs, for some reason, to have both Windows 10 and Linux running on his or her computer. In that circumstance, the user can install a virtual host operating system and then install both Windows 10 and Linux on top of it. In that way, the user can have both systems on the same hardware. VMWare Workstation is a popular PC virtualization product that can run both Windows and Linux operating systems.

With **server virtualization**, a server computer hosts one or more other server computers. Users can log onto virtual machines and they will appear as normal servers. Server virtualization plays a key role for cloud vendors, as you learned in Chapter 3.

PC virtualization is interesting and sometimes quite useful, and server virtualization is key to cloud economics. Desktop virtualization, on the other hand, has the potential to be revolutionary. With **desktop virtualization**, a server hosts many versions of desktop operating systems. Each of those desktops has a complete user environment and appears to the user to be just another PC. However, the desktop can be accessed from any computer to which the user has access. Thus, you could be at an airport, go to an airport computer, and access your virtualized desktop. To you, it appears as if that airport computer is your own personal computer. Later, you could do the same to a utility computer sitting in your hotel room. Meanwhile, many other users could have accessed the computer in the airport, and each thought he or she had his or her personal computer. Virtualization hides the location of the software from the user, a detail most users do not want or need to know.

QE2-6 ▸ What Are Native and Web Apps, and How Are They Different?

Apps can be categorized as **native apps**, which are those that can run on just one operating system, or as **Web apps**, which can run in browsers on many different operating systems. Figure CE2-9 contrasts native and Web apps on their important characteristics. Many popular apps have both native and Web versions such as Facebook and Microsoft Word. Native apps are more commonly used on smartphones. Popular smartphone native apps include Uber, Facebook, and YouTube; Web apps include Google docs, Skype, and Google search. Consider the native apps column first.

	Native Apps	**Web Apps**
Development languages	Objective-C Java C#, VB.net (object-oriented languages)	html5 CSS3 JavaScript (scripting languages)
Developed by	Professional programmer only	Professional programmers and technically oriented Web developers and business professionals
Skill level required	High	Low to high
Difficulty	High	Easy to hard, depending on application requirements
Developer's degree	Computer science	Computer science Information systems Graphics design
User experience	Can be superb, depending on programming quality	Simple to sophisticated, depending on program quality
Possible applications	Whatever you can pay for…	Some limits prohibit very sophisticated applications
Dependency	iOS, Android, Windows	Browser difference only
Cost	High. Difficult work by highly paid employees, multiple versions required	Low to medium … easier work by lesser-paid employees, only multiple browser files necessary. Sophisticated applications may require high skill and pay
Application distribution	Via application stores (e.g., Apple iTunes store)	Via Web sites
Example	Vanguard iPad application (free in Apple's iTunes store)	Seafood Web site: *www.brownfamilyseafood.com* Picozu editor: *www.picozu.com/editor*

FIGURE CE2-9

Characteristics of Native and Web Applications

Native Apps

Native apps are developed using serious, heavy-duty, professional programming languages. macOS and iOS apps are constructed using Objective-C or Swift. Linux (Android) apps are constructed using Java, and Windows apps are constructed using C#, VB.Net, C++, and others. All of these languages are object-oriented, which means they can be used to create difficult, complex apps and, if used properly, will result in high-performance code that is easy to alter when requirements change.

The benefit of object-oriented languages is that they give programmers close control over the assets of the computing device and enable the creation of sophisticated and complex user interfaces. If the programs are well written, they perform fast and use memory efficiently, and to the user they "feel right." The limits on native apps are usually budgetary and not technological.

The downside of native apps is that they are, well, native. They only run on the operating system for which they are programmed. An iOS app must be completely recoded in order to run on Android and recoded again to run on Windows.[2] Thus, to reach all users, an organization will need to support and maintain three separate versions of the same app. It will also have to staff and manage three different development teams with three different skill sets.

An example of a native app is the Microsoft Office products resident on your laptop. Microsoft has spent millions to build this highly functional app, and there are different versions for a MacBook Air than a Surface Pro. Microsoft also makes a version of Office available via a browser called Office Online. This Web app version runs in a browser with fewer functions, but only one version exists. We summarize Web apps next.

Web Apps

Web apps run inside a browser such as Firefox, Chrome, Opera, Safari, Internet Explorer (IE), and Edge. The browser handles the idiosyncrasies of the operating system and underlying hardware. In a perfect world, an organization could develop a single app and have it run flawlessly on all browsers on all devices. Unfortunately, there are some differences in the way that browsers implement the Web app code and some app features do not work in some browsers.

As shown in the first row of Figure CE2-9, Web app development languages are html5, CSS3, and JavaScript. These are not object-oriented languages and hence are much easier to learn. Html5 is the latest version of html; CSS3 is used with html5 to specify the appearance of content coded in html. JavaScript is a scripting programming language that is much easier to learn than object-oriented languages. It is used to provide the underlying logic of the app.

Web apps can be written by professional programmers, and, indeed, most are. However, it is possible for technically oriented Web developers and business professionals to develop them as well. The entry-level technical skill required is low, and simple apps are relatively easy to develop. Sophisticated user experiences are difficult. Web app developers may have degrees in computer science, information systems, or graphic design.

The user experience provided by a Web app varies considerably. Some are simply fancy Web-based brochures with no interaction; others are quite sophisticated, such as Microsoft Office. Web apps are limited by the capabilities of the browser. Thus, Web apps are unable to support specialized and complex apps, though this becomes less true each year.

Because Web apps can be developed by less-skilled, lesser-paid employees and because only one code base and one development team are necessary, they are considerably cheaper to develop than native apps.

Which is better? You know the answer to that question. If it were clear-cut, we'd only be discussing one alternative. It's not. The choice depends on your strategy, your particular goals, the requirements for your app, your budget, your schedule, your tolerance for managing technical projects, your need for app revenue, and other factors. In general, Web apps are cheaper to develop and maintain, but they may lack the wow factor. But, how much is "wow!" worth? You and your organization have to decide for yourselves!

In this extension, we presented the key attributes and vocabulary used to describe the most essential aspects of hardware and software. A complete understanding of them is as valuable as knowing all your options at Chipotle or Subway. When you choose your options at Chipotle or Subway you enjoy what you get because you know what all the ingredients do. A good foundation with hardware and software will also allow you to observe key disruptive technologies like the Internet of Things or a new app and help your future business adapt to these changes.

ACTIVE REVIEW

Use this Active Review to verify that you understand the ideas and concepts in this extension.

QE2-1 How do the main components of computer hardware work?

What are the four main hardware components? Where does most of the input and output from computers go to and come from? Explain the Internet of Things. Describe input devices and provide three examples. Describe output devices and provide examples. Explain how 3D printing is done. How is secondary storage different from primary storage? Describe three options for storage and what type of storage is expected to be the most common. Explain what a CPU does and the two types of memory it works with.

QE2-2 What are the types of computer hardware and their capacities?

Describe three types of wearable computers. What types of computers are included with the term *personal computer*? Provide examples of tablets and explain the attributes of a tablet. Explain what a server does and what a server farm is. Define *bit* and *byte* and describe the relationship between them. Explain how the speed of a CPU is expressed and the speed range of a typical CPU.

QE2-3 What is operating system software?

Explain what an operating system does and its functions. Describe the four nonmobile client operating systems and how they differ. Explain the three mobile operating systems and

their chief characteristics. Describe the most common server operating systems. Explain the functions of utility software.

QE2-4 What are the types of software apps, and how do organizations obtain them?

Explain the difference between a horizontal app and a vertical app and give an example of each. Describe a one-of-a-kind app. Explain each of the four sources of apps. Describe the challenges of a custom development. Explain licensing and site licenses. Define *open source software* and list three examples. Contrast the differences between machine code and source code.

QE2-5 What is virtualization?

Explain the basic concept of virtualization and list the three types. Describe PC virtualization and provide an example. Explain the relationship between server virtualization and the cloud. Describe desktop virtualization and why a university might use it.

QE2-6 What are native and Web apps, and how are they different?

Describe native apps and compare native and Web apps. Explain at least three ways native apps and Web apps differ and provide an example of each. Most generally, describe the advantages of each.

KEY TERMS

Android   385
Bit   382
Byte   383
Central processing unit (CPU)   381
Client   382
Custom-developed software   386
Desktop virtualization   389
Dual-processor   381
Horizontal-market app   386
Internet of Things (IoT)   381
iOS   385
Linux   385
macOS   385

Machine code   387
Main memory   382
Microsoft Windows   385
Native app   389
Off-the-shelf software   386
Off-the-shelf with alterations   386
One-of-a-kind app   386
Operating system (OS)   384
PC virtualization   388
Personal computers   382
RAM   382
Server   382
Server farm   382

Server virtualization   388
Site license   387
Source code   387
Tablet   382
Unix   385
Utility software   385
Vertical-market app   386
Virtual machine (vm)   388
Wearables   382
Web app   389
Windows Server   385
Windows 10 mobile   385

USING YOUR KNOWLEDGE

E2-1. Microsoft offers free licenses of certain software products to students at colleges and universities that participate in its Imagine program (formerly known as Dreamspark). If your college or university participates in the program you have the opportunity to obtain hundreds of dollars of software for free. Here is a partial list:

Microsoft Visual Studio	OneNote 2016
Visio 2016	SQL Server 2016
Project 2016	SharePoint Server

   a. Search online to find out the function of each of these software products.

   b. Which of these programs is an operating system? Which is a database program?

   c. Which of these programs should you download and install?

   d. For your academic major or a major you select, describe how a professional in that job would use three of these apps.

   e. Does Imagine provide an unfair competitive advantage for Microsoft? Why or why not?

E2-2. Visit the Open Source Initiative's Web site at *http://opensource.org*. Summarize the mission of this nonprofit corporation. Find the definition of *open source* on this site and summarize that definition in your own words. Explain this corporation's role with regard to open source licenses. Summarize the process for having a license approved by OSI. Describe the advantage of having OSI's approval.

E2-3. Visit your school or college alumni giving Web page on a laptop and on a mobile device. Suppose that you are the leader of the team redesigning that page. List five criteria you would use in helping to decide whether the school should develop a native or a Web app. Justify your criteria.

E2-4. Using the Internet, shop for a laptop you would like to buy upon graduation. Specify two choices. For each choice list the input and output options, the CPU speed, and the RAM storage capacity. Also list for each choice the software that comes with the laptop. Also specify the weight, battery life, and screen size. Find two additional criteria to use to compare the two options and list these.

E2-5. Microsoft Office and Outlook apps can be used as native or Web apps. When do you use each and which functions of the native apps do you miss when using the Web app versions?

EXTENSION RESOURCES

[1]"Unlocking the Cloud," *The Economist*, last modified May 28, 2009, www.economist.com/node/13740181.

[2]Not quite true. Much of the design and possibly some of the code can be reused between native applications. But for your planning, assume that it all must be redone. Not enough will carry over to make it worth considering.

Process Management and Information Systems Development

Every organization today needs to adapt to new technologies and new opportunities. Businesses that do not adapt cannot thrive, and they may not even be able to survive. Organizations can adapt by changing their strategy or, if the strategy remains the same, updating their processes or information systems. As a business professional you will often participate in process or system change.

To help you help your organization adapt, we will consider two structured processes in this extension: business process management, which is a process for managing other processes, and systems development, which is a process for creating and maintaining information systems. Both processes heavily rely on collaboration between analysts and end users; and as a future end user, your assistance will be vital.

QE3-1 What Are the Activities of Business Process Management?

As we have stated repeatedly, business processes provide the key means by which businesses accomplish work. Because this is so, it is not surprising that businesses use a process to manage processes. The most important of such processes is known as business process management (BPM). In this question, we will describe the primary activities of the BPM process. BPM and its principles not only are useful in large organizations with many processes but also have been applied to nonprofits, government agencies, and small organizations. We also discuss the topic of business processes in Chapter 6. Here we discuss the general topic of business processes in a broad and general framework that would be common in a non-MIS textbook. In Chapter 6, we focus on how to improve business processes with IS in a way unique to this textbook.

Figure CE3-1 shows the four basic activities in **business process management (BPM)**, a structured, cyclical process for systematically monitoring, modeling, creating, and implementing business processes. In Figure CE3-1, note how the activities of monitor/model/create/implement form a loop. As each activity is completed, it feeds into the next activity.

During the monitoring activity, managers evaluate process measures against their objectives and respond to changes in the business climate, as described below. Next, models and other forms of requirements for changes in the business process are developed. Components for implementing those requirements are then created, and the process changes are implemented. That implementation activity leads to the monitoring activity of the next cycle. Consider each activity in more detail.

FIGURE CE3-1
BPM Process

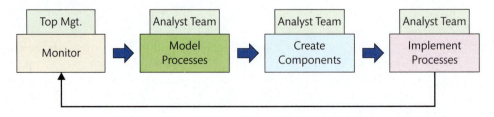

The BPM Monitor Activity

Organizations are dynamic, and processes within organizations need to be adapted. The need for process change arises from two sources:

- The process itself—the process does not consistently meet its objectives
- The environment of the process—a change in technology or business

Managers can learn that a process needs to be adapted in one of two ways. They can ignore the process and possible need for change until trouble ensues or they can continually monitor the process and proactively make changes before problems occur.

Organizations that engage in process management take the latter approach. To do so, they create targets for process objectives and frequently, sometimes continuously, measure the process against those objectives.

MONITORING PROCESS PERFORMANCE BY ITS OBJECTIVES As you have learned, process objectives are either effective or efficient. Effectiveness assesses how well the process helps the organization achieve its strategy. For example, the shipping department of an organization that differentiates based on high-quality service will set high objectives for the percent of orders shipped on time, the percent of orders that are accurate, and the percent of orders that are delivered to the correct address. Measures of efficiency objectives determine how well the process uses its resources. For shipping, efficiency measures include the average cost of preparing a shipment, the number of trucks required to deliver shipments, the cost per item of packaging, and so forth. These process measures are often called key performance indicators (KPIs). A KPI is a measure of particular importance used by a business to measure an activity in a critical process.

MONITORING FOR CHANGES IN THE ENVIRONMENT Business processes need to be monitored against changes in technology. For example, 3D printing, the Internet of Things, and driverless vehicles will require businesses to reassess their processes. A second source of change in a process's environment is the business itself. A substantial change in any of the following factors can signal a need to modify business processes:

- Market (e.g., new customer category, change in customer characteristics)
- Product lines
- Supply chain
- Company policy
- Company organization (e.g., merger or acquisition)
- Internationalization
- Business environment

To provide an example, consider the process of closing a computer lab for the night at your university. A change in the environment is the nighttime theft at a nearby school of computers from a similar lab. To adapt, your school appoints a small team of process analysts to evaluate your school's lab closing processes.

The BPM Model Processes Activity

At some point, either because a process is not meeting its performance objectives or because of changes in the environment, processes will need to be changed. During the modeling activity, it is often necessary to document how the process currently works. To accomplish this, business users who have expertise and are involved in the process (this could be you!) adjust and evaluate those models. Process analyst teams build an as-is model that documents the current situation and then make adjustments to that model to solve process problems. A common way to construct an as-is model is with a BPMN document. During the modeling activity, the analyst team also assesses objectives and goals for the new process. To read more about how processes are adjusted and improved, read Chapter 6, which describes how IS can be used to improve processes. Returning to the example of the computer lab closing process, in the modeling step the team will build an as-is BPMN of the steps the school currently takes—turn off machines, engage security alarm, and ensure door is locked.

FIGURE CE3-2

SDLC Process Within the Create
Components Activity of the BPM
Process

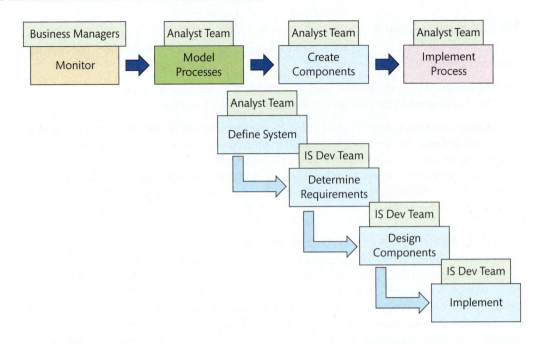

The BPM Create Components Activity

The third major BPM activity is to create process components. In this activity, the team designs changes to the business process at a depth sufficient for implementation. One component of the process may be an information system; if so, the systems development life cycle in Q2 may be used. In addition to IS components, the analyst team develops procedures and training for activities that do not involve information systems. For the computer lab process, new activities such as manually ensuring windows are locked were added to the closing process, and changes were made to the IS that maintained key codes for each lab door.

The BPM Implement Process Activity

Implementation activities make process changes operational. During this activity, process actors are trained on the activities they will perform and the IS procedures they will use. Activities to perform here are similar to implementation activities for the systems development life cycle (SDLC), and we will defer discussion of them to the SDLC discussion in Q2. For processes, however, note that if the new version of the business process involves considerable change for employees, there is likely to be resistance to the new system. If the new lab closing process at the school requires twice as many activities, workers will be less than enthused. We discuss employee resistance to change in Chapters 6 through 9, and we won't repeat that discussion here. However, it is important to remember the need for addressing resistance to change.

The four activities of BPM are cyclical. Once a process change has been implemented, it is monitored. If it needs improvement, it is remodeled, and components are created and implemented. Many large firms label this ongoing cycle of process improvement a **continuous improvement process (CIP)**.

As mentioned, if the create components activity suggests an IS needs to change, the four activities listed under the create components activity in Figure CE3-2 are executed. These steps are discussed next.

QE3-2 What Are the Activities of the Systems Development Life Cycle (SDLC) Development Process?

Some systems you use are terrific and easy to use—your smartphone, wireless headphones, Google Drive—but other IS are a nightmare. The differences often come down to how the products were developed, and in this question and the next we examine how IS are developed. Development is a significant challenge and our hope is that by the end of this chapter extension you will be able to appreciate why.

Systems development is the process of creating and maintaining an information system. Just like the BPM process, systems development is a structured process, and in this question, we describe each of its activities.

As stated in Chapter 2, the relationship between a business process and an information system is many-to-many. A given business process may use one or more information systems, and a given information system may be used by more than one process. Because this is so, organizations can begin with BPM and, in the context of process management, create an IS. Or organizations can begin with an IS and back into the processes that will use it.

Several processes can be used to create information systems. The most common process is called the **systems development life cycle (SDLC)**. The SDLC is a structured process composed of activities; some organizations define five activities, some seven, and some even more, that creates an IS. The activities in these different versions are more or less the same; they are just grouped differently. Several of the steps are similar to BPM. While organizations use SDLC to create new systems, SDLC can also be used to improve existing systems. For simplicity most of our discussion addresses the creation of a new IS.

In this text, we discuss the SDLC as having the following five activities:

1. Define the system.
2. Determine requirements.
3. Design system components.
4. Implement system.
5. Maintain the system.

Figure CE3-2 shows how the first four activities are related; the maintenance activity occurs last but is not shown for simplicity. The SDLC begins when a business planning process identifies a need for a new system. Consider each of the SDLC activities.

Define System

As shown in Figure CE3-3, in response to the need for the new system, the analyst team will define the new system, assess its feasibility, make outsourcing suggestions, and form the IS development team.

DEFINE SYSTEM GOALS AND SCOPE As shown in Figure CE3-3, the first step is to define the goals and scope of the new information system. Is the goal of the new system to support one or two processes, or is the new system broader in scope? The team must specify the scope of the new system and examine who will use it, when it will be done, and what it will do.

ASSESS FEASIBILITY Given the goals and scope of the new system, the next task is to assess feasibility. "Does this project make sense?" The aim here is to eliminate impractical projects before forming a project development team and investing significant labor. Impractical projects are those that cost more than they're worth, are technically too challenging, or may take too long to accomplish.

The feasibility of a project has several dimensions. **Cost feasibility** determines if the benefits of the new system are worth the cost of developing it. **Schedule feasibility** assesses whether the project can be accomplished by the estimated completion date. **Technical feasibility** determines if the planned technology can deliver the project's requirements and whether the firm has the expertise to use this technology.

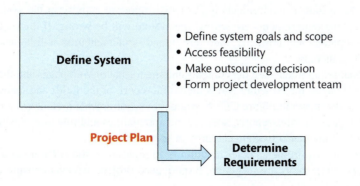

FIGURE CE3-3
SDLC Systems Definition Activity

FIGURE CE3-4

Key Advantages and Disadvantages
of Outsourcing

Advantages
- Cost reduction
- Better accountability
- Focus on core competency
- Reduces overhead

Disadvantages
- Reduces control
- Increases dependence on other firms
- Sensitive data less secure

MAKE OUTSOURCING DECISION During this activity, the analyst team and senior organizational leaders will need to decide whether the system will be developed by the organization's employees or outsourced to another firm. **Outsourcing** is obtaining goods or services from an outside or foreign supplier. The related term, **offshoring** means that the goods or services are obtained from a foreign supplier. Because of the abundance of low-cost, well-educated, English-speaking professionals in India, many organizations have chosen to offshore some steps in the development of the system to India. Outsourcing and offshoring are choices not only for systems development; companies can outsource or offshore all types of activities, such as marketing, customer support and manufacturing. Advantages and disadvantages of outsourcing are listed in Figure CE3-4.

FORM A PROJECT DEVELOPMENT TEAM The next step is to form the IS development team. Normally, the team consists of both IT personnel and user representatives. Typical personnel on a development team are a manager (or managers for larger projects), business analysts, IT analysts, programmers, software testers, and users. A **business analyst** is someone who is well versed in the Porter models, organizational strategy, and models such as COBIT that are designed to align information systems with strategy and processes.

IT analysts, also called systems analysts, are IS professionals who understand both business and technology. They are active throughout the systems development process and play a key role in moving the project through the process. Systems analysts integrate the work of the programmers, testers, and users. Depending on the nature of the project, the team may also include hardware and communications specialists, database designers and administrators, and other IT specialists.

User involvement is critical throughout the systems development process. Users are involved in many different ways. Users help the development team understand the specifications and requirements for the new system, how they intend to use the system, and how the new system interacts with other processes and systems within the organization. *The important point is for users to have active involvement and to take ownership of the project throughout the entire development Process.*

The first major task for the IS development team is to plan the project. Members of the team specify tasks to be accomplished, assign personnel, determine task dependencies, and set schedules. Development teams often use Microsoft Project as shown in Figure CE3-5 and activity planning tools such as Gantt charts, PERT, and the Critical Path Method (CPM).

Determine Requirements

Determining the system's requirements is the most important activity in the systems development process. If the requirements are wrong, the system will be wrong. If the requirements are determined completely and correctly, then design and implementation will be easier and more likely to result in success.

Examples of requirements are the contents and the format of Web pages and the functions of buttons on those pages, the structure and content of a report, or the fields and menu choices in a data entry form. As shown in Figure CE3-6, sources of requirements include existing systems as well as the Web pages, forms, reports, queries, and app features and functions desired in the new system. Security is another important category of requirements.

Sometimes the requirements determination is so focused on the software and data components that other components are forgotten. Experienced project managers ensure consideration

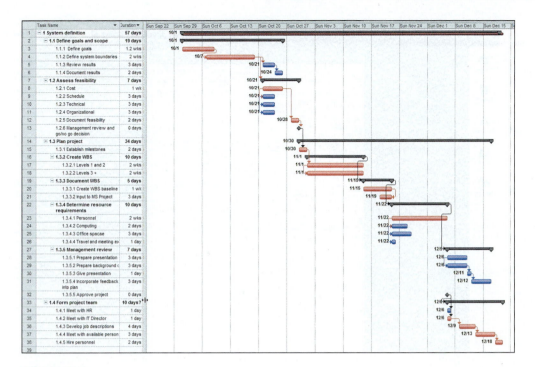

FIGURE CE3-5
Project Gantt Chart in Microsoft Project

of requirements for all five IS components, not just for software and data. Regarding hardware, the team might ask: Are there special needs or restrictions on hardware? Is there an organizational standard governing what kinds of hardware can, or cannot, be used? Must the new system use existing hardware? What requirements are there for communications and network hardware?

Similarly, the team should consider requirements for procedures and personnel: Do accounting controls require procedures that separate duties and authorities? Are there restrictions that some actions can be taken only by certain departments or specific personnel? Are there policy requirements or union rules that restrict activities to certain categories of employees? Will the system need to interface with information systems from other companies and organizations? In short, requirements need to be considered for all of the components of the new information system. These questions are examples of the kinds of questions that must be asked and answered during requirements analysis.

Because requirements are difficult to specify, building a working prototype can be quite beneficial. A **prototype** is a scaled-down but functional version of a system that is built to help evaluate a system. A prototype helps analysts and users collaborate on the initial or basic requirements of the system. A user should be able to interact with the prototype and tell the analyst what they like and do not like about it. Whereas future systems users often struggle to understand and relate to requirements expressed as word descriptions and sketches, working with a prototype provides a more direct experience.

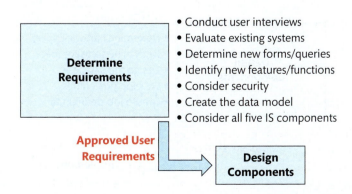

FIGURE CE3-6
SDLC Requirements Analysis Activity

FIGURE CE3-7
Sales Order Prototype in SAP Build

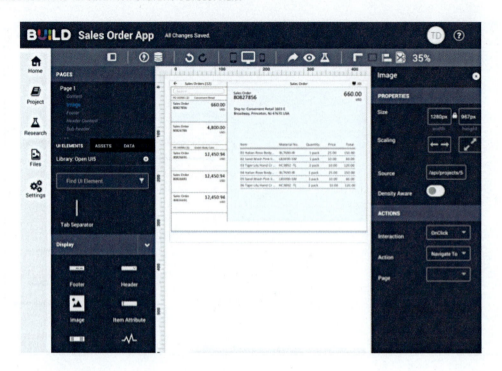

To support the creation of prototypes, the development team can use several apps to create low cost, realistic prototypes. Figure CE3-7 shows SAP Build, a new cloud-based app that enables development teams to build interactive prototypes, share them with end users and collect feedback, all without writing code. The Build example in Figure CE3-7 shows a prototype of a sales order screen.

The requirements activity ends with a sign-off. A **sign-off** is the user's signatures that indicate approval of the stated requirements.

Design Components

Each of the five components of an IS is designed and created in this activity. Typically, the team designs each component by developing alternatives, evaluating each of those alternatives against the requirements, and then selecting from among those alternatives. Accurate requirements are critical here; if they are incomplete or wrong, then they will be poor guides for evaluation.

Figure CE3-8 shows that design tasks pertain to each of the five IS components. For hardware, the team determines specifications for the hardware that it wants to acquire. (The team is not designing hardware in the sense of building a CPU or a disk drive.) Program design depends on the source of the programs. For off-the-shelf software, the team must determine candidate products and evaluate them against the requirements. For off-the-shelf with alteration programs, the team identifies products to be acquired off-the-shelf and then determines the alterations required. For custom-developed programs, the team produces design documentation for writing program code.

If the project includes constructing a database, then during this activity database designers convert the data model to a database design using techniques like those described in Chapter 4.

FIGURE CE3-8
SDLC Component Design Activity

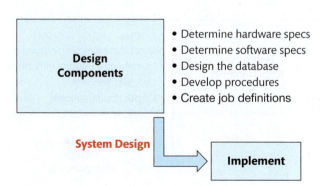

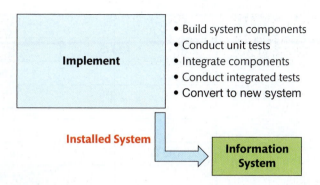

If the project involves off-the-shelf programs, then little database design needs to be done; the programs will have been coded to work with a preexisting database design.

Procedure design differs depending on whether the project is part of a BPM process (processes first) or a systems development process (systems first). If the former, business processes will already be designed, and all that is needed is to create procedures for using the app. If the latter, then procedures for using the system need to be developed, and it is possible that business processes that surround the system need to be developed as well.

With regard to people, design involves developing job descriptions. These descriptions will detail responsibilities, skills needed, training required, and so forth.

Implement

The term *implementation* has two meanings for us. It means to implement the information systems components only, or it means to implement the information system and the business processes that use the information system. As you read the following task descriptions, keep in mind that the tasks can apply to both interpretations of implementation. Tasks in the implementation activity are to build and test system components and to convert users to the new system and any new business processes (see Figure CE3-9).

TESTING Developers construct each of the components independently. They obtain, install, and test hardware. They license and install off-the-shelf programs. They write adaptations and custom programs as necessary. They construct a database and fill it with data. They document, review, and test procedures, and they create training programs. Finally, the organization hires and trains needed personnel.

Testing the system is important, time consuming, and expensive. A **test plan**, which is a formal description of the system's response to use and misuse scenarios, is written. Professional test engineers, called product quality assurance (PQA) test engineers, are hired for this task. Often teams of professional test engineers are augmented by users as well.

SYSTEM CONVERSION Once the system has passed testing, the organization installs the new system. The term **system conversion** is often used for this activity because it implies the process of *converting* business activity from the old system to the new. Again, conversion can be to the new system only, or it can be to the new system including new business processes.

Four types of conversion are possible: pilot, phased, parallel, and plunge as shown in Figure CE3-10. Any of the first three can be effective. In most cases, companies should avoid the fourth—"taking the plunge"!

With **pilot installation**, the organization implements the entire system/business processes on a limited portion of the business. An example would be for a college to use a new lab door locking system to secure only one of its computer labs. The advantage of pilot implementation is that if the system fails, the failure is contained within a limited boundary.

As the name implies, with **phased installation**, the new system/business process is installed in phases across the organization(s). Once a given piece works, then the organization installs and tests another piece of the system, until the entire system has been installed. Some systems are so tightly integrated that they cannot be installed in phased pieces. Such systems must be installed using one of the other techniques.

FIGURE CE3-10

Four Conversion Options

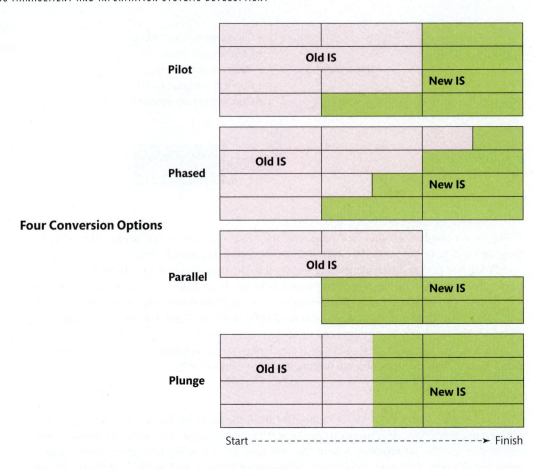

Four Conversion Options

With **parallel installation**, the new system/business process runs in parallel with the old one until the new system is tested and fully operational. Parallel installation is expensive because the organization incurs the costs of running both existing and new systems/business processes. Users must work double time, if you will, to run both systems. Then considerable work is needed to reconcile results of the new with the old. Twice the work, half the risk.

The final style of conversion is **plunge installation** (sometimes called *direct installation*). With it, the organization shuts off the old system and starts the new one. The best aspect of plunge is that the organization does not have to maintain both systems during the installation activity. However, if the new system/process fails, the organization is in trouble: Nothing can be done until either the new system/process is fixed or the old system/process is reinstalled. Because of the risk, organizations should avoid this conversion style if possible. The one exception is if the new system is providing a new capability that will not disrupt the operation of the organization if it fails.

A final challenge with any implementation is managing the impact of the new IS. Every new IS impacts a variety of processes and other information systems that affect other processes and systems, a ripple effect of impacts. In addition, often more than one IS is changed during development, and their impacts on each other are difficult to anticipate.

Not all new IS survive the implementation activity. Some systems are so poorly designed and managed that their failure is only evident after implementation is attempted. In these cases, deciding whether to throw good money after bad in order to keep the implementation alive can be a very difficult decision for executives. Disasters look like challenges to be overcome when they begin.

Figure CE3-11 summarizes the tasks for each of the five components during the design and implementation activities. Use this figure to test your knowledge of the tasks in each activity.

Maintain the System

The term **maintenance** is a misnomer; the work done during this activity is either to *fix* the system so that it works correctly or to *adapt* it to changes in requirements.

	Hardware	**Software**	**Data**	**Procedures**	**People**
Design	Determine hardware specifications.	Select off-the-shelf programs. Design alterations and custom programs as necessary.	Design database and related structures.	Design user and operations procedures.	Develop user and operations job descriptions.
Implementation	Obtain, install, and test hardware.	License and install off-the-shelf programs. Write alterations and custom programs. Test programs.	Create database. Fill with data. Test data.	Document procedures. Create training programs. Review and test procedures.	Hire and train personnel.

Unit test each component

Integrated Test and Conversion

FIGURE CE3-11

Design and Implementation for the Five IS Components

Figure CE3-12 shows tasks during the maintenance activity. First, there needs to be a means for tracking both failures and requests for enhancements to meet new requirements. For small systems, organizations can track failures and enhancements using word processing documents. As systems become larger, however, and as the number of failure and enhancement requests increases, many organizations find it necessary to develop a tracking database. Such a database contains a description of the failure or enhancement. It also records who reported the problem, who will make the fix or enhancement, what the status of that work is, and whether the fix or enhancement has been tested and verified by the originator.

A failure is a difference between what the system does and what it is supposed to do. Sometimes you will hear the term *bug* used instead of failure. As a future user, call failures *failures* because that's what they are. Don't have a bugs list, have a failures list. Don't have an unresolved bug, have an unresolved failure. A few months of managing an organization that is coping with a serious failure will show you the importance of this difference in terms.

Because an enhancement is an adaptation to new requirements, developers usually prioritize update requests separate from failures. The decision to make an enhancement includes a business decision that the enhancement will generate an acceptable rate of return. An organization needs a **configuration control** process, a method to ensure all changes to the new system are approved by management.

When changes are made to maintain a system, often those changes are first evaluated in a sandbox. A **sandbox** is a testing environment that isolates new code while replicating enough of it to see how the new code will work with existing code.

As mentioned, the SDLC process is similar to the BPM process described in Q1. One difference is that the BPM process occurs much more frequently than the SDLC; changes to processes are more common than changes to IS. One reason is that the SDLC process typically takes

FIGURE CE3-12

SDLC Maintenance Activity

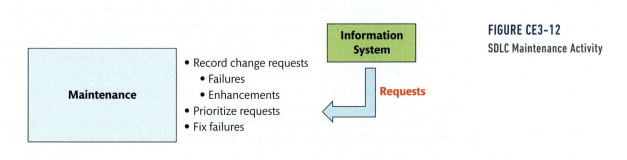

longer to accomplish than the BPM process. Because it is longer, it is typically more expensive. One attempt to shorten the process of building or updating an IS is to create a new process that replaces the SDLC. One of these new ways is the scrum process discussed next.

QE3-3 ▶ How Can Agile Development and the Scrum Process Overcome the Problems of the SDLC?

In this question, we present an alternative process to develop systems called agile development. We explain why it is needed, the principles of agile development, and the scrum process—a particularly useful version of agile development. We conclude the question and chapter extension by highlighting the challenges of system development for both SDLC and agile.

Why Agile Development Is Needed

The systems development life cycle (SDLC) process is falling out of favor in the systems development community. While it is still used for the largest projects, it is difficult to execute quickly and requirements are fuzzy and difficult to obtain. Requirements also frequently change as more is known about the project, users change their minds about what they want after they use part of the system, business needs change, or new technology offers other new possibilities.

According to the SDLC, however, progress goes in a linear sequence from requirements to design to implementation. Sometimes this is called the waterfall method because the assumption is that once you've finished an activity, you never go back; you go over the waterfall into the pool of the next stage. Requirements are done. Then you do design. Design is done; then you implement. However, experience has shown that it just doesn't work that way.

In the beginning, systems developers thought the SDLC might work for IS because processes like the SDLC work for building physical things. If you're going to build a runway, for example, you specify how long it needs to be, how much airplane weight the surface must support, and so forth. Then you design it, and then you build it. Here waterfall processes work.

However, business processes and information systems are not physical; as stated, they're abstract, made of thought-stuff. When you build a physical thing like a runway or a bridge, you can build a mock-up or replica that reveals most of the key features and can elicit feedback; building a replica of a thought isn't possible, so getting feedback on what you think you're building is much harder. Information systems are also social; they exist for people to inform themselves and achieve their goals. But people and social systems are incredibly malleable; they adapt. That characteristic enables humans to do many amazing things, but it also means that requirements change and the waterfall development process cannot work.

SDLC is risky not only are the requirements changed but because the people for whom the system is being constructed cannot see what they have until the very end. At that point, if something is wrong, all the money and time have already been spent. Furthermore, what if, as frequently happens, the project runs out of money or time before it is completed?

In short, the SDLC assumes that requirements are clear and don't change, which everyone who has ever been within 10 feet of a development project knows is false.

What Are the Principles of Agile Development?

Over the past 45 years, numerous alternatives to the SDLC have been proposed, including *rapid application development,* the *unified process, joint application design, extreme programming, Rational Unified Process, scrum*, and others. All of these techniques addressed the problems of the SDLC, and by the turn of the last century, their philosophy had coalesced into what has come to be known as **agile development**, which means a development process that conforms to the principles in Figure CE3-13. Scrum is an increasingly popular agile process that conforms to these principles.

First, scrum and the other agile techniques expect and even welcome change. Given the nature of social systems, *expect* is not a surprise, but why *welcome*? Isn't welcoming requirements changes a bit like welcoming a bad case of the flu? No, because systems are created to help organizations and people achieve their strategies, and the more the requirements change, the closer they come to facilitating strategies. The result is better and more satisfying for both the users and the development team.

Second, scrum and other agile development processes are designed to frequently deliver a *working* version of some part of the product. Frequently means 1 to 8 weeks, not longer.

> - Expect, even welcome, changes in requirements
> - Frequently deliver *working* version of the product
> - Work closely with customer for the duration
> - Design as you go
> - Test as you go
> - Team knows best how it's doing/how to change
> - Can be used for business processes, information systems, and applications development

FIGURE CE3-13
Principles of Agile (Scrum) Development

This frequency means that management is at risk only for whatever costs and time have been consumed in that period. And, at the end of the period, it will have some usable product piece that has at least some value to the business.

Thus, unlike the SDLC, agile techniques deliver benefits early and often. The initial benefits might be small, but they are positive and increase throughout the process. With the SDLC, no value is generated until the very end. Considering the value of time, this characteristic alone makes agile techniques more desirable.

The third principle in Figure CE3-13 is that the development team will work closely with the customer until the project ends. Someone who knows the business requirements must be available to the development team and must be able and willing to clearly express, clarify, and elaborate on requirements. Also, customers need to be available to test the evolving work product and provide guidance on how well new features work.

The fourth principle is a tough one for many developers to accept. Rather than design the complete, overall system at the beginning, only those portions of the design that are needed to complete the current work are done. Sometimes this is called just-in-time design.

Test as you go, the next principle, is obvious if the team is going to be delivering working versions. Testing is initially conducted among members of the team but involves the business customer as well.

Development teams know how well they're doing. You could go into any development environment today and ask the team how it's doing, and once team members understood you were not about to inflict a new management program on them, you would find they know their strengths, weaknesses, bottlenecks, and process problems quite well. That principle is part of agile development methodologies. At the end of every deliverable or some other (short) milestone, the team meets to assess how it's doing and how it can improve.

Agile development methodologies are generic. They can be applied to the creation of both business processes and information systems. They are applicable to other team projects as well, but that subject is beyond the scope of this text.

It may be tempting to think of agile development as a dynamic process, but it is structured. In each agile development, the activities occur in the same order. The key difference with structured SDLC is that in agile development the activities are much shorter. The fixed structure of these short activities is evident in the scrum process described next.

What Is the Scrum Process?

In rugby, a *scrum* is a gathering of a team into a circle to restart play after a foul or other interruption. Think of it as a huddle in American football. As stated, scrum is an agile development process with the characteristics shown in Figure CE3-14. First, the process is driven by a prioritized list of requirements that is created by the users and business sponsors of the new system. Scrum work periods can be as short as 1 week but, as with all agile processes, never longer than 8. Two to 4 weeks is recommended. Each work period, the team selects the top-priority items that it will commit to delivering that period.

Each workday begins with a **stand-up**, which is a 15-minute meeting in which each team member states:

- What he or she has done in the past day.
- What he or she will do in the coming day.
- Any factors that are blocking his or her progress.

- Requirements list drives process
- Each work period (1 to 4–8 weeks):
  - Select requirements to consider
  - Determine tasks to perform—select requirements to deliver
  - Team meets daily for 15 minutes (stand-up)
    - What I did yesterday
    - What I'm going to do today
    - What's blocking me
  - Test frequently
  - Paired work possible
  - Minimal documentation
  - Deliver (something) that works
  - Evaluate team's work process at end of period (and say thanks)
- Rinse and repeat until
  - Customer says we're done
  - Out of time
  - Out of money
- Three principal roles
  - Product owner (business professional)
  - Scrum master
  - Team members (7 ± 2 people)

The purpose of the stand-up is to achieve accountability for team members' progress and to give public forum for blocking factors. Often, one team member will have expertise to help a blocked team member resolve the problem.

Testing is done frequently, possibly many times per day. Sometimes the business owner of the project is involved in daily testing as well. In some cases, team members work in pairs; in **paired programming**, for example, two team members share the same computer and write a computer program together. Sometimes, one programmer will provide a test, and the other will either demonstrate that the code passes that test or alter the code so that it will.

Minimal documentation is prepared. The result of the team's work is not design or other documents but rather a working version of the requirements that were selected at the start of the scrum period.

At the end of the scrum period, the working version of the product is delivered to the customer, who can, if desired, put it to use at that time, even if it is not fully finished. After the product is delivered, the team meets to evaluate its own process and to make changes as needed. Figure CE3-15 summarizes the scrum process.

Work continues in a repeating cycle of scrum periods until one of three conditions is met:

- The customer is satisfied with the product created and decides to accept the work product, even if some requirements are left unsatisfied.
- The project runs out of time.
- The project runs out of money.

Unlike the SDLC, if a scrum project terminates because of time or budget limitations, the customer will have some useful result for the time and money expended. It may not be the fully functioning version that was desired, but it is something that can generate value for the project sponsors, assuming requirements are defined and prioritized correctly.

The success of scrum is that it improves collaboration between the development team and end users. As mentioned in Chapter 10, collaboration is iteration with feedback, and scrum creates feedback within an iterating cycle of development. Part of the system is built, feedback is obtained, another part is added, feedback is obtained, and on and on. Scrum's main advantage over SDLC are these many iterations with good feedback. However, this improved collaboration requires colocation of users and the development team, which can be expensive for the firm and distracting for busy users.

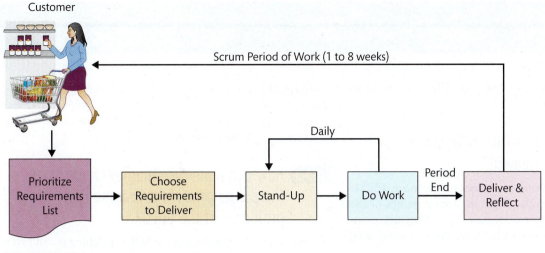

FIGURE CE3-15
Scrum Process

Challenges to Systems Development Both SDLC and Agile

Before closing, consider the challenges facing the analysts developing a new IS. While SDLC, agile, and scrum seem like they would create success projects, the history of system's development is littered with project failures both epic and small scale that have cost firms millions of dollars and countless headaches. Figure CE3-16 lists some of these challenges.

Busy executives fail to give the project a clear definition or fail to link the new IS to business strategy or processes, and they allow scope creep after the project begins. At times, this creep becomes very risky as executives escalate their commitment to a project and throw good money after bad. Users are not engaged—they either don't see the value in their participation or are poor collaborators. Some users resist accepting the new system because careers are changed, implementation is done poorly, or processes are not changed to take advantage of the new system. Planning by the development team is difficult as every project is unique and the technology is often new to many on the team. As a result, the development team fails to define a realistic schedule, fails to coordinate the project activities, or misses too many milestones. A second issue for the development team is failure to maintain adequate collaboration with end users. Systems development can be a daring venture.

As you can imagine, much more can be said and learned about processes for developing business processes and information systems. If you want to learn more, take a course in systems development. But as you look to your future, expect to be involved in process or IS development, and realize much of the success of these projects depend on your ability to collaborate with project analysts. What's more, one day you may want to lead such a change project. That job, often called project management, is both rewarding and lucrative, and is frequently done by professionals with some technical background.

Top Management
· Fail to limit project scope
· Allow scope creep after start

End Users
· Not engaged
· Resist new system

IS Development Team
· Poor planning
· Limited collaboration with users

FIGURE CE3-16

Challenges of Systems Development

ACTIVE REVIEW

Use this active review to verify that you understand the ideas and concepts in this extension.

QE3-1 ▶ What are the activities of business process management?

Describe the need for business process management (BPM) and explain why it is a cycle. Name the four activities of the BPM process and summarize the tasks in each. Summarize two reasons why business processes need to be changed and give an example of each.

QE3-2 ▶ What are the activities of the systems development life cycle (SDLC) development process?

Name five basic systems development activities. Describe tasks required for the definition, requirements, and design components activities. Explain the role of business analysts and IT analysts. Describe prototyping and why it is used. Explain the tasks required to implement and maintain the system and assess the process. Describe four types of process/system conversion. Explain configuration control.

QE3-3 ▶ How can agile development and the scrum process overcome the problems of the SDLC?

Explain the three reasons that the SDLC is falling out of favor. In your own words, explain the meaning and importance of each of the principles in Figure CE3-13. Explain how each of the scrum essential items in Figure CE3-14 is implemented in the scrum process shown in Figure CE3-15. Explain the challenges of systems development.

KEY TERMS AND CONCEPTS

Agile development   404
Business analyst   398
Business process management
   (BPM)   394
Configuration control   403
Continuous improvement process
   (CIP)   396
Cost feasibility   397
IT analyst   398
Maintenance   402

Offshoring   398
Outsourcing   398
Paired programming   406
Parallel installation   402
Phased installation   401
Pilot installation   401
Plunge installation   402
Prototype   399
Sandbox   403
Schedule feasibility   397

Sign-off   400
Stand-up   405
System conversion   401
Systems development   397
Systems development life cycle
   (SDLC)   397
Technical feasibility   397
Test plan   401

USING YOUR KNOWLEDGE

E3-1. Search Google or Bing for the phrase *what is a business analyst*. Investigate several of the links that you find and answer the following questions:
   a. What are the primary job responsibilities of a business analyst?
   b. What knowledge do business analysts need?
   c. What skills/personal traits do business analysts need?
   d. Would a career as a business analyst be interesting to you? Explain why or why not.

E3-2. Specify a popular app that you use frequently, it could be Uber, Canvas, Snapchat, for example. For this app put yourself on the IS development team that is charged with improving the system, a significant update is required. Answer the following questions from the SDLC activities:
   a. Define System: What are the goals and scope of the improved system?

b. Determine Requirements: What are two new features and two new outputs (screens)?

c. Design Components: What new data needs to be collected to make the new requirements possible?

d. Implementation: Which of the four system conversion option do you suggest, and why?

e. Maintenance: Draw the activities in a configuration control process you would use to address changes in the new system.

E3-3. Which step in the SDLC contains the most risk? Explain your answer.

E3-4. Reread the system conversion section of the Implementation phase. For new or improved apps at your school or for apps you commonly use, for each conversion method suggest an app that should use that method and explain why.

E3-5. Using the Internet, find descriptions of scrum and agile development processes. What two ideas about these development processes would you add to this chapter extension? Why are those two important for students to know?

AI and Robots

Artificial intelligence (AI) and robots are always in the news. Amazon's Alexa, IBM's Watson, drones, and driverless vehicles make daily headlines. These innovations are as old as computers themselves, and their promise, potential, and peril have long stoked the imagination of authors, futurists, technologists, and moviemakers. What once was only imagination is rapidly becoming our reality today.

These innovations are beguiling and clever, and it is captivating, even fun, to study how they work. However, as businesspeople, we are interested in what they can do for business processes. But you should be interested for another reason. AI and robots will also will have a significant impact on the job market. For you to compete in that changing labor market, you'll need to understand what they are good at doing and what they are not so good at doing. Know your competition.

In this extension, we first introduce the intelligence process and then the AI that support it. We conclude our discussion of AI by considering the business processes AI supports. We then consider robots, a particular type of computer that mimics human actions. Before we begin, one distinction is helpful. Most people use *AI* and *robots* rather loosely to mean the same thing. Here we emphasize a simple distinction—AI thinks like us and robots act like us. While many robots also use AI, AI does not need a robot.

QE4-1 What Is the Intelligence Process?

Intelligence is power in the information economy. **Intelligence**, the ability to acquire, store, and apply knowledge, has been the holy grail of your protracted school crusade. With intelligence, businesses can optimize their supply chains, more accurately price their products, and hire the best people, to name just three benefits.

The intelligence process has three activities—acquire, store, and apply knowledge—as shown in Figure CE4-1. This is a dynamic process, as the activities do not always follow the same order. For example, many applications can occur after data is stored, and new acquisitions of knowledge can be added after storing has occurred. The goal of these activities, of the intelligence process, is effective behavior by the user or by the AI.

The substance of the intelligence process is knowledge. Most fundamentally, **knowledge** is justified beliefs. For example, I know a stop sign means I must stop my vehicle—my belief that I should stop is justified by the law; I know we landed on the Moon in 1969 because my belief is justified by historical evidence.

FIGURE CE4-1

Main Intelligence Process Activities and Roles

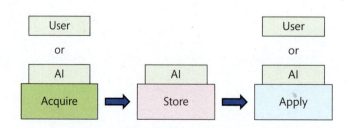

We can see the activities of Figure CE4-1 played out in Google's new driverless car. Google software engineers acquire the knowledge of car driving, that knowledge is stored in computers, and AI in the car applies that knowledge as it drives. The goal of the process, intelligent behavior by the car, is achieved by successfully acquiring, storing, and applying knowledge.

The intelligence process is very similar to another process called the knowledge management process. **Knowledge management** also acquires, stores, and applies knowledge, but it broadens the Acquire activity to include creation. An example of creating knowledge is asking an HR expert what key attributes each candidate for a position should provide on an application. This step of asking the expert creates new knowledge that subsequently leads to acquiring knowledge about each candidate.

Having described the Intelligence process, we next consider how AI can support these activities in the Intelligence process "artificially."

▶ QE4-2 ▶ What Is Artificial Intelligence?

Intelligence is a tantalizing prize for our machine friends where we call it **artificial intelligence**, or **AI**. AI is software that enables an IS to mimic or simulate human intelligence. As shown in Figure CE4-1, when AI software mimics how a user acquires, stores, or applies knowledge, it is called AI. With artificial intelligence, a computer can drive a car, diagnose an illness, spot a fraudulent credit card transaction, and beat us at our own games—*Jeopardy!*, chess, and even matchmaking.

Three Common AI Techniques

To explain how AI can acquire, store, and apply knowledge, we consider three of its most common techniques of AI as shown in Figure CE4-2. Each AI techniques acquires, stores, and applies knowledge in different ways.

Expert Systems

The earliest AI technique, called expert systems, attempted to capture employee expertise directly. **Expert systems** are rule-based systems that encode *data from* human knowledge in the form of **If/Then rules**. Such rules are statements that specify that if a particular condition exists, then some action should be taken. One example is the rules that could be part of a medical expert system for diagnosing heart disease.

To create the system of rules, the expert system development team interviews human experts in the domain of interest. The rules to diagnose heart disease are *acquired* for an expert system by interviewing cardiologists who are known to be particularly adept at diagnosing cardiac disease. These rules are *stored* in the expert system, sometimes referred to as a knowledge base, until a user asks the system to *apply* those rules to a particular heart patient.

Unlike a conventional computer program, expert systems rely on an **inference engine**. An inference engine applies logical rules to the knowledge base to derive new knowledge. For the

FIGURE CE4-2
Three AI Techniques

Expert Systems

If/Then Rules Inference Engine

Content Management

Management and Delivery of Documents (SharePoint)

Neural Networks

Nodes and Connections That Learn

heart patient, the inference engine takes inputs from the user and chains through a series of If/ Then statements to create new knowledge—a diagnosis for this patient.

Content Management

Another AI technique is designed to address knowledge that is encoded in documents. **Content management systems (CMS)** support the management and delivery of documents including reports, Web pages, and other expressions of employee knowledge. Typical users of content management systems are companies that sell complicated products and want to share their knowledge of those products with employees and customers. Someone at Toyota, for example, knows how to change the timing belt on the four-cylinder 2016 Toyota Camry. Toyota wants to share that knowledge with car owners, mechanics, and Toyota employees.

Content management systems face serious challenges. First, most content databases are huge; some have thousands of individual documents, pages, and graphics. Second, CMS content is dynamic. Imagine the frequency of Web page changes at Apple or Google or Amazon that must occur each day! Another complication for content management systems is that documents do not exist in isolation from each other. Documents refer to one another, and when one changes, others must change as well. A fourth complication is that document contents are perishable. Documents become obsolete and need to be altered, removed, or replaced. Consider, for example, what happens when a new product is announced. Figure CE4-3 shows the main page for Microsoft.com less than 2 hours after its announcement of Surface. Finally, content is provided in many languages. 3M has tens of thousands of products, some of which are harmful when used improperly. 3M must publish product safety data for all such products in all the languages shown. Every document, in whatever language it was authored, must be translated into all languages before it can be published on 3M's site. And when one of them changes, all of the translated versions must change as well. CMS can be expensive to maintain.

Due to the expense of custom applications, many organizations today use *off-the-shelf* CMS software. Microsoft SharePoint provides generalized facilities to acquire, store, and apply knowledge in documents and other content types. Such off-the-shelf products have considerably more functionality than most in-house systems, and they are far less expensive to maintain.

To see how a content management system might be used, consider a large multinational energy firm seeking to acquire a wind energy company in Japan. The large energy firm needs to assemble a team to determine the value of the wind energy company. The team needs individuals with appropriate backgrounds and experiences, but the multinational firm has thousands of employees. Who among them knows Japanese, has lived in Japan, or is familiar with wind energy consumption, production, or valuation?

Now consider how the content management system can help. First, a CMS can *acquire* knowledge about employees by asking each of them to specify language skills, work experience,

FIGURE CE4-3

Microsoft Main Page Less than
2 Hours after Surface Announcement

and other unique talents in a personal database that it then *stores*. Later, employees are able to ask the CMS to *apply* its knowledge of employees and produce a list of employees with particular language and work experiences in order to assemble a team.

Neural Networks

A neural network is a technique of AI inspired by the networks of neurons in our brains and central nervous systems. A **neural net** is an adaptive system of nodes and connections that learn. These neural nets are also called artificial neural nets (ANN). Common domains for neural nets are Google's language translator, spell checkers, and vehicle control, game playing, and speech recognition systems like Apple's Siri and Amazon's Alexa.

A simple three-level network designed to recognize handwritten numbers is shown in Figure CE4-4. Much like the collection of neurons in our bodies, each node in a neural network connects to many other nodes, and working together the network of nodes produces an output. This neural net compares the output to a right answer, and the network adjusts how the neurons fire and influence each other in order to produce a better output the next time.

In Figure CE4-4, the four input nodes are "Have a stem?," "Have a diagonal?," "Have a loop?," and "Have crossing lines?" Each of these input nodes has a weight; if we think the diagonal is the most telling characteristic of a 7, it gets the highest weight. Then the middle nodes start with even weights and the output node is "It is a 7?" or "Is it not a 7?"

Once the initial parameters are set up, the network is shown a trial run of, say, 100 cases and the right answer for each; perhaps 60 of those shown are 7s. The network itself decides new values for the node weights and reruns the 100 cases with new weights. It continues to try new weights until it can no longer improve its accuracy. Then the system is ready for use. The special aspect of a neural network is that it can continue to learn how to distinguish a 7 or anything else as long as it is in operation. Like us, neural networks learn as they go.

The neural network technique is one method of **machine learning**, a broader term that encompasses all techniques that use algorithms to discover patterns in data. With machine learning, a subset of AI, the computer is more autonomous and can find patterns without as much structure as typical AI; give the computer access to data and let it learn for itself. One example of machine learning is an email spam filter. A machine learning approach would direct the computer to observe which emails users ignore and which ones they don't and figure out a pattern so that future emails can be filtered more accurately.

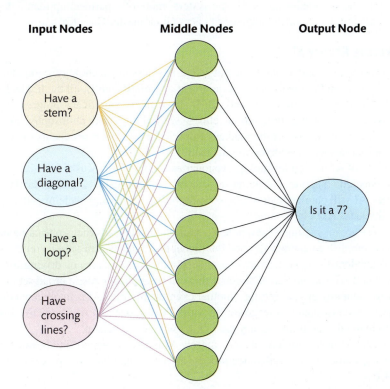

FIGURE CE4-4

Simple Three-Level Neural Network for Recognizing a 7

Five Components of IS	Artificial Intelligence IS
Hardware	Traditional computing system or a robotic device
Software	Unconventional algorithms that learn, are goal centered, and are narrow and specific
Data	Domain specific, often rules or statements (e.g., "faces are round," "dogs are animals")
Procedures	Methods for converting implicit expertise or the steps to get expertise
People	Experts and end users

Five Common Components

While these three AI techniques differ in how they acquire, store, and apply knowledge, they do so with similar components. Each of the three techniques has the same five components as other IS: hardware, software, data, procedures, and people. However, what makes AI IS distinct is their software. The five components of an AI IS are summarized in Figure CE4-5.

A list of the key aspects of AI systems begins with hardware. Hardware can be traditional computer systems of all sizes, but it can also be robotic hardware. Robots are discussed in the second half of the extension, and oftentimes they use AI systems to mimic human thinking. AI software is unconventional—a processor does not typically execute it in sequence or as objects but using an inference engine or neural network algorithm. This software also has the distinguishing attribute of improvement; the system is designed to become more intelligent. The data for an AI system is often specific rules or statements about a domain such as "faces are round" or "dogs are animals." The procedures, the steps for humans to interact with AI systems, are often for making knowledge explicit. These procedures enable the AI system to put data *in* the system; procedures also enable users to interact with the AI system to get the intelligence data *out*. Finally, people are the experts or others with knowledge that the AI system is using or the end users seeking to obtain intelligence from the system. People, at times, can play a more interactive role with the knowledge stored by the system, more of a partnership than a dependence, creating a Centaur in the colorful language of chess Grandmaster Gary Kasparov.

Broad AI Versus Narrow AI

AI is a 60-year-old term and a vital topic outside of business in psychology, computer engineering, and philosophy and in media and entertainment as well. Recently, all the big tech players—Amazon, Apple, Google, Microsoft, and IBM—have made significant progress in AI. This growth in AI has raised questions about ethics, warfighting, and philosophy. For example, should a driverless car swerve off the road and imperil the lives of its occupants to avoid striking a group of pedestrians who wandered into its path?

The growth of AI has led technology visionaries such as Elon Musk, Bill Gates and Steven Hawking to conclude that one day, perhaps too soon, an event called the **singularity** will occur. At singularity, AI will gain enough intelligence to initiate a runaway cycle of self-improvement that eventually leads AI to turn on us.

While these are interesting issues, here we restrict ourselves to what some call a **narrow AI**: using AI to accomplish a narrowly defined intelligent task such as generating a recommendation, spotting a fraudulent financial transaction, understanding a sentence, or driving a car. On the other hand, **broad AI** is a general intelligence that can be applied across a broad set of tasks such as counseling, planning, or goal setting. Another example of broad AI is intelligent conversation, and a famous conversational challenge for AI is the **Turing test**. An AI passes the Turing test if it can fool individuals into thinking they are talking with a real person.

While broad AI may soon have its day, narrow AI is already supporting business processes. The relationships among AI, Intelligence process activities, and business processes is shown in Figure CE4-6.

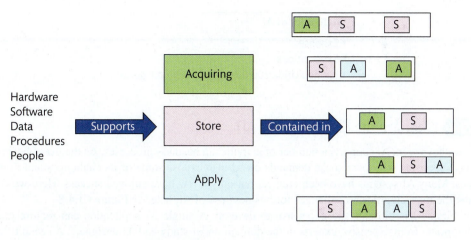

FIGURE CE4-6
AI Components, Activities, and
Business Processes

Hardware
Software
Data
Procedures
People

Five Components of IS   Three Intelligence Activities   Business Processes*

* White space represents other activities in the business process.

QE4-3 ▶ What Business Processes Are Supported by AI?

Many business processes are supported by AI systems. In Figure CE4-7, we list some of the most common. We briefly outline the first four processes as examples of processes supported by AI.

Process: Medical Diagnosis

Patients can use AI expert systems to diagnose and better understand their own illnesses. One expert system, the Web site WebMD, asks the patient a series of questions about their ailment, runs their answers through its expert system, and produces a diagnosis.

Process: Locating Expertise

Microsoft uses SharePoint to help its coders write software. Coders frequently update their SharePoint profiles with software applications they helped develop. For example, Cal Smith helped write the code for Word tables in Word 2013. If during the development of Word 2020 a coder at Microsoft runs into a problem with the autowidth function of tables, she can use Share-Point to find and communicate with Cal.

Process: Fraud Detection

Credit card companies use neural network AI to identify fraudulent transactions. Nodes in the neural net include "has this card been used more than three times in the last 15 minutes," "is this transaction near where the cardholder resides," "is this transaction online," and "is this transaction for a high-risk item." The output from the neural network is a yes/no decision, and the network is provided the feedback on its decision so it can update its weights.

Process: Human Authentication

Facebook built a neural network to recognize and authenticate human faces. This program, called DeepFace, can accurately differentiate human faces about 97 percent of the time.

| Medical Diagnosis |
| Locating Expertise |
| Fraud Detection |
| Human Authentication |
| Image Classification |
| Web Advertisement Placement |

FIGURE CE4-7
Business Processes Supported
by AI

FIGURE CE4-8

Challenges of AI

> **Challenges of AI**
>
> • Expense
> • Expectations
> • Limited Understanding of Human Intelligence

QE4-4 ▸ What Are the Challenges of AI?

As we have seen, AI supports a number of activities in business processes. As the list of business processes using AI grows, these demands on AI also expose some of its challenges and limitations. Many AI systems have been created, but only a few have enjoyed success. Here we consider the most significant challenges for business use of AI, listed in Figure CE4-8.

First, AI is difficult and expensive to develop. A single AI application can require many labor hours from expensive experts in the domain under study and AI designers. A second challenge is the high expectations of AI. Proponents of AI hoped to be able to duplicate the performance of highly trained experts, like doctors. It turned out, however, that no AI has the same diagnostic ability as knowledgeable, skilled, and experienced doctors. Even when AI came close in ability, changes in medical technology required constant changing of the AI, and the problems caused by such changes are very expensive to correct. Third, while AI can mimic the human mind, our scientific understanding of the mind is still limited. As a result, progress in AI, even narrow AI, is limited. As one AI expert put it: saying that AI thinks like a human mind is like saying submarines swim. A sub moves through water, but that is a limited understanding of swimming. Submarines and swimmers are good at different things. AI can do what people find hard, such as consistently applying a large rule set, but is poor at what we find easy, such as being creative or asking new questions.

While these perils of AI are significant, the promise of AI suggests that this field will continue to grow. Robots, like AI, also show promise. We examine robots, their attributes, and their challenges next.

QE4-5 ▸ How Are Robots Used in Business?

Now that we have discussed AI, machines that think like us, consider robots, machines that act like us. Robots seem to be everywhere now—moving inventory in warehouses, driving vehicles and airplanes, building cars in an assembly line, and disposing of hazardous material. These and other examples are shown in Figure CE4-9. In the figure are current examples; soon drones will

FIGURE CE4-9

Examples of Robots and Their Common Attributes

Source: Chesky/Shutterstock, WENN Ltd/Alamy Stock Photo, WENN Ltd/Alamy Stock Photo, Polaris/Newscom, Photomontage/Shutterstock, Michael Fitzsimmons/Shutterstock, USAF/Science Source

Name of Robot	Attributes of Robots			Example
	Autonomy	**Lifelikeness**	**Physical Motion**	
Warehouse AGV	Fully autonomous	Like ants	Moves inventory	
Honda ASIMO	Semiautonomous	Very humanlike	Answers questions	
Big Dog	Fully autonomous	Like dogs	Carries equipment	
Amazon drone	Fully autonomous	Like birds	Delivers packages	
Telesurgeon	Semiautonomous	Like human arms/hands	Performs surgery	
Haz	Fully autonomous	Not humanlike	Disposes of waste, delivers ordinance	
Military drone	Fully autonomous	Like birds	Surveils	

Attributes of Robots	• Autonomy • Lifelike • Physical Motion

fly in building hallways at 40 mph, and robots will cook our food, fight our battles, and care for our kids and our elderly.

Here we examine how business processes use robots and their current challenges. However, we begin by considering their attributes—what makes a robot a robot.

As mentioned earlier, many discussions of AI and robots mash them together under a breathless title like "The Rise of the Machines." Instead, we encourage you to keep them separate—an AI supports processes, and robots are physical machines that do work, often replacing people. Think of robots as actors in a process playing a role. As an actor, they can be used as substitutes for human actors.

Attributes

A **robot** is an autonomous, lifelike machine that performs an action in place of a person. The three main characteristics of robots are listed in Figure CE4-10. **Autonomy** means the ability to operate, at least in part, without direct human intervention. Most robots are also lifelike; many of them perform an action like humans or animals. Finally, all robots move and create action. These attributes are also incorporated in Figure CE4-10, a figure that includes examples of the variety of work done by robots.

Limited Here to Business

Robots, like AI, have a life outside of the business domain. This general domain is called robotics and includes engineering and computer science fields. In this domain, **robotics** is the design, construction, and use of autonomous machines that mimic human or animal actions.

For business purposes, the best way to think about robots is their impact on business processes. They are a substitute for human actors in activities in business processes. Several examples of these activities, their processes, and the objectives of the processes are listed in Figure CE4-11.

As suggested by the variety of processes and objectives shown in Figure CE4-11, robots are important to businesses because they can do an increasingly wide variety of activities in pursuit of a wide variety of process objectives. Figure CE4-11 also shows that robots typically perform roles that are dirty, dangerous, dull, or distant. These four D's are a good way to determine if a role might be more suitable for a robot than a person.

Challenges for Robotics

Robots are increasingly attractive to business; however, businesses are finding out that robots bring some of their own troubles to work. These challenges are listed in Figure CE4-12. A number of studies suggest that robots contribute to unemployment; they take jobs away from people.

Name of Robot

	Activity	Process	Objective	Role: 4D
Warehouse AGV	Move inventory	Packing	Speed	Dull
Honda ASIMO	Answer questions	Customer service	Cost and service	Dull
Big Dog	Carry equip	Mil/police ops	More weight	Dirty
Amazon drone	Deliver	Sales	Lower cost	Dull
Telesurgeon	Cutting	Surgery	Availability	Distant
Haz	Dispose	Removal	Safety	Dirty
Military drone	Surveillance	Surveillance	Loiter, exposure	Dangerous

FIGURE CE4-12

Challenges of Robots

Challenges of Robots
• Human Unemployment
• Harm to Human Life
• Vulnerable to Threats

Others are concerned about the ethics of automated machines executing military or police activities that have the potential of harming human life. Finally, some are concerned that as we grow dependent on machine slaves, we become vulnerable to threats to these robots such as hacking, viruses, or electromagnet pulses (EMPs).

While these challenges limit robot use, our lack of imagination also limits their use. We often fail to imagine how we might use a robot in a different way than a person to accomplish the same objective. Most savings and process improvement occur when the robot does activities in different ways but still accomplishes the same goal. For example, a Google car is better if a humanoid robot in a driver seat does not do the steering. In warehouses, the goal is to move inventory; humans do this by driving forklifts, but some robots would rather lift and move inventory by sliding underneath it first. Different strokes for different—robot—folks.

Impact on Your Career

Before we close, reconsider a topic from the beginning of the extension. You will be competing in a labor market with AI and robots. Clearly, machines have many advantages—productivity, speed, quality, scale, consistency, and reduction of human injury. People have their advantages too—lower development cost, better security, and greater flexibility. These advantages are summarized in Figure CE4-13.

The last human strength in Figure CE4-13 is particularly important. People are much better than machines when judgment is required. Machines can only understand inputs that are objective, repeatable, and programmed measures. They excel with objective inputs like the timing inputs to a robot on an assembly line, altitude inputs to an autopilot, and completeness of inputs of every box on a web form. Objective inputs, routine actions.

Humans, on the hand, are uniquely able to deal with uncertain or ambiguous inputs. For example, machines can measure the length, sound variety, and rating of a movie, but only humans can assess its quality, as an assessment of quality is based on ambiguous inputs. Where inputs are ambiguous, rely on people for activities like diagnosis and treatment of illness, risk assessment, human communication and interaction, and learning. Be good in ambiguity where judgment is required; your career may depend on it.

In this extension, we introduced AI and the business processes it can support. We also described robotics and the types of activities robots do in business processes. For both AI and robotics, we also highlighted the challenges of using them effectively. While these business opportunities and challenges are worth identifying, the impact of AI and robots on our society will greatly exceed their impact on business processes. These are disruptive technologies.

FIGURE CE4-13

Strengths of AI & Robots; Strengths of Humans

Strengths

AI and Robots	Humans
• Productivity	• Low Development Cost
• Speed	• Better Security
• Quality	• Flexibility
• Scale	• Judge Ambiguity
• Consistency	
• Few Injuries	

ACTIVE REVIEW

Use this active review to verify that you understand the ideas and concepts in this extension.

QE4-1 ▶ What is the intelligence process?

Describe the Intelligence process. Explain each of the three Intelligence process activities. Define knowledge and give a specific example of how that knowledge is justified. Describe knowledge management and how it differs from the Intelligence process.

QE4-2 ▶ What is artificial intelligence?

Explain AI. Describe the three general AI techniques. Describe how expert systems work. Give an example of an If/Then rule. Explain how an inference engine works. Explain content management systems and the type of knowledge they are typically used with. Describe several of the content management system challenges. Explain neural networks and how they work. Describe how nodes work and how they are updated. Describe the five components of an AI IS. Explain the difference between broad and narrow AI. Describe the Turing test.

QE4-3 ▶ What business processes are supported by AI?

List several business processes supported by AI. Explain how AI supports a particular business process and how AI improves that process.

QE4-4 ▶ What are the challenges of AI?

Explain why AI can be expensive to develop. Describe why AI often fails to meet high expectations. Explain how the limited understanding of the mind limits progress.

QE4-5 ▶ How are robots used in business?

How are robots different than AI? Explain each of the three attributes of robots. Give an example of a robot, an activity the robot does, and the objective of the process. Explain what each of the four D's means. Explain the challenges of using robots. Describe advantages of AI and robots and advantages of humans.

KEY TERMS AND CONCEPTS

Artificial intelligence (AI)   411
Autonomy   416
Broad AI   414
Content management systems
   (CMS)   412
Expert systems   411

If/Then rules   411
Inference engine   411
Intelligence   410
Knowledge   410
Knowledge management   410
Machine learning   413

Narrow AI   414
Neural net   413
Robot   416
Robotics   417
Singularity   414
Turing test   414

USING YOUR KNOWLEDGE

E4-1. Search online to read about a common AI system such as Amazon's Alexa or IBM's Watson. Give an example of how that system acquires, stores, and applies knowledge. Specify the knowledge in your example.

E4-2. Visit WebMD.com and navigate to the main Symptom Checker page. Enter some symptoms and observe how the expert system presents a general diagnosis.

E4-3. Go to the Wikipedia entry for "artificial neural networks" and read the introduction about neural networks. Describe an example listed on the page of a successful neural network.

E4-4. Refer to Figure CE4-7 for examples and describe a business process your university or college uses and how AI could make that process more effective.

E4-5. Read about one of the robots listed in Figure CE4-10 online. Explain how it is used. Which of the challenges in Figure CE4-12 apply to your robot description?

Extension 5

Location-Based Data Information Systems: Mobile Devices and Geographic Information Systems

Location matters. Location dictates your choices, the people you interact with, the businesses you use. Your location influences almost all of your food, travel, entertainment, and social decisions. Think about how often you view your location on Google Maps. Businesses use location just as much. The location of their customers matters, as does the location of all the items in their supply chain. Location data provides the answer to every business "where" question.

Location-based data (LBD), also called spatial data, is spatially referenced data; it identifies where an object or person is located on a map or reference system. In this extension, we introduce you to two IS that use LBD—mobile devices and geographic information systems (GIS), as shown in Figure CE5-1. A **geographic IS (GIS)** is, most simply, an organizational IS that captures, analyzes, and presents LBD.

The goal of this extension is to help you understand how businesses use these two LBD IS to support their processes. We first examine the activities of the location-based process—capture, analyze, and present—and how the two types of location IS—mobile devices and GIS—support those activities before we close with challenges and limitations.

With your smartphone, you are already a willing participant in location processes. In this extension, we do not want you to take the perspective of a student but rather a businessperson and understand the different options, opportunities, and challenges presented by mobile devices and GIS systems as well as the wide variety of business processes they support.

QE5-1 ▶ How Fast Is LBD Growing?

Mobile devices include smartphones, tablets, smartwatches, and other wearable devices. They are everywhere. Your smartphone is one of 2 billion smartphones in the world, your mobile subscription one of about 4 billion, and your mobile purchases a part of $113 billion a year global market. When you bought your first smartphone, you contributed to the fastest adoption technology boom in history, faster than the adoption of TV, laptops, or the Internet.

Traditional mobile devices and GIS have been creating and using LBD for years. Now, new mobile devices are joining the act. Cars now create and share their location data with other cars,

FIGURE CE5-1
Two Types of LBD and LBD Activities

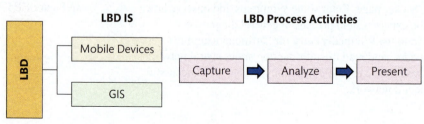

LBD IS   LBD Process Activities

LBD — Mobile Devices / GIS

Capture → Analyze → Present

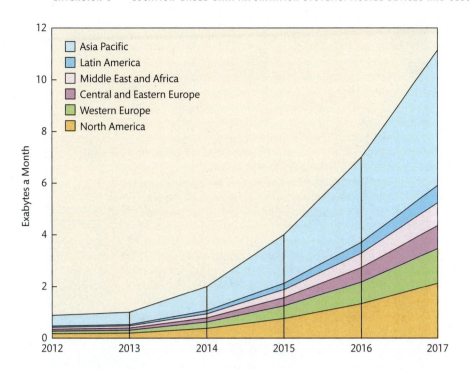

FIGURE CE5-2
Growth in LBD

open parking spaces share their location data with desperate drivers, and robots share location data about goods in a warehouse with a database. In the coming years, the growth of the Internet of Things will make location data about many, many more items available—products in a supply chain, food containers in the home, and virtually every consumer item sold in a mall or grocery store. The growth in LBD is shown in Figure CE5-2.

As shown, LBD is growing by as much as 20 percent per year, and these gains will translate to impressive savings in business efficiency. Boston Consulting expects LBD will help create $2.6 trillion in efficiency gains worldwide over the next 5 years due to the key role that LBD plays in logistics and marketing. Businesses profit, but so do consumers; LBD is expected to save consumers more than $600 billion annually by 2020.

QE5-2 ▶ How Are Mobile Devices and GIS Different?

Figure CE5-3 contrasts the two LBD information systems. We first describe mobile devices and then GIS.

As shown in Figure CE5-3, mobile devices differ from GIS on each of the LBD process activities. The data captured by a mobile device is about itself; it creates data about its own location. An individual carrying the device analyzes that data. The device owner analyzes data presented on the device itself. For example, when you use your smartphone to find a Starbucks, your device determines and captures its location, and then you analyze your location relative to the Starbucks; you do this on your smartphone's small screen.

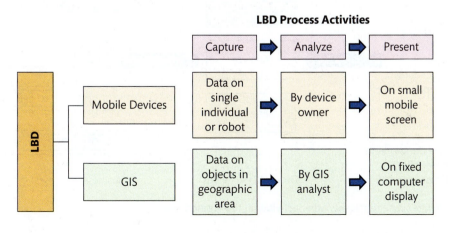

FIGURE CE5-3

LBD, Mobile Devices, GIS, and LBD Process Activities

FIGURE CE5-4

GIS of Possible Store Location Data

In contrast, a business might use a GIS to determine the best location of a new store within a geographic area. An analyst would capture data about vehicle traffic on nearby roads and analyze that data on a map using a large, nonmoving computer display as shown in Figure CE5-4.

Note: Mobile technology and how mobile networks work are discussed in Chapter 3.

QE5-3 ▶ What Is a Location-Based Process?

A location-based process is a type of dynamic process that captures, analyzes, and presents LBD. The objective of a location-based process is typically to present location-based data in a way that individuals using mobile devices or GIS analysts can use to inform themselves about location-relevant issues in a timely fashion. The main components of the LBD process are shown in Figure CE5-5.

FIGURE CE5-5

LBD IS Components and Business Processes

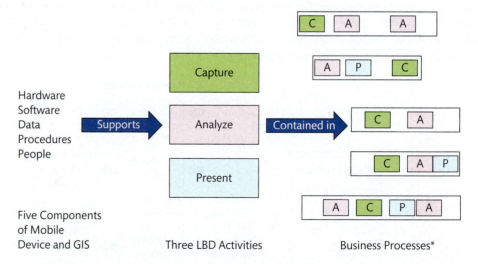

* White space represents other activities in the business process.

That figure depicts the relationship between the two LBD IS, these three LBD process activities, and business processes. On the left of the figure are the five components of an LBD IS, in the middle are the three activities in an LBD process, and on the right are business processes containing the LBD activities. In the next two questions, we examine each of the three LBD activities in more detail. We first consider those activities of mobile devices and then for GIS. We then will be able to discuss the wide variety of business processes these LBD activities support.

First, consider the components of the LBD IS. While mobile devices and GIS have the five components of all information systems, the unique type of data they use makes them distinct from other IS. While location data is their defining characteristic, both mobile devices and GIS also use non-location data. Both include non-location data such as the serial number of the device, the name of person, or a product number. The real value of a location-based IS is that it combines location data with non-location data. For example, you create value by combining the location data of the Starbucks nearest you with the non-location data of its hours of operation.

QE5-4 ▶ How Do Mobile Devices Support the Location-Based Process?

In this question, we examine the three activities in the location-based process we just described and how mobile devices support each. We begin our discussion with the Capture activity.

Capture

To capture mobile device LBD two items are needed—a mobile device and a fixed receiver system, as shown in Figure CE5-6. Also shown in the figure is the useful range or distance between device and receiver and the four most common combinations for outdoor and indoor use, which are described next.

The most common outdoor combination of devices is a smartphone and cell tower. When you take a photo, your cell phone photo app requests location data that your phone obtains by interrogating fixed nearby cell towers. Using local towers is faster and requires less energy than using GPS, which is another method that your phone can use to determine its location.

The second common outdoor combination uses an RFID tag on a person or a moving object and an RFID receiver. An **Radio-frequency identification (RFID)** tag is a small electronic tag composed of a chip and antenna that can exchange data with an RFID reader by using a radio frequency. This combination is typically more accurate than smartphones and cell towers because its receivers cover a smaller area. Disney uses RFID to track your movements in its parks. The RFID chip is in the MagicBand you wear to gain admission, as shown in Figure CE5-7. The band communicates with RFID receivers throughout the park, allowing the receivers to capture a continuous stream of LBD. In a similar way, Walmart uses RFID technology to help track its inventory as it moves in its supply chain and in its warehouses, and highway tollbooths track cars and vehicles that carry in-car RFID tags as they move past toll readers.

When indoors, two other combinations are more commonly used as the outdoor combinations have limitations. The Smartphone-Cell Tower combination is not helpful indoors as it is not very accurate and it consumes considerable battery power. The RFID Tag-Receiver combination solves these problems, but individuals often do not want to obtain a device or allow themselves to be tracked in a public place.

Mobile Device	Stationary Receiver	Range
Outdoors		
Smartphone	Cell Tower	Up to 5 Miles
RFID Tag	RFID Receiver	Up to 700 Meters
Indoors		
Smartphone	Bluetooth Receiver	Up to 100 Meters
Smartphone	NFC Receiver	Less than 4 Centimeters

FIGURE CE5-6

LBD Capture Combinations of Device, Receiver, and Range for Mobile Devices

FIGURE CE5-7
Disney's MagicBands

One common indoor solution is a third combination: a smartphone Bluetooth private network system. **Bluetooth** is a standard for short-range wireless connections. While the accuracy and reduced energy use are helpful, this combination requires the moving individual to activate a Bluetooth device or the Bluetooth option on their smartphone. Bluetooth determines only proximity, not direction or location. A Bluetooth receiver used in a car is shown in Figure CE5-8. Bluetooth is commonly used to connect smartphones to car audio devices and to wireless headphones.

The fourth and newest combination uses Near Field Communication (NFC) technology. **NFC** is a standard for very short-range communication between devices, typically under 4 cm. Like Bluetooth, NFC-equipped smartphones can connect to NFC receivers using an NFC network. Again, like Bluetooth, NFC does not know where the mobile device is exactly, just that it is near the receiver. Even less power is required, and security is improved as NFC devices must be very near to each other to connect. One common application of NFC is Apple Pay; another is hotel room key cards that unlock a door when the card is held near to the card reader in the door lock.

These four combinations are the most common for people or small objects. Larger objects like vehicles or robots share data using **vehicle-to-vehicle (V2V)**, a communication network of vehicles and roadside units that provide each other data about their own location, accidents, road congestion, rerouting opportunities, and weather conditions. V2V systems use special vehicle transmitters and communicate via Wi-Fi using a new wireless standard, 802.11p.

Analyze

Once mobile LBD is captured, it can be analyzed. In this section, we examine how individuals with mobile devices analyze their location data to inform themselves about location relevant issues.

Individuals, while driving, use their mobile device to analyze route options, the impact of road construction, and the distance to and location of restaurants along their driving route. Individuals also use their devices to analyze nearby movie options, the proximity of friends, and notes posted in augmented reality, as shown in Figure CE5-9. In that figure, a tourist is pointing a mobile device at a geotagged church in Torino that generates a short description of it at the bottom of the screen.

FIGURE CE5-8
Bluetooth In-Car Receiver

Individuals also use their smartphones to analyze LBD-generated business offers and discounts. For example, a restaurant owner is facing a difficult night. The weather is brutally cold, and as a result, his restaurant is depressingly empty. Looking at his reservation list for the night distresses him further; it's going to be very slow. Unfortunately, he has a kitchen full of perishable food and a waitstaff that has already arrived for work. Rather than face a certain financial loss for the day, he turns to his geomarketing app, which allows him to analyze location data of his participating customers to offer them discounts if they are currently within walking distance of the restaurant, are driving nearby, or live close to the restaurant. If the discount is right, a crowd soon arrives, the waiters are happy, his valuable customers are enjoying a discounted meal, and—icing on the cake—the owner makes enough revenue to break even for the night. All from analyzing location data.

While these examples show the value of analyzing the location data of people, objects that move are also analyzed. For example, driverless cars analyze location and proximity data to avoid collisions as they move, and warehouse robotic forklifts analyze location data about pallets, inventory, and other objects as they scurry about the warehouse.

Present

The output of a mobile device is often a geographic display or map. One example is shown in the Figure CE5-10, a smartphone display that shows a number of geotagged restaurants superimposed on a map.

The restaurant display in Figure CE5-10 highlights several key features of a mobile location presentation. These key features are listed in Figure CE5-11.

Presentation of location-based data on a small screen like a mobile phone is challenging and even more difficult on smaller surfaces such as watches. Users analyzing these displays are often distracted and interrupted. They quickly need to understand where they are relative to other points of interest. These displays must prioritize essentials, keep tasks simple, and be self-contained—requiring no other screens. Finally, mobile presentations must minimize typing inputs by the user. These factors make small screen presentations problematic.

Having discussed how mobile devices support the three activities of the location-based process, next we examine how GIS support each activity.

FIGURE CE5-11

Necessary Elements for Effective
Presentations on Mobile Devices

Know the audience is often distracted
Expect interruptions, make return to display easy
Make orientation of observer to the world simple
Prioritize essentials
Keep tasks simple
Do not require other screens
Require few typing inputs

QE5-5 How Do GIS Support the Location-Based Process?

Unlike the more recent development of mobile devices, traditional GIS have been using LBD for almost 50 years. When GIS were first introduced, they helped analysts create digital maps; with the recent explosion in location data generated by mobile devices, GIS increasingly merge digital maps with LBD generated by mobile devices onto full-sized screens or displays. Here we examine how GIS support the creation, analysis, and presentation of LBD.

Capture

The most common method used by a GIS to capture LBD is from maps and photographic images. First, a map or image is compiled and formatted into a digital form, a process called **digital mapping** or digital cartography. Then the digital map is geotagged. **Geotagging** is a process that assigns quantitative location measures, like longitude and latitude, to the map and the objects on the map. Another common coordinate system is the Universal Transverse Mercator (**UTM**) that divides the world into a series of zones and specifies coordinates within each zone. An example is shown in Figure CE5-12.

Maps and aerial photographic images were, in the past, satellite or airplane based. However, with the growth of drones, remotely piloted vehicles now capture a number of digital maps.

In addition to a geotag, a GIS can record whether objects are discrete or continuous (rainfalls and elevation). In addition, the GIS can classify the type of object; it can be a point, line, or area. Figure CE5-13 shows examples of these three types of data. A point represents objects with no dimensions such as a device or stoplight, a line shows objects with one dimension such

FIGURE CE5-12

UTM Coordinates

FIGURE CE5-13

Points, Lines, and Areas on a
GIS Presentation

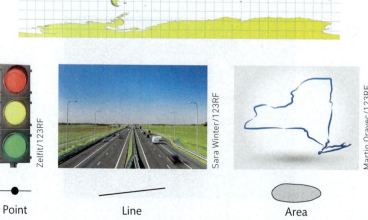

Zelfit/123RF   Sara Winter/123RF   Martin Oravec/123RF

Point   Line   Area

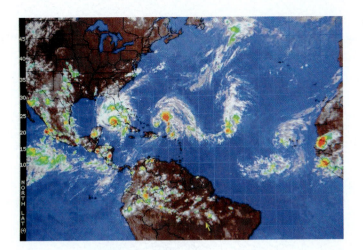

FIGURE CE5-14
Weather Remote Sensing, Eastern
United States

as a road or fence, and a polygon represents objects with two dimensions such as state, zip code, precinct, county, or building.

Another source for generating LBD, in addition to maps and photographic images, is **remote sensing**. Remote sensing measures the amount of energy reflected off an object on the ground, more precisely the wavelengths of the reflected light off the target. Weather disturbances emit unique wavelengths as shown in Figure CE5-14. Another example of satellite remote sensing systems helped identify a dangerous growth of toxic algae in Lake Erie. The lake had developed an algae allergy, as toxic algae blooms grew to alarming levels in recent summers. By remotely measuring infrared emissions off the lake, government analysts could track algae growth and treatment efforts in attempts to reverse this trend.

Analyze

Users of mobile devices typically analyze where they are relative to nearby objects. On the other hand, GIS analysts typically evaluate LBD to see movement patterns in groups of objects or people in a geographic area. This type of analysis, also called **spatial analysis**, examines the locations, attributes, and relationships of features in LBD through overlay and other analytical techniques.

For example, a spatial analysis can display location-relevant issues such as trends in real estate prices in a neighborhood, the size and movement of a forest fire, or travel distances of potential customers to a new restaurant location. Another example of GIS analysis tracks movement of customers. The Disney MagicBand device mentioned earlier creates LBD for park visitors that analysts at Disney can aggregate and analyze to reduce waiting times, use park space more wisely, enhance safety, and improve service.

GIS are also used by government agencies to improve services for constituents. In Figure CE5-15, subway planners are able to analyze population density to plan future subway changes.

Present

Presenting LBD on a GIS occurs on a full-sized screen, unlike small screen mobile presentations. As a result, the creation of an effective display presents different challenges. The presentation designer must choose what will be included and omitted, the type of audience that will view

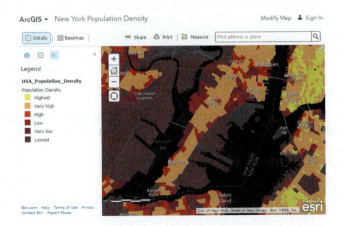

FIGURE CE5-15
New York Population Density
Interactive Display

FIGURE CE5-16
GIS Twitter Output in UK

the presentation and whether the presentation will stand on its own or be a part of a larger set of displays, and the types of interaction an analyst or end user might need. Further, the designer must choose symbols to indicate key features, how the data is classified, and the resolution of the display. In Figure CE5-16, the display shows tweets on a given day in the UK. The symbols are the areas and names, the data is the color of the area, and the resolution was chosen to show the entire country.

In this question and the previous one, we highlighted how mobile and GIS systems support the three location activities: creating, analyzing, and presenting location data. While it is helpful to understand the activities of the generic location-based process, it is also important to recognize the variety of business processes supported by these activities. We describe these activities next.

QE5-6 ▸ What Business Processes Are Supported by LBD?

Businesses first began to use LBD in the 1980s with the first commercial use of GPS satellite data. Recently, business use of LBD has been rapidly expanding as smartphones, low-cost sensors, and the Internet of Things make the measurement and communication of LBD cheaper and more widespread. As a result, LBD IS support a wide variety of business and government processes. A sample of these processes is listed in Figure CE5-17 in two sections. The top section presents processes that use moving LBD while the bottom section shows static LBD.

Earlier in the extension, we provided examples from Disney and how its MagicBands helped improve customer service and park planning processes as well as a restaurant discount example that improved its marketing process. These examples are just the tip of the iceberg.

Netflix has collected data on movie rentals by zip code. Interestingly, people in different zip codes seem to like different movies. These geographical differences are used to improve the movie recommendation process for Netflix viewers.

Walmart uses a GIS to predict product sales in the path of impending weather disasters. Not surprisingly, GIS predict sales spikes of flashlights, water, beer, and batteries prior to these events. Remarkably, other products also spike, such as strawberry Pop Tarts, in one weather disaster over 700 percent.

Mobile payment options such as Square, as shown in Figure CE5-18, and Stripe enable sellers to take customer payment with mobile devices. Other payment options such as Apply Pay and Google Wallet allow individuals to send or receive money instantly. These mobile payment options improve entertainment, banking, retail, and sales processes.

Government and nonbusiness organizations also use LBD. Law enforcement agencies use location data to push Amber Alerts to smartphones and to record the location of moving vehicles

Industry	Process Supported by LBD	Goal
Moving LBD		
Marketing	Generate real-time ads based on location	Increase sales
Checkout	Enable self-service checkout with phone	Reduce payment inefficiency
Parking	Display open parking spaces in cars	Reduce time and fuel use
Disaster warning	Warn people of impending crisis	Improve public safety
Entertainment	Track movement of customers in parks	Improve use of limited space
Wearables	Display LBD to people on the move	Improve knowledge in context
Sports	Analyze player speeds, movements	Improve player training and selection
Banking	Analyze transaction location	Improve fraud analysis
Media/enter	Map physical world to virtual	Improve game play
Supply chain	Track weather impacts of supplies	Improve fleet management
Mass transit	Display arriving vehicles on mobile app	Reduce customer wait time
Transportation	Share traffic, hazard data among vehicles	Reduce congestion, improve safety
Packaging	Robotic forklifts moving warehouse goods	Reduce conflicts, collisions
STATIC LBD		
Retail	Analyze store location opportunities	Improve new store location
Marketing	Track lifestyle demographics	Improve sales
Sales	Increase products before bad weather	Improve sales
911 Dispatch	Display LBD on caller of 911	Reduce delay
War relief	Track location of supplies & relief efforts	Save lives
Insurance	Identify location of disasters	Claims process
Real Estate	Identify properties values	Investment process
Public Works	Monitor forests, waste collection	More efficiency
Farming	Deploy fertilizer inch by inch segments	Increase crop yield, reduce fertilizer
Utilities	Map underground cables and pipes	Reduce mistakes
Climate	Map changes to climate	Better awareness of change

FIGURE CE5-17

LBD Supporting Business Process Goals

using automated license plate readers. Farmers deploy fertilizer in inch-by-inch segments to optimize plant growth and minimize fertilizer expense and runoff. Finally, the Department of Defense is using LBD about crowds collected by drones to predict unrest and increase security. Data on crowd size, location, and movement are analyzed and risk projections are presented on GIS to help security supervisors plan responses to civil disturbances.Here we described only five of the many ways business and government agencies are using LBD. We expect this list to continue to grow in the coming years. While we are optimistic about the growth of mobile devices and GIS, they do have limitations, and we consider these challenges next.

QE5-7 ▶ What Are the Limitations and Challenges of LBD?

While individuals, businesses, and government agencies enjoy many advantages associated with mobile devices and GIS, there are several significant limitations and challenges that currently limit greater widespread adoption. We list the most significant challenges in Figure CE5-19.

FIGURE CE5-18

Using Square to Process a Credit Card Payment

FIGURE CE5-19

Mobile Devices and GIS Challenges

Technical
- Lagging Standards
- Power Consumption
- Measurement Errors
- Small Screen

People
- Privacy
- Funding
- Security

Technical

While great technical progress has been made, many challenges remain. One challenge is that the technical standards needed for interoperability of LBD are still emerging. The industry needs widely accepted technical standards to overcome LBD information silos. With adequate standards, LBD will be able to move more efficiently between databases and among applications, devices, and networks. A second technical problem is measurement errors in LBD that arise from mapping a round world onto a two-dimensional flat coordinate system as well as accurately measuring moving objects. Power requirements on mobile devices are also a challenge. Finally, screen size is still an issue—the challenges of creating meaningful outputs on a small screen continue to limit adoption. LBD technology challenges, like challenges with other rapidly emerging technology, take time to overcome, but LBD people challenges, discussed next, will take even longer to overcome.

People

LBD processes that use data about people always generate privacy concerns. For example, a business might tweet shopping coupons and discounts to customers nearby. While some customers would welcome such opportunities, others would view it as a violation of their privacy. While business use of LBD generates privacy concerns, government use of LBD also bumps up against privacy concerns. One government LBD application is monitoring the movements of criminals on probation. A new mobile LBD app will enable law enforcement to track the location of offenders using a wearable device that continually emits their location and alerts the public of their presence. Another app allows any individual to see the home locations of registered child predators. Again the challenge is balancing privacy of individuals, albeit criminal individuals, with the efficiency of public processes.

Another LBD challenge is funding for LBD services. Mobile network providers can collect revenue from their consumers, but should they share some of that revenue with LBD app developers? In other words, should these network providers "tax" their users for location services to raise funds for improved LBD services such as Amber Alerts, weather warnings, 911, and other emergency services? The same issue applies to remote sensing. Both government agencies and private enterprises rely on remote sensing, but who should pay for it, and how should it be funded?

LBD use also poses new security concerns. It is helpful for you and for businesses to know where you are and where your stuff is, but if you know, then others might be able to overcome security and find you and your stuff as well. For example, several soldiers posted on a social network a picture of helicopters arriving in Iraq. The geotag attached to the photo gave insurgents the location where one of the soldiers took the picture, and they launched a mortar attack that destroyed four of the newly arrived helicopters. Further, law enforcement agencies have requested that Waze discontinue displaying active police location data, as they believe it places their officers at risk. According to some reports, the killer of two New York City police officers in 2014 used Waze to locate the police in the shooting. In addition to threats to property, LBD security also includes vulnerabilities such as theft of mobile device, unsecure apps, rogue Wi-Fi access points, and eavesdropping.

These technical and people-oriented challenges are considerable. However, businesses will increasingly rely on location-based processes and the mobile devices and GIS that support them. As with many technologies over the years, the technology will continue to improve, and using it to capture, analyze, and present LBD is sure to become even more widespread.

ACTIVE REVIEW

Use this active review to verify that you understand the ideas and concepts in this extension.

QE5-1 ▶ How fast is LBD growing?

Describe LBD and GIS. Summarize the types of devices that are considered mobile devices. Explain new types of mobile devices that generate and use LBD. Describe how fast LBD is growing and two industries in which it plays a key role.

QE5-2 ▶ How are mobile devices and GIS different?

Explain the three main activities in the LBD process. Describe how these activities are done first with first a mobile device and then with a GIS.

QE5-3 ▶ What is a location-based process?

Is the location-based process a dynamic or static process? Describe the objective of the location-based process. Describe the types of data used in a location-based process.

QE5-4 ▶ How do mobile devices support the location-based process?

Describe how smartphones and cell towers can be used to generate LBD. Explain RFID tags and how RFID tags create LBD. Describe Bluetooth, its common uses, and the type of LBD it

creates. Explain NFC, its common uses, and the type of LBD it creates. Provide examples of how mobile devices are used by individuals to analyze LBD. Describe the necessary elements for effective presentations on a small screen.

QE5-5 ▶ How do GIS support the location-based process?

Explain a digital map. Describe how LBD are assigned to digital maps. Explain the three different types of objects on a GIS. Describe spatial analysis and provide several examples. Explain the types of choices a presentation designer must make to create a LBD presentation.

QE5-6 ▶ What business processes are supported by LBD?

Explain several examples of business processes that are supported by LBD and the objectives they seek. Describe how government and nonbusiness organizations use LBD.

QE5-7 ▶ What are the limitations and challenges of LBD?

Describe the technical challenges faced by LBD. Explain how privacy affects the use of LBD. Describe the problem with funding for LBD services. Explain the security challenges that confront LBD.

KEY TERMS AND CONCEPTS

Bluetooth 424	Location-based data (LBD) 420	Remote sensing 426
Digital mapping 426	Near Field Communication	Spatial analysis 426
Geographic information system	(NFC) 424	UTM 426
(GIS) 420	Radio-frequency identification	Vehicle-to-vehicle (V2V) 424
Geotagging 426	(RFID) 423	

USING YOUR KNOWLEDGE

E5-1. Make a list of the most common types of locations you use Google Maps to find (e.g., gas stations, restaurants). Also list the most common types of locations you believe other college students use Google Maps to find.

E5-2. For two of the business processes listed in Figure CE5-17, specify what data is captured, who analyzes that data, and how it is presented (the three activities in Figure CE5-2).

E5-3. Provide examples from your own experiences where Bluetooth and NFC devices are used by businesses.

Also provide an example of a business use of an RFID tag not included in the text.

E5-4. Using the list of necessary elements for effective mobile device presentations (Figure CE5-10), evaluate a popular mobile app presentation that uses LBD—what does that app do well, and what could it improve?

E5-5. Of the people challenges shown in Figure CE5-19, which most affect your use of LBD, and why? For a government process that uses LBD about its citizens, which of these people problems is most significant, and why?

APPENDIX A PRODUCTION TUTORIAL

In this tutorial, Chuck's Bikes will be producing a batch of off-road bicycles by executing three main activities: Plan, Produce, and Store, as shown in Figure A-1. First it creates a Planned Order, a plan that specifies how many bikes it expects to sell over the upcoming months. This Planned Order is created by Sally, who works in the company headquarters in a supply chain role. Once this Planned Order is complete, it is converted to a Production Order by Wally a warehouse manager in Dallas. In this tutorial, we will only produce one batch of bicycles, even though the original Planned Order creates a whole series of Production Orders. Once our order is produced, the production run is confirmed, and the finished bikes must be moved to storage. In sum, the main activities—Plan, Produce, and Store.

FIGURE A-1

Production Process and SAP Screens

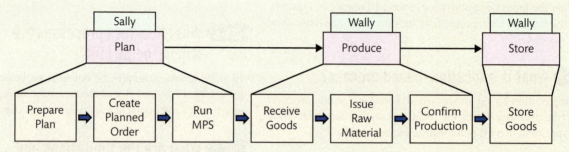

1. **Change Master Material Record**
2. **Change Routing**
3. **Create Sales and Production Plan**
4. **Transfer SOP to Demand Management**
5. **Execute MPS with MRP**
6. **Convert Planned Order to Production Order**
7. **Receive Goods in Inventory**
8. **Issue Goods to Production Order**
9. **Confirm Production Completion**
10. **Receive Goods**

This tutorial follows the Production process shown in Figure A-1. The top of Figure A-1 shows the three main Production activities—Plan, Produce, Store—and their subactivities. At the bottom of Figure A-1, we show the 10 SAP screens that are completed during the Production process. This tutorial directs you through the procedures for completing each screen. Other companies may use some other screens; these 10 screens were chosen to keep this tutorial simple and because they are common to most production processes.

1. Change Material Master Record

To begin, Sally, a supply chain professional at CBI with the job title Production Supervisor, has decided to create a new Planned Order for off-road bikes. She has created a forecast of sales for the off-road bike, but before she can input that order, she needs to update the Material Master record for the off-road bike. From the SAP Easy Access Screen, she navigates to the Change Material screen by selecting

Logistics > Production > Master Data > Material Master > Material > Change > Immediately

The Change Material (Initial Screen) will appear as shown in Figure A-2.

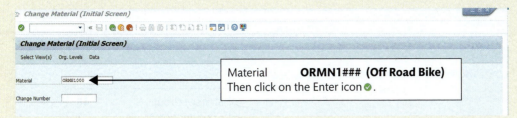

FIGURE A-2
Change Material (Initial Screen)

The Select Views pop-up screen appears as shown in Figure A-3. Sally wants to adjust some of the material master data on the MRP3 screen, so she selects MRP3.

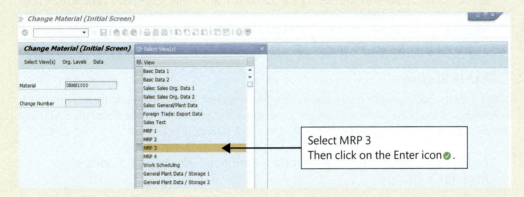

FIGURE A-3
Select View(s) Screen

The next screen is the Organizational Levels pop-up screen as shown in Figure A-4. Sally specifies that she wants to change the material record about the off-road bike that is to be produced at the Dallas warehouse and that after the production runs the bikes will be stored in Finished Goods.

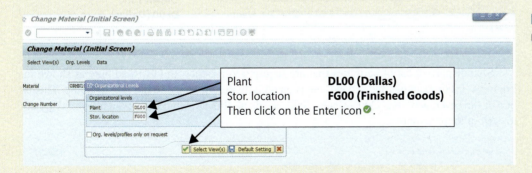

FIGURE A-4
Organizational Levels Screen

The MRP3 screen now loads, as shown in Figure A-5. On this screen, Sally changes the material master for the off-road bike. She changes the planning strategy, the consumption mode, and the backward consumption period. The planning strategy of 40 means Sally is creating a plan that will create a final assembly, not an intermediate assembly—a complete bike, not just a sub-assembly of a seat to a frame. Consumption mode and bwd.consumption per. mean that raw materials will be consumed prior to expected sales date. This means CBI wants to make the bikes before they are needed in order to build inventory rather than making bikes after they are requested.

FIGURE A-5

MRP3 Screen

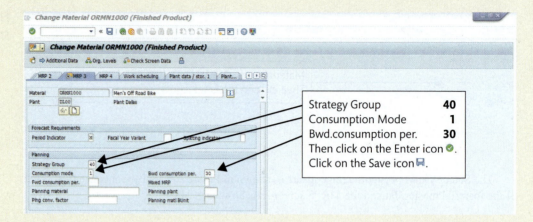

If you receive an information message at the bottom left of the screen that says "Check consumption periods," click Enter.

After the system updates the Material Master record for the off-road bike, click on Exit to return to the Easy Access Menu.

2. Change Routing

In this activity, Sally assigns bike components, like seats and wheels, to assembly activities such as Attach Seat to Frame. Sally will assign 10 components to seven activities. From the SAP Easy Access screen, Sally navigates to the Change Material screen by selecting

> *Logistics > Production > Master Data > Routings > Routings > Standard Routings > Change*

The Change Routings: Operational Overview screen as shown in Figure A-6 appears. Once again Sally specifies that this production will use the off-road bike material and will be done at the Dallas warehouse.

FIGURE A-6

Change Routing: Initial Screen

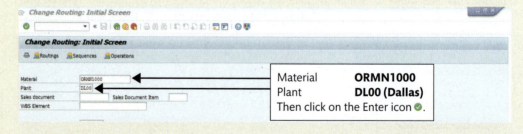

SAP displays a list of activities that are required to produce an Off Road bike as shown in Figure A-7. For example, the second line is an activity described as Attach seat to frame. This is one of the seven activities. At this step, Sally needs to allocate which components are assigned to each of these activities.

FIGURE A-7

Change Routing Operation Overview

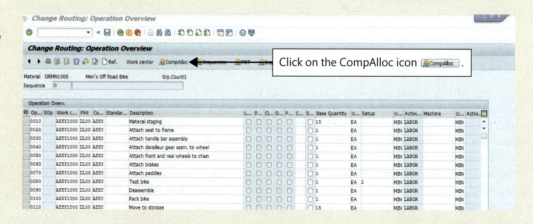

To begin, Sally wants to assign two components to one activity. She selects two components, the frame and seat, and assigns them to activity 20 as shown in Figures A-8 and A-9.

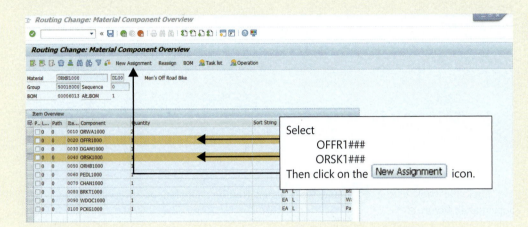

FIGURE A-8

Routing Change: Material Component Overview Screen

The New Assignment pop-up screen loads, as shown in Figure A-9. Here Sally can assign these two components to one activity, activity 20.

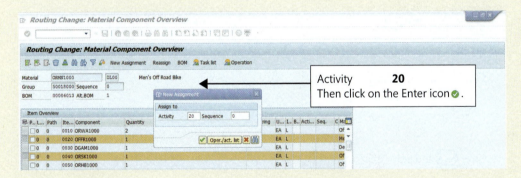

FIGURE A-9

Routing Change: Material Component Overview Screen

After the check mark is clicked, the pop-up New Assignment disappears, and Sally can select the off-road handlebars for the next assignment. Sally repeats the process of assigning other components to other activities according to the following table. The result will be the Item Overview screen as shown in Figure A-10.

COMPONENT (Material)		ACTIVITY
ORHB1###	Off-road handlebars	0030
ORWA1###	Off-road aluminum wheel assembly	0040
DGAM1###	Derailleur gear assembly	0040
CHAN1###	Chain	0050
BRKT1###	Brake kit	0060
PEDL1###	Pedal assembly	0070
WDOC1###	Warranty document	0100
PCKG1###	Packaging	0100

When finished with the final assignment, the Routing Change: Material Component Overview screen looks like Figure A-10. Notice now the activity (shown as Acti… in Figure A-10) column is complete compared to how it appeared in Figure A-9.

FIGURE A-10

Routing Change: Material Component
Overview Completed Screen

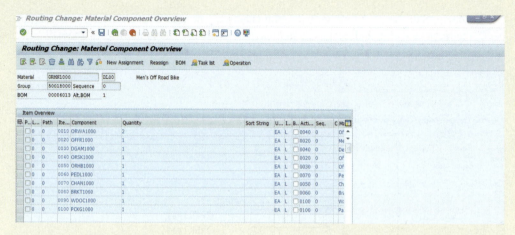

Click the back button 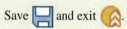, and the Change Routing: Operations Overview screen will appear as in Figure A-11.

FIGURE A-11

Change Routing: Operations
Overview Screen

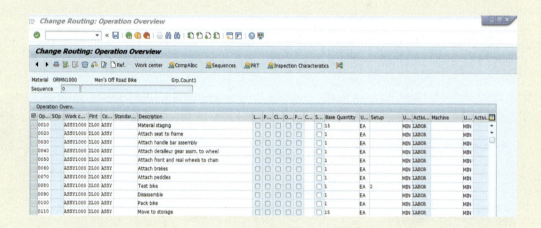

Save 💾 and exit 🔼.

3. Create Sales and Production Plan

Now that material details have been prepared, Sally can work on making a Planned Order. In this activity, Sally inputs sales forecast data for the off-road bike. This sales forecast is then converted to a Planned Order.

Logistics > Production > SOP > Planning > For Material > Change

To begin, the Change Plan Initial screen loads, as shown in Figure A-12.

FIGURE A-12

SOP Create Plan Initial Screen

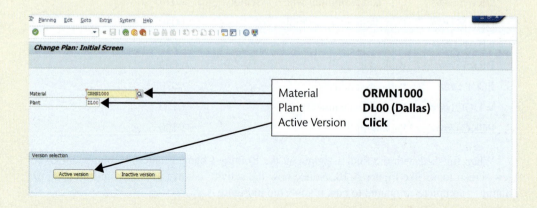

Sally can later make several versions of a sales plan and eventually select one to convert to the Production Order. We will make just one version of this sales plan in this tutorial.

The Create Rough Cut Plan screen loads, as shown in Figure A-13. Here Sally inputs Sales forecasts beginning two months from now in the third column. The Target Days' Supply is a measure of safety stock; a higher number will shift production so that more bicycles are produced early on and inventory rises before demand kicks in.

FIGURE A-13
Create Rough-Cut Plan Screen

From the System menu at the top of the current SAP screen, select the drop-down options as shown in Figure A-14:

Edit > Create productn plan > Target days' supply

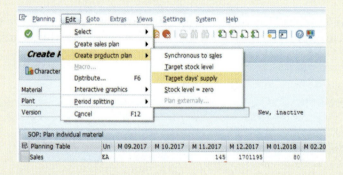

FIGURE A-14
Production Plan Dropdown Option

SAP will create a Production Plan based on the Sales Plan and the value in the Target days' supply cells. After Target days' supply is clicked, SAP creates the Production Plan, and you can see the stock levels and production values in the new Change Rough-Cut Plan screen, as shown in Figure A-15.

FIGURE A-15
Create Rough-Cut Plan Screen

Click on Save . Click on Exit to return the SAP Easy Access Screen.

4. Transfer SOP to Demand Management

In this activity, Sally creates a Demand Management document. This document is used by the warehouse to assemble the bikes. In the overall process, this step is a part of the transition from a Planed Order, which extends over a period of months, to creating specific Production Orders that will be executed on specific days.

Logistics > Production > SOP > Disaggregation > Transfer Material to Demand Management

This activity begins with the Transfer Planning Data to Demand Management screen as shown in Figure A-16. Here enter version A00 and deselect Invisible transfer.

FIGURE A-16

Transfer Planning to Demand Management Screen

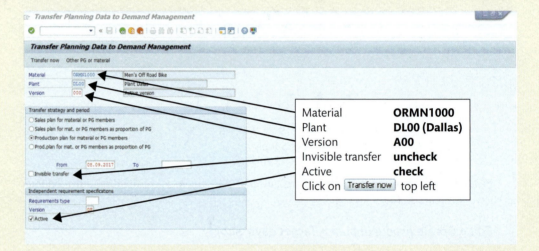

SAP will produce the Planned Independent Requirements screen as shown in Figure A-17. If Sally wanted to edit the order, she could do that on this screen. We will not make any changes.

FIGURE A-17

Plnd Ind. Reqmts: Planning Table Screen

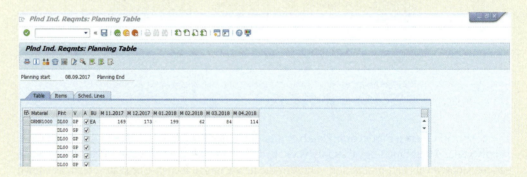

Click on Save 💾. Click on Exit 🔶 to return to the SAP Easy Access Screen

5. Execute MPS with MRP

This step continues the transition from a forecasting plan to creating specific production orders for specific days.

Logistics > Production > Production Planning > MPS > MPS > Single Item, Multi-Level

In this activity, Sally executes the Master Production Schedule (MPS). Single-Item refers to the production of one output—the off-road bike. Multi-Level means the BOM for the bike has multiple stages (levels). In stage 1, the seat and frame are connected, and then in stage 2, the other components are added to the stage 1 output (creating two levels for a single item). The Single-Item, Multi-Level screen appears as shown in Figure A-18.

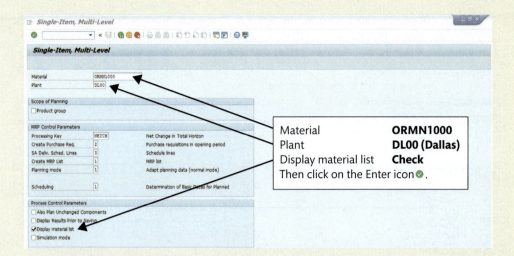

FIGURE A-18

Single-Item, Multi-Level Screen

A warning message will appear asking you to check input parameters. Press Enter. A Planned Order is created as shown in Figure A-19. No saving is needed.

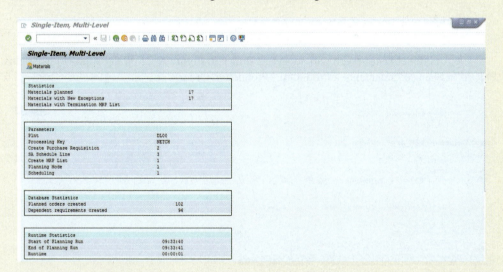

FIGURE A-19

List Display Screen

Sally ensures the details here are correct and then clicks on Exit to return to the SAP Easy Access Screen.

6. Convert Planned Order to Production Order

To this point, Sally has generated a Planned Order. In the next several steps, the activities are accomplished by the role Warehouse Manager. In our example, Wally is the actor playing the Warehouse Manager role. In this step, he converts the Planned Order for the next 6 months into just one Production Order that will be accomplished today in the warehouse.

Logistics > Production > MRP > Evaluations > Stock/Requirements List

The Stock/Requirements List: Initial Screen appears as shown in Figure A-20.

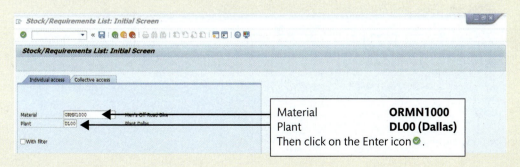

FIGURE A-20

Stock/Requirements List: Initial Screen

The Stock/Requirements List shown in Figure A-21 appears. Wally will select just one of the many Planned Orders (PldOrd) in the MRP Element Column (shown as MRP... in Figure A-21).

FIGURE A-21

Stock/Requirements List: Initial Screen

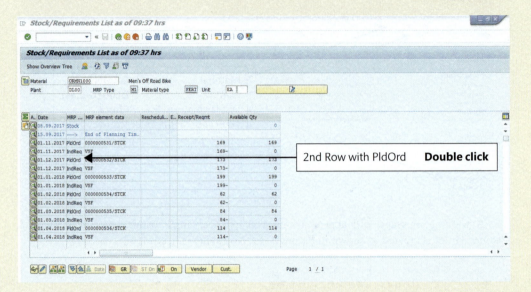

The Additional Data screen will appear as shown in Figure A-22. Wally wants to make this PldOrd (a Planned Order) into a Prod. Ord. (Production Order).

FIGURE A-22

Additional Data for MRP Element Screen

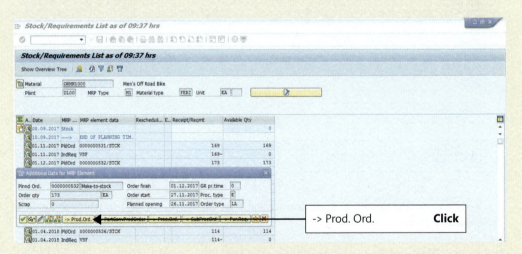

The Production order Create: Header screen will appear as shown in Figure A-23.

FIGURE A-23

Production Order Create: Header Screen

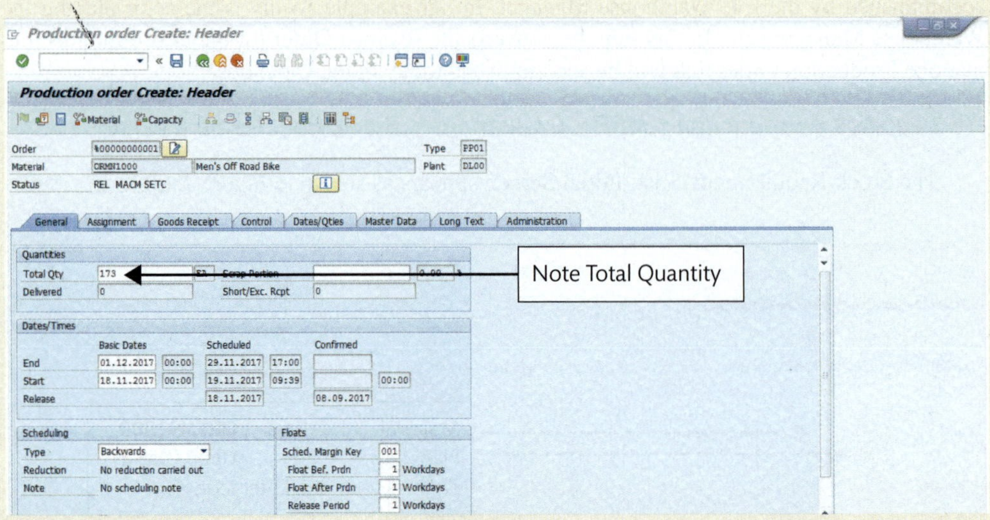

For later steps, it will be important to remember the Total Qty (Quantity) this Production Order will create. This is the number of bikes that will be produced by this first Production Order.

_____ Total Quantity

Click on Save 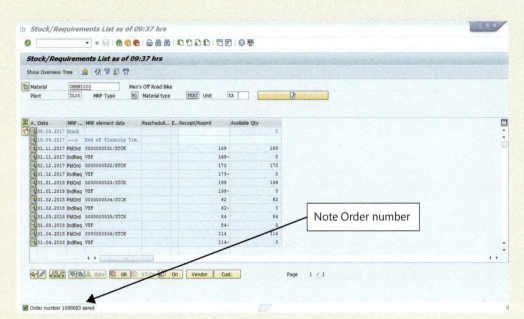. After saving a Production Order, the S/R list reappears as shown in Figure A-24. The Production Order number is created and displayed at the bottom of the screen. Write this down for future use.

_____ Production Order Number

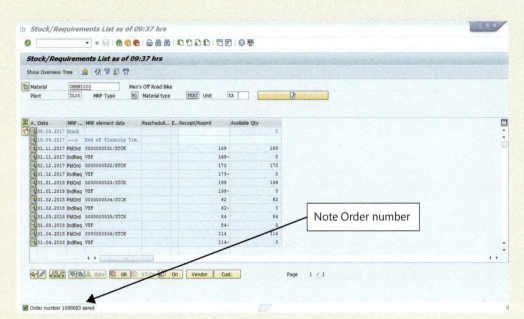

FIGURE A-24
Production Order Create: Header Screen

Click on Exit to return to the SAP Easy Access Menu

7. Receive Goods in Inventory

Before Wally can start the tasks that assemble the bicycles, he must have enough inventory of raw materials on hand in the Dallas warehouse such as bike frames and seats. To make things simple on Wally, just now a shipment arrived with all the materials needed for this production order. In this step, he is receiving those materials.

Logistics > Material Management > Inventory Management > Goods Movement > Goods Receipt > Other

The Enter Other Goods Receipts: Initial Screen will appear as shown in Figure A-25.

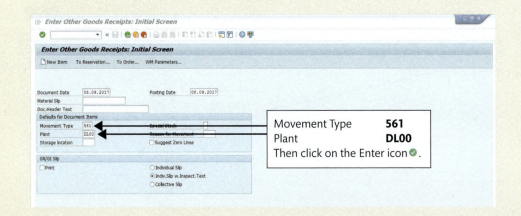

FIGURE A-25
Enter Other Goods Receipts: Initial Screen

Wally entered 561 in the Movement Type. This type of movement means that the material being received in inventory is available for production.

The Enter Other Goods Receipts: New Item screen appears as shown in Figure A-26. All 10 items will be stored as raw materials except the first item, the Wheel assembly, which is a semi-finished good. It is semi-finished because it was assembled from a tire, tube, and aluminum wheel in a previous activity that was not a part of this tutorial.

FIGURE A-26

Blank Enter Other Goods Receipts: New Items Screen

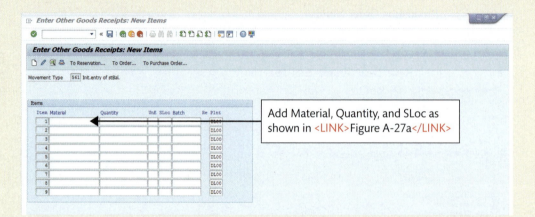

Input the Material, Quantity, and SLoc (storage location) with the data in the following table. When finished, your inputs will look like Figure A-27a and b. Note: You may only have room for the first nine materials on the screen. If so, after inputting the first nine as shown in Figure A-27a, click on New Items as shown in Figure A-27a, and Figure A-27b will appear.

	MATERIAL	QUANTITY	SLOC
Off-road aluminum wheel assembly	ORWA1###	500	SF00
Off-road frame	OFFR1###	500	RM00
Derailleur gear assembly	DGAM1###	500	RM00
Off-road seat kit	ORSK1###	500	RM00
Off-road handlebars	ORHB1###	500	RM00
Pedal assembly	PEDL1###	500	RM00
Chain	CHAN1###	500	RM00
Brake kit	BRKT1###	500	RM00
Warranty document	WDOC1###	500	RM00
Packaging	PCKG1###	500	RM00

FIGURE A-27a

Completed Enter Other Goods Receipts: New Item Screen, Items 1–9

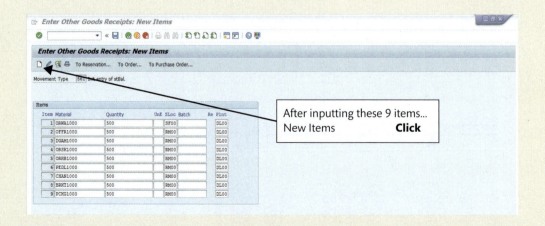

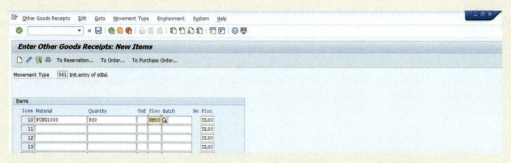

If all is correct, click on Save ![save] . Notice the document number in the lower left part of the screen that confirms these goods have been received. Exit ![exit] to return to the SAP Easy Access Screen.

8. Issue Goods to Production Order

With this step, Wally instructs SAP that the specific materials received into inventory in the previous activity will be used to satisfy the Production Order developed in the earlier steps of this tutorial. During this step, SAP will decrease inventory and allocate costs of production to this Production Order.

> **Logistics > Production> Shop Floor Control > Goods Movements > Goods Issue**

The Enter Goods Issue: Initial Screen will appear as shown in Figure A-28.

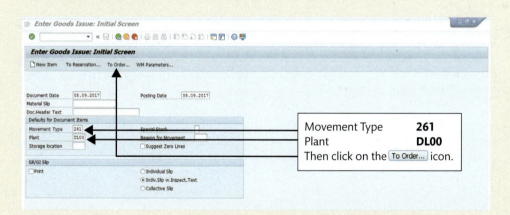

FIGURE A-28
Enter Goods Issue: Initial Screen

Wally entered 261 in the Movement Type. This identifies the material and the quantities of material in inventory that will be allocated to a specific Production Order.

The Reference Order pop-up screen appears as shown in Figure A-29. On this screen, you input your Production Order number from the end of step 6, Figure A-24.

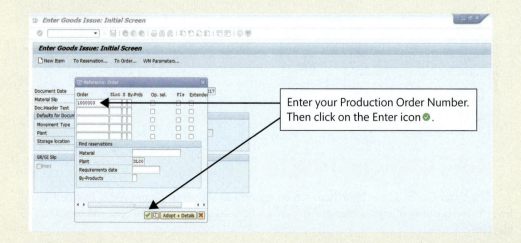

FIGURE A-29
Reference: Order Pop-Up Screen

The Enter Goods Issue: Selection Screen appears as shown in Figure A-30a. On this screen, we need to tell SAP where the material needed for production is currently stored. Enter SF00/ RM00 for the first nine materials as shown in Figure A-31. Then, as shown, click on Next Page to enter RM00 for the 10th material as shown in Figure A-30b. By doing this, we are identifying the quantity of each material and where that material is coming from for this Production Order.

FIGURE A-30A

Enter Goods Issue Selection Screen, First 9 Materials

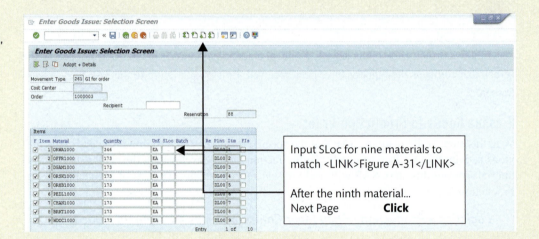

FIGURE A-30B

Enter Goods Issue Selection Screen, 10th Material

FIGURE A-31

Enter Goods Issue Selection Screen with SLoc Input

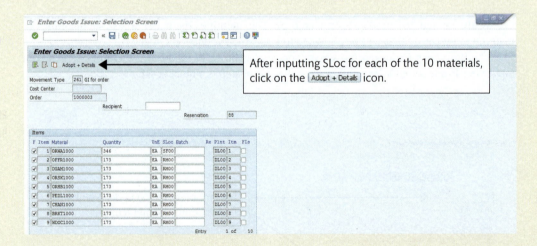

The Enter Goods Issue: New Item screen appears as shown in Figure A-32. Notice Unit of Entry is the quantity of each material (346 shown here, as two wheels are required to make 173 bicycles).

FIGURE A-32

Enter Goods Issue: New Item 0001 Screen

After adopting each of the 10 items, SAP will load the Enter Goods Issue: Overview screen as shown in Figure A-33. This screen is a summary of the adopted requirements.

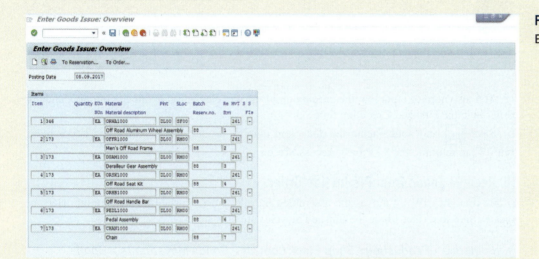

FIGURE A-33

Enter Goods Issue: Overview Screen

Click on Save ![save icon], and note the document number in the bottom left of the screen that confirms that the goods have been issued to the Production Order. Exit ![exit icon] and return to the SAP Easy Access Screen.

9. Confirm Production Completion

After the previous step, the actual production of the bicycles takes place in the Dallas location. In this step, Wally updates the SAP Production Order to reflect that the Production Order is now complete.

Logistics > Production> Shop Floor Control > Confirmation > Enter > For Order

The Enter Production Order Confirmation: Initial Screen appears as shown in Figure A-34.

FIGURE A-34

Confirmation of Production Order Enter: Actual Data Screen

The Enter PO Confirmation of Production Order Enter: Actual Data screen appears as shown in Figure A-35. Wally simply inputs the number of bicycles planned for this order. You wrote down this number near the end of step 6.

FIGURE A-35

Confirmation of Production Order Enter: Actual Data Screen

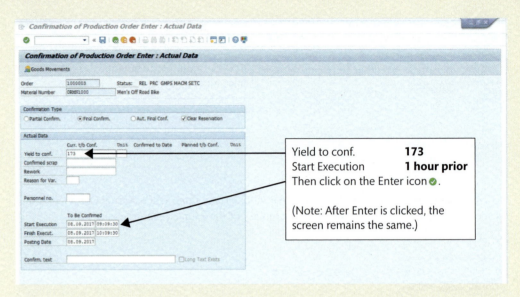

You also need to input that the production of the bicycles began about an hour ago, an hour earlier than the Finished Execution time.

Save ![save icon], and notice again the document number produced that production is complete. Exit ![exit icon] to return to the SAP Easy Access Screen.

10. Receive Goods from Production Order

In this final step, Wally moves the assembled bicycles into Finished Goods storage. Here he updates SAP to reflect where the finished bicycles are now stored.

Logistics > Production> Shop Floor Control > Goods Movements > Goods Receipt

The Goods Receipt for Order: Initial Screen will appear as shown in Figure A-36.

FIGURE A-36

Goods Receipt for Order: Initial Screen

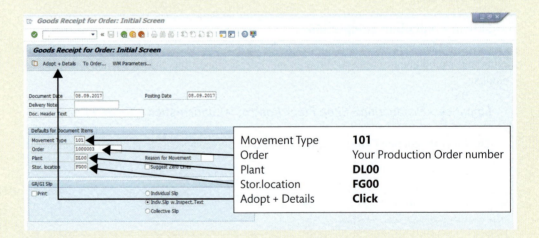

Wally entered 101 in the Movement Type and Prod Order # and storage location. This type of movement means that the assembled bikes are moved from assembly to a Finished Goods location.

The Goods Receipt for Order: New Items 0001 screen appears as shown in Figure A-37. Ensure that the order quantity is correct (173 shown).

Click on Save 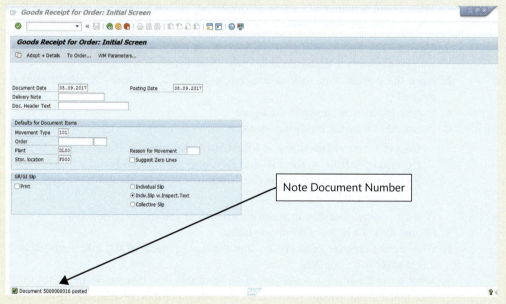. Write down the document number at the end as shown in Figure A-38.

Having acknowledged that the goods have now moved to Finished Goods, you have finished the tutorial.

Please note that all exercise files can be found on the following Web site: *www.pearsonhighered.com/kroenke*.

PART 1

Chapter 1

1-1. Figure AE-1 shows an Excel spreadsheet that the resort bicycle rental business, discussed in Chapter 1, uses to value and analyze its bicycle inventory. Examine this figure to understand the meaning of the data. Now use Excel to create a similar spreadsheet. Note the following:

- The top heading is in 20-point Calibri font. It is centered in the spreadsheet. Cells A1 through H1 have been merged.
- The second heading, *Bicycle Inventory Valuation*, is in 18-point Calibri, italics and red. It is centered in cells A2 through H2, which have been merged.
- The column headings are set in 11-point Calibri, bold. They are centered in their cells, and the text wraps in the cells.

a. Make the first two rows of your spreadsheet similar to those in Figure AE-1. Choose your own colors for background and type, however.

b. Place the current date so it is centered in cells C3, C4, and C5, which must be merged.

c. Outline the cells as shown in the figure.

d. Figure AE-1 uses the following formulas:

> **Cost of Current Inventory = Bike Cost × Number on Hand**
> **Revenue per Bike = Total Rental Revenue/Number on Hand**
> **Revenue as a Percent of Cost of Inventory = Total Rental Revenue/Cost of Current Inventory**

Please use these formulas in your spreadsheet, as shown in Figure AE-1.

e. Format the cells in the columns as shown.

f. Give three examples of decisions that the management of the bike rental agency might make from this data.

g. What other calculation could you make from this data that would be useful to the bike rental management? Create a second version of this spreadsheet in your worksheet document that has this calculation.

1-2. In this exercise, you will learn how to create a query based on data that a user enters and how to use that query to create a data entry form.

a. Download the Microsoft Access file **Ch01Ex02**. Open the file and familiarize yourself with the data in the Customer table.

FIGURE AE-1

Resort Bicycle Rental							
Bicycle Inventory Valuation							
Wednesday September 5, 2018							
Make of Bike	Bike Cost	Number on Hand	Cost of Current Inventory	Number of Rentals	Total Rental Revenue	Revenue per Bike	Revenue as Percent of Cost of Inventory
Wonder Bike	325	12	$3,900	85	$6,375	$531	163.5%
Wonder Bike 2	385	4	$1,540	34	$4,570	$1,143	296.8%
Wonder Bike Supreme	475	8	$3,800	44	$5,200	$650	136.8%
LiteLift Pro	655	8	$5,240	25	$2,480	$310	47.3%
LiteLift Ladies	655	4	$2,620	40	$6,710	$1,678	256.1%
LiteLift Racer	795	3	$2,385	37	$5,900	$1,967	247.4%

b. Click *Create* in the Access ribbon and select *Query Design*. Select the *Customer* table as the basis for the query. Drag *CustomerName, CustomerEmail, DateOfLastRental, BikeLastRented, TotalNumberOfRentals*, and *TotalRentalRevenue* into the columns of the query results pane (the table at the bottom of the query design window).

c. In the *CustomerName* column, in the row labeled *Criteria*, place the following text:

[Enter Name of Customer:]

Type this exactly as shown, including the square brackets. This notation tells Access to ask you for a customer name to query.

d. In the ribbon, click the red exclamation mark labeled *Run*. Access will display a dialog box with the text "Enter Name of Customer:" (the text you entered in the query *Criteria* row). Enter the value *Scott, Rex* and click OK.

e. Save your query with the name *Parameter Query*.

f. Click the Home tab on the ribbon and click the *Design View* (upper left-hand button on the Home ribbon). Replace the text in the *Criteria* column of the *CustomerName* column with the following text. Type it exactly as shown:

Like "*" & [Enter part of Customer Name to search by:] & "*"

g. Run the query by clicking *Run* in the ribbon. Enter *Scott* when prompted *Enter part of Customer Name to search by*. Notice that the two customers who have the name Scott are displayed. If you have any problems, ensure that you have typed the phrase above *exactly* as shown into the *Criteria* row of the *CustomerName* column of your query.

h. Save your query again under the name *Parameter Query*. Close the query window.

i. Click *Create* in the Access ribbon. Under the Forms group, choose *Form Wizard* (if using an older version of Access you need to select the down arrow to the right of *More Forms*). In the dialog that opens, in the Tables/Queries box, click the down arrow. Select *Parameter Query*. Click the double chevron (>>) symbol and all of the columns in the query will move to the Selected Fields area.

j. Click *Next* two or three times (depending on your version of Access) until you come to the Finish option. In the box under *What title do you want for your form?* enter *Customer Query Form* and click *Finish*.

k. Enter *Scott* in the dialog box that appears and click OK. Access will open a form with the values for Scott, Rex. At the bottom of the form, click the right-facing arrow and the data for Scott, Bryan will appear.

l. Close the form. Select *Object Type* and *Forms* in the Access Navigation Pane. Double-click on Customer Query Form and enter the value *James*. Access will display data for all six customers having the value James in their name.

Chapter 2

2-1. The spreadsheet in Microsoft Excel file **Ch02Ex01** contains records of employee activity on special projects. Open this workbook and examine the data that you find in the three spreadsheets it contains. Assess the accuracy, relevancy, and sufficiency of this data to the following people and problems.

a. You manage the Denver plant, and you want to know how much time your employees are spending on special projects.

b. You manage the Reno plant, and you want to know how much time your employees are spending on special projects.

c. You manage the Quota Computation project in Chicago, and you want to know how much time your employees have spent on that project.

d. You manage the Quota Computation project for all three plants, and you want to know the total time employees have spent on your project.

e. You manage the Quota Computation project for all three plants, and you want to know the total labor cost for all employees on your project.

f. You manage the Quota Computation project for all three plants, and you want to know how the labor-hour total for your project compares with the labor-hour totals for the other special projects.

    g. In the Denver plant, what is the average number of hours worked per employee?

    h. Sort the Denver spreadsheet by Department. What is the total number of hours worked by Accounting employees?

2-2. The database in the Microsoft Access file **Ch02Ex02** contains the same records of employee activity on special projects as in Application Exercise 2-1. Before proceeding, open that database and view the records in the Employee Hours table.

    a. Seven queries have been created that process this data in different ways. Using the criteria of accuracy, relevancy, and sufficiency, select the single query that is most appropriate for the information requirements in Application Exercise 2-1, parts a–f.

    b. If a query contains the data but needs to be modified to make the data meaningful (sort, filter, add total row, etc.), describe the actions you should take on the current queries to easily find the information requested in Application Exercise 2-1, parts a–f.

    c. If no current query meets the requirements for the information requested in Application Exercise 2-1, parts a–f, explain why. For these questions, design a query that will provide the desired information. If a query cannot be designed because the appropriate data is not in the database, describe the data that is needed to answer the question.

    d. What conclusions can you make from this exercise?

    e. Comparing your experiences on these two projects, what are the advantages and disadvantages of spreadsheets and databases?

PART 2

Chapter 3

3-1. Sometimes you will have data in one Office application and want to move it to another Office application without rekeying it. Often this occurs when data were created for one purpose but then are used for a second purpose. For example, Figure AE-2 presents a portion of an Excel spreadsheet that shows the assignment of computers to employees. Lucas, at Chuck's Bikes, might use such a spreadsheet to track who has which equipment.

    Suppose that you (or Lucas) want to use this data to help you assess how to upgrade computers. Let's say, for example, that you want to upgrade all of the computers' operating systems to Windows 10. Furthermore, you want to first upgrade the computers that most need upgrading, but you have a limited budget. To address this situation, you would like to query the data in Figure AE-2 to find all computers that do not have Windows 10 and then select those with slower CPUs or smaller memory as candidates for upgrading. To do this, you need to move the data from Excel and into Access.

FIGURE AE-2

	A	B	C	D	E	F	G	H
1	EmpLastName	EmpFirstName	Plant	Computer Brand	CPU (GHz)	Memory (	Disk (GB)	OS
2	Ashley	Jane	Denver	Dell	3	4	400	Windows 10
3	Davidson	Kaye	Denver	Dell	2	3	120	Vista
4	Ching	Kam Hoong	Denver	HP	2	3	100	Vista
5	Collins	Giovanni	Denver	Dell	1	1	80	Windows 8
6	Corning	Sandra	Denver	HP	1.2	1	120	Vista
7	Scott	Rex	Denver	HP	1.8	2	100	XP
8	Corovic	Jose	Denver	Dell	3	2	250	Windows 10
9	Lane	Brandon	Denver	Lenova	2	1.512	250	Vista
10	Wei	Guang	Denver	IBM	2	1	120	Windows 10
11	Dixon	Eleanor	Denver	IBM	1	1.512	120	Vista
12	Lee	Brandon	Denver	Dell	0.5	2	80	XP
13	Duong	Linda	Denver	Dell	0.5	2	40	XP
14	Bosa	Victor	Denver	HP	1	2	30	Vista
15	Drew	Richard	Denver	HP	1	3	100	Windows 8
16	Adams	James	Denver	HP	1	1	80	XP
17	Lunden	Haley	Denver	Lenova	2	0.512	80	Windows 10
18	Utran	Diem Thi	Denver	Dell	2	0.512	120	Windows 10
19								
20		Primary Contact:	Kaye Davidson					

Once you have analyzed the data and determined the computers to upgrade, you want to produce a report. In that case, you may want to move the data from Access back to Excel or perhaps into Word. In this exercise, you will learn how to perform these tasks.

a. To begin, download the Excel file **Ch03Ex01** into one of your directories. We will import the data in this file into Access, but before we do so, familiarize yourself with the data by opening it in Excel. Notice that there are three worksheets in this workbook. Close the Excel file.

b. Create a blank Access database. Name the database *Ch03Ex01_Answer*. Place it in some directory; it may be the same directory into which you have placed the Excel file, but it need not be. Close the default table that Access creates and delete it.

c. Now, we will import the data from the three worksheets in the Excel file **Ch03Ex01** into a single table in your Access database. In the ribbon, select *External Data* and *Excel* in the Import and Link group. Start the import. For the first worksheet (Denver), you should select *Import the source data into a new table in the current database*. Be sure to click *First Row Contains Column Headings* when Access presents your data. You can use the default Field types and let Access add the primary key. Name your table *Employees* and click *Finish*. There is no need to save your import script.

For the second and third worksheets, again click *External Data* and *Excel*, but this time select *Append a copy of the records to the table Employees*. Import all data.

d. Open the *Employee* table and examine the data. Notice that Access has erroneously imported a blank line and the Primary Contact data into rows at the end of each data set. This data is not part of the employee records, and you should delete it (in three places—once for each worksheet). The *Employee* table should have a total of 40 records.

e. Now, create a parameterized query on this data. Place all of the columns except *ID* into the query. In the *OS* column, set the criteria to select rows for which the value is not *Windows 10*. In the *CPU* (GHz) column, enter the criterion: <=*[Enter cutoff value for CPU]*. In the *Memory* (GB) column, enter the criterion: <=*[Enter cutoff value for Memory]*. Test your query. For example, run your query and enter a value of 2 for both CPU and memory. Verify that the correct rows are produced.

f. Use your query to find values of CPU and memory that give you as close to a maximum of 15 computers to upgrade as possible.

g. When you have found values of CPU and memory that give you 15, or nearly 15, computers to upgrade, leave your query open. Now, click *External data, Export group, More down arrow* and *Word* to create a Word document that contains the results of your query. Adjust the column widths of the created table so it fits on the page. Write a memo based on this table explaining that these are the computers you believe should be upgraded.

3-2. Assume that you have been asked to create a spreadsheet to help make a local-versus-cloud decision for the servers on your organization's Web farm. Assume that you are considering the servers for a 5-year period, but you do not know exactly how many servers you will need. Initially, you know you will need five servers, but you might need as many as 50, depending on the success of your organization's e-commerce activity.

a. For the local-alternative calculations, set up your spreadsheet so you can enter the base price of the server hardware, the price of all software, and a maintenance expense that is some percentage of the hardware price. Assume that the percent you enter covers both hardware and software maintenance. Also assume that each server has a 3-year life, after which it has no value. Assume straight-line depreciation for computers used less than 3 years and that at the end of the 5 years you can sell the computers you have used for less than 3 years for their depreciated value. Also assume that your organization pays 2 percent interest on capital expenses. Assume the servers cost $5,000 each and the needed software costs $750. Assume that the maintenance expense varies from 2 to 7 percent.

b. For the cloud-alternative calculations, assume that the cloud vendor will lease the same computer hardware as you can purchase. The lease includes all the software you need as well as all maintenance. Set up your spreadsheet so you can enter various cloud costs, which vary according to the number of years of the lease (1, 2, or 3).

Assume the cost of a 3-year lease is $285 per machine per month, a 2-year lease is $335 per machine per month, and a 1-year lease is $415 per machine per month. Also, the cloud vendor offers a 5 percent discount if you lease from 20 to 30 computers and a 10 percent discount if you lease from 31 to 50 computers.

c. Using your spreadsheet, compare the costs of local versus cloud under the following situations. (Assume you use either the local or cloud option. You cannot use the cloud for some and local for others.) Make assumptions, as necessary, and state those assumptions.

(1) Your organization requires 20 servers for 5 years.

(2) Your organization requires 20 servers for the first 2 years and 40 servers for the next 3 years.

(3) Your organization requires 20 servers for the first 2 years, 40 servers for the next 2 years, and 50 servers for the last year.

(4) Your organization requires 10 servers the first year, 20 servers the second year, 30 servers the third year, 40 servers the fourth year, and 50 servers the last year.

(5) For the previous case, does the cheaper alternative change if the cost of the local servers is $4,000? If it is $8,000?

3-3.   Numerous Web sites are available that will test your Internet data communications speed. A good one is available at www.speakeasy.net/speedtest/. (If that site is no longer active, Google or Bing "What is my Internet speed?" to find another speed-testing site. Use it.)

a. While connected to your university's network, go to Speakeasy and test your speed against servers in Seattle, New York City, and Atlanta. Compute your average upload and download speeds. Compare your speed to the speeds listed in Figure AE-3.

b. Go home or to a public wireless site and run the Speakeasy test again. Compute your average upload and download speeds. Compare your speed to those listed in Figure AE-3. If you are performing this test at home, are you getting the performance you are paying for?

c. Contact a friend or relative in another state. Ask him or her to run the Speakeasy test against those same three cities.

d. Compare the results in parts a, b, and c. What conclusion, if any, can you make from these tests?

Type	Topology	Transmission Line	Transmission Speed	Equipment Used	Protocol Commonly Used	Remarks
Local area network	Local area network	UTP or optical fiber	Common: 10/100/1000 Mbps Possible: 1 Gbps	Switch NIC UTP or optical	IEEE 802.3 (Ethernet)	Switches connect devices, multiple switches on all but small LANs.
	Local area network with wireless	UTP or optical for non-wireless connections	Up to 600 Mbps	Wireless access point Wireless NIC	IEEE 802.11n	Access point transforms wired LAN (802.3) to wireless LAN (802.11).
Connections to the Internet	DSL modem to ISP	DSL telephone	Personal: Upstream to 1 Mbps downstream to 40 Mbps (max 10 likely in most areas)	DSL modem DSL-capable telephone line	DSL	Can have computer and phone use simultaneously. Always connected.
	Cable modem to ISP	Cable TV lines to optical cable	Upstream to 1 Mbps Downstream 300 Kbps to 10 Mbps	Cable modem Cable TV cable	Cable	Capacity is shared with other sites; performance varies depending on others' use.
	WAN wireless	Wireless connection to WAN	500 Kbps to 1 Mbps	Wireless WAN modem	One of several wireless standards.	Sophisticated protocol enables several devices to use the same wireless frequency.

FIGURE AE-3

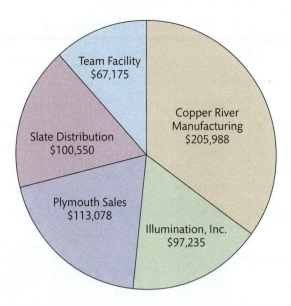

Chapter 4

4-1. A common scenario in business is to combine the processing of Microsoft Access and Excel. A typical scenario is for users to process relational data with Access, import some of the data into Excel, and use Excel's tools for creating professional-looking charts and graphs. You will do exactly that in this exercise.

Download the Access file **Ch04Ex01**. Open the database, and select *Database Tools/Relationships*. As you can see, there are three tables: *Product, Vendor Product Inventory,* and *Vendor.* Open each table individually to familiarize yourself with the data.

For this problem, we will define *Inventory Cost* as the product of *Industry Standard Cost* and *Quantity On Hand.* The query *Inventory Cost* computes these values for every item in inventory for every vendor. Open that query and view the data to be certain you understand this computation. Open the other queries as well so that you understand the data they produce.

a. Sum this data by vendor and display it in a pie chart like that shown in Figure AE-4. Proceed as follows:

(1) Open Excel and create a new spreadsheet.
(2) Click *Data* on the ribbon and select *From Access* in the *Get External Data* group.
(3) Navigate to the location in which you have stored the Access file **Ch04Ex01**.
(4) Select the query that contains the data you need for this pie chart.
(5) Import the data into a table.
(6) Format the appropriate data as currency.
(7) Select the range that contains the data, press the function key, and proceed from there to create the pie chart. Name the data and pie chart worksheets appropriately.

b. Follow a similar procedure to create the bar chart shown in Figure AE-5. Place the data and the chart in separate worksheets and name them appropriately.

4-2. Suppose you are hired by an auto dealer to create a database of customers and their interests. Salespeople have been keeping data in a spreadsheet, and you have been asked to convert that data into a database. Because the dealer's data is so poorly structured, it will be a challenge, as you will see.

a. Download the Excel file named **Ch04Ex02**. Open the spreadsheet and examine the data. It's a mess!
b. Download the Access file with the same name, **Ch04Ex02**. Open the database, select *Database Tools*, and click *Relationships*. Examine the four tables and their relationships.

FIGURE AE-5

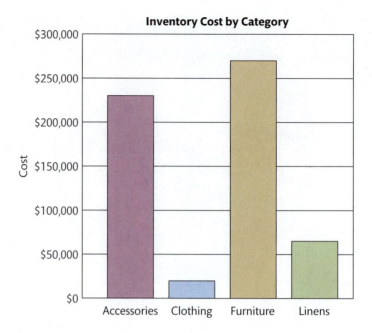

Inventory Cost by Category

c. Somehow, you have to transform the data in the spreadsheet into the table structure in the database. Because so little discipline was shown when creating the spreadsheet, this will be a labor-intensive task. To begin, import the spreadsheet data into a new table in the database; call that table *Sheet1* or some other name.

d. Copy the *Name* data in *Sheet1* onto the clipboard. Then open the *Customer* table and paste the column of name data into that table.

e. Unfortunately, the task becomes messy at this point. You can copy the *Car Interests* column into *Make or Model of Auto*, but then you will need to straighten out the values by hand. Phone numbers will need to be copied one at a time.

f. Open the *Customer* form and manually add any remaining data from the spreadsheet into each customer record. Connect the customer to his or her auto interests.

g. The data in the finished database has much more structure than that in the spreadsheet. Explain why that is both an advantage and a disadvantage. Under what circumstances is the database more appropriate? Less appropriate?

4-3.   In this exercise, you will create a two-table database, define relationships, create a form and a report, and use them to enter data and view results.

a. Download the Excel file **Ch04Ex03**. Open the spreadsheet and review the data in the *Employee* and *Computer* worksheets.

b. Create a new Access database with the name *Ch04Ex03_Solution*. Close the table that Access automatically creates and delete it.

c. Import the data from the Excel spreadsheet into your database. Import the *Employee* worksheet into a table named *Employee*. Be sure to check *First Row Contains Column Headings*. Select *Choose my own primary key* and use the ID field as that key.

d. Import the *Computer* worksheet into a table named *Computer*. Check *First Row Contains Column Headings*, but let Access create the primary key.

e. Open the relationships window and add both *Employee* and *Computer* to the design space. Drag ID from *Employee* and drop it on *EmployeeID* in *Computer*. Check *Enforce Referential Integrity* and the two checkmarks below. Ensure that you know what these actions mean.

f. Open the Form Wizard dialog box (under *Create tab, Forms group, Form Wizard*), and add all of the columns for each of your tables to your form. Select *View your data by Employee*. Title your form *Employee* and your subform *Computer*.

g. Open the *Computer* subform and delete *EmployeeID* and *ComputerID*. These values are maintained by Access, and it is just a distraction to keep them. Your form should appear like the one shown in Figure AE-6.

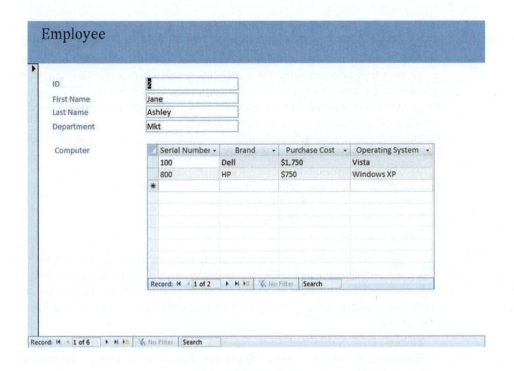

h. Use your form to add two new computers to *Jane Ashley*. Both computers are Dells, and both use Vista; one costs $750, and the second costs $1,400.

i. Delete the Lenovo computer for Rex Everest.

j. Use the Report Wizard (under *Create*) to create a report having all data from both the *Employee* and *Computer* tables. Play with the report design until you find a design you like. Correct the label alignment if you need to.

Chapter 5

5-1. Develop a spreadsheet model of the cost of a virus attack in an organization that has three types of computers: employee workstations, data servers, and Web servers. Assume that the number of computers affected by the virus depends on the severity of the virus. For the purposes of your model, assume that there are three levels of virus severity: *Low-severity* incidents affect fewer than 30 percent of the user workstations and none of the data or Web servers. *Medium-severity* incidents affect up to 70 percent of the user workstations, up to half of the Web servers, and none of the data servers. *High-severity* incidents can affect all organizational computers.

a. *Assumptions* for your model include:
- 40 percent of incidents are low severity.
- 35 percent of incidents are medium severity.
- 25 percent of incidents are high severity.
- Employees are able to remove viruses from their own workstations.
- Trained technicians are required to repair servers.
- The time to eliminate a virus from an infected computer depends on the computer type.
- When employees remove the virus themselves, they are unproductive for twice the time require for the removal.

b. *Inputs* for your model include:
- Severity level (low, medium, high)
- Percentage of computers affected
- The time it takes to remove the virus from each type of computer
- Average employee hourly labor cost for virus removal
- Average cost of a technician to remove a virus from servers
- Total number of user computers, data servers, and Web servers affected by the virus

c. Run your simulation 10 times. Use the same inputs for each run, but draw a random number (assume a uniform distribution for all random numbers) to determine the severity level. Then draw random numbers to determine the percentage of computers of each type affected, using the constraints detailed earlier. For example, if the attack is of medium severity, draw a random number between 0 and 70 to indicate the percentage of infected user workstations and a random number between 0 and 50 to indicate the percentage of infected Web servers.

d. Calculate the following data and show the results for each run, and then calculate the average costs and hours for the 10 runs combined:
- Total lost employee hours
- Total dollar cost of lost employee hours
- Total hours of technicians to fix the servers
- Total cost of technician labor
- Total overall cost

5-2. Suppose you have just been appointed manager of a help desk with an IS department. You have been there for just a week, and you are amazed to find only limited information to help you manage your employees. In fact, the only available data concerns the processing of particular issues, called *Tickets*. The following data are kept:

> **Ticket#, Date_Submitted, Date_Opened, Date_Closed, Type (new or repeat), Reporting_Employee_Name, Reporting_Employee_Division, Technician_Name, Problem_System, and Problem_Description**

You can find sample Ticket data in the Excel file **Ch05Ex02**.

As a manager, you need more data. Among your needs are data that will help you learn who are your best- and worst-performing technicians, how different systems compare in terms of number of problems reported and the time required to fix those problems, how different divisions compare in terms of problems reported and the time required to fix them, which technicians are the best and worst at solving problems with particular systems, and which technicians are best and worst at solving problems from particular divisions.

a. Using either Access or Excel or a combination of the two, produce the information listed previously from the data in the Excel file **Ch05Ex02**. In your answer, you may use queries, formulas, reports, forms, graphs, pivot tables, pivot charts, or any other type of Access or Excel display. Choose the best display for the type of data you are producing.
b. Explain how you would use these different types of data to manage your department.
c. Specify any additional data you would like to record to help you manage your department.
d. Use either Access or Excel or a combination to produce the data in part c.

PART 3

Chapter 6

6-1. Assume that you have been hired to develop an Access database for a facilities reservation system at CBI's exercise facility. You have been given the following design for implementation:

FACILITY   (FacilityID, FacilityName, Description, StandardRentalFee)

RESERVATION   (ReservationNumber, *FacilityID*, Date, StartTime, EndTime)

Where FacilityID and ReservationNumber are AutoNumber primary keys and RESERVATION FacilityID is a foreign key to FACILITY. Use the appropriate data types for the other columns.

a. Create these tables in Access.
b. Create the appropriate relationship in Access.

c. Import the data in the file **Ch06Ex01.txt** into the FACILITY table.
d. Create a reservation form for creating and viewing specific reservations.
e. Create a parameterized query for finding a reservation by value of ReservationNumber.
f. Create a report that shows all of the reservations for all facilities.
g. Create a parameterized report that shows all of the reservations for a particular date.

6-2.   You are the manager of the pizza shop described in Chapter 6. Recently, you provided your drivers with handheld GPS devices that display real-time traffic data. The owner of another franchise has asked you to give a presentation to the other franchise owners about the usefulness of the devices. To make your case, you collected data on 50 deliveries before and 50 deliveries after installing the devices at the end of June 2018. The data is located in the file **Ch06Ex02**.

In this spreadsheet, you have made two main sections. On the left is data from before the GPS devices were added, and on the right is data from after the GPS devices were added. There are four drivers, and each makes deliveries to four zones—A, B, C, and D. Zone A is composed of students in dorms at the campus; the other three zones are located in different geographic regions around the town. Also included in each of the two sections are time for delivery and the price of the delivery.

a. Format the labels at the top of each section using font size and color, fill color, and cell merging to make your spreadsheet look more professional.
b. Format the price data in currency format.
c. Calculate the average time and price before and after the GPS devices were used.
d. Calculate the average time and price before and after the GPS devices were used for zone A (dorm students).
e. How much time did the GPS devices save overall (all four zones combined)?
f. How much time did the GPS devices save per order for nonstudent deliveries?
g. Sort the data in the After GPS area by driver; what is the average price for driver Green?
h. If you are one of the managers considering adopting GPS devices, what factors might be different between your restaurant and the restaurant in this exercise that might affect your willingness to invest in GPS?

Chapter 7

7-1.   Your university is considering consolidating all purchasing functions into one central office. To assess the cost savings of such a move, the university collected data about the purchasing costs in three departments. These data are shown in the file **Ch07Ex01**.

The data show the number of orders and the total price of the orders for each of the three departments. The file also includes data on the monthly fixed costs of operating a purchasing office. Fixed costs include the cost of the purchasing agent(s) for that month; the estimated cost of the office space; and the approximate cost of other fixed costs, such as insurance and supervision. These three departments were chosen for data collection because they represent typical small, medium, and large purchasing offices.

a. If each purchasing agent costs the university $7,500 per month, calculate the total fixed cost for each of the offices.
b. Calculate the average fixed cost per order for each of the three departments.
c. Create a bar chart with appropriate labels and titles that shows the average fixed cost per order for each of the three departments.
d. The university estimates that it has 15 small, 5 medium, and 3 large departments. If each of these departments has the same number and price of orders as the three departments shown in the file, calculate the total number and total price for the entire university.
e. The university estimates that the fixed cost data for these other departments will be the same as the three departments shown in the file; that is, each small department will have the same data as the Athletics department, each medium department is like the Student Services department, and each large department is like the Bookstore. Calculate the total fixed costs for the entire university.

f. The university assumes that when purchasing is consolidated in one office, the average cost per order will be about the same as the Bookstore's average cost per order. Using the total number of orders for the university from part d and the average fixed cost per order of a large department from part b, how much will the university save if it consolidates purchasing in one location?

7-2. Figure AE-7 is a sample bill of materials, a form that shows the components and parts used to construct a product. In this example, the product is a child's wagon. Such bills of materials are an essential part of manufacturing functional applications as well as ERP applications.

This particular example is a form produced using Microsoft Access. Producing such a form is a bit tricky, so this exercise will guide you through the steps required. You can then apply what you learn to produce a similar report. You can also use Access to experiment on extensions of this form.

a. Create a table named *PART* with columns *PartNumber, Level, Description, QuantityRequired,* and *PartOf. Description* and *Level* should be text, *PartNumber* should be AutoNumber, and *QuantityRequired* and *PartOf* should be numeric. Add the *PART* data shown in Figure AE-7 to your table.

b. Create a query that has all columns of *PART*. Restrict the view to rows having a value of 1 for *Level*. Name your query *qLevel1*.

c. Create two more queries that are restricted to rows having values of 2 or 3 for *Level*. Name your queries *qLevel2* and *qLevel3*, respectively.

d. Create a form that contains *PartNumber, Level,* and *Description* from *qLevel1*. You can use a wizard for this if you want. Name the form *Bill of Materials*.

e. Select the Subform/Subreport tool in the Controls section of the Design ribbon and create a subform in your form in part d. Set the data on this form to be all of the columns of *qLevel2*. After you have created the subform, ensure that the Link Child Fields property is set to *PartOf* and that the Link Master Fields property is set to *PartNumber*. Close the *Bill of Materials* form.

f. Open the subform created in part e and create a subform on it. Set the data on this subform to be all of the columns of *qLevel3*. After you have created the subform,

FIGURE AE-7

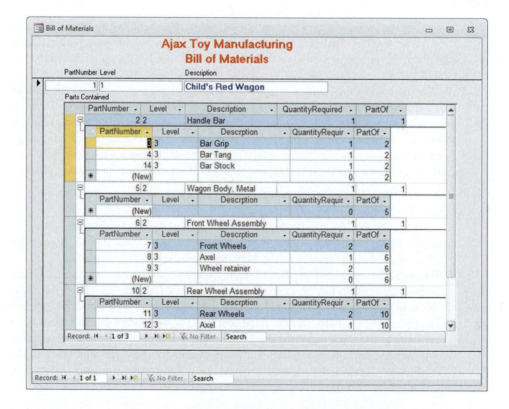

ensure that the Link Child Fields property is set to *PartOf* and that the Link Master Fields property is set to *PartNumber*. Close the *Bill of Materials* form.

   g. Open the *Bill of Materials* form. It should appear as in Figure AE-7. Open and close the form and add new data to the table. Using this form, add sample BOM data for a product of your own choosing.

   h. Following the process similar to that just described, create a *Bill of Materials Report* that lists the data for all of your products.

   i. (**Optional, challenging extension**) Each part in the BOM in Figure AE-7 can be used in at most one assembly (there is space to show just one *PartOf* value). You can change your design to allow a part to be used in more than one assembly as follows: First, remove *PartOf* from PART. Next, create a second table that has two columns: *AssemblyPartNumber* and *ComponentPartNumber*. The first contains a part number of an assembly and the second a part number of a component. Every component of a part will have a row in this table. Extend the views described previously to use this second table and to produce a display similar to Figure AE-7.

Chapter 8

8-1. ![X SAP] SAP Your firm, a small bike manufacturing outfit, is considering the possibility of adding a new item to its product line. This bike accessory is a 3rd Wheel, a trailer designed to carry children or, in a different configuration, goods and equipment (see Figure AE-8).

Your firm will procure and build the 3rd Wheel in-house if the labor costs for assembly are sufficiently less than the cost of procuring the 3rd Wheel already assembled. You are asked to estimate the labor cost of producing this new accessory. You have downloaded labor cost data from your ERP system into an Excel spreadsheet. This data file is **Ch08Ex01**. (To see how to download the data directly from SAP, see the end of this exercise.)

At the East plant there are four hourly wage rates for assembly workers and there are two possible unions that hourly pay is based upon—U001 and U002. To assemble the 3rd Wheel, the engineering department has developed several options. Each of the options requires a different set of hours for the pay rates, as shown below:

| | Labor Hours | | |
Pay Scale	Option A	Option B	Option C
0	5	3	7
1	3	4	2
2	2	2	1
3	2	1	2

FIGURE AE-8
3rd Wheel

Source: Jim West/Alamy Images

a. Calculate the total labor cost for options A, B, and C for Union 001 and Union 002 using the minimum wage rate in each pay grade. Which option is lowest cost?

b. Calculate the total labor cost for options A, B, and C for Union 001 and Union 002 using the maximum wage rate in each pay grade. Which option is lowest cost?

c. Create a chart with appropriate labels and titles that shows all six options in the previous two parts.

d. Another option for your firm is to outsource the payscale 0 work. If the bottom payscale work is removed, does the lowest cost option change?

e. The analysis in part d is a common one. This interactive analysis is also called "what-if" analysis. In part d you were asked, "What if payscale 0 work is outsourced?" If you expect to do "what-if" analysis on a spreadsheet, how does that change how you set up the original spreadsheet, its data, functions, and equations?

To download the data directly from SAP:[1]

(1) Log in to SAP as before.

(2) On the SAP Easy Access Screen, select:

> *Information Systems > General Report Selection > Human Resources > Personal Management > Compensation Management > Pay Structure > Display Pay Scale Structure*

(3) Enter *10* in Country Grouping (for USA), then click the *Execute* icon above Key date, as shown in Figure AE-9.

(4) On the Display Pay Scale Structure screen, click the *Local* file icon (ninth icon from left) and specify a file name and location for the file to be saved on the local machine, as shown in Figure AE-10.

(5) Open Excel. Navigate to the downloaded Excel file and open it. Inspect your spreadsheet. It should look like Figure AE-11.

8-2. Assume that you have been given the task of compiling evaluations that your company's purchasing agents make of their e-commerce vendors. Each month, every purchasing agent evaluates all of the vendors that he or she has ordered from in the past month on three factors: price, quality, and responsiveness. Assume the ratings are from 1 to 5, with 5 being the best. Because your company has hundreds of vendors and dozens of purchasing agents, you decide to use Access to compile the results.

a. Create a database with three tables: VENDOR (*VendorNumber, Name, Contact*), PURCHASER (*EmpNumber, Name, Email*), and RATING (*EmpNumber, VendorNumber, Month, Year, PriceRating, QualityRating, ResponsivenessRating*). Assume that *VendorNumber* and *EmpNumber* are the keys of VENDOR and PURCHASER, respectively. Decide what you think is the appropriate key for RATING.

b. Create appropriate relationships.

c. Import the data in the Excel file **Ch08Ex02**. Note that the data for Vendor, Purchaser, and Rating are stored in three separate worksheets.

FIGURE AE-9

Source: Copyright © SAP AG

[1]This example uses the Global Bike Inc SAP client set. See Appendix 8A for instructions on how to access this client set.

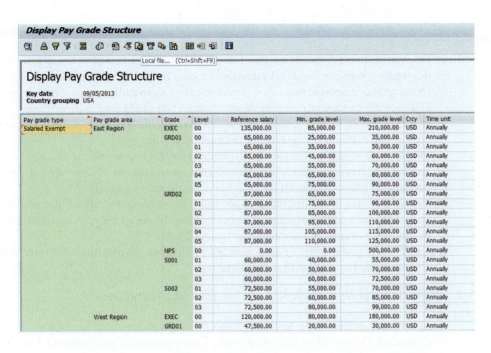

FIGURE AE-10

Source: Copyright © SAP AG

d. Create a query that shows the names of all vendors and their average scores.

e. Create a query that shows the names of all employees and their average scores. *Hint: In this and in part f, you will need to use the Group By function in your query.*

f. Create a parameterized query that you can use to obtain the minimum, maximum, and average ratings on each criterion for a particular vendor. Assume you will enter *VendorName* as the parameter.

g. Using the data created by your queries, what conclusions can you make about vendors or purchasers?

Chapter 9

9-1. Suppose your manager asks you to create a spreadsheet to compute a production schedule. Your schedule should stipulate a production quantity for seven products that is based on sales projections made by three regional managers in your company's three sales regions.

a. Create a separate worksheet for each sales region. Use the data in the Word file **Ch09Ex01**. This file contains each manager's monthly sales projections for the past year, actual sales results for those same months, and projections for sales for each month in the coming quarter.

FIGURE AE-11

b. Create a separate worksheet for each manager's data. Import the data from Word into Excel.

c. On each of the worksheets, use the data from the prior four quarters to compute the discrepancy between the actual sales and the sales projections. This discrepancy can be computed in several ways: You could calculate an overall average, or you could calculate an average per quarter or per month. You could also weight recent discrepancies more heavily than earlier ones. Choose a method that you think is most appropriate. Explain why you chose the method you did.

d. Modify your worksheets to use the discrepancy factors to compute an adjusted forecast for the coming quarter. Thus, each of your spreadsheets will show the raw forecast and the adjusted forecast for each month in the coming quarter.

e. Create a fourth worksheet that totals sales projections for all of the regions. Show both the unadjusted forecast and the adjusted forecast for each region and for the company overall. Show month and quarter totals.

f. Create a bar graph showing total monthly production. Display the unadjusted and adjusted forecasts using different-colored bars.

9-2. Do Application Exercise 5-1, if you have not already done so.

a. Add a Status column to the RESERVATION table, where Status can have values of *Not Confirmed*, *Confirmed*, or *Cancelled*. A reservation guarantees a customer a locker and access to all equipment. Explain why CBI might wish to track cancelled reservations.

b. Create a data entry form that would be appropriate to make a reservation at a facility.

c. Create a data entry form that would be appropriate to confirm a reservation at a facility.

d. Create a Daily Facility Use Report. Assume the report has a parameterized query to produce all reservations for a given date.

e. Input data and test your database. Use the Windows 7 Snipping Tool or some other tool to capture screen shots of your data entry screens and your report.

PART 4

Chapter 10

10-1. Suppose that you have been asked to assist in the managerial decision about how much to increase pay in the next year. Assume you are given a list of the departments in your company, along with the average salary for employees in that department for major companies in your industry. Additionally, you are given the names and salaries of 10 people in each of three departments in your company.

Assume you have been asked to create a spreadsheet that shows the names of the 10 employees in each department, their current salary, the difference between their current salary and the industry average salary for their department, and the percent their salary would need to be increased to meet the industry average. Your spreadsheet should also compute the average increase needed to meet the industry average for each department and the average increase, company-wide, to meet industry averages.

a. Use the data in the file **Ch10Ex01** and create the spreadsheet.

b. How can you use this analysis to contribute to the employee salary decision? Based on this data, what conclusions can you make?

c. Suppose other team members want to use your spreadsheet. Name three ways you can share it with them, and describe the advantages and disadvantages of each.

10-2. Suppose that you have been asked to assist in the managerial decision about how much to increase pay in the next year. Specifically, you are tasked to determine if there are significant salary differences among departments in your company.

You are given an Access database with a table of employee data with the following structure:

EMPLOYEE (Name, Department, Specialty, Salary)

where *Name* is the name of an employee who works in a department, *Department* is the department name, *Specialty* is the name of the employee's primary skill, and *Salary* is the employee's current salary. Assume that no two employees have the same name. You have been asked to answer the following queries:

(1) List the names, department, and salary of all employees earning more than $100,000.
(2) List the names and specialties of all employees in the Marketing department.
(3) Compute the average, maximum, and minimum salary of employees in your company.
(4) Compute the average, minimum, and maximum salary of employees in the Marketing department.
(5) Compute the average, minimum, and maximum salary of employees in the Information Systems department.
(6) *Extra credit:* Compute the average salary for employees in every department. Use *Group By*.

a. Design and run Access queries to obtain the answers to these questions, using the data in the file **Ch10Ex02**.
b. Explain how the data in your answer contributes to the salary increase decision.
c. Suppose other team members want to use your Access application. Name three ways you can share it with them, and describe the advantages and disadvantages of each.

Chapter 11

11-1. For the following exercises, tutorials and help are available from each social media platform and also by using a search engine.

a. **Facebook:** Create a Facebook page for a small local business, a student organization, or a team. Use a search engine to find instructions.
b. **Twitter:** Create an account and follow several of your classmates (and have them follow you). Tweet and send them a direct message. Make a tweet with a #hashtag, and then use Twitter's search function to find this tweet. Find your classmates' hashtag tweets. Find and follow popular accounts or accounts of individuals or organizations in an area of interest to you.
c. **LinkedIn:** Create an account and begin to fill out your profile. Create or extend the data in your profile (if you already had an account). Connect to your classmates. Add a photo. Find and follow companies, and explore the site and learn new options in Groups, Jobs, and Contacts.
d. **Blogger:** Create a blog about the use of social media in small business or another topic of interest to you. Embed a YouTube video in your blog. Follow other blogs.

11-2. For the following exercises, tutorials and help are available from each social media platform and also by using a search engine.

a. **Wikipedia:** Create your own user account and log in. Go to your *User talk* page and click *Edit source*. You will be creating a page called *User talk:Yourusername*. Write a paragraph about social media. Find a classmate's user talk entry and edit his or her paragraph. Go back to your talk page and click *View History* to see how your page has been edited. Finally, find an entry on Wikipedia that you can contribute to and edit that page. Use a search engine and find instructions to play Wiki Races (an example is *http://wikibin.org/articles/wiki-races.html*).
b. **Delicious, Digg, and StumbleUpon:** Create accounts at these sites. Share your list of bookmarks in Delicious with a classmate.
c. **Klout.com:** Go to Klout.com or another social media monitoring site. Sign in with your Twitter account name and see the impact of your tweets. Read about how your clout is determined.
d. **Google Drive:** Create or use an existing Gmail account. Discover how to make a Google document, and share that document with your classmates. Edit the document simultaneously with classmates.

e. **Tumblr and Pinterest**: Create accounts on these platforms. Find three businesses that use them well and write a blog entry about what these organizations are doing right.

Chapter 12

12-1. OLAP cubes are very similar to Microsoft Excel pivot tables. For this exercise, assume that your organization's purchasing agents rate vendors similar to the situation described in Application Exercise 8-2.

a. Open the Excel file **Ch12Ex01**. The spreadsheet has the following column names: *VendorName, EmployeeName, Date, Year*, and *Rating*.
b. Under the *Insert* ribbon in Excel, click *Pivot Table*.
c. When asked to provide a data range, drag your mouse over the data you imported so as to select all of the data. Be sure to include the column headings. Excel will fill in the range values in the open dialog box. Place your pivot table in a separate spreadsheet.
d. Excel will create a field list on the right-hand side of your spreadsheet. Drag and drop the field named *VendorName* under the word "Rows" at the bottom of the field list. Drag and drop *EmployeeName* under the word "Columns." Now drag and drop the field named *Rating* under the word "Values." Voilà! You have a pivot table.
e. To see how the table works, drag and drop more fields onto the various sections of your pivot table. For example, drop *Year* on top of *Employee*. Then move *Year* below *Employee*. Now move *Year* below *Vendor*. All of this action is just like an OLAP cube, and, in fact, OLAP cubes are readily displayed in Excel pivot tables. The major difference is that OLAP cubes are usually based on thousands or more rows of data.

12-2. It is surprisingly easy to create a market basket report using table data in Access. To do so, however, you will need to enter SQL expressions into the Access query builder. Here you can just copy SQL statements to type them in. If you take a database class, you will learn how to code SQL statements like those you will use here.

a. Create an Access database with a table named *Order_Data* having columns *OrderNumber, ItemName*, and *Quantity*, with data types Number, Short Text, and Number, respectively. Define the key as the composite (*OrderNumber, ItemName*).
b. Import the data from the Excel file **Ch12Ex02** into the *Order_Data* table.
c. Now, to perform the market basket analysis, you will need to enter several SQL statements into Access. To do so, click the queries tab and select *Query Design* in Design view. Click *Close* when the Show Table dialog box appears. Right-click in the gray section above the grid. Select *SQL View*. Enter the following expression exactly as it appears here:

SELECT	**T1.ItemName as FirstItem,**
	T2.ItemName as SecondItem
FROM	**Order_Data T1, Order_Data T2**
WHERE	**T1.OrderNumber=**
	T2.OrderNumber
AND	**T1.ItemName<>**
	T2.ItemName;

Click the red exclamation point in the toolbar to run the query. Correct any typing mistakes and, once it works, save the query using the name *TwoItemBasket*.
d. Now enter a second SQL statement. Again, click the queries tab and select *Query Design* in Design view. Click *Close* when the Show Table dialog box appears. Right-click in the gray section above the grid. Select *SQL View*. Enter the following expression exactly as it appears here:

SELECT	TwoItemBasket.FirstItem,
	TwoItemBasket.SecondItem,
	Count(*) AS SupportCount
FROM	TwoItemBasket
GROUP BY	TwoItemBasket.FirstItem,
	TwoItemBasket.SecondItem;

Click *Run* and correct any typing mistakes and, once it works, save the query using the name *SupportCount*.

e. Examine the results of the second query and verify that the two query statements have correctly calculated the number of times that two items have appeared together. Explain further calculations you need to make to compute support.

f. Explain the calculations you need to make to compute lift. Although you can make those calculations using SQL, you need more SQL knowledge to do it, and we will skip that here.

g. Explain, in your own words, what the query in part c seems to be doing. What does the query in part d seem to be doing? Again, you will need to take a database class to learn how to code such expressions, but this exercise should give you a sense of the kinds of calculations that are possible with SQL.

Glossary

3D printing. Also called *additive manufacturing*; a process of depositing successive layers of material to manufacture objects. Just as current printers deposit ink in two dimensions, 3D printing deposits material in three dimensions, layering material in the third dimension as it dries. **p. 206**

A/B testing. Also called split testing; an analysis technique in which a Web site developer builds two identical pages with slight changes in design to determine the better conversion rate for each design. **p. 351**

Abstract reasoning. The ability to make and manipulate models. **p. 6**

Access. A popular personal and small workgroup DBMS product from Microsoft. **p. 76**

Activity. A task within a business process. **p. 26 and 132**

Actor. A person or computer who performs a subset of activities in a business process. **p. 26 and 132**

Advanced Persistent Threat (APT) A sophisticated, possibly long-running computer hack that is perpetrated applications, and services, many of which without requiring human input. **p. 110**

Agile development. A systems development process that conforms to specific principles designed to welcome change and deliver working versions of the product frequently. **p. 404**

Analysis. A method of breaking a thing down to examine its details in order to discover or reveal its essential features. **p. 342**

Android. A mobile operating system licensed by Google. **p. 385**

Artificial intelligence (AI) Software that enables an IS to mimic or simulate human intelligence. **p. 411**

As-is diagram. A diagram that represents the current situation and processes. **p. 145**

Assessment. To be informed about current conditions. **p. 338**

Asymmetric encryption. An encryption method whereby different keys are used to encode and to decode the message; one key encodes the message, and the other key decodes the message. Symmetric encryption is simpler and much faster than asymmetric encryption. **p. 115**

Asynchronous communication. Information exchange that occurs when all members of a work team do not meet at the same time, such as those who work different shifts or in different locations. **p. 287**

Attribute. (1) A variable that provides properties for an html tag. Each attribute has a standard name. For example, the attribute for a hyperlink is *href*, and its value indicates which Web page is to be displayed when the user clicks the link. (2) Characteristics of an entity. Example attributes of *Order* would be *OrderNumber, OrderDate, SubTotal, Tax, Total*, and so forth. Example attributes of *Salesperson* would be *SalespersonName, Email, Phone*, and so forth. **p. 59**

Auction. Application that matches buyers and sellers by using an e-commerce version of a standard, competitive-bidding auction process. **p. 248**

Auditing process. The official, unbiased examination of an organization's financial accounts. **p. 355**

Augmented reality (AR). Technology that superimposes data or graphics onto a computer-generated display of the physical environment. **p. 205**

Authentication. The process whereby an information system verifies (validates) a user. **p. 114**

Automation. A system in which a computer does an activity or part of an activity that was once done by a person. **p. 141**

Autonomy. The ability to operate, at least in part, without direct human intervention. **p. 416**

Availability check. Determines if the promised delivery quantity can be met by the promised delivery date. **p. 238**

Barriers to entry. Factors that make it difficult for a new business to begin operating in an industry. **p. 12**

Big Data. Data collections that differ from relational databases by their huge volume, rapid velocity, and great variety. **p. 352**

Bill of material (BOM). A structure or description that specifies the raw materials, quantities, and subassemblies to create a product. **p. 170**

Biometric authentication. The use of personal physical characteristics, such as fingerprints, facial features, and retinal scans, to verify users. **p. 114**

Bit. The smallest unit of data with a single binary value of 0 or 1. **p. 382**

Blockchain. Overcomes the need for a trusted third party and verifies records by maintaining data on a distributed database that is public and difficult to hack. **p. 249**

Bluetooth. A common wireless protocol designed for transmitting data over short distances, replacing cables. **p. 53 and 424**

Bottleneck. When a limited resource greatly reduces the output of an integrated series of activities or processes. **p. 144 and 201**

Bring your own device (BYOD). A policy that allows employees to use their own personal mobile device to conduct company activities. **p. 121**

Broad AI. A general intelligence that can be applied across a broad set of tasks such as counseling, planning, or goal setting. **p. 414**

Brute force. Attack that uses a trial-and-error method to obtain passwords or a personal identification number. **p. 107**. By large, well-funded organizations such as governments. **p. 109**

Bullwhip effect. Phenomenon in which the variability in the size and timing of orders increases at each stage up the supply chain, from customer to supplier. **p. 201**

Business analyst. Someone who is well versed in the Porter models, organizational strategy, and systems alignment theory such as COBIT and who also understands the proper role for technology. **p. 398**

Business intelligence. A process of acquiring, analyzing, and publishing data with an objective of discovering or revealing patterns in data that will inform a business person. **p. 336**

Business intelligence system. An information system that supports business processes by consolidating and analyzing data in a large database to help users create information. **p. 336**

Business process. A sequence of activities for accomplishing a function. **p. 26 and 132**

Business process management (BPM). A systematic process of modeling, creating, implementing, and assessing business processes. **p. 394**

Business Process Model and Notation (BPMN) standard. A standard set of terms and graphical notations for documenting business processes. **p. 26**

Business-to-business (B2B). Sales between companies. **p. 233**

Business-to-consumer (B2C). Sales between a supplier and a retail customer (the consumer). **p. 233**

Business-to-government (B2G). Sales between companies and governmental organizations. **p. 247**

Buy-in. A term for selling a product or system for less than its true price. **p. 209**

Byte(s). (1) A character of data. (2) An 8-bit chunk. **p. 73**

Cable line. A type of WAN connection that provides high-speed data transmission using cable television lines. Because up to 500 user sites can share a cable line, performance varies depending on how many other users are sending and receiving data. **p. 54**

Capital. The investment of resources with the expectation of future returns in the marketplace. **p. 319**

CAPTCHA. A pseudo acronym for "Completely Automated Public Turing test to tell Computers and Humans Apart," which uses a simple challenge-response exercise to determine if the user is a human or a computer program such as a brute force attacker. **p. 114**

Cascading Style Sheet (CSS). Defines the fonts and layout of all the elements on pages on a Web site so that the site has one consistent look and feel. **p. 59**

Categorical imperative. An ethical principle developed by the German philosopher Immanuel Kant. The categorical imperative states that one should behave only in a way that one would want the behavior to be a universal law. **p. 18**

Cause marketing. Using social media to promote social issues, hoping that this will result in profit for the business. **p. 317**

Cellular network. Also called a mobile network or wireless WAN (WWAN), is a communication network that uses radio signals to send and receive data to mobile users. **p. 53**

Central processing unit (CPU). The CPU selects instructions, processes them, performs arithmetic and logical comparisons, and stores results of operations in memory. **p. 381**

Certification. A designation earned by an individual that assures the individual can perform a particular job or task. **p. 375**

Chief information officer (CIO). The principal manager of the IS department **p. 374**

Chief information security officer (CISO). Designs and leads the organization's information security program while managing IS security personnel. **p. 375**

Chief technology officer (CTO). Heads the technology group. The CTO evaluates new technologies. **p. 374**

Clearinghouse. Entity that provides goods and services at a stated price and arranges for the delivery of the goods, but never takes title to the goods. **p. 248**

Click-through rate. The number of clicks on an ad divided by the number of times the ad is displayed. **p. 316**

Clickstream data. Web site data that describes a customer's clicking behavior. Such data includes everything the customer does at the Web site. **p. 357**

Client. A computer that provides word processing, spreadsheets, database access, and usually a network connection. **p. 382**

Collaboration. A dynamic process in which a group of people work together to achieve common objectives via communication and iteration. **p. 280**

Collaboration information system. An information system that supports collaboration; this system needs to support iteration and communication among team members. **p. 285**

Collaborative consumption. Mutual access to products and services rather than individual and exclusive ownership. **p. 326**

Columns. Also called *fields*, or groups of bytes. A database table has multiple columns that are used to represent the attributes of an entity. Examples are *PartNumber*, *EmployeeName*, and *SalesDate*. **p. 73**

Competitive strategy. The strategy an organization chooses as the way it will succeed in its industry. According to Porter, there are four fundamental competitive strategies: cost leadership across an industry or within a particular industry segment and product differentiation across an industry or within a particular industry segment. **p. 12**

Computer forensics. Disaster or incident, determine cause of computer disasters or incidents. **p. 123**

Computer science graduates. Skilled programmers who take many highly technical classes. **p. 372**

Computer-based information system. An information system that includes a computer. **p. 29**

Configuration. The process of adapting ERP software to conform to customer requirements without changing program code. **p. 164**

Configuration control. A method to ensure all changes to the new system are approved by management. **p. 403**

Connection data. Data about relationships. **p. 312**

Content data. User-generated content and the responses to that content contributed by other users. **p. 312**

Content management systems (CMS). Support the management and delivery of documents including reports, Web pages, and other expressions of employee knowledge. **p. 412**

Continuous improvement process (CIP). An ongoing cycle of process improvement; the process includes component creation, implementation, monitoring, and remodeling. **p. 369**

Control. A method used in a process to limit behavior. **p. 140**

Conversion rate. A measure of Web site traffic involving the ratio of the number of customers who eventually purchased divided by the number who visited. **p. 316 and 351**

Cookie(s). (1) Data that a Web site stores on your computer to record something about its interaction with you. (2) Small files that your browser stores on your computer when you visit Web sites. **p. 111**

Cooperation. A process where a group of people work together, all doing essentially the same type of work, to accomplish a job. **p. 280**

Cost feasibility. Determines if the benefits of the new system are worth the cost of developing it. **p. 397**

Cross-selling. The sale of related products; salespeople try to get customers who buy product *X* to also buy product *Y*. **p. 347**

Cross-site scripting (XSS). A technique used to compromise database data in which Web page scripting is injected into the server. **p. 109**

Crow's feet. Lines on an entity-relationship diagram that indicate a 1:N relationship between two entities. **p. 85**

Crow's-foot diagram. A type of entity-relationship diagram that uses a crow's foot symbol to designate a 1:N relationship. **p. 86**

Crowdsourcing. Outsourcing a task to a large number of users. **p. 318**

Culture. The day-to-day work habits and practices that workers take for granted. **p. 171**

Custom-developed software. Tailor-made software. **p. 386**

Customer relationship management (CRM). A system that integrates customer-facing processes and manages all the interactions with customers. **p. 231**

Customer service. the series of activities before, during, or after a sale with the goal of increasing customer satisfaction. **p. 317**

Customization. Writing new code to supplement an ERP system. **p. 164**

Darknet. Part of the Internet that is intentionally hidden and inaccessible from traditional search engines. **p. 251**

Dashboards. Easy to read, concise, up-to-the-minute displays of process KPIs. **p. 168** A viz customized for a particular user. **p. 349**

Data. Recorded facts or figures. One of the five fundamental components of an information system. **p. 29**

Data broker. Also called a *data aggregator*; a company that acquires and purchases consumer and other data from public records, retailers, Internet cookie vendors, social media trackers, and other sources and uses it to create business intelligence that it sells to companies and the government. **p. 362**

Data integrity problem. In a database, the situation that exists when data items disagree with one another. An example is two different names for the same customer. **p. 87**

Data mart. A subset of read-only data in a data warehouse that is packaged for subsequent analysis by a particular client within the firm. **p. 342**

Data mining. A type of Informing process that uses sophisticated statistical analyses to uncover patterns in a large database of data in order to improve prediction. **p. 346**

Data model. A logical representation of the data in a database that describes the data and relationships that will be stored in the database. Akin to a blueprint. **p. 83**

Data sharing. The practice of distributing the same data to multiple processes. **p. 200**

Data warehouse. A facility that prepares, stores, and manages data specifically for reporting and data mining. **p. 339**

Database. A self-describing collection of integrated records. **p. 73**

Database administration (DBA). The management, development, operation, and maintenance of the database so as to achieve the organization's objectives. This staff function requires balancing conflicting goals: protecting the database while maximizing its availability for authorized use. In smaller organizations, this function usually is served by a single person. Larger organizations assign several people to an office of database administration. **p. 78**

Database application. Forms, reports, queries, and application programs for processing a database. A database can be processed by many different database applications. **p. 79**

Database application system. Applications, having the standard five components, that make database data more accessible and useful. Users employ a database application that consists of forms, formatted reports, queries, and application programs. Each of these, in turn, calls on the database management system (DBMS) to process the database tables. **p. 76**

Database management systems (DBMS). A program for creating, processing, and administering a database. A DBMS is a large and complex program that is licensed like an operating system. Microsoft Access and Oracle are example DBMS products. **p. 76**

DB2. A popular, enterprise-class DBMS product from IBM. **p. 76**

Decision Making process. The selection of a choice among available options; can be done individually or in a groaup. **p. 350**

Decision support systems (DSS). An information system used in support of decision making. **p. 337**

Deep web. The extended Internet with addresses that are not indexed by search engines such as academic resources, members-only Web sites, dynamic pages that are created when users visit a site, government agencies and records, and corporate internal networks. **p. 251**

Denial of service (DOS). A security problem in which users are not able to access an information system; can be caused by human errors, natural disaster, or malicious activity. **p. 110**

Desktop virtualization. A desktop operating system hosted by a server that can be accessed from any computer to which the user has access. **p. 389**

Digital mapping. A process where a map or image is compiled and formatted into a digital form. **p. 426**

Digital subscriber line (DSL). A communications line that operates on the same lines as voice telephones, but does so in such a manner that its signals do not interfere with voice telephone service. **p. 54**

Dimension. A characteristic or attribute of data. **p. 344**

Dirty data. Problematic data. Examples are a value of *B* for customer gender and a value of *213* for customer age. All these values are problematic when data mining. **p. 356**

Discussion forums. A form of asynchronous communication in which one group member posts an entry and other group members respond. A better form of group communication than e-mail, because it is more difficult for the discussion to go off track. **p. 288**

Disintermediation. Elimination of one or more middle layers in the supply chain. **p. 248**

Document library. A named collection of documents in SharePoint. **p. 295**

Domain name. A worldwide-unique name that is affiliated with a public IP address. The process of changing a name into its IP address is called *resolving the domain name*. **p. 57**

Drill down. With an OLAP report, to further divide the data into more detail. **p. 345**

Dual processor. A computer with two CPUs. **p. 381**

Dynamic processes. A process whose structure is fluid and dynamic. Contrast with structured processes. Collaboration is a dynamic process; SAP order entry is a structured process. **p. 33**

Economies of scale. The principle that the average cost of production decreases as the size of the operation increases. **p. 62**

E-commerce. A multifirm process of buying and selling goods and services using Internet technologies. **p. 246**

Effectiveness. A process objective that helps achieve organizational strategy. **p. 134**

Efficiency. A resource-oriented process objective; a process is efficient if it creates more output with the same inputs or the same output with fewer inputs. **p. 134**

Elastic. (1) The amount of resources leased in the cloud can be increased or decreased dynamically, programmatically, in a short span of time; organizations pay for just the resources that they use. (2) The number of servers can dynamically increase and decrease without disrupting performance. **p. 61**

Electronic exchange. Site that facilitates the matching of buyers and sellers; the business process is similar to that of a stock exchange. Sellers offer goods at a given price through the electronic exchange, and buyers make offers to purchase over the same exchange. Price matches result in transactions from which the exchange takes a commission. **p. 248**

Encryption. The process of transforming clear text into coded, unintelligible text for secure storage or communication. **p. 115**

Enterprise 2.0. When businesses employ social media internally to facilitate cooperative work. **p. 310**

Enterprise DBMS. A product that processes large organizational and workgroup databases. These products support many users, perhaps thousands, and many different database applications. Such DBMS products support 24/7 operations and can manage databases that span dozens of different magnetic disks with hundreds of gigabytes or more of data. IBM's DB2, Microsoft's SQL Server, and Oracle's Oracle are examples of enterprise DBMS products. **p. 81**

Enterprise resource planning (ERP) system. A suite of software, a database, and a set of inherent processes for consolidating business operations into a single, consistent, information system. **p. 158**

Entity. In the E-R data model, a representation of some thing that users want to track. Some entities represent a physical object; others represent a logical construct or transaction. **p. 83**

Entity-relationship (E-R) data model. A popular technique for creating a data model whereby developers define the things that will be stored and identify the relationships among them. **p. 83**

Entity-relationship (E-R) diagrams. A type of diagram used by database designers to document entities and their relationships to each other. **p. 85**

Ethernet. Another name for the IEEE 802.3 protocol, Ethernet is a network protocol that operates at Layers 1 and 2 of the TCP/IP–OSI architecture. Ethernet, the world's most popular LAN protocol, is used on WANs as well. **p. 55**

Evil twin. A spoofed wireless access point that is similar to a legitimate access point; it is then used to eavesdrop on an unsuspecting user who mistakes the spoofed access point for the legitimate one. **p. 109**

Exceptions. Unexpected or unwelcome outputs from a process that require an action—the parts don't arrive, the employee performs poorly, the budget is overspent. **p. 141**

Executive support systems (ESS). Information systems that support strategic processes. **p. 134**

Experimentation. A careful and reasoned analysis of an opportunity, envisioning potential products or solutions or applications of technology, and then developing those ideas that seem to have the most promise, consistent with the resources you have. **p. 7**

Expert system. A rule-based system that acquires and stores human knowledge in the form of if/then rules. **p. 411**

Feedback. The return of a part of the output of process to the input. **p. 144**

Fields. Also called *columns*; groups of bytes in a database table. A database table has multiple columns that are used to represent the attributes of an entity. Examples are *PartNumber*, *EmployeeName*, and *SalesDate*. **p. 73**

File. A group of similar rows or records. In a database, sometimes called a *table*. **p. 73**

File server. A computer that stores files. **p. 290**

Finished goods inventory. Completed products awaiting delivery to customers. **p. 187**

Firewall. A computing device that prevents unauthorized access to parts of a network. **p. 116**

Five-component framework. The five fundamental components of an information system—computer hardware, software, data, procedures, and people—that are present in every information system, from the simplest to the most complex. **p. 29**

Five forces model. Model, proposed by Michael Porter, that assesses industry characteristics and profitability by means of five competitive forces—bargaining power of suppliers, threat of substitution, bargaining power of customers, rivalry among firms, and threat of new entrants. **p. 11**

Folksonomy. An emergent classification of content structure based on the processing of many user tags. **p. 312**

Foreign keys. A column or group of columns used to represent relationships. Values of the foreign key match values of the primary key in a different (foreign) table. **p. 75**

Form. Data entry forms are used to read, insert, modify, and delete database data. **p. 79**

Gap analysis. A study that highlights the differences between the business requirements that emerge from strategic planning and the capabilities of the ERP system. **p. 166**

General Data Protection Regulation (GDPR). Regulates the business use of personal data in the EU. **p. 361**

Geographic information system (GIS). An organizational IS that captures, analyzes, and presents LBD. **p. 420**

Geotagging. Process that assigns quantitative location measures, like longitude and latitude, to the map and the objects on the map. **p. 426**

Google Drive. A free thin-client application for sharing documents, presentations, spreadsheets, drawings, and other data. **p. 291**

Granularity. The level of detail in data. Customer name and account balance is large-granularity data. Customer name, balance, and the order details and payment history of every customer order is smaller granularity. **p. 357**

Hacking. Occurs when a person gains unauthorized access to a computer system. Although some people hack for the sheer joy of doing it, other hackers invade systems for the malicious purpose of stealing or modifying data. **p. 109**

Hadoop. An open-source program supported by the Apache Foundation that implements MapReduce on potentially thousands of computers. **p. 354**

Handover. In a cellular network when a user moves out of the original cell a **handover** or handoff is accomplished which switches the end user to an adjoining cell base station automatically. **p. 54**

Hardware. The physical parts of a computer, includes input and output devices as well as the computer processor and internal storage system. **p. 29**

Hash. A scrambled series of characters generated from a string of text, a unique digital fingerprint used in identification procedures. **p. 114**

Hashtag. A user-created tag that adds the prefix # to a word; this makes it easier to search for that term or keyword. **p. 312**

Horizontal-market application. Software that provides capabilities common across all organizations and industries; examples include word processors, graphics programs, spreadsheets, and presentation programs. **p. 386**

html (Hypertext Markup Language). A language that defines structure and layout of Web page content. An html tag is a notation used to define a data element for display or other purposes. **p. 58**

http (Hypertext Transport Protocol). A protocol used between browsers and Web servers. **p. 56**

https. A secure version of http. **p. 56**

Human capital. The investment in human knowledge and skills with the expectation of future returns in the marketplace. **p. 320**

Human resource processes. Organizational processes that assess the motivations and skills of employees; create job positions; investigate employee complaints; and staff, train, and evaluate personnel. **p. 136**

Human safeguards. Safeguards that result when authorized users follow appropriate procedures for system use and recovery. **p. 119**

Identifier. An attribute (or group of attributes) whose value is associated with one and only one entity instance. **p. 84**

IEEE 802.11 protocol. A protocol standard used for wireless LAN connections. **p. 55**

IEEE 802.3 protocol. A protocol standard used for wired LAN connections that specifies hardware characteristics, such as which wire carries which signals, and describes how messages are to be packaged and processed for wired transmission over the LAN. **p. 55**

If/then rule. A rule that specifies *if* a particular condition exists, *then* to take some action. **p. 411**

Inbound logistics processes. Processes that receive, store, and disseminate product input. **p. 136**

Index. A large database with links and keywords for billions of Web pages. **p. 350**

Industry-specific platform. An ERP system configuration that is appropriate for a particular industry, such as retail, manufacturing, or health care. **p. 176**

Information. (1) Knowledge derived from data, where *data* is defined as recorded facts or figures; (2) data presented in a meaningful context; (3) data processed by summing, ordering, averaging, grouping, comparing, or other similar operations; (4) a difference that makes a difference. **p. 35**

Information Age An era where production, distribution, and control of information are the primary drivers of the economy. **p. 5**

Information silo. An island of automation; information systems that work in isolation from one another. **p. 147**

Information system (IS). A group of components that interact to produce information. **p. 29**

Information systems security. The process of protecting information systems vulnerabilities from threats by creating appropriate safeguards. **p. 106**

Infrastructure as a service (IaaS). The cloud hosting of a bare server computer or disk drive. **p. 65**

Infrastructure processes. Essential supporting processes in the organization that enable day-to-day operations, such as processes in accounting, administration, quality assurance, and legal and financial areas. **p. 137**

Inherent processes. Process designs included in an ERP product that may be implemented by the organization. **p. 166**

Intelligence. The ability to acquire, store, and apply knowledge. **p. 410**

Internal control. Systematically limiting the actions and behaviors of employees, processes, and systems within the organization to safeguard assets and to achieve objectives. **p. 191**

Internet. The collection of networks that is used to send e-mail or access a Web site. **p. 52**

Internet of Things (IoT). A vision of everyday objects connected to the Internet and interacting with other devices. **p. 381**

Internet protocols and standards. Additions to TCP/IP that enable cloud-hosting vendors to provide processing capabilities in flexible yet standardized ways. **p. 62**

Internet service provider (ISP). An ISP provides users with Internet access. An ISP provides a user with a legitimate Internet address; it serves as the user's gateway to the Internet; and it passes communications back and forth between the user and the Internet. ISPs also pay for the Internet. They collect money from their customers and pay access fees and other charges on the users' behalf. **p. 54**

Interorganizational IS. Information systems that support processes and activities that span two or more independent organizations. **p. 247**

Intranet. A private internet used exclusively within an organization. **p. 52**

Invoice. An itemized bill. **p. 188**

iOS. The operating system used on the iPhone, iPad, and iPod Touch. **p. 385**

IP address. A number that uniquely identifies a computer's location on the Internet. **p. 57**

IS graduates. Business school graduates who apply collaboration skills and business knowledge to technical challenges. **p. 372**

IP spoofing. A type of spoofing whereby an intruder uses another site's IP address as if it were that other site. **p. 109**

IT analysts. Also called *systems analysts*; Individuals with specialized training or education that enables them to support, maintain, and adapt a system after it has been implemented. **p. 398**

Iteration control. A collaboration tool that limits, and sometimes even directs, user activity. **p. 292**

Iteration management. A system that tracks changes to documents and provides features and functions to accommodate concurrent work; examples are Google Drive and Microsoft SkyDrive. **p. 291**

Just in time (JIT). A delivery method that synchronizes manufacturing and supply so that materials arrive just as the manufacturing process requires them. **p. 163**

Key. (1) A column or group of columns that identifies a unique row in a table. Also referred to as a Primary Key. (2) A number used to encrypt data. The encryption algorithm applies the key to the original message to produce the coded message. Decoding (decrypting) a message is similar; a key is applied to the coded message to recover the original text. **p. 74 and 115**

Key escrow. A control procedure whereby a trusted party is given a copy of a key used to encrypt database data. **p. 118**

Knowledge. Justified beliefs. **p. 410**

Knowledge Management (KM) process. A process in an organization that creates value from intellectual capital and shares that knowledge with employees, managers, suppliers, customers, and others. **p. 410**

KPI. Key performance indicators; quantities assigned to attributes that are used to measure the success of a process. **p. 138**

Lead time. The time required for a supplier to deliver an order. **p. 188**

Libraries. In version-control collaboration systems, shared directories that allow access to various documents by means of permissions. **p. 292**

Linkages. Process interactions across value chains. Linkages are important sources of efficiencies and are readily supported by information systems. **p. 16**

Linux. A version of Unix that was developed by the open source community. The open source community owns Linux, and there is no fee to use it. Linux is a popular operating system for Web servers. **p. 385**

Local area network (LAN). A network that connects computers that reside in a single geographic location on the premises of the company that operates the LAN. The number of connected computers can range from two to several hundred. **p. 52**

Location-based data (LBD) Also called spatial data, is spatially referenced data; it identifies where an object or person is located on a map or reference system. **p. 420**

Lost update problem. An issue in multiuser database processing in which two or more users try to make changes to the data but the database cannot make all those changes because it was not designed to process changes from multiple users. **p. 81**

Mac OS. An operating system developed by Apple Computer, Inc., for the Macintosh. The current version is Mac OS X Mountain Lion. Macintosh computers are used primarily by graphic artists and workers in the arts community. Mac OS was developed for the PowerPC, but as of 2006 runs on Intel processors as well. **p. 385**

Machine code. Code that has been compiled from source code and is ready to be processed by a computer. **p. 387**

Machine learning. All techniques that use algorithms to discover patterns in data. **p. 413**

Main memory. A set of cells in which each cell holds a byte of data or instruction; each cell has an address, and the CPU uses the addresses to identify particular data items. **p. 382**

Maintenance. In the context of information systems, (1) to fix the system to do what it was supposed to do in the first place or (2) to adapt the system to a change in requirements. **p. 402**

Malware. A term used to describe a variety of software that damages or disables computers. **p. 109**

Management information systems (MIS). An information system that helps businesses achieve their goals and objectives. **p. 9 and 134**

Management (of MIS). The creation, monitoring, and adapting of processes, information systems, and information. **p. 134**

Managerial processes. Processes that concern resource use; includes planning, assessing, and analyzing the resources used by the company in pursuit of its strategy. **p. 134**

Manufacturing resource planning (MRPII). A manufacturing information system that schedules equipment and facilities and provides financial tracking of activities. **p. 163**

Many-to-many (N:M) relationship. Relationships involving two entity types in which an instance of one type can relate to many instances of the second type, and an instance of the second type can relate to many instances of the first. For example, the relationship between Student and Class is N:M. One student may enroll in many classes, and one class may have many students. Contrast with *one-to-many relationships*. **p. 85**

MapReduce. A technique used for harnessing the power of thousands of computers working in parallel. **p. 353**

Margin. The difference between the value that an activity generates and the cost of the activity. **p. 14**

Market Basket Analysis (MBA). An unsupervised data mining analysis that helps determine sales patterns. It shows the products that customers tend to buy together. **p. 347**

Marketing. The activity, set of institutions, and processes for creating, communicating, delivering, and exchanging offerings that have value for customers, clients, partners, and society at large. **p. 231**

Markup language The most common language for defining the structure and layout of Web pages **p. 57**

Mashup. The combining of output from two or more Web sites into a single user experience. **p. 314**

Master data. Also called *reference data*; data used in the organization that don't change with every transaction. **p. 164**

Material requirements planning (MRP). Software used to efficiently manage inventory, production, and labor. **p. 163**

Maximum cardinality. The maximum number of entities that can be involved in a relationship. Common examples of maximum cardinality are 1:N, N:M, and 1:1. **p. 86**

Measure(s). (1) Also called metrics or KPIs; quantities that are assigned to attributes; in the process context, measures help assess achievement of process objectives. (2) A data item of interest that can be summed, averaged, or otherwise processed. **p. 138 and 344**

Merchant company. In e-commerce, a company that takes title to the goods it sells. The company buys goods and resells them. **p. 247**

Metadata. Data that describe data. **p. 75**

Metrics. Also called measures or KPIs; quantities that are assigned to attributes; in the process context, measures help assess achievement of process objectives. **p. 138**

Microsoft Dynamics. A suite of ERP products licensed by Microsoft. The suite is composed of four ERP products, all obtained via acquisition: AX, Nav, GP, and SL. AX and Nav have the most capability, GP is smaller and easier to use. Although Dynamics has over 80,000 installations, the future of SL is particularly cloudy; Microsoft outsources the maintenance of the code to provide continuing support to existing customers. **p. 175**

Microsoft Skype. Videoconferencing software for collaboration. **p. 288**

Microsoft OneDrive. Collaboration software that stores and shares Office documents and other files and offers free storage. **p. 291**

Microsoft Windows. The most popular nonmobile client operating system for personal computers. **p. 385**

Minimum cardinality. The minimum number of entities that must be involved in a relationship. **p. 86**

Module. A suite of similar applications in an ERP system; examples include manufacturing and finance. **p. 176**

Moore's Law. A law, created by Gordon Moore, stating that the number of transistors per square inch on an integrated chip doubles every 18 months. Moore's prediction has proved generally accurate in the 40 years since it was made. Sometimes this law is stated that the performance of a computer doubles every 18 months. Although not strictly true, this version gives the gist of the idea. **p. 4**

Multiple instances. A separate ERP implementation for each country, business unit, or region. **p. 174**

Mutinous movement. An extension of bad reviews where prosumers revolt and use an organization's site in damaging ways. **p. 324**

Multi-user processing. When more than one users is processing a database. **p. 80**

MySQL. A popular open source DBMS product that is license-free for most applications. **p. 76**

Narrow AI. Using AI to accomplish a narrowly defined intelligent task such as generating a recommendation, spotting a fraudulent financial transaction, understanding a sentence, or driving a car. **p. 414**

Native applications. Applications that can run on just one operating system. **p. 389**

Near Field Communication (NFC). A standard for very short-range communication between devices, typically under 4 cm. **p. 424**

Net neutrality. An approach where all data moving on the Internet is treated equally. **p. 60**

Network. A collection of computers that communicate with one another over transmission lines. **p. 52**

Neural net. An adaptive system of nodes and connections that learn, also called artificial neural nets (ANN). **p. 413**

Next Best Offer (NBO) process. A targeted offer or proposed action for customers based on the data patterns in the customer's history and preferences, context, and attributes of the product or service. **p. 350**

Nonmerchant company. An e-commerce company that arranges for the purchase and sale of goods without ever owning or taking title to those goods. **p. 247**

Normal forms. A classification of tables according to their characteristics and the kinds of problems they have. **p. 88**

Normalization. The process of converting poorly structured tables into two or more well-structured tables. **p. 86**

noSQL databases. A catchall category that includes many different types of DBMS. It means no processing of SQL at all; and it means Not only SQL, meaning the DBMS will process both SQL and something else, where something else is not standard. **p. 91**

Object-relational database. A type of database that stores both object-oriented programming objects and relational data. Rarely used in commercial applications. **p. 103**

Objective. A goal that people in an organization have chosen to pursue. In the process context, managers develop and measure objectives for each process. Objectives fall into two categories: effectiveness and efficiency. **p. 134**

Off-the-shelf software. Generic application software that is used without customization. **p. 386**

Off-the-shelf with alterations software. Generic application software that is customized before use. **p. 386**

Office Web Apps. License-free Web application versions of Word, Excel, PowerPoint, and OneNote available on Sky-Drive. **p. 291**

Offshoring Means that the goods or services were obtained from a foreign supplier. **p. 398**

One-of-a-kind application. Software that is developed for a specific, unique need. **p. 386**

One-to-many (1:N) relationship. Relationships involving two entity types in which an instance of one type can relate to many instances of the second type, but an instance of the second type can relate to at most one instance of the first. For example, the relationship between *Department* and *Employee* is 1:N. A department may relate to many employees, but an employee relates to at most one department. **p. 85**

Online analytical processing (OLAP). An interactive type of reporting analysis that provides the ability to sum, count, average, and perform other simple arithmetic operations on groups of data. Such reports are interactive because users can change the format of the reports while viewing them. **p. 340**

Online transactional processing (OLTP). An operational process that uses an information system for the processing and reporting of day-to-day operational events. Order processing is a common OLTP example. **p. 340**

Operating system (OS). A computer program that controls the computer's resources. It manages the contents of main memory, processes keystrokes and mouse movements, sends signals to the display monitor, reads and writes disk files, and controls the processing of other programs. **p. 384**

Operational database. A data store that contains data produced and consumed by operational processes. **p. 339**

Operational processes. Common, routine, everyday business processes such as Procurement and Sales. **p. 133**

Oracle Database. A popular, enterprise-class DBMS product from Oracle Corporation. **p. 76**

Order to cash (O2C). Also called the sales process or the order-to-cash cycle. **p. 233**

Organizational data. Data about an organization, such as the location of its warehouses, the mailing addresses of the buildings, and the names of its financial accounts. **p. 164**

Ought-to-be diagram. A diagram of suggested improvements to a current process. **p. 145**

Outbound logistics processes. Processes that collect, store, and distribute products to buyers. **p. 136**

Outsourcing. Obtaining goods or services from an outside or foreign supplier. **p. 398**

Overflow attack. The hacker presents malicious code to a computer's operating system or application that deliberately overflows the capability of the software. The overflowing code contains damaging instructions that are later executed. **p. 110**

Paired programming. Two team members share the same computer and write a computer program together. **p. 406**

Parallel installation. A type of system conversion in which the new system runs in parallel with the old one for a while. Parallel installation is expensive because the organization incurs the costs of running both systems. **p. 402**

Parallel workflow. The condition that exists when two or more workers perform a task concurrently. A common example is concurrent review of a document. **p. 295**

PC virtualization. Using a personal computer to host several different operating systems. **p. 388**

Peering. Agreements that specify how the data will move among Tier 1 network providers. **p. 60**

People. As part of the five-component framework, one of the five fundamental components of an information system; includes those who operate and service the computers, those who maintain the data, those who support the networks, and those who use the system. **p. 29**

Personal area network (PAN). A network that connects devices around a single person. **p. 52**

Personal computer (PC). A classic computing device that is used by an individual. **p. 382**

Personal DBMS. DBMS products designed for smaller, simpler database applications. Such products are used for personal or small workgroup applications that involve fewer than 100 users, and normally fewer than 15. Today, Microsoft Access is the only prominent personal DBMS. **p. 81**

Phased installation. A type of system conversion in which the new system is installed in pieces across the organization(s). Once a given piece works, then the organization installs and tests another piece of the system, until the entire system has been installed. **p. 401**

Phisher. An individual or organization that spoofs legitimate companies in an attempt to illegally capture personal data, such as credit card numbers, e-mail accounts, and driver's license numbers. **p. 109**

Phishing. A technique for obtaining unauthorized data that uses pretexting via e-mail. The *phisher* pretends to be a legitimate company and sends an e-mail requesting confidential data, such as account numbers, Social Security numbers, account passwords, and so forth. **p. 109**

Pilot installation. A type of system conversion in which the organization implements the entire system on a limited portion of the business. The advantage of pilot implementation is that if the system fails, the failure is contained within a limited boundary. This reduces exposure of the business and also protects the new system from developing a negative reputation throughout the organization(s). **p. 401**

Platform as a service (PaaS). A category of cloud hosting in which vendors provide hosted computers, an operating system, and possibly a DBMS. **p. 64**

Plunge installation. A type of system conversion in which the organization shuts off the old system and starts the new system. If the new system fails, the organization is in trouble: Nothing can be done until either the new system is fixed or the old system is reinstalled. Because of the risk, organizations should avoid this conversion style if possible. Sometimes called *direct installation*. **p. 402**

Pooled. Physical hardware resources that are shared by many different organizations. **p. 61**

Posting. When the legal ownership of a material that has been sold is transferred from the seller to the buyer. **p. 240**

Power curve. A graph that shows the relationship of the power, or the utility that one gains from a software product, as a function of the time using that product. **p. 298**

Prediction. To look at something in order to be informed about the likelihood of future events. **p. 338**

Prescriptive procedures Clearly delimit what the users of the information system can do and under what conditions they can do it. **p. 34**

Pretexting. A technique for gathering unauthorized information in which someone pretends to be someone else. A common scam involves a telephone caller who pretends to be from a credit card company and claims to be checking the validity of credit card numbers. Phishing is also a form of pretexting. **p. 109**

Primary activities. In Porter's value chain model, the fundamental activities that create value: inbound logistics, operations, outbound logistics, marketing/sales, and service. **p. 14**

Primary key. Also called a *key*; a column or group of columns that identifies a unique row in a table. **p. 74**

Privacy. Controlling how one's personal information is acquired and analyzed. **p. 323**

Private cloud. In-house hosting, delivered via Web service standards, that can be configured dynamically. **p. 65**

Procedures. Instructions for humans. One of the five fundamental components of an information system. **p. 29**

Process blueprint. In an ERP application, a comprehensive set of inherent processes for all organizational activities, each of which is documented with diagrams that use a set of standardized symbols. **p. 166**

Process improvement. A method used to help a process better achieve its objectives based on its measures. **p. 138**

Procure-to-pay (P2P) Also called the procurement process or the procure-to-pay cycle. **p. 187**

Procurement. Obtaining goods and services. **p. 136 and 186**

Project data. Data that is part of the collaboration's work product, such as design documents. **p. 285**

Project management. The process of applying principles and techniques for planning, organizing, and monitoring temporary endeavors. **p. 293**

Project metadata. Data that is used to manage a project, such as schedules, tasks, budgets, and other managerial data. **p. 285**

Promotion. The process of sharing data about a product or service with the objective to improve awareness and sales. **p. 316**

Prosumer. A user who contributes to a Web site. **p. 319**

Protocol. A standardized means for coordinating an activity between two or more entities. **p. 55**

Prototype. A scaled-down but functional version of a system that is built to help evaluate a system. **p. 399**

Public key/private key. A special version of asymmetric encryption that is popular on the Internet. With this method, each site has a public key for encoding messages and a private key for decoding them. **p. 115**

Purchase order (PO). A written document requesting delivery of a specified quantity of a product or service in return for payment. **p. 187**

Purchase requisition (PR). An internal company document that issues a request for a purchase. When accepted, data from the purchase requisition is used in the purchase order. **p. 194**

Query. A request for data from a database. **p. 80**

Quotation. A binding agreement to sell a product at a specific price to a customer on a specific date. **p. 234**

R/3. One of the best-known versions of SAP. It was the first truly integrated system that was able to support most of organizations' major operational processes. **p. 177**

Radio-frequency identification (RFID). Computer chips that help identify and track items. As small as, and soon to be as cheap as, a postage stamp, RFID chips broadcast data to receivers that can display and record the broadcast data. **p. 360**

RAM (random access memory). Main memory consisting of cells that hold data or instructions. Each cell has an address that the CPU uses to read or write data. Memory locations can be read or written in any order, hence the term *random access*. RAM memory is almost always volatile. **p. 382**

Ransomware Blocks access to a computer until the victim pays money to the attacker. **p. 109**

Raw material The basic material used in the manufacturing or primary production of goods. **p. 186**

Raw materials inventory. A repository of parts and subassemblies procured from suppliers that are used to produce products to be stored in the finished goods inventory. **p. 187**

Real-time price discount. A discounted price offered during a sales call. **p. 235**

Record. Also called a *row*, a group of columns in a database table. **p. 73**

Reddit. Very popular social news Web site built on crowdpolling and anonymous posting. **p. 325**

Regression analysis. Supervised data mining analysis that estimates the values of parameters in a linear equation. Used to determine the relative influence of variables on an outcome and also to predict future values of that outcome. **p. 346**

Relation. The more formal name for a database table. **p. 75**

Relational database. A database that carries its data in the form of tables and that represents relationships using foreign keys. **p. 75**

Relationship. An association among entities or entity instances in an E-R model or an association among rows of a table in a relational database. **p. 84**

Remote sensing. Measures the amount of energy reflected off an object on the ground. **p. 426**

Report. A presentation of data in a structured or meaningful context. **p. 79**

Reporting. A process that uses simple statistical analysis to uncover patterns in a large database of data in order to improve assessment. **p. 343**

Repository. A collection of records, usually implemented as a database. **p. 28**

Resources. The items, such as people, computers, and data and document collections, necessary to accomplish an activity. **p. 132**

Return on investment (ROI). A method of measuring costs and benefits based on the amount earned by an investment as a percentage. **p. 322**

Returns Management process. A process that manages the returns of faulty products for businesses. **p. 200**

RFM analysis. A type of reporting analysis that ranks customers according to the recency, frequency, and monetary value of their purchases. **p. 343**

Risk. Simply the chance of loss; if the likelihood of a hack is greater than the chance of a virus, we would say the risk of a hack is greater than the risk of a virus. **p. 106**

Robot. An autonomous, lifelike machine that performs an action in place of a person. **p. 416**

Robotics. The design, construction, and use of autonomous machines that mimic human or animal actions. **p. 417**

Role. A subset of activities in a business process that is performed by a particular actor; resources are assigned to roles. **p. 26 and 132**

Roll up. To compile, total, and summarize data. For example, daily sales are "rolled up" into monthly sales. In accounting systems, transactions are "rolled up" into common accounting reports such as balance sheets and income statements. **p. 191**

Rows. Also called *records*, a group of columns in a database table. **p. 73**

Safeguard. Measure that individuals or organizations take to block a threat from obtaining an asset. **p. 107**

Sales. An operational outbound process comprised of three main activities—Sell, Ship, and Payment. **p. 232**

Sales process. An operational outbound process that records the sales order, ships the product, and bills the customer. **p. 136**

Salesforce. The preeminent cloud-based CRM vendor. **p. 236**

Sandbox. A testing environment that isolates new code while replicating enough of it to see how the new code will work with existing code. **p. 403**

SAP AG. The world's most successful ERP vendor. SAP AG is the third largest software company in the world. The core business of SAP AG is selling licenses for its SAP software solutions and related services. In addition, it offers consulting, training, and other services for its software solutions. **p. 176**

SAP HANA. An in-memory database in SAP that is exceptionally fast. **p. 354**

Sarbanes-Oxley Act (SOX). A federal law requiring companies to exercise greater control over their financial processes. **p. 163**

Schedule feasibility. Assesses whether the project can be accomplished by the estimated completion date. **p. 397**

Screen-sharing application. Applications that enable virtual meeting members to view the same whiteboard, application, or other display. **p. 288**

Security audit. a systematic evaluation of security by assessing how well the security safeguards conform to established criteria. **p. 122**

Self-efficacy. A person's belief that he or she can be successful at his or her job. **p. 171**

Self-service BI. When users do business intelligence analysis by themselves. **p. 339**

Sentiment analysis. Classifies opinions about a business, product, or service, typically as either positive or negative. **p. 347**

Sequential workflow. The condition that exists when two or more workers perform a task one at a time. A common example is the sequential review of a document. **p. 295**

Server(s). A computer that provides some type of service, such as hosting a database, running a blog, publishing a Web site, or selling goods. Server computers are faster, larger, and more powerful than client computers. **p. 382**

Server farm. A large collection of server computers that coordinates the activities of the servers, usually for commercial purposes. **p. 382**

Server tier. In the three-tier architecture, the tier that consists of computers that run Web servers to generate Web pages and other data in response to requests from browsers. Web servers also process application programs. **p. 72**

Server virtualization. A system in which a server computer hosts one or more other server computers. **p. 388**

Service. In SOA, a repeatable task that a business needs to perform. **p. 136**

Service-oriented architecture (SOA). The use of standard protocols to publish a menu of services that an application provides, the structure of data that it expects to receive, the structure of data that it will produce, and the ways in which services can be requested. **p. 59**

Session hijacking. When a hacker steals an encryption key that client is using to access a secure site and reuses that key to impersonate the legitimate user. **p. 109**

Sharing economy. Firms that enable peer-to-peer exchanges via online communities, where individuals can rent assets or obtain services offered by others. **p. 326**

Showrooming. When someone visits a brick-and-mortar store to examine and evaluate products without the intention of buying them at the store. **p. 66**

Sign-off. The user's signatures that indicate approval of the stated requirements. **p. 400**

Single instance. The use of one large ERP implementation to consolidate all the operations of an international firm. **p. 174**

Singularity. AI will gain enough intelligence to initiate a run-away cycle of self-improvement that eventually leads AI to turn on us. **p. 414**

Site license. A flat fee that authorizes the company to install a product, such as an operating system or application, on all of that company's computers or on all of the computers at a specific site. **p. 387**

Six Sigma. A popular strategy for process improvement that seeks to improve process outputs by removing causes of defects and minimizing variability in the process. **p. 145**

Slack. The time an activity is idle. **p. 145**

Slicing and dicing. The repeated use of basic analysis operations such as sorting, grouping, filtering, and calculating. **p. 343**

Small office/home office (SOHO). A business office with usually fewer than 10 employees; often located in the business professional's home. **p. 52**

Smart card. A plastic card similar to a credit card that has a microchip loaded with identifying data; requires a PIN to be authenticated. **p. 114**

Sniffing. A technique for intercepting computer communications. With wired networks, sniffing requires a physical connection to the network. With wireless networks, no such connection is required. **p. 109**

Social capital. The investment in social relations with expectation of future returns in the marketplace. **p. 320**

Social CRM. An information system that helps a company collect customer data from social media and share it among their customer facing processes. **p. 250**

Social engineering. A category of threats that involve manipulating a person or group to unknowingly release confidential information. **p. 108**

Social graph. A network of personal interdependencies, such as friendships, common interests, or kinship, on a social media application. **p. 312**

Social media. Any Web application that depends on usergenerated content. **p. 308**

Social media information system. An information system that supports the two activities in the social media process: creating and sharing user-generated content. **p. 308**

Social media policy. A statement that delineates employees' rights and responsibilities when using social media for business purposes. **p. 323**

Software. As part of the five-component framework, one of the five fundamental components of an information system; includes computer programs used to record and process data. **p. 29**

Software as a service (SaaS). An organization that provides not only hardware infrastructure but also an operating system and application programs on top of that hardware. **p. 64**

Source code. Computer code as written by humans and that is understandable by humans. Source code must be translated into machine code before it can be processed. **p. 387**

Source list. A list of all approved vendors for a business. **p. 194**

Spatial analysis. Examines the locations, attributes, and relationships of features in LBD through overlay and other analytical techniques. **p. 426**

Spoofing. When someone pretends to be someone else with the intent of obtaining unauthorized data. If you pretend to be your professor, you are spoofing your professor. **p. 109**

SQL injection attacks. A technique used to compromise database data in which SQL code is unknowingly processed by a Web page. **p. 110**

SQL Server. A popular enterprise-class DBMS product from Microsoft. **p. 76**

Stand-up. A component of the scrum process; a 15-minute meeting in which each team member states what he or she has done in the past day, what he or she will do in the coming day, and any factors that are blocking his or her progress. **p. 405**

STEM. Academic programs in science, technology, engineering, and math. **p. 372**

Strategic processes. Business processes that seek to resolve issues that have a long-range impact on the organization. These processes have a broad scope and impact most of the firm. **p. 134**

Strength of a relationship. In the theory of social capital, the likelihood that a person or other organization in a relationship will do something that will benefit the organization. **p. 321**

Structured processes. Formally defined, standardized processes that support day-to-day operations such as accepting a return, placing an order, computing a sales commission, and so forth. **p. 33**

Structured Query Language (SQL). An international standard language for processing database data. **p. 77**

Substitute. In the five forces model, a competing product that performs the same or similar function as an industry's product by another means. **p. 12**

Supervised data mining. A form of data mining in which data miners develop a model prior to the analysis and apply statistical techniques to data to estimate values of the parameters of the model. **p. 347**

Supplier Evaluation process. A strategic process that determines the criteria for supplier selection and adds and removes suppliers from the list of approved suppliers. **p. 200**

Supplier Relationship Management (SRM) process. A process that automates, simplifies, and accelerates a variety of supply chain processes. SRM is a management process that helps companies reduce procurement costs, build collaborative supplier relationships, better manage supplier options, and improve time to market. **p. 199**

Supply chain Is a network of people, organizations, resources, and processes that create and distribute a particular product from the delivery of raw materials at the supplier to final delivery to consumer. **p. 186**

Supply chain management (SCM). The design, planning, execution, and integration of all supply chain processes. SCM uses a collection of tools, techniques, and management activities to help businesses develop integrated supply chains that support organizational strategy. **p. 200**

Support activities. In Porter's value chain model, the activities that contribute indirectly to value creation: procurement, technology, human resources, and the firm's infrastructure. **p. 15**

Supportive procedures. Allow end users to determine how to best use an IS. **p. 34**

Swimlane. A long column in a BPMN diagram; each column contains all the activities for a particular role. **p. 27**

Switch. A special-purpose computer that receives and transmits data across a network. **p. 52**

Symmetric encryption. An encryption method whereby the same key is used to encode and to decode the message. **p. 115**

Synchronous communication. Information exchange that occurs when all members of a work team meet at the same time, such as face-to-face meetings or conference calls. **p. 287**

System. A group of components that interact to achieve some purpose. **p. 29**

System conversion. The process of converting business activity from the old system to the new. **p. 401**

Systems development. The process of creating and maintaining information systems. It is sometimes called *systems analysis and design.* **p. 397**

Systems development life cycle (SDLC). The classical process used to develop information systems. These basic tasks

of systems development are combined into the following phases: system definition, requirements analysis, component design, implementation, and system maintenance (fix or enhance). **p. 397**

Systems thinking. The mental process of making one or more models of the components of a system and connecting the inputs and outputs among those components into a sensible whole, one that explains the phenomenon observed. **p. 7**

Table. Also called a *file*, a group of similar rows or records in a database. **p. 73**

Tablets. Also called *slates*; computers that receive input via a touch screen rather than a keyboard or mouse. **p. 382**

Tag. In markup languages such as html and XML, notation used to define a data element for display or other purposes. **p. 58**

Target. An asset that is desired by a threat. **p. 107**

TCP/IP (Transmission Control Protocol/Internet) Protocol architecture. A protocol architecture having four layers; forms the basis for the TCP/IP–OSI architecture used by the Internet. **p. 56**

Team survey. A form of asynchronous communication in which one team member creates a list of questions and other team members respond. Microsoft SharePoint has built-in survey capability. **p. 289**

Technical feasibility. Determines if the planned technology can deliver the project's requirements and whether the firm has the expertise to use this technology. **p. 397**

Technical safeguard. Safeguard that involves the hardware and software components of an information system. **p. 113**

Technology development processes. A support activity in the value chain; includes designing, testing, and developing technology in support of the primary activities of an organization. **p. 136**

Test plan. A formal description of a system's response to use and misuse scenarios. **p. 401**

Text mining. The analytical technique that extracts insights from unstructured data sources, typically textual documents. **p. 347**

Threat. A challenge to information systems security. **p. 106**

Three-tier architecture. Architecture used by most e-commerce server applications. The tiers refer to three different classes of computers. The user tier consists of users' computers that have browsers that request and process Web pages. The server tier consists of computers that run Web servers and in the process generate Web pages and other data in response to requests from browsers. Web servers also process application programs. The third tier is the database tier, which runs the DBMS that processes the database. **p. 60**

Three-way match. The activity within the procurement process that ensures that the data on the invoice matches the data on the purchase order and the goods receipt. **p. 189**

Traditional capital. Investments into resources such as factories, machines, manufacturing equipment, and the like with the expectation of future returns in the market. **p. 320**

Train the trainer. Training sessions in which vendors train the organization's employees to become in-house trainers in order to improve training quality and reduce training expenses. **p. 165**

Transaction processing system (TPS). An information system that supports operational decision making. **p. 134**

Transactional data. Data related to events such as a purchase. **p. 164**

Turing test. An AI passes the Turing test if it can fool individuals into thinking they are talking with a real person. **p. 414**

Unicorn. Startup companies valued in excess of $1 billion. **p. 326**

Unix. An operating system developed at Bell Labs in the 1970s. It has been the workhorse of the scientific and engineering communities since then. **p. 385**

Unsupervised data mining. A form of data mining whereby the analysts do not create a model or hypothesis before running the analysis. Instead, they apply the data mining technique to the data and observe the results. With this method, analysts create hypotheses after the analysis to explain the patterns found. **p. 347**

User-generated content. Publicly available content created by end users. **p. 308**

Usurpation Unauthorized control of some part of an IS. It occurs when criminals replace a legitimate user or software program with their own access or illegitimate software program to give the attacker unauthorized control of some part of the IS. **p. 110**

Utilitarianism. An ethics theory in which the morality of an act is determined by its outcome; acts are judged to be moral if they result in the greatest good to the greatest number or if they maximize happiness and reduce suffering; founders of the modern theory are Jeremy Bentham and John Stuart Mill. **p. 43**

Utility software. Helps optimize and configure the computer and provide additional functionality for the OS. **p. 385**

UTM. A common coordinate system that divides the world into a series of zones and specifies coordinates within each zone. **p. 426**

Value. According to Porter, the amount of money that a customer is willing to pay for a resource, product, or service. **p. 14**

Value chain. A network of value-creating activities. **p. 14**

Vehicle-to-vehicle (V2V). A communication network of vehicles and roadside units that provide each other data about their own location, accidents, road congestion, rerouting opportunities, and weather conditions. **p. 424**

Version lock. Customizing software so heavily that the software cannot be upgraded when the ERP vendor upgrades their system to a new version. **p. 173**

Vertical-market application. Software that serves the needs of a specific industry. Examples of such programs are those used by dental offices to schedule appointments and bill

patients, those used by auto mechanics to keep track of customer data and customers' automobile repairs, and those used by parts warehouses to track inventory, purchases, and sales. **p. 386**

Videoconferencing. A technology that combines a conference call with video cameras. **p. 288**

Viral. User-generated content, typically a video, that is shared and promoted by individuals on social media outlets in greater than expected volume. **p. 314**

Virtual machines (vm). In the process of virtualization, a hosted operating system. **p. 388**

Virtual meeting. A meeting in which participants do not meet in the same place and possibly not at the same time. **p. 288**

Virtual private network (VPN). Software or a dedicated computer to create a private network over the public Internet. **p. 118**

Visualization. The use of images, or diagrams, for communicating a message. Simple examples include bar charts and infographics. **p. 348**

Vulnerability. A weakness in an information system that provides an opportunity for threats to gain access to individual and organizational assets. **p. 107**

Wearables. Small electronic devices worn on the body. The most common examples include headsets, glasses, and wristbands. **p. 382**

Web app. Run in browsers on many different operating systems. **p. 389**

Web farm. A facility that runs multiple Web servers. Work is distributed among the computers in a Web farm so as to maximize throughput. **p. 61**

Web page. A document encoded in html that is created, transmitted, and used using the World Wide Web. **p. 61**

Web server. A program that processes the http protocol and transmits Web pages on demand. Web servers also process application programs. **p. 61**

Web storefront. In e-commerce, a Web-based application that enables customers to enter and manage their orders. **p. 247**

Wide area network (WAN). A network that connects computers located at different geographic locations. **p. 52**

Windows 10 mobile. Microsoft's attempt to unify OS across both mobile and nonmobile platforms. **p. 385**

Windows Server. A version of Windows that has been specially designed and configured for server use. **p. 385**

Workflow. A process or procedure by which content is created, edited, used, and disposed. **p. 295**

XML. A markup language like html but is machine readable and was designed to enable the exchange of structured data over the Web. **p. 59**

Index